MOTOCOURSE

THE WORLD'S LEADING GRAND PRIX & SUPERBIKE ANNUAL

icon
PUBLISHING LIMITED

RALLIES / MXGP
FREESTYLE /

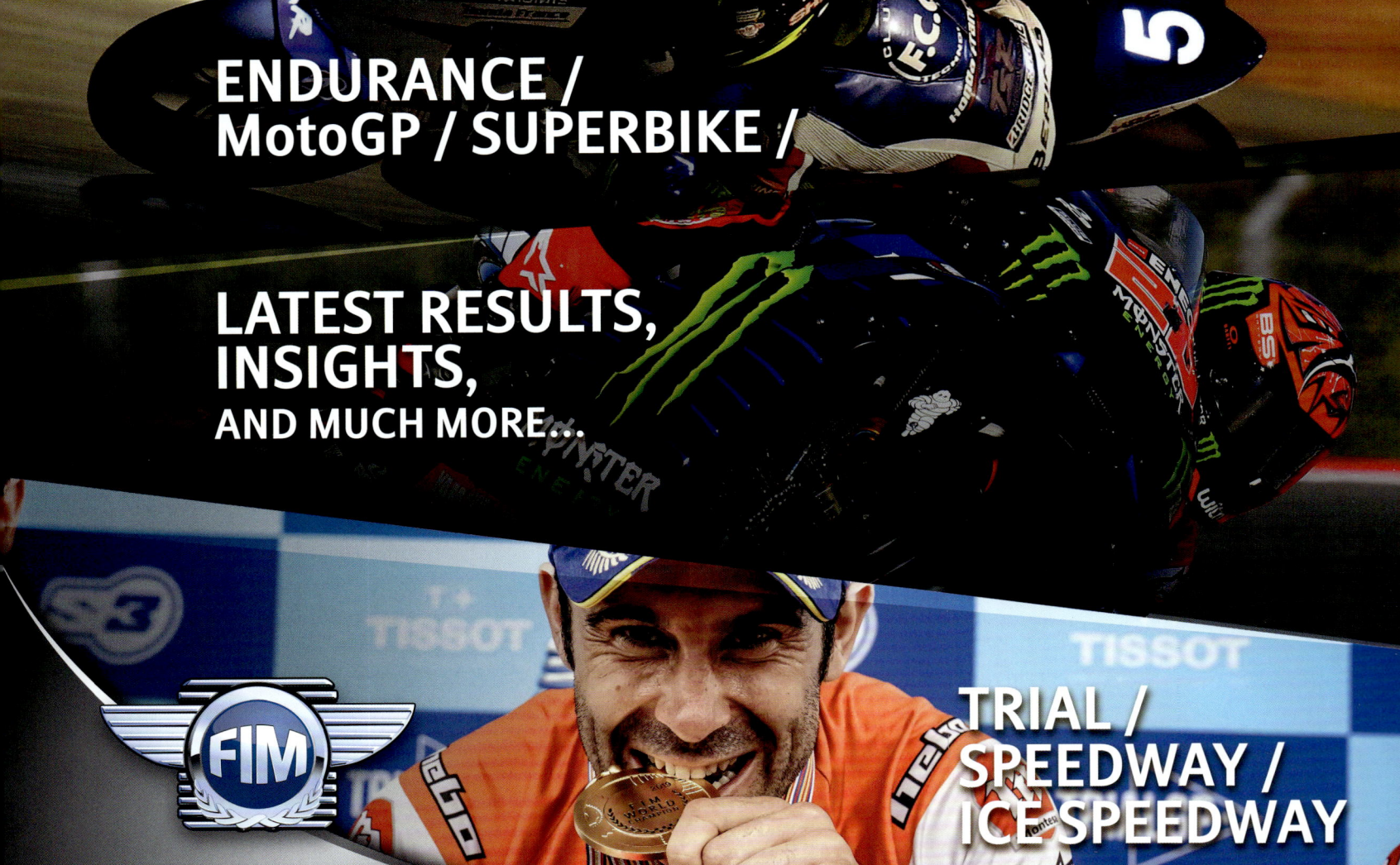

GET CONNECTED

FIM-MOTO.COM
THE OFFICIAL WEBSITE

ENDURANCE /
MotoGP / SUPERBIKE /

LATEST RESULTS,
INSIGHTS,
AND MUCH MORE...

TRIAL /
SPEEDWAY /
ICE SPEEDWAY

CONTENTS

MOTOCOURSE 2021–2022

is published by:
Icon Publishing Limited
4 Suffolk Villas
Suffolk Road,
Cheltenham
Gloucestershire
GL50 2AX
United Kingdom

Tel: +44 (0)1242 245329

Email: info@motocourse.com
Website: www.motocourse.com

Printed in the United Kingdom by
Gomer Press Ltd
Llandysul Enterprise Park
Llandysul
Ceredigion
SA44 4JL
Tel: 01559 362371
email: sales@gomer.co.uk

© Icon Publishing Limited 2021.
No part of this publication may be reproduced, stored in a retrieval system or transmitted, in any form or by any means, electronic, mechanical, photocopying, recording or otherwise, without prior permission in writing from Icon Publishing Limited.

ISBN: 978-1910584-47-7

DISTRIBUTORS

Gardners Books
1 Whittle Drive, Eastbourne,
East Sussex, BN23 6QH
Tel: +44 (0)1323 521555
email: sales@gardners.com

Chaters Wholesale Ltd
25/26 Murrell Green Business Park,
Hook, Hampshire, RG27 9GR
Tel: +44 (0)1256 765443
Fax: +44 (0)1256 769900
email: books@chaters.co.uk

NORTH AMERICA
Quayside Publishing Group
400 First Avenue North, Suite 300,
Minneapolis, MN 55401, USA
Tel: (612) 344 8100
Fax: (612) 344 8691

Dust jacket: Yamaha's Fabio Quartararo became France's first ever premier-class world champion at the age of 22.
Photo: Monster Energy Yamaha MotoGP

Title page: Toprak Razgatlioglu, WorldSBK's 2021 champion.
Photo: Gold & Goose

FOREWORD by 2021 MotoGP World Champion Fabio Quartararo	4
EDITOR'S INTRODUCTION	6
THE TOP TEN RIDERS OF 2021 Ranked by the Editor	8
THE STATE OF RACING by Michael Scott	14
APPRECIATIONS	20
LOOKING BACK AT A LEGEND… Michael Scott reflects on the record-breaking career of Valentino Rossi	22
THE TYRE WHISPERERS Kevin Cameron examines the complex relations between riders and tyres	30
BROTHERS AT WAR Neil Morrison meets the latest siblings about to square up in MotoGP	36
ELECTRO DUKE! Neil Spalding looks at the development of the electric bike in racing	42
IN THE SHADOW OF THE RULES The MotoGP machines of 2021 analysed by Simon Crafar	46
MOTOGP RIDERS AND TEAMS Guide to the grid by Matthew Birt	52
MOTO2 RIDERS AND TEAMS by Peter McLaren	76
MOTO3 RIDERS AND TEAMS by Peter McLaren	80
2021 GRANDS PRIX by Michael Scott and Neil Morrrison	84
WORLD CHAMPIONSHIP RIDERS' POINTS TABLES Compiled by Peter McLaren	230
MOTOE REVIEW by Oliver Barstow	234
RED BULL ROOKIES CUP REVIEW by Peter Clifford	236
SUPERBIKE WORLD CHAMPIONSHIP REVIEW by Gordon Ritchie	240
SUPERBIKE WORLD CHAMPIONSHIP RESULTS AND POINTS TABLES Compiled by Peter McLaren	276
SUPERSPORT WORLD CHAMPIONSHIP REVIEW by Gordon Ritchie	284
BRITISH SUPERBIKE REVIEW by Oliver Barstow	290
SIDECAR CHAMPIONSHIP REVIEW by John Mackenzie	314
US RACING REVIEW by Larry Lawrence	316
MAJOR RESULTS WORLDWIDE compiled by Peter McLaren	324

Acknowledgements

The Editor and staff of MOTOCOURSE wish to thank the following for their assistance and support: Maider Barthe, Matt Birt, Peter Clifford, Simon Crafar, Steve Day, Matt Dunn, William Favero, Michael Guy, Isabelle Lariviere, Hector Martin, Neil Morrison, Mat Oxley, David Pato, Ignacio Sagnier, Paolo Scalera, Federico Tonelli, Mike Trimby, Frine Vellila, Mike Webb and Gunther Wiesinger, as well as numerous others. The usual apologies to colleagues and friends for generally ignoring their comments and advice.

Photographs published in MOTOCOURSE 2021–2022 have been contributed by:
Chief photographers: Gold & Goose.
Other photographs contributed by: Agni, Clive Challinor Motorsport Photography, Simon Crafar, Ducati Corse, ECSTAR Suzuki, Ian Hopgood Photography, HRC/Repsol Honda, Monster Energy, MotoAmerica/Brian J. Nelson, MotoCzysz, Monster Energy Yamaha MotoGP, Pramac Ducati, Red Bull KTM, Neil Spalding, www.suzuki-racing.com, Mark Walters, Barry White, Bryn Williams.

---

publisher
STEVE SMALL
steve.small@iconpublishinglimited.com

commercial director
BRYN WILLIAMS
bryn.williams@iconpublishinglimited.com

editor
MICHAEL SCOTT

text editor
IAN PENBERTHY

results and statistics
PETER McLAREN

chief photographers
GOLD & GOOSE
David Goldman
Gareth Harford
David 'Chippy' Wood
www.goldandgoose.com
Tel: +44 (0)208 444 2448

MotoGP bike and circuit illustrations
ADRIAN DEAN
f1artwork@blueyonder.co.uk

MOTOCOURSE
www.motocourse.com

FOREWORD
by FABIO QUARTARARO

BECOMING a MotoGP World Champion, that's what we riders all chase after, right? It's what motivates us to train, what drives us to dig deeper and do better. It takes years of work. But, speaking from experience, nothing can prepare you for that moment when you finally make it happen.

I crossed the finish line in Misano, and so many thoughts were rushing through my head. Among them were all those moments when, as a kid, I had dreamed of becoming a MotoGP rider. I also thought about all the sacrifices my parents had made to help me make my dream come true.

In 2021, I stepped up to the Yamaha Factory Team. That was already a massive achievement and milestone for me. I was taking over from my idol, Valentino Rossi, so the pressure was on. There were high expectations, and I had to deliver.

MotoGP is so competitive. The fastest time from today will be too slow tomorrow. That constant striving for improvement makes MotoGP an inspiring sport. I find it a real honour to put my name among the champions of this sport, whom I admire so much. Now I, Fabio Quartararo, am one of those riders who made it all the way to the top. And I'm the first French rider to do it in the premier class – that's just amazing!

I was able to do it because I brought something extra in 2021. I managed to stay calm and focused, and made the best of every situation. That's partially thanks to Yamaha and my team. They have worked so hard for this World Championship title too. Together, we always gave it our all and never gave up. But I also couldn't have done it without my family and my friends. They have supported me for more than ten years and have helped me get to this point.

MOTOCOURSE is the top-quality record of this year, and of every year since before I was born. It is a pleasure to write this Foreword, to see my image on the front cover, and to dedicate it to all those who share our passion.

This championship title is hopefully just the start…

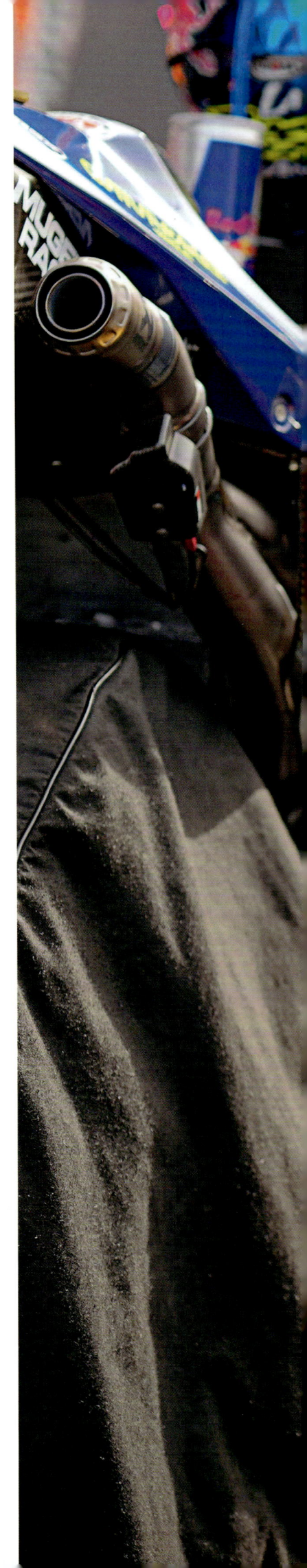

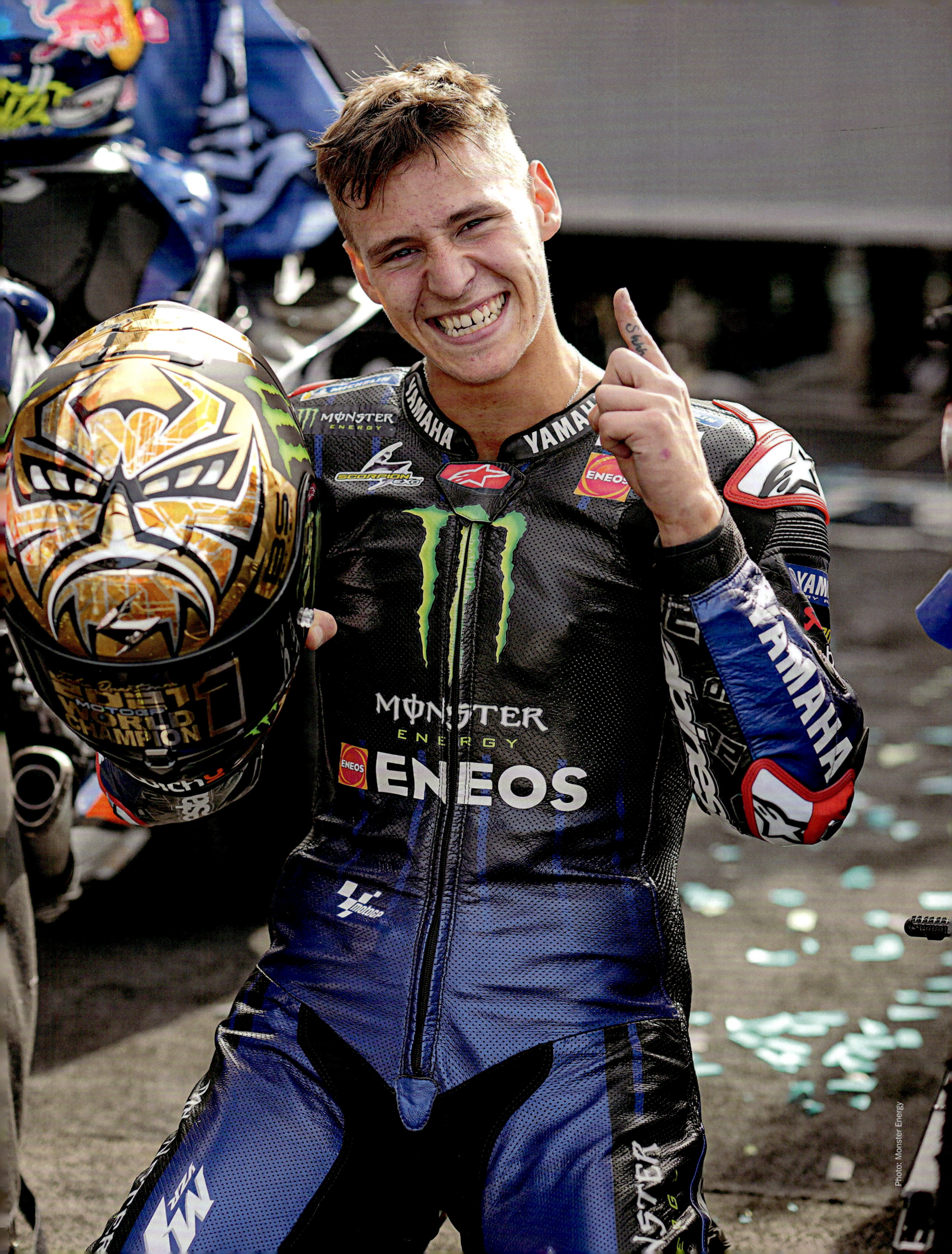

Photo: Monster Energy

EDITOR'S INTRODUCTION
A TRIUMPH OF HUMANITY

Above: Ring out the old, ring in the new. Marquez helped Quartararo celebrate his title.
Photo: Repsol Honda

Top right: Jake Gagne, utterly dominant in MotoAmerica.
Photo: MotoAmerica/Brian J. Nelson

Top far right: Final chapter. Racing legend Valentino Rossi retired after 26 great grand prix years.

Above right: Participants only. Paddocks were mainly empty throughout the season.
Photos: Gold & Goose

Above far right: Tarran Mackenzie triumphed in a compelling BSB series.
Photo: Bryn Williams

Right: Toprak Ragatlioglu finally toppled the mighty Jonathan Rea in World Superbikes.
Photo: Gold & Goose

BY the start of 2021, everybody everywhere was thoroughly sick and tired of the pandemic.

In all theatres of competition, motorcycle racing provided a healthy antidote. It continued, and if in some regards that continuation was not quite as normal, that only served to emphasise its humanity.

No other major motorsport is as human.

At the simplest level, this is shown by the riders' athleticism. Their body weight is a major component of the total weight of their projectiles. A rider's speed, agility, anticipation and sense of balance are vital components of the dynamic equation.

Humanity is evident also in the courage, the rivalry, the humour, even the vainglory of the task of arriving back where you had started before anyone else.

Also in the tragedy – and there was more of that in 2021 than anyone should be prepared to tolerate.

Cruel fate struck at the junior levels of the sport with fatal results.

As a welcome contrast, the upper echelons celebrated a year when young newcomers crowded the podiums. Astonishingly talented rookies and relative beginners elbowed the old-timers aside.

This was evident in every championship class. In the year when Valentino Rossi, the not-quite-undisputed Greatest Of All Time, hung up his leathers, and his nemesis Marc Marquez suffered sadly from human frailty, the likes of Quartararo, Bagnaia, Martin, Raul Fernandez and Acosta in MotoGP, and Razgatlioglu and Mackenzie in Superbikes proved that there is vigour aplenty for a sustained future.

Dorna, the FIM and the various national racing authorities are to be thanked and congratulated for keeping racing healthy at this difficult time. So, too, the riders, team staff, engineers, photographers and journalists…

Over more than 40 years, MOTOCOURSE has not only chronicled motorcycle racing – the broad sweeps of history and the minutiae of its detail. It has striven to do so with a level of excellence that those who risk their lives in their own pursuit of excellence deserve.

That is why it is regarded as the leading motorcycle racing annual.

That is why we hope you will enjoy this book, now and in better years to come.

MICHAEL SCOTT
West Sussex, November, 2021

PETRONAS
SEPANG RACING TEAM
Beta
Green Power
monitor
PETRONAS
Sprinta
YAMAHA

DUNLOP

Arai
SHOWA
SHOEI
BRIXX.COM
PATA
54
BMP
YAMAHA

FIM WORLD CHAMPIONSHIP 2021

TOP TEN RIDERS

THE EDITOR'S CHOICE

Rider Portraits by Gold & Goose

1 FABIO QUARTARARO

QUARTARARO was much fancied when brought into Moto3 under age in 2015. But his first four seasons were patchy at best, only partly because of injury, and rewarded with one race win, in his second year in Moto2 in 2018.

That made him a surprise choice for Yamaha's new MotoGP team.

Also inspired.

In his first year, he was fast at once, frequently closest challenger to Marquez. In 2020, he started out as a serious title contender. But in spite of three wins, his campaign was undermined by fits of temperament. On bad days, he slumped.

Sessions with a sports psychiatrist and a much-improved Yamaha changed all that in 2021. Five wins and five more podiums in 16 races secured an early title, while when things went against him, he kept calm and carried on. Even his bad days were good, and he finished every race but one in the points.

Clearly the best, all year, with a true champion's performance. The 2022 season might be harder.

2 PECCO BAGNAIA

HAVING Rossi in your corner would always be an asset. Having the best ever Ducati between your legs likewise. Bagnaia completed a worthy trinity by studiously addressing the weak points that had hampered his first two seasons, and repaid Ducati's faith in signing him to a full factory seat in spite of them.

He learned from Miller how to attack early on to bring the front tyre up to temperature, and most significantly, he learned how to remain calm under pressure.

In this way, he not only resisted Marquez's attacks at Aragon, but also put pressure on Quartararo as the season drew to a close.

There were still a few errors – falling out of the lead at Mugello and Misano the worst of them. But his end-of-season charge, with four wins in the last six races, marked a clear improvement for a rider who was already pretty darned good.

3 MARC MARQUEZ

A TALLY of three wins is a worst-ever for the eight-times champion – but he did it with one hand. More or less.

Marquez's injury in July, 2020, and subsequent complications (including a third eight-hour operation in December) kept him off motorcycles altogether for almost nine months; and he was still not back to full strength even by the end of the season. Weakness in his right arm and shoulder left him unable to heave the bike around as he likes.

Nor was the 2021 RC213V the bike he needed. His prolonged absence had cost HRC dear in terms of development, and it showed in the problems faced by all the Honda riders.

Marc demonstrated that his old talent and aggression were undimmed, however, although full expression of them was still a work in progress. The ability to win races in this condition speaks volumes.

His season ended with a worrying injury again. If he recovers completely, the others should watch out for him in 2022.

4 JORGE MARTIN

WAS the Pramac Ducati MotoGP rookie's pole position and podium finish, in only his second race, the biggest surprise of the season?

Only until he went on to take a first win at the first of two rounds in Austria, and another podium at the second – both from pole position.

There were other occasions when the 23-year-old former Moto3 champion demonstrated his inexperience; but the biggest setback was a relatively innocent cold-tyres fall at round three in Portugal, which left him with several fractures and ruled him out of four races.

The speed with which Martin meshed with the Ducati showed not only a depth of talent and a quantum of courage, but also the ability to learn very quickly.

With youngsters of this calibre – a product of the system that spots pre-teen talent, then polishes it via the Red Bull Rookies Cup – MotoGP demonstrates rude if somewhat risky health.

5 JACK MILLER

IT was a patchy year for Miller: two consecutive wins early on (including his first in a dry race) seemed to flatter to deceive.

But that didn't tell the whole story.

Jack seemed particularly cursed with the occasional blips in the Michelin tyres, and there were other mishaps and misfortunes that were not necessarily all his fault. And in the final races, he was ready to sacrifice his own interests to help the broader championship chances of team-mate Bagnaia and employers Ducati.

By then, Bagnaia was his biggest problem, several times denying him pole position, and setting a high bar for the older and more experienced rider.

Halfway through the year, Ducati extended Miller's contract, which unusually had been for just a single year. That gives the popular Aussie the chance to fight for himself rather than support his team-mate in 2022.

6 JOAN MIR

MIR had won the 2020 championship with an element of stealth – only a single win. It was his consistent podium presence, achieved by ghosting through in the latest stages, that had garnered the points. It was a high-class demonstration on a Suzuki that offered stable responses rather than dazzling speed.

He did much the same in 2021, but it wasn't good enough for more than a token title defence.

The Suzuki had changed very little, the rivals – Yamaha, Ducati and even Aprilia – by quite a lot.

Mir was still able to move forward unobtrusively, but not to set the qualifying times he required for this to deliver great rewards. He managed the second row just once, the third row on another five occasions, but often was stuck in a highly-competitive midfield.

In consequence, sometimes he resorted to desperate lunges, which won him few friends and no races. Seven podiums equalled his 2020 tally, but it was not enough.

7 ENEA BASTIANINI

IN a year of fast rookies in all classes, the reigning Moto2 champion was another one. Bastianini seemed to have few advantages, riding a supposedly flawed two-year-old motorcycle in the most junior Ducati team. He didn't seem to notice.

He suffered only in qualifying, being only twice in Q2 and once in the top ten. Most times, he was on the fifth row, or even worse, in a year when it was common cause that overtaking was difficult, and that bad starting positions would generally ruin your race.

Then he would spend his Sunday afternoons picking cleanly and steadily past much more experienced riders, becoming stronger as the season wore on. By the 18th race, he had finished nine times in the top ten, with two podiums at his home circuit of Misano.

For 2022, only three of eight Ducati riders will not get the latest bike. Bastianini is one of them. He probably won't notice that either.

8 REMY GARDNER

IF it were possible to share this position, it would be jointly held with the son-of-a-champion's team-mate, Raul Fernandez, who actually won more races and pole positions. But it's not possible to share a championship either, and Remy Gardner takes the spoils.

Championship success is about sustained strength, and this is where the the Australian, who lives in Spain, showed his mettle.

In the past, Gardner has been volatile, prone to temperamental outbursts. The 2021 season showed how the 23-year-old had achieved maturity, growing into the role of team leader and remaining calm even as the pressure ramped up.

He made only one slip, crashing in America. Raul crashed three times. It made all the difference.

Both are in the deep end in 2022, team-mates again in MotoGP. The pressure will be on once more.

12 TOP TEN RIDERS

9 BRAD BINDER

IT was an unobtrusive year for KTM, facing sundry technical stumbling blocks, in particular a changed tyre construction that undermined their major strength.

Miguel Oliveira seemed to overcome them best, with three successive podiums, including a win early on. But consistency eluded the Portuguese rider, and not only because of injury.

Instead, it was team-mate Binder who dug deeper, race after race, as the year wore on.

His uplifting single victory, on slicks in the rain in Austria, was something of a freak event, requiring boundless courage and the daring of a gambler.

Elsewhere, he showed the true depth of his racing intelligence and the strength of his talent, gaining places especially later in races. Only eight times in Q2, he claimed 13 top-tens, often in the upper reaches.

In the end, he achieved sixth overall, ousting the (admittedly absent) Marc Marquez. A fine reward for his efforts.

10 PEDRO ACOSTA

ONE swallow does not make a summer, nor one winning season a racing legend. Yet it's impossible not to predict a gigantic future for the Spanish teenager.

Even if his results did tail off in the latter half of the year, by then Moto3's pre-eminent rookie had won five of the first ten races, including the unforgettable epic run from the pit lane to victory in Qatar, in only his second GP.

After Austria, Acosta didn't win again until the penultimate round at Portimao, but he never lost that jaunty look that speaks of the pleasure of racing, rather than a pathological need to win. The Red Bull Rookie champion had a mantra he never abandoned – to have fun.

At that Portuguese race, he showed his spirit with cheeky pre-race exchanges with Dennis Foggia, whose own brilliant efforts seriously threatened to upend the Spaniard's dream year.

Acosta's debut possessed all the hallmarks of the budding genius.

THE STATE OF RACING
CARRYING ON REGARDLESS

MotoGP gave every appearance of thriving in spite of it all in 2021. MICHAEL SCOTT looks into the ups and downs behind the scenes...

Above: Assen was one favourite track back on the calendar, with spectators socially distanced.

Right: Carmelo Ezpeleta and his star turn, Valentino Rossi. How much will racing feel his loss?
Photos: Gold & Goose

IN a second year of worldwide pandemic, MotoGP coped rather better than in the first. Racing was spread over a longer period, from March to November, rather than from July. And there were 18 full rounds, up from fourteen-and-a-half (the Qatar round only for the smaller classes). And while the premier class had made no trips outside Europe the previous year, in 2021 there were two – to Qatar and the USA.

Dorna are to be congratulated for not only keeping the show on the road, but also expanding it. At the same time, some easing of restrictions during the course of the season reinstated at least a semblance of normality, with crowds returning in ever increasing numbers, including full grandstands for the finale at Valencia.

And with technical development frozen for another year, the racing was ultra-close and reliably thrilling again, with all three GP titles, WorldSBK and BSB finalised over the last three races of the year.

There were fraught moments, and shifting sands on a calendar that had started out with 21 rounds when announced in November, 2020. Revisions came in January, July and August, with the final calendar confirmed only in September. This was thanks to postponement and cancellations, especially to the flyaway rounds.

The original calendar included not only Finland's Kymiring, which had come and gone the previous year and would do so again in 2021, but also Argentina, the USA, Japan, Thailand, Australia and Malaysia. Of these, only the US round survived.

The lost races were replaced with doubled-up events at Losail, Portugal, the Red Bull Ring and Misano. Portugal had not even been on the first calendar, but subsequently had races at the start and end of the year, at the popular Portimao circuit.

There were welcome returns to Assen, Mugello, Silverstone and the Sachsenring, as well as CoTA.

Also welcomed by some, obliged to spend long periods away from home because of quarantine restrictions, the longest ever midsummer break – a yawning five-weekend gap between the Dutch TT in June and the Styrian GP in August. This was less popular with the riders, who feared race rustiness in a year when testing was strictly restricted, with one day each after the rounds at Jerez and Catalunya, and two after the first Misano race.

The outlook for 2022 was far from certain when a provisional calendar was announced in November. Doubts notwithstanding, Dorna essayed the longest and the most ambitious calendar yet: expanded to 22 races, with all the events missed in 2021 back on the card, plus a new one at Mandalika in Indonesia, and (again) Finland.

Missing in 2021 and for the foreseeable future, Brno, no longer considered financially viable, given the need for a full resurfacing. The loss of a fine sweeping track with fast corners is just that – a loss, and while the Kymiring is no substitute, there are hopes that Mandalika will offer MotoGP bikes a new place to stretch their legs.

The ambition counters the negative aspect of a signal event: finally, the long-deferred retirement of Valentino Rossi. On the one hand, the former nine-times champion's retention of a factory saddle had been blocking the path for younger riders – including the ever increasing number benefiting from training in his burgeoning VR46 team structure and training ranch. On the other, his continued presence guaranteed the maintenance of MotoGP's unprecedented fan base, cutting across barriers of class, gender, geography and predilection.

Rossi's departure was celebrated with reverence and sadness. Now it is time for racing to face a question that has been waiting in the wings ever since there was a threat that he might switch to F1, after testing with Ferrari on several occasions between 2004 and 2010. What will happen when Valentino goes?

Now we will find out. But Dorna's hope mirrors that of Rossi himself, when he switched from dominant Honda to underdogs Yamaha in 2004, to prove that "the rider is more important than the motorcycle". The need now is to prove that the sport matters more than the rider.

Danger on the Road to MotoGP

An uncomfortable undercurrent pervaded the latter half of the 2021 season – deep disquiet, already fostered by Moto3 racing so close as to be frightening to watch, and driven home by a trio of fatal accidents. The victims were all just teenagers, two of them still on the lower rungs of the ladder that Dorna had put together over recent years – the so-called Road to MotoGP.

This occasioned sombre soul searching, and a hasty rewrite of rules and protocol for all levels of racing. It was a sobering reminder of the serious perils that accompany the racing of motorcycles for fun.

Dorna's Road to MotoGP programme gathered extra strength during 2021. The various feeder series – CEV Repsol Moto3 'Junior World Championship', Red Bull Rookies Cup, Idemitsu Asia Talent Cup, the Northern Talent Cup and the Honda British Talent Cup – gained a junior sibling.

In January, the FIM MiniGP series was announced. This is open to riders between the ages of 10 and 14, racing identical Ohvale GP-0 160 bikes – shrunken track-racers with 155.5cc engines and four-speed gearboxes. A minimum of eight races on karting tracks culminated in a final at the Valencia GP. The title went to 11-year-old Spaniard Izan Rodriguez Alvarez.

Some three weeks earlier, shock and dismay at a third fatal accident involving a teenage rider had triggered a special Permanent Bureau meeting, which announced limitations in the opposite direction – raising minimum age limits and limiting grid sizes over the forthcoming two years.

The contrast spoke clearly of a real dilemma.

There is the wish to find and nurture talent for the future. Beyond this, a belief that giving young riders the chance to race on fully-fledged circuits, on high-level machines and under professional supervision, and with comprehensive medical facilities, is a safer and more responsible approach than leaving it to, for example, local clubs. Or leaving them to discover their own risks – tombstoning, midnight parkour, base-jumping...

On the other hand, the pressure to perform on GP circuits, under the gaze of TV cameras, race fans and (eventually) the full MotoGP establishment, with a future career hanging in the balance, puts a heavy burden on young shoulders.

Overlying everything is a racing ethos, heavily fostered by Dorna. In recent years, all the technical regulations have been strongly biased towards equalising the level of machinery. The pay-off is the show: very close racing with unpredictable results – typified by Moto3, but apparent not only in the senior grand prix classes, but also in the junior feeder series.

High entertainment value is beyond doubt. High risk, however, goes hand in hand. Large packs of riders desperate to find elusive advantage over identically-mounted rivals, while in very close company, is a recipe for serious danger.

It could be argued that by putting show business above all other considerations, Dorna and the FIM are neglecting their duty of care. For while adults must be trusted to take responsibility for their own safety, extending this facility to those not yet considered old enough to vote, to have sex or (at the most junior level) even to have criminal responsibility needs to be seriously questioned.

Typically in these junior races, gangs of 15 or more circulate on the ragged edge within touching distance. Some call these tactical battles "high-speed games of chess". They are more like skittles. One down, and it's pure chance that he doesn't take several more with him. What happens next is a matter of blind luck. In the Moto3 race at CoTA, by sheer miracle, Pedro Acosta, Jeremy Alcoba and Andrea Migno collided at top speed, and all walked away unhurt.

It's not always like that.

Above: Back in the USA! MotoGP broke out of Europe and the Middle East to return to CoTA in Texas.

Top right: Riders gather to pay tribute to Jason Dupasquier, fatally injured at Mugello.

Above right: When is close racing too close? This clash decided the Moto3 title.

Right: Punished by a pit-lane start, Pedro Acosta (37) still won in Qatar, suggesting that lap-time grid formations might be somewhat irrelevant in Moto3.

Photos: Gold & Goose

The 2021 victims were 18-year-old Jason Dupasquier, a Moto3 rider killed in qualifying for the Italian GP at Mugello; 14-year-old Hugo Millan at Aragon Motorland in a European Talent Cup round; and 15-year-old Supersport 300 rider Dean Berta Vinales at Jerez.

In each case, the rider fell and then was hit by at least one following rider. This is how most racing fatalities occur. Of the past four in GP racing – Shoya Tomizawa (2010), Marco Simoncelli (2011), Luis Salom (2016) and Dupasquier (2021), only Salom was not struck by following bikes. The one thing the safety equipment cannot mitigate.

Several suggestions surfaced in the wake of these tragedies. Allowing more engine tuning would create a difference that good riders could exploit; going further, engines with narrower power bands (reminiscent of the old two-strokes) would be more difficult to ride, again giving better riders a chance not only to shine, but also to escape from lesser-talented rivals presently able to stay with them.

Former MotoGP rider Jurgen van den Goorbergh, presently shepherding 15-year-old son Zonta through the Spanish national Moto3 'Junior World Championship', offered a more detailed solution.

Interviewed in *Motor Sport* magazine by MOTOCOURSE contributor Mat Oxley, he proposed closer-ratio upper gearing to reduce the need for slipstreaming. Presently, he explained, Moto3 bikes have the first four gears set for the corners (a choice of two different ratios is available for each gear), but fifth and sixth widely spaced. Sixth is essentially too tall, except for slipstreaming, making it essential for ultra-close company in races, and more especially in qualifying. Technical regulations could reduce this tendency, the Dutch rider suggested.

The FIM and Dorna did respond, with a special meeting of the Permanent Bureau after the third fatal accident. The result was a series of higher minimum age limits, and other regulations intended to reduce the dangers. A step in the right direction, though it is somewhat oxymoronic that while a rider below the age of 18 is considered too young for the Moto3 world championship, it is acceptable for 14-year-olds to race Moto3 bikes on the same circuits in feeder series.

As well as plans to research improved impact protection, particularly for the chest and neck, and upgrading communication to riders to warn of a crash ahead the grist of the new regulations was as follows:

In 2022:

- Talent Cups and junior Moto3 races will raise minimum age to 13, with a maximum of 30 on each grid.

- The minimum age for the Red Bull Rookies Cup raised to 14.

- The Junior World Championship age raised from 14 to 15, with a maximum grid of 32.

- World Supersport 300 minimum age from 15 to 16; 32 grid maximum.

- Airbags compulsory in all FIM championships.

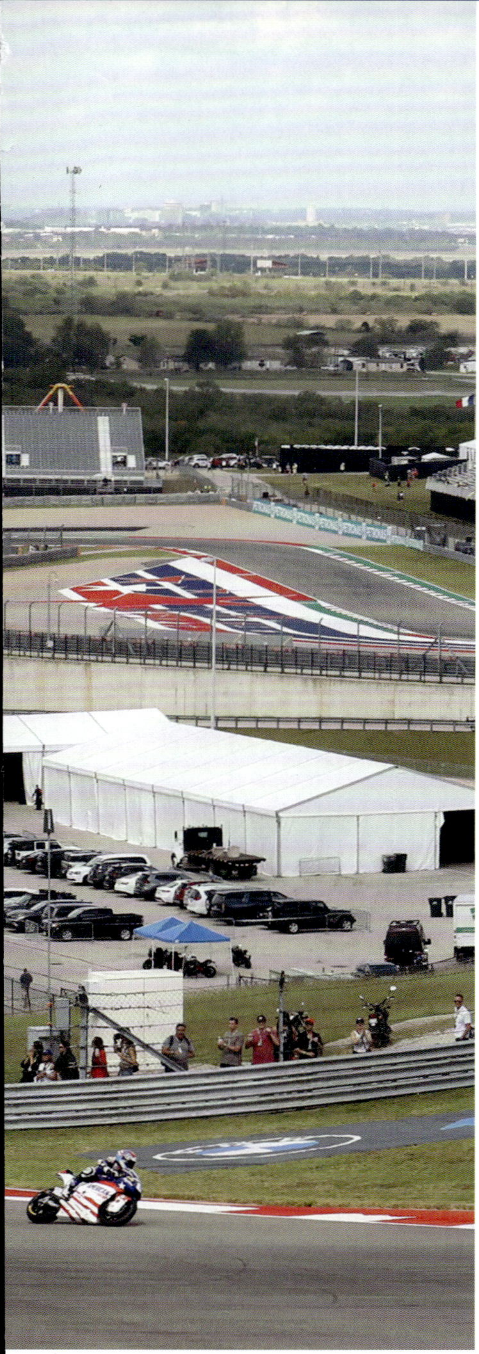

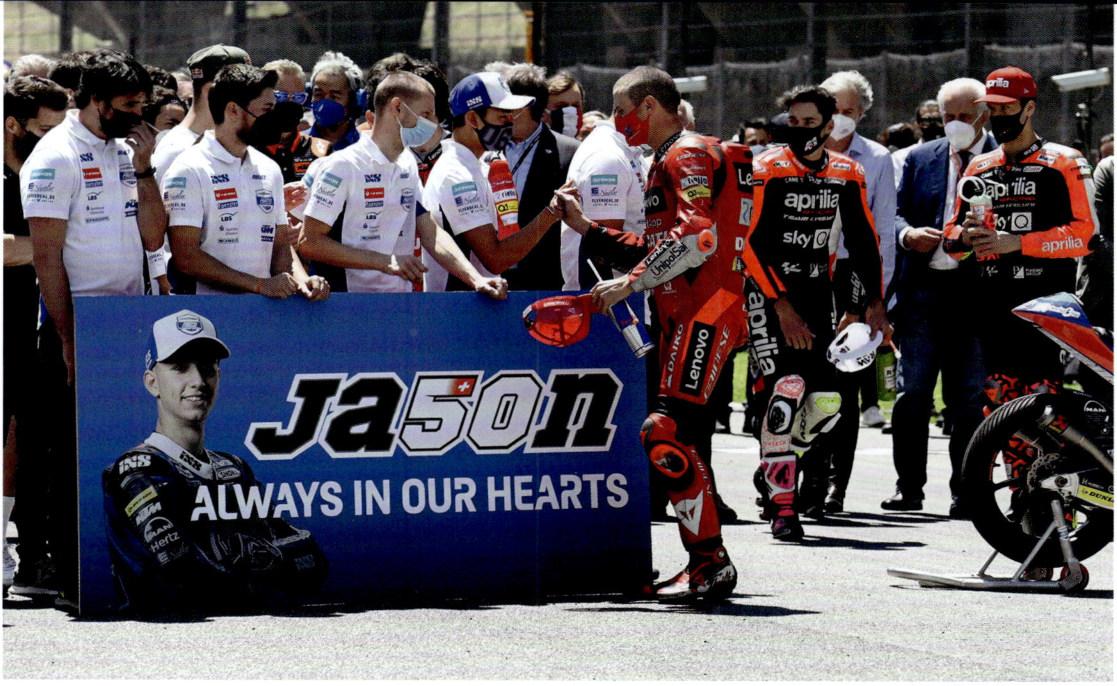
Ja50n
ALWAYS IN OUR HEARTS

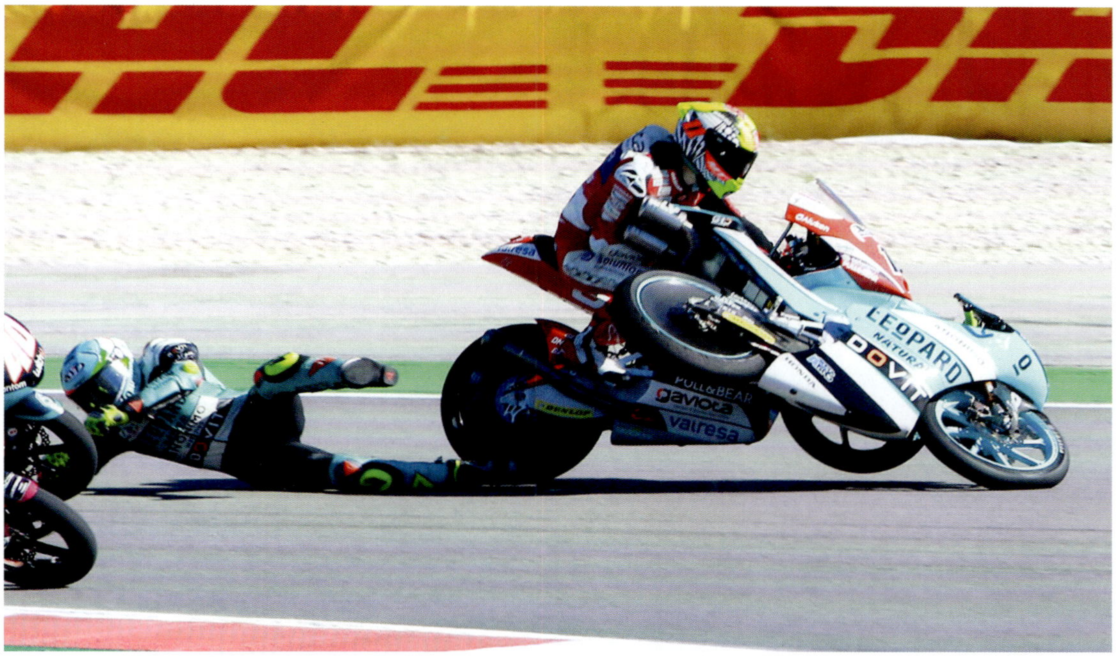

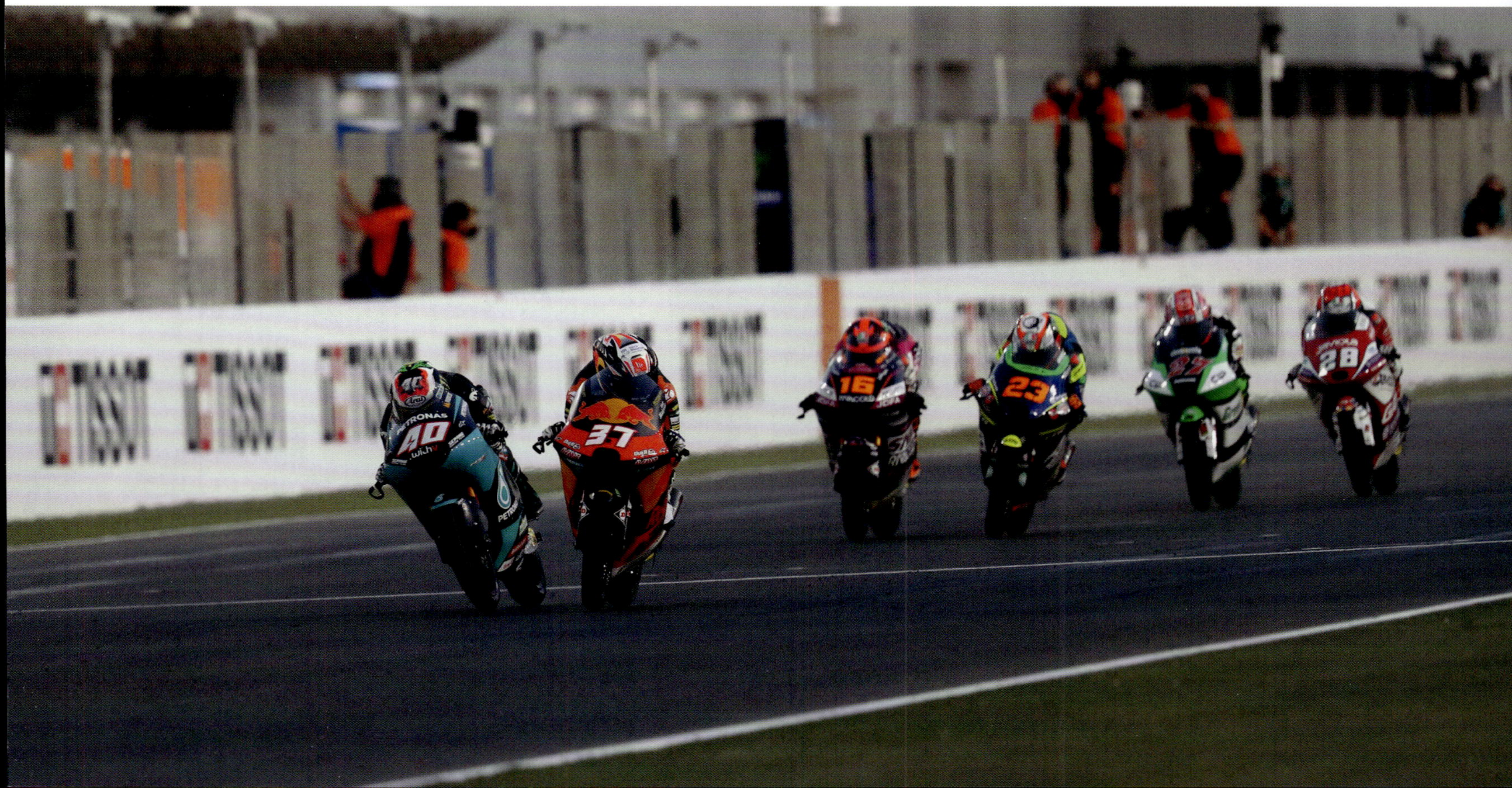

Above: Mind the green paint! Moto3 riders use all the track and more at the start of the Styrian Grand Prix.

Right: Darryn Binder (40), Deniz Oncu (53) and Andrea Migno (16) lead the slipstreaming Moto3 pack at Aragon. All three riders had on-track incidents during 2021. Binder was disqualified, Oncu suspended for two races.
Photos: Gold & Goose

18   THE STATE OF RACING

In 2023:

- Minimum age of 14 for all racing at any grand prix-type circuits.
- Minimum age for all MotoGP World Championship classes raised to 18; Motos 2 and 3 currently 16.
- Moto3 Junior World Championship and Moto2 European Championship minimum age 16.
- Red Bull Rookies Cup minimum age increased to 15.
- World Supersport Championship minimum age increased to 18.

Results by decree

For several years, improving safety in Moto3 has exercised on-track race direction, and in 2021, there was a further escalation in attempts to reduce the intrinsic risk, with heavier penalties, including a handful of disqualifications and suspensions. All part of a pattern of increased intervention by the FIM Stewards Panel, now in its third year of operation.

This intervention was seldom popular and often derided, especially when it altered the results of races, which happened frequently. Only once was a seemingly nonsensical decision reversed, after Miguel Oliveira was demoted from second place in the Italian GP for a somewhat notional infringement of track limits on the last lap, then restored after it was decided that he had gained no advantage. Other cases that seemed to fit the same criterion were left uncorrected, however, and accusations of inconsistency (always a bugbear for racing authorities) ensued.

Critics keenly appreciated the irony that Freddie Spencer, permanent head of the panel, would have been denied his classic 1983 500-class championship win over Kenny Roberts had he been in place to enforce the rules that are currently applied so rigidly. He had gained advantage by exceeding track limits in the Swedish Grand Prix, in the process forcing Roberts off the track. He effectively gained six points from Roberts with his race win, and won the championship by just two.

Riders' hopes that Spencer, with his depth of experience, might have brought some empathetic latitude to the interpretation of the rules were dashed once again.

There were two main areas where authority was exercised – exceeding track limits, and (for Moto3) going slow and bunching up in qualifying.

Exceeding track limits was always going to be controversial. In earlier times, straying over the paint had imposed its own penalties – up to and often including crashing. Modern track design, however, provides an area of green-painted hard paving beyond the kerbs, an effective safety measure for a rider running wide, but potentially also offering faster cornering lines or overtaking opportunities. It is to prevent this exploitation that track-limits rules were introduced, and tightened up still further in 2021.

Previously, the verdicts had followed judgement by Race Direction and/or the stewards looking at TV images, increasingly from cameras "placed and dedicated specifically for track-limits policing" at trouble spots, according to a statement from Race Direction. Until the end of 2020, the criterion had been that both tyres had to be completely on the green. If only one tyre had touched the kerb, no punishment.

By then, a system of using a pressure-detection tube installed in the track, at particularly sensitive points, was already being tested. The difference was that it reacted as soon as a tyre touched it. "Due to this change, it was decided, for consistency and uniformity, to change the criteria of Track Limits" for 2021. Now, if any part of a tyre just touched the green, that was enough.

The result was qualifying laps being scrubbed for the most minor of transgressions, while in races, an accumulation of transgressions would earn a long-lap or a time penalty. Most controversially, transgressions on the final lap would earn an automatic penalty, generally losing one place. There was room for exceptions, as for example when a rider was pushed over the edge through no fault of his own. In general, however, it was felt that more personal rather than purely electronic judgement calls would have been welcomed.

As for trying to stop Moto3 riders loitering in the hope of picking up a slipstream, this continued to have much in common with trying to herd cats. Partly because of the technical reasons of gearing outlined earlier, and partly by the nature of the beast, gaining a slipstream was more or less essential for a good qualifying position. Riders were unable to stop themselves. In consequence, the authorities started hitting the cats progressively harder.

Punishments of single or double long-lap penalties were dished out liberally, with stronger sanctions always available. Just to underline that, at only the second GP in Qatar, seven Moto3 riders were given starts from the pit lane. That one of them, Pedro Acosta, went on to win the race only served to prove that risking sanction in search of a better qualifying position was not necessarily very worthwhile – but the practice continued.

Calls to change the qualifying system also continued, one suggestion being that grid positions could be determined by an average of each rider's best laps over free practice sessions. Only slightly less effective, if essentially facetious, was the notion that riders could be arranged in alphabetical order, with the front row initial changing race by race to give everyone – from Pedro Acosta to Kaito Toba (2021's alphabetical extremes) a chance up front.

The other punishments concerned dangerous riding, and the most salutary was a two-race suspension applied to Deniz Oncu, after his swerve on the main straight at CoTA caused a terrifying three-rider crash. The rider was aggrieved, and the notion that this was somewhat random was reinforced by footage showing that one of the crash victims, Jeremy Alcoba, had swerved in apparently an even more deliberate and dangerous manner earlier in the race, but had escaped unpunished.

APPRECIATIONS

FAUSTO GRESINI 1961–2021

FAUSTO GRESINI did not make it. Hospitalised on 27th December, he passed away on 23rd February in Bologna, following complications caused by the coronavirus. The disease had caused a severe lung infection, and after a worsening of his condition, the former rider had to surrender.

It is difficult to define Fausto Gresini. A superlative rider, twice world champion, he was also a perceptive talent scout and exemplary team manager. His passion for motorcycling united all the moments of his life like a thin red line.

Born in Imola in 1961, he first set foot in the world championship paddock in 1982, on an MBA. It was not a particularly fortunate debut it has to be said, but he had the right stuff and would soon prove it as a 125 protagonist for more than a decade.

In 1985, he won his first title with Garelli. The following year, he was beaten by his team-mate, Luca Cadalora, but Fausto made a comeback (with interest) in 1987, taking his second world championship by winning ten consecutive races out of the 11 on the calendar, only because in the GP of Portugal (curiously held in Spain), he was forced to retire due to a puncture.

Out injured in 1988, he subsequently moved to Aprilia, scoring one podium. In 1990, he changed bikes again, to Honda, the company with which he would finish his racing career. He shared his pit with a very young Loris Capirossi, but suffered an early injury. Loris won the championship in the last race, thanks also to help from Fausto, who did everything he could to slow down Dutch rival Hans Spaan.

Over the next two years, Fausto was runner-up in the championship; then after two more years, he retired. In 132 races, he took two championships, 21 wins, 47 podiums and 17 pole positions.

The best was yet to come, however. While Fausto had been a magician of the small-displacement categories, his debut as a team manager took place in the 500 class, with Honda and Alex Barros in 1997. The first podium came immediately.

In 1999, the Gresini team made its debut in the 250 class, with reigning champion Capirossi.

In the following year came the arrival of a rider whom Honda cared a lot about: Daijiro Kato, a pure talent who won four races that season, and Gresini Racing's first title. The partnership continued in MotoGP in 2002, with the Japanese rider winning the Rookie of the Year title.

Then, in the first race of 2003, at Suzuka, Fausto had to face a terrible moment when Kato lost his life.

Sete Gibernau took up the baton for the team, and in subsequent years, the Spaniard became one of Valentino Rossi's main rivals, even though he raced for a private team. Marco Melandri was also able to get to grips with the Honda, and the Gresini team became one of the benchmarks in the premier class.

Many riders raced in Fausto's team, including Colin Edwards, Toni Elias, Alex de Angelis, Alvaro Bautista and, of course, Marco Simoncelli.

The understanding between Fausto and Sic was immediately perfect, and together they thrilled many fans worldwide, before the tragic accident in Sepang in 2011.

Simoncelli's death was another hard blow for Fausto, who nevertheless found the strength to continue, and in 2015, Aprilia chose his structure for its return to MotoGP.

By now, the Gresini team had expanded to operate in all three categories, with success in each. In addition to taking the 250 title with Kato, it won the debut Moto2 title in 2010 with Toni Elias, its first world title in Moto3 with Jorge Martin in 2018, and the MotoE crown with Matteo Ferrari in 2019.

The Gresini family have continued the team in his name, a legacy that Fausto has left to the entire world of motorcycling – a priceless gift.

Paolo Scalera
Founder, GPOne.com

PAUL SMART 1943–2021

MOTORCYCLE racing was going through profound changes in the early 1970s. The burgeoning Japanese industry was beginning to build a new generation of power-crazed big two-strokes that were ripping into the establishment, and road-racing was taking off in the United States, presaging an invasion of American riders..

Englishman PAUL SMART was in the thick of the action, and a significant contributor not only to machine development, but also the changes in riding style required to accommodate motorcycles whose tyres, frames and suspension were no match for the new levels of horsepower.

Where old-school racers sat firmly in the seat and essayed smooth, sweeping cornering lines, Smart could take credit for initiating the knee-out (and subsequently knee-down) style, of hanging off, shifting body weight inboard to reduce lean angles; and of exploiting point-and-squirt cornering to ride around handling weaknesses.

Already a successful short-circuit, endurance and TT rider, developing this new technique, Smart won major races in Britain, Europe and the USA, where he rode F750 Suzuki and Kawasaki tyre-shredding monsters to great effect. Ironically, among the two-strokes' prominent victims were the BSA/Triumph three-cylinder 750s. Smart had played an important role in these bikes' earlier success, as a Triumph factory rider.

He rode for Triumph in the UK and at Daytona, and subsequently for Suzuki and Kawasaki also in the US. Yet his most memorable achievement came in Italy.

Smart took the then-new 750 V-twin Ducati, which had evolved from an unsuccessful 500cc GP racer, to victory in the inaugural Imola 200 race in Italy, thereby playing a pivotal role in establishing the Bologna firm's credentials as pre-eminent sports-bike manufacturers.

That iconic machine, with its desmodromic valve gear and distinctive glass-fibre fuel tank with transparent sighting strip down the side, was the basis for every road-going Ducati V-twin ever since.

Smart was delighted when the factory created a limited-edition Paul Smart Replica in 2006, and further tribute bikes thereafter, and the grateful factory supplied him with motorcycles ever after.

The Imola classic took place in 1972. That same year, among other successes, Smart won the Mallory Park Race of the Year, riding a Seeley-Kawasaki, and on the same machine, the Ontario Classic in the USA. The next year, he joined Suzuki, and in 1974, with Barry Sheene, helped to race-develop the new and then very fast, but very unreliable, square-four RG500 Suzuki GP bike.

Like all British racers in that era, Smart rode in the shadow of Sheene, his brother-in-law, for he had married Barry's older sister, Maggie. The natural rivalry between them did not overcome the family ties.

Smart was riding his Ducati Monster when he was killed instantly in a road collision on 27th October. The crash occurred not far from his home in Kent, near Brands Hatch, where he had first started racing in the mid-1960s.

He is survived by his wife Maggie, daughter Paula and son Scott, who became technical director of WorldSBK after pursuing his own national and international racing career.

REINHOLD ROTH 1953–2021

TRIPLE 250 grand prix winner REINHOLD ROTH, riding a works HB Honda NSR250 in 1990 at the Rijeka GP, was fighting in a typically close seven-strong lead pack when they ran into Australian straggler Darren Milner, who was cruising back to the pits because it had started to rain. The front-runners swerved off the racing line, but Roth's view was blocked. He crashed into the rear of Milner's Aprilia at around 170km/h. The 37-year-old German suffered a fractured skull base and a third-degree traumatic brain injury..

Primitive medical equipment, including a lack of oxygen, delayed Roth's resuscitation, leaving him in a coma for days. In spite of severe brain damage, thanks to constant nursing and the care of his wife, Elfriede, he survived for 31 years.

Roth suffered several health setbacks. "Reinhold was mostly in a good mood; he liked to laugh and call out to everyone he saw on the street. He often fought for his life. And I fought with him for 31 years, but his strength had run out," said his widow.

Championship runner-up in 1987 and 1989, in the wake of the success of five-times world champion Toni Mang, Roth played a significant role in the revival of motorcycle sport in Germany.

Popular with everyone, Roth had no enemies and many fans, having worked his way to the top of the world from privateer through the German and European championships to the 250 world championship. He also made his mark in the 500cc world championship in 1984, with a best of seventh in Austria, riding his own three-cylinder Honda RS500.

Nicknamed 'Jointie' because he smoked one cigarette after another for years, he gave up the habit after coming second in the championship for the first time – but sometimes he puffed a whistle in its place.

Rest in peace, Reinhold. And forgive me that we didn't visit you as often in the last 30 years as we wanted to.

Gunther Wiesinger
Editor, speedweek.com

LOOKING BACK AT A LEGEND…

Massively talented, impish, a deadly on-track rival, Valentino Rossi retired in 2021 after a record-breaking career that spanned 26 years and delivered 115 wins. MICHAEL SCOTT considers the man who was synonymous with motorcycle racing…

Above: Rossi at 42 – a legend in his own lifetime.
Photo: Monster Energy

Top right: In the big league. A young Rossi with his mentors at Honda: Jeremy Burgess (*left*) and his father, Graziano.
Photo: Gold & Goose

Above right: The Doctor is in the house. Yellow-clad fans flock whenever Rossi appears.
Photo: Monster Energy

Above far right: Unforgettable image. Rossi's pit board was forever young.

Right: Rossi and his M1 – he made the number '46' his own.
Photos: Gold and Goose

LEGENDS are not born. They are made. In this case, self-made. The raw material was already exceptional. Son of grand prix winner Graziano Rossi, Valentino had speed in his genes. What he did with it was quite exceptional. Without precedent. And likely to remain unique.

Valentino Rossi was always a brilliant racer – one of the best ever, natural talent combined with an iron will. Just look at the results.

But so much more than that: Rossi is a gigantic character – unpredictable, witty, self-assured, mischievous. A one-off, with a rascally sense of fun, able to share his *joie de vivre* and his devilment without giving any of it away.

Earning admiration with his prowess, then deploying his effortless charm, he not only elevated motorcycle racing and expanded it worldwide, but he also illuminated the sport.

As *The Times* newspaper put it, after he had announced his retirement: "It is hard to think of a more playful maverick, with wit, wickedness and a wildness that is out of kilter with media-trained mores and bores. All of this would be frippery if it were not for the breathtaking talent that made it fabulous."

Clever and astute, and commanding the brains and loyalty of his close circle – the original *Tribu dei Chihuaha* – in his home village of Tavullia, he also monetised it. With apparently natural inspiration, he built the yellow VR46 logo and 'The Doctor' nickname into a brand. It is now a comprehensive bike-racing business. Rossi became one of the top-earning sportsmen of his era.

But it doesn't go only one way. Questioned in recent years for prolonging his career beyond its natural span, blocking the way for young riders, Rossi and his cohorts at the same time created an all-new pathway to stardom for those coming behind. There are highly successful Spanish rider development programmes, but his VR46 Academy, with its training ranch near his home town, is unique, and the world's best racer training foundation. It has developed and continues to develop a legacy of Italian racing talent to perpetuate his legend.

Pecco Bagnaia is probably the most prominent graduate, but he is just one of many. Look at the top Italian riders in all three classes, and it is odds-on that they are his protégés.

Along with the new VR46 MotoGP team, which has grown through Motos 3 and 2 to a fully-fledged MotoGP squad for 2022, this echoes the sun-moon helmet logo he has espoused almost throughout his career. It speaks, he explained, of the light and dark sides of his character. So also does his legacy. Take, and once you've done so, also give.

His retirement (as one of several deadly rivals, Jorge Lorenzo, put it on the day it was announced) is epochal. Writing on Twitter, Jorge (who twice beat him to the title) said, "End of an era. On the track the four of us were just as fast, but in terms of charisma or transcendence @valeyellow46 is at the level of Jordan, Woods, Ali or Senna."

This was one of a torrent of tributes from far and wide, from fans and rivals, from all branches of motorsport, from show business and beyond. Even from the Olympic village in Tokyo…

Valentino's primrose path to glory might have been written in the stars. It had been gilded, thanks to prescient support from Aprilia and the Italian racing establishment, and also thanks to the support of Graziano.

And it had been rapid. As well as those assets, indeed, giving rise to them, was massive talent. Give him a machine –

Nastro Azzurro
ENERGIE

YAMAHA

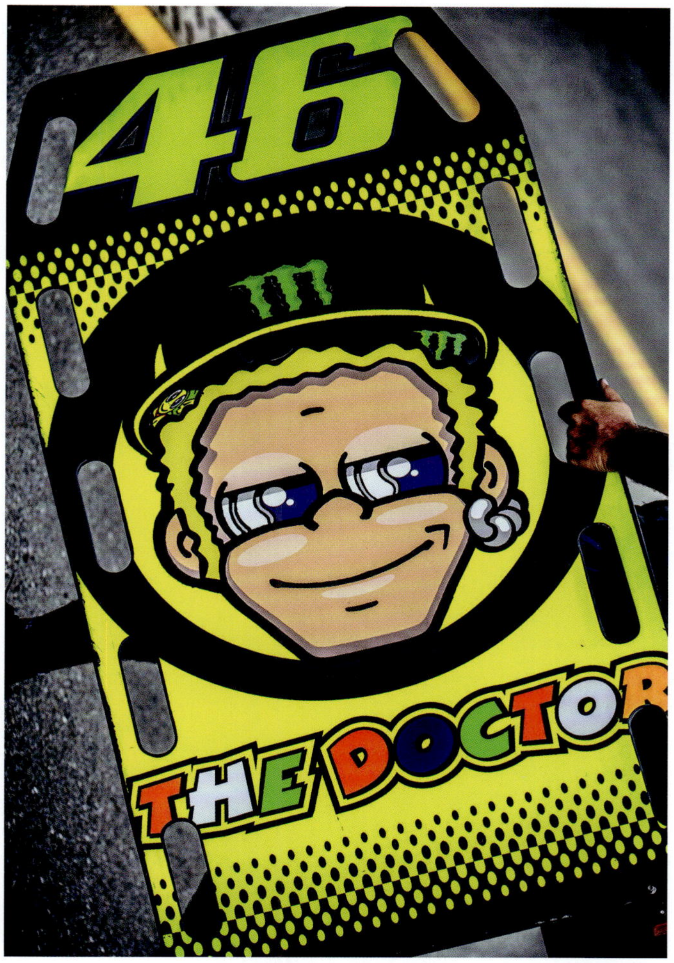
46
THE DOCTOR

YAMAHA
ENEOS
46
MONSTER ENERGY
YAMALUBE

Above: Gimlet-eyed Rossi and Biaggi in Catalunya, 2001. They had come to blows minutes before.

Above right: Preventing Gibernau from ever winning again, Jerez, 2005.

Above centre right: With Angel Nieto at Le Mans in 2008, after equalling his 90 wins.

Above centre far right: Intense. Battling team-mate Lorenzo in 2009.

Top: Welkom, 2004, and Gibernau can only watch as Rossi and Biaggi fight it out.

Top right: With Burgess during the difficult Ducati years.

Right: Downing Marquez in Malaysia in 2015.

Photos: Gold & Goose

motorcycle, go-kart, car or even (in his youth) a three-wheel two-stroke delivery 'Ape' – and he will get the best from it, without even appearing to try.

More importantly, he had the killer instinct. In spades. A ruthless streak that the cheerful charm couldn't quite conceal.

I asked him once if he had ever felt even an ounce of empathy with any beaten rival. He threw back his head and gave his trademark cackling laugh. Clearly, it had never occurred to him. Rather the reverse. He preferred to crush his rivals on and off the track.

As he said at his retirement press conference, "A real racer doesn't go racing for fun. You are there for the results. To win."

No other rider suffered quite as much at Rossi's hands as Max Biaggi, a target even before they met in the 500 class. Still on a 250, Rossi liked to poke fun at Max. When they met, it was bitter. In a physical confrontation on the steps of the podium at Catalunya in 2001, Rossi hit Max and drew blood. Max explained: "A mosquito bit me." Earlier spats paled in comparison – as when Rossi and his chums upended Max's Smart Car in the paddock one night; or his slow-down lap with a blow-up doll on the pillion, with a shirt labelled 'Claudia Schiffer' (mocking rumours that Max was dating rival super-model Naomi Campbell).

Another victim was 250 champion and MotoGP race winner Marco Melandri. They had been friends, practising motocross together and (as Marco told me) "hanging our socks to dry together on the radiator afterwards." Then Melandri made the mistake of beating Valentino on a couple of occasions. End of friendship.

A once-cordial relationship with Sete Gibernau came badly unstuck when Rossi was penalised in Qatar after his team had used scooter wheelspin to lay down rubber on his starting position. Rossi blamed Gibernau, called him a spy and announced, "He will never win another race." This was true – though he had to barge into him in the last corner at Jerez to make sure.

There were uneasy times with Yamaha team-mate Jorge Lorenzo. At first, they were on different tyre brands – Michelin and Bridgestone, and the French company insisted on a wall down the middle of the pit. Both riders were pleased to keep it there after they both began using Bridgestones, and Rossi laughed like a drain when Jorge won the 2010 US Grand Prix, but organisers played the Italian national anthem by mistake. Jorge got the last laugh, though, winning the title, then clearly the Yamaha team's number-one when Rossi rejoined in 2013.

More of a nemesis: Marc Marquez, who had professed himself a fan, but the admiration turned out to be rather one sided when Rossi unaccountably accused the Spaniard of conspiring with Lorenzo against him in 2015, then barged him off the

24 VALENTINO ROSSI PROFILE

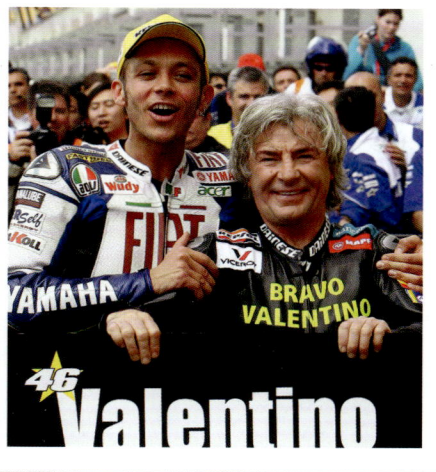

track at Sepang. The back-of-the-grid start he earned as punishment arguably cost him the championship.

The need to prevail was just an outward manifestation of a drive that had propelled him from his first outings on a go-kart, then as a pre-teen switching to minimotos, until beyond his last win in 2017 at Assen.

If it is possible to pick a defining moment from the longest world championship grand prix career (on two or four wheels), it happened not even a third of the way through.

It was a sunny afternoon outside the dusty gold-mining town of Welkom in South Africa, the fifth visit to the Phakisa Freeway race-track, for what would turn out to be the last South African Grand Prix there. Valentino – aged 24 – was already five times a champion, once each in 125 and 250, thrice in the premier class.

He was already wildly popular – his speed, skill and showmanship unsurpassed; his charm and trademark put-downs to his rivals and his post-race pantomime celebrations had made him so. But now he had taken the greatest gamble of a high-risk life. Feeling undervalued at Honda, whose engineering-bent management valued machinery more than manpower, he had jumped ship and switched to underdogs Yamaha.

"I wanted to show that it was the rider that made the difference, not the motorbike," he said.

The move, accomplished after clandestine negotiations, had been a 'do or die mission' for Yamaha, long-standing head of the racing department Lin Jarvis explained in 2021: "We hadn't won a championship for 12 years [actually 11]; we were getting beaten up by Honda. But if you take the best rider in the world and you don't succeed…"

Throughout the negotiations, Rossi had spoken about how he wanted to have fun again in racing. Yamaha responded with a hastily reconfigured M1, raised on its suspension after his early tests, powered by a crucially redesigned in-line-four engine, with revised firing intervals that emulated the more tyre-friendly power stream of a V4. This was the 'cross-plane-crank' engine conceived by engineering chief Masao Furusawa, which has been the basis of racing M1s and the sports street-bike R1 ever since.

Rossi's move was carefully managed, and one demand was that his pit crew, led by Australian Jeremy (Jerry) Burgess should accompany him. Burgess, who shepherded Valentino to all his titles, takes up the story:

"He didn't go to Yamaha without observing the Yamaha for a great part of the 2003 season, so he sort of had an idea of what he was going to be getting on." But the team staff were in a state of confusion. "None of the Italian staff had any belief … all they kept saying was, 'You'll never beat Honda, you'll never beat Honda.' Myself and the other Australians said, 'How do you know? You've never been at Honda.' Typical Italians, they'd given up before they'd even tried. And the poor Japanese were putting more and more rider aids on the bikes for riders who didn't understand anything, and making the bike far more difficult to ride.

"We sort of stripped the bike back to basics in 2004 and started again – with attitude. We didn't know where we were going to be, other than that I said to Valentino, 'If we give it our best shot, it'll force Honda to bring out everything they've got in the library, that they've been stacking away for years.'"

The simplified M1 brought a new growling exhaust note to the tracks for the opening round of 2004. And new rider Rossi put it on pole position. But the race was far from easy. He had to fight every inch of the way with bitter rival Max Biaggi, culminating in a bare-knuckle last lap. Rossi won it by less than half a second.

On the slow-down lap, he stopped, leaned the bike against the barrier and slumped on to the ground, bent forward, shoulders tumbling. It looked as though he was weeping. He took most of the rest of the year to correct that impression.

"I was laughing," he eventually disclosed gleefully.

As well he might. The achievement was far greater than one race win, and one more humiliation of Biaggi. Yamaha's Jarvis said, "He gave the faith back to all in Yamaha Racing."

VALENTINO ROSSI PROFILE 25

VALENTINO ROSSI – A CAREER IN NUMBERS

IN the longest active career ever recorded in grand prix racing, Valentino Rossi claimed 115 wins in all classes. Only fellow Italian Giacomo Agostini has more, 122.

Agostini (15) and Angel Nieto (13) exceed his total of nine championships; Mike Hailwood and Carlo Ubbiali are equal on nine.

His record of 230 consecutive race starts ended when he missed the Mugello GP after breaking his leg in 2010, and it was broken by compatriot Andrea Dovizioso six years ago.

He leads all his motorcycle rivals in all other significant statistics:
- 89 premier-class wins – to Agostini's 68
- 432 grand prix starts
- 372 premier-class starts
- First to take back-to-back premier-class victories with different manufacturers (Honda and Yamaha, 2003 and 2004).
- 199 premier-class podiums
- 235 podiums in all classes
- 6,357 points scored in all classes
- On four wheels, he is seven times winner of the Monza Rally Show.

Above: Osvaldo the Chicken rides pillion in 1998. Just one of Rossi's pantomime co-stars.

Above right: Fresh-faced and dangerous – Valentino in 1996.
Photos: Gold & Goose

Above far right: En route to the 250 title in 1999.

Facing page:
Top: Rossi on the way to his first GP win at Brno in 1996.

Centre: On the 500cc Honda in 2001 – Rossi took the first of seven premier-class titles.

Bottom: It's a carve-up. Rossi needed extra track to beat Stoner's Ducati at Laguna Seca in 2008.
Photos: Gold & Goose

A faith that the factory generously repaid with their long continued support in the later unsuccessful years of his career.

Rossi had come to MotoGP in 1996, riding a factory-backed 125 Aprilia and taking his first win at Brno (narrowly beating multi-champion 'Aspar' Martinez, now a team owner), then the championship in 1997. His big personality had already made an impact. He was noticeable from the first moment, scootering around, flowing locks blowing in the wind, constantly laughing with his rivals, a frequent presence in the press room.

On to 250 in 1998 for two years with Aprilia, and more of the same: race wins in his first year, the championship in the second. By now, he was an accomplished entertainer, but he'd learned one other thing – to be more careful with the press. His fellow Italian journalists might have seemed friendly, but they would not hesitate to bite.

It was one aspect of a growing worldliness that he kept well hidden behind his growing penchant for post-race play acting, and beneath an ever changing variety of hairstyles and colours – including a memorable half white/half black version.

In 2000, the big time welcomed the burgeoning new star. Riding in an independent Honda team, inheriting not only the mighty NSR Honda that had taken Mick Doohan to five successive titles but also the highly successful, Jerry Burgess-led pit crew (left at a loose end by Mick's career-ending crash in 1999), Rossi had arrived where he was meant to be.

Again, one year to learn – the first of two 2000 race wins coming in Britain – and one year to win. But that was just the start of it. Those were the first of 89 race wins, 2001 the first of seven championships – four more over the coming years,

a further two in 2008 and 2009. The first three were with Honda, the next four with Yamaha.

To list his achievements would take pages. A small selection draws a clear picture.

There was his domination at two of the fastest classic tracks, where a rider can really give a MotoGP bike its head. At Mugello, Rossi won every year from 2002 to 2008; at Australia's Phillip Island, he owned the circuit from 2001 to 2005.

He also bestraddled the transition from two-stroke to four-stroke, taking the last ever 500cc title on the formidable Honda NSR honed and polished by Doohan; then the first MotoGP on the mighty 990cc V5 Honda RC211V.

One could go on, but for this writer, present at every one of his 115 race wins in all three classes, as well as the 2004 South African GP, two more achievements stand out.

The first followed on from Welkom, when he won the 2004 championship for Yamaha to add to three won on a Honda. Only three riders in history have won the premier title on different makes of motorcycle, and all three were legends: Geoff Duke, Giacomo Agostini and Eddie Lawson. Only Lawson did so in consecutive years. And now also Rossi.

The other was the Australian GP of 2003. Valentino was already champion, so he could afford to relax, but he planned to win. It was the wake of Barry Sheene's death, and Rossi acknowledged Barry as his true predecessor – a gifted entertainer who had taken bike racing beyond its niche boundaries. He planned a celebration in the event that he won, taking one of the bed sheets from his hotel and painting Sheene's number '7' on it. "Sorry, hotel," he said afterwards.

He took control of the race, a little clear of a big brawl behind him, comprising Hayden, Melandri, Capirossi, Gibernau, and briefly also Troy Bayliss and Max Biaggi, before the former knocked the latter off. But one of his passes to get there had inadvertently been under a yellow flag. Ten-second penalty.

That forced him to show the full measure of his ability. Where usually he was content at least to make races look close, in the interests of entertainment, now he needed to make a margin. It was, he said later, the first race that he had ridden flat out for the full distance. He won by a country mile, adding almost another five seconds to the ten he needed to make sure Capirossi was only second, and he could display his painted bed sheet.

On and off the track, Rossi was always an entertainer. The value of pleasing the crowd was something that he not only understood better than any successful rider before him, and probably since, but also was able to accomplish. He had a real gift. He was already working on the cult of personality from his earliest GP years, on a 125 in 1996 and 1997.

In his first years in 125, in a nod to his many Japanese rivals and an early demonstration of his awareness of the importance of branding, he adopted the nickname 'Rossifumi'. Later, this was changed to 'Valentinik', after a Disney character, before he adopted his permanent nickname, 'The Doctor', in 2001.

Entertainment was something he celebrated at the announcement of his retirement: "The difference between me and other great riders – I was able to bring a lot of people close to motorcycle racing. I did things to switch on the emotion, and I entertain a lot of people on Sunday. I am very proud. I think for this, I am a legend."

Some of that entertainment came just from the way he raced. He was never less than committed and spectacular. Classic overtaking moves were a hallmark. Some were especially memorable:

• On Max Biaggi at Suzuka, after his rival had ridden him on to the grass on the main straight, Vale went around the outside at the first corner and flipped him the bird as he went by.

• On Casey Stoner at Laguna Seca, where he took the second apex at the Corkscrew a metre or two inside the white line, on the dirt. A bitter Stoner commented, "I lost some respect for Valentino today."

• On Jorge Lorenzo at Catalunya, after he had seemed beaten on a breathtaking last lap, with an unprecedented inside swerve into the last corner…

• On Sete Gibernau at Jerez, barging his rival wide at the last hairpin, then laughing at his discomfort on the podium.

Sometimes it was pre-planned and heavily orchestrated postrace pantomime, devised with his fan club. These were often painfully cheesy, but unfailingly crowd pleasing – whether it be putting a man in a chicken suit on the pillion, rushing to the lavatory, being given a mock speeding ticket or miming working on a chain gang. Other riders have imitated, none has come close (though Lorenzo had to be rescued from drowning after jumping into a lake at Jerez in 2010).

All of it built his brand, but also benefited all of racing. Rossi's fame spread far beyond the fans who would have been dedicated with or without him. Cal Crutchlow summed it up: "No matter where you are in the world, when you say motorbikes, people just say, 'Valentino Rossi'."

And vice versa. In this way, Rossi made a huge one-man contribution to the growth of MotoGP. Among the riders, he took the lion's share of the benefit – as Barry Sheene had done before him. But he pulled the rest along behind him; everybody's earning power increased. More importantly, he helped Dorna to get racing through the perilous financial times after the loss of tobacco sponsorship and in the 2008 financial crisis, making it possible for the series to expand internationally

VALENTINO ROSSI PROFILE 27

Above: Rossi's last premier-class podium came at Jerez in 2020, leaving him just one short of the magic 200.
Photo: Monster Energy Yamaha MotoGP

Top centre: Third at Le Mans in 2011 was a rare podium for Rossi with Ducati.

Above centre right: Rossi's only major injury was breaking his leg at Mugello in 2010.

Centre right: Valencia, 2006, and a last-race crash hands the championship to Nicky Hayden.
Photos: Gold & Goose

Right: A second career on four wheels beckons for Rossi, "but not at the same level."
Photo: Monster Energy

Top far right: The eyes have it.
Photo: Whit Bazemore Photography

as never before. Be it in Rio de Janeiro or Australia, China or the USA, the instantly recognisable figure on the publicity posters always wore the number '46'.

It wasn't all plain sailing, which underlines his persistence and makes the unprecedented length of his career all the more remarkable.

Most ghastly, the accident that killed Marco Simoncelli in Malaysia in 2011. Marco was a friend and protégé, but he fell right under the wheels of Rossi's Ducati and Colin Edwards's Yamaha.

There were well-publicised tax problems in 2007/8, concerning his somewhat mythical residence in London in 2000. These were settled by negotiation with the Italian authorities, for a payment variously reported as between 18 million and 51 million euros.

There was the blight on his charmed injury-free life, when he broke his leg in practice at Mugello in 2010. It was a double fracture, but he was back in action just 41 days later, setting a record for the forced pace of his recovery and missing only four races. He suffered a lesser leg fracture in a training crash in 2017, but otherwise has had a remarkable ability to bounce back from crashes.

Then, in 2008/9, there was the perceived betrayal by Yamaha, when they signed up Jorge Lorenzo as his team-mate. Famously, there was a wall down the middle of the factory pit box, nominally because they were on different tyre brands, but also because Rossi refused to share data. He announced that if they kept Lorenzo, he would leave – and that is what happened.

His move to Ducati for 2011 and 2012 was contrived as revenge, and as a chance to prove to 2007 Ducati champion Casey Stoner that the subsequent lack of success for the Desmosedici could be fixed, with the right rider and pit crew developing the bike. That plan went badly wrong. While Stoner smashed the title on his new Honda, Valentino struggled to make the podium on the recalcitrant beast.

At his retirement conference, however, he declined to express any regret: "The Ducati was very difficult, but it was a great challenge – an Italian rider on an Italian bike."

He was, he said, "a little bit sad not to win ten championships. I lose two times in the last race, so I think I deserve ten."

He was also regretful that he would not have the chance to race alongside his half-brother, Luca Marini, in the new VR46 team in 2022, but the decision to retire was irrevocable: "To ride in the team next year … would be a good project for two or three years. But for just one year, it could be dangerous."

The decision had been some time in the making.

"In 2018, I didn't win a race, but I was strong. 2019 started well, but then something changed. And in 2020, after the end of the season, I was in trouble. It was hard to stay with the young guys. Now the guys are athletes, they change a lot.

"During this season, the results were less than I thought. But I feel like a rider or driver all life long, so I think I will race cars for the next years … though not at the same level.

"I will miss the life of an athlete, to get up every morning to train. I will miss the team and the emotion of Sunday morning, the two hours after you wake up and feel nervous for the coming race.

"But especially, I will miss to ride a MotoGP bike – it really is a great feeling."

Racing will miss him more: the armies of fans, the yellow-draped grandstands, the Doctor-clad intergenerational devotees to whom Rossi is everything about MotoGP. We move on to a new era. It won't necessarily be worse, and in many ways it will be better.

But it definitely won't be quite the same without him.

28 VALENTINO ROSSI PROFILE

WHAT STOPPED VALENTINO?

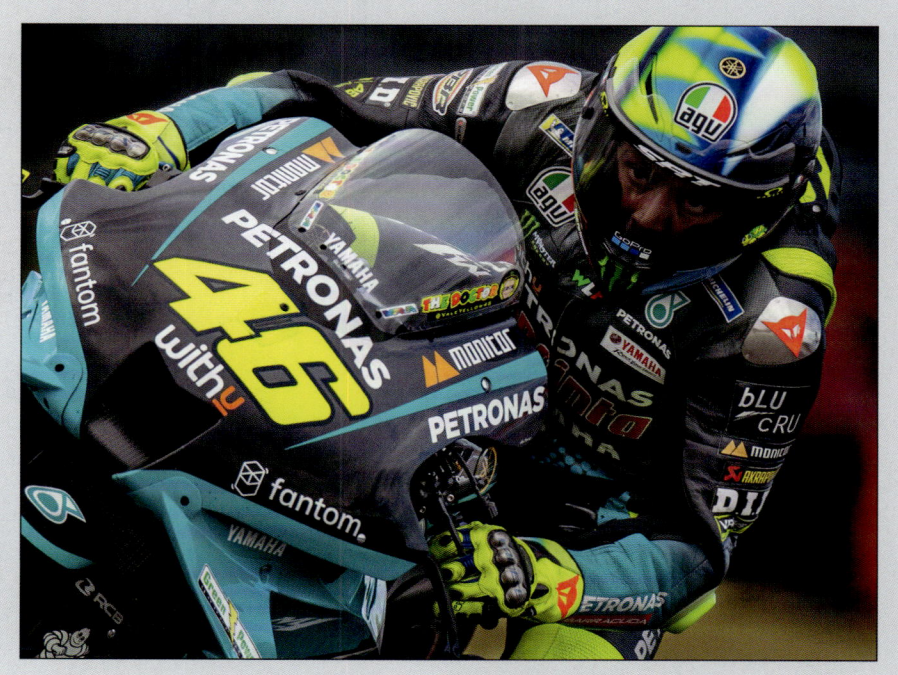

Grand prix winner and racing analyst SIMON CRAFAR explains…

SO what happened to Valentino in 2021? Age finally caught up with him, like it does us all. And by that, I mean he no longer has the ability to change and adapt like he has done so brilliantly so many times over the decades.

People who have worked with Valentino for many years point to the following attributes: passion for the sport and his job, dedication, humility in the pit box and listening to everyone before making his decision. And never giving up. Many times, he found what he needed to win at the last possible moment.

Valentino showed the ability to change and adapt brilliantly, many times over – champion on 125, 250 and 500cc two-strokes, the first four-stroke MotoGP champion, from the more upright two-stroke style to hanging right off, elbow down, he's learned how to race and to beat the best.

To me, winning first time out on the Yamaha, proving without doubt that the rider is the most important element, was a great day for all riders of all ages.

He also won on Dunlop tyres in the smaller classes, and on both Michelin and Bridgestone in the premier class. Changing tyre manufacturers means having to change both bike set-up and the way of riding it.

From my experience, I rode on Michelin from the start all the way to my first World Superbike podiums. Then at 26, I changed to Dunlop, which demanded I adapt my style. Once I had figured it out and gained more success, I received an offer to move to 500GPs, on Dunlops. The transition wasn't easy, but after a half-dozen races, I was standing on the podium next to my hero, Mick Doohan.

The year was incredible, three podiums, including a win. We changed to Michelin the next year. As the current world champion's tyre, surely it was the right move? But I was now 29. From the first test, I struggled. Everything I'd learned to get the most from the Dunlops did not work. The Michelins had to be used in a different way, with a very different bike set-up. I found I could no longer change. I realised it was the end when my team manager told me, "Simon, it's easier to change the rider than the tyres."

The ability to change and adapt becomes more difficult with age, but still Valentino surprised us, and did it right when we thought it was the end for him. Like Peter Pan, forever young. I believe that he'd be retiring with ten or even eleven championships if he hadn't dropped Jerry Burgess as crew chief in 2013. The subsequent two years when he became lost set-up-wise, yet still managed to fight for the championship, must have taken their toll. It wasn't too long after that we saw the first signs of real cracks, the beginning of the end.

Young sportsmen have wonderful natural ability and talent to adapt. Their minds are not yet set in what worked best before. They are ready and willing to invent the best ways of the future.

In 2020, MotoGP winners Danilo Petrucci and Andrea Dovizioso struggled to be consistently competitive on Michelin's new-construction rear tyre, while young Pramac riders Pecco Bagnaia and Jack Miller figured out how to adapt themselves and their machine set-up.

In recent years, the younger Yamaha riders have been able to adapt to different bike set-ups that allow the tyres to work better. Valentino, the incredible motorcycle racing chameleon, struggled to do the same.

I believe we finally saw him come to the end of his ability to fully adapt and change his style.

He admitted that he found he needed to train harder. His natural ability no longer ensured the win, and he started to see the danger – what might look dry to an 18-year-old looks wet to a 40-year-old.

Time slowly caught up with Valentino, but don't be sad. He beat all the modern-era records, including the age at which a rider can still adapt and win.

VALENTINO ROSSI PROFILE 29

TECHNICAL ESSAY

THE TYRE WHISPERERS

It's not just how a bike treats its tyres as they change during a race, but how the rider understands and exploits these nuances. KEVIN CAMERON examines why different riders obtain wildly different results from identical motorcycles…

Above: Marc Marquez quickly developed the knack of making his tyres last better.

Top right: Jorge Lorenzo earned respect for adjusting his riding style to win on a Ducati, at Mugello in 2018. Similar adjustments take place all race long.

Above right: Johann Zarco pushed the envelope a little too far in Portugal: "If it feels like you will crash, you crash."
Photos: Gold & Goose

Right: Zarco showed one-lap prowess to take pole at the Sachsenring, but was eighth in the race.
Photo: Pramac Racing

EACH make of bike in MotoGP now has just one rider capable of consistently strong finishes. Many riders have won races owing to the very high levels of skill and equipment, but few can do it consistently. Why?

For years, Ducati had only Andrea Dovizioso who could finish races, despite the Ducati's tyre-burning power, and accumulate serious points. From 2004 to 2009, Yamaha had only Valentino Rossi, for team-mate Colin Edwards never connected with the M1. Ducati were famous only for making enough power to scare Honda, until Casey Stoner arrived in 2007 to win ten races and the championship.

By mid-season in 2021, Yamaha could have sent all its riders but Fabio Quartararo home, as he was leading the championship and uniquely was able to win on the motorcycle. Ditto Honda with Marc Marquez. Takaaki Nakagami and Pol Espargaro are both skilled riders, but only Marc had been able to put the Honda first.

Ducati had a squad of excellent riders, but at that halfway point, Jorge Martin was looking as though he could be consistent enough to succeed, while the current series champion, Joan Mir, had won through sheer consistency.

In 2004, Rossi's then crew chief, Jerry Burgess, had commented that a manufacturer had not done the whole job until its motorcycle could win races in the hands of more than one rider. While an attractive goal, the present facts suggest otherwise. Have motorcycles, riding styles and bike set-up all become so intensely personal and specialised that only one rider can truly connect with a given motorcycle?

In 2018, Andrea Dovizioso (Ducati rider from 2013 to 2020) said, "In MotoGP, every rider is really, really fast, but less than half the grid is able to be fast and save the tyres." Speaking of the Honda in 2019, he said, "That bike with Marc works. With other riders, it doesn't work. But the other riders aren't bad."

One aspect that can cause a talented rider to suffer poor results is the possibility of a clash between riding style and the style for which a bike has been developed. Colin Edwards, a double World Superbike champion and Superbike point-and-shoot stylist, achieved little on the corner-speed Yamaha between 2005 and 2011. That clash of styles effectively ended his career. Johann Zarco, sent to ride an immature KTM in 2019, accomplished nothing. Valentino Rossi got nowhere at Ducati – he is a corner-speeder, but the bike was a point-and-shooter. Jorge Lorenzo made the same move and adapted his style over 18 months, winning three races in 2018, only to leave the team when the relationship soured.

Poor finishes can spring from tyres lacking a sufficiently wide operating temperature range. They might work well for one group of riders, but hardly at all for another. At one Laguna Seca MotoGP, Edwards's tyres refused to come to temperature, while team-mate Rossi, staying down on his tyre edges through long corners, could generate temperature easily. Around 2010, some riders, including Lorenzo, found themselves arriving from a straight into a corner with tyres that had cooled enough to lose significant grip. Yamaha riders, compelled to draft faster bikes by lack of top speed, lost front grip as tyre temperature rose in the lead bike's hot slipstream.

Zarco, riding for Ducati in 2021, spoke of front tyre feedback: "The tyre warns you before you crash, so if it's warning you and you keep pushing, then for sure you will crash. The feedback from the tyre has changed since I first came to

30 TECHNICAL ESSAY

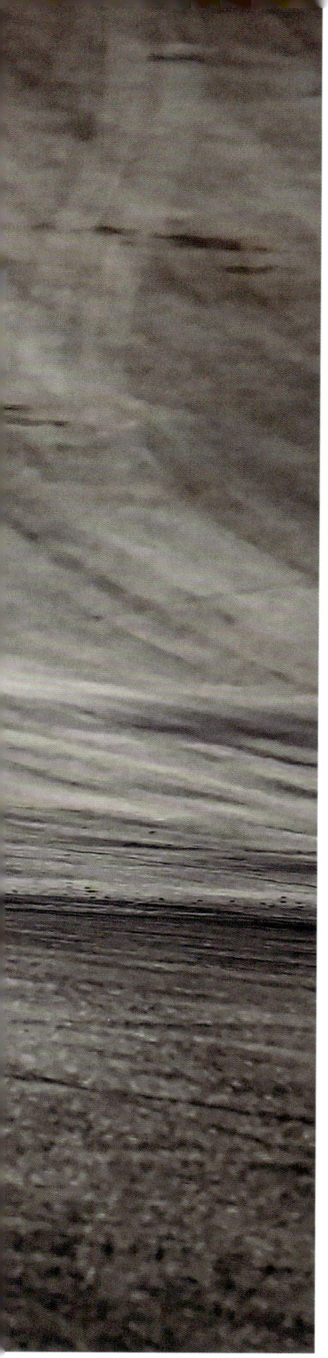

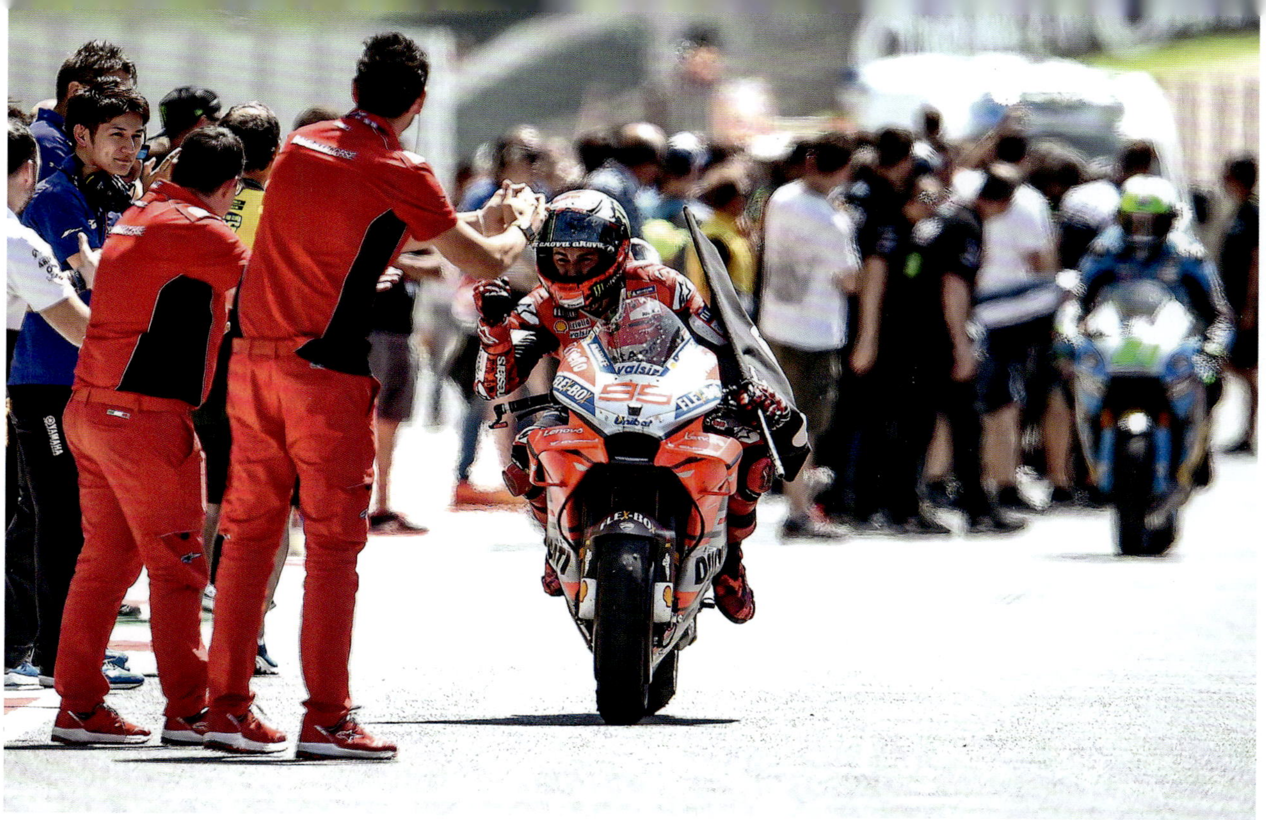

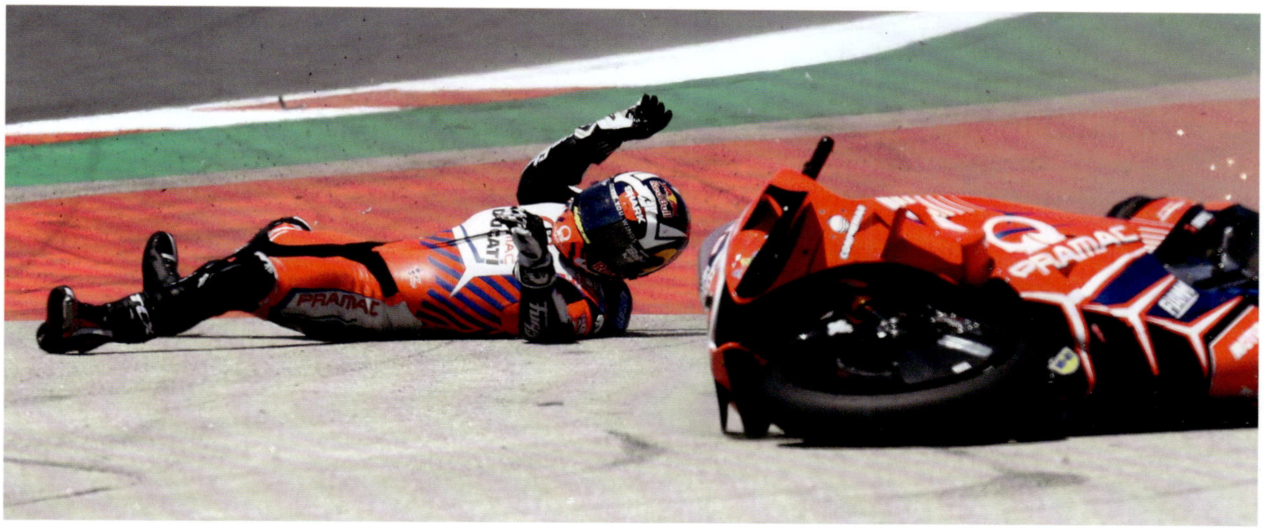
PRAMAC

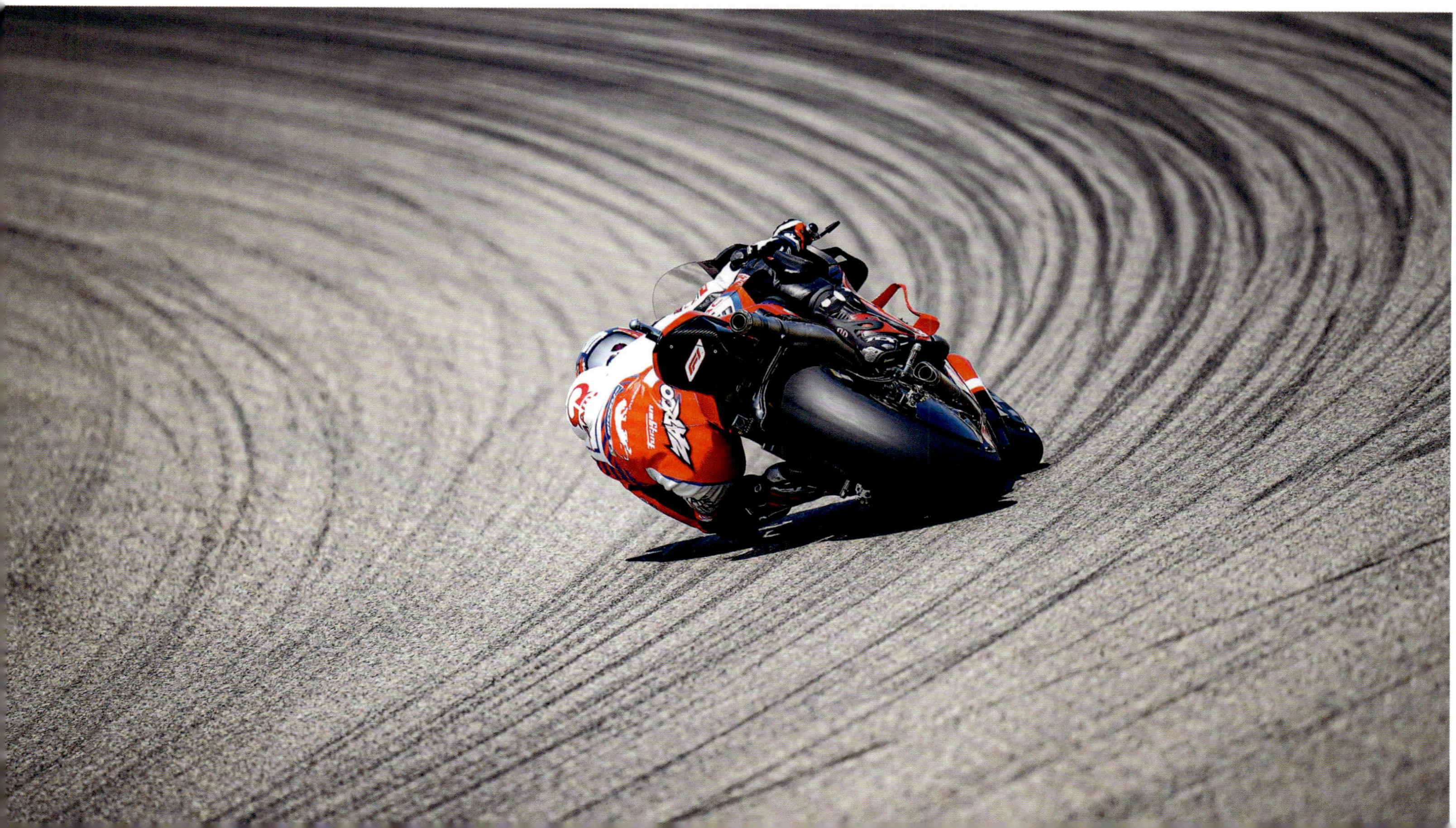

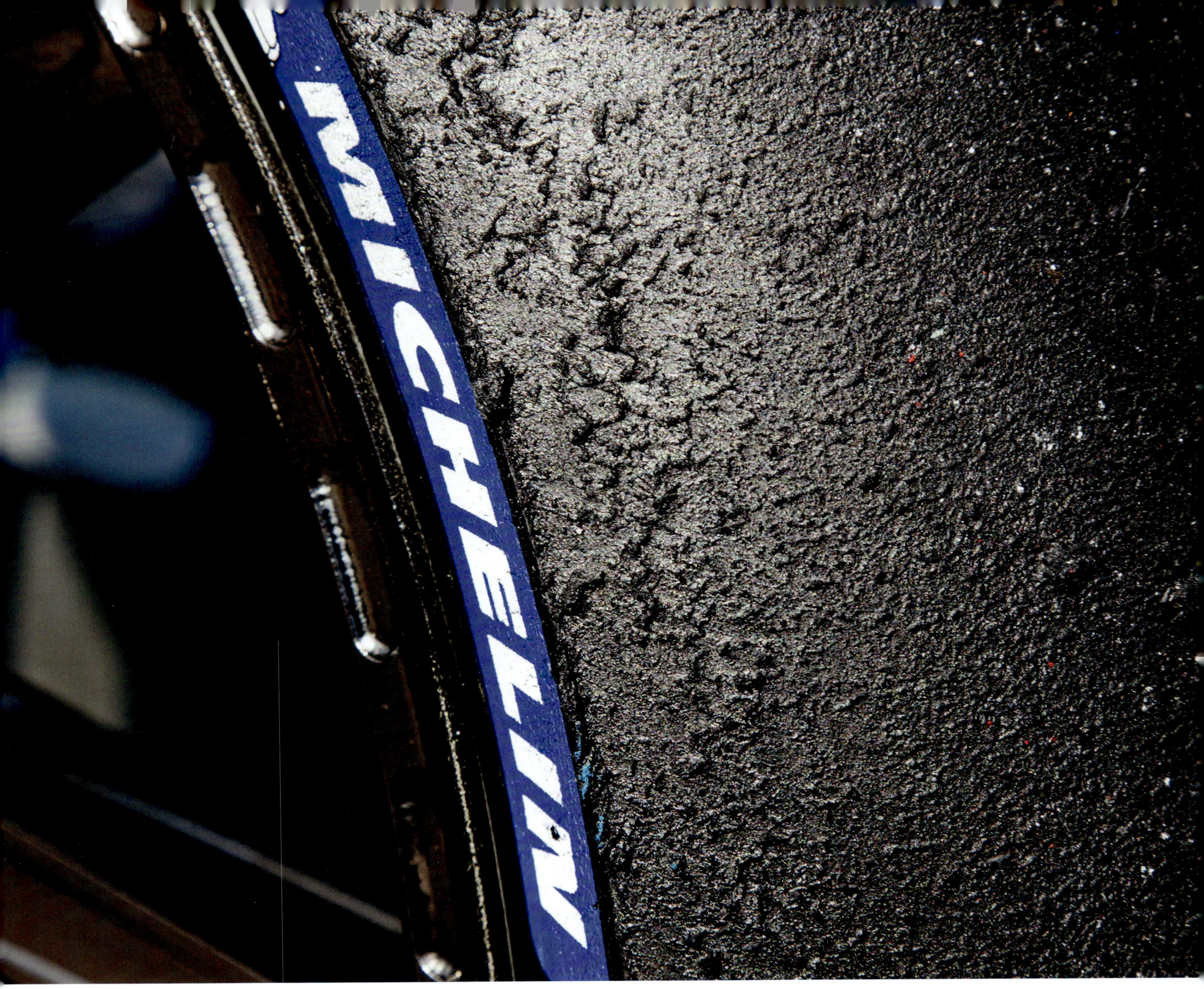
MICHELIN

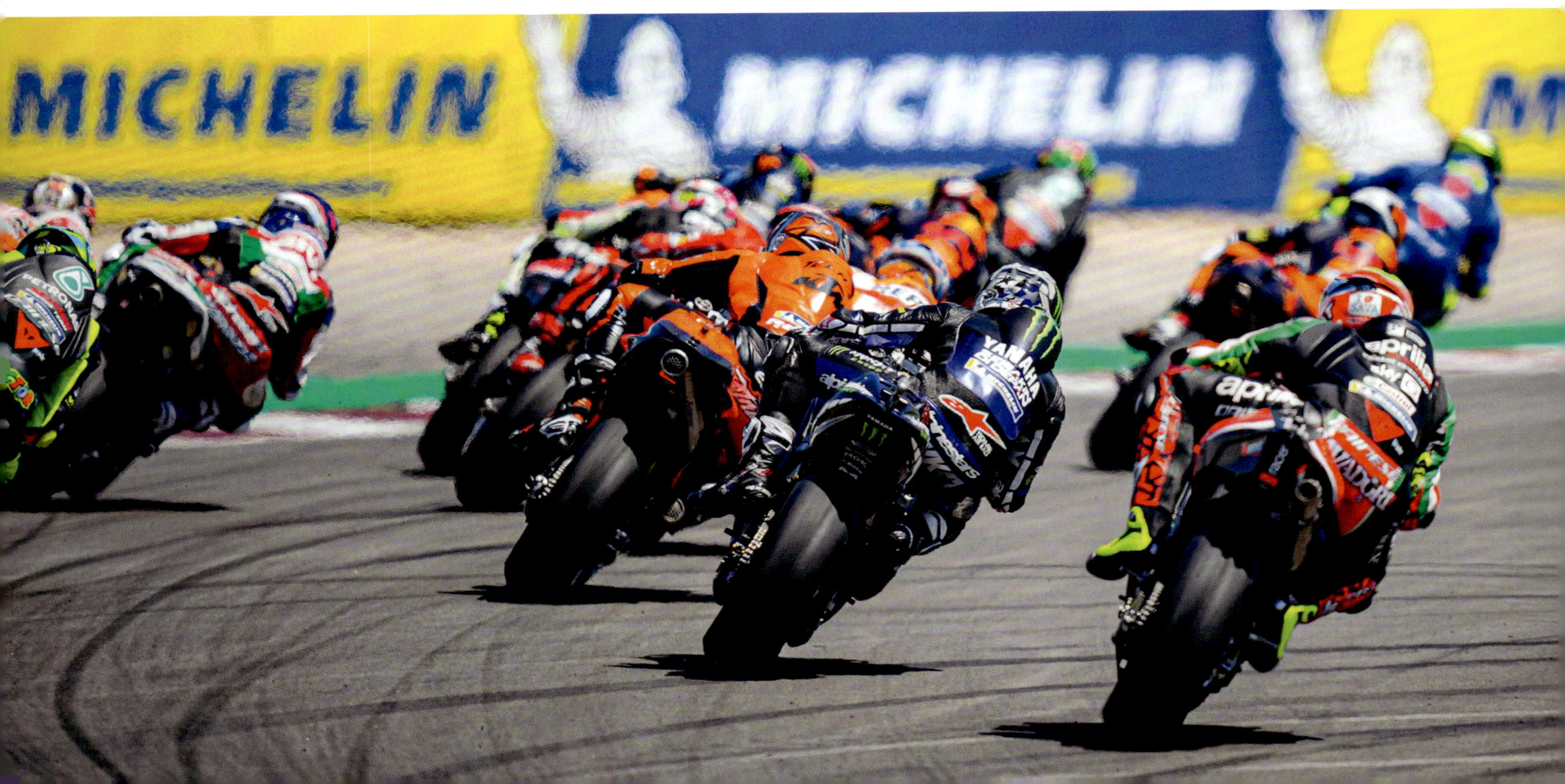
MICHELIN
MICHELIN

MotoGP." Speaking of the rear tyre, he said, "You don't have the same feeling, the perfect feeling, all the way through the race, so you must adapt. When you brake, enter the corner and use your corner speed. It's almost the same feeling with new or used tyres, but still I need to adapt quicker when the rear tyre drops."

Cal Crutchlow has said that although he can see what Marquez does on the Honda to achieve the results he does, he can't reproduce them with a similar result. All who have ridden the Honda have said that it is very physical, meaning that great strength is required to make it perform. In 2021, as Marquez returned to racing after his 2020 injury, often he found that he lacked that strength.

It has been quite common for newcomers to MotoGP to lay down hot single laps in free practice and qualifying, then get a poor start, waste the tyres trying to regain positions and fall back to undistinguished finishes. Or they start well, but are slowed and sent downfield by tyre drop that can't be explained.

This level of culling can be quite obvious, as it was for Kenny Roberts's younger son, Kurtis. Very talented, he would typically go to the front and then burn his tyres down with ingrained habits that could not be trained out of him.

When I asked five-times Daytona 200 winner Scott Russell how he conserved tyres, he said only that he had the discipline to keep the rear tyre from spinning. Suzuki's Alex Rins noted that "once the tyre starts to spin, it's very difficult to stop it spinning, which affects the lap time and also tyre life." Franco Morbidelli said the same: "Once you get a lot of wheelspin, it's difficult to recover, very difficult."

This leads to a belief that all a rider has to do to conserve tyres is to go easy – and the casual language used by many riders encourages this. Not so. Don't imagine that once the tyres are hot all is well. Tyres cool down on a long straight, then the centre of the front tyre heats up during braking, while the shoulder about to carry the cornering force remains cool and might provide reduced grip. Maverick Vinales's corner entry style, perhaps developed in response to the early weakness of the Michelin fronts, is to brake hard while upright, then quickly flick the bike over into cornering attitude. Trying, as Andrea Iannone did, to ride the Michelin front in Bridgestone style – trail-braking at high lean angle all the way to the apex – resulted in crashes.

Yet trail-braking has the potential to heat the tyre's shoulder progressively, rather than just slapping lukewarm rubber straight to full lean and hoping for grip. Tyre temperature goes up and down, and must be considered at times other than the risky first three laps, when a cold-tyre crash is most likely.

Yet so often a quite distinguished rider will start well only to find himself going irrevocably backwards, despite having finished well recently and riding with his customary respect for tyre management. A defective tyre? A subtle and unconscious change in riding? A slight, but significant difference in stressing the rubber? Conspiracy theorists propose that tyre distribution is somehow selective.

Next comes the idea that the rider can actively do something about tyre deterioration. Decades ago, Kenny Roberts spoke of switching from the "tired rubber" in one band of the tyre's width to fresh rubber in an adjacent band. This made the tyre better able to provide competitive acceleration over the race distance. On Marc Marquez's first visit to Austin, Texas's CoTA track, he spoke of being vigilant lest the tyres became "hard and bouncy" from overheating, which would have raised their inflation pressure. This relates to the previous remarks about it being difficult to recover from wheelspin – if a tyre that is becoming hard and bouncy is immediately rested for a period, it might recover its grip. But it can also spin more and more readily, quickly becoming useless and delivering a down-field finish.

Very soon after his arrival in MotoGP from two years in Moto2, Marquez demonstrated his tyre management ability by making more laps before tyre drop than even the most experienced riders.

What riders call tyre drop is a stress-driven softening of rubber described in 1962 by English rubber scientist A.R. Payne. Sometimes the result is loss of grip; at other times, the tyre's behaviour changes, but fast laps are still possible by altering technique. Racing tyre rubber is black or grey because it is loaded with reinforcing fillers, such as fine particles of carbon black or silica. Because the long molecular chains of rubber polymer are either attracted to or chemically bonded to these particles, they have the effect of increasing tensile strength and abrasion resistance. They are present in the form of clusters of particles that clump into larger agglomerates.

When rubber is stressed by flexing and undergoing shear as it passes through a tyre footprint at 20 or more revolutions per second, the clusters of filler particles are gradually separated – forced to move in relation to one another. Given time and enough stress cycles, they may migrate through the rubber to

Above: Fair wear and tear. A dozen laps of CoTA have left their mark on this Michelin.
Photo: Whit Bazemore

Left: The MotoGP pack shares the same tyres, but individual bikes use them differently.
Photo: Monster Energy Yamaha MotoGP

Right: Some bikes are easier on tyres, likewise some riders. Joan Mir and his Suzuki are both known for it.
Photo: www.suzuki-racing.com

TECHNICAL ESSAY 33

a distance from one another at which some of their stiffening effect as anchor points is lost. This stress softening has been given the name Payne Effect by tyre engineers.

As made clear by Pirelli compounder Fabio Meni, this stress-driven migration of filler particle clusters is reversible to some extent. This explains how a given tyre today can do a total race simulation over more than one practice session. This was impossible during the 1970s and '80s, when a race tyre was permanently altered chemically by a single use and then had to be discarded.

To obtain the peak properties from such filler, it must be mixed into the rubber in such a way that the desired sizes and spatial distribution of particle clumps and agglomerates are achieved. Is this easy to achieve reliably? Maverick Vinales has spoken of having wasted time in trying to adapt his set-up to a tyre that ultimately proved to be simply non-typical.

We know from what occurs during tyre testing that certain riders are able to accurately identify specific compounds from their track behaviour, while others are not. Tyre engineers check this by putting a previously tested tyre type back into the sequence to see if the rider identifies it.

Dovizioso added a fresh layer of complexity to this picture, saying, "The way to win races is different now, and it's not always the same story. Sometimes you have to save the tyres from the start of the race, sometimes you can push harder from the start. Every time it's different. It depends on which tyres Michelin bring."

In 2020, he said, "The new Michelins work differently, and you have to adapt your way of braking, entering corners, coming off the brakes and opening the gas. They are really small differences, but it is not easy [to adapt to such changes]. It is not even clear what we have to do. It is difficult to manage the rear tyre. In each phase of the curve, there is a different behaviour to interpret."

As to recent changes in tyre behaviour, he said, "We had all been riding for years in a way that now it is no longer possible to replicate."

The Italian had developed a turning style based on sliding the rear in "harmony" with the front, but subsequently Michelin softened its rear tyre carcass with the intent of laying down a larger footprint of increased grip. That extra grip put an end to Dovi's use of his carefully developed in-corner turning style.

Top riders observe the smallest details, search for the pattern that may exist within them and then intentionally alter their riding to adapt. This is like periodically taking the sheet music from a musician during a concert, putting an amended copy in its place and expecting the music to gracefully continue uninterrupted.

Dovizioso continued, "At some tracks, you can't use the best potential of the rear tyre because if you enter and exit the corners with full force, you won't have enough tyre to finish the race, so you can't open the throttle when you want. You have to wait to open the throttle. The difference is very small, but when you are on the limit, small things can be big things.

"You never have the perfect feeling, so you use the feedback from the tyres to tell you if it's better to do this or that."

Even the apparently simple act of releasing the front brake upon having entered a corner can present major problems. Danilo Petrucci noted, "One of the problems now is that when you are trying to pass someone on the brakes, you cannot hold your line when you release the front brake, so you go a bit wide and the other rider comes past on the inside."

Spectators are frequently treated to the sight of this cross-over pass and repass.

Dovizioso explained: "If you're very hard on the front tyre all the way to the middle of the corner, then you must be very, very, very slow when you release the brake, turn the bike and open the throttle, because the change between loading the tyres and unloading the tyres is very bad with the Michelins."

By neglecting this slow transition, a rider loses grip and runs wide, opening the inside line to a pass attempt.

We are fortunate that Dovizioso is so articulate in describing this 'conversation' between tyres and rider, but surely the others who are now uniquely getting the most from the bikes they ride employ similar tyre feedback to tell them how best to use their tyres from moment to moment? In American dirt-track, it is the track itself that changes from minute to minute: in MotoGP, it is the tyres that are always changing.

By contrast, Johann Zarco has said that he prefers not to be too analytical lest somehow it confuses the connection he has with what the machine and tyres are doing.

Kenny Roberts is another who has contributed to our understanding by discussing such things, but when I sought such analysis from Eddie Lawson, he said, "The more I think about things like that, the slower I go."

This large number of details is a lot to remember, to hold in readiness for rapid use and to constantly update as tyres change, the paddock moves on to new tracks and the weather unfolds. Even harder is integrating subtle adjustments into riding technique. We admire Lorenzo for eventually adapting to the Ducati, but the small and continuing adaptations required moment by moment on the track must be equally demanding.

Established habits resist change. I can think of several riders I have seen go faster in practice by consciously fighting their natural habit of rushing corners, only to snap back to their natural style in the race – and go slower. Perhaps this is why, in 1980, Roberts said, "I think of my mind as this big Velcro board, and hanging from it are all these little packets, one for each situation. My reflexes aren't all that fast, so I have to get a lot of my thinking done ahead of time. When something comes up, I grab the packet for that situation and do it."

Would it be surprising that a small minority of riders not only are fast, but also can handle so much information, so rapidly – especially with the changes occurring in tyres? When a rider learns to read the subtle and changing signals being sent by the tyres, he can more closely adapt his riding to what the tyres actually need to perform at their best.

This is a conversation. Relationships of this kind, because they are mysterious and unseen, appear as magic. People who seem to communicate mysteriously well with horses have been called 'horse whisperers'. Must we regard these extraordinary riders as 'tyre whisperers'?

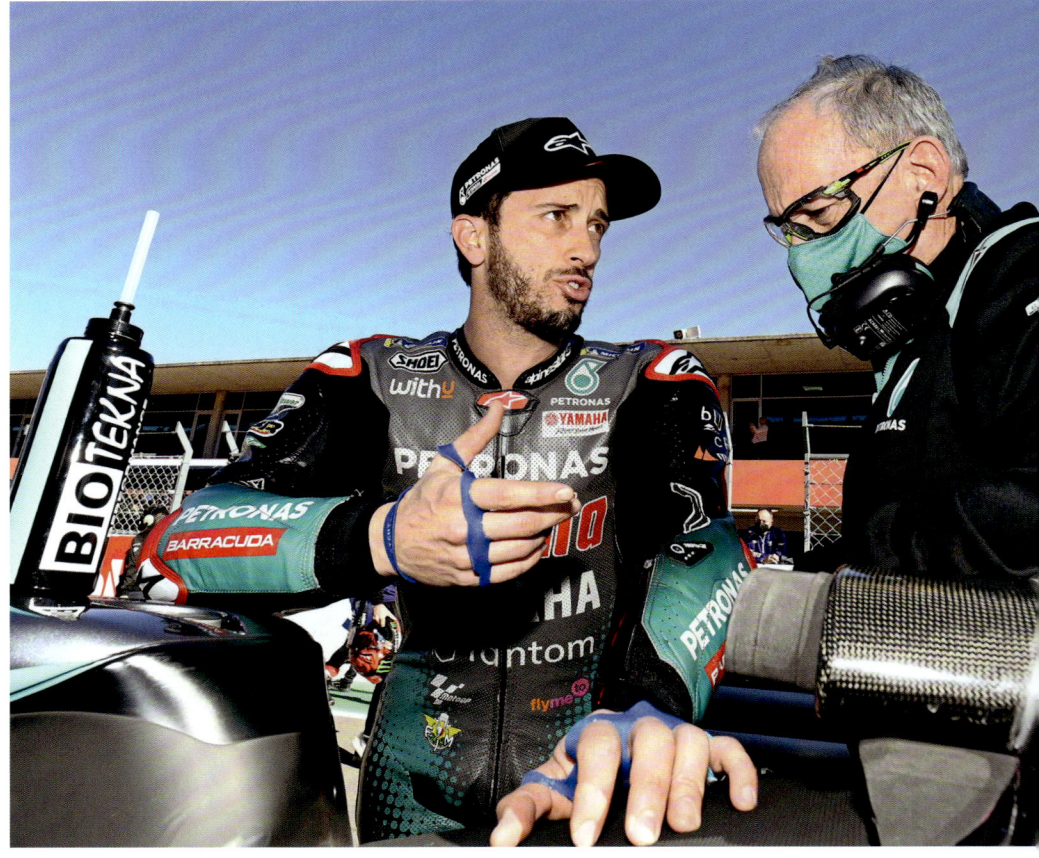

Above: "Small things are big things." Dovizioso, here leading Miller and Suzuki's Mir in Austria in 2020, is articulate in describing – and exploiting – nuances of tyre performance.
Photo: Ducati Corse

Far left: Dovizioso was dubbed 'The Professor' at Ducati. Now he has taken his huge depth of knowledge to Yamaha for 2022.
Photo: Gold & Goose

Left: Quartararo did best when out alone. When following other bikes, their high-temperature wake can overheat a front tyre, with complicated consequences.
Photo: Monster Energy Yamaha MotoGP

TECHNICAL ESSAY 35

BROTHERS AT WAR

Grand prix winners Brad and Darryn Binder are the latest brothers to square up to one another in MotoGP. NEIL MORRISON spoke to the South African siblings about the pleasures and perils of keeping it in the family…

THE MotoGP field might not know it yet, but if they thought they had their hands full trying to contain Brad Binder, South Africa's first grand prix champion in 27 years, then 2022 could be doubly as tricky. All-action brother Darryn, known for roughing up the best Moto3 has to offer, makes the unenviable jump from junior class to premier class for that season, capping an unlikely career path for MotoGP's latest brother pairing.

This outcome might have seemed unlikely in the extreme when the Binder brothers were riding together in junior motocross events around their home town of Krugersdorp, on the outskirts of Johannesburg. But two brothers fighting each other in the premier class is nothing new. Following the Espargaro, Marquez and Rossi/Marini siblings in recent years, the Binders make for unlikely MotoGP rivals, after Darryn's surprise appointment in the all-new RNF Yamaha team.

Off their bikes, there are traits that single them out as unmistakable siblings. Three years apart, they are approachable, well mannered and, on the surface, laid back to the point of being horizontal, that nonchalant South African twang adding humour to most situations. And both share a clinical, aggressive streak on the bike that, on occasion, has earned them the ire of their peers. In Brad's case, from Valentino Rossi no less.

But their difference in achievements until now couldn't be starker. Thanks, in part, to a dominant Moto3 title in 2016, as well as an unlikely championship challenge in the Moto2 class of 2019, Brad is the darling of KTM, signed up to an almost unique long-term contract all the way to the end of 2024. He has the distinction of having won the Austrian factory's first premier-class race, and over ten decorated years of riding at world level, he has amassed 17 wins and 37 podiums. In 2021, he brought KTM a level of consistency that otherwise it was missing. Sixth in the championship bodes well for the future.

While he now has a place among the 24 best riders in the world, Darryn is still awaiting that breakthrough season. And 2022 could be it, as he becomes only the second rider since the 1990s to bypass Moto2 to go straight to the premier class, thanks to exercising his contractual right to a seat with his team (originally, he had been meant to move Moto2, only for the team to pull its efforts in the intermediate class). He does so after a solitary triumph in Moto3 and six podiums after seven full seasons.

The brothers were inseparable when they were growing up. "It's a family effort," explained Brad. "Everything you do revolves around racing. If you have two siblings, then the whole family is behind that." Their father, Trevor, was a motorsport obsessive and raced himself. And despite initially competing in go-karts, Brad switched to two wheels when he was ten years old. Three junior national titles followed before it dawned on the family that the next step would involve longer trips to Europe.

Despite full backing from Trevor, the head of a goldmine management company, the road to the world championship was long, costly and lonely for the Binder brothers. On the back of two successful years in the Red Bull Rookies class, Brad moved to Spain with mother Sharon for his first full season in Moto3 in 2012, leaving his dad and Darryn – still at school – at home.

"In 2012, my mum and I moved to live in Spain when I was 16," Brad recalled. "My dad and brother were back in South Africa. That was how we did it for the first couple of years. It was tough. It wasn't easy to figure out how to do all of that. I was just a kid wanting to race a bike. It was my parents' job to sort out the rest. At that stage, you don't realise

Opposite: Brad (*top*) and younger brother Darryn were set to race against one another in MotoGP in 2022, with Darryn skipping straight from Moto3.

Below: On the way up. After a long apprenticeship, Brad joined the Red Bull Ajo Moto3 team, and in 2016, he dominated the championship.

Photos: Gold & Goose

Above: Learning how to brawl. Darryn Binder (40) triumphed in Catalunya in 2020. The top five passed the flag inside four-tenths.

Top right: Shake on it. In 2015, the Binder brothers met in Moto3. Brad (*left*) was third in Spain; rookie Darryn finished his fourth GP 24th, one place ahead of Remy Gardner.

Above right: Brad with father Trevor after winning at Le Mans in 2016.

Above far right: A young Brad found his feet after joining Red Bull Ajo's Moto3 team in 2015.

Right: Brad flies the South African flag after securing the 2016 Moto3 title at Aragon, with seven wins and four races to spare.

Below right: A late charge in 2019 resulted in Brad winning the last three races and closing to within three points of eventual champion Alex Marquez, here in hot pursuit.

Sidebar
Top: The Espargaro brothers have been racing across the MotoGP classes since 2006.

Bottom: Luca Marini has half-brother Valentino Rossi to guide his fortunes.

Photos: Gold & Goose

what went into it, but now I really appreciate how important all of these small moments were."

With certain seats in the Moto3 world championship costing in the region of 200,000–300,000 euros, it took a tremendous financial sacrifice on the part of Trevor to help his sons get a foothold on the grand prix ladder. "I was always aware it was costing a ton of money," said Brad. "It's only really later in life, when you start to make your own money, that you really understand what my parents did was insane. The amount of money it costs to become a MotoGP rider, I don't even want to know. I don't think my dad wants to know either! I've been very fortunate to have such amazing parents that paved the way for me."

And without his younger brother around, it was a lonely existence for a teenager nearly 7,000 miles from home. "It was a bit boring," said Brad. "I didn't have too much to do. I was used to having my brother around, just to go riding. But it was just me and my mum. All we could do was wait until the next grand prix. It was difficult, more so for my brother. He was young – still in primary school – and he was the one running the house. My dad was at work all day, and he was at home. It was hectic, a big sacrifice for the whole family."

That burden was eased in 2013, when Darryn followed Brad's path to Spain, competing in the Red Bull Rookies Cup. "My brother and I are super-close," said the younger sibling. "I'm really fortunate to have him overseas, and I think he would say the same about having me there. Leaving South Africa, we left everything behind. It's difficult to go off on your own, and always easier to do it with someone you know around."

After two years in the Red Bull Rookies Cup, Darryn finally made it into the world championship in 2015. It was around then that Brad's career was really taking off. Two years spent riding Mahindra's sweet-handling, but dog-slow Moto3 machine in 2013 and '14 had equipped him with the necessary skills to scrape time in the turns. "You had to make up your time somewhere, because it wasn't on the straight," he said.

Promotion to Aki Ajo's KTM-backed Moto3 team was an education at first. "That first year with Aki was a huge struggle. You have an idea of what you want to achieve, and I really wasn't ready for it. I was still not riding the bike properly. I was just looking at the time sheets wanting to be on top, but not doing my weekend's work properly. Aki taught me a huge amount that year."

The Finn's schooling streamlined Brad's working methods. When he returned for a second try in 2016, he cleaned up. Even in a year when he had racked up seven wins, tied up his first world title with four races to spare and had a record-breaking points margin for the class come the end of it – he finished the year 142 points ahead of Enea Bastianini in second – there was one clear standout moment: a staggering back-to-front victory at Jerez, where he had scored his first win after gaining 34 positions. "When you win a race like that, you look back on it and think, 'You know what? I managed to beat these guys starting last.'" He made everything look easy from there.

A rookie season in Moto2 showcased another element of the elder Binder's make-up: grit. The then 21-year-old spent his winter in operating theatres, hospital wards and on his sofa when he ought to have been celebrating a Moto3 title triumph. A high-side while testing at Valencia in November, 2016, had resulted in his 135kg Moto2 machine landing on his left arm. A fracture-dislocation of the forearm was the result, but that wasn't the end of it. The bone failed to knit, meaning he soon went under the knife again. The arm was plated for a second time and a bone graft was required to aid growth.

Still it wasn't right. Arriving in Argentina for his second race as a Moto2 rookie, aboard KTM's new chassis, Brad was in some pain. A high-speed wobble during qualifying broke the arm again. A third operation in five months awaited. Before then, however, there was still the small matter of racing. Despite his team's concerns, he finished ninth, an astonishing feat when 16 men behind him had the luxury of two working arms. Brad talked about the ordeal as though it was nothing. "I was taught from a young age that if you have a problem, you say nothing, just deal with it. If things aren't okay, no problem, just carry on. Whether I'm hurt or not hurt, I'll be happier riding," he said.

Brad won three races in 2018, but his most impressive campaign was the following year. Moto2 was adapting to Triumph's new 765cc triple-cylinder engine. Some chassis manufacturers – Kalex, Speed Up – nailed the new configuration from the off; KTM, however, got its calculations badly wrong. As it tried revamped and completely new chassis most weekends, Brad lost sight of the title contenders. Only from Assen did he have a package to finish on the podium. With six races to go, he was out of touch, 62 points adrift of Alex Marquez. But an inspired late run took him to within

38 BINDER BROTHERS PROFILE

FAMOUS BROTHERS IN THE SPORT

THE Binders join a fairly long line of brothers to come up against one another in motorcycle racing's premier class. The Rossis (Luca Marini, Valentino's half-brother, raced against his sibling throughout 2021), the Aokis (Nobuatsu raced Takuma in 1997, and Haruchika in 1999), the Sarrons (Christian and Dominique duelled in 1989), the Garcias (Bernard and Marc made an unlikely privateer combination in the mid-1990s) as well as the Robertses (Kenny Junior and Kurtis competed against one another on track for spells in 2001, '04, '05 and '07) are siblings who raced one another.

And with the Espargaros, and Marc and Alex Marquez currently on the MotoGP grid, how come there are so many brothers now racing at the elite level of motorcycle racing?

In each case, the siblings have grown up in the same bike-mad family. Take the Espargaros for example: constant competition from within the same household drove them both forward. "All of our life, we were competing to be faster than the other one," Aleix said.

When discussing racing alongside his older brother, Marini expressed his belief in the value of having that familiar figure on hand to offer advice at home and during the race weekend: "I think there are more positive aspects than the negative. I can learn a lot from him. I can speak a lot with him and he can give me a lot of advice, and this is very important."

BINDER BROTHERS PROFILE 39

three points of the eventual champion. "The way I look at it is I did my best," he said, unfazed. "If things had gone different, I know where I would have been. But second is still second."

The best was yet to come. After a shaky start in his first test as a MotoGP rider, Brad was second fastest in his opening race. Then he won his third, a barely believable outing at Brno. "I was terrible at the first test. Like really, really slow," he recalled. "Then from Valencia to the first official day of testing at Jerez [which preceded the opening], I was tenth in the morning and third in the afternoon. Something clicked that day." If anything, it was a bigger challenge matching that initial burst. "It's been a struggle to try and stay there," he explained. "I look back and ask, 'What did I do to stay there? How do I get back?' The reality is that the class has changed since the beginning of last year. I've just got to keep adapting."

The 2021 season had some sensational highs, notably the daring victory at KTM's home GP, when he tackled a wet track on slick tyres for two laps. Qualifying was an issue, but Brad scored points in every race bar one, showing he can nearly always deliver on Sunday. That, and his long-term deal with the Austrian factory, gives him confidence for the future. "I can't really explain how much I hate when you've given your best and you're not where you want to be. I look at this as an opportunity to grow together," he said.

During this time, Darryn was cultivating a fierce reputation as a no-holds-barred brawler in Moto3, a class known for having no shortage of such riders. Like Brad, he first cut his teeth on a painfully slow Mahindra, hamstrung by a lack of top speed. He first started showing flashes when his Platinum Bay Real Estate team switched to KTM machinery in 2017. Still, results were erratic, even if he followed Brad's lead again by moving into the Ajo set-up for 2018. That move, however, produced less success. Instead, he flourished in the less-pressured reaches of CIP KTM.

By 2019, Darryn could regularly be seen riding through the pack at breakneck speed, barging riders out of the way. Brad wasn't exactly a stranger to this kind of reputation. His final year in Moto2 had been aboard a dog of a KTM chassis, which led him to regularly override his package. Barging riders out of the way became the norm, until chassis improvements arrived. Soon he was roughing up the best in MotoGP, with Rossi providing something of a verbal slap after 2021's season-opening GP. "There are a lot of riders that ride with more respect for their opponents, and there are others like Binder that don't care about the rival," said the Italian.

The elder Binder was unmoved: "What was really strange was going out the pits for the first time at Valencia and seeing Dovi [Andrea Dovizioso], [Marc] Marquez and Rossi next to you. But when you're on track, you don't think about who they are or what they've done. You just want to get past them. Their reputation doesn't change anything."

Having recognised that this kind of daring was winning him few friends, Darryn changed tack for 2020. Aside from the unfortunate incident in 2021's Algarve GP, when he took down title contender Dennis Foggia, he was less lairy than before. It is in issues like this that older brother Brad is always on hand to offer direction. "I think it's one of the best things, having my older brother with me overseas," said Darryn. "If you look at what my brother has done, it only motivates me to do better. He's been through where I am now. I always go to him for advice.

"He'll say, 'You didn't listen to me! I told you to do this!' We're just a normal family. We don't fight too much. We might have an argument once in a blue moon. He'll tell me, 'You're stupid, why did you do that?' Even after a race. Like recently we were watching a rerun of the Qatar [Moto3] race from last year. I led across the line and went to the left of the track. Then I got hit and had nowhere to go and crashed. [Brad was like,] 'Your first mistake was you shouldn't have gone left, that's where you went wrong!' We're always talking about stuff. It's free advice."

A switch to the Petronas Sprinta Team was supposed to be the final piece of the jigsaw. But the team hit financial issues through the year. His Honda was down on speed. And his weight – Darryn was one of the heavier riders in the class – contributed to it being an underwhelming campaign, with just two podium finishes. "It's not too difficult to get to the front of races from further back at the beginning of races," Darryn said "As a bit of a heavier rider, I struggle to lead. When I get to the front, I just get swallowed up on the next straight, and it just becomes that dogfight."

That shouldn't be an issue in 2022, when Yamaha's rookie-friendly M1 will be his machine of choice. "It'll be a huge learning experience," he conceded, "but an opportunity you can't turn down, a no-brainer." Once again, he'll be calling on that brotherly advice to see him through: "I'll be asking my brother a lot of questions! I'll be following his footsteps training over the winter to get ready for the bigger bike."

Above: Brad Binder after his amazing slicks-in-the-wet win in Austria in 2021.
Photo: Red Bull KTM

Left: Darryn Binder's size and weight proved to be obstacles in an up-and-down final Moto3 season.

Right: Thumbs-up from the younger brother after claiming second at Doha in 2021.
Photos: Whit Bazemore Photography

Far right: Darryn was the first to congratulate Brad on his maiden MotoGP win at Brno, in only his third race in the premier class.
Photo: Gold & Goose

BINDER BROTHERS PROFILE 41

ELECTRODUKE!

For three years, MotoE has given close racing over short distances – but failed to thrill. In 2023, Ducati takes over as sole supplier, with a view to developing electric superbikes. Can the Italian racing stalwarts elevate the class, and what does it mean for motorcycling? NEIL SPALDING investigates...

Above: Close, but underwhelming: Alessandro Zaccone leads Dominique Aegerter and Lukas Tulovic at Le Mans in the seven-round 2021 MotoE World Cup.
Photo: Pramac Racing

Top right: Early sophistication from the MotoCzysz, four-times winner of the Isle of Man TT Zero race.
Photo: MotoCzysz

Above right: Early days – the 2009 Agni TT bike mounted motor and massive battery in a Suzuki GSXR750 chassis.
Photo: Agni

Right: MotoE bikes lined up for testing at Valencia in 2019.
Photo: Neil Spalding

Far right, top: A weighty matter. Riders struggle to pick up current MotoE bikes after minor spills. Ducati have promised a lighter machine.
Photo: Gold & Goose

Far right, bottom: Spaghetti junction – wiring on the Agni's battery pack.
Photo: Agni

THE first electric bike race in the modern era was the TTXGP at the Isle of Man TT in 2009 – a single lap around the TT circuit, a distance of 37.75 miles. A small company called Agni turned up with a very large battery and two electric motors bolted into a GSXR750 chassis and, against some fairly serious competition, won the race.

The brain behind the bike was Cedric Lynch, a long-term Battery Vehicle Society regular. Lynch understood that the game wasn't about power; it was all about using the stored energy as carefully and efficiently as possible. He had developed his own high-efficiency, permanent-magnet DC motor, and the bike was powered by versions further developed by Agni. The motors were unusual at that time in being of an axial-flux design, offering plenty of torque, but sensitive if over-revved.

In the years that followed, the technology level for the renamed TT Zero jumped several notches. In Portland in the USA, Michael Czysz changed his locally-built electric motorcycle from an Agni axial-flux design to radial-flux motors; then long-term Honda satellite racing operation Mugen also entered a bike.

Energica, which was developing a sports bike on which the subsequent MotoE racers were based, also became involved in 2010. The manufacturer won many races in that year's TTXGP European Championship and was runner-up in the 2011 World Championship.

In 2019, Dorna launched the MotoE series as a support race for MotoGP, with the full sanction of the FIM.

Rather than allow a technical competition, with all the accompanying costs, Dorna decided on a single-make series, and Energica was persuaded to provide the bikes. Thus the MotoE championship was equipped with well-developed, but heavy race bikes based closely on the Italian company's range-topping Ego electric sports bike, itself based on the earlier Energica race bikes. Weighing a hefty 280kg, compared with MotoGP's 157kg, this led to the frequent spectacle of riders being unable to pick up the bikes after sliding off.

The motor is a permanent-magnet AC (alternating current) unit, oil-cooled with an air-cooled lithium-ion battery pack providing a maximum of 20kWh of storage. Power has never been an issue, with over 200Nm of torque and a maximum power output of 80kW.

The weight required Michelin to develop special tyres, and problems in the first few races led to a shortening of the race distance. However, 2022 will be Energica's last year. Thereafter, Ducati will take the series forwards.

Ducati CEO Claudio Domenicali's initial announcement focused immediately on lighter weights. We will have to wait and see what he has in mind, but of course Ducati will have access to the VW Group's technologies if it wishes to create something more technically advanced than the current MotoE bikes.

There are many options in a fast developing automotive field. To look at things that might better reflect an electric race bike in 2023, it is still necessary to bear in mind that this snapshot was taken in late 2021. The rate of change is such that things might be very different in just a year or two.

To reduce weight, the logical starting point is the battery. Any new system will need to be liquid-cooled, the only way to keep the batteries near optimum temperature, most likely just over 20°C. Tesla and several other car manufacturers use aluminium 'micro channel' strips through the battery pack, routing coolant through the core and then passing it through a heat exchanger (radiator) of some sort.

If the batteries themselves are conventionally cylindrical, they can be fixed together to become a 'brick' to achieve the desired power density. Batteries can also be made up of lightweight packs and boxed together (prismatic batteries) or heavier-duty pouch cells, which are simply clipped to one another. For a simple, relatively light and efficient solution, Tesla is the class leader, with its cylindrical batteries glued and wired together into one rigid structure.

All batteries need management units to monitor their efficiency and heat levels. Overheating requires rapid shutdown – a thermal runaway isn't good for anyone or anything in close proximity. As batteries are improving so too is the accuracy of the management programs, so that fewer cells need to be taken out of service if things start to get too hot.

If the shapes of the batteries vary enormously so does their chemistry. Lithium-ion batteries are simple in concept, but as ever the devil is in the detail. Each cell has a positive electrode (cathode) and a negative electrode (anode) submerged in an electrolyte. As the battery is charged, lithium ions move from the cathode to the anode and energy is stored. The reverse happens on discharge.

The materials used in the cathode and anode are critical to the performance of the battery. Current batteries use several different cathode materials, each with slightly different performance characteristics. They include, among others, lithium iron phosphate (LFP) and lithium cobalt oxide (LCO), both paired with a graphite anode. Tesla uses a nickel-cobalt-aluminium (NCA) cathode in its 'bricks', but has announced a range-wide change to LFP cells. Development is bringing other improved material pairings. Until recently, it was accepted that higher power densities are typically accompanied by reductions in the number of charging and discharging cycles. Now, however, we are seeing changes that could dramatically improve the power density.

The commonest anode design employs a graphite coating, and this is one of the limiting factors in battery performance. Sulphur-coated anodes increase battery power density, each sulphur atom reacting with two lithium ions during discharge. This compares with traditional lithium-ion anodes only being able to react with 0.5–0.7 lithium ions per host atom.

US firm Lyten has announced a mass-production lithium-sulphur battery. This combines the repeatability and stability of a graphite anode with the increased efficiency of a sulphur anode. Lyten also says that its design eliminates the possibility

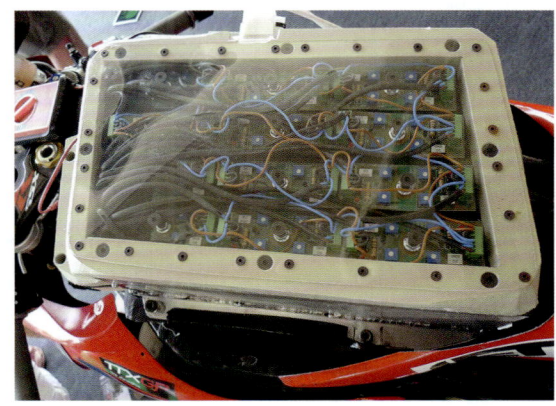

ELECTRODUKE! 43

Above: Charging stations. The Avintia squad spark up their bikes for the 2021 Spanish GP outing.

Top right: A peek behind the bodywork of an Energica MotoE bike.
Photos: Gold & Goose

Above right: All smiles. Dorna's Carmelo Ezpeleta with Ducati's Claudio Domenicali. The Bologna firm takes over in MotoE from 2023.
Photo: Ducati Corse

Right: Future friendly? Ex-Ducati designer Pierre Terblanche showed his BST Hypertek electric-bike prototype at the Milan show in 2019.
Photo: Barry White

of a thermal event. It claims three times the energy density of a conventional battery. For motorcycling (indeed for the world), this could be a game changer.

Mahle and its partner Alltrope Energy have also announced a new generation of lithium-carbon batteries, which combine the 'best bits' of a super-capacitor and a normal lithium-ion battery. The result is a battery that will allow fast recharging (a full charge in 90 seconds!) and which doesn't degrade with regular use. They also don't require any of the rare earth metals that make conventional battery designs expensive.

If the VW Group can be persuaded to experiment in MotoE, we could not only benefit from these developments, but also play a role in taking them forward.

Motor designs also offer options.

The Energica uses a well-developed radial-flux motor. That's in line with what a lot of other companies have been doing: Triumph's TE-1 prototype employs a particularly efficient British-developed unit from Integral Power. But older designs, like the axial flux, are being re-examined.

A radial-flux design is quite compact and typically revs quite high. The magnets are clustered close to the centre of the armature, and the coils set immediately next to them. This limits the maximum torque simply because the 'leverage' from the coils to the magnets and armature is so short.

An axial-flux motor has a different layout, mounting the coils and magnets as if on the outer edge of a set of dinner plates. Thus the 'leverage' from magnets to armature is longer, increasing the torque dramatically. Most current axial-flux designs use two outer rotors with rare-earth magnets and an inner stator, with all the windings on it. This layout also brings benefits to the way the wires are wound, improving the magnetic flux flows and the manner in which the whole assembly can be cooled.

While radial-flux motors are often run up to 20,000rpm, axial-flux units rev lower, say 9,000rpm. But even at these lower speeds, there can be issues related to keeping the magnets in place. There is a lot of energy involved, which is capable of distorting the different components, especially lightweight items. A lot of current design effort is concentrated on developing a stiff rotor that can hold the magnets accurately while maintaining the close running tolerances that improve efficiency.

Next, there is the question of the accurate control of the power – particularly crucial for the 'feel' of the throttle of a racing motorcycle.

Theoretically, an electric motor is capable of producing 100 per cent of its torque instantaneously, but that isn't what users typically want or need. So a controller also has to provide the power levels the operator is expecting. For that, you need a controller that 'chops' the power going in to a level that the motor can take, that doesn't cause overheating and that gives you a 'feel' closer to that which you get from an internal-combustion engine. It is important to control the current so it gives torque that is proportional to how far you turn the throttle.

Controllers also need careful temperature management to ensure predictable performance.

There has been tremendous progress since the original TTXGP bikes, but this is still a developing science, and one of critical importance in MotoE.

Finally, there is the overall architecture of the bike to be considered and refined.

An axial-flux motor needs to sit in a motorcycle chassis somewhat differently, simply because of its larger diameter. However, although axial-flux motors won't rev as quickly as the radial-flux alternative, they will still have an effect on motorcycle dynamics, with both torque reactions and gyroscopic effects contributing to the way the bike feels and acts. As with the current generation of MotoGP bikes, it is possible to have the weightier parts of the motor rotating in either direction, which will have to be considered.

An electric motorcycle doesn't have to look like an internal-combustion bike with a big box of batteries levered vertically into the space where the engine used to sit. This is where big changes are possible. As we have seen, batteries can be packaged in different ways. The trick will be to find the compromise that optimises performance, weight position and packaging with a bike that still feels 'normal'. Motorcycle racers brought up on conventional machines aren't going to welcome something that feels radically different to what they are used to.

While we will have to wait to see what the current Ducati designers come up with, we do have one recent view from former Ducati design chief Pierre Terblanche. Now operating as a freelance designer, he launched a new electric bike design at the Milan show in 2019 – the BST Hypertek. Commissioned by MD Gary Turner, the bike features a minimalist carbon-fibre frame and a longitudinally-mounted DHX Hawk water-cooled radial-flux permanent-magnet synchronous motor, putting out 107bhp and 120Nm of torque.

Although not designed as a dedicated racing bike, it does postulate a new generation of electric bikes. The start point was "What does an electric bike design require?" The battery is rolled 90 degrees to the norm and shaped to fit between the rider's legs. There is a neo-honeycomb water radiator above the battery for cooling the controller and motor, with priority for the controller.

The motor is set in line between the rider's feet, and the bike has a clutch, giving the rider greater control of the power train and the potential to add a gearbox. All the electronics are in the 'tank' area between the rider's knees.

With its roller-supported forks and the shock absorber built into the swing-arm, the bike is significantly more avant-garde than would have been possible if the design had had to be talked through the boardroom of a conservative manufacturer.

Now we will have to wait and see what Terblanche's former Ducati colleagues come up with for 2023.

ELECTRODUKE! 45

2021 MOTOGP · BIKE BY BIKE

IN THE SHADOW OF THE RULES

The pandemic enforced another year of frozen engine and aerodynamic development, but designers managed to find improvements all the same. SIMON CRAFAR held a close watching brief...

THE shadow of Covid 19 lingered over MotoGP's engineers in 2021, with restrictions extended and all but detailed technical development stalled. In particular, engine development was frozen for a second year, the engines used being as homologated at the start of 2020. Normally, engineers would be free to make any changes within the basic rules during the off-season, with designs only frozen and engines sealed at the start of the new season. Only Aprilia, the sole remaining Concession Team, was permitted to make engine changes.

Thus battle lines remained as before, with the six manufacturers split four-to-two in favour of V4 engines versus in-line fours – essentially a contest between greater horsepower, and better handling and control.

The horsepower was unchangeable. Ducati, Honda, KTM and Aprilia use the V4 option, where benefits include a narrower (shorter) crankshaft. With no balance shaft required, internal friction is reduced, one reason why V4s are generally more powerful. This is despite some restrictions to space on the intake side within the vee and compromised exhaust design for the rear cylinders.

Yamaha and Suzuki remain faithful to the in-line architecture. Different inertial and gyroscopic influences of the wider (longer) crankshaft confer greater stability and more predictable handling, and the shorter fore-and-aft cylinder block allows more favourable engine positioning for weight distribution, and less compromised intake and exhaust design. The negative is less power.

Aero rules were as before, with one aero-body update allowed per rider during the season. That left little room for manoeuvre, except in the areas of chassis and suspension, where the signature of the season was the now-universal adoption of rear ride-height devices, pioneered in 2020 by Ducati.

By the start of the 2021 season, all six manufacturers had front ride-height devices, also known as holeshot devices, by means of which front forks could be compressed for the launch off the start line, lowering the centre of gravity to reduce wheelies.

By the end of the season, all had added similar devices to lower the rear. This squatting action is used not only off the start line, but also during the race on corner exit, again to lower the centre of gravity.

Above: Looking for improvements. New rider Pol Espargaro's Honda at pre-season tests.
Photo: Gold & Goose

Right: The Ducati Desmosedici GP21. Aero bodywork remained unchanged all season.

Top right: Rider's eye view of Ducati handlebars. Note ride-height device controls on carbon-fibre section.
Photos: Ducati Corse

Above right: Front wheel detail shows ride-height sensor and mechanism, connections for tyre temperature monitor and carbon fork shroud, which smoothes airflow to the radiator.
Photo: Simon Crafar

Above far right: Jack Miller chassis section was flattened to change stiffness ratios for rider preference. Bagnaia's chassis lacked this feature.
Photo: Ducati Corse

DUCATI DESMOSEDICI GP21

DUCATI continued in their way of constant improvement in 2021. Moving two young guns into the factory team was a risk, but understandable. It was the young riders in 2020 who had proved they could adapt their riding style to suit the new-construction rear tyre and the altered settings that were needed to get the best performance from it.

Already the most powerful bike on the grid, the Desmosedici GP21 arrived at Qatar with chassis modifications, new suspension parts, new downforce aero ducts on the lower fairing, a choice of engine flywheels and a new front holeshot device. The 2020 Ducati had been good, but the impression at the start of 2021 was that the new machine was a step better, especially in their weaker area – turning.

Jack Miller mentioned that never before had he been able to release the front brake with so much speed, and still retain front feel and turning. So now the Ducati was the machine to beat.

The factory Ducatis did not change in appearance through the year, once Pramac riders received enough of the new belly-pan aero. They tried variations of suspension and geometry settings, but the base bike, fairings/aero, exhausts, in fact everything visible stayed pretty much the same, apart from an updated chassis for Jack Millar. Of course, there was a freeze on engine development until the end of 2021, but the lack of chassis parts, exhausts, etc did point towards Ducati and their riders being relatively content. In fact, in the latter part of the year, even the bike geometry settings remained relatively unchanged.

With MotoGP closer than ever, grid position became more important and qualifying brutally competitive. Nobody made more of qualifying than Ducati. When their riders dug deep, they had Ducati's famous 'mechanical grip', so they could try to squeeze every last drop of rear grip from the tyre. When up off the edge, they had the benefit of the grid's most advanced rear ride-height device; when out of a corner, they had what Ducati is most famous for: engine power. Then, at the end of the straight, Ducati's braking stability – and for the first time ever, Ducati riders were able to release the brake and turn the bike without losing all that they had gained.

Actuation of the rear ride-height device was particularly clever. Riders could pre-select operation on a preceding straight, when they were not quite so occupied, and it would kick into action the next time the bike was in the full acceleration phase, possibly triggered by full extension of the front forks.

The Desmosedici might not be the easiest bike to ride, needing to be used in a very specific way, but in 2021, Ducati engineers, together with the new generation of riders, were awesome. Bagnaia was the biggest threat to Quartararo, and even without further improvements, the Ducati should remain the bike to beat in 2022. But Gigi Dall'Igna and his team never rest, so it will be interesting to see what changes come for when the engine freeze is lifted.

YAMAHA

YAMAHA knew they had to make some changes if they were going to fix the inconsistency problems of 2020 and become serious title contenders in 2021. The main complaints were lack of acceleration/top speed, and a lack of competitiveness at wet races and especially on drying tracks.

None of this was new. What was new was that Fabio Quartararo could make the bike turn and have good front feel at one circuit, then have problems in this area at the next.

Yamaha arrived at the Qatar test with a bike that looked very similar to the 2020 machine, but on closer inspection, it had a modified chassis that was very different around the steering-head area. To me, it looked similar to the Ducati steering head.

This new chassis held an engine that produced more acceleration and was different from the 2020 motor because it could not be bolted into the 2020 chassis. This could be because of a number of things (engine mounts for example), but most likely because of the updated air intake running through the steering-head area.

This completely revised machine was wrapped in a slightly changed fairing, with a different air intake aperture and slightly improved aerodynamics.

By the close of the final test at Qatar, all the factory riders said that the 2021 Yamaha M1 was an improvement, but management was left to wonder whether it would also be better at the European tracks (the downside of a very limited test schedule).

The only thing obviously missing compared to the opposition was the front holeshot device to compress the front forks for the launch off the line. All other manufacturers were using this to good effect at the Qatar test. Suzuki did not yet have the rear ride-height device, but did not seem to be suffering much in the race start phase. The Yamaha riders obviously were fighting a losing battle with the wheelie most of the way to the first turn: proof that the front holeshot device really did have a positive effect on race start performance.

Why had it taken so long for engineers to adopt the device in MotoGP when it had been in use for decades in motocross, drag racing and even national Superbike championships? It is hard to understand.

Yamaha already had the rear ride-height device from 2020. Depending on rider preference, machines could be fitted with left-thumb or forefinger activation levers.

The updated M1 proved to be a considerable improvement at the opening races. It was also more consistent in the hands of French wonder-boy Quartararo. For him, Yamaha had come up trumps development-wise. He no longer had the front feel complaints of 2020, but at least part of this new-found consistency can be attributed to his own improvements and maturity.

In engine performance, Yamaha still lost out to the V4s on long straights, but they were losing less in acceleration over the first few hundred metres. Better late than never.

Eventually, Yamaha introduced their own version of the front holeshot device. No point Quartararo risking all for pole, only to lose a row of the grid to the first turn. Yamaha gave him what he needed, and he did the rest.

As in 2020, Yamaha continued to experiment with carbon-fibre and aluminium swing-arms, but in the latter half of the year, all 2021 factory machines settled on aluminium.

Yamaha were the winners in 2021 and really did improve where needed. It was difficult to spot any weaknesses in Quartararo's game, but I believe Yamaha had at least a couple of weak areas that they (and Fabio) will want to work on and improve for 2022. First, they need greater strength on the long straights, and last, but not least, better wet- and drying-track performance. The latter is a particular Achilles heel that could lose them a championship if the weather doesn't go their way. Whenever the circuit conditions were mixed (damp, no standing water), the Yamahas were absolutely nowhere. In the wet, Quartararo held his own, but I think he was lucky not to have had more races in such conditions. Maybe he won't be so lucky in 2022.

A big part of Quartararo's winning game in 2021 was his brilliance in qualifying. His ability to put together a special lap that gave him 14 front-row starts was key to his success. Without a good start position, the Yamaha, much like the Suzuki, was weak in the race battle, losing ground on exits and having to rely on the rider pushing the entry to the point where the front tyre cried no more (Rins regularly, Quatararo in Portimao, and Mir every time he faded or made contact with another rider on entry).

If Yamaha are going to have a chance of challenging Ducati in 2022, they will need to step up in the engine department.

HONDA

AFTER a very tough year in 2020 without Marc Marquez, due to injury, and also a lack of rear grip in every phase – corner entry, mid-turn and exit – Honda arrived at the Qatar pre-season tests with a range of new parts, to be tested back to back with the old ones. These included a number of old and new chassis, exhausts, front wings, rear shocks and linkages, and a front holeshot device to complement the rear ride-height device they had been developing since mid-2020.

They also had an exciting new signing, Pol Espargaro. This was a master stroke by team manager Alberto Puig. Espargaro is an experienced and highly motivated rider who had already proved he could handle a less-than-perfect, relatively difficult-to-ride V4 MotoGP bike in the shape of the early KTMs.

Honda could not test engine parts due to the development freeze, as a frustrated Puig pointed out to me pre-season. The mighty HRC had been struggling to fix their rear grip problem for a year or so, and I had already come to the conclusion that it could have something to do with their engine's characteristics. Puig's despondent comments only reinforced my thoughts.

From the start, it was clear that even though Honda had put a big effort into fixing their problems, they were still struggling. Over the following races, I saw them go back to earlier exhausts and chassis. This was a clear sign that they were not making the progress they had hoped for.

Espargaro took on the new chassis almost immediately. Marquez started many FP1s with both an old (2020) chassis and the all-new version, but he always raced the old chassis (winning at Sachsenring and Austin on it), until Misano 2, where finally he had a version of the new chassis that he liked (Honda brought something like five versions over the season). He used it to win, with Espargaro finishing second, also on a new chassis. Misano seemed to be where Marc finally decided that it offered an advantage. Alex Marquez also opted for the new chassis in the second Misano race, for the first time.

Was it a big step forward? I don't think so, more like a small step. But I do think Honda were learning ways of improving grip, and no doubt this knowledge will be very useful in 2022 with their new machine, which will also receive engine updates.

Thinking back to Marc's injurious crash at Jerez in 2020, his crash at Assen 2021 in free practice and Pol Espargaro's crash at Valencia's final round, they were all huge on-throttle high-sides. This points to a failure of the electronics that are meant to help prevent such a situation. Although KTM had something similar in Austria with Miguel Olivera, no other manufacturer has repeatedly suffered from this.

With Marc absent throughout 2020, Honda were left behind by the opposition and suffered greatly in 2021, despite Marc demonstrating that he was still a huge force to be reckoned with. If he is in good shape physically in 2022, and given the might of HRC when backed into a corner, as they have been, we should see Honda again prove to be a serious title contender.

Above: Marc Marquez used this 2020 Honda chassis until later in the season.
Photo: Simon Crafar

Left: Front forks on Nakagami's Honda show the fittings that operate the hole-shot device.
Photo: Gold & Goose

Top: Honda's RCV213. The hangover of Marquez's absence in 2020 cast a shadow on development.
Photo: Repsol Honda

Top far left: Yamaha's complex working environment.

Far left: The 2021 M1 looked much the same as the previous model.
Photos: Monster Energy Yamaha MotoGP

TECHNICAL ROUND-UP

Above: KTM tested this wing on the rear seat, but did not race it.
Photo: Simon Crafar

Left: Suzuki was slow to catch up with ride-height developments.

Centre, from left: Suzuki chassis offered refined handling; curved chassis members controlled flex ratios; Aprilia reveals ride-height switch below left handlebar.
Photos: www.suzuki-racing.com/Simon Crafar

Top: All-new Aprilia benefited from free engine and aero development.
Photo: Simon Crafar

Right: KTM chased chassis changes to accommodate differing tyre characteristics.
Photo: Red Bull KTM

APRILIA

APRILIA were significantly the biggest improvers in 2021. With Aleix Espargaro on board, they were competitive everywhere, securing 11 top-ten finishes, including one podium in the first 14 races, until the abnormally bumpy CoTA circuit in Texas interrupted their impressive run. Then they also suffered with rear grip when it became cold in the autumn.

Free from the restrictions that hampered the non-concession teams, the 2021 version of the RS-GP had been developed and improved in every area over the winter, especially in braking and corner-entry phases, and it arrived at the Qatar pre season tests looking like the all-new bike that it was – new front wing, fairing, chassis, carbon-fibre swing-arm, radical new exhausts, front holeshot device and new seat unit.

Other bonuses, as the only team able to take advantage of official concessions, included less restricted testing and free engine development. The 90-degree V4 that had replaced the narrower-angle V4 in 2020 now had increased power and rpm – when it had first appeared, rpm had been restricted to avoid risking reliability.

Espargaro was full of praise, and after some races, even opposition riders were impressed by the competitiveness of the Aprilia. Then, no sooner had they perfected their rear ride-height device, than they started work on its automated activation, at a time when only Ducati had such a feature. A clear example of innovation and motivation.

The Aprilia was now competitively fast and stable on the brakes. But often with stability comes heavy handling, forcing riders to use more energy in muscling the machine from side to side.

Aprilia could be very proud of what they had achieved in the 12 months to the end of the 2021 season. Now, with Maverick Vinales aboard and showing signs of making friends with the first V4 he has ever ridden, these are exciting times for the Noale factory. The question is how much will the other manufacturers progress in 2022, when the freeze on engine development lifts?

SUZUKI

THE 2020 world champions and their riders had a tough time in 2021. Not as tough as Honda, but well short of what they would have been hoping for in their title defence.

The Suzuki was still a very good machine, but when Yamaha, Ducati, Aprilia and even KTM had made some clear progress, Suzuki had not, and the riders paid dearly. Joan Mir was every bit as good as he had been in 2020, possibly even more skilled, but no longer was he able to make big inroads into the opposition in the second half of a race.

At this level, losing two- or three-tenths on each long acceleration area alone (due to the lack of a rear ride-height device in the first half of the straight, and engine speed in the second) is something that riders just can't be expected to make up for. Both riders made mistakes. Rins tended to crash on corner entry, while Mir made several imperfect overtaking attempts. But that's what happens when a rider is being forced to find a way to make up ground on the entry that he's lost on the exit.

Suzuki finally debuted their version of the rear ride-height device in Austria, but it was too little, too late. As for every team, acquisition of prototype equipment is only the first step. Then the hard work begins in trying to perfect it, so that it drops at the right moment and at the right rate, then disengages correctly and smoothly again in the braking phase. It took other manufacturers at least half a season to get the device working, closer to a year to perfect it, so it seemed doubtful that we would see the Suzuki device working perfectly in 2021, and we didn't.

At Austin, we briefly saw a new carbon-fibre-reinforced chassis for Mir, and again at Misano. I believe this was aimed at improving braking stability.

Suzuki's overall weakness in qualifying continued in 2021, though it improved at the last two rounds. They seem to have great rear grip that clearly helps them in the later stages of races, but the riders find it impossible to squeeze something extra – something special from a shiny new soft tyre – for a time attack. Poor grid positions are an extreme handicap in this championship, especially when you no longer have an advantage in any other areas.

Suzuki are close. Mir finished third in 2021, only bettered by Quartararo and Bagnaia. With only a small amount of progress, they could very well be fighting for the championship again in 2022, but they will need to pull out all the stops.

KTM

AFTER having their best season in 2020, KTM would have been expecting to hit the ground running in 2021, but yet again, the brutal reality of MotoGP hit them hard from day one at the Qatar test, and subsequent race results were a big disappointment.

This class never stands still. Yamaha, Ducati and Aprilia had made steps forward, and that progress, combined with a different front tyre construction, adversely affected KTM. The bike's strong point is in the braking zone, and to exploit this advantage, they need a very strong front tyre. Thus they were disappointed that the front tyre they favoured was no longer in the allocation. Once again, the KTMs were fighting for the lower places.

Those who follow MotoGP closely will be familiar with the rapid response and depth of KTM development, and they did not take this bad start to 2021 lying down. An attitude of disappointment quickly changed to one of, "How can we get the most from the tyres we have available?" (This being a key in racing.)

After regrouping, they arrived at Mugello, a couple of races later, with a new chassis and a new synthetic fuel, and they came out swinging. Race boss Pit Beirer admitted surprise at such an effect, after mixed reviews at brief tests. But with rider confidence and the new fuel, results improved. Binder's small stature and big bravery allowed him to equal Zarco and Ducati's new outright Doha speed record of 225.5mph. Oliveira finished a strong second, then at Catalunya, another high-speed track, won convincingly. Given struggles at tight circuits like Valencia, I wonder if KTM concentrated on top-end power at the expense of a little low-end torque.

Again, KTM did not stand still. They went straight to work on another version of the chassis, going further in the same direction. This was delivered at Aragon, seven races later. They played musical chassis over the next few races. Some confusion was caused at least in part by Oliveira's injury in Austria, where a TC glitch caused him to be launched into the air. The subsequent drop in confidence from such an event always affects otherwise clear feedback when testing new items.

Overall in 2021, KTM machines kept their trait of being strong in braking, though they regularly suffered front tyre locking, which was average in the turning phase, but showed a distinct weakness in the acceleration phase due to a lack of rear grip. Probably it is not a complete coincidence that the Honda and the KTM shared these traits, considering that the basic technical specs of these two machines are very similar.

During the season, one difference from the Honda (and the Aprilia) was revealed. Rather than being a 90-degree V4, the KTM is actually configured at 86 degrees. The aim of this design was to improve packaging with a slightly more compact design, while retaining the basic advantages of a V4 without having to add a balance shaft. Engineers admitted that they'd probably opt for 90 degrees if they had their time again.

In line with the opposition, KTM developed a rear ride-height device. They tested a couple of different rear drop heights with this. In the end, once all the different machines had the device, it was back to a relatively even playing field, with only Ducati out on their own in terms of acceleration and top speed.

Overall, KTM were very close, but they trailed most of the Japanese manufacturers and Ducati. A fruitful winter will be needed to discover the small refinements that will make a big difference.

TECHNICAL ROUND-UP 51

D. PEDROSA
A. MARQUEZ
L. LECUONA
L. SAVADORI
D. PETRUCCI
L. MARINI
M. PIRRO
S. GUINTOLI
Y. TEST1
J. MARTIN
Y. TEST3
E. BASTIANINI
YAMAHA
MONSTER ENERGY
ENEOS

TEAM-BY-TEAM
2021 MOTOGP REVIEW

Teams and Riders
MATTHEW BIRT

Bike Illustrations
ADRIAN DEAN

Bike Specifications
SIMON CRAFAR

Photo: Monster Energy Yamaha MotoGP

DUCATI LENOVO TEAM

TEAM STAFF

Luigi DALL'IGNA: Ducati Corse General Manager
Paolo CIABATTI: Ducati Corse Sporting Director
Davide BARANA: Ducati Corse Technical Director
Davide TARDOZZI: Team Manager
Riccardo SAVIN: Chassis & Vehicle Dynamics Engineer
Gabriele CONTI: Electronic Systems Manager
Massimo BARTOLINI: Vehicle Performance Engineer
Leonardo SIMONCINI: Track Technical Co-ordinator
Michele MUZZI: Team Technical Co-ordinator
Andrea GIAVARINI: Data Analyst
Artur VILALTA: MotoGP Press Manager
Julie GIOVANOLA: MotoGP Press Officer
Mauro GRASSILLI: Marketing & Sponsorship Manager
Paola BRAIATO: Operations Manager
Davide GIBERTINI: Team Co-ordinator
Davide BARALDINI: Warehouse

JACK MILLER PIT CREW

Cristian PUPULIN: Track Engineer
Andrea MATTIOLI: Electronics Engineer
Michele PERUGINI: Chief Mechanic
Marco POLASTRI, Fabio MORANDINI,
Pedro RIVERA CRESPO, Giuliano POLETTI: Mechanics
Rhys HOLMES: Öhlins Suspension Technician

FRANCESCO BAGNAIA PIT CREW

Cristian GABARRINI: Track Engineer
Tommaso PAGANO: Electronics Engineer
Marco VENTURA: Chief Mechanic
Ivan BRANDI, Massimo TOGNACCI,
Lorenzo CANESTRARI, Tommaso PELI: Mechanics
Giacomo MASSAROTTO: Öhlins Suspension Technician

JACK MILLER
Born: 18 January, 1995 – Townsville, Queensland, Australia
GP Starts: 172 (117 MotoGP, 55 Moto3/125cc)
GP Wins: 9 (3 MotoGP, 6 Moto3)

FRANCESCO BAGNAIA
Born: 14 January, 1997 – Torino, Italy
GP Starts: 152 (47 MotoGP, 36 Moto2, 69 Moto3)
GP Wins: 14 (4 MotoGP, 8 Moto2, 2 Moto3)
World Championships 1 Moto2

Photos: Ducati Corse

DUCATI might have unleashed a new Italian factory star in Pecco Bagnaia in 2021, but its long quest for an elusive second MotoGP crown rumbles on into 2022. For the fourth time in five years, a Ducati rider finished second in the World Championship.

With triple runner-up Andrea Dovizioso off the scene, it was Bagnaia's turn to pick up the baton for the Bologna brand. The Valentino Rossi protégé was more than a match for the task. A pole and podium on his factory-team debut was followed by a stunning fight back from 11th to second in Portimao.

A crash out of the lead in an emotionally draining home race at Mugello was one of only two DNFs of a breakthrough campaign. Second to 11th in Styria, and to 14th with grip problems in Britain dented his title challenge, but his maiden premier-class victory will live long in the memory.

Bagnaia survived seven late overtakes by Marc Marquez in Aragon to take Italy's 250th premier-class win. It was also the first time in 21 years that six different nationalities had won in the premier class in the same season.

Then he withstood late pressure from title rival Fabio Quartararo in Misano to become just the sixth Ducati rider in history to win back-to-back races.

The 2018 Moto2 world champion was again under the guidance and calming influence of track engineer Cristian Gabbarini, who had masterminded Ducati's

DUCATI Desmosedici GP21

Engine: 1000cc liquid-cooled 90-degree V4, counter-rotating crankshaft, DOHC, 4-valves per cylinder, desmodromic valve gear
Power: More than 250bhp
Ancillaries: Magneti Marelli ECU, Dorna software, ride-by-wire fuel injection, active Akrapovic titanium 4-into-2 exhaust • *Lubrication:* Shell Advance
Transmission: Six-speed seamless-shift cassette-type gearbox, dry clutch, DID chain
Frame: Aluminium-alloy twin-spar chassis, carbon-fibre swing-arm, front and rear ride-height devices
Suspension: Öhlins inverted front fork, carbon outer tubes, Öhlins rear shock absorber
Tyres: Michelin • *Brakes:* Brembo 340mm carbon-fibre twin front discs, single stainless steel rear disc, thumb and foot levers

MICHELE PIRRO
Born: 5 July, 1986 – San Giovanni Rotondo, Italy
GP Starts: 107 (60 MotoGP, 18 Moto2, 29 125cc)
GP Wins: 1 Moto2

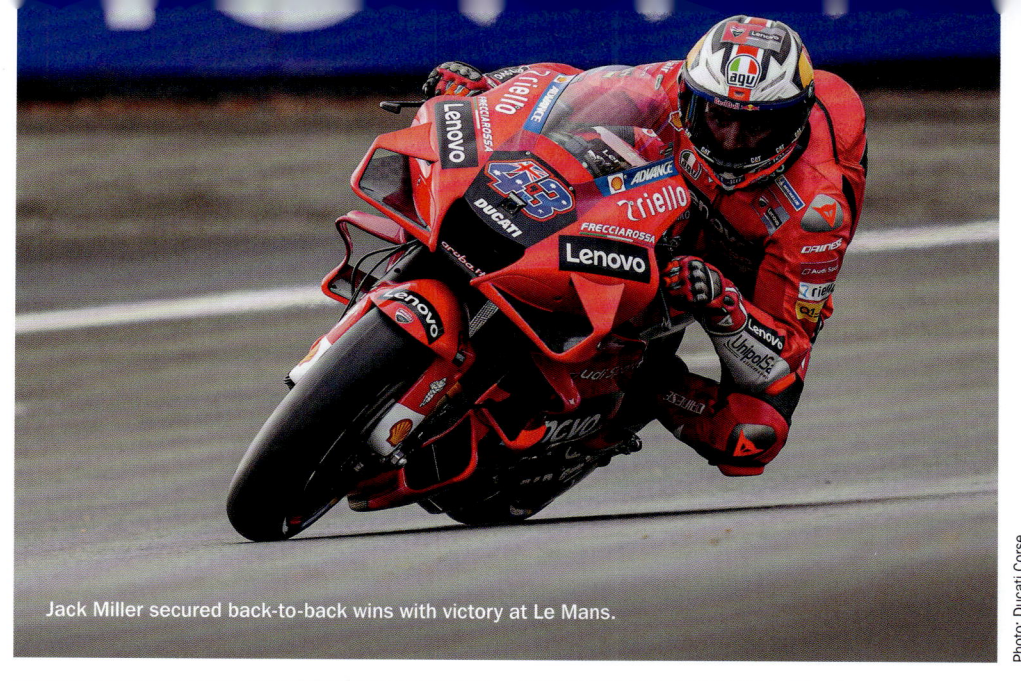

Jack Miller secured back-to-back wins with victory at Le Mans.

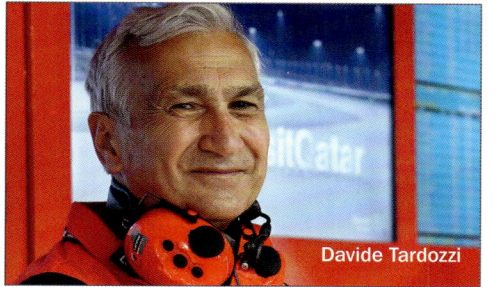

Davide Tardozzi

Paulo Ciabatti

Francesco Bagnaia winning at Aragon.

Celebrating a Ducati 1-2 finish at Jerez.

only MotoGP title success in 2007 with Casey Stoner, and had nurtured Bagnaia in the Pramac team in 2019 and 2020.

Also back in the factory team was electronics engineer Tommaso Pagano. In addition, Bagnaia worked with the ex-Petrucci crew, comprising chief mechanic Marco Ventura and mechanics Ivan Brandi, Massimo Tognacci, Lorenzo Canestrari and Tommaso Peli.

Unusually, Ducati had completely cleared its factory rider line-up, bringing in Bagnaia's Pramac teammate Jack Miller. The Australian was also allowed to bring two key members of his Pramac staff with him – track engineer Cristian Pupulin and electronics engineer Andrea Mattioli.

Miller's crew was also changed by mechanic Marco Polastri transferring from Pramac. The only personnel retained from Dovizioso's farewell campaign on a Desmosedici were chief mechanic Michele Perugini, and mechanics Pedro Crespo and Giuliano Poletti.

Two underwhelming ninth places in the Qatar double-header were followed by a DNF in Portimao. With pressure mounting, Miller's response was emphatic. He won in Jerez after capitalising on Quartararo's arm-pump, to help Ducati claim four podiums in the opening four races for the first time in its history. He backed that with another win in a dramatic flag-to-flag race success in France, the first Australian to take back-to-back wins since Stoner in 2012.

His title challenge petered out, however, with only three more podiums coming after France. But Miller had emerged as a constant top-six contender, and it was no surprise when Ducati took up an option on him for 2022 just before its home round in Mugello in late May.

Individual glory may have escaped Ducati again, but the consolation came in the fact that it successfully defended the constructors' title and won the teams' championship.

The upper echelons of Ducati featured a very familiar line-up. Ducati Corse general manager Gigi Dall'Igna was backed again by sporting director Paolo Ciabatti, technical director Davide Barana and team manager Davide Tardozzi.

Riccardo Savin (chassis and vehicle dynamics engineer), Gabriele Conti (electronic systems manager) and Massimo Bartolini (vehicle performance engineer) were also back in key roles. Andrea Giavarini was recruited in the new position of data analyst.

Ducati welcomed a new title backer in 2021, and for the first time it appeared on the official entry list at the Ducati Lenovo Team, after an alliance with the computer company since 2018. The expansion to full naming rights will last until at least the end of 2024.

With restrictions eased, wild-cards returned in 2021, and Ducati brought in test rider Michele Pirro for three appearances. He finished with a best of 11th in the first of two Misano races.

MONSTER ENERGY YAMAHA MOTOGP

TEAM STAFF

Hiroshi ITO: President, Yamaha Motor Racing & General Manager, Motorsports Development

Lin JARVIS: Managing Director, Yamaha Motor Racing & Team Principal

Takahiro SUMI: MotoGP Group Leader, Yamaha Motor Racing

Massimo MEREGALLI: Team Director

William FAVERO: Marketing & Communications

MAVERICK VINALES/CAL CRUTCHLOW/ FRANCO MORBIDELLI PIT CREW

Silvano GALBUSERA: Crew Chief

Federico GIOVANNINI: Yamaha Engineer

Davide MARELLI: Data Engineer

Ian GILPIN, Jurij PELLEGRINI, Julien ARMENGAUD, Juan MADURGA REVILLA: Mechanics

FABIO QUARTARARO PIT CREW

Diego GUBELLINI: Crew Chief

Shinya YADA: Yamaha Engineer

Pablo GUILLIEM: Data Engineer

Bernard ANSIAU, Achim KARIGER, Daniele GRELLI, Mark ELDER: Mechanics

Julian SIMON: Rider Performance Analyst

MAVERICK VINALES
Born: 12 January, 1995 – Figueres, Spain
GP Starts: 187 (120 MotoGP, 18 Moto2, 49 Moto3/125cc)
GP Wins: 25 (9 MotoGP, 4 Moto2, 12 Moto3/125cc)
World Championships: 1 Moto3

FABIO QUARTARARO
Born: 20 April, 1999 – Nice, France
GP Starts: 118 (51 MotoGP, 36 Moto2, 31 Moto3)
GP Wins: 9 (8 MotoGP, 1 Moto2)
World Championships: 1 MotoGP

YAMAHA'S official factory squad had plenty to celebrate in its 60th grand prix anniversary. New golden boy Fabio Quartararo had filled the sizeable void left by Valentino Rossi with consummate ease, the formidable Frenchman delivering a first title for the Iwata factory since Jorge Lorenzo in 2015.

Quartararo was the star pupil in a high-calibre class of 2021, and he became France's first premier-class world champion, with statistics that emphasised his superiority. He scored points in every race bar one, and five wins, ten podiums, five poles and 14 front-row starts meant that almost single-handedly he had made it a triple crown for Yamaha, although ultimately the constructors' and teams' accolades were claimed by Ducati.

The title might have been wrapped up sooner than in the Algarve, had a chronic arm-pump issue not robbed him of a win in Jerez. And then there was the bizarre 'zip-gate' business in Catalunya, where he finished third, but was demoted to sixth after racing without his mandatory chest protector and with his Alpinestars leathers not correctly fastened.

He also missed the top six in Austria and Aragon, and crashed at Portimao, but those blips apart, he was a supreme and deserving champion.

His win in round two at Doha put him on the top

YAMAHA YZR-M1

Engine: 1000cc liquid-cooled in-line 4, counter-rotating cross-plane crankshaft, DOHC, 4 valves per cylinder, pneumatic valve return system
Power: More than 240bhp
Ancillaries: Magneti Marelli ECU, Dorna software, ride-by-wire fuel injection, active Akrapovic titanium 4-into-2-into-1 exhaust
Transmission: Six-speed seamless-shift cassette-type gearbox, dry clutch
Frame: Aluminium twin-spar chassis, aluminium or carbon-fibre swing-arm, front and rear ride-height devices
Suspension: Öhlins inverted front fork, Öhlins rear shock absorber • *Wheels:* Forged magnesium, 17in diameter • *Tyres:* Michelin
Brakes: Brembo 320 or 340mm carbon-fibre twin front discs; single steel rear disc, thumb and foot levers

CAL CRUTCHLOW
Born: 29 October, 1985 – Coventry, England
GP Starts: 172 MotoGP
GP Wins: 3 MotoGP
World Championships: 1 World Supersport

FRANCO MORBIDELLI
Born: 4 December, 1994 – Rome, Italy
GP Starts: 133 (62 MotoGP, 71 Moto2)
GP Wins: 11 (3 MotoGP, 8 Moto2)
World Championships: 1 Moto2

The Yamaha team celebrate their championship success.

Fabio Quartararo recorded five wins in his championship year.

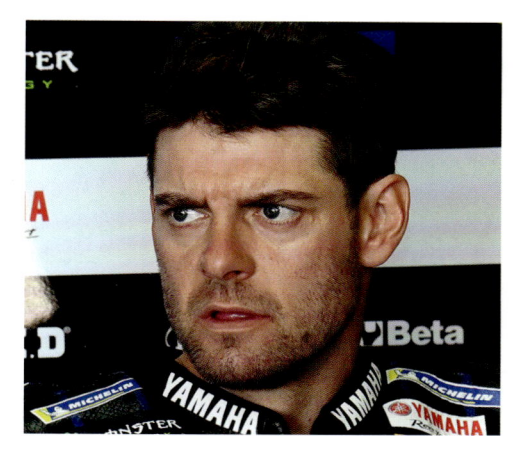

Vinales was victorious in Qatar.

step of the first podium to feature two Frenchman in the premier class since 1954, the first ever top-class one, two.

It took him just eight races in 2021 to better his points tally from 14 outings in a Covid-19 hit 2020, and when he finished second in Misano, he overtook Christian Sarron as the most successful Frenchman in terms of podiums in the premier class.

Quartararo's arrival as replacement for fading star Rossi led to Yamaha instigating wholesale changes to its garage workforce. He brought crew chief Diego Gubellini and data engineer Pablo Guilliem from Petronas in his slipstream, while mechanics Achim Kariger and Daniele Grelli also made the switch.

The only evidence of Rossi's past was that Bernard Ansiau and Mark Elder remained. Long-serving and loyal Rossi crew members Alex Briggs and Brent Stephens had departed, having been at the Italian's side throughout his glory years at Yamaha. Both found jobs in the domestic Australian Superbike series, with Briggs working for Michelin. Stephens joined the Gold Coast DesmoSport Ducati team, working for Mike Jones, who had raced three times in MotoGP in 2017 and 2018 as a Ducati replacement rider for Avintia and Angel Nieto.

Yamaha's senior management structure remained as before. Hiroshi Ito was president of Yamaha Motor Racing (YMR) and general manager of Yamaha Motor Company's (YMC) Motorsports Development Division. Lin Jarvis also filled a dual role of YMR managing director and principal of the Monster Energy Yamaha MotoGP Team. Takahiro Sumi was YMC MotoGP group leader, and Monster Energy Yamaha Team director was again the remit of Massimo Meregalli.

Yamaha kicked off its 60th anniversary celebrations by confirming on 15th February that it had agreed a new five-year deal with Dorna.

Quartararo revelled in his elevated status in the factory team, but Yamaha's 2021 season was also a whirlwind of controversy, chaos and crisis.

There was little hint of the turbulent times that lay ahead when Maverick Vinales won the opening round in Qatar. He was paired with crew chief Esteban Garcia; Davide Marelli returned as data engineer, and Ian Gilpin, Jurij Pellegrini and Juan Revilla were back as mechanics, too. Julien Armengaud came in as replacement for Javier Ullate.

Garcia, crew chief for Vinales's Moto3 title in 2013, had been chosen by the rider in 2019, after he had dispensed with the experienced Ramon Forcada. There were no obvious signs of issues with their relationship when it was revealed that he was being replaced by Silvano Galbusera from the Catalan round onwards.

Galbusera had been the chosen one to replace Jerry Burgess when Rossi had unceremoniously dumped the legendary Aussie at the end of 2013. Then Rossi had fired Galbusera at the end of 2019, but he was retained by Yamaha in the test team that worked initially with Lorenzo in 2020 and newly hired test rider Cal Crutchlow for 2021.

The crew change masked a significant erosion in an increasingly fraught relationship between Vinales and Yamaha. Inexplicably, he qualified second last and finished last in Sachsenring, before a week later starting from pole and finishing second in Assen, ahead of extremely awkward podium celebrations. Immediately after Assen, it was confirmed that Yamaha had agreed to release Vinales from his two-year deal at the end of 2021, which triggered ultimately correct gossip that he was heading to Aprilia for 2022.

The relationship went into an irreversible meltdown during a remarkable Styrian GP at the Red Bull Ring in Austria. Vinales was last again, but in a shock plot twist, he was suspended from the second Austrian race due to "unexplained irregular use of the motorcycle". In other words, he deliberately attempted to blow up his YZR-M1 engine in a moment of madness that not only threatened his own safety, but those of his peers on track.

Less than a week later, Yamaha announced that they had reached a "mutual decision" with Vinales to split forthwith. He quickly found a new home at Aprilia, but the complete breakdown in his relationship with Yamaha created a huge headache for the Japanese manufacturer, which also had significant implications for its Petronas-supported Independent Team.

Cal Crutchlow substituted at Silverstone and Motorland Aragon, but the unexpected vacancy alongside Quartararo gave Yamaha the opportunity to upgrade Franco Morbidelli and fast-track him into the factory team when the Italian returned from major surgery to his left knee at Misano. Simultaneously, Yamaha confirmed a two-year factory deal for 2022 and 2023.

MotoGP · TEAM REVIEW 57

TEAM SUZUKI ECSTAR

TEAM STAFF
Shinichi SAHARA: Project Leader
Ken KAWAUCHI: Technical Manager
Atsushi KAWASAKI: Chassis Engineer
Jordi MELENDO: Parts Manager
Roberto BRIVIO, Mitia DOTTA: Team Co-ordinators
Alberto GOMEZ: Marketing & Communication Manager
Federico TONDELLI: Press Officer & Media Co-ordinator
Hatsumi TSUKAMOTO: Marketing Operations & Relations
Adriana PINTO: Digital Co-ordinator
Emanuele MAZZINI: Test Team Co-ordinator
Massimo TOMASONI: Truck Driver

ALEX RINS CREW
Jose Manuel CAZEAUX: Crew Chief
Yuta SHIMABUKURO: Engine Management Engineer
Davide MANFREDI, Massimo MIRANO, Kevin LOUSSOUARN, Paco NOGUEIRA: Mechanics

JOAN MIR PIT CREW
Frankie CARCHEDI: Crew Chief:
Claudio RAINATO: Engine Management Engineer
Tsutomu MATSUGANO, Jacques ROCA, Marco Rosa GASTAIDO, Fernando MENDEZ PICON: Mechanics

JOAN MIR
Born: 1 September, 1997 – Palma de Mallorca, Spain
GP Starts: 104 (49 MotoGP, 18 Moto2, 37 Moto3)
GP Wins: 12 (1 MotoGP, 11 Moto3)
World Championships: 2 (1 MotoGP, 1 Moto3)

ALEX RINS
Born: 8 December, 1995 – Barcelona, Spain
GP Starts: 168 (80 MotoGP, 36 Moto2, 52 Moto3)
GP Wins: 15 (3 MotoGP, 4 Moto2, 8 Moto3)

Photos: www.suzuki-racing.com

SUZUKI'S hopes of launching a successful MotoGP title defence were dealt a crushing blow before a wheel had even turned in anger in 2021. The Hamamatsu factory had won its first premier-class crown in two decades in 2020, but was rocked to its core on 7th January with the bombshell news that influential and respected team manager Davide Brivio was quitting.

Brivio had joined Suzuki in 2013 and had masterminded its full-time return to MotoGP in 2015. This was after Suzuki had opted to take a three-year break at the end of 2011 because of the ongoing impact of the global recession.

His success had gained widespread acclaim in MotoGP, but crucially his impressive accomplishments were becoming known outside the two-wheeled motorsport arena. Within days of his resignation, he was confirmed as racing director of the Alpine Formula 1 team, which was a rebrand of Renault F1 for 2021. He would oversee the return to F1 of Spanish legend Fernando Alonso to race alongside Esteban Ocon in a deal he said he simply couldn't refuse.

SUZUKI GSX-RR

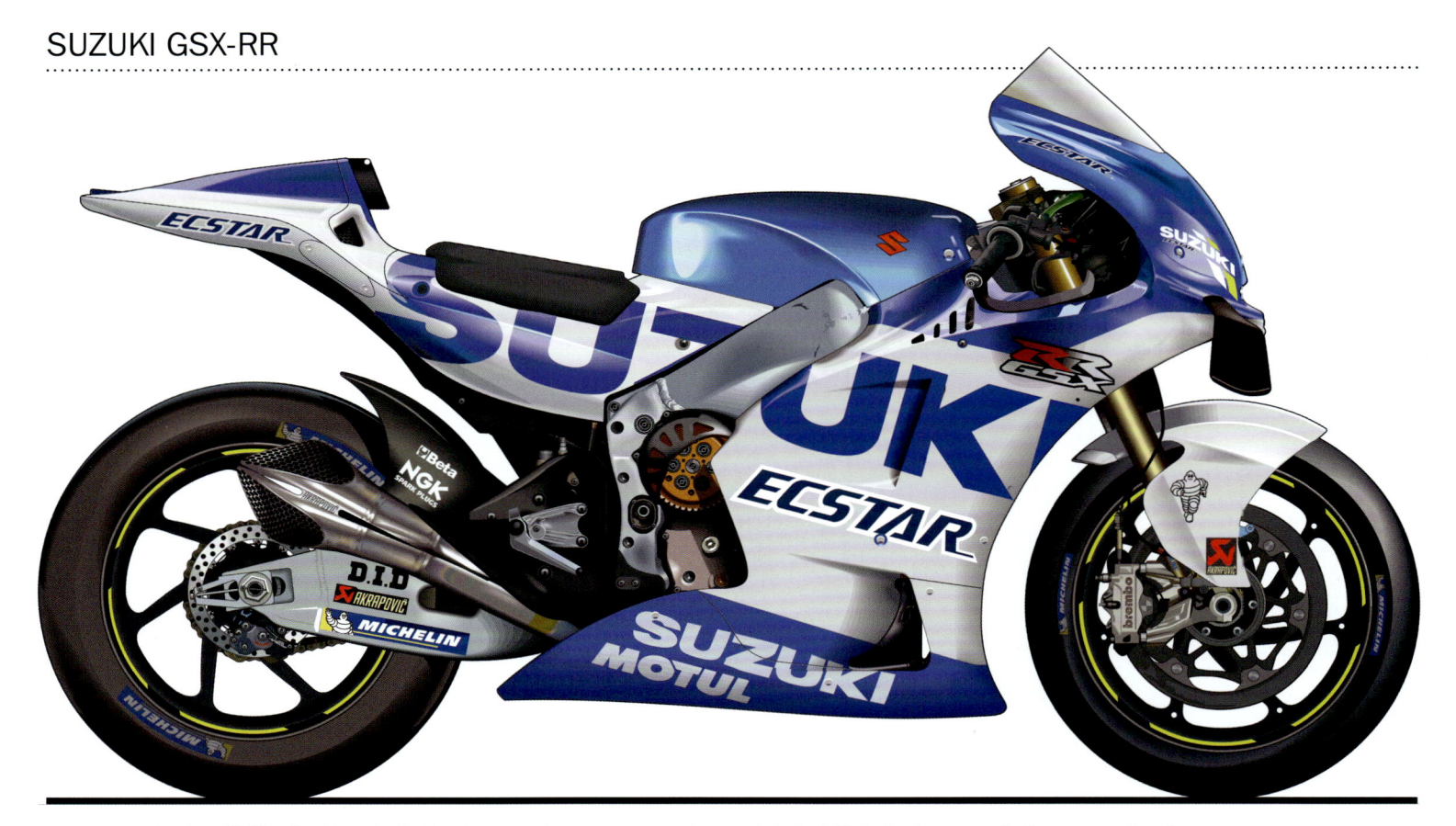

Engine: 1000cc liquid-cooled in-line 4, cross-plane counter-rotating crankshaft, DOHC, 4 valves per cylinder, pneumatic valve return system
Power: More than 240bhp
Ancillaries: Magneti Marelli ECU, Dorna software, ride-by-wire fuel injection, active Akropovic titanium 4-into-2 exhaust
Transmission: Six-speed seamless-shift cassette-type gearbox, dry clutch
Frame: Aluminium twin-spar chassis, aluminium or carbon-fibre swing-arm, front and rear ride-height devices
Suspension: Öhlins inverted front fork, Öhlins rear shock absorber
Brakes: Brembo carbon-fibre twin front discs, single steel rear disc, thumb and foot levers

Mir and Suzuki were unable to challenge for victory in 2021.

Second place in Styria for Mir.

Brivio's decision had come as a bolt from the blue for Suzuki's management. Alex Rins even thought he was being pranked when first informed of the news. The timing of his departure meant that it was nigh on impossible for Suzuki to find a suitable replacement in time for the start of Joan Mir's title defence in Qatar on 28th March. The interim solution was the formation of a committee made up of seven current key members of the project.

The most senior member of the 'magnificent seven' was team director Shinichi Sahara. Technical manager Ken Kawauchi was a member, as was Mir's crew chief, Frankie Carchedi, and Rins's crew chief, Jose Manuel Cazeaux. Also selected were team co-ordinators Roberto Brivio – brother of departed Davide – and Mitia Dotta. Completing the committee was marketing and communications manager Alberto Gomez.

One of the most important decisions taken over the heads of the committee was confirmed in late April, when it was announced that Suzuki had signed a new five-year contract with Dorna to remain in MotoGP until the end of 2026.

The committee was only ever seen as a stopgap measure, and by the end of the season, Sahara had made it clear that Suzuki was actively seeking to hire a team manager for 2022.

Pre-season upheaval aside, Suzuki's title defence never looked like gaining any serious momentum, although that certainly wasn't for a lack of effort on the part of Mir, who blended skill and aggression, often outclassing Rins. He felt that he was riding better than when he had been crowned world champion, but the factory GSX-RR appeared to stagnate.

Suzuki certainly didn't develop its bike at the same rate as some of its rivals, with Yamaha, Ducati and Aprilia making clear progress. An example was its rear ride-height device, which didn't appear until round ten in Styria, despite the fact that this was now essential technology – Ducati had been experimenting with it since the tail end of 2019.

Mir's reign as world champion ended with three rounds remaining, a low-key eighth in Austin making it mathematically impossible for him to overhaul Fabio Quartararo and Pecco Bagnaia.

The Spaniard was certainly never dull to watch. However, Suzuki's failure to make significant strides with its time-attack performance meant that frequently he had to fight for the podium from the third or fourth row of the grid; surprisingly, he still secured a top-three overall finish, despite never leading a single lap in the entire season.

Unsurprisingly, he didn't tinker with a winning line-up, and under crew chief Carchedi, his staff remained the same: Claudio Rainato was retained as engine management engineer, while Tsutomu Matsugano, Jacques Roca, Marco Gastaldo and Fernando Picon stayed as mechanics.

Any hopes of retaining the teams' championship prize were blown off course by a lacklustre season for Rins, who endured his worst campaign since an injury-blighted rookie season in 2017. Like Mir, his support crew, under crew chief Cazeaux, was untouched: Yuta Shimabukuro was back as engine management engineer, while mechanics were Davide Manfredi, Massimo Mirano, Kevin Loussouarn and Paco Nogueira.

Top-six finishes in the opening two races were a steady, rather than spectacular, start before the Spaniard capitulated in the next four rounds. He was a close second to Quartararo from a rare Suzuki front row in Portimao when he crashed, and then he jumped off again in Jerez, Le Mans and Mugello. It was the first time in his career that Rins had gone four races in a row with no points, but even worse was to follow on the eve of his home race in Barcelona.

In a prime candidate for MotoGP's most bizarre accident, Rins was distracted by his mobile phone while cycling the track and ploughed headfirst into a stationary service vehicle. The outcome was a broken radius bone in his right arm, and a hugely frustrating season ended with a solitary podium at Silverstone's British Grand Prix.

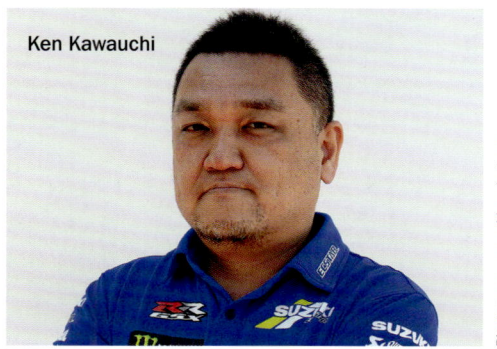

Alex Rins

Shinichi Sahara

Ken Kawauchi

MotoGP · TEAM REVIEW 59

PRAMAC RACING

TEAM STAFF

Paolo CAMPINOTI: Team Principal
Francesco GUIDOTTI: Team Manager
Felix RODRIGUEZ: Team Co-ordinator
Iacopo MICANGELI/Jacopo MENGHETTI: Marketing Manager
Rita SIMONINI: Media & Press Officer
Alex GHINI: Hospitality Manager

JOHANN ZARCO PIT CREW

Marco RIGAMONTI: Crew Chief
Erik CHIARVESIO: Data Engineer
Fabrizio MALAGUTI: Chief Mechanic
Carlo CORRADINI, Adriano CABRAS, Simone ZERBONIA: Mechanics
Moris GRASSI: Fuel & Tyres
Andrea DENARO: Warehouse Spare Parts

JORGE MARTIN PIT CREW

Daniele ROMAGNOLI: Crew Chief
Cristian BATTAGLIA: Data Engineer
Nicola MANNA: Chief Mechanic
David GALACHO, Daniele PENZO, Jarno POLASTRI: Mechanics
Riccardo PEPE: Fuel & Tyres
Andrea DENARO: Warehouse Spare Parts

JOHANN ZARCO
Born: 16 July, 1990 – Cannes, France
GP Starts: 222 (84 MotoGP, 88 Moto2, 50 125cc)
GP Wins: 16 (15 Moto2, 1 125cc)
World Championships: 2 Moto2

JORGE MARTIN
Born: 29 January, 1998 – Madrid, Spain
GP Starts: 113 (14 MotoGP, 32 Moto2, 67 Moto3)
GP Wins: 11 (1 MotoGP, 2 Moto2, 8 Moto3)
World Championships: 1 Moto3

Photo: Gold & Goose

THE status of Ducati's principal independent team was further cemented at the end of another hugely impressive season. In 18 years, no non-factory Ducati rider had ever managed to win. That all changed courtesy of rookie sensation Jorge Martin's stunning debut success from pole position in a restarted Styrian Grand Prix.

Martin was one of the major success stories of 2021, although it certainly wasn't a pain-free exercise for the former Moto3 world champion. His stock rose immediately when he powered to pole position in Qatar in just his second appearance, and he led for 18 laps before finishing a strong third, the first rookie to podium on a Ducati since Ruben Xaus in 2004.

The best was yet to come, but all the early-season momentum vanished in a cloud of dust when he suffered a terrifying high-speed crash in FP3 at round three at Portimao. He was diagnosed with a total of eight fractures and needed surgery to his right thumb, right ankle and left knee.

He missed the following three races, triggering the recall of former Moto2 world champion Tito Rabat, who had switched to WorldSBK. He came in at Jerez and Le Mans, where he scored a single point. Ducati's long-serving test and development rider, Michele Pirro, replaced Martin at Mugello and finished 13th.

On the eve of his return in early June, Ducati announced that Martin's option for 2022 had been

DUCATI Desmosedici GP21 – Pramac

Engine: 1000cc liquid-cooled 90-degree V4, counter-rotating crankshaft, DOHC, 4-valves per cylinder, desmodromic valve gear
Power: More than 250bhp
Ancillaries: Magneti Marelli ECU, Dorna software, ride-by-wire fuel injection, active Akrapovic titanium 4-into-2 exhaust • *Lubrication:* Shell Advance
Transmission: Six-speed seamless-shift cassette-type gearbox, dry clutch, DID chain
Frame: Aluminium-alloy twin-spar chassis, carbon-fibre swing-arm, front and rear ride-height devices
Suspension: Öhlins inverted front fork, carbon outer tubes, Öhlins rear shock absorber
Tyres: Michelin • *Brakes:* Brembo 340mm carbon-fibre twin front discs, single stainless steel rear disc, thumb and foot levers

TITO RABAT
Born: 25 May, 1989 – Barcelona, Spain
GP Starts: 238 (79 MotoGP, 83 Moto2, 76 125cc)
GP Wins: 13 Moto2
World Championships: 1 Moto2

MICHELE PIRRO
Born: 5 July, 1986 – San Giovanni Rotondo, Italy
GP Starts: 107 (60 MotoGP, 18 Moto2, 29 125cc)
GP Wins: 1 Moto2

Second at Le Mans for Johann Zarco.

Paolo Campinoti

Francesco Guidotti

taken up, and once close to full fitness, in Austria, he became Ducati's ninth winner, and only the fifth rookie to have won in the modern four-stroke era, after Marc Marquez, Dani Pedrosa, Jorge Lorenzo and Brad Binder.

Martin, who rode the latest-spec GP21, was paired with crew chief Daniele Romagnoli. The former factory Yamaha crew chief was back in the Pramac fold after moving to Ducati's works squad to lead Danilo Petrucci's crew for 2019 and 2020.

Data engineer Cristian Battaglia made the same transfer back to Pramac; chief mechanic Nicola Manna and mechanic David Galacho kept their roles as long-serving members of the squad.

Early in the year, it had appeared a realistic prospect that a Pramac Ducati rider would contend for the title in 2021. Rescued from oblivion by Ducati at the end of 2019, after his shock decision to quit KTM halfway through a two-year deal, Johann Zarco's promotion to Pramac and the latest-spec GP21 reaped instant rewards.

Second in both Qatar races were the double Moto2 champion's first back-to-back MotoGP podiums, further runner-up spots were secured in Le Mans and Catalunya. Zarco's outstanding early form earned him a 2022 contract renewal, announced at the same time as Martin's extension on the eve of the Barcelona battle. But his title tilt disappeared without trace thereafter. A crash in the chaos of Austria's flag-to-flag triggered the unexpected and alarming collapse.

In the four races that followed, Zarco scored just nine points. His cause certainly wasn't helped by an aggravated arm-pump issue that required surgery pre-Austin, but for all his great moments in 2021, he was the only one of the quartet on board Ducati's vastly improved GP21 not to win, and he remained without a victory in his five-year MotoGP career.

Zarco had been enticed to Ducati for 2020 by the promise of factory staff being assigned to him for a short stint in the underdog Esponsorama Racing Team. He worked with Marco Rigamonti as crew chief and Erik Chiarvesio as data engineer, who were parachuted into Pramac with Zarco as well.

The rest of the crew had worked with rising star Bagnaia in 2020, with chief mechanic Fabrizio Malaguti, and mechanics Carlo Corradini, Adriano Cabras and Simone Zerbonia all remaining.

Pramac Racing's hierarchy continued unchanged. Team principal Paolo Campinoti was backed by team manager Francesco Guidotti. Post-season came surprise news: that Guidotti was joining KTM

The Pramac alliance with Ducati had been formed originally in 2005, and in recent years the Bologna factory had clearly identified Campinoti's project as its prime Independent team. So it came as no surprise, on the eve of their home race in Mugello, that Pramac and Ducati announced the continuation of their collaboration for at least another three years. They will have the latest equipment again.

Martin's maiden MotoGP win in Styria, ahead of Mir.

Zarco and Martin celebrate second and third in Doha.

REPSOL HONDA TEAM

TEAM STAFF

Tetsuhiro KUWATA: HRC Director, General Manager Race Operations

Shigehisa FUJITA: HRC Director, General Manager Business Support

Shinichi KOKUBU: HRC Director, General Manager Technology Development

Takeo YOKOYAMA: HRC Technical Manager

Alberto PUIG: Team Manager

MARC MARQUEZ/STEFAN BRADL PIT CREW

Santi HERNANDEZ: Chief Engineer

Carlo LUZZI: Electronics Engineer

Jenny ANDERSON: Data Engineer

Carlos LINAN: Chief Mechanic

Roberto CLERICI, Jordi CASTELLA, Javier ORTIZ, Koji KAMINAKABEPPU: Mechanics

POL ESPARGARO PIT CREW

Ramon AURIN: Chief Engineer

Ricardo CARRASCOSA: Electronics Engineer

Marco BARBIANI: Data Engineer

Masashi OGO: Chief Mechanic

Emanuel BUCHNER, Carles LURBE, Felix KERTZSCHER, Juan LLANSA: Mechanics

POL ESPARGARO
Born: 10 June, 1991 – Granollers, Spain
GP Starts: 257 (135 MotoGP, 51 Moto2, 71 125cc)
GP Wins: 15 (10 Moto2; 5 125cc)
World Championships: 1 Moto2

MARC MARQUEZ
Born: 17 February, 1993 – Cervera, Spain
GP Starts: 220 (142 MotoGP, 32 Moto2, 46 125cc)
GP Wins: 85 (59, MotoGP, 16 Moto2, 10 125cc)
World Championships: 8 (6 MotoGP, 1 Moto2, 1 125cc)

FEW racing comebacks have been met with such huge anticipation and trepidation as the return of MotoGP's mercurially talented Marc Marquez. The severity of the injury to his right arm, which had sidelined the eight-times world champion for the whole of 2020, became obvious when he needed a third major operation in early December to treat an infection of the humerus bone. That was five months after the initial crash in Jerez, where MotoGP had finally kicked off a Covid-19-delayed 2020 campaign.

An eight-hour surgery, carried out by five specialists at the Hospital Ruber Internacional in Madrid, had ended with the insertion of a new plate and bone graft taken from his hip. Marquez needed a further ten days in hospital, but it was less than a week prior to the season's curtain-raiser in Qatar when the Spaniard confirmed that he would be out of the Doha double-header.

On 10th April, he was given the all-clear to return to racing at Portugal's roller-coaster Portimao. A short statement from HRC concluded by saying, "Marquez can return to competition, assuming the reasonable risk implicit in his sporting activity."

His incalculable value to Honda became appar-

HONDA RC213V – Repsol

Engine: 1000cc liquid-cooled 90-degree V4, counter-rotating crankshaft, DOHC, 4 valves per cylinder, pneumatic valve return system
Power: More than 240bhp
Ancillaries: Magneti Marelli ECU, Dorna software, ride-by-wire fuel injection, non-active Arrow 4-into-2 exhaust
Transmission: Six-speed seamless-shift cassette-type gearbox, dry clutch
Frame: Aluminium twin-spar chassis, carbon-fibre swing-arm, front and rear ride-height devices
Suspension: Öhlins front and rear
Tyres: Michelin • *Brakes:* Brembo twin carbon-fibre front discs, Yutaka single steel rear disc, thumb and foot levers

STEFAN BRADL

Born: 29 November, 1989 – Augsburg, Germany
GP Starts: 198 (111 MotoGP, 33 Moto2, 54 125cc)
GP Wins: 7 (5 Moto2, 2 125cc)
World Championships: 1 Moto2

ent immediately. He finished top Honda on his return, with an emotional seventh place. But his lack of strength and mobility in his right arm were also painfully exposed.

For the first time in his MotoGP career, he failed to score in three races in succession, when he fell out of the lead in a flag-to-flag battle in Le Mans, and crashed out in Mugello and Catalunya.

There were tears of joy and relief, though, at Germany's Sachsenring, where Marquez claimed an astonishing 11th successive victory – 581 days since his previous triumph at Valencia in 2019. The reduced stress on his right arm and shoulder on the anti-clockwise track meant that he was like his old superb self, so it was no surprise when he was a close second in a thriller against Pecco Bagnaia in Motorland Aragon, and then won for the seventh time in eight attempts in Austin, both also anti-clockwise.

These flashes of brilliance showed precisely what Honda had been lacking in 2020. A training accident curtailed his season, however, meaning that eventually he missed a total of four races, and he didn't finish in four others, yet he was still comfortably the top-ranked HRC rider in the classification.

He also ended the year as MotoGP's second most prolific crasher, which proved four key points. First, he was still racing's ultimate risk taker. Second, his recovering right arm could withstand repeated bashings, including bone-crunching high-speed practice spills in Assen and Silverstone. Third, Honda's latest version of the wild RC213V was hard to manage, even for a rider of his unrivalled skill. And finally, the lack of strength and mobility in his right arm meant that he was no longer able to frequently rescue himself with gravity-defying saves.

Marquez's return featured a surprise change to his crew. Since 2014, the Spaniard had barely altered his dominant squad, but for 2021, he had sought the services of Pol Espargaro's KTM data engineer, Jenny Anderson. She replaced Gerold Bucher, a member of the Marquez crew since his arrival in Moto2 back in 2011. Bucher was a paddock veteran, having first worked with Dirk Raudies in the 125cc category three decades earlier, and his career had also taken him to D'Antin and Kawasaki. He moved to the HRC test team with Stefan Bradl, run by former 250cc rider and Bridgestone engineer Klaus Nohles.

Bradl replaced Marquez in the two Doha races and the Algarve GP, and wild-carded in Jerez and Misano. The German scored points in all five events.

The rest of the Marquez crew had a very familiar appearance, with Santi Hernandez working as chief engineer again, supported by chief mechanic Carlos Linan, and mechanics Roberto Clerici, Koji Kaminakabeppu, Jordi Castella, and Javier Ortiz. Carlo Luzzi returned as electronics engineer.

A Repsol Honda one-two at Misano.

Alberto Puig

Tetsuhiro Kuwata

Marc Marquez returned to a record victory at the Sachsenring.

The senior management was also unchanged for 2021, with Tetsuhiro Kuwata overseeing proceedings with the impressive title of HRC Director – General Manager Race Operations Management Division. There were also director roles for Shigehisa Fujita, who was general manager of the Business Support Division, and Shinichi Kokubu in the role of general manager of the Technology Development Division. Once again, team manager duty was the remit of Alberto Puig, while Takeo Yokoyama continued as HRC technical manager.

It was no surprise in early February to learn that HRC had inked a new five-year deal with Dorna. What was a surprise was new recruit Pol Espargaro's major struggle to adapt to the RC213V. He had inherited all but one of the crew allocated to Alex Marquez in 2020, the only change being the arrival of Ricardo Carrascosa as electronics engineer in place of Arlan Holterman. Once again, that side of the garage was led by chief engineer Ramon Aurin, with Masashi Ogo as chief mechanic.

Highlights were few and far between for Espargaro. His outstanding weekends were at Silverstone's British GP, where he took pole, and a season-best second place at Misano in October. But that was his lone visit to the podium, and he was left to pin his hopes on a radically revised 2022 RC213V that broke cover in a post-race test session in Misano in September.

RED BULL KTM

TEAM STAFF

Stefan PIERER: KTM CEO
Pit Beirer: KTM Motorsport Director
Jens HAINBACH: KTM Vice President Road Racing
Mike LEITNER: MotoGP Race Manager
Fabiano STERLACCHINI: MotoGP Head of Technology
Sebastian RISSE: MotoGP Technical Co-ordinator
Sebastian KUHN: MotoGP PR Manager
Beatriz GARCIA: Team Co-ordinator

MIGUEL OLIVEIRA PIT CREW

Paul TREVATHAN: Crew Chief
Christophe LEONCE: Chief Mechanic
Andreas RIEGER, Xavi QUEIXALOS,
Mark BARNETT: Mechanics
Stefano SIGNORETTI: Tyres
Alessio CAPUANO: Strategy Engineer
Peter SCHLAEGER: Data Recording Engineer
Manuel OLIVENZIA: WP Suspension Technician

BRAD BINDER PIT CREW

Andres MADRID: Crew Chief
Mark LLOYD: Chief Mechanic
Daniel PETAK, John EYRE,
Florian FERRACCI: Mechanics
Craig BURTON: Tyre Mechanic
Errki SIUKOLA: Strategy Engineer
Tex GEISSLER: Data Recording Engineer
Gerald PERDON: WP Suspension Technician

BRAD BINDER
Born: 11 August, 1995 – Potchefstroom, South Africa
GP Starts: 177 (32 MotoGP, 52 Moto2, 93 Moto3/125cc)
GP Wins: 17 (2 MotoGP, 8 Moto2, 7 Moto3)
World Championships: 1 Moto3

MIGUEL OLIVEIRA
Born: 4 January, 1995 – Pragal, Portugal
GP Starts: 177 (48 MotoGP, 50 Moto2, 79 Moto3/125cc)
GP Wins: 15 (3 MotoGP, 6 Moto2, 6 Moto3)

Photos: Gold & Goose

CONSISTENTLY inconsistent is probably an appropriate way to summarise the 2021 MotoGP campaign for KTM's official factory effort. When Miguel Oliveira and Brad Binder were good, they looked like world beaters on the RC16, in its fifth season in the premier class. But when they weren't, KTM vanished to mid-pack obscurity and sometimes worse. The RC16 seemed to operate in a much narrower window than rivals like Yamaha and Ducati.

Off track at least, the year started in positive fashion. As early as 13th January, KTM became the first of the six major factories competing in MotoGP to ink a new five-year deal with rights holders Dorna until the end of 2026.

Senior management at the Austrian manufacturer remained unchanged, with forthright CEO Stefan Pierer at the helm. Again, Pit Beirer's influence across all of KTM's efforts in the road-racing and off-road sectors was pivotal, and he continued in the prominent role of motorsport director.

Jens Hainbach was a senior figure as well, with a slightly altered title. Previously, he had worked as road racing manager, but for 2021, he was officially listed as KTM road racing vice president.

Once again, vital technical roles were performed by Mike Leitner and Sebastian Risse, who oversaw development of the RC16 as MotoGP race manager and technical co-ordinator respectively.

KTM carried out two significant recruitments, both from the upper echelons of Ducati. First Fabi-

KTM RC16

Engine: 1000cc liquid-cooled 86-degree V4, counter-rotating crankshaft, DOHC, 4 valves per cylinder, pneumatic valve return system

Ancillaries: Magneti Marelli ECU, Dorna software, ride-by-wire fuel injection, non-active Akropovic titanium 4-into-2 exhaust

Transmission: Six-speed seamless-shift cassette-type gearbox, dry clutch

Frame: Steel-tube chassis, carbon-fibre swing-arm, front and rear ride-height devices

Suspension: WP front and rear

Tyres: Michelin • *Brakes:* Brembo carbon-fibre twin front discs, single steel rear disc

DANI PEDROSA
Born: 29 September, 1985 – Sabadell, Spain
GP Starts: 296 (218 MotoGP, 32 250cc, 46 125cc)
GP Wins: 54 (31 MotoGP, 15 250cc, 8 Moto3)
World Championships 3 (2 250cc, 1 125cc)

Oliveira's only win of the year in Catalunya.

Brad Binder

Miguel Oliveira

Dani Pedrosa

Binder won an amazing Austrian Grand Prix.

biano Sterlacchini, until 2019 considered Ducati boss Dall'Igna's right-hand man, joined as the new factory-based head of MotoGP technology. Post-season, Francesco Guidotti came in to replace Mike Leitner, who moved to a consulting role.

Miguel Oliveira was another high-profile recruit, rewarded for his two stunning wins in 2020 with a prized seat in the factory squad. He slotted into the team that had previously worked with Pol Espargaro. Paul Trevathan continued as crew chief, and Christophe Leonce as chief mechanic. The only change was the introduction of Alessio Capuano, promoted from the KTM test team, where he'd worked with Dani Pedrosa and Mika Kallio.

Oliveira and KTM struggled at the start of the season with a revised Michelin front tyre allocation, the softer asymmetric compounds robbing both riders of confidence on braking and corner entry.

Prior to chassis changes for Mugello, Oliveira had a dismal return of nine points from the opening five rounds. Then he hit a stunning purple patch. Second at Mugello was followed by a nerveless win in Catalunya and another excellent second at Sachsenring. Fifth in Assen, prior to the summer break, led to talk of Oliveira emerging as a dark horse for the title.

Any such prospect quickly evaporated, however, when a disastrous double-header in KTM's backyard at the Red Bull Ring sparked a shocking slump. A nasty FP1 high-side in the Stryian race left him with a painful injury to his right wrist, and a defective front tyre forced retirement from the race.

That proved the catalyst for another bleak spell, and he collected just seven points from the following six races. There was no great relief in the remaining rounds either.

In his second season in MotoGP, Binder emerged as the leading KTM rider on points. The undisputed highlight was the South African's outrageously skillful and daring win of an Austrian flag-to-flag race, on slick tyres on a soaked surface.

The consistent podium challenge he craved, though, was missing and not helped by his struggles to exploit optimum one-lap grip from a new soft Michelin rear tyre. He qualified in the top ten in only three races.

Binder's crew was largely unchanged for 2021. Chief mechanic duty went again to Mark Lloyd, with Daniel Petak, John Eyre, and Florian Ferracci back as mechanics. Errki Siukola and Tex Geissler returned as strategy and data engineers respectively, and the only revision to the crew came at the top. The former Moto3 world champion was reunited with Andres Madrid, having completed his rookie season under the guidance of Sergio Verbena. Madrid had been Binder's crew chief during his stint with the Red Bull KTM Ajo squad in Moto2, and his most recent engagement had been in the same squad with Japan's Tetsuta Nagashima.

Binder is a prime example of the importance of Red Bull and KTM's hugely successful feeder system. He was a graduate of the Red Bull MotoGP Rookies Cup and had ridden for Red Bull and KTM in both Moto3 and Moto2, before earning his big break in the premier class. Their appreciation and loyalty were further demonstrated in early June when he was handed a new three-year contract, until the end of 2024.

KTM's World Championship programme is heavily geared towards future talent, but there was a blast from the past in Styria, where test rider Dani Pedrosa appeared as a wild-card for the first time since retiring at the end of 2018. Working with former MotoGP and Moto2 World Championship-winning crew chief Pete Benson, Pedrosa finished a very respectable tenth in a race restarted after he'd crashed on lap three; the race was red-flagged when his KTM and Lorenzo Savadori's Aprilia burst into flames.

MotoGP · TEAM REVIEW 65

LCR HONDA

TEAM STAFF

Lucio CECCHINELLO: CEO
Martine FELLONI: Administration & Legal
Elisa PAVAN: Logistics
Maria Victoria RAMOS: Press Officer
Elena CECCHINELLO: Hospitality Manager/Workshop Manager

ALEX MARQUEZ PIT CREW

Christophe BOURGUIGNON: Chief Engineer
Jaume CARRAU: Engine Mapping
David GARCIA: Data Recording
Joan CASA, Christopher RICHARDSON, Michele ANDREINI: Mechanics
Sergi SANGRA LLUCH: Tyres
Jose CARRIO: Rider's Associate
Yuji KIKUCHI: HRC Technician
Katsuhiko IMAI: HRC Staff

TAKAAKI NAKAGAMI PIT CREW

Giacomo GUIDOTTI: Chief Engineer
Alessandro DAMIA: Engine Management
Eric PEREZ SALVA: Data Recording
Filippo BRUNETTI, Marc CANELLAS, Federico VICINO: Mechanics
Willbrord KLEINE: Tyres
Enrique PINTOR: Rider's Associate
Oscar HARO TASENDE: Team Staff
Yuichiro SEGAWA: HRC Technician

ALEX MARQUEZ
Born: 23 April, 1996 – Cervera, Spain
GP Starts: 167 (32 MotoGP, 89 Moto2, 46 Moto3)
GP Wins: 12 (8 Moto2, 4 Moto3)
World Championships: 2 (1 Moto2, 1 Moto3)

TAKAAKI NAKAGAMI
Born: 9 February, 1992 – Chiba, Japan
GP Starts: 205 (66 MotoGP, 105 Moto2, 34 125cc)
GP Wins: 2 Moto2

Photos: Gold & Goose

THERE was much to celebrate off track in 2021 for the LCR Honda squad, as Lucio Cecchinello's Monaco-based project marked its 25th year in the World Championships.

Formed in 1996 to compete in the 125cc class, the team had expanded rapidly into the 250s by 2002. Four years later, LCR made its first foray into MotoGP as a new Honda customer team, with precociously talented young Australian Casey Stoner.

Since 2006, LCR Honda has been a mainstay of the premier class, and recently it enjoyed its most successful and productive spell, with Briton Cal Crutchlow delivering three wins and 12 podiums.

Cecchinello's commitment to MotoGP prompted more celebrations in late January, 2021, when the Italian signed a new five-year deal with Dorna and IRTA to remain on the grid until the end of 2026. Hopes that celebrations off track would be matched on it were undermined, however, by Honda's unforgiving RC213V.

Optimism and expectation had been high, with new recruit Alex Marquez retaining full factory support after he had made way in the Repsol-backed factory squad for compatriot Pol Espargaro.

A revelation in 2020, Taka Nakagami had earned an elevation in status, too, and he was also supplied

HONDA RC213V – LCR

Engine: 1000cc liquid-cooled 90-degree V4, counter-rotating crankshaft, DOHC, 4 valves per cylinder, pneumatic valve return system
Power: More than 240bhp

Ancillaries: Magneti Marelli ECU, Dorna software, ride-by-wire fuel injection, non-active Arrow 4-into-2 exhaust

Transmission: Six-speed seamless-shift cassette-type gearbox, dry clutch

Frame: Aluminium twin-spar chassis, carbon-fibre swing-arm, front and rear ride-height devices • *Suspension:* Öhlins front and rear

Tyres: Michelin • *Brakes:* Brembo carbon-fibre twin front discs, single steel rear disc, thumb and foot levers ('scooter' lever operation for Crutchlow)

Lucio Cecchinello

Nakagami – Idemitsu Honda 213CV

Alex Marquez had his best race of the season in the Algarve.

Takaaki Nakagami

Photos: Gold & Goose

with a current-spec factory RC213V. The Japanese rider had been a rare ray of light in a bleak 2020 campaign for Honda. In 14 races, he had claimed 12 top-ten finishes, with half a dozen inside the top six; and he had made four front-row starts. But his fourth season at LCR Honda, with title backing from Japan's petroleum giant, Idemitsu, didn't deliver.

Crew chief responsibility again went to Italian Giacomo Guidotti, brother of Pramac Ducati team boss Francesco Guidotti. Alessandro Damia and Eric Salva handled engine mapping and data recording once more. The only changes to Nakagami's crew were the arrival of Marc Canellas as mechanic to replace Carlos Salvador, and installation of Yuichiro Segawa as new HRC technician in place of Naoki Komoto.

Nakagami finished in the top six in only two races, with a best of fourth place at round four in Jerez, where he was only 0.7 of a second off the podium. On six occasions, he finished outside the top ten, and twice even out of the points. Add in three race crashes, and it is clear to see how much Honda's ill-handling and aggressive RC213V seriously blunted his progress.

It was an equally uphill battle on the Castrol-backed side of LCR Honda for former Moto3 and Moto2 world champion Marquez. He had performed admirably in trying circumstances at Repsol Honda in 2020, and had ended a tough rookie season with two podium finishes. The Spaniard was also undone by the bike's erratic nature, however.

Three crashes in the first four races did little to inspire confidence on the morale-sapping RC213V, and Marquez's only visits to the top six were in the tricky flag-to-flag race at Le Mans and a morale-boosting fourth-place finish in the Algarve after a mighty battle with the Ducati of Jack Miller. However, Marquez endured an ongoing struggle to capitalise on the grip of a new soft Michelin rear tyre, painfully evident from 19 crashes, a tally exceeded only by fellow Honda riders Marc Marquez (22) and Pol Espargaro (20), and Iker Lecuona (KTM, 26). Alex qualified in the top ten only once.

The younger Marquez inherited most of Crutchlow's 2020 crew. Chief engineer duty went to Christopher 'Beefy' Bourguignon, while engine mapping was once again the remit of Jaume Carrau, who had previously worked with Marquez during his pre-GP days in Spanish domestic racing.

David Garcia was drafted in to oversee data recording in place of Andrea Albanese. Garcia had worked with Marquez as crew chief during his Moto2 title-winning campaign with Marc VDS Racing in 2019 and was also a former HRC data technician, who had worked with Dani Pedrosa at the end of his MotoGP career with Repsol Honda. Yuji Kikuchi had switched from a mechanic's role to that of HRC technician in place of Katsuhiko Imai.

MotoGP · TEAM REVIEW 67

AVINTIA ESPONSORAMA/ SKY VR46 DUCATI

TEAM STAFF

Raul ROMERO: General Manager

Ruben XAUS: Sports Manager

Jordi RUBIO: Team Co-ordinator

Marc VIDAL: Logistics Co-ordinator

Jiaxin TANG: Press Manager

ENEA BASTIANINI PIT CREW

Alberto GIRIBUOLA: Ducati Crew Chief

Dario MASSARIN: Ducati Data Engineer

Rafa LOPEZ, Jesus MORENO, Joan TORTOSA, David CASTANEDA, Luca BELLOSI: Mechanics

Luca DAVID: Ducati Spare Parts

LUCA MARINI PIT CREW

Luca FERRACCIOLI: Ducati Crew Chief

Mattia SERENI: Ducati Data Engineer

Christian DIONIGI, Gianluca FALCONI, Federico PECCI, Edoardo CIFERRI, Guillem RODRIGUEZ: Mechanics

Luca DAVID: Ducati Spare Parts

LUCA MARINI
Born: 10 August, 1997 – Urbino, Italy
GP Starts: 106 (18 MotoGP, 87 Moto2, 1 Moto3)
GP Wins: 6 Moto2

ENEA BASTIANINI
Born: 30 December, 1987 – Rimini, Italy
GP Starts: 139 (18 MotoGP, 33 Moto2, 88 Moto3)
GP Wins: 6 (3 Moto2, 3 Moto3)
World Championships: 1 Moto2

VALENTINO ROSSI'S influence on track might have seriously diminished in 2021, but his influence behind the scenes was undoubtedly on an upward spiral, as the year marked his first taste of management in MotoGP. He had made his managerial debut in Moto3 in 2014, with Romano Fenati and Pecco Bagnaia, a year after the formation of his now-revered VR46 Academy, created to nurture Italian talent.

Rossi shut down his Moto3 squad in 2021 to channel funds into his first foray into MotoGP, where Sky supported a one-man VR46 effort for his half-brother, Luca Marini.

Marini raced a two-year-old Ducati GP19 alongside compatriot Enea Bastianini. The pair operated out of the same garage, but they were separate entities, with 2020 Moto2 world champion Bastianini riding under the banner of Avintia Esponsorama Racing.

Raul Romero remained as general manager of the Andorran-based Esponsorama Racing project, and former WorldSBK and MotoGP rider Ruben Xaus returned as sports manager. Pablo Nieto, son of late Spanish motorcycling legend Angel Nieto, was very much a hands-on presence, though on Marini's side. Nieto also continued to oversee Rossi's Moto2 squad, with Marco Bezzecchi and Celestino Vietti.

Luca Ferraccioli, previously Ducati's eyes and ears at Esponsorama, was Marini's crew chief, with only one crewman, data engineer Mattia Sereni, remaining from Esponsorama's 2020 line-up. Mechanics Christian Dionigi and Gianluca Falconi came with

DUCATI Desmosedici GP19 – Esponsorama

Engine: 1000cc liquid-cooled 90-degree V4, counter-rotating crankshaft, DOHC, 4 valves per cylinder, desmodromic valve gear

Power: More than 250bhp

Ancillaries: Magneti Marelli ECU, Dorna software, ride-by-wire fuel injection, active Akropovic titanium 4-into-2 exhaust

Transmission: Six-speed seamless-shift cassette-type gearbox, dry clutch

Frame: Aluminium-alloy twin-spar chassis, carbon-fibre swing-arm, front and rear ride-height devices

Suspension: Öhlins inverted front forks, Öhlins rear shock absorber

Tyres: Michelin • *Brakes:* Brembo carbon-fibre twin front discs, single steel rear disc, thumb and foot levers

Two MotoGP podiums for Bastianini.

Luca Marini on the Sky VR46 Ducati.

Marini from the Sky Moto2 squad, while Federico Pecci, Edoardo Ciferri and Guillem Rodriguez were new arrivals.

It was a baptism of fire for Marini, who finished inside the top ten just twice, fifth after risking remaining on slicks when the heavens opened during the Austrian Grand Prix, and ninth at Misano in October.

Bastianini opened with two top-tens in his first three races, then hit a purple patch late in the season, which included a sensational charge through to a maiden podium in the first of two Misano battles. He had been given a huge boost when Ducati paired him with Andrea Dovizioso's former crew chief, Alberto Giribuola. His backroom squad included mechanics Rafa Lopez, Jesus Moreno, Joan Tortosa, David Casteneda and Luca Bellosi who, during the previous season, had been part of the Esponsorama set-up, with either Rabat or Johann Zarco.

Persistent pre-season rumours that Rossi would acquire the Esponsorama Racing grid places and run his own two-rider squad from 2022 onwards came true in late June, when the veteran rider confirmed that he had signed a five-year contract with Dorna. Also, he had opted to run Ducatis, with a three-year deal, boosting the Bologna marque's grid numbers to eight. In 2022, Marini would race the latest-spec GP22, and rookie Bezzecchi a secondhand GP21.

Thereafter, the waters became properly muddied.

On the eve of the Spanish GP in April, a statement from Tanal Entertainment Sport and Media, a Saudi Arabian holding company belonging to former deputy foreign minister Prince Abdulaziz bin Abdullah Al Saud, declared a new partnership with Saudi state-owned oil giant Aramco. The new team would be known as Aramco Racing Team VR46. This sparked accusations of sports-washing, given Saudi Arabia's record on human rights.

Then, within days of the Tanal announcement, Aramco denied that any deal had been concluded. The situation became even murkier in Assen, at the end of June, when Aramco Overseas CEO Talal Al-Marri, who was in attendance as a guest of Pramac Ducati, was coy in the extreme about any potential partnership with VR46.

The issue dragged on well into the autumn, as serious doubts plunged Rossi into a frantic hunt for fresh funding. Had he fallen victim to an elaborate hoax? Where was the due diligence before the 2022 plans were announced?

The sponsorship saga didn't threaten Rossi's place on the grid in 2022, but in another bizarre twist, when the list of 2022 Moto2 teams was revealed in late September, Rossi's squad appeared under the banner of Aramco VR46 Team, and not long-term backers Sky. A new addition to the Moto2 grid also featured Rossi's name: the Yamaha VR46 Master Camp Team. The Master Camp, where hand-picked youngsters are trained at the VR46 Riders Academy, is Yamaha's new development programme.

Bastianini on the Esponsorama Racing Ducati.

Ruben Xaus

Marini displayed Rossi tribute livery at Misano.

Marini – Sky VR46 Ducati GP19

MotoGP · TEAM REVIEW 69

APRILIA RACING TEAM GRESINI

TEAM STAFF

Massimo RIVOLA: Aprilia Racing CEO
Romano ALBESIANO: Aprilia Racing Technical Manager
Paolo BONORA: Race Manager
Fabrizio CECCHINI: Technical Co-ordinator
Michele MASINI: Team Co-ordinator
Stefano ROMEO: Electronics Engineer
Michele FANTINI: Engine Engineer
Elena DE CIA: Strategy Engineer
Michele BERTELLI: Vehicle Engineer
Andrea ROSTAGNO: Performance Engineer
Massimo MENEGHIN: Spare Parts
Mike WATT: Öhlins Technician
Andrea ZOCCARATO: Press Officer

LORENZO SAVADORI/MAVERICK VINALES PIT CREW

Giovanni MATTAROLLO: Crew Chief
Luca CONTI: Electronics Engineer
Nicolo CECCATO: Data Engineer
Matteo FRIGO: Suspension Engineer
Roberto SIMIONATO, Gianluca PERETTI, Simone ALESSANDRINI, Filippo TOGNONI: Mechanics
Garcia INIGO: Tyres & Fuel

ALEIX ESPARGARO PIT CREW

Antonio JIMENEZ: Crew Chief
Renato PENNACCHIO: Electronics Engineer
Guido FONTANA: Data Engineer
Oscar BOLZONELLA: Suspension Engineer
Carlo TOCCAFONDI, Franco SALVA, Alberto PRESUTTI, Jose BARBER: Mechanics
Oscar MARTINEZ: Tyres & Fuel

ALEIX ESPARGARO
Born: 30 July, 1989 – Granollers, Spain
GP Starts: 281 (197 MotoGP, 61 Moto2/250cc, 23 125cc)

LORENZO SAVADORI
Born: 4 April, 1993 – Cesena, Italy
GP Starts: 43 (12 MotoGP, 31 125cc)

Photos: Gold & Goose

TRIUMPH and tragedy combined to make 2021 a rollercoaster final year of collaboration between Aprilia and Gresini Racing.

In mid-December, 2020, Fausto Gresini had confirmed that he would return to Independent Team status for 2022 in what would be the Italian squad's 26th anniversary in the premier class since an initial entry with Alex Barros in 1997.

Just two weeks later, the double 125cc world champion was hospitalised in Bologna and placed in a medically induced coma, having contracted Covid-19. Gresini's critical condition improved in January and he was brought out of the coma, but complications due to the virus forced medical staff to put him back into a coma in mid-February. The treatment failed, however, and on 23rd February, Gresini Racing issued a short statement confirming that the former champion and longstanding team owner had died just over a month after his 60th birthday.

The Gresini family vowed to honour him by pressing ahead with plans to continue his legacy. During the Jerez Grand Prix weekend, it was confirmed that his widow, Nadia Padovani, would assume his role. His son, Lorenzo, took on a lead administrative role, and his brother, Luca, would also be heavily involved.

Gresini's dream of returning with his own privately-

APRILIA RS-GP

Engine: 1000cc liquid-cooled 90-degree V4, counter-rotating crankshaft, DOHC, 4 valves per cylinder, pneumatic valve return system

Ancillaries: Magneti Marelli ECU, Dorna software, ride-by-wire fuel injection, active Akrapovic titanium 4-into-2 exhaust

Transmission: Six-speed seamless-shift cassette-type gearbox, dry clutch

Frame: Aluminium twin-spar chassis, aluminium swing-arm, front and rear ride-height devices

Suspension: Öhlins front and rear

Tyres: Michelin • *Brakes:* Brembo carbon-fibre twin front discs, single steel rear disc, thumb and foot levers

MAVERICK VINALES
Born: 12 January, 1995 – Figueres, Spain
GP Starts: 187 (120 MotoGP, 18 Moto2, 49 Moto3/125cc)
GP Wins: 25 (9 MotoGP, 4 Moto2, 12 Moto3/125cc)
World Championships: 1 Moto3

Massimo Rivola

Maverick Vinales

Lorenzo Savadori

Aleix Espargaro

run project was fulfilled on the eve of the German GP in mid-June. The relationship with Aprilia had always been a marriage of convenience, however, facilitating the factory's MotoGP return in 2015 with a ready-made infrastructure, while there had been no major financial burden on Gresini to bankroll the team.

Expectations that Gresini Racing would help Aprilia expand to a four-rider presence proved wide of the mark, and at the Sachsenring, it was announced that the team had clinched a two-year deal with Ducati, with an all-Italian line-up of Enea Bastianini and Gresini Moto3/Moto2 rider Fabio Di Giannantonio. Both would race year-old Ducati GP21 machinery. Long-serving Gresini team co-ordinator Michele Masini would take up the position of sporting director.

A week later, at Assen, it was announced that shipping-container developer and manufacturer Flex-Box would be the title sponsor. Flex-Box is well known in the GP paddock as an official partner of Ducati, and the company would continue to back Sito Pons's Moto2 project with Aron Canet and Jorge Navarro for the 2022 season.

The familiar Aprilia team hierarchy was led by CEO Massimo Rivola, with Romano Albesiano as technical director. Key roles remained for race manager Paolo Bonora and technical co-ordinator Fabrizio Cecchini.

Aprilia's radically revamped RS-GP was a prime candidate for most improved bike on the grid, and it became common to see Aleix Espargaro fighting for the top six.

Espargaro was paired with crew chief Antonio Jimenez for his fifth season with Aprilia, and the only alteration to his squad was that Renato Pennachio took the role of electronics engineer.

Aprilia had only ever mustered five top-six finishes in the modern four-stroke era. Espargaro delivered a total of four in 2021, including a memorable third place at Silverstone – his first podium since 2014, on the Forward Yamaha. It was a first for the Noale factory since Jeremy McWilliams had finished third at Donington Park's British Grand Prix in 2000. Espargaro was eighth in the championship.

Aprilia started the season with ex-test rider Lorenzo Savadori on the second bike. Three points finishes in nine races came before he suffered a broken right ankle in a fireball crash with KTM wild-card Dani Pedrosa in Austria. Little did he know that it would be his final appearance as a full-time RS-GP racer.

Aprilia were the chief benefactors of the Maverick Vinales meltdown at Yamaha. He had already signed a deal with them for 2022 when it was decided to bring him in for the final six races of the season, following a positive two-day test at Misano.

Vinales was immediately paired with crew chief Giovanni Mattarollo, hauled out of Aprilia's test team in place of Pietro Caprara, who previously had headed Savadori's side of the garage.

More tragedy hit the Aprilia camp in late September, when Dean Berta Vinales, the 15-year-old cousin of Maverick, was killed in a Supersport 300 championship race at Jerez. Vinales withdrew from the Circuit of The Americas race in Austin the following weekend.

Savadori returned for a wild-card ride in the second Misano race, but withdrew after the first day, still suffering injury, and he was signed again by Aprilia as a development rider – a position filled for a large part of 2021 by Andrea Dovizioso, until his sabbatical was ended by Yamaha.

Photos: Gold & Goose

MotoGP · TEAM REVIEW 71

PETRONAS YAMAHA SRT

TEAM STAFF

Razlan Ahmad RAZALI: Team Principal
Johan STIGEFELT: Team Director
Wilco ZEELENBERG: MotoGP Team Manager
Cyril FRANCIS: Head of Partnerships & Hospitality
Andy STOBART: Head of Communications
Pol BERTRAN: Senior Media Manager
Heather MACLENNAN: Team Co-ordinator
Roger VD BORGHT: Logistics Manager
Mats MELANDER: MotoGP Parts Manager

FRANCO MORBIDELLI/CAL CRUTCHLOW/ GARRETT GERLOFF/JAKE DIXON/ ANDREA DOVIZIOSO PIT CREW

Ramon FORCADA: Crew Chief
Andy GRIFFITH: Electronics Engineer
Stewart MILLER, Matt LLOYD, Ben FRY: Mechanics
Calum WILLEY: Tyres & Fuel
Torleif HARTELMAN: Rider Analyst

VALENTINO ROSSI PIT CREW

David MUNOZ: Crew Chief
Matteo FLAMIGNI: Electronics Engineer
Daniel SWYER, Miguel PERURENA,
Robin SPIJKERS: Mechanics
Martin ZABALA: Tyres & Fuel
Idalio GAVIRA: Rider Analyst

VALENTINO ROSSI
Born: 16 February, 1979 – Urbino, Italy
GP Starts: 432 (372 MotoGP/500cc, 30 250cc, 30 125cc)
GP Wins: 115 (89 MotoGP/500cc, 14 250cc, 12 125cc)
World Championships: 9 (6 MotoGP, 1 500cc, 1 250cc, 1 125cc)

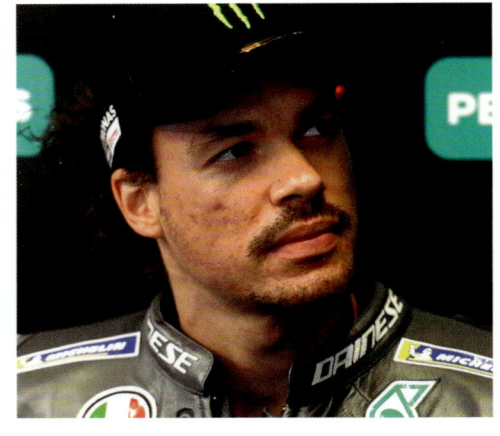

FRANCO MORBIDELLI
Born: 4 December, 1994 – Rome, Italy
GP Starts: 133 (62 MotoGP, 71 Moto2)
GP Wins: 11 (3 MotoGP, 8 Moto2)
World Championships: 1 Moto2

Photos: Gold & Goose

IT'S hard to recall any team in recent history going from a startling rise to prominence to a shocking decline into oblivion quite as quickly as the high-profile Petronas Yamaha SRT project.

A glittering 2019 debut season had ended with the Malaysian-backed squad taking the Rookie of the Year and top Independent Team rider awards, with Fabio Quartararo having claimed seven podiums and six poles. And it had easily defeated several established teams to claim the Top Independent Team award.

That team honour had been successfully defended in 2020, when Franco Morbidelli had been crowned top Independent Team rider. Petronas Yamaha SRT had also finished second to Suzuki in the teams' championship, and its tally of six wins had been the most of any team on the grid.

Yet by the end of 2021, Petronas Yamaha SRT had been banished to the history books – gone almost as quickly as it had emerged after taking over the defunct Marc VDS Honda grid slots in 2019. In its current guise, the team was doomed in mid-August when Malaysian oil giant Petronas announced that it would cease its title sponsorship at the end of 2021.

That announcement had far reaching ramifications, with the collapse of the Petronas-backed Moto3 and Moto2 teams. Just over a month later, the plot took

YAMAHA YZR-M1 – Petronas

Engine: 1000cc liquid-cooled in-line 4, counter-rotating cross-plane crankshaft, DOHC, 4 valves per cylinder, pneumatic valve return system
Power: More than 240bhp
Ancillaries: Magneti Marelli ECU, Dorna software, ride-by-wire fuel injection, active Akrapovic titanium 4-into-2-into-1 exhaust
Transmission: Six-speed seamless-shift cassette-type gearbox, dry clutch
Frame: Aluminium twin-spar chassis, aluminium or carbon-fibre swing-arm, front and rear ride-height devices
Suspension: Öhlins inverted front fork, Öhlins rear shock absorber • *Wheels:* Forged magnesium, 17in diameter • *Tyres:* Michelin
Brakes: Brembo 320 or 340mm carbon-fibre twin front discs; single steel rear disc, thumb and foot levers

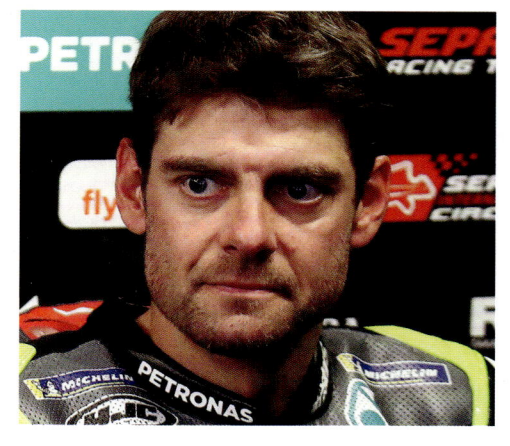

CAL CRUTCHLOW
Born: 29 October, 1985 – Coventry, England
GP Starts: 172 MotoGP
GP Wins: 3 MotoGP
World Championships: 1 World Supersport

GARRETT GERLOFF
Born: August 1, 1995 – Spring, Texas, USA
GP Starts: 1 (1 MotoGP)

JAKE DIXON
Born: 15 January, 1996 – Dover, England
GP Starts: 47 (2 MotoGP, 45 Moto2)

ANDREA DOVIZIOSO
Born: 23 March, 1986 – Forlimpopoli, Forli, Italy
GP Starts: 332 (234 MotoGP, 49 250cc, 49 125cc)
GP Wins: 24 (15 MotoGP, 4 250cc, 5 125cc)
World Championships: 1 125cc

Optimism abounded for the SRT Team in pre-season testing at Qatar.

another dramatic twist when team principal Razlan Razali confirmed that he'd signed a new five-year deal with Dorna to run an Independent Team, rebranded and relaunched as RNF Racing.

Speculation as to the meaning of RNF was confirmed when Razali revealed it to be the first initials of his three children. Clearer was mounting tension between Razali and team director Johan Stigefelt. They were the two very public and most senior on-site figures of Petronas SRT, yet it was not clear if Stigefelt was to have any role in the new RNF Racing outfit.

Team manager Wilco Zeelenberg appeared to be joining Razali's new venture, despite rumoured interest from Suzuki in him taking on the role vacated by Davide Brivio.

This turbulent season wasn't helped by major disruption and upheaval on track. It had started full of great expectations with an all-star Italian line-up of Valentino Rossi and Franco Morbidelli, but soon it turned into a nightmare.

Rossi had no intention of 2021 being his last season, but that's how it turned out. The 42-year-old was still impressively fast, but simply not fast enough. He finished in the top ten only four times, crashed three times, and five times missed the points.

Rossi knew the game was up, and during the Styrian Grand Prix in early August, he announced that his 26th season as one of history's greatest racers and personalities would be his last.

Crew chief David Munoz and electronics engineer Matteo Flamigni were the only survivors of Rossi's last factory Yamaha crew. Mechanic Miguel Perurena moved up from Rossi's Sky-backed Moto2 squad, while Robin Spijkers had worked with Quartararo in 2020, and Daniel Sawyer was promoted from within Petronas SRT.

Franco Morbidelli had been a star performer for Petronas SRT in 2020, finishing only 13 points behind world champion Joan Mir on a year-old Yamaha YZR-M1. He was not rewarded with an upgrade in machinery, however, and his discontent was obvious from the get-go. In response, Yamaha repeatedly insisted that the team was supplied with the machinery spec they'd paid for. A higher-grade M1 could have been provided had the lease costs been met.

The former Moto2 champion's strong 2020 meant that it was no surprise he worked with the same crew, led by vastly experienced Ramon Forcada, with electronics engineer Andy Griffith, and mechanics Stewart Miller, Matt Lloyd, and Ben Fry.

Morbidelli claimed just three top-ten finishes in the opening eight races, but they included an excellent third in Jerez. Then a serious ligament injury in his left knee, suffered in a training incident, sidelined him for three months, and he missed five races.

On his return to action for the first of two home races in Misano, he was seconded to the factory team and reunited with former Petronas SRT stablemate Quartararo for the remainder of 2021.

Morbidelli's lengthy absence meant that Yamaha and Petronas SRT struggled to provide cover. American GRT Yamaha World Superbike rider Garrett Gerloff subbed for Assen, and then test rider Cal Crutchlow came out of retirement to fill the breach in both Austrian rounds. Next, Jake Dixon was given his dream premier-class break for the Silverstone and Motorland Aragon rounds, but none of that trio managed to score a single point.

Then a deal was struck to tempt Andrea Dovizioso out of his self-imposed exile for the final five races, and he scored a best of 12th in Valencia.

The shock departure of Maverick Vinales from Yamaha's factory team pushed Petronas into a selection crisis. Although Morbidelli was under contract for 2022, he was the obvious and natural replacement for Vinales.

Yamaha's Independent Team was linked with Gerloff, Dixon, Moto2 starlet Raul Fernandez, Dani Pedrosa, multiple World Superbike champion Jonathan Rea and his new nemesis, tenacious Turk Toprak Razgatlioglu, to name but a few.

Shortly before the news that Petronas SRT would operate as a completely new entity, Yamaha announced that it had signed Dovizioso on a factory contract for 2022 during the opening Misano encounter on the latest-spec YZR-M1. The signing of the second RNF Racing rider proved to be a protracted saga.

With top picks Fernandez committed to KTM in MotoGP and Razgatlioglu inking a new Yamaha WorldSBK contract in mid-July, the seat went to Petronas Moto3 rider Darryn Binder, who was under contract to the team for 2022. The initial plan had been to move the South African into Moto2, but with that team folding, he'll copy Aussie Jack Miller, who had made the huge leap from Moto3 into MotoGP in 2015 with Honda.

TECH3 KTM FACTORY RACING

TEAM STAFF

Herve PONCHARAL: Team Manager
Fabien ROPERS: Parts/Design Manager
Amelie JOURDAIN: Team Co-ordinator
Mathilde PONCHARAL: Press Officer/Communication
Maria POHLMANN: Social Media Co-ordinator
Laurence COTTIN: Secretary

IKER LECUONA PIT CREW

Nicolas GOYON: Crew Chief
Maxime REYSZ: Strategy Engineer
Kylian SAUVAGE: Data Engineer
Eric LABORIE, Thomas RUBANTEL,
David LIEBERT: Mechanics
Jerome PORCHET: Fuel & Tyres Manager

DANILO PETRUCCI PIT CREW

Sergio VERBENA: Crew Chief
Alexandre MERHAND: Strategy Engineer
Guillaume DUMAS: Data Engineer
Jerome PONCHARAL, Brice GROSSIN,
Steve BLACKBURN: Mechanics
Pascal AUBEROUX: Fuel & Tyres Manager

IKER LECUONA
Born: 6 January, 2000 – Valencia, Spain
GP Starts: 85 (30 MotoGP, 55 Moto2)

DANILO PETRUCCI
Born: 24 October, 1990 – Terni, Italy
GP Starts: 169 MotoGP
GP Wins: 2 MotoGP

A BREAKTHROUGH and success-rich 2020 campaign rapidly became a distant memory for the Tech3 KTM Racing squad by the end of 2021.

In its second season of a new partnership with KTM, Herve Poncharal's French-based squad had won two races with Miguel Oliveira, a feat it hadn't managed once in nearly two decades of operating as Yamaha's sole Independent Team. The 2021 campaign never once threatened to get remotely close to those dizzy heights, and by the end of 2021, Tech3 had made only two visits to the top six.

Tech3 was different in name and appearance for 2021, after global energy drinks colossus Red Bull had withdrawn its sponsorship. KTM agreed to pick up the financial slack, and the result was a striking bright orange livery for the new line-up of Danilo Petrucci and Iker Lecuona.

Any fears that the disappearance of Red Bull backing would taint Tech3 and KTM's relationship was quickly dispelled when they signed a new long-term agreement until the end of the 2026 campaign on race day at Jerez.

Team manager Poncharal remained very much the public figurehead of Tech3, and he also continued in

KTM RC16 – Tech3

Engine: 1000cc liquid-cooled 86-degree V4, counter-rotating cross-plane crankshaft, DOHC, 4 valves per cylinder, pneumatic valve return system
Power: Approximately 265bhp, rev limit 18,500rpm
Ancillaries: Magneti Marelli ECU, Dorna software, ride-by-wire throttle, Akrapovic exhaust • *Lubrication:* Elf
Transmission: Six-speed seamless-shift cassette-type gearbox, dry clutch
Frame: Steel-tube chassis, carbon-fibre swing-arm, front and rear ride-height devices
Suspension: WP front and rear
Tyres: Michelin • *Brakes:* Brembo carbon-fibre twin front discs, single steel rear disc

Danilo Petrucci

Iker Lecuona

Mike Leitner, Herve Poncharal and Pit Beirer sign Remy Gardner for the 2022 MotoGP season.

the prominent position as president of the International Race Teams Association.

There was one significant backroom change, with legendary engineer and tuner Guy Coulon stepping aside from his long-standing role as crew chief. Coulon had been a founder member of Tech3 in 1990 with Poncharal and Bernard Martignac, and he remained a frequent presence around the garage in an advisory capacity.

This was the only revision to the team working with new arrival Petrucci. Sergio Verbena came in as crew chief for the Italian, having worked in KTM's factory squad as the head of Brad Binder's technical crew in 2020.

Strategy engineer and data engineer roles went again to Alexandre Merhand and Guillaume Dumas respectively, while Jerome Poncharal, Brice Grossin and Steve Blackburn continued as mechanics.

Petrucci endured a gruelling year on the RC16, a rare highlight being a fighting fifth from 17th in a flag-to-flag encounter at Le Mans. He finished in the top ten in only two other races, and by the end of a frustrating and disappointing season, his career was heading off on a new trajectory. With no options in MotoGP or World Superbikes, he struck a deal with KTM to race in the 2022 Dakar Rally, and he planned to compete in several other rally and enduro events in the future.

Lecuona also lost his place on the grid in 2022, despite showing glimpses of promise and potential in just his second season in MotoGP. Three top-tens, including a MotoGP best of sixth in Austria's wet and wild flag-to-flag race, weren't enough to save the Spaniard, and he would move to Honda's factory World Superbike squad in 2022. Lecuona had the unenviable statistic of the most crashes, at 26.

Lecuona's crew was completely untouched for 2021. Nicolas Goyon worked as crew chief, with strategy and data tasks falling to Maxime Reysz and Kylian Sauvage. Eric Laborie, Thomas Rubantel and David Liebert continued as mechanics.

Petrucci and Lecuona were frozen out by a new wave of exciting and emerging talent coming through KTM's stacked young rider development system. Remy Gardner and Raul Fernandez were utterly dominant in the Red Bull KTM Moto2 squad run by renowned king-maker Aki Ajo.

Gardner had just won his first Moto2 race of the season at Mugello when his promotion to MotoGP with Tech3 was announced in early June. The son of 1987 500cc world champion Wayne Gardner, Remy was no stranger to Tech3, having ridden for Poncharal on the team's self-built Mistral 610 chassis in Moto2 in 2017 and 2018.

Promotion for Fernandez was not so seamless. His signature was widely sought following a scintillating rookie season in Moto2 that garnered eight wins in 18 starts, which bettered even the great Marc Marquez's back in 2011. He did match his predecessor's championship position, in second.

Under contract to KTM for 2022, Fernandez was handcuffed to his current deal unless a hefty 500,000-euro buy-out clause could be met. After fending off mounting interest from Yamaha, a switch to Tech3 for Fernandez was bizarrely announced during the MotoGP FP4 session in the first of a Red Bull Ring double-header in August.

That was before Petrucci and Lecuona had been informed, and unsurprisingly they voiced their disapproval at the way such a delicate matter had been handled. Even Fernandez seemed aggrieved at the situation, having strongly hinted that his preference was to remain for one more season in Moto2.

MotoGP · TEAM REVIEW 75

FIM MOTO2 WORLD CHAMPIONSHIP

2021 TEAMS AND RIDERS

By PETER McLAREN

THIRTY-FOUR years after his father Wayne had stormed to 500cc glory, Remy Gardner joined the list of grand prix world champions with a tense title victory in Moto2.

The championship battle between Ajo team-mates Gardner and rookie Raul Fernandez was a situation not seen in the intermediate category since Tech3's Olivier Jacque and Shinya Nakano had fought over the 250cc crown in 2000 – a contest that also had gone down to the final round.

On the technical front, the Covid freeze meant that chassis, swing-arms and aerodynamic parts remained at Qatar 2020 specification.

The third year of 765cc Triumph engines (a deal extended until 2024) resulted in another clean sweep of victories for the Kalex chassis. Speed Up became Boscoscuro after a winter name change and repeated occasional podiums, while MV Agusta and NTS again played for points.

Just five riders tasted victory, down from eight in the previous year. Among them was an emotional Fabio Di Giannantonio, who dedicated his first Moto2 win to much-missed team owner Fausto Gresini.

While Fernandez exceeded even Marc Marquez's rookie Moto2 win tally, Ai Ogura was the only other newcomer to make a podium as Celestino Vietti, Tony Arbolino and Cameron Beaubier featured in the top six.

Joining Gardner and Fernandez (Tech3 KTM) in moving to MotoGP in 2022 would be Di Giannantonio (Gresini Ducati) and Marco Bezzecchi (VR46 Ducati). Sam Lowes was again the highest-ranked rider to remain in the class.

Also bidding farewell at the end of the season was former 125cc world champion Thomas Luthi, a veteran of 318 GP starts and holder of the most Moto2 podiums (53). He retired to become sporting director of PrustelGP. The 2022 grid places vacated by Petronas SRT would be filled by a second VR46 entry for Yamaha Master Camp riders. RW Racing would end its NTS chassis partnership and switch to Kalex.

2021 MOTO 2 RIDERS

No.	Rider	Team
5	Alonso Lopez	Speed Up Racing - Boscoscuro
5	Yari Montella	Speed Up Racing - Boscoscuro
6	Cameron Beaubier	American Racing - Kalex
7	Lorenzo Baldassarri	MV Agusta Forward Racing - MV Agusta
9	Jorge Navarro	Speed Up Racing - Boscoscuro
10	Tommaso Marcon	MV Agusta Forward Racing - MV Agusta
		NTS RW Racing GP - NTS
11	Nicolo Bulega	Federal Oil Gresini Moto2 - Kalex
12	Thomas Luthi	Pertamina Mandalika SAG Team - Kalex
13	Celestino Vietti	Sky Racing Team VR46 - Kalex
14	Tony Arbolino	Liqui Moly Intact GP - Kalex
16	Joe Roberts	American Racing - Kalex
18	Xavier Cardelus	Esponsorama Racing - Kalex
19	Lorenzo Dalla Porta	Italtrans Racing Team - Kalex
20	Dimas Ekky Pratama	Pertamina Mandalika SAG Team - Kalex
21	Fabio Di Giannantonio	Federal Oil Gresini Moto2 - Kalex
22	Sam Lowes	ELF Marc VDS Racing Team - Kalex
23	Marcel Schrotter	Liqui Moly Intact GP - Kalex
24	Simone Corsi	MV Agusta Forward Racing - MV Agusta
25	Raul Fernandez	Red Bull KTM Ajo - Kalex
27	Mattia Casadei	Italtrans Racing Team - Kalex
29	Taiga Hada	Pertamina Mandalika SAG Teluru - Kalex
32		NTS RW Racing GP - NTS
35	Somkiat Chantra	IDEMITSU Honda Team Asia - Kalex
37	Augusto Fernandez	ELF Marc VDS Racing Team - Kalex
40	Hector Garzo	Flexbox HP 40 - Kalex
42	Marcos Ramirez	American Racing - Kalex
44	Aron Canet	Aspar Team Moto2 - Boscoscuro
45	Tetsuta Nagashima	Italtrans Racing Team - Kalex
54	Fermin Aldeguer	+Ego Speed Up - Boscoscuro
		Termozeta Speed Up - Boscoscuro
55	Hafizh Syahrin	NTS RW Racing GP - NTS
62	Stefano Manzi	Flexbox HP 40 - Kalex
64	Bo Bendsneyder	Pertamina Mandalika SAG Team - Kalex
70	Barry Baltus	Pertamina Mandalika SAG Euvic - Kalex
72	Marco Bezzecchi	Sky Racing Team VR46 - Kalex
74	Piotr Biesiekirski	NTS RW Racing GP - NTS
75	Albert Arenas	Aspar Team Moto2 - Kalex
77	Miquel Pons	MV Agusta Forward Racing - MV Agusta
79	Ai Ogura	IDEMITSU Honda Team Asia - Kalex
81	Keminth Kubo	VR46 Master Camp Team - Kalex
87	Remy Gardner	Red Bull KTM Ajo - Kalex
89	Fraser Rogers	NTS RW Racing GP - NTS
96	Jake Dixon	Petronas Sprinta Racing - Kalex
97	Xavi Vierge	Petronas Sprinta Racing - Kalex

Raul Fernandez

Remy Gardner

Joe Roberts

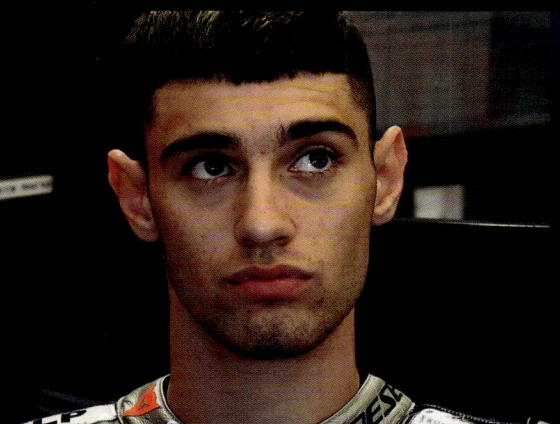

Tony Arbolino

Cameron Beaubier

Marcos Ramirez

Bo Bendsneyder

Somkiat Chantra

Augusto Fernandez

Fabio Di Giannantonio

MOTO2 TEAMS AND RIDERS OF 2021

Marco Bezzecchi

Celestino Vietti

Thomas Luthi

Fermin Aldeguer

Nicolo Bulega

Barry Baltus

Lorenzo Baldassarri

Hector Garzo

Marcel Schrotter

Sam Lowes

Aron Canet

Xavi Vierge

Stefano Manzi

Albert Arenas

Jake Dixon

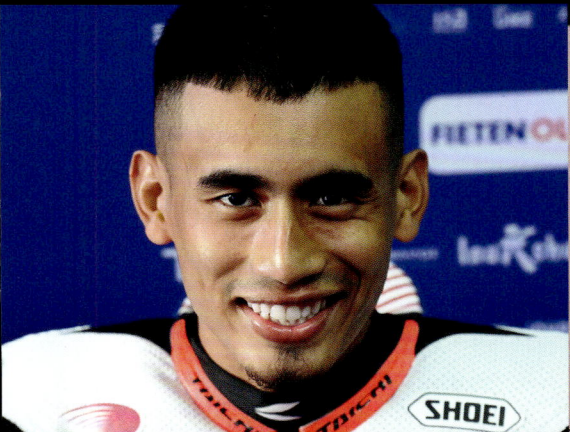

Hafizh Syahrin

Simone Corsi

Lorenzo Dalla Porta

Jorge Navarro

Ai Ogura

MOTO2 TEAMS AND RIDERS OF 2021 79

FIM MOTO3 WORLD CHAMPIONSHIP

2021 TEAMS AND RIDERS

By PETER McLAREN

PEDRO ACOSTA made history as the first rookie to win the Moto3 title, ending a drought of junior-class debutants that stretched back to Loris Capirossi in the 1990 125cc world championship.

A near-perfect opening run, topped by victory from a pit-lane start, made Acosta's crown seem a formality. But the KTM Ajo star flipped the usual rookie form on its head by starting strong, then stumbling, shedding 76 points to Dennis Foggia in the space of six races.

The lottery of a Valencia title showdown remained on the cards until a dramatic last lap in Portimao.

KTM retained the constructors' title, despite its points margin over Honda being diluted by five other wins for the RC4 machine attributed to rebadged GASGAS and Husqvarna entries. The Austrian firm would expand its branding programme to include bikes badged for Chinese partner CFMoto in 2022.

Full-time grid numbers were trimmed to 28 in 2021, after the departure of the Estrella Galicia 0,0 and VR46 teams, while Avintia expanded its entry to two riders.

The second season of the Covid technical freeze prevented major upgrades to the 250cc four-stroke machines, as sealed at Qatar 2020.

With racing as close as ever, and budgets uncertain, it was decided to extend the technical freeze until 2023. From 2024, a minimum two-year 'rolling period' for bike design will be introduced, plus a more sustainable fuel.

Acosta, Foggia and Sergio Garcia won 14 of the 18 races. Seven different riders featured on the top step, compared to ten the year before, with Izan Guevara and Xavier Artigas joining Acosta as rookie race winners.

2021 MOTO3 RIDERS

#	Rider	Team
2	Gabriel Rodrigo	Indonesian Gresini Racing Moto3 - Honda
5	Jaume Masia	Red Bull KTM Ajo - KTM
6	Ryusei Yamanaka	CarXpert PruestelGP - KTM
7	Dennis Foggia	Leopard Racing - Honda
11	Sergio Garcia	Gaviota GASGAS Aspar Team - GASGAS
12	Filip Salac	CarXpert PruestelGP - KTM
16	Andrea Migno	Rivacold Snipers Team - Honda
17	John McPhee	Petronas Sprinta Racing - Honda
18	Matteo Bertelle	Bardahl VR46 Riders Academy - KTM
19	Andi Farid Izdihar	Honda Team Asia - Honda
20	Lorenzo Fellon	SIC58 Squadra Corse - Honda
22	Elia Bartolini	Avintia VR46 - KTM Bardahl VR46 Riders Academy
23	Niccolo Antonelli	Avintia VR46 - KTM
24	Tatsuki Suzuki	SIC58 Squadra Corse - Honda
27	Kaito Toba	CIP Green Power - KTM
28	Izan Guevara	Gaviota GASGAS Aspar Team - GASGAS
31	Adrian Fernandez	Sterilgarda Max Racing Team - Husqvarna
32	Takuma Matsuyama	Honda Team Asia - Honda
37	Pedro Acosta	Red Bull KTM Ajo - KTM
38	David Salvador	Rivacold Snipers Team - Honda
40	Darryn Binder	Petronas Sprinta Racing - Honda
43	Xavier Artigas	Leopard Racing - Honda
50	Jason Dupasquier	CarXpert PruestelGP - KTM
52	Jeremy Alcoba	Indonesian Gresini Racing Moto3 - Honda
53	Deniz Oncu	Red Bull KTM Tech3 - KTM
54	Riccardo Rossi	BOE Owlride - KTM
55	Romano Fenati	Sterilgarda Max Racing Team - Husqvarna
63	Syarifuddin Azman	Petronas Sprinta Racing - Honda
64	Mario Aji	Honda Team Asia - Honda
66	Joel Kelso	CIP Green Power - KTM
67	Alberto Surra	Rivacold Snipers Team - Honda
71	Ayumu Sasaki	Red Bull KTM Tech3 - KTM
73	Maximilian Kofler	CIP Green Power - KTM
80	David Alonso	Gaviota GASGAS Aspar Team - GASGAS
82	Stefano Nepa	BOE Owlride - KTM
92	Yuki Kunii	Honda Team Asia - Honda
95	Jose Antonio Rueda	Indonesian Gresini Racing Moto3 - Honda
96	Daniel Holgado	CIP Green Power - KTM Red Bull KTM Tech3
99	Carlos Tatay	Avintia Esponsorama Moto3 - KTM

80 MOTO3 TEAMS AND RIDERS OF 2021

Pedro Acosta

Dennis Foggia

Ayumu Sasaki

Andrea Migno

Jeremy Alcoba

Deniz Oncu

John McPhee

Tatsuki Suzuki

Sergio Garcia

Jaume Masia

MOTO3 TEAMS AND RIDERS OF 2021   81

Romano Fenati	Niccolo Antonelli
Gabriel Rodrigo	Filip Salac	Kaito Toba
Carlos Tatay	Riccardo Rossi	Adrian Fernandez
Daniel Holgado	Andi Farid Izdihar	Syarifuddin Azman

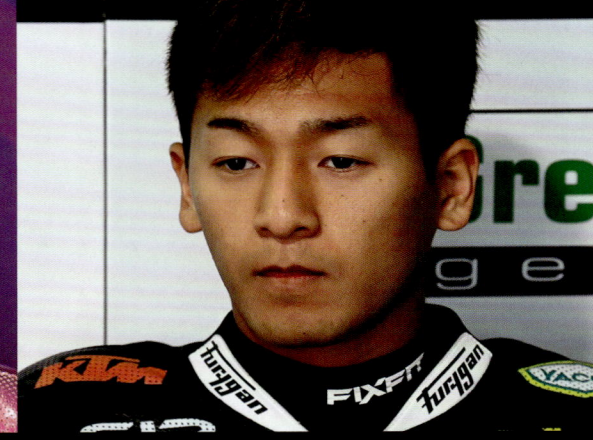

Darryn Binder	Izan Guevara
Xavier Artigas	Ryusei Yamanaka	Stefano Nepa
Kunii Yuki	Maximilian Kofler	Elia Bartolini
Joel Kelso	Alberto Surra	Lorenzo Fellon

Photo: www.suzuki-racing.com

MOTOGP · MOTO2 · MOTO3
GRANDS PRIX 2021
Reports by MICHAEL SCOTT & NEIL MORRISON

Statistics compiled by PETER McLAREN

It was a dream start for Maverick Vinales, here showing the way to Mir and Zarco.
Photo: Gold & Goose

FIM WORLD CHAMPIONSHIP · ROUND 1

QATAR GRAND PRIX
LOSAIL INTERNATIONAL CIRCUIT

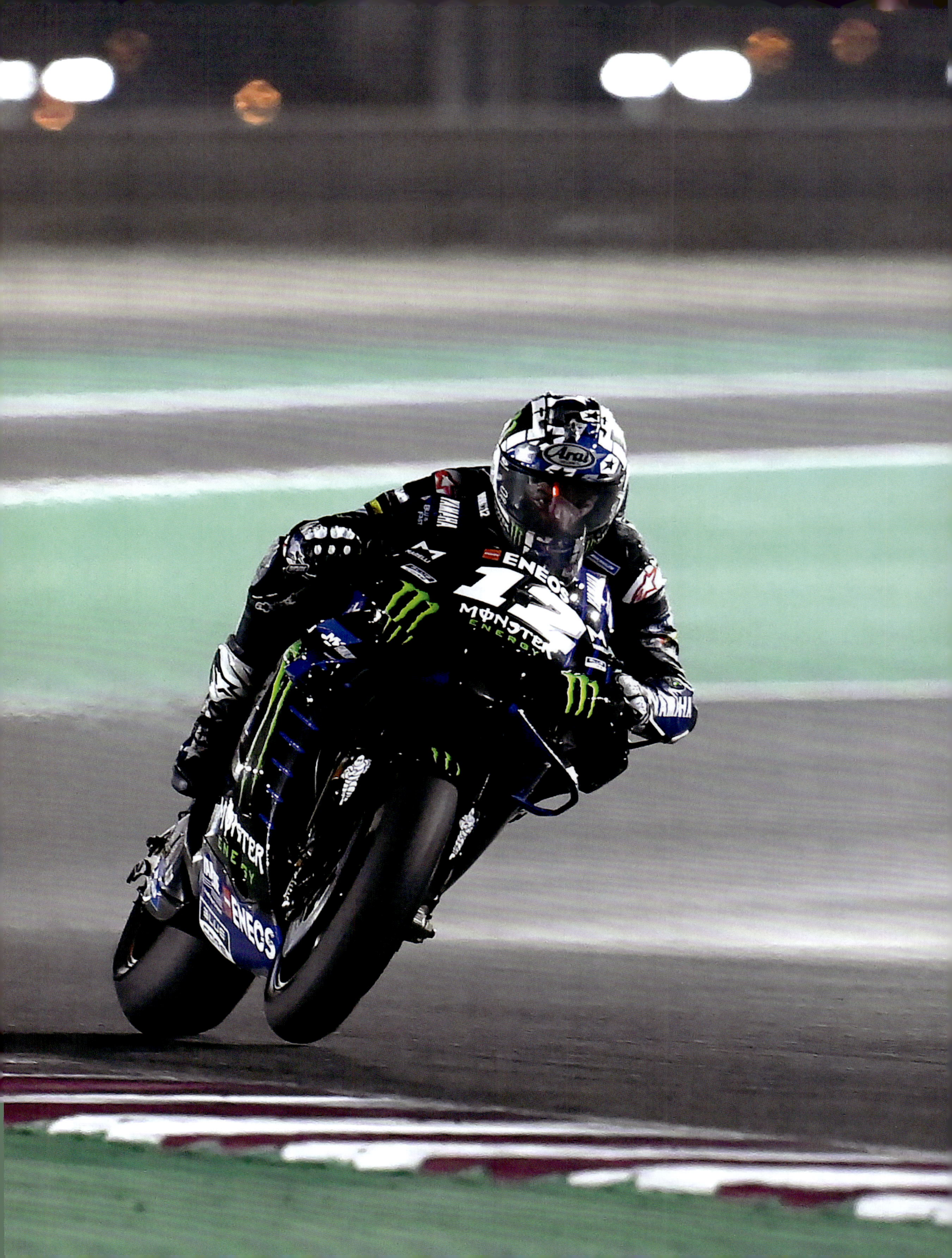
Arai
ENEOS
12
ENERGY
ENEOS

Above: A maiden pole augured well for Bagnaia in his first race for the factory Ducati team.
Photo: Ducati Corse

Top and above right: MotoGP's Italian new boys, Luca Marini (*top*) and Enea Bastianini.
Photos: Gold & Goose

Right: Eyes watering? Johann Zarco set a blistering new 225mph top speed record in Saturday's FP4.
Photo: Pramac Racing

FOREWARNED and thus forearmed, MotoGP began again on schedule under the desert lights – not as usual, but as had become usual in the preceding abbreviated season, masked and socially distanced, and eager to get under way with the first of what, at this stage, was the only planned double-header on a calendar that still had several question marks hanging over it.

The race did not disappoint. By the flag, five manufacturers were in the top eight places, with just 5.9 seconds in it.

The final round of tests at Qatar had pricked the interest, with the factory Ducatis and Yamahas setting the pace, and the all-new Aprilia up with them, just ahead of the Suzukis. Honda? Well, no Marc Marquez, but new Repsol signing Pol Espargaro only seven-tenths slower with minimal time on the bike and placed tenth on combined times.

There were no fewer than four rookies: Luca Marini, Enea Bastianini and Lorenzo Savadori from Italy; plus ex-Moto3 champion Jorge Martin from Spain. Marini and Bastianini were team-mates in the third Ducati squad, the former in the SKY VR46 colours of half-brother Valentino Rossi, a first toe in the water of the premier class; Bastianini was in Esponsorama livery, and both were on older bikes. Martin and Pramac team-mate Zarco had 2021 bikes.

Savadori was now full time at Aprilia, having subbed three times in 2020 for Andrea Iannone during the latter's doping trials. The GP winner's situation had gone from bad to worse after his appeal, with the original 18-month suspension extended to four years from December, 2019; his replacement was in at the deep end.

With younger brother Alex now in the satellite LCR team, hopes that the elder Marquez might be there for the race were dashed: recuperation from a third major operation in December was taking its time. Mindful of the destructive effect of his premature return the previous July, the Spaniard had complied with those urging caution. Later, he revealed that he had feared not that he might not be able to race a motorcycle again, but that he might never regain full use of his arm. Once again, his place was taken by factory test rider Stefan Bradl.

Losail's long straight gave the Ducatis a chance to stretch their legs in practice, before Sunday's headwind. Zarco posted an eye-watering 225.184mph (362.4km/h), a new record. He was ably backed by rookie Martin (358) and Miller (357), with Ducatis posting six of the top ten speeds. Pol Espargaro's Honda was fifth at 355.2, Marquez's long-serving replacement, Bradl, sixth; Iker Lecuona's KTM was tenth, at 350.6. This, however, flattered the KTMs; while proof that top speed is not everything would come, this weekend and the following, with a pair of race wins from Yamaha. These were seriously slower, Rossi's significantly the best with a fast reading of 348.3.

For Vinales, this was proof that the new hiring of Cal Crutchlow as test rider was paying early dividends: "We ride very similar. In the last day of testing, I tried his bike, and it was fantastic for me." He promised a totally different mentality from the previous year, but it would not last.

KTM's difficulties, at the far end of the points, took everyone by surprise after their strong finish to the previous season, although underwhelming testing performance had sounded a warning. For Binder, it was a matter of lack of confidence in the front of the RC16, "on a track where you are not using a lot of front brake and trying to keep the bike flowing". Oliveira went further, criticising Michelin's front tyre allocation and explaining that the options didn't suit their machine. The soft front – used by everyone in the race – was too soft for KTM's riders, but the medium, an asymmetric tyre, was as bad. He'd pointed out the problems in pre-season tests, but with no response. "The combination between the carcase and the rubber from the medium is just wrong, and we communicated that from day one of testing here, and in fact nobody used it. So we use the hard when it's hot, and we're competitive. We cannot spend six months developing a bike to a certain kind of tyre and then just have this tyre removed from the allocation. We feel that the result today is not any kind of reflection of a bike issue."

Pecco Bagnaia's debut pole (a new track record) and second podium followed an impressive, measured pre-season of testing. The 2018 Moto2 world champion had been blindingly fast on occasion in 2020, but inconsistencies had wrecked his campaign. Analysis over the winter had suggested that problems generating heat in Michelin's fickle front caused problems on cooler tracks, "crashing without pushing". He studied the technique of team-mate Miller – a master at quickly getting his front tyre up to temperature – and appeared to have cured this previous weakness: "I had luck to have Jack as team-mate. He's very good with this temperature. I have to push without feeling to warm the tyre."

New strength for Aprilia came from a complete redesign. Further news was that Dovizioso had been enlisted for a private test in April. Speculation went into overdrive as to whether he might be drafted in to replace new signing Savadori, who was still struggling. Dovi's manager, Simone Battistella, poured cold water on that dream. "I don't think there is a chance [he will race] this season," he said. "There may be another test or more testing." This proved correct.

There was testing also for Covid, for anyone hoping to enter the paddock. Two team crew chiefs were missing on Friday, after reactive test results: Vinales's Esteban Garcia and Alex Marquez's veteran LCR chief, Christophe 'Beefy' Bourguignon. They directed Friday's sessions via Zoom – said Alex: "It was like he was here." Better still, both were cleared to return on Saturday.

The Stewards Panel began the year as they would go on, issuing several penalties. Moto3's Xavier Artigas earned a post-race double long-lap penalty for causing a crash, deferred until the following weekend's Doha GP; Mir was fined 1,000 euros and had his first qualifying lap cancelled (for leaving the pit lane early); Moto2's Dixon was dropped three grid places for riding slowly in qualifying and causing a crash; and Moto3's Toba and Tatay each one place for exceeding track limits on the last race lap. Tatay had already served a long-lap for irresponsible riding, and Romano Fenati a double long-lap for jumping the start.

MOTOGP RACE – 22 laps

Bagnaia's first pole set a new all-time record for the circuit; mentor Rossi took the benefit of his slipstream for fourth, leading row two for his first race for the satellite Yamaha team. The factory bikes of Quartararo and Vinales were ahead, the Ducatis of Miller and Zarco alongside. Champion Mir was tenth, on row four, having come through from Q1 with 11th-fastest Nakagami.

Four Ducatis swarmed into the first turn in an almost laughable show of strength, Bagnaia from Miller, Zarco and rookie Martin, sensationally up from the fifth row.

But a strong headwind on the long straight nullified their top-speed advantage, and as the race wore on, an unusually decisive and aggressive Vinales disposed of all four. But for an unexpected last-corner blunder, Mir might have left only Zarco still on a podium the Bologna bikes had been expected to dominate.

Mindful of Losail's notoriously high fuel consumption, Bagnaia adopted a conservative approach as he led the early laps, an orderly queue forming behind.

Quartararo and Vinales had pounced on Martin on lap three, then closed on the front three. The expectation that top speed could keep the Ducatis safe proved false, and Quartararo's lap-six lunge on Miller at Turn 15 announced that they would not have this all their own way. The Aussie responded on the main straight, but the Frenchman's braking prowess kept him in third. Two laps on, and Vinales was also by, producing a glorious pass at Turn Ten to take fourth.

Above: The early laps were frenetic. Repsol Honda's new boy, Pol Espargaro, leads Binder, Marquez substitute Bradl, Nakagami, Lecuona and Alex Marquez.

Top right: Yamaha's Vinales overcame a significant top-speed deficit to defeat the Ducati pair of Bagnaia and Zarco.

Above right: Fabio di Giannantonio eventually just held off compatriot Bezzecchi for third in Moto2. Rookie Raul Fernandez and Joe Roberts give chase.

Centre right: Sam Lowes started the season in dominant form.

Centre far right: Five times US champion Cameron Beaubier about to stake his reputation in Moto2. He made an impressive start.

Right: Moto2 2021 was reliably scarily close. Winner Masia leads the brawl from Binder (40), Acosta and Sasaki (hidden), Garcia (11), Guevara, Toba, Salac (12), Yamanaka (6), Antonelli (23), Rodrigo (2), Dupasquier (50) and Suzuki (24).
Photos: Gold & Goose

By now, it wasn't just Yamaha that looked capable of challenging. Six laps in, the Suzukis of Rins and Mir had climbed four places apiece, to sixth and seventh, as Martin continued to fade. By half-distance, Rins was just behind Miller, with just over a second covering the top six. A couple of seconds further back, Mir headed the Espargaro brothers, Aleix's Aprilia ahead of the factory Honda.

On that lap, Vinales's superiority began to tell as Quartararo ran into grip trouble. First, the Spaniard coolly slotted past at Turn One. Next lap, he swooped under Zarco at Turn Ten. And by lap 15, he had put the same move on Bagnaia to lead – a five-lap blitz that was more Marquez than Vinales. The ex-Moto3 champ hadn't looked this convincing since the start of 2017.

By lap 15, Quartararo was not the only one struggling with tyre life, Bagnaia especially as the leading Yamaha stretched clear. Vinales credited "working really well in FP4 to understand how to get grip when the tyre was used." He crossed the line better than a second ahead, and with the lap record to boot.

Mir was also flying, having taken some time to warm up. On lap 13, he was the fastest out there, and he made short work of Miller, Quartararo and Rins to move into fourth.

As the laps ticked down, the champion homed in on Bagnaia and Zarco, displaying trademark late-laps pace. With three laps left, he took Bagnaia, and by the last lap, he had slashed the 0.8-of-a-second deficit to Zarco. He was poised for a remarkable second as he passed the Frenchman at the penultimate turn.

A rare mistake at the next was costly. He missed the apex and ran wide; immediately, both 'rockets' flashed by, with Zarco nabbing second, Bagnaia third, 0.13 of a second covering them all at the flag.

Exasperated by the drop in rear tyre performance, Quartararo labelled fifth place disastrous. Rins was sixth, again overshadowed by his team-mate. Forgetting to engage his bike's launch control had left him with too much to do. "I pushed a lot to recover this time and destroyed the tyres," he rued.

Aleix Espargaro made good on a weekend of promise for the new Aprilias with seventh, just 5.9 seconds behind Vinales – the closest Aprilia had been to a race winner in the four-stroke era. Brother Pol was a place behind on his Honda debut, while Miller had dropped to a disappointing ninth, also stricken with rear grip problems.

Bastianini was the best of the rookies, in tenth, a second clear of Bradl. Another half a second away, Rossi's 12th marked a bad afternoon for the Petronas team, with Morbidelli out of the points after encountering problems with his holeshot device.

Thirteenth and 14th were disappointing for the factory KTM pair of Oliveira and Binder; fast-starter Martin had faded to 15th, comfortably clear of Lecuona. Second satellite KTM rider Petrucci fell on the first lap; satellite Honda pair Nakagami and Marquez also fell.

MOTO2 RACE – 20 laps

After strong testing results, the season proper began perfectly for Sam Lowes, with pole position, alongside class rookie Raul Fernandez – serving early notice of being the quickest of learners – and first-timer Bendsneycer.

Bezzecchi led row two from Roberts, in his first race as replacement for departed champion Bastianini at Italtrans, and Remy Gardner, in his first outing in the equally high-ranking Ajo Red Bull colours.

Bezzecchi led away, but from the moment Lowes breezed past on lap three, the outcome was in no doubt. The Englishman took total control for a seventh class win.

It might not have been so easy had Gardner not come into contact with Jake Dixon, who had qualified well on row three, at only the second corner. Gardner was pushed wide on to the dirty part of the track, to finish the first lap eighth.

At once, he began picking his way through with assurance, while up front Fernandez had got ahead of Bezzecchi. Bendsneyder was already falling back, but Dixon was hanging on behind, Roberts and Di Giannantonio tracking him close.

By lap nine, Gardner had passed them all for second, Fernandez still close, with a little gap to Bezzecchi. Then came Roberts, Di Giannantonio and Dixon, with Navarro a couple of seconds adrift.

Gardner now set about closing the 1.4-second gap to

FIM WORLD CHAMPIONSHIP

Lowes, but he could make no impression, and at around three-quarters-distance, he chose to settle for second.

Fernandez faded over the last three laps, leaving it to Bezzecchi and Di Giannantonio to contest third place, the latter taking it by a hundredth with a finally successful attack two corners from the flag.

Fernandez was fifth, ahead of Roberts. Dixon was a couple of seconds off; then Marcel Schrotter was clear of Bendsneyder and the fading Navarro, on the renamed Boscoscuro (formerly Speed Up), the first non-Kalex.

US multi-champion Cameron Beaubier made an impressive Moto2 debut, in his first GP since 2009, but not quite his first time at Qatar. He had qualified 22nd, but picked his way through steadily to take 11th on the last lap, less than half a second behind Navarro, but ahead of several notables. Fellow class rookie Vietti was his last victim, from Canet, Fernandez and Luthi. Three more ex-Moto3 rookies – Arbolino, Ogura and Dalla Porta – were close behind, but out of the points.

Baldassarri, Garzo, Vierge and Chantra crashed out; Syahrin and Ramirez retired.

MOTO3 RACE – 18 laps

The year began with a typically nerve-wracking Moto3 brawl – a seething leading group of 13 still within one second at half-distance, seven surviving in the same interval at the finish. Close contact had caused several crashes and near misses, setting the tone for a fraught year to come.

Three standout rookies and a couple of notable team changes played their part.

New boys were Izan Guevara on the Gas Gas (formerly KTM) and Pedro Acosta (KTM), who looked entirely at home at the front of the pack; less so Xavi Artigas, who skittled fellow Honda riders and likely challengers John McPhee, Jeremy Alcoba and Andrea Migno on lap three, earning a double long-lap penalty for the next race.

Among veterans, Darryn Binder had switched to Honda and claimed pole position; Jaume Masia had made the reverse trip to KTM.

Eight different riders led across the line, the pack constantly shuffling. On the final lap, Masia pipped Sasaki for the lead at the first turn before the Japanese rider binned it in anger a corner later.

That left rookie Acosta to chase down the leader, foiling Binder's final efforts. Masia just held on after a typical drag race from the final corner to beat Acosta by 0.04 of a second, with Binder 0.09 of a second further back in third.

Sergio Garcia was fourth, ahead of Rodrigo, Antonelli and Guevara. A second back, Suzuki, Toba and Jason Dupasquier completed the top ten, the last named's first points.

Foggia crashed on the first lap; Oncu a little later.

FIM WORLD CHAMPIONSHIP: ROUND 1

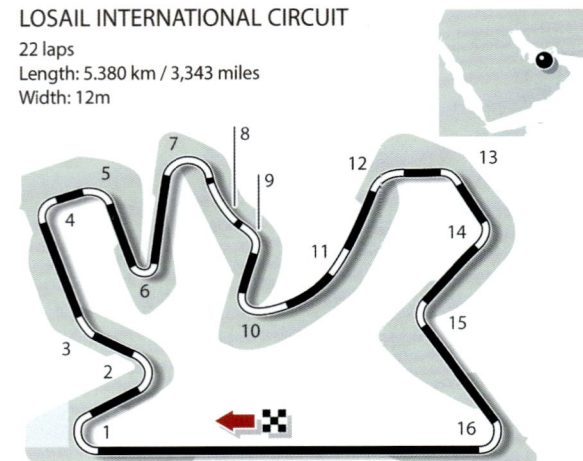

BARWA GRAND PRIX OF QATAR

26–28 MARCH, 2021

LOSAIL INTERNATIONAL CIRCUIT
22 laps
Length: 5.380 km / 3,343 miles
Width: 12m

MotoGP

RACE DISTANCE: 22 laps, 73.545 miles/118.360km · RACE WEATHER: Dry (air 20°, humidity 60%, track 22°)

Pos.	Rider	Nat.	No.	Entrant	Machine	Tyres	Race tyre choice	Laps	Time & speed
1	Maverick Vinales	SPA	12	Monster Energy Yamaha MotoGP	Yamaha YZR-M1	M	F: Soft/R: Soft	22	42m 28.663s / 103.8mph / 167.1km/h
2	Johann Zarco	FRA	5	Pramac Racing	Ducati Desmosedici	M	F: Soft/R: Soft	22	42m 29.755s
3	Francesco Bagnaia	ITA	63	Ducati Lenovo Team	Ducati Desmosedici	M	F: Soft/R: Soft	22	42m 29.792s
4	Joan Mir	SPA	36	Team SUZUKI ECSTAR	Suzuki GSX-RR	M	F: Soft/R: Soft	22	42m 29.885s
5	Fabio Quartararo	FRA	20	Monster Energy Yamaha MotoGP	Yamaha YZR-M1	M	F: Soft/R: Soft	22	42m 31.693s
6	Alex Rins	SPA	42	Team SUZUKI ECSTAR	Suzuki GSX-RR	M	F: Soft/R: Soft	22	42m 32.020s
7	Aleix Espargaro	SPA	41	Aprilia Racing Team Gresini	Aprilia RS-GP	M	F: Soft/R: Soft	22	42m 34.597s
8	Pol Espargaro	SPA	44	Repsol Honda Team	Honda RC213V	M	F: Soft/R: Soft	22	42m 34.653s
9	Jack Miller	AUS	43	Ducati Lenovo Team	Ducati Desmosedici	M	F: Soft/R: Soft	22	42m 35.721s
10	Enea Bastianini	ITA	23	Esponsorama Racing	Ducati Desmosedici	M	F: Soft/R: Soft	22	42m 37.951s
11	Stefan Bradl	GER	6	Repsol Honda Team	Honda RC213V	M	F: Soft/R: Soft	22	42m 38.962s
12	Valentino Rossi	ITA	46	Petronas Yamaha SRT	Yamaha YZR-M1	M	F: Soft/R: Soft	22	42m 39.405s
13	Miguel Oliveira	POR	88	Red Bull KTM Factory Racing	KTM RC16	M	F: Soft/R: Soft	22	42m 40.120s
14	Brad Binder	RSA	33	Red Bull KTM Factory Racing	KTM RC16	M	F: Soft/R: Soft	22	42m 42.763s
15	Jorge Martin	SPA	89	Pramac Racing	Ducati Desmosedici	M	F: Soft/R: Soft	22	42m 45.085s
16	Luca Marini	ITA	10	SKY VR46 Esponsorama	Ducati Desmosedici	M	F: Soft/R: Soft	22	42m 49.579s
17	Iker Lecuona	SPA	27	Tech 3 KTM Factory Racing	KTM RC16	M	F: Soft/R: Soft	22	42m 49.689s
18	Franco Morbidelli	ITA	21	Petronas Yamaha SRT	Yamaha YZR-M1	M	F: Soft/R: Soft	22	42m 52.555s
19	Lorenzo Savadori	ITA	32	Aprilia Racing Team Gresini	Aprilia RS-GP	M	F: Soft/R: Soft	22	43m 15.009s
	Alex Marquez	SPA	73	LCR Honda CASTROL	Honda RC213V	M	F: Soft/R: Soft	13	DNF-crash
	Takaaki Nakagami	JPN	30	LCR Honda IDEMITSU	Honda RC213V	M	F: Soft/R: Soft	6	DNF-crash
	Danilo Petrucci	ITA	9	Tech 3 KTM Factory Racing	KTM RC16	M	F: Soft/R: Soft	0	DNF-crash

Fastest lap: Maverick Vinales, on lap 4, 1m 54.624s, 104.9mph/168.9km/h.
Lap record: Jorge Lorenzo, 1m 54.927s, 104.7mph/168.5km/h (2016).
Event maximum speed: Johann Zarco, 225.2mph/362.4km/h (free practice).

Qualifying

Weather: Dry
Air Temp: 28° Humidity: 34%
Track Temp: 29°

1	Bagnaia	1m 52.772s
2	Quartararo	1m 53.038s
3	Vinales	1m 53.088s
4	Rossi	1m 53.114s
5	Miller	1m 53.215s
6	Zarco	1m 53.286s
7	Morbidelli	1m 53.313s
8	A. Espargaro	1m 53.315s
9	Rins	1m 53.490s
10	Mir	1m 53.682s
11	Nakagami	1m 53.721s
12	P. Espargaro	1m 53.930s

Q1

13	Bastianini	1m 53.733s
14	Martin	1m 53.840s
15	Oliveira	1m 53.915s
16	A. Marquez	1m 53.958s
17	Bradl	1m 53.995s
18	Marini	1m 54.122s
19	Binder	1m 54.240s
20	Petrucci	1m 54.443s
21	Lecuona	1m 54.627s
22	Savadori	1m 55.183s

Fastest race laps

1	Vinales	1m 54.624s
2	Quartararo	1m 54.890s
3	Zarco	1m 54.896s
4	Rins	1m 54.912s
5	Miller	1m 55.074s
6	Bagnaia	1m 55.084s
7	P. Espargaro	1m 55.159s
8	A. Espargaro	1m 55.160s
9	A. Marquez	1m 55.161s
10	Mir	1m 55.178s
11	Oliveira	1m 55.178s
12	Bastianini	1m 55.244s
13	Rossi	1m 55.253s
14	Binder	1m 55.293s
15	Martin	1m 55.338s
16	Lecuona	1m 55.354s
17	Bradl	1m 55.382s
18	Nakagami	1m 55.439s
19	Marini	1m 55.688s
20	Morbidelli	1m 55.815s
21	Savadori	1m 57.111s

Championship Points

1	Vinales	25
2	Zarco	20
3	Bagnaia	16
4	Mir	13
5	Quartararo	11
6	Rins	10
7	A. Espargaro	9
8	P. Espargaro	8
9	Miller	7
10	Bastianini	6
11	Bradl	5
12	Rossi	4
13	Oliveira	3
14	Binder	2
15	Martin	1

Constructor Points

1	Yamaha	25
2	Ducati	20
3	Suzuki	13
4	Aprilia	9
5	Honda	8
6	KTM	3

Grid order / Lap-by-lap

Grid order		1	2	3	4	5	6	7	8	9	10	11	12	13	14	15	16	17	18	19	20	21	22	
63	BAGNAIA	63	63	63	63	63	63	63	63	63	63	63	63	63	63	12	12	12	12	12	12	12	12	1
20	QUARTARARO	5	5	5	5	5	5	5	5	5	5	5	12	12	12	63	63	5	5	5	5	5	5	2
12	VINALES	43	43	43	43	43	20	20	20	20	20	12	5	5	5	5	5	63	63	63	36	36	63	3
46	ROSSI	89	89	20	20	20	43	43	12	12	12	20	43	43	42	42	42	42	36	36	63	63	36	4
43	MILLER	20	20	12	12	12	12	12	43	43	43	43	42	42	43	43	36	36	42	42	20	20	20	5
5	ZARCO	12	12	89	89	42	42	42	42	42	42	42	20	20	20	36	43	20	20	20	42	42	42	6
21	MORBIDELLI	46	46	42	42	89	36	36	36	36	36	36	36	36	36	20	20	43	43	41	41	41	41	7
41	A. ESPARGARO	41	42	46	36	36	89	89	89	41	41	41	41	41	41	41	41	41	41	43	44	44	44	8
42	RINS	42	36	36	46	46	46	41	41	89	89	44	44	44	44	44	44	44	44	44	43	43	43	9
36	MIR	36	41	41	41	41	41	46	88	88	88	89	88	88	88	23	23	23	23	23	23	23	23	10
30	NAKAGAMI	88	88	88	88	88	88	46	46	44	88	33	33	23	88	88	88	6	6	6	6	6	6	11
44	P. ESPARGARO	44	44	44	44	44	44	44	44	46	46	89	23	33	33	6	6	6	88	88	88	88	46	12
23	BASTIANINI	6	33	33	33	33	33	33	33	33	23	6	6	89	33	33	46	46	46	46	46	88	13
89	MARTIN	33	6	6	6	6	6	6	6	6	73	46	89	33	46	46	33	33	33	33	33	14
88	OLIVEIRA	30	30	30	27	27	73	27	73	73	73	46	89	46	46	89	89	89	89	89	89	15
73	A. MARQUEZ	21	27	27	30	30	27	73	23	73	73	23	46	89	10	10	10	10	10	10	10	
6	BRADL	27	73	73	73	73	30	23	10	10	10	10	10	21	21	27	27	27	27	27	27	
10	MARINI	73	23	23	23	23	23	10	27	27	27	27	21	10	27	21	21	21	21	21	21	
33	BINDER	23	21	21	10	10	10	21	21	21	21	21	27	27	32	32	32	32	32	32	32	
9	PETRUCCI	10	10	10	21	21	21	32	32	32	32	32	32	32								
27	LECUONA	32	32	32	32	32																
32	SAVADORI																					

Moto2

RACE DISTANCE: 20 laps, 66.860 miles/107.600km · **RACE WEATHER:** Dry (air 21°, humidity 56%, track 23°)

Pos.	Rider	Nat.	No.	Entrant	Machine	Laps	Time & Speed
1	Sam Lowes	GBR	22	Elf Marc VDS Racing Team	Kalex	20	40m 03.123s
							100.1mph/
							161.1km/h
2	Remy Gardner	AUS	87	Red Bull KTM Ajo	Kalex	20	40m 05.383s
3	Fabio Di Giannantonio	ITA	21	Federal Oil Gresini Moto2	Kalex	20	40m 08.351s
4	Marco Bezzecchi	ITA	72	SKY Racing Team VR46	Kalex	20	40m 08.364s
5	Raul Fernandez	SPA	25	Red Bull KTM Ajo	Kalex	20	40m 09.268s
6	Joe Roberts	USA	16	Italtrans Racing Team	Kalex	20	40m 09.909s
7	Jake Dixon	GBR	96	Petronas Sprinta Racing	Kalex	20	40m 11.844s
8	Marcel Schrotter	GER	23	Liqui Moly Intact GP	Kalex	20	40m 14.034s
9	Bo Bendsneyder	NED	64	Pertamina Mandalika SAG Team	Kalex	20	40m 15.616s
10	Jorge Navarro	SPA	9	MB Conveyors Speed Up	Boscoscuro	20	40m 19.923s
11	Cameron Beaubier	USA	6	American Racing	Kalex	20	40m 20.270s
12	Celestino Vietti	ITA	13	SKY Racing Team VR46	Kalex	20	40m 20.412s
13	Aron Canet	SPA	44	Inde Aspar Team	Boscoscuro	20	40m 20.650s
14	Augusto Fernandez	SPA	37	Elf Marc VDS Racing Team	Kalex	20	40m 20.663s
15	Thomas Luthi	SWI	12	Pertamina Mandalika SAG Team	Kalex	20	40m 20.939s
16	Tony Arbolino	ITA	14	Liqui Moly Intact GP	Kalex	20	40m 21.334s
17	Ai Ogura	JPN	79	IDEMITSU Honda Team Asia	Kalex	20	40m 22.266s
18	Lorenzo Dalla Porta	ITA	19	Italtrans Racing Team	Kalex	20	40m 22.343s
19	Stefano Manzi	ITA	62	Flexbox HP40	Kalex	20	40m 28.929s
20	Yari Montella	ITA	5	MB Conveyors Speed Up	Boscoscuro	20	40m 33.787s
21	Albert Arenas	SPA	75	Inde Aspar Team	Boscoscuro	20	40m 33.831s
22	Nicolo Bulega	ITA	11	Federal Oil Gresini Moto2	Kalex	20	40m 35.887s
	Somkiat Chantra	THA	35	IDEMITSU Honda Team Asia	Kalex	19	DNF-crash
	Xavi Vierge	SPA	97	Petronas Sprinta Racing	Kalex	14	DNF-crash
	Hector Garzo	SPA	40	Flexbox HP40	Kalex	9	DNF-crash
	Hafizh Syahrin	MAL	55	NTS RW Racing GP	NTS	9	DNF-technical
	Lorenzo Baldassarri	ITA	7	MV Agusta Forward Racing	MV Agusta	6	DNF-crash
	Marcos Ramirez	SPA	42	American Racing	Kalex	0	DNF-injured

Fastest lap: Remy Gardner, on lap 13, 1m 59.491s, 100.7mph/162.0km/h.
Lap record: Thomas Luthi, 1m 58.711s, 101.3mph/163.1km/h (2019).
Event maximum speed: Marcos Ramirez, 183.8mph/295.8km/h (free practice).

Qualifying:
Weather: Dry
Air: 28° Track: 32°
Humidity: 48%

1	Lowes	1m 58.726s
2	R. Fernandez	1m 58.866s
3	Bendsneyder	1m 58.959s
4	Bezzecchi	1m 59.052s
5	Roberts	1m 59.168s
6	Gardner	1m 59.197s
7	Dixon	1m 59.203s
8	Di Giannantonio	1m 59.241s
9	Navarro	1m 59.420s
10	Vietti	1m 59.439s
11	Bulega	1m 59.454s
12	Canet	1m 59.477s
13	Schrotter	1m 59.487s
14	Dalla Porta	1m 59.531s
15	Vierge	1m 59.620s
16	Chantra	1m 59.899s
17	Luthi	1m 59.908s
18	Arbolino	1m 59.925s

Q1
19	Ogura	1m 59.498s
20	Ramirez	1m 59.638s
21	A. Fernandez	1m 59.667s
22	Beaubier	1m 59.673s
23	Arenas	1m 59.710s
24	Manzi	1m 59.819s
25	Garzo	2m 00.015s
26	Baldassarri	2m 00.135s
27	Montella	2m 00.173s
28	Syahrin	2m 00.644s
29	Corsi	2m 02.566s

Fastest race laps
1	Gardner	1m 59.491s
2	Lowes	1m 59.502s
3	Di Giannantonio	1m 59.590s
4	R. Fernandez	1m 59.710s
5	Roberts	1m 59.745s
6	Bezzecchi	1m 59.758s
7	Dixon	1m 59.764s
8	Schrotter	1m 59.771s
9	Arbolino	1m 59.866s
10	Ogura	1m 59.950s
11	Navarro	1m 59.954s
12	Dalla Porta	2m 00.022s
13	Beaubier	2m 00.045s
14	Luthi	2m 00.105s
15	Canet	2m 00.124s
16	A. Fernandez	2m 00.130s
17	Bendsneyder	2m 00.170s
18	Vierge	2m 00.183s
19	Bulega	2m 00.196s
20	Vietti	2m 00.241s
21	Chantra	2m 00.248s
22	Manzi	2m 00.382s
23	Garzo	2m 00.597s
24	Montella	2m 00.635s
25	Arenas	2m 00.674s
26	Baldassarri	2m 00.987s
27	Syahrin	2m 02.158s

Championship Points
1	Lowes	25
2	Gardner	20
3	Di Giannantonio	16
4	Bezzecchi	13
5	R. Fernandez	11
6	Roberts	10
7	Dixon	9
8	Schrotter	8
9	Bendsneyder	7
10	Navarro	6
11	Beaubier	5
12	Vietti	4
13	Canet	3
14	A. Fernandez	2
15	Luthi	1

Constructor Points
| 1 | Kalex | 25 |
| 2 | Boscoscuro | 6 |

Moto3

RACE DISTANCE: 18 laps, 60.174 miles/96.840km · **RACE WEATHER:** Dry (air 23°, humidity 48%, track 28°)

Pos.	Rider	Nat.	No.	Entrant	Machine	Laps	Time & Speed
1	Jaume Masia	SPA	5	Red Bull KTM Ajo	KTM	18	38m 29.620s
							93.8mph/
							150.9km/h
2	Pedro Acosta	SPA	37	Red Bull KTM Ajo	KTM	18	38m 29.662s
3	Darryn Binder	RSA	40	Petronas Sprinta Racing	Honda	18	38m 29.714s
4	Sergio Garcia	SPA	11	GASGAS Gaviota Aspar	GASGAS	18	38m 30.055s
5	Gabriel Rodrigo	ARG	2	Indonesian Racing Gresini Moto3	Honda	18	38m 30.500s
6	Niccolo Antonelli	ITA	23	Avintia Esponsorama Moto3	KTM	18	38m 30.519s
7	Izan Guevara	SPA	28	GASGAS Gaviota Aspar	GASGAS	18	38m 30.585s
8	Tatsuki Suzuki	JPN	24	SIC58 Squadra Corse	Honda	18	38m 31.834s
9	Kaito Toba	JPN	27	CIP Green Power	KTM	18	38m 31.570s
10	Jason Dupasquier	SWI	50	CarXpert PruestelGP	KTM	18	38m 31.839s
11	Romano Fenati	ITA	55	Sterilgarda Max Racing Team	Husqvarna	18	38m 31.936s
12	Carlos Tatay	SPA	99	Avintia Esponsorama Moto3	KTM	18	38m 31.918s
13	Filip Salac	CZE	12	Rivacold Snipers Team	Honda	18	38m 31.965s
14	Ryusei Yamanaka	JPN	6	CarXpert PruestelGP	KTM	18	38m 32.054s
15	Maximilian Kofler	AUT	73	CIP Green Power	KTM	18	38m 44.388s
16	Yuki Kunii	JPN	92	Honda Team Asia	Honda	18	38m 44.454s
17	Adrian Fernandez	SPA	31	Sterilgarda Max Racing Team	Husqvarna	18	38m 51.807s
18	Stefano Nepa	ITA	82	BOE Owlride	KTM	18	38m 51.897s
19	Lorenzo Fellon	FRA	20	SIC58 Squadra Corse	Honda	18	38m 57.902s
20	Deniz Oncu	TUR	53	Red Bull KTM Tech 3	KTM	18	39m 10.903s
21	Andi Farid Izdihar	INA	19	Honda Team Asia	Honda	18	39m 14.596s
	Ayumu Sasaki	JPN	71	Red Bull KTM Tech 3	KTM	17	DNF-crash
	Xavier Artigas	SPA	43	Leopard Racing	Honda	7	DNF-crash
	John McPhee	GBR	17	Petronas Sprinta Racing	Honda	2	DNF-crash
	Andrea Migno	ITA	16	Rivacold Snipers Team	Honda	2	DNF-crash
	Jeremy Alcoba	SPA	52	Indonesian Racing Gresini Moto3	Honda	2	DNF-crash
	Riccardo Rossi	ITA	54	BOE Owlride	KTM	1	DNF-crash
	Dennis Foggia	ITA	7	Leopard Racing	Honda	0	DNF-crash

Fastest lap: Xavier Artigas, on lap 2, 2m 6.557s, 95.1mph/153.0km/h.
Lap record: Romano Fenati, 2m 5.403s, 95.9mph/154.4km/h (2019).
Event maximum speed: Ryusei Yamanaka, 152.1mph/244.8km/h (free practice).

Qualifying:
Weather: Dry
Air: 22° Track: 28°
Humidity: 59%

1	Binder	2m 04.075s
2	Guevara	2m 04.278s
3	McPhee	2m 04.358s
4	Alcoba	2m 04.437s
5	Masia	2m 04.498s
6	Toba	2m 04.673s
7	Rodrigo	2m 04.780s
8	Garcia	2m 04.870s
9	Rossi	2m 04.889s
10	Antonelli	2m 04.959s
11	Acosta	2m 05.058s
12	Dupasquier	2m 05.065s
13	Foggia	2m 05.115s
14	Tatay	2m 05.729s
15	Sasaki	2m 05.761s
16	Kofler	2m 05.887s
17	Migno	2m 13.160s
18	Fenati	No Time

Q1
19	Oncu	2m 05.804s
20	Kunii	2m 05.901s
21	Yamanaka	2m 06.169s
22	Fernandez	2m 06.356s
23	Salac	2m 06.414s
24	Artigas	2m 06.487s
25	Nepa	2m 06.735s
26	Izdihar	2m 07.143s
27	Fellon	2m 07.787s
	Suzuki	No Time

Fastest race laps
1	Artigas	2m 06.557s
2	Acosta	2m 06.718s
3	Masia	2m 06.792s
4	Dupasquier	2m 06.838s
5	Binder	2m 06.946s
6	Antonelli	2m 06.947s
7	Guevara	2m 06.985s
8	Sasaki	2m 06.999s
9	Salac	2m 07.009s
10	Garcia	2m 07.054s
11	Fenati	2m 07.078s
12	Rodrigo	2m 07.147s
13	Suzuki	2m 07.147s
14	Tatay	2m 07.158s
15	Kofler	2m 07.199s
16	Toba	2m 07.214s
17	Yamanaka	2m 07.286s
18	Migno	2m 07.337s
19	McPhee	2m 07.474s
20	Fernandez	2m 07.548s
21	Alcoba	2m 07.549s
22	Kunii	2m 07.618s
23	Nepa	2m 08.028s
24	Fellon	2m 08.514s
25	Oncu	2m 08.583s
26	Izdihar	2m 09.382s

Championship Points
1	Masia	25
2	Acosta	20
3	Binder	16
4	Garcia	13
5	Rodrigo	11
6	Antonelli	10
7	Guevara	9
8	Suzuki	8
9	Toba	7
10	Dupasquier	6
11	Fenati	5
12	Tatay	4
13	Salac	3
14	Yamanaka	2
15	Kofler	1

Constructor Points
1	KTM	25
2	Honda	16
3	GASGAS	13
4	Husqvarna	5

الدولية
LOSAIL INTERNAT
READY TO RACE
Red Bull
KTM
READY TO RACE
33
Red Bull
KTM
MARINI
TISSOT
TISSOT
TISSOT
ENEOS
20
MONSTER

FIM WORLD CHAMPIONSHIP · ROUND 2

DOHA GRAND PRIX
LOSAIL INTERNATIONAL CIRCUIT

THE MotoGP riders had now spent some four weeks in Qatar, including pre-season tests and the first race of the year. Familiarity bred a kind of content, with some of the closest margins ever seen in the premier class. Maverick Vinales summed it up: "After a lot of laps – a lot, everyone can go fast."

And how. First came a sensational pole position for rookie Jorge Martin, followed by an equally sensational race to the podium. Over the course of a week, he cut his race time over the same distance by a remarkable 19 seconds.

He was just a member of the pack. The podium trio, covered by 1.50 of a second, was close enough – the closest in history had been in the 500 class at Phillip Island in 1999, with Okada, Biaggi and Laconi inside 0.124 of a second. But everybody else had been even closer: the top 15 inside 8.928 seconds was a historic landmark, more than a second inside the premier-class record set in Austria in 2020.

As well as surprises, the proximity led to some conflict, in particular between champion Joan Mir and Jack Miller, with the former quietly seething on Sunday evening, believing the Ducati rider had intentionally run into his side. It had started with Mir's aggressive pass six turns before, which sat Miller up. "It was the only place I could overtake," explained Mir, while Miller replied that "I got hit I think three times already before that." At the final corner, Mir was wide on the exit. "I saw Jack. He moved his head like he saw me ... but he just came across over me and we both touched. We almost crashed on the straight. It was super-dangerous." Had it been deliberate? Miller didn't exactly deny it. "It was the way the race was going," he shrugged. But the FIM stewards decided not to penalise the Australian, and eventually Suzuki elected not to protest that decision.

There was disappointment for Valentino Rossi, now aged 42, in his 26th season, and down in the satellite squad. The second race of the year set the pace for a downward trend that would continue. Qualification in 21st was the worst of his career, and he earned no points in a lone 16th, worst of the Yamahas, while Fabio Quartararo won a second race in a row for the marque. Was it because he had yet to gel with his new crew, the old faithfuls having been dropped? Was it his extra height that upset the balance, robbing him of rear grip? Or was this the beginning of the end?

Nonetheless, the racing legend managed a robust defence when 1981 500cc champion Marco Lucchinelli added his voice to a growing chorus, suggesting Vale should step aside and give a younger rider a chance on a factory bike. Lucchinelli was quoted on Italian website Tutto Motori as saying that while Rossi could race on until he was 50, "something important has changed. He was a genius, a Martian. But now he is back on earth ... takes the bike off a young man. He always competed to win. Now it is just to finish."

Rossi responded with his trademark brutal charm, ear finely tuned for the stinging sound bite. "I hope I am not like that when I get old," he said, adding that he was surprised

96 DOHA GRAND PRIX

Left: Zarco leads Rins, the factory Ducatis and Mir in pursuit of early leader Martin. He left Qatar heading the championship.

Below far left: It was this close for Martin in the battle for second with team-mate Zarco.
Photos: Pramac Racing

Below centre left: Under fire 1. Rossi's moribund start to the season put him firmly under the microscope.

Below left: Under fire 2. Michelin's Piero Taramasso faced complaints about reheated tyres.
Photos: Gold & Goose

Below: Less than two seconds separated seventh from 14th. Mir leads Binder, Miller, Aleix Espargaro, Bastianini, Morbidelli, Pol Espargaro and Bradl over the line.
Photo: Suzuki ECSTAR

Opening spread, main: Quartararo opened a comfortable gap over his closest rivals, Martin, Zarco, Vinales and Rins.
Photo: Gold & Goose

Opening spread, inset: First of the season – Quartararo would have many more chances to celebrate.
Photo: Monster Energy Yamaha

because hitherto Lucchinelli had always "kissed my arse".

The rider denied a factory bike by Rossi's presence was his own protégé, Franco Morbidelli, second overall in 2020 on a year-old M1, and still on the same machine, to his growing consternation. He'd complained after the previous weekend's race, when he had been second-last, blaming problems with his launch control and saying, "I don't know with what rush Yamaha will take this problem. I know I'm not on the top of Yamaha's list at the moment." Subsequently, he softened his attitude, saying, "I explained myself a bit roughly. Finally, the timing of their help was great … everything is fine." His reward was a return to the points, but far from the glory of the previous year, and he too faced a troubled season ahead.

Riders seldom stop complaining about tyres, but there was a different dimension on this weekend, the consequence of back-to-back races at a track where the MotoGP field had also conducted pre-season testing. It meant unusual recycling: tyres that teams hadn't used had been returned to Michelin and then redistributed. But having been heated to working temperature (around 90°C) in tyre warmers, when they were allocated for a second (or third) time, their grip characteristics had changed. Piero Taramasso, head of Michelin motorsport, explained that the reallocation was normal practice and insisted that there was no drop in performance. Several riders disagreed – especially Pol Espargaro, who insisted, "The grip level is lower … they are very different. So when we put the proper one to make the time attack, the bike changes a little and this makes me do a lot of mistakes."

The stewards made good on the promise of harsher penalties for those naughty teenagers in Moto3, with seven riders punished for riding slowly in FP2, seeking a tow down the long straight – potentially worth well over a second a lap. Sergio Garcia, Romano Fenati, Dennis Foggia, Pedro Acosta, Deniz Oncu, Stefano Nepa and Riccardo Rossi were handed pit-lane starts for Sunday's race. But while the value of a slipstream for a good qualifying position is obvious, just how important is that position? Not so much, apparently, with the typical big lead groups slowing one another down. Acosta was able to win the race from the pit lane.

But the need to punish remained a driving force in the control tower, and when in the race John McPhee and Jeremy Alcoba came to blows in the gravel trap after the latter had knocked the former down, they were handed not only pit-lane starts for the next round, but also a further time penalty: five seconds for Alcoba and ten for the original aggressor, McPhee. At 26, the Scotsman is the oldest rider in the class, and reliably the most mature, but falling innocent victim for a second race in a row was enough to destroy his usual equilibrium.

MOTOGP RACE – 22 laps

Qualifying portended close racing, the top ten inside seven-tenths, the front row covered by less than two. And at the head of it, rookie Martin, in just his second MotoGP race and making good on glowing tributes to his talent from within his Pramac team and beyond.

Zarco alongside made it two Ducatis on the front row, with two more on the second. Vinales completed row one; Miller led the second from Quartararo and Bagnaia; the elder Espargaro impressed again on the revitalised Aprilia, heading row three from the Suzukis. Mir, in ninth, was through (along with 12th-placed Oliveira) from Q1. Rossi was 21st and second-last, his struggles continuing.

It was frenetic from the start, Martin leading away confidently from Zarco, Aleix Espargaro and Oliveira, who had jumped ten places off the line. Then came the Suzukis, with Miller sandwiched between the Monster Yamahas, Quartararo ahead.

One lap later, the Ducati had powered past, and on lap four, Bagnaia, whose start device had failed off the line, was ahead of both Yamahas as well, now lying ninth and tenth as they started lap five.

The gang stayed close, only Oliveira gradually dropping away, out of touch by half-distance and suffering a malfunctioning dashboard.

The moves came thick and fast. Rins split the Pramac Ducatis to sit second on lap five, while the Aprilia's top speed deficit meant that Espargaro gradually dropped down the order. Mir appeared desperate, lacking the conviction so evident the week before. His second-lap move on Quartararo at Turn Six was rough and pushed both wide. Then he dived under Miller at Turn Ten on lap 13 as both factory Ducatis were advancing. "I understand it was risky," he said later, "but not over the limits." The Australian was incensed. As the Suzuki ran wide at the final turn, Miller attempted to muscle it wider and force Mir to shut the throttle. An ugly tangle resulted in much fist shaking while Quartararo and Espargaro breezed by.

All the while, Martin was calm and consistent, belying his inexperience. Zarco, sitting behind, expected him to slow: "I thought, 'He's a rookie and maybe he will get some stress or something.' It never came." The Frenchman contented himself with acting as a buffer: "Every time someone passed and maybe tried to attack Jorge, thanks to the engine, I was able to get second again."

The pace was stretching some, Rins's unreal front save through Turn Nine on lap 13 a case in point. And with eight to go, the Ducatis were perfectly placed to make good on their pre-season promise. Bagnaia was now third. But the Yamahas were coming.

Quartararo passed Rins on lap 15, then Bagnaia a lap later at the penultimate turn. From nowhere, Vinales was fourth, passing Zarco for third after his team-mate's quick one-two to reach first. But now his confidence from round one deserted him. First, he nearly tailgated Martin while braking for the final turn, dropping to fourth. Then a mistake at Turn One on the final lap allowed Rins through. He wasn't alone. Bagnaia had done the same on lap 17.

His costly haste was triggered by the way Quartararo had bolted in the final three laps. No one could live with this. In his wake, it was left to Zarco to pick off Martin with two corners remaining. A second runner-up position in eight days gave him the championship lead.

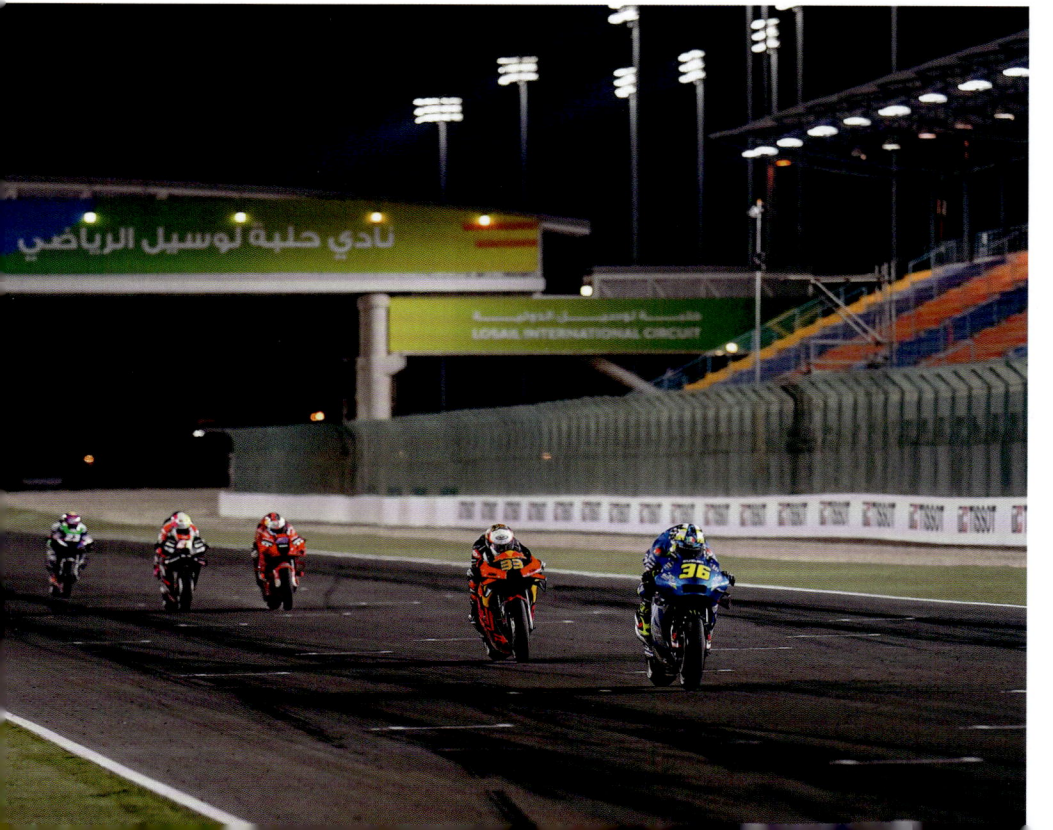

DOHA GRAND PRIX 97

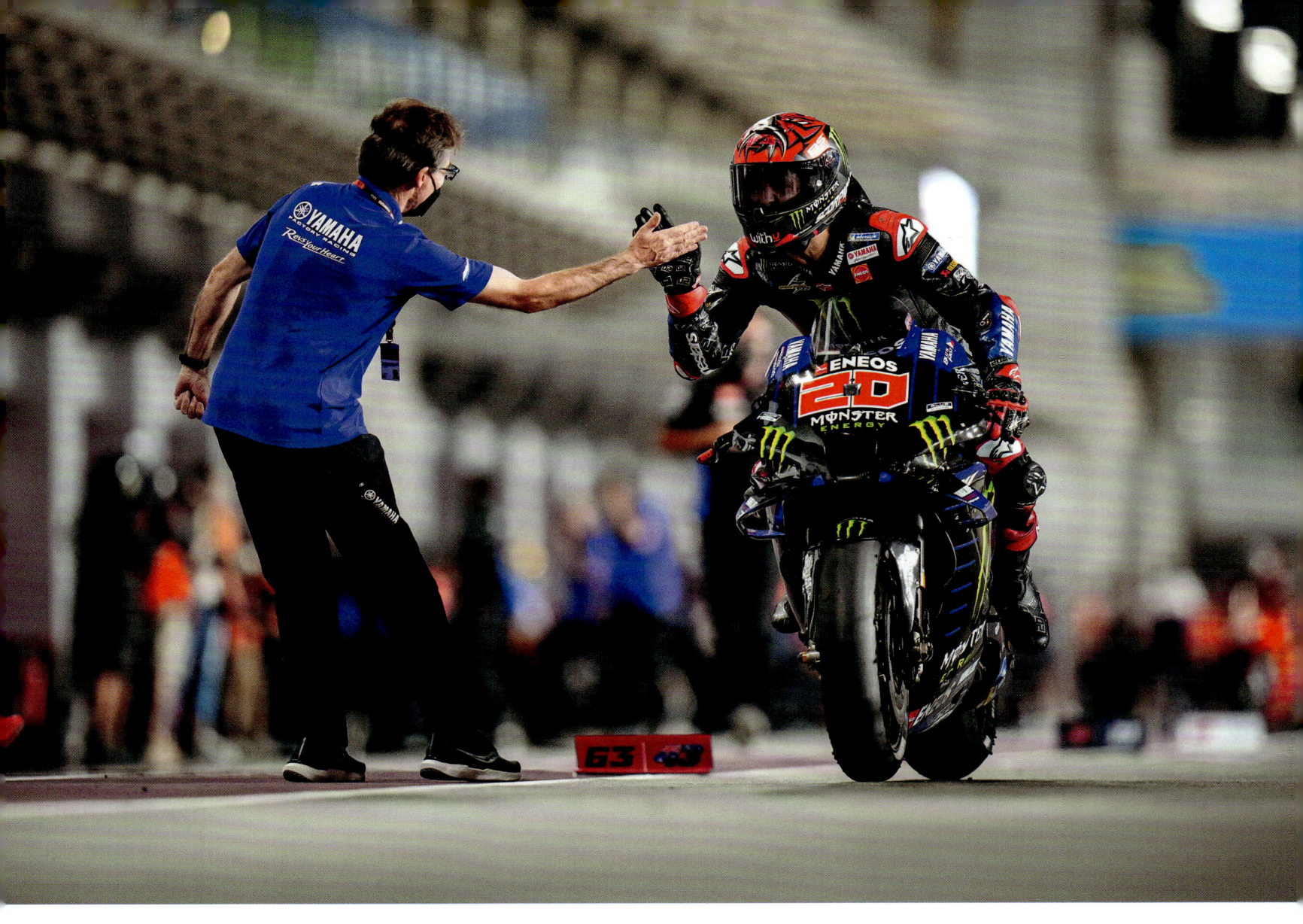

Top: High five. Yamaha Racing chief Lin Jarvis greets his winning rider in the pit lane.
Photo: Monster Energy Yamaha

Top right: Joy for the Pramac pair, Martin and Zarco, on the podium.
Photo: Pramac Racing

Above right: Lowes just held off Gardner for the Moto2 win.

Right, clockwise from top left: Two out of two for Sam Lowes; Alcoba leads the Moto3 brawl before falling; Binder was one of many to briefly lead Moto3; even a pit-lane start couldn't stop rookie winner Pedro Acosta.
Photos: Gold & Goose

Martin's third was a landmark. "Even if I was a bit nervous, I could control it well and do a great job," he said. "The pace was great."

Rins was fourth, then came Vinales and Bagnaia, both ruing mistakes. A late dash allowed Mir to mug Miller for seventh on the final lap, with angry gestures on the slow-down lap. Binder joined in, nabbing eighth off the Australian at the flag, through from 18th on the grid and underlining his 'Sunday-man' credentials. Miller had been slowed by arm-pump issues that undermined his tactics.

Espargaro's Aprilia eventually dropped to tenth, with Enea Bastianini a solid 11th in his second race, despite his long hair obstructing his view in the later laps.

Morbidelli capped another miserable weekend for Petronas SRT Yamaha in 12th, ahead of Pol Espargaro, after a Turn One braking mistake on lap 17 had dashed the Spaniard's hopes. He called it a disgusting result, but he was barely six seconds off the winner.

Bradl and Oliveira wrapped up the points; Rossi was another eight seconds away; then Nakagami led Marini and Petrucci for the next pointless trio. Alex Marquez and Lecuona crashed out.

MOTO2 RACE – 20 laps

Sam Lowes's picture-perfect start to the season survived a second race, with the same top two over the line. It was closer this time, though: Remy Gardner peering over his shoulder, but holding back from a last-lap attack in the interests of the war rather than the battle.

The British rider had taken pole for a second race in succession, from Gardner and Bezzecchi; with Red Bull Ajo rookie Raul Fernandez heading the second row from Jake Dixon and the other hot rookie, Ogura. Dixon was through from Q1.

Bezzecchi got the jump to lead away, but once Lowes had outbraked the Italian on lap four, the second Moto2 outing mirrored the first, with Fernandez completing a lead group of four.

By lap six, the Ajo team-mates were past Bezzecchi, but soon only Gardner could match the leader's pace. Twice Lowes tried to break his pursuer, posting personal best times on laps 13 and 18. And twice the Australian responded. The gap over the line would never exceed half a second.

On the final lap, Gardner was lining up a move on the exit from Turn 14 when he feared that his rear wheel had edged over track limits. That moment of hesitancy, and the knowledge that a long season lay ahead, meant that there was no banzai manoeuvre at the final turn. "I wasn't going to do anything silly for five points," he said.

Lowes won by less than two-tenths, both riders being ten seconds faster than the previous weekend and both setting their fastest laps on the last. "I was surprised by the pace," said Lowes.

Raul Fernandez capped another impressive display with a debut Moto2 podium, 3.3 seconds back. Bezzecchi settled for a lonely fourth.

Some way behind by the end, there was a lively gang. It had been led at first by Roberts, who had got ahead of Canet, until the American slipped off on lap seven. Canet would last another eight laps, falling back in the group, before he too crashed out.

Ogura had been running at the front of the group until displaced before half-distance by Di Giannantonio, while others tagged on behind.

By the finish, fifth to eleventh was covered by just 1.5 seconds, with Ogura impressively at the front from Augusto Fernandez, Celestino Vietti (up from 18th on the grid), Manzi, Vierge, Di Giannantonio and Arbolino. Ogura, Vietti and Arbolino were more fast class rookies up from Moto3.

Along the way, Dixon and Schrotter had tangled and crashed out of the group, two laps before Canet; while Bendsneyder, Navarro and Dalla Porta had slipped off the back of the gang.

98 DOHA GRAND PRIX

Arenas took the final point; both veteran Luthi and class rookie Beaubier slipped off and out, the American lying 14th, which matched his qualifying position.

MOTO3 RACE – 18 laps

The FIM stewards made good on their threat to crack down on Moto3 riders with seven pit-lane starts; one of those riders responded with an epic ride to make fools of the disciplinarians. Having taken second, his first podium, the week before, Red Bull Rookies champion Acosta went one better, after making up a first-lap deficit of more than 11 seconds.

He was helped by a chaotic battle up front, where 17 riders were slicing away at each other and tripping one another up, slowing the pace.

There were innumerable changes of lead over the line, with front-men at that point including Binder, Toba, Suzuki, Migno, Salac, McPhee and (with three laps left) Masia. But they were down five or even more places by the entry to the first corner, and for McPhee it was worst – innocent victim of an overenthusiastic Jeremy Alcoba, with whom he came to blows.

All the while, Acosta, followed by pit-lane companions Fenati and Garcia, was closing on the front. The last-named lost his chance, slipping off and remounting, while Fenati ended up mired in tenth. But Acosta's tactics were perfect, dealing a hammer blow also to his senior team-mate, Masia, in the final scramble.

Binder was best of the rest, less than four-hundredths behind, from Antonelli, Bigno, Toba and rookie Guevara, barely half a second away.

Another second away, Sasaki led Yamanaka, the displaced Masia and Fenati, still less than two seconds from the leader. The front pack of 15 was covered by 2.2 seconds.

What a thriller. And what a way for the teenage Acosta to extend his championship lead.

DOHA GRAND PRIX 99

FIM WORLD CHAMPIONSHIP: ROUND 2

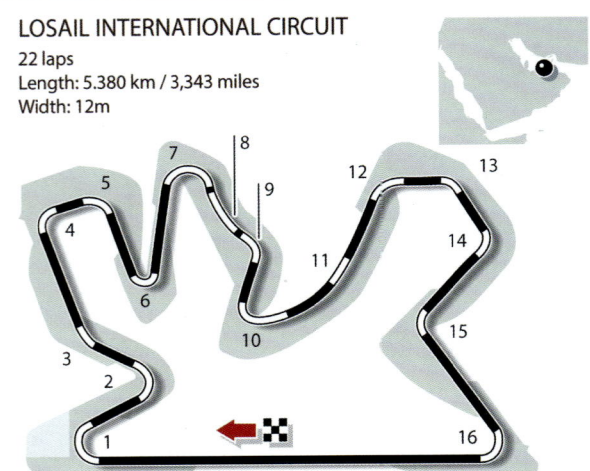

TISSOT GRAND PRIX OF DOHA

2–4 APRIL, 2021

LOSAIL INTERNATIONAL CIRCUIT
22 laps
Length: 5.380 km / 3,343 miles
Width: 12m

MotoGP

RACE DISTANCE: 22 laps, 73.545 miles/118.360km · RACE WEATHER: Dry (air 21°, humidity 62%, track 22°)

Pos.	Rider	Nat.	No.	Entrant	Machine	Tyres	Race tyre choice	Laps	Time & speed
1	Fabio Quartararo	FRA	20	Monster Energy Yamaha MotoGP	Yamaha YZR-M1	M	F: Soft/R: Soft	22	42m 23.997s 104.0mph/167.4km/h
2	Johann Zarco	FRA	5	Pramac Racing	Ducati Desmosedici	M	F: Soft/R: Soft	22	42m 25.454s
3	Jorge Martin	SPA	89	Pramac Racing	Ducati Desmosedici	M	F: Soft/R: Soft	22	42m 25.497s
4	Alex Rins	SPA	42	Team SUZUKI ECSTAR	Suzuki GSX-RR	M	F: Soft/R: Soft	22	42m 26.085s
5	Maverick Vinales	SPA	12	Monster Energy Yamaha MotoGP	Yamaha YZR-M1	M	F: Soft/R: Soft	22	42m 26.107s
6	Francesco Bagnaia	ITA	63	Ducati Lenovo Team	Ducati Desmosedici	M	F: Soft/R: Soft	22	42m 26.639s
7	Joan Mir	SPA	36	Team SUZUKI ECSTAR	Suzuki GSX-RR	M	F: Soft/R: Soft	22	42m 28.865s
8	Brad Binder	RSA	33	Red Bull KTM Factory Racing	KTM RC16	M	F: Medium/R: Soft	22	42m 28.976s
9	Jack Miller	AUS	43	Ducati Lenovo Team	Ducati Desmosedici	M	F: Soft/R: Soft	22	42m 29.362s
10	Aleix Espargaro	SPA	41	Aprilia Racing Team Gresini	Aprilia RS-GP	M	F: Soft/R: Soft	22	42m 29.379s
11	Enea Bastianini	ITA	23	Avintia Esponsorama	Ducati Desmosedici	M	F: Soft/R: Soft	22	42m 29.547s
12	Franco Morbidelli	ITA	21	Petronas Yamaha SRT	Yamaha YZR-M1	M	F: Soft/R: Soft	22	42m 29.784s
13	Pol Espargaro	SPA	44	Repsol Honda Team	Honda RC213V	M	F: Soft/R: Soft	22	42m 30.060s
14	Stefan Bradl	GER	6	Repsol Honda Team	Honda RC213V	M	F: Soft/R: Soft	22	42m 30.450s
15	Miguel Oliveira	POR	88	Red Bull KTM Factory Racing	KTM RC16	M	F: Medium/R: Soft	22	42m 32.925s
16	Valentino Rossi	ITA	46	Petronas Yamaha SRT	Yamaha YZR-M1	M	F: Soft/R: Soft	22	42m 38.243s
17	Takaaki Nakagami	JPN	30	LCR Honda IDEMITSU	Honda RC213V	M	F: Soft/R: Soft	22	42m 40.238s
18	Luca Marini	ITA	10	SKY VR46 Avintia	Ducati Desmosedici	M	F: Soft/R: Soft	22	42m 40.469s
19	Danilo Petrucci	ITA	9	Tech 3 KTM Factory Racing	KTM RC16	M	F: Medium/R: Soft	22	42m 40.776s
20	Lorenzo Savadori	ITA	32	Aprilia Racing Team Gresini	Aprilia RS-GP	M	F: Soft/R: Soft	22	43m 02.772s
	Alex Marquez	SPA	73	LCR Honda CASTROL	Honda RC213V	M	F: Soft/R: Soft	12	DNF-crash
	Iker Lecuona	SPA	27	Tech 3 KTM Factory Racing	KTM RC16	M	F: Medium/R: Soft	12	DNF-crash

Fastest lap: Francesco Bagnaia, on lap 7, 1m 54.491s, 105.1mph/169.1km/h.
Lap record: Maverick Vinales, 1m 54.624s, 104.9mph/168.9km/h (2021).
Event maximum speed: Johann Zarco, 221.5mph/356.4km/h (free practice).

Qualifying

Weather: Dry
Air Temp: 23° **Humidity:** 45%
Track Temp: 24°

1	Martin	1m 53.106s
2	Zarco	1m 53.263s
3	Vinales	1m 53.267s
4	Miller	1m 53.303s
5	Quartararo	1m 53.469s
6	Bagnaia	1m 53.654s
7	A. Espargaro	1m 53.705s
8	Rins	1m 53.745s
9	Mir	1m 53.785s
10	Morbidelli	1m 53.794s
11	Bradl	1m 54.224s
12	Oliveira	1m 55.096s

Q1

13	Marini	1m 54.228s
14	A. Marquez	1m 54.261s
15	P. Espargaro	1m 54.402s
16	Nakagami	1m 54.481s
17	Petrucci	1m 54.528s
18	Binder	1m 54.555s
19	Bastianini	1m 54.632s
20	Lecuona	1m 54.731s
21	Rossi	1m 54.881s
22	Savadori	1m 55.823s

Fastest race laps

1	Bagnaia	1m 54.491s
2	A. Espargaro	1m 54.798s
3	Miller	1m 54.807s
4	Vinales	1m 54.832s
5	Zarco	1m 54.919s
6	Rins	1m 54.923s
7	Quartararo	1m 54.973s
8	Mir	1m 54.985s
9	Morbidelli	1m 54.992s
10	Marini	1m 55.016s
11	Martin	1m 55.026s
12	Bastianini	1m 55.057s
13	Binder	1m 55.074s
14	Bradl	1m 55.106s
15	A. Marquez	1m 55.132s
16	P. Espargaro	1m 55.134s
17	Oliveira	1m 55.227s
18	Lecuona	1m 55.266s
19	Petrucci	1m 55.341s
20	Nakagami	1m 55.374s
21	Rossi	1m 55.383s
22	Savadori	1m 56.468s

Championship Points

1	Zarco	40
2	Quartararo	36
3	Vinales	36
4	Bagnaia	26
5	Rins	23
6	Mir	22
7	Martin	17
8	A. Espargaro	15
9	Miller	14
10	P. Espargaro	11
11	Bastianini	11
12	Binder	10
13	Bradl	7
14	Rossi	4
15	Morbidelli	4
16	Oliveira	4

Constructor Points

1	Yamaha	50
2	Ducati	40
3	Suzuki	26
4	Aprilia	15
5	KTM	11
6	Honda	11

Grid order / lap-by-lap positions

Grid order		1	2	3	4	5	6	7	8	9	10	11	12	13	14	15	16	17	18	19	20	21	22
89	MARTIN	89	89	89	89	89	89	89	89	89	89	89	89	89	89	89	89	89	20	20	20	20	1
5	ZARCO	5	5	5	5	42	42	5	42	42	5	5	5	5	5	5	5	20	89	89	89	5	2
12	VINALES	41	41	42	42	5	5	42	5	5	42	42	42	63	63	63	63	5	5	5	5	89	3
43	MILLER	42	42	41	41	41	41	41	41	41	63	63	63	42	42	20	20	43	12	12	12	12	4
20	QUARTARARO	36	88	88	36	36	36	36	63	63	43	43	43	20	20	42	42	42	43	42	42	42	5
63	BAGNAIA	88	36	36	88	88	63	63	36	36	41	36	36	41	41	41	43	12	42	43	63	63	6
41	A. ESPARGARO	20	43	43	43	43	88	43	43	43	36	41	20	43	43	43	12	63	63	63	43	43	7
42	RINS	43	20	20	63	63	20	20	20	20	20	20	41	12	12	12	41	41	41	41	41	36	8
36	MIR	12	63	63	20	20	43	12	12	12	12	12	12	36	36	36	36	36	36	36	36	41	9
21	MORBIDELLI	33	33	12	12	12	12	88	88	88	33	33	33	44	44	44	33	33	33	33	33	33	10
6	BRADL	63	12	33	33	33	33	33	33	33	88	88	44	44	33	33	23	23	23	23	23	23	11
88	OLIVEIRA	44	44	44	44	44	21	21	21	21	44	88	23	23	23	23	21	21	21	21	21	21	12
10	MARINI	21	21	21	21	21	44	44	44	44	44	23	88	88	21	21	44	44	44	44	44	44	13
73	A. MARQUEZ	30	30	30	30	30	23	23	23	23	23	21	21	88	6	6	6	6	6	6	6	6	14
44	P. ESPARGARO	73	23	23	23	23	30	6	6	6	6	6	6	6	88	88	88	88	88	88	88	88	15
30	NAKAGAMI	10	73	73	6	6	6	30	30	30	10	10	10	10	10	10	46	46	46	46			
9	PETRUCCI	23	10	6	73	10	10	10	73	73	73	10	30	30	30	30	30	46	10	10	30		
33	BINDER	6	6	10	10	73	73	73	27	27	27	46	46	46	46	46	30	30	30	30	10		
23	BASTIANINI	9	9	9	9	9	27	27	9	9	9	9	9	9	9	9	9	9	9	9	9		
27	LECUONA	27	27	27	27	27	9	9	46	46	46	32	32	32	32	32	32	32	32	32	32		
46	ROSSI	46	46	46	46	46	46	46	9														
32	SAVADORI	32	32	32	32	32	32	32	32	32													

Moto2

RACE DISTANCE: 20 laps, 66.860 miles/107.600km · **RACE WEATHER:** Dry (air 21°, humidity 56%, track 24°)

Pos.	Rider	Nat.	No.	Entrant	Machine	Laps	Time & Speed
1	Sam Lowes	GBR	22	Elf Marc VDS Racing Team	Kalex	20	39m 52.702s 100.1mph/161.1km/h
2	Remy Gardner	AUS	87	Red Bull KTM Ajo	Kalex	20	39m 52.892s
3	Raul Fernandez	SPA	25	Red Bull KTM Ajo	Kalex	20	39m 56.073s
4	Marco Bezzecchi	ITA	72	SKY Racing Team VR46	Kalex	20	39m 59.491s
5	Ai Ogura	JPN	79	IDEMITSU Honda Team Asia	Kalex	20	40m 09.342s
6	Augusto Fernandez	SPA	37	Elf Marc VDS Racing Team	Kalex	20	40m 09.589s
7	Celestino Vietti	ITA	13	SKY Racing Team VR46	Kalex	20	40m 09.956s
8	Stefano Manzi	ITA	62	Flexbox HP40	Kalex	20	40m 09.985s
9	Xavi Vierge	SPA	97	Petronas Sprinta Racing	Kalex	20	40m 10.217s
10	Fabio Di Giannantonio	ITA	21	Federal Oil Gresini Moto2	Kalex	20	40m 10.869s
11	Tony Arbolino	ITA	14	Liqui Moly Intact GP	Kalex	20	40m 10.882s
12	Bo Bendsneyder	NED	64	Pertamina Mandalika SAG Team	Kalex	20	40m 13.398s
13	Jorge Navarro	SPA	9	MB Conveyors Speed Up	Boscoscuro	20	40m 14.718s
14	Lorenzo Dalla Porta	ITA	19	Italtrans Racing Team	Kalex	20	40m 14.745s
15	Albert Arenas	SPA	75	Solunion Aspar Team	Boscoscuro	20	40m 18.968s
16	Hector Garzo	SPA	40	Flexbox HP40	Kalex	20	40m 21.241s
17	Nicolo Bulega	ITA	11	Federal Oil Gresini Moto2	Kalex	20	40m 22.012s
18	Yari Montella	ITA	5	MB Conveyors Speed Up	Boscoscuro	20	40m 25.852s
19	Somkiat Chantra	THA	35	IDEMITSU Honda Team Asia	Kalex	20	40m 32.540s
20	Lorenzo Baldassarri	ITA	7	MV Agusta Forward Racing	MV Agusta	20	40m 37.663s
21	Hafizh Syahrin	MAL	55	NTS RW Racing GP	NTS	20	40m 48.825s
	Aron Canet	SPA	44	Solunion Aspar Team	Boscoscuro	14	DNF-crash
	Jake Dixon	GBR	96	Petronas Sprinta Racing	Kalex	12	DNF-crash
	Marcel Schrotter	GER	23	Liqui Moly Intact GP	Kalex	12	DNF-crash
	Thomas Luthi	SWI	12	Pertamina Mandalika SAG Team	Kalex	12	DNF-crash
	Cameron Beaubier	USA	6	American Racing	Kalex	8	DNF-crash
	Tommaso Marcon	ITA	10	MV Agusta Forward Racing	MV Agusta	8	DNF-crash
	Joe Roberts	USA	16	Italtrans Racing Team	Kalex	6	DNF-crash

Fastest lap: Sam Lowes, on lap 20, 1m 58.954s, 101.2mph/162.8km/h.
Lap record: Thomas Luthi, 1m 58.711s, 101.3mph/163.1km/h (2019).
Event maximum speed: Lorenzo Dalla Porta, 182.8mph/294.2km/h (free practice).

Qualifying
Weather: Dry
Air: 23° Track: 25°
Humidity: 43%

1	Lowes	1m 59.055s
2	Gardner	1m 59.192s
3	Bezzecchi	1m 59.327s
4	R. Fernandez	1m 59.441s
5	Dixon	1m 59.443s
6	Ogura	1m 59.692s
7	Di Giannantonio	1m 59.696s
8	Roberts	1m 59.727s
9	Canet	1m 59.785s
10	A. Fernandez	1m 59.809s
11	Manzi	1m 59.870s
12	Arenas	1m 59.885s
13	Bulega	2m 00.012s
14	Beaubier	2m 00.040s
15	Bendsneyder	2m 00.077s
16	Schrotter	2m 00.108s
17	Navarro	2m 00.142s
18	Vietti	2m 00.532s
Q1		
19	Vierge	2m 00.091s
20	Arbolino	2m 00.092s
21	Luthi	2m 00.131s
22	Montella	2m 00.232s
23	Chantra	2m 00.448s
24	Dalla Porta	2m 00.581s
25	Baldassarri	2m 00.738s
26	Garzo	2m 00.929s
27	Syahrin	2m 01.466s
28	Marcon	2m 03.113s

Fastest race laps

1	Lowes	1m 58.954s
2	Gardner	1m 58.991s
3	R. Fernandez	1m 59.175s
4	Bezzecchi	1m 59.399s
5	Beaubier	1m 59.456s
6	Vietti	1m 59.543s
7	Schrotter	1m 59.551s
8	Roberts	1m 59.562s
9	Ogura	1m 59.603s
10	Di Giannantonio	1m 59.692s
11	Arbolino	1m 59.718s
12	Vierge	1m 59.762s
13	Garzo	1m 59.773s
14	Dixon	1m 59.779s
15	A. Fernandez	1m 59.794s
16	Bendsneyder	1m 59.810s
17	Dalla Porta	1m 59.830s
18	Manzi	1m 59.863s
19	Canet	1m 59.878s
20	Bulega	1m 59.887s
21	Navarro	1m 59.975s
22	Arenas	2m 00.112s
23	Montella	2m 00.380s
24	Luthi	2m 00.508s
25	Baldassarri	2m 00.510s
26	Chantra	2m 01.006s
27	Syahrin	2m 01.384s
28	Marcon	2m 03.575s

Championship Points

1	Lowes	50
2	Gardner	40
3	R. Fernandez	27
4	Bezzecchi	26
5	Di Giannantonio	22
6	Vietti	13
7	A. Fernandez	12
8	Ogura	11
9	Bendsneyder	11
10	Roberts	10
11	Dixon	9
12	Navarro	9
13	Manzi	8
14	Schrotter	8
15	Vierge	7
16	Arbolino	5
17	Beaubier	5
18	Canet	3
19	Dalla Porta	2
20	Arenas	1
21	Luthi	1

Constructor Points

1	Kalex	50
2	Boscoscuro	9

Moto3

RACE DISTANCE: 18 laps, 60.174 miles/96.840km · **RACE WEATHER:** Dry (air 23°, humidity 45%, track 26°)

Pos.	Rider	Nat.	No.	Entrant	Machine	Laps	Time & Speed
1	Pedro Acosta	SPA	37	Red Bull KTM Ajo	KTM	18	38m 22.430s 94.1mph/151.4km/h
2	Darryn Binder	RSA	40	Petronas Sprinta Racing	Honda	18	38m 22.469s
3	Niccolo Antonelli	ITA	23	Avintia Esponsorama Moto3	KTM	18	38m 22.912s
4	Andrea Migno	ITA	16	Rivacold Snipers Team	Honda	18	38m 22.944s
5	Kaito Toba	JPN	27	CIP Green Power	KTM	18	38m 23.081s
6	Izan Guevara	SPA	28	GASGAS Gaviota Aspar Team	GASGAS	18	38m 23.138s
7	Ayumu Sasaki	JPN	71	Red Bull KTM Tech 3	KTM	18	38m 24.235s
8	Ryusei Yamanaka	JPN	6	CarXpert PruestelGP	KTM	18	38m 24.287s
9	Jaume Masia	SPA	5	Red Bull KTM Ajo	KTM	18	38m 24.305s
10	Romano Fenati	ITA	55	Sterilgarda Max Racing Team	Husqvarna	18	38m 24.397s
11	Jason Dupasquier	SWI	50	CarXpert PruestelGP	KTM	18	38m 24.424s
12	Tatsuki Suzuki	JPN	24	SIC58 Squadra Corse	Honda	18	38m 24.664s
13	Gabriel Rodrigo	ARG	2	Indonesian Racing Gresini Moto3	Honda	18	38m 24.665s
14	Maximilian Kofler	AUT	73	CIP Green Power	KTM	18	38m 24.679s
15	Yuki Kunii	JPN	92	Honda Team Asia	Honda	18	38m 24.690s
16	Stefano Nepa	ITA	82	BOE Owlride	KTM	18	38m 27.789s
17	Dennis Foggia	ITA	7	Leopard Racing	Honda	18	38m 33.482s
18	Deniz Oncu	TUR	53	Red Bull KTM Tech 3	KTM	18	38m 33.515s
19	Riccardo Rossi	ITA	54	BOE Owlride	KTM	18	38m 38.426s
20	Lorenzo Fellon	FRA	20	SIC58 Squadra Corse	Honda	18	38m 39.560s
21	Carlos Tatay	SPA	99	Avintia Esponsorama Moto3	KTM	18	38m 40.910s
22	Andi Farid Izdihar	INA	19	Honda Team Asia	Honda	18	38m 48.302s
23	Sergio Garcia	SPA	11	GASGAS Gaviota Aspar Team	GASGAS	18	39m 04.344s
	John McPhee	GBR	17	Petronas Sprinta Racing	Honda	14	DNF-crash
	Jeremy Alcoba	SPA	52	Indonesian Racing Gresini Moto3	Honda	14	DNF-crash
	Adrian Fernandez	SPA	31	Sterilgarda Max Racing Team	Husqvarna	14	DNF-crash
	Filip Salac	CZE	12	Rivacold Snipers Team	Honda	12	DNF-crash
	Xavier Artigas	SPA	43	Leopard Racing	Honda	11	DNF-crash

Fastest lap: Stefano Nepa, on lap 5, 2m 6.232s, 95.3mph/153.4km/h.
Lap record: Romano Fenati, 2m 5.403s, 95.9mph/154.4km/h (2019).
Event maximum speed: Izan Guevara, 149.8mph/241.0km/h (free practice).

Qualifying:
Weather: Dry
Air: 25° Track: 27°
Humidity: 39%

1	Masia	2m 05.913s
2	Garcia	2m 06.012s
3	Alcoba	2m 06.158s
4	Rodrigo	2m 06.346s
5	Suzuki	2m 06.407s
6	Migno	2m 06.619s
7	Binder	2m 06.643s
8	McPhee	2m 06.646s
9	Acosta	2m 06.829s
10	Guevara	2m 06.833s
11	Dupasquier	2m 06.967s
12	Antonelli	2m 07.025s
13	Toba	2m 07.108s
14	Fenati	2m 07.145s
15	Nepa	2m 07.197s
16	Artigas	2m 07.252s
17	Yamanaka	2m 07.429s
18	Foggia	2m 07.498s
Q1		
19	Fernandez	2m 07.541s
20	Salac	2m 07.661s
21	Fellon	2m 07.749s
22	Sasaki	2m 07.948s
23	Rossi	2m 07.994s
24	Tatay	2m 08.011s
25	Kunii	2m 08.011s
26	Kofler	2m 08.233s
27	Izdihar	2m 08.469s
	Oncu	No Time

Fastest race laps

1	Nepa	2m 06.232s
2	Fenati	2m 06.263s
3	Acosta	2m 06.317s
4	Garcia	2m 06.361s
5	Salac	2m 06.398s
6	Masia	2m 06.464s
7	Rodrigo	2m 06.497s
8	Toba	2m 06.497s
9	Tatay	2m 06.540s
10	Antonelli	2m 06.589s
11	Migno	2m 06.609s
12	Fernandez	2m 06.615s
13	Artigas	2m 06.639s
14	Dupasquier	2m 06.658s
15	Binder	2m 06.686s
16	McPhee	2m 06.715s
17	Sasaki	2m 06.746s
18	Yamanaka	2m 06.755s
19	Kunii	2m 06.762s
20	Alcoba	2m 06.853s
21	Rossi	2m 06.953s
22	Foggia	2m 06.974s
23	Oncu	2m 07.030s
24	Guevara	2m 07.071s
25	Kofler	2m 07.159s
26	Suzuki	2m 07.192s
27	Izdihar	2m 07.263s
28	Fellon	2m 07.324s

Championship Points

1	Acosta	45
2	Binder	36
3	Masia	32
4	Antonelli	26
5	Guevara	19
6	Toba	18
7	Rodrigo	14
8	Garcia	13
9	Migno	13
10	Suzuki	12
11	Fenati	11
12	Dupasquier	11
13	Yamanaka	10
14	Sasaki	9
15	Tatay	4
16	Salac	3
17	Kofler	3
18	Kunii	1

Constructor Points

1	KTM	50
2	Honda	36
3	GASGAS	23
4	Husqvarna	11

DOHA GRAND PRIX

FIM WORLD CHAMPIONSHIP · ROUND 3
PORTUGUESE GRAND PRIX
ALGARVE INTERNATIONAL CIRCUIT

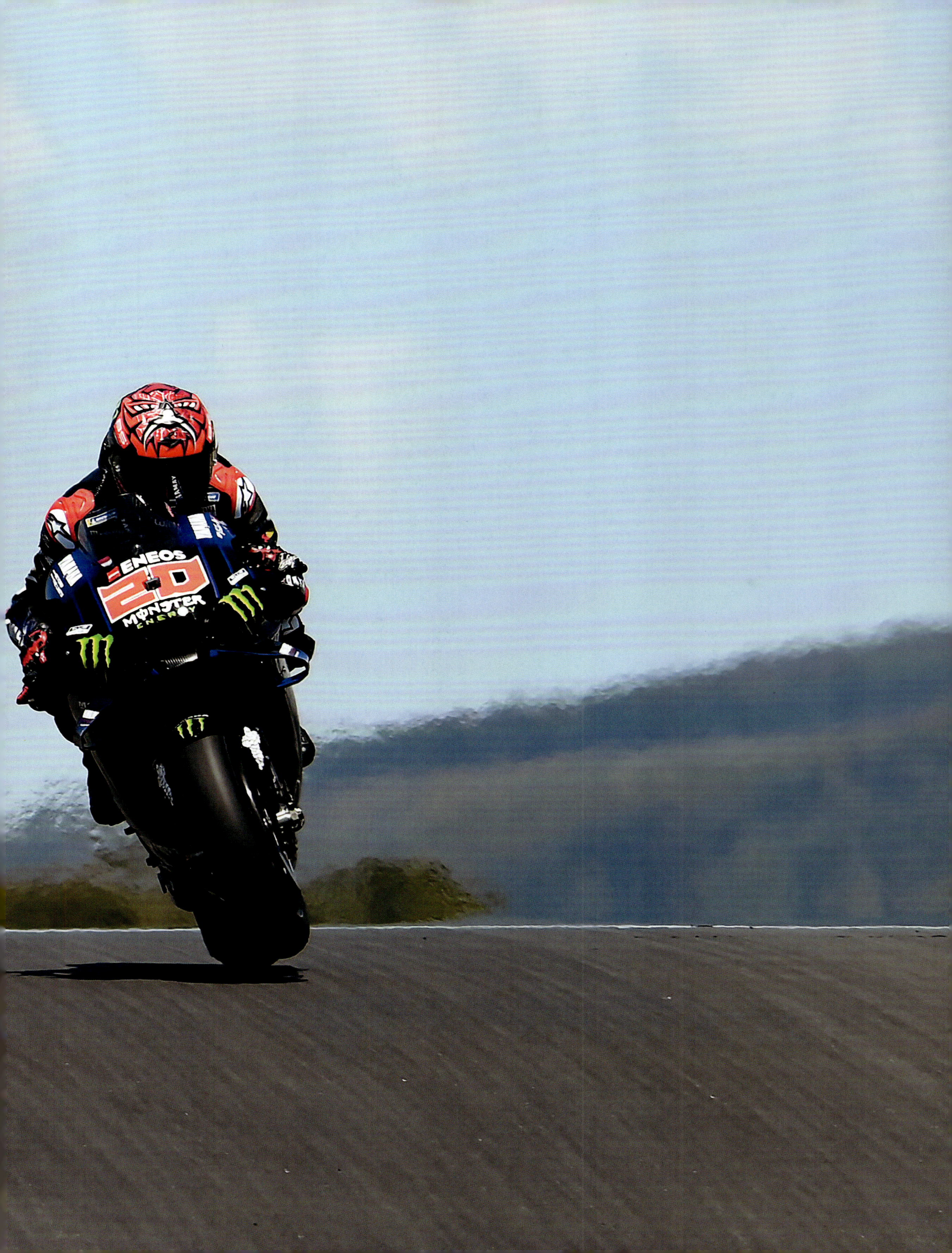
ENEOS
20
MONSTER
ENERGY

AFTER Covid forced the abandonment of the original plans to continue the start of the season transatlantic, in Argentina and the USA, for the second year running, the Portuguese Circuit of the Algarve was shoehorned on to the calendar as a substitute – and a mighty popular one, given the fast corners, sinuous layout, and interesting swoops and climbs.

There were no fans, but something extra special for 2021: the return of Marc Marquez after 265 days away.

The Spaniard's previous time on a MotoGP bike had been in FP4 at Jerez for the Andalusian GP. Since then, he'd been out twice on Honda's road-legal RC213V-S, including a familiarisation outing at Portimao. Now, the real thing.

Was anybody surprised when he was fast from the start, a close third in FP1? His own pronouncements sounded a more realistic note. He had spoken to his team, who were "so motivated … immediately, I said, 'We don't have a target this weekend. I will not be the same Marc.'" On the eve of practice, he added, "I have some butterflies in my stomach, that aren't normal for me."

The weekend ended with an outpouring of emotion after a race in which seventh place, under the circumstances, was close to heroic.

As Valentino Rossi said on Sunday evening: "On this evidence, he'll be contesting podiums come May." It took only a little longer for his first win.

It hadn't taken long for his fighting instincts to show. In Q1, after placing 15th in combined FP times (one slot behind new team-mate Pol Espargaro), he started working on the man who had benefited most from his absence, defending champion Joan Mir, also looking to go into Q2. He slowed up to slot in behind the Suzuki, then set fastest time. Mir, second and not amused, accused Marc of "playing games. In Moto3, they penalise you for this." The multi-champion was unabashed, pointing out that other riders had followed him to improve their qualifying times often enough. Normal tactics, and coincidental that he'd chosen Mir for the reference.

There were other peeved riders after qualifying.

Pecco Bagnaia had set a time that was good enough for pole, only to have it cancelled because there had been a yellow flag after Miguel Oliveira had fallen. He was pushed back to 11th on the grid. He insisted that he hadn't seen the flag, prompting a reopening of the debate on the time-cancelled rule, and highlighting the new practice, compulsory from this race on, of illuminated LED trackside boards in addition to flag signals.

Likewise angry at being dispossessed was Maverick Vinales, knocked back from a potential pole to 12th and last in Q2, on the far end of row four. His transgression had been a little run over the edge of the kerb, and if he felt that the punishment was massively disproportionate, he was not alone.

New-for-2021 regulations had changed two aspects. No longer would there be any subjective judgement (from studying TV images) as to whether a rider had strayed on to the green area beyond track limits, with the introduction of a pressure-sensitive tube on the track edge. More crucially, whereas previously both wheels had needed to be fully beyond track limits to incur a penalty, now the slightest touch of even only one wheel would be enough. But in this case, on that particular corner, it had not been possible to fit the tube. Vinales's penalty was the result of old-school observation. Given the new razor-edge margin, it is perhaps not surprising that he was dismayed at a punishment that (given his well-known early-lap difficulties) effectively destroyed his race.

Such destruction would continue to be a theme of this and future meetings. Moto3 miscreants John McPhee and Jeremy Alcoba were each handed a pit-lane start (and a 1,000-euro fine) for their trackside fracas in Qatar, but given Pedro Acosta's win there from the pit lane, there was added severity, five seconds extra delay for Alcoba, ten for McPhee. Joining them in the pit lane, for slow riding in practice, were Darryn Binder and Deniz Oncu, the latter with an additional five seconds for his second offence. Only Alcoba and Oncu were able to recover enough to trouble the bottom end of the points.

The stewards are not racing's only jarring hazard, as demonstrated with sickening violence by Jorge Martin, fresh from triumph at Losail. Saturday morning's FP3 was red-flagged 40 minutes in after he had crashed heavily. On an out-lap, and with tyres not up to temperature, the 23-year-old had lost the front of his Pramac Ducati on the run to Turn Nine and was clipped by the bike as the pair looped through the gravel. Worryingly, he came to rest in a position of supplicant prayer, not moving. Concussion, however, was the least of his injuries, which included several fractures – to his right thumb, right ankle and left knee. Surgery was delayed until later in the week due to the blow to his head; he would return after missing the next three races.

There was happier news from Aprilia, after the resting Andrea Dovizioso had undertaken his first tests of the RS-GP at Jerez. They'd been spoiled by bad weather, but familiarisation had proved encouraging enough for the veteran to agree to further tests in the future. This triggered a frenzy of speculation that he might be due back in the paddock before the end of the year, in place of Savadori, who responded by scoring his first points on Sunday.

Jack Miller was hoping for relief after surgery to counter arm-pump ten days before. An early error caused him to crash out, unable to test the success of the procedure over full race distance and tearing stitches out of the wound.

The best news belonged to Fabio Quartararo, whose mas-

104 PORTUGUESE GRAND PRIX

terful second win in a row came off his first pole position of the year, at a track where in 2020 he had struggled to 14th, his second-worst of the season. It was also the first back-to-back win for anyone since Jerez that year, 14 races before.

He was glowing as he explained how he believed the inconsistency that had wrecked his 2020 campaign might now be forgotten. More important than an air of calmness endowed by consultation with a psychologist over the winter were clear improvements to the Yamaha: "I feel better with the new chassis. I have a little bit more feedback that actually is one thing that is making me faster. If I don't feel the front, I'm lost. Now I have a really great feeling on the front."

MOTOGP RACE – 25 laps

Quartararo's first pole of the year headed 12 riders all within one second, positions hard won. Rins was second from Zarco, but Suzuki team-mate Mir (through from Q1) was ninth, on the third row. Miller led the second from Morbidelli and the remarkable Marc Marquez; Aleix Espargaro's Aprilia was strong again in seventh; Rossi in trouble once more in 17th, in spite of improving his lap time from just over four months before by better than a tenth.

For one lap, it looked as though Marquez might be contesting the podium. Taking advantage of Quartararo's poor start, he was third – behind Zarco and Rins on the exit of Turn Five. But even for a man of his talent, this was too much, too soon. "I was not in my place and didn't have the pace," he admitted, like "when you play football with the older guys in school. They overtook [me] where they wanted."

Soon the moves came. And how. First Mir barged through at Turn 11, retribution for Marquez's antics in Q1. The Honda man nearly took them both down at Turn Three on the next lap. Mir survived, but Quartararo sensed his opportunity, jumping two places to fourth. Then Miller, Morbidelli, Bagnaia, Binder and Aleix Espargaro on laps two and three.

By then, Rins had moved by Zarco with the Suzuki's turning prowess at Turn 13. Mir followed suit. Miller was out after crashing at Turn Three on lap six, likewise home hero and 2020 winner Oliveira, who fell from 15th on lap six. But the danger lay elsewhere. From Friday afternoon, it had been apparent that Quartararo was the reference. He took little time in disposing of Zarco and Mir before pouncing on Rins at Turn One the ninth time around.

Then it was on. Quartararo immediately lowered his times, trying to break the field. Mir, Zarco and Morbidelli had no answer, but to the leader's surprise, Rins did. In nine laps, Quartararo bettered his previous best five times, a devastat-

Above: He's back. After eight months away and not yet fully fit, Marquez commanded the fullest attention.

Left: Marquez shadows Mir in qualifying, much to the reigning champion's chagrin.
Photos: Repsol Honda

Above left: Under pressure, Aprilia's rookie, Lorenzo Savadori, scored his first points.

Opening spread: Rins matched Quartararo's escape bid, but did not make it all the way.
Photos: Gold & Goose

PORTUGUESE GRAND PRIX 105

Above: Exhausted and emotional, Marquez slumped in his pit after a gritty ride to seventh.
Photo: Repsol Honda

Top: Having just lost second to Bagnaia, Zarco's attempt to respond went wrong.

Top right: Raul Fernandez tasted victory in Moto2 at only his third attempt.

Above right: Joe Roberts, Aron Canet and Remy Gardner were hammer and tongs for second. Canet took it, the Boscoscuro chassis ahead of Kalex for once.

Right: Float like a butterfly… Acosta enjoyed his perfectly judged second straight Moto3 win.
Photos: Gold & Goose

ing pace in the mid-1m 39s, edging the pair clear. Still, the Suzuki man hung on. Not that it led to a great deal of panic. "I was pushing so hard," said Fabio. "I was expecting Alex to make a mistake."

Eventually he did. Rins had just posted the race's fastest lap on the 18th time around when he tucked the front at Turn Five. "It's a big shame because we analysed the crash and data, and I did nothing wrong on that corner. Same braking point, same pressure on brakes. But sometimes it happens," he shrugged. It was his third crash from the victory fight in his previous 14 races.

That left Quartararo free to cruise home, 4.8 seconds clear, for a fifth premier-class win, two days before his 22nd birthday. Only Marquez (19), Casey Stoner (9) and Freddie Spencer (8) had won more so early in their careers.

The four-way battle for third now became the struggle for second. Bagnaia was fighting a sense of grievance at starting 11th – it took four laps for him to start climbing. But his pace was similar to the leaders'; quick-fire moves on Morbidelli (lap 17), Mir (19) and Zarco (20) pushed him to second, before Zarco crashed out at Turn Ten while trying to launch an immediate response, citing "a little issue with the gearbox".

On lap 18, Mir was in danger of fading, his front tyre giving him cause for concern. But he rallied late on in trademark style to push Bagnaia all the way, at the same time holding Morbidelli at bay, securing third by less than two tenths.

Binder was a sensational fifth from 15th on the grid, in spite of Michelin's decision to drop KTM's favoured front tyre for this track from the weekend's allocation. Aleix Espargaro matched Aprilia's best four-stroke result with a fine sixth; a tearful Marc Marquez was exhausted in seventh, ahead of brother Alex; then came top rookie Bastianini.

Nakagami had succumbed to Bastianini with four laps to go, but held off a dispirited Vinales after a heroic ride. The Japanese had suffered a huge FP2 crash that injured his right collarbone, leaving him a doubtful starter.

Marini and Petrucci battled over 12th to the end, the rookie holding the veteran at bay. Savadori and Lecuona trailed in, followed by the remounted Oliveira, a lap down.

Pol Espargaro's Honda troubles continued. Having qualified 14th, he made no progress before dropping away and pitting to retire with rear brake failure.

With Zarco having failed to score, Quartararo took over the championship lead.

MOTO2 RACE – 23 laps

Any notion that Moto2 might settle into a familiar pattern was blown apart at the very first turn, where double winner Lowes high-sided out of second place. One difference was that, unusually, this was the last race of the day, with the highest temperatures of the weekend rendering tyre preconceptions invalid.

Soon after the start, it became apparent that the previous November's winner and pre-race favourite, Gardner, was thus affected and didn't have the pace to break clear.

106 PORTUGUESE GRAND PRIX

FIM WORLD CHAMPIONSHIP | 3

Instead, Bezzecchi, Roberts and Canet (the only one not on a Kalex) enjoyed spells at the front, with Raul Fernandez, Augusto Fernandez and Vierge joining Gardner in a vintage seven-rider fight.

Lowes had claimed a third pole in a row, with Gardner and Vierge alongside; rookie Ogura led Bezzecchi and Augusto Fernandez on row two. Another rookie, Arenas, headed the third row from Roberts and Canet, and only then came Raul Fernandez. Impressively, American champion and Moto2 rookie Beaubier, through from Q1 and still finding his feet back in Europe, led the fourth row.

Raul Fernandez had got past Gardner for third on lap 17, then swooped by Canet's Boscoscuro on the run to Turn One with four laps to go. No one could live with his late-race pace and he scorched to a first victory in the class in just his third appearance. "I have no words," he said. "I'm happy with how the race went, especially the final part, which is what we had been finding most difficult so far."

As he broke clear, it was left to Canet, Roberts and Gardner to contest the final podium places on the last lap, in a furious game of tactics and determination. The American took second from Canet at Turn 11, only for the Spaniard to retaliate two turns later. Gardner then barged Roberts wide at Turn 14 to secure a third straight podium.

Augusto Fernandez, Bezzecchi and Vierge were still together, three seconds back by the end; then came Garzo in a lone eighth.

Beaubier took benefit from his good qualifying and, as usual, better Sunday performance for ninth, stealing it from Schrotter on the last lap, with Di Giannantonio and Dalla Porta up close. Arenas was a lone 13th; Baldassarri and Ramirez claimed the last points, Arbolino missing out by a couple of tenths.

Ogura was knocked off after just four laps, tangling with another rider; Dixon also crashed out – each had been lying ninth at the time. Other fallers in a race of some attrition included Manzi, Chantra, Navarro (who remounted), Bendsneyder, Bulega and Vietti.

Lowes's crash cost him the title lead, Gardner taking over, just four points ahead of precocious Ajo Red Bull team-mate Raul Fernandez.

MOTO3 RACE – 21 laps

At the previous round, Acosta had produced one of the great performances in Moto3 history. In Portugal, he added lustre to his title credentials, winning a fearsome eight-rider battle.

On pole was Migno, at the head of what would have been an all-Honda front row, if third-fastest Alcoba had not been starting from the pit lane. Instead, GasGas- (née KTM) mounted Garcia moved up to third, next to Foggia. Rodrigo led row two, and would have had McPhee and Oncu alongside and Binder behind, had they not suffered the same fate as Alcoba. Artigas and Sasaki took advantage; Acosta now in the middle of row three, alongside team-mate Masia.

Migno led the first lap, then Artigas for two heady laps before tumbling out, with Fernandez taking over on the fourth. On the fifth, Foggia seized the lead and appeared to be in control. But Acosta was right behind throughout, studying his strengths and weakness. Foggia appeared to have done enough, pulling clear by three bike lengths out of Turn 11, but Acosta's late braking prowess allowed him to nip underneath the Honda two corners later, to win by five-hundredths.

Half a second behind, Migno claimed third, a hair's breadth ahead of Sasaki, Rodrigo, Antonelli and Fenati; with Garcia less than half a second adrift.

Masia had crashed out of third early on the final lap while chasing the leading pair, but had hastily remounted to save ninth, two-hundredths ahead of Yamanaka and the rest of the still-close pursuit pack, ninth to 15th inside 1.3 seconds, with pit-lane starters Alcoba and Oncu at the back of it.

Acosta now had a massive 31-point championship lead over supposedly senior Ajo Red Bull team-mate Masia.

PORTUGUESE GRAND PRIX 107

FIM WORLD CHAMPIONSHIP: ROUND 3

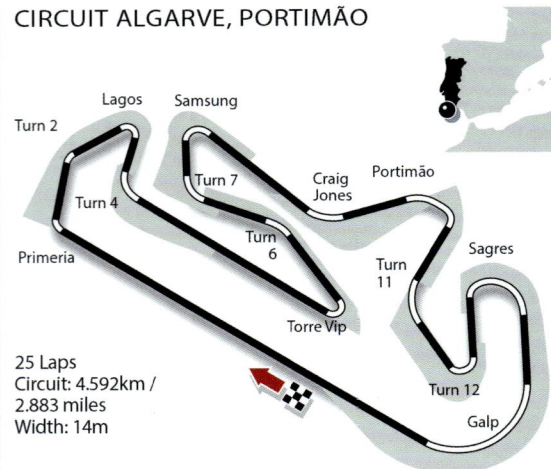

GRANDE PREMIO 888 DE PORTUGAL

CIRCUIT ALGARVE, PORTIMÃO

25 Laps
Circuit: 4.592km / 2.883 miles
Width: 14m

16–18 APRIL, 2021

MotoGP

RACE DISTANCE: 25 laps, 71.333 miles/114.800km · RACE WEATHER: Dry (air 25°, humidity 30%, track 41°)

Pos.	Rider	Nat.	No.	Entrant	Machine	Tyres	Race tyre choice	Laps	Time & speed
1	Fabio Quartararo	FRA	20	Monster Energy Yamaha MotoGP	Yamaha YZR-M1	M	F: Medium/R: Hard	25	41m 46.412s / 102.4mph / 164.8km/h
2	Francesco Bagnaia	ITA	63	Ducati Lenovo Team	Ducati Desmosedici	M	F: Med/R: Med	25	41m 51.221s
3	Joan Mir	SPA	36	Team SUZUKI ECSTAR	Suzuki GSX-RR	M	F: Med/R: Med	25	41m 51.360s
4	Franco Morbidelli	ITA	21	Petronas Yamaha SRT	Yamaha YZR-M1	M	F: Med/R: Hard	25	41m 51.539s
5	Brad Binder	RSA	33	Red Bull KTM Factory Racing	KTM RC16	M	F: Med/R: Hard	25	41m 53.080s
6	Aleix Espargaro	SPA	41	Aprilia Racing Team Gresini	Aprilia RS-GP	M	F: Med/R: Med	25	41m 55.297s
7	Marc Marquez	SPA	93	Repsol Honda Team	Honda RC213V	M	F: Med/R: Med	25	41m 59.620s
8	Alex Marquez	SPA	73	LCR Honda CASTROL	Honda RC213V	M	F: Med/R: Med	25	42m 04.404s
9	Enea Bastianini	ITA	23	Avintia Esponsorama	Ducati Desmosedici	M	F: Med/R: Med	25	42m 08.781s
10	Takaaki Nakagami	JPN	30	LCR Honda IDEMITSU	Honda RC213V	M	F: Med/R: Med	25	42m 10.088s
11	Maverick Vinales	SPA	12	Monster Energy Yamaha MotoGP	Yamaha YZR-M1	M	F: Hard/R: Hard	25	42m 10.173s
12	Luca Marini	ITA	10	SKY VR46 Avintia	Ducati Desmosedici	M	F: Med/R: Med	25	42m 16.072s
13	Danilo Petrucci	ITA	9	Tech 3 KTM Factory Racing	KTM RC16	M	F: Med/R: Hard	25	42m 16.248s
14	Lorenzo Savadori	ITA	32	Aprilia Racing Team Gresini	Aprilia RS-GP	M	F: Med/R: Hard	25	42m 25.353s
15	Iker Lecuona	SPA	27	Tech 3 KTM Factory Racing	KTM RC16	M	F: Med/R: Hard	25	42m 37.054s
16	Miguel Oliveira	POR	88	Red Bull KTM Factory Racing	KTM RC16	M	F: Med/R: Med	24	42m 03.588s
	Johann Zarco	FRA	5	Pramac Racing	Ducati Desmosedici	M	F: Med/R: Med	19	DNF-crash
	Alex Rins	SPA	42	Team SUZUKI ECSTAR	Suzuki GSX-RR	M	F: Med/R: Med	18	DNF-crash
	Valentino Rossi	ITA	46	Petronas Yamaha SRT	Yamaha YZR-M1	M	F: Med/R: Hard	14	DNF-crash
	Jack Miller	AUS	43	Ducati Lenovo Team	Ducati Desmosedici	M	F: Med/R: Med	5	DNF-crash
	Pol Espargaro	SPA	44	Repsol Honda Team	Honda RC213V	M	F: Med/R: Med	4	DNF-technical
	Jorge Martin	SPA	89	Pramac Racing	Ducati Desmosedici	M	-	-	DNS-injured

Fastest lap: Alex Rins, on lap 18, 1m 39.450s, 103.3mph/166.2km/h.
Lap record: Miguel Oliveira, 1m 39.855s, 102.8mph/165.5km/h (2020).
Event maximum speed: Johann Zarco, 218.5mph/351.7km/h (race).

Qualifying

Weather: Dry
Air Temp: 23° Humidity: 61%
Track Temp: 36°

1	Quartararo	1m 38.862s
2	Rins	1m 38.951s
3	Zarco	1m 38.991s
4	Miller	1m 39.061s
5	Morbidelli	1m 39.103s
6	M. Marquez	1m 39.121s
7	A. Espargaro	1m 39.169s
8	Marini	1m 39.386s
9	Mir	1m 39.398s
10	Oliveira	1m 39.445s
11	Bagnaia	1m 39.482s
12	Vinales	1m 39.807s

Q1

13	A. Marquez	1m 39.530s
14	P. Espargaro	1m 39.710s
15	Binder	1m 39.776s
16	Bastianini	1m 39.855s
17	Rossi	1m 39.943s
18	Petrucci	1m 40.202s
19	Lecuona	1m 40.408s
20	Savadori	1m 40.444s
	Nakagami	No Time
	Martin	No Time

Fastest race laps

1	Rins	1m 39.450s
2	Bagnaia	1m 39.468s
3	Quartararo	1m 39.472s
4	Zarco	1m 39.700s
5	Binder	1m 39.850s
6	A. Espargaro	1m 39.854s
7	Mir	1m 39.855s
8	Morbidelli	1m 39.939s
9	M. Marquez	1m 40.001s
10	Vinales	1m 40.006s
11	Bastianini	1m 40.126s
12	Oliveira	1m 40.148s
13	Rossi	1m 40.365s
14	Miller	1m 40.411s
15	A. Marquez	1m 40.428s
16	Nakagami	1m 40.524s
17	Marini	1m 40.693s
18	Petrucci	1m 40.734s
19	Lecuona	1m 40.955s
20	Savadori	1m 40.997s
21	P. Espargaro	1m 41.166s

Championship Points

1	Quartararo	61
2	Bagnaia	46
3	Vinales	41
4	Zarco	40
5	Mir	38
6	A. Espargaro	25
7	Rins	23
8	Binder	21
9	Bastianini	18
10	Martin	17
11	Morbidelli	17
12	Miller	14
13	P. Espargaro	11
14	M. Marquez	9
15	A. Marquez	8
16	Bradl	7
17	Nakagami	6
18	Marini	4
19	Rossi	4
20	Oliveira	4
21	Petrucci	3
22	Savadori	2
23	Lecuona	1

Constructor Points

1	Yamaha	75
2	Ducati	60
3	Suzuki	42
4	Aprilia	25
5	KTM	22
6	Honda	20

Grid order / Lap chart

Grid order	1	2	3	4	5	6	7	8	9	10	11	12	13	14	15	16	17	18	19	20	21	22	23	24	25	*
20 QUARTARARO	5	5	5	42	42	42	42	42	20	20	20	20	20	20	20	20	20	20	20	20	20	20	20	20	20	1
42 RINS	42	42	42	5	20	20	20	20	42	42	42	42	42	42	42	42	42	42	5	63	63	63	63	63	63	2
5 ZARCO	36	36	36	20	5	36	36	36	36	36	36	36	36	36	5	5	5	5	63	36	36	36	36	36	36	3
43 MILLER	93	20	20	36	36	5	5	5	5	5	5	5	5	5	36	36	36	36	36	21	21	21	21	21	21	4
21 MORBIDELLI	43	43	43	43	41	41	21	21	21	21	21	21	21	21	21	63	63	21	33	33	33	33	33	33	33	5
93 M. MARQUEZ	20	41	41	41	43	21	33	33	33	33	33	63	63	63	63	21	21	33	41	41	41	41	41	41	41	6
41 A. ESPARGARO	21	93	21	21	21	33	33	63	63	63	63	33	33	33	33	33	33	41	93	93	93	93	93	93	93	7
10 MARINI	41	21	33	33	33	93	63	41	41	41	41	41	41	41	41	41	41	93	73	73	73	73	73	73	73	8
36 MIR	33	33	93	93	93	63	93	93	93	93	93	93	93	93	93	93	93	73	30	30	23	23	23	23	23	9
88 OLIVEIRA	10	10	10	10	63	10	10	10	73	73	73	73	73	73	73	73	73	30	23	23	30	30	30	30	30	10
63 BAGNAIA	63	63	63	63	10	73	73	73	10	10	10	46	10	10	10	30	30	23	12	12	12	12	12	12	12	11
12 VINALES	88	88	88	88	73	46	46	46	46	46	46	10	30	30	30	23	10	10	10	10	10	10	10	10	10	12
73 A. MARQUEZ	73	73	30	73	46	30	30	30	30	23	30	30	23	23	23	10	23	12	9	32	32	32	32	32	32	13
44 P. ESPARGARO	30	30	73	30	30	23	23	23	23	30	23	23	12	12	12	12	12	9	32	9	9	9	9	9		14
33 BINDER	44	44	46	46	88	9	9	9	9	9	9	9	9	9	9	9	9	32	27	27	27	27	27	27		15
23 BASTIANINI	27	46	23	23	23	27	32	32	12	12	12	12	32	32	32	32	32	27	88	88	88	88	88			
46 ROSSI	46	23	44	9	9	32	27	27	32	32	32	32	27	27	27	27	27	88								
9 PETRUCCI	23	9	9	27	27	12	12	12	27	27	27	27	27	88	88	88	88									
27 LECUONA	9	9	27	32	32	88	88	88	88	88	88	88	88													
32 SAVADORI	12	12	32	12	12																					
30 NAKAGAMI	32	32	12	44																						

44 Pit stop · 88 Lapped rider

108 PORTUGUESE GRAND PRIX

Moto2

RACE DISTANCE: 23 laps, 65.627 miles/105.616km · **RACE WEATHER:** Dry (air 25°, humidity 29%, track 44°)

Pos.	Rider	Nat.	No.	Entrant	Machine	Laps	Time & Speed
1	Raul Fernandez	SPA	25	Red Bull KTM Ajo	Kalex	23	39m 47.377s 98.9mph/159.2km/h
2	Aron Canet	SPA	44	Solunion Aspar Team	Boscoscuro	23	39m 48.977s
3	Remy Gardner	AUS	87	Red Bull KTM Ajo	Kalex	23	39m 49.345s
4	Joe Roberts	USA	16	Italtrans Racing Team	Kalex	23	39m 49.774s
5	Augusto Fernandez	SPA	37	Elf Marc VDS Racing Team	Kalex	23	39m 52.999s
6	Marco Bezzecchi	ITA	72	SKY Racing Team VR46	Kalex	23	39m 53.721s
7	Xavi Vierge	SPA	97	Petronas Sprinta Racing	Kalex	23	39m 54.737s
8	Hector Garzo	SPA	40	Flexbox HP40	Kalex	23	39m 59.917s
9	Cameron Beaubier	USA	6	American Racing	Kalex	23	40m 02.366s
10	Marcel Schrotter	GER	23	Liqui Moly Intact GP	Kalex	23	40m 02.617s
11	Fabio Di Giannantonio	ITA	21	Federal Oil Gresini Moto2	Kalex	23	40m 02.898s
12	Lorenzo Dalla Porta	ITA	19	Italtrans Racing Team	Kalex	23	40m 03.044s
13	Albert Arenas	SPA	75	Solunion Aspar Team	Boscoscuro	23	40m 06.890s
14	Lorenzo Baldassarri	ITA	7	MV Agusta Forward Racing	MV Agusta	23	40m 10.524s
15	Marcos Ramirez	SPA	42	American Racing	Kalex	23	40m 10.871s
16	Tony Arbolino	ITA	14	Liqui Moly Intact GP	Kalex	23	40m 11.016s
17	Thomas Luthi	SWI	12	Pertamina Mandalika SAG Team	Kalex	23	40m 14.847s
18	Hafizh Syahrin	MAL	55	NTS RW Racing GP	NTS	23	40m 44.376s
19	Miquel Pons	SPA	77	MV Agusta Forward Racing	MV Agusta	23	40m 47.794s
20	Fraser Rogers	GBR	89	NTS RW Racing GP	NTS	23	41m 09.343s
21	Somkiat Chantra	THA	35	IDEMITSU Honda Team Asia	Kalex	23	41m 12.537s
22	Jorge Navarro	SPA	9	Lightech Speed Up	Boscoscuro	20	40m 30.633s
	Jake Dixon	GBR	96	Petronas Sprinta Racing	Kalex	14	DNF-crash
	Celestino Vietti	ITA	13	SKY Racing Team VR46	Kalex	11	DNF-crash
	Nicolo Bulega	ITA	11	Federal Oil Gresini Moto2	Kalex	11	DNF-crash
	Bo Bendsneyder	NED	64	Pertamina Mandalika SAG Team	Kalex	7	DNF-crash
	Ai Ogura	JPN	79	IDEMITSU Honda Team Asia	Kalex	4	DNF-crash
	Yari Montella	ITA	5	Lightech Speed Up	Boscoscuro	3	DNF-crash
	Stefano Manzi	ITA	62	Flexbox HP40	Kalex	3	DNF-crash
	Sam Lowes	GBR	22	Elf Marc VDS Racing Team	Kalex	0	DNF-crash

Fastest lap: Raul Fernandez, on lap 21, 1m 42.864s, 99.9mph/160.7km/h.
Lap record: Remy Gardner, 1m 42.504s, 100.2mph/161.2km/h (2020).
Event maximum speed: Lorenzo Dalla Porta, 183.8mph/295.8km/h (race).

Qualifying: Weather: Dry; Air: 23°; Track: 39°; Humidity: 56%

1	Lowes	1m 42.901s
2	Gardner	1m 42.924s
3	Vierge	1m 43.075s
4	Ogura	1m 43.121s
5	Bezzecchi	1m 43.170s
6	A. Fernandez	1m 43.259s
7	Arenas	1m 43.304s
8	Roberts	1m 43.314s
9	Canet	1m 43.359s
10	R. Fernandez	1m 43.389s
11	Chantra	1m 43.454s
12	Garzo	1m 43.472s
13	Beaubier	1m 43.475s
14	Dixon	1m 43.664s
15	Bulega	1m 43.676s
16	Di Giannantonio	1m 43.744s
17	Ramirez	1m 43.841s
18	Montella	1m 44.003s

Q1
19	Schrotter	1m 43.523s
20	Manzi	1m 43.772s
21	Dalla Porta	1m 43.778s
22	Luthi	1m 43.993s
23	Vietti	1m 44.195s
24	Baldassarri	1m 44.269s
25	Arbolino	1m 44.462s
26	Bendsneyder	1m 44.773s
27	Syahrin	1m 44.908s
28	Pons	1m 46.176s
29	Rogers	1m 46.753s
30	Navarro	1m 49.000s

Fastest race laps

1	R. Fernandez	1m 42.864s
2	Gardner	1m 42.943s
3	Canet	1m 43.105s
4	Roberts	1m 43.280s
5	Vierge	1m 43.386s
6	A. Fernandez	1m 43.461s
7	Beaubier	1m 43.540s
8	Chantra	1m 43.559s
9	Bezzecchi	1m 43.575s
10	Di Giannantonio	1m 43.639s
11	Bulega	1m 43.662s
12	Garzo	1m 43.677s
13	Schrotter	1m 43.782s
14	Dixon	1m 43.800s
15	Dalla Porta	1m 43.841s
16	Navarro	1m 43.908s
17	Ogura	1m 43.913s
18	Vietti	1m 43.931s
19	Luthi	1m 43.980s
20	Manzi	1m 44.048s
21	Bendsneyder	1m 44.057s
22	Arbolino	1m 44.059s
23	Baldassarri	1m 44.077s
24	Ramirez	1m 44.086s
25	Arenas	1m 44.090s
26	Montella	1m 44.110s
27	Syahrin	1m 45.226s
28	Pons	1m 45.739s
29	Rogers	1m 46.239s

Championship Points

1	Gardner	56
2	R. Fernandez	52
3	Lowes	50
4	Bezzecchi	36
5	Di Giannantonio	27
6	Canet	23
7	Roberts	23
8	A. Fernandez	23
9	Vierge	16
10	Schrotter	14
11	Vietti	13
12	Beaubier	12
13	Ogura	11
14	Bendsneyder	11
15	Dixon	9
16	Navarro	9
17	Garzo	8
18	Manzi	8
19	Dalla Porta	6
20	Arbolino	5
21	Arenas	4
22	Baldassarri	2
23	Luthi	1
24	Ramirez	1

Constructor Points

1	Kalex	75
2	Boscoscuro	29
3	MV Agusta	2

Moto3

RACE DISTANCE: 21 laps, 59.920 miles/96.432km · **RACE WEATHER:** Dry (air 23°, humidity 32%, track 35°)

Pos.	Rider	Nat.	No.	Entrant	Machine	Laps	Time & Speed
1	Pedro Acosta	SPA	37	Red Bull KTM Ajo	KTM	21	38m 01.773s 94.5mph/152.1km/h
2	Dennis Foggia	ITA	7	Leopard Racing	Honda	21	38m 01.824s
3	Andrea Migno	ITA	16	Rivacold Snipers Team	Honda	21	38m 02.357s
4	Ayumu Sasaki	JPN	71	Red Bull KTM Tech 3	KTM	21	38m 02.388s
5	Gabriel Rodrigo	ARG	2	Indonesian Racing Gresini Moto3	Honda	21	38m 02.448s
6	Niccolo Antonelli	ITA	23	Avintia Esponsorama Moto3	KTM	21	38m 02.502s
7	Romano Fenati	ITA	55	Sterilgarda Max Racing Team	Husqvarna	21	38m 02.546s
8	Sergio Garcia	SPA	11	GASGAS Valresa Aspar Team	GASGAS	21	38m 03.018s
9	Jaume Masia	SPA	5	Red Bull KTM Ajo	KTM	21	38m 14.260s
10	Ryusei Yamanaka	JPN	6	CarXpert PruestelGP	KTM	21	38m 14.281s
11	Stefano Nepa	ITA	82	BOE Owlride	KTM	21	38m 14.314s
12	Jason Dupasquier	SWI	50	CarXpert PruestelGP	KTM	21	38m 14.366s
13	Filip Salac	CZE	12	Rivacold Snipers Team	Honda	21	38m 14.606s
14	Jeremy Alcoba	SPA	52	Indonesian Racing Gresini Moto3	Honda	21	38m 15.516s
15	Deniz Oncu	TUR	53	Red Bull KTM Tech 3	KTM	21	38m 15.561s
16	Yuki Kunii	JPN	92	Honda Team Asia	Honda	21	38m 17.007s
17	Carlos Tatay	SPA	99	Avintia Esponsorama Moto3	KTM	21	38m 19.805s
18	Andi Farid Izdihar	INA	19	Honda Team Asia	Honda	21	38m 22.057s
19	Riccardo Rossi	ITA	54	BOE Owlride	KTM	21	38m 22.116s
20	Darryn Binder	RSA	40	Petronas Sprinta Racing	Honda	21	38m 35.147s
21	Maximilian Kofler	AUT	73	CIP Green Power	KTM	21	38m 35.183s
22	Lorenzo Fellon	FRA	20	SIC58 Squadra Corse	Honda	21	38m 38.275s
23	John McPhee	GBR	17	Petronas Sprinta Racing	Honda	21	38m 39.313s
24	Izan Guevara	SPA	28	GASGAS Valresa Aspar Team	GASGAS	21	39m 10.325s
	Kaito Toba	JPN	27	CIP Green Power	KTM	15	DNF-crash
	Adrian Fernandez	SPA	31	Sterilgarda Max Racing Team	Husqvarna	16	DNF-crash
	Tatsuki Suzuki	JPN	24	SIC58 Squadra Corse	Honda	15	DNF-crash
	Xavier Artigas	SPA	43	Leopard Racing	Honda	4	DNF-crash

Fastest lap: Gabriel Rodrigo, on lap 13, 1m 47.610s, 95.4mph/153.6km/h.
Lap record: Raul Fernandez, 1m 47.858s, 95.2mph/153.2km/h (2020).
Event maximum speed: Ayumu Sasaki, 155.0mph/249.4km/h (race).

Qualifying: Weather: Dry; Air: 24°; Track: 38°; Humidity: 50%

1	Migno	1m 47.423s
2	Foggia	1m 47.572s
3	Alcoba	1m 47.702s
4	Garcia	1m 47.900s
5	Rodrigo	1m 47.909s
6	McPhee	1m 48.362s
7	Oncu	1m 48.486s
8	Binder	1m 48.513s
9	Artigas	1m 48.546s
10	Sasaki	1m 48.615s
11	Masia	1m 48.622s
12	Acosta	1m 48.711s
13	Suzuki	1m 48.749s
14	Fenati	1m 48.769s
15	Guevara	1m 48.865s
16	Fernandez	1m 49.814s
17	Antonelli	1m 49.834s
18	Salac	1m 50.096s

Q1
19	Izdihar	1m 49.153s
20	Kunii	1m 49.435s
21	Toba	1m 49.613s
22	Yamanaka	1m 49.618s
23	Kofler	1m 49.636s
24	Tatay	1m 49.723s
25	Nepa	1m 49.744s
26	Rossi	1m 49.842s
27	Dupasquier	1m 49.970s
28	Fellon	1m 50.234s

Fastest race laps

1	Rodrigo	1m 47.610s
2	Oncu	1m 47.915s
3	Alcoba	1m 47.946s
4	Fenati	1m 47.978s
5	Antonelli	1m 48.030s
6	Fernandez	1m 48.054s
7	Dupasquier	1m 48.081s
8	Sasaki	1m 48.152s
9	Migno	1m 48.158s
10	Garcia	1m 48.169s
11	Masia	1m 48.191s
12	Yamanaka	1m 48.196s
13	Salac	1m 48.196s
14	Nepa	1m 48.257s
15	Suzuki	1m 48.267s
16	Acosta	1m 48.320s
17	Foggia	1m 48.326s
18	McPhee	1m 48.442s
19	Guevara	1m 48.480s
20	Toba	1m 48.495s
21	Binder	1m 48.513s
22	Kunii	1m 48.618s
23	Rossi	1m 48.924s
24	Izdihar	1m 49.007s
25	Kofler	1m 49.012s
26	Tatay	1m 49.045s
27	Artigas	1m 49.230s
28	Fellon	1m 49.432s

Championship Points

1	Acosta	70
2	Masia	39
3	Binder	36
4	Antonelli	36
5	Migno	29
6	Rodrigo	25
7	Sasaki	22
8	Garcia	21
9	Foggia	20
10	Fenati	20
11	Guevara	19
12	Toba	18
13	Yamanaka	16
14	Dupasquier	15
15	Suzuki	12
16	Salac	6
17	Nepa	5
18	Tatay	4
19	Kofler	3
20	Alcoba	2
21	Kunii	1
22	Oncu	1

Constructor Points

1	KTM	75
2	Honda	56
3	GASGAS	31
4	Husqvarna	20

PORTUGUESE GRAND PRIX

Lenovo
SUOMY
motorola
riello
FASSI
SUOMY
Lenovo
NetApp
DUCATI
DAIKO
43
DUCATI
Lenovo
DESMOSEDICI
Audi Sport

FIM WORLD CHAMPIONSHIP · ROUND 4
SPANISH GRAND PRIX
JEREZ-ANGEL NIETO CIRCUIT

Above: Team-mates Miller and Bagnaia share the podium after Quartararo's mid-race decline.
Photo: Ducati Corse

Above right: Innocence and experience. Entering his 26th season, Valentino Rossi displays a photo of the lank-haired 17-year-old rookie of 1996.

Right: Two years on and what do you get? For Franco Morbidelli, a 2021 podium on his 2019-model Yamaha.

Opening spread: Ducati's one-two. Miller took his first dry-weather win since 2016, Bagnaia the championship lead.
Photos: Gold & Goose

SURPRISINGLY to grand prix veterans, nowadays Jerez itself is something of a veteran. Not like Assen, perhaps, or Mugello, but the circuit outside the sherry capital of Andalusia predates the Spanish accession to the MotoGP throne, and this was the 34th visit to the track. It was showing its age, not in facilities, but in character.

What once was merely challenging is now scary, and in some places, notably the fast left-hand Turn Seven, clearly dangerous. Previously, this corner had not been a trouble spot, and perhaps six falls there is not that many, but given the speed, the severity was notable. Three bikes – both factory Repsol Hondas and Jake Dixon's Moto2 Kalex – went all the way to the air-fence, while Celestino Vietti's Moto2 bike went right over it. The calibre of the riders was also concerning, since one of them was Marc Marquez, who body-slammed the air-fence and credited it with preventing any injury. Moto3 riders Darryn Binder and Gabriel Rodrigo also crashed there.

One problem was the nature of the gravel – coarser than usual, according to Jack Miller, so that bikes scooted across the top rather than digging in. Another aspect was simpler – not enough run-off for bikes that become faster year by year. As Joan Mir opined, "For a MotoGP bike, if you want a super-safe track, they have to make a lot of changes. Turn One, Turn Ten … and also Turn Seven is really on the limit. I hit the wall there [in a testing crash in 2019]. But it's the same story. They don't change until something happens."

The physical strain of the all-action layout is another aspect, which overturned what had seemed a foregone conclusion in the MotoGP race, when clear leader Fabio Quartararo dropped away to an eventual 13th. He was the latest of several riders in 2021 suffering from severe arm-pump. Weakened and in pain, he gave way first to steadfast pursuer Miller and kept losing ground.

He was mystified. He had had surgery for the condition the previous year, then suffered a severe bout at the season-closing Portuguese GP. But this time at Portimao, there was no trouble, and no warning at Jerez either. He left hotfoot for France for another surgical intervention.

By some natural justice, winner Miller was actually recovering from surgery for arm-pump, which had spoiled his Doha race (his crash in Portugal then popped his stitches). There was no problem on this day, however, as he went on to his first dry-weather MotoGP win, indeed his first such since 2014 in Moto3. It followed a bleak spell during which he had picked up only 14 points from his first three races as a factory Ducati rider. Battered by social-media trolls, his confidence was shot, and on Friday he spoke frankly: "We're in the shit. I'm trying everything I can to turn the ship around. I've never been so desperate to do that in my life." Support from the factory was boosted by a series of frankly worded pep-talk calls and texts through the weekend from Lucy Crutchlow, wife of Cal. "It feels good to hear stuff like this sometimes. We're all human. We all have doubts," he said after the win.

Maverick Vinales had been another to close his Twitter account after a series of abusive messages, while Aleix Espargaro had his own view: "With this hate that we see on social media, the only thing people will gain is the athletes' profiles will be in the charge of big companies. There will not be any more personal ones." It was not clear how much of a sacrifice this would be, for fans or riders.

Valentino Rossi put himself in line for plenty of questions, with the long expected announcement of his independent VR46 MotoGP team from 2022 to 2026, taking over the slot currently shared with Esponsorama Ducati. The surprise was the sponsorship – not their long-standing SKY, but an all-new package in the name of Saudi petroleum company Aramco. It was under the auspices of Tanal Entertainment Sport & Media, the holding company of Saudi Prince Abdulaziz bin Abdulla Al Saud, who expressed the hope that Rossi might be persuaded to ride for the team, along with his half-brother, Luca Marini.

Now came the speculation – which bikes? Suzuki was one

112 SPANISH GRAND PRIX

favoured candidate, with the factory's hitherto lukewarm interest in a satellite squad; Rossi's long-term allies Yamaha likewise, putting him in competition with his current Petronas-backed team; but even now, Ducati seemed the most likely, as would soon be confirmed.

Honda was neither on the menu nor the wish list, given the current results slump afflicting racing's most decorated manufacturer. They had won premier-class races every year from 1982 to 2019, but the current bike seemed no more promising than 2020's, with Marquez using a 2019/20 hybrid, leaving new team-mate Pol Espargaro baffled and frustrated, bemoaning not only the enforced shortage of pre-season testing, but also the lack of sharing information in the pit: "I don't know if I'm good, if I'm bad, if it's the bike, if it's the package I'm using, if it's my riding style. I don't know what's going on, and I'm a little bit confused because there is the same confusion inside the factory at the moment."

A familiar face returned to Moto2, in the American Racing pit of multi-US champion Cameron Beaubier – veteran crew chief Stuart Shenton. The Englishman's CV included illustrious names going all the way back to four-times champion Kork Ballington. He had also worked with Freddie Spencer and deserved much credit for Kevin Schwantz's 1993 championship win. Shenton had also been crew chief to the Moto2 team's race director, John Hopkins, during his entire MotoGP career at Suzuki. "It's really cool having him back," said the former rider.

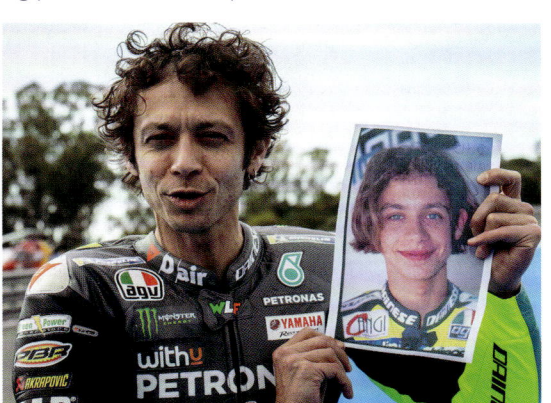

MOTOGP RACE – 25 laps

By common consent, Jerez is not 'a Ducati track': no fast straights or hard braking, too many long corners. Honda and Yamaha have shared the wins since Capirossi's single Desmo victory in 2006. Qualifying suggested things might be different. The Yamahas of Quartararo and Morbidelli led the front row, but Miller's Duke was alongside, having taken the benefit of a tow from team-mate Bagnaia, who led row two.

Nakagami was fourth, top Honda, then Zarco. Mir was tenth, one down on team-mate Rins; Pol Espargaro and Marc Marquez 13th and 14th, unable to escape from Q1.

Miller assumed early control, bolting past Morbidelli on the run to Turn One. Bagnaia rose from fourth to third; Quartararo was fourth. Aleix Espargaro's Aprilia, Nakagami, the Suzukis of Mir and Rins, then Vinales made an early lead group. Possible podium challengers Binder and Rins crashed out of tenth and seventh on the second and third laps respectively.

Quartararo made light work of those ahead. His corner speed through Turns 11 and 12 was spectacular, taking him to within touching distance for the final left, where, coolness personified, he picked off Bagnaia (lap two), Morbidelli (three) and Miller (four) in quick succession. "I knew I was fastest today," he said. From there, he showed exactly that. Within a lap, he was half a second clear, and on lap nine more than a second.

But by lap 14, it was clear that something wasn't right. Miller had halved his deficit, and at the start of lap 16, the Australian breezed by. Quartararo continued to plummet, to finish a desperately disappointed 13th. It was a recurrence of arm-pump, for the first time since the final race of 2020. "I had no power," he said between tears. "I had to brake with four fingers, and normally I brake with one. I couldn't even go full gas on the straight."

Miller faced a long nine laps out front. His pursuer was Bagnaia, 2.6 seconds back, having passed Aleix Espargaro and Morbidelli, The Australian simply had to hold his nerve, a difficult task while the gap gradually shrank. "I saw on the pit board he dropped it down from 2.8 to 1.8," said Miller. "I was thinking, 'Surely not on the last lap. Come on!' I didn't even know how close he was. I buried it up the inside of the last corner like I was protecting, like a Moto3 race and I had three bikes behind me, but it was just me on my own. I felt a bit of a wuss!"

He won by 1.9s, injecting new life into a season in danger of going limp: "I've never ridden that precise, that well in my whole entire life. I don't think I've ever done 25 laps in a row like that."

Bagnaia was delighted with a third podium in four races, enough to take the championship lead by two points.

Morbidelli was third, 2.5s off the winner, an achievement on a two-year-old bike. "There is this shadow of frustration around us," he'd admitted, referring to Yamaha's decision not to update his package. A frank exchange with boss Lin Jarvis over the weekend cleared the air. "This podium tastes fantastically sweet," he said. "I'm really, really happy because you all know the situation and that this is really difficult. Still, here we are."

Nakagami was the top Honda, in fourth, equalling his best MotoGP result, having held off a sustained challenge from Mir. The Suzuki had been within four-tenths on lap 20, more than double that behind at the end. He explained the difficulties of riding in a train in hot conditions: "Half a second behind a rider there is a wall. You overheat the front tyre and you can't stop the bike. It's frustrating."

Both had passed Aleix Espargaro's Aprilia on lap 19, the Spaniard also suffering arm-pump in the final laps, bravely battling on for sixth, another second off Mir and five off the winner. Vinales was just behind and, like Mir, lacking top speed, but unable to overtake in braking.

Zarco recovered from a poor start for eighth, ahead of the factory Hondas of Marquez and Pol Espargaro. It was an impressive result for Marquez, just ten seconds from the winner in his second race back, a day on from that heavy 140mph crash at Turn Seven.

Oliveira was a lone 11th after another undistinguished weekend, lacking the harder front tyre the KTM preferred; Bradl, Quartararo, Petrucci and Lecuona tied up the points, the last pair fending off Marini by less than a second.

Alex Marquez crashed out on the first lap; Bastianini also tumbled out.

MOTO2 RACE – 23 laps

Di Giannantonio started from the middle of the front row, took the lead on the first lap and was untouchable. By lap six, he was better than 1.5 seconds clear; by lap eight, he had added another second, and he was able to control it from there for his first victory in the class in his third year of trying.

The switch from Speed Up to a Kalex chassis in the Gresini team clearly suited his style. He dedicated his win to team boss Fausto Gresini, who had succumbed to Covid in May, and with whose squad Di Giannantonio had taken his two Moto3 wins in 2018. "It's quite emotional," he said.

Title leader Gardner was on pole, his first of the year; Bezzecchi on the far end of the front row. Lowes, chastened by his Portuguese misadventure, was in the middle of row two, between super-rookie Raul Fernandez and Vierge.

The excitement came in a feisty pursuit group of four – Bezzecchi, Raul Fernandez, Lowes and Gardner, who at first was in front of it. His precocious team-mate took over from lap eight to 16.

Then Bezzecchi got through and tried in vain to reel in the leader.

From mid-distance, it was the turn of Fernandez to feel the

Above: Nakagami was top Honda, in fourth, ahead of Mir, Aleix Espargaro and Vinales.

Above right: Heading Gardner and Augusto Fernandez, Di Giannantonio dominated Moto2 for Gresini.

Right: Chasing the leaders, Tatay (99) heads Alcoba (52), Dupasquier (50), Antonelli, Garcia and Yamanaka (6).

Below: How could they all possibly finish? Oncu, Migno, Binder and Suzuki go four abreast ahead of eventual winner Acosta. Sasaki, Fenati, Tatay and Guevara follow on.

Below right: After the last-corner shambles, Alcoba inherited second. He was delighted.
Photos: Gold & Goose

effects of arm-pump. Lowes pushed past on the penultimate lap; Gardner followed suit, demoting the rookie to fifth. "Finishing fourth on a difficult day is a good thing, and we also picked up some important points," said the Australian, his advantage over Lowes now three points.

Vierge, 12 seconds adrift, was never in contention, but managed to stay narrowly ahead of rookie Ogura and Joe Roberts in a close, but unvarying battle that lasted most of the race, with the order across the line unchanged throughout. They were covered by less than four-tenths at the flag.

Canet was alone in ninth by the finish on the first Boscoscuro chassis in the points, having escaped from the next gang, still close over the line. Schrotter was in front, ahead of Marcos Ramirez and Navarro on the second Boscoscuro.

Beaubier had been in this group and had pushed through to ninth, ahead of team-mate Ramirez, when he slipped off on the final lap.

Manzi, Baldassarri and Bendsneyder were another close trio and took the last points; Dalla Porta was four seconds off the back.

As well as Beaubier, several other riders crashed out, including Augusto Fernandez, Chantra, Garzo, Arenas, Corsi and Bulega. The last named fell before he had been able to take the long-lap penalty imposed for causing a crash in Portugal, discharging his duty in the process.

MOTO3 RACE – 22 laps

For the third race in succession, rookie Pedro Acosta made his rivals look like the beginners, prevailing over a 14-bike thriller for his third straight win, after qualifying 13th, on the fifth row of the grid.

Hondas dominated qualifying, with Suzuki, Alcoba and Migno on the front row, Rodrigo and McPhee straddling Fenati's Gas Gas on the second. But Suzuki, Rodrigo and McPhee would crash out, the last named on the first lap.

From lap six, Acosta had joined Oncu and Fenati in a frenetic fight up front, Oncu looking wild in his first time leading. Binder, Masia and Migno were prominent in the big gang.

Another rash of stewards' penalties also complicated matters, with Alcoba serving a double long-lap. Foggia and Toba, among five others, received single long-laps, while rookie Adrian Fernandez had to run three of them.

Oncu led on to the final lap, but Acosta's trademark late braking was impossible to resist as he nipped past both Masia and the Turk at Turn Six. He defended his line into the final hairpin, leaving Oncu to make a desperate lunge, tucking the front and taking the hapless Masia and Binder down with him. Fenati and Alcoba inherited second and third; Migno was two-hundredths behind for fourth.

The next gang was still close: Sasaki, Tatay, Dupasquier. Antonelli, Artigas and Yamanaka – sixth to tenth covered by 0.625 of a second!

Dispossessed, Masia and Binder remounted for 21st and 22nd, and zero points; Foggia was another to crash out.

Acosta was now 51 points clear (of Antonelli) in the championship chase.

SPANISH GRAND PRIX 115

FIM WORLD CHAMPIONSHIP: ROUND 4

GRAN PREMIO RED BULL DE ESPAÑA

30 APRIL–2 MAY, 2021

CIRCUITO DE JEREZ - ANGEL NIETO
25 laps
Length: 4.423 km. / 2.748 miles
Width: 11m

MotoGP

RACE DISTANCE: 25 laps, 68.708 miles/110.575km · RACE WEATHER: Dry (air 22°, humidity 36%, track 41°)

Pos.	Rider	Nat.	No.	Entrant	Machine	Tyres	Race tyre choice	Laps	Time & speed
1	Jack Miller	AUS	43	Ducati Lenovo Team	Ducati Desmosedici	M	F: Med/R: Med	25	41m 05.602s 100.3mph/161.4km/h
2	Francesco Bagnaia	ITA	63	Ducati Lenovo Team	Ducati Desmosedici	M	F: Med/R: Med	25	41m 07.514s
3	Franco Morbidelli	ITA	21	Petronas Yamaha SRT	Yamaha YZR-M1	M	F: Med/R: Med	25	41m 08.118s
4	Takaaki Nakagami	JPN	30	LCR Honda IDEMITSU	Honda RC213V	M	F: Med/R: Med	25	41m 08.808s
5	Joan Mir	SPA	36	Team SUZUKI ECSTAR	Suzuki GSX-RR	M	F: Soft/R: Med	25	41m 09.858s
6	Aleix Espargaro	SPA	41	Aprilia Racing Team Gresini	Aprilia RS-GP	M	F: Med/R: Med	25	41m 10.766s
7	Maverick Vinales	SPA	12	Monster Energy Yamaha MotoGP	Yamaha YZR-M1	M	F: Soft/R: Med	25	41m 11.253s
8	Johann Zarco	FRA	5	Pramac Racing	Ducati Desmosedici	M	F: Med/R: Med	25	41m 12.763s
9	Marc Marquez	SPA	93	Repsol Honda Team	Honda RC213V	M	F: Med/R: Med	25	41m 16.096s
10	Pol Espargaro	SPA	44	Repsol Honda Team	Honda RC213V	M	F: Med/R: Med	25	41m 17.378s
11	Miguel Oliveira	POR	88	Red Bull KTM Factory Racing	KTM RC16	M	F: Med/R: Med	25	41m 20.368s
12	Stefan Bradl	GER	6	Honda HRC	Honda RC213V	M	F: Med/R: Med	25	41m 22.845s
13	Fabio Quartararo	FRA	20	Monster Energy Yamaha MotoGP	Yamaha YZR-M1	M	F: Med/R: Med	25	41m 24.509s
14	Danilo Petrucci	ITA	9	Tech 3 KTM Factory Racing	KTM RC16	M	F: Med/R: Med	25	41m 25.697s
15	Iker Lecuona	SPA	27	Tech 3 KTM Factory Racing	KTM RC16	M	F: Med/R: Med	25	41m 25.879s
16	Luca Marini	ITA	10	SKY VR46 Avintia	Ducati Desmosedici	M	F: Med/R: Med	25	41m 26.524s
17	Valentino Rossi	ITA	46	Petronas Yamaha SRT	Yamaha YZR-M1	M	F: Med/R: Med	25	41m 28.333s
18	Tito Rabat	SPA	53	Pramac Racing	Ducati Desmosedici	M	F: Med/R: Med	25	41m 26.524s
19	Lorenzo Savadori	ITA	32	Aprilia Racing Team Gresini	Aprilia RS-GP	M	F: Med/R: Med	25	41m 43.514s
20	Alex Rins	SPA	42	Team SUZUKI ECSTAR	Suzuki GSX-RR	M	F: Med/R: Med	25	41m 43.836s
	Brad Binder	RSA	33	Red Bull KTM Factory Racing	KTM RC16	M	F: Med/R: Med	11	DNF-crash
	Enea Bastianini	ITA	23	Avintia Esponsorama	Ducati Desmosedici	M	F: Soft/R: Med	11	DNF-crash
	Alex Marquez	SPA	73	LCR Honda CASTROL	Honda RC213V	M	F: Med/R: Med	0	DNF-crash

Fastest lap: Fabio Quartararo, on lap 8, 1m 37.770s, 101.2mph/162.8km/h.
Lap record: Marc Marquez, 1m 38.051s, 100.8mph/162.3km/h (2019).
Event maximum speed: Johann Zarco, 186.9mph/300.8km/h (race).

Qualifying
Weather: Dry
Air Temp: 20° Humidity: 41%
Track Temp: 42°

1	Quartararo	1m 36.755s
2	Morbidelli	1m 36.812s
3	Miller	1m 36.860s
4	Bagnaia	1m 36.960s
5	Nakagami	1m 37.008s
6	Zarco	1m 37.054s
7	Vinales	1m 37.070s
8	A. Espargaro	1m 37.085s
9	Rins	1m 37.124s
10	Mir	1m 37.154s
11	Binder	1m 37.467s
12	Bradl	1m 37.502s

Q1
13	P. Espargaro	1m 37.407s
14	M. Marquez	1m 37.489s
15	Bastianini	1m 37.675s
16	Oliveira	1m 37.746s
17	Rossi	1m 37.915s
18	Marini	1m 37.925s
19	Petrucci	1m 38.065s
20	A. Marquez	1m 38.069s
21	Lecuona	1m 38.139s
22	Savadori	1m 38.325s
23	Rabat	1m 38.641s

Fastest race laps
1	Quartararo	1m 37.770s
2	Miller	1m 37.908s
3	Morbidelli	1m 37.993s
4	Rins	1m 38.028s
5	Bagnaia	1m 38.059s
6	Nakagami	1m 38.101s
7	M. Marquez	1m 38.122s
8	Vinales	1m 38.148s
9	Zarco	1m 38.165s
10	Mir	1m 38.239s
11	A. Espargaro	1m 38.262s
12	P. Espargaro	1m 38.356s
13	Bradl	1m 38.399s
14	Binder	1m 38.430s
15	Bastianini	1m 38.508s
16	Oliveira	1m 38.520s
17	Marini	1m 38.639s
18	Petrucci	1m 38.677s
19	Rossi	1m 38.792s
20	Lecuona	1m 38.869s
21	Rabat	1m 38.901s
22	Savadori	1m 39.220s

Championship Points
1	Bagnaia	66
2	Quartararo	64
3	Vinales	50
4	Mir	49
5	Zarco	48
6	Miller	39
7	A. Espargaro	35
8	Morbidelli	33
9	Rins	23
10	Binder	21
11	Nakagami	19
12	Bastianini	18
13	Martin	17
14	P. Espargaro	17
15	M. Marquez	16
16	Bradl	11
17	Oliveira	9
18	A. Marquez	8
19	Petrucci	5
20	Marini	4
21	Rossi	4
22	Savadori	2
23	Lecuona	2

Constructor Points
1	Yamaha	91
2	Ducati	85
3	Suzuki	53
4	Aprilia	35
5	Honda	33
6	KTM	27

Grid order / Lap-by-lap

Grid order	1	2	3	4	5	6	7	8	9	10	11	12	13	14	15	16	17	18	19	20	21	22	23	24	25	
20 QUARTARARO	43	43	43	20	20	20	20	20	20	20	20	20	20	20	20	43	43	43	43	43	43	43	43	43	43	1
21 MORBIDELLI	21	21	20	43	43	43	43	43	43	43	43	43	43	43	43	20	20	63	63	63	63	63	63	63	63	2
43 MILLER	63	20	21	21	21	21	21	21	21	21	21	21	21	21	21	63	63	21	21	21	21	21	21	21	21	3
63 BAGNAIA	20	63	41	41	41	41	41	63	63	63	63	63	63	63	21	21	21	20	30	30	30	30	30	30	30	4
30 NAKAGAMI	41	41	63	63	63	63	63	41	41	41	41	41	41	41	41	36	36	36	36	36	36	36	36	36	36	5
5 ZARCO	36	36	30	30	30	30	30	30	30	30	30	30	30	30	30	41	41	41	41	41	41	41	41	41	41	6
12 VINALES	30	42	36	36	36	36	36	36	36	36	36	36	36	36	36	20	12	12	12	12	12	12	12	12	12	7
41 A. ESPARGARO	42	30	12	12	12	12	12	5	12	12	12	12	12	12	12	12	5	5	5	5	5	5	5	5	5	8
42 RINS	12	12	5	5	5	5	5	12	5	5	5	5	5	5	5	5	93	93	93	93	93	93	93	93	93	9
36 MIR	33	5	44	44	44	44	44	44	44	93	93	93	93	93	93	93	20	44	44	44	44	44	44	44	44	10
33 BINDER	5	44	6	6	6	93	93	93	93	44	44	44	44	44	44	44	44	20	20	88	88	88	88	88	88	11
6 BRADL	93	6	93	93	93	6	23	23	23	6	6	6	6	6	6	6	6	88	88	6	6	6	6	6	6	12
44 P. ESPARGARO	44	23	23	23	23	23	6	6	6	88	88	88	88	88	88	88	88	6	6	20	20	20	20	20	20	13
93 M. MARQUEZ	6	93	88	88	88	88	88	88	88	9	9	9	9	9	9	9	9	9	9	9	9	9	9	9	9	14
23 BASTIANINI	23	88	9	9	9	9	9	9	9	27	27	27	27	27	27	27	27	27	27	27	27	27	27	27	27	15
88 OLIVEIRA	88	9	27	27	27	27	27	27	27	46	46	46	46	46	46	10	10	10	10	10	10	10	10	10	10	
46 ROSSI	9	27	46	46	46	46	46	10	10	10	10	10	10	10	10	46	46	46	46	46	46	46	46	46	46	
10 MARINI	27	46	32	32	32	10	10	10	53	53	53	53	53	53	53	53	53	53	53	53	53	53	53	53	53	
9 PETRUCCI	46	32	53	10	53	32	53	53	32	32	32	32	32	32	32	32	32	32	32	32	32	32	32	32	32	
73 A. MARQUEZ	32	53	10	53	10	53	32	32	42	42	42	42	42	42	42	42	42	42	42	42	42	42	42	42	42	
27 LECUONA	10	10	33	33	33	33	33	33	23	42																
32 SAVADORI	53	33	42	42	42	42	42	42	42	23										23 Pit stop						
53 RABAT																										

116 SPANISH GRAND PRIX

Moto2

RACE DISTANCE: 23 laps, 63.211 miles/101.729km · **RACE WEATHER:** Dry (air 20°, humidity 40%, track 38°)

Pos.	Rider	Nat.	No.	Entrant	Machine	Laps	Time & Speed
1	Fabio Di Giannantonio	ITA	21	Federal Oil Gresini Moto2	Kalex	23	39m 07.396s 96.9mph/156.0km/h
2	Marco Bezzecchi	ITA	72	SKY Racing Team VR46	Kalex	23	39m 09.118s
3	Sam Lowes	GBR	22	Elf Marc VDS Racing Team	Kalex	23	39m 09.625s
4	Remy Gardner	AUS	87	Red Bull KTM Ajo	Kalex	23	39m 10.415s
5	Raul Fernandez	SPA	25	Red Bull KTM Ajo	Kalex	23	39m 15.967s
6	Xavi Vierge	SPA	97	Petronas Sprinta Racing	Kalex	23	39m 19.577s
7	Ai Ogura	JPN	79	IDEMITSU Honda Team Asia	Kalex	23	39m 19.709s
8	Joe Roberts	USA	16	Italtrans Racing Team	Kalex	23	39m 19.919s
9	Aron Canet	SPA	44	Inde Aspar Team	Boscoscuro	23	39m 21.803s
10	Marcel Schrotter	GER	23	Liqui Moly Intact GP	Kalex	23	39m 24.548s
11	Marcos Ramirez	SPA	42	American Racing	Kalex	23	39m 25.467s
12	Jorge Navarro	SPA	9	Lightech Speed Up	Boscoscuro	23	39m 26.116s
13	Stefano Manzi	ITA	62	Flexbox HP40	Kalex	23	39m 33.171s
14	Lorenzo Baldassarri	ITA	7	MV Agusta Forward Racing	MV Agusta	23	39m 33.292s
15	Bo Bendsneyder	NED	64	Pertamina Mandalika SAG Team	Kalex	23	39m 34.722s
16	Lorenzo Dalla Porta	ITA	19	Italtrans Racing Team	Kalex	23	39m 38.755s
17	Hafizh Syahrin	MAL	55	NTS RW Racing GP	NTS	23	39m 43.241s
18	Celestino Vietti	ITA	13	SKY Racing Team VR46	Kalex	23	39m 43.829s
19	Thomas Luthi	SWI	12	Pertamina Mandalika SAG Team	Kalex	23	39m 45.593s
20	Yari Montella	ITA	5	Lightech Speed Up	Boscoscuro	23	39m 47.185s
21	Tony Arbolino	ITA	14	Liqui Moly Intact GP	Kalex	23	39m 47.479s
22	Taiga Hada	JPN	32	NTS RW Racing GP	NTS	23	40m 10.376s
23	Tommaso Marcon	ITA	10	MV Agusta Forward Racing	MV Agusta	23	40m 27.940s
	Cameron Beaubier	USA	6	American Racing	Kalex	22	DNF-crash
	Simone Corsi	ITA	24	MV Agusta Forward Racing	MV Agusta	13	DNF-crash
	Albert Arenas	SPA	75	Inde Aspar Team	Boscoscuro	11	DNF-crash
	Hector Garzo	SPA	40	Flexbox HP40	Kalex	5	DNF-crash
	Somkiat Chantra	THA	35	IDEMITSU Honda Team Asia	Kalex	3	DNF-crash
	Augusto Fernandez	SPA	37	Elf Marc VDS Racing Team	Kalex	2	DNF-crash
	Nicolo Bulega	ITA	11	Federal Oil Gresini Moto2	Kalex	2	DNF-crash

Fastest lap: Sam Lowes, on lap 3, 1m 41.313s, 97.6mph/157.1km/h.
Lap record: Lorenzo Baldassarri, 1m 41.539s, 97.4mph/156.8km/h (2019).
Event maximum speed: Hector Garzo, 159.8mph/257.1km/h (race).

Qualifying
Weather: Dry
Air: 20° Track: 42°
Humidity: 39%

1	Gardner	1m 40.667s
2	Di Giannantonio	1m 40.738s
3	Bezzecchi	1m 40.753s
4	R. Fernandez	1m 40.808s
5	Lowes	1m 40.833s
6	Vierge	1m 41.038s
7	A. Fernandez	1m 41.210s
8	Roberts	1m 41.235s
9	Ogura	1m 41.251s
10	Dixon	1m 41.266s
11	Canet	1m 41.329s
12	Navarro	1m 41.458s
13	Bulega	1m 41.521s
14	Ramirez	1m 41.704s
15	Bendsneyder	1m 41.714s
16	Beaubier	1m 41.736s
17	Arenas	1m 41.933s
18	Schrotter	1m 41.945s
Q1		
19	Manzi	1m 41.483s
20	Garzo	1m 41.521s
21	Baldassarri	1m 41.557s
22	Chantra	1m 41.601s
23	Dalla Porta	1m 41.636s
24	Arbolino	1m 41.675s
25	Corsi	1m 41.705s
26	Luthi	1m 41.841s
27	Montella	1m 41.974s
28	Syahrin	1m 42.124s
29	Vietti	1m 42.159s
30	Hada	1m 43.014s
31	Marcon	1m 43.271s

Fastest race laps

1	Lowes	1m 41.313s
2	Bezzecchi	1m 41.371s
3	R. Fernandez	1m 41.394s
4	Di Giannantonio	1m 41.505s
5	Gardner	1m 41.597s
6	A. Fernandez	1m 41.787s
7	Vierge	1m 41.824s
8	Ogura	1m 41.939s
9	Roberts	1m 42.065s
10	Ramirez	1m 42.080s
11	Beaubier	1m 42.143s
12	Canet	1m 42.155s
13	Garzo	1m 42.195s
14	Schrotter	1m 42.233s
15	Navarro	1m 42.245s
16	Bulega	1m 42.385s
17	Manzi	1m 42.396s
18	Bendsneyder	1m 42.403s
19	Baldassarri	1m 42.404s
20	Dalla Porta	1m 42.554s
21	Vietti	1m 42.620s
22	Corsi	1m 42.631s
23	Luthi	1m 42.645s
24	Syahrin	1m 42.691s
25	Chantra	1m 42.811s
26	Montella	1m 42.868s
27	Arbolino	1m 42.919s
28	Arenas	1m 43.033s
29	Hada	1m 43.678s
30	Marcon	1m 44.554s

Championship Points

1	Gardner	69
2	Lowes	66
3	R. Fernandez	63
4	Bezzecchi	56
5	Di Giannantonio	52
6	Roberts	31
7	Canet	30
8	Vierge	26
9	A. Fernandez	23
10	Ogura	20
11	Schrotter	20
12	Vietti	13
13	Navarro	13
14	Beaubier	12
15	Bendsneyder	12
16	Manzi	11
17	Dixon	9
18	Garzo	8
19	Ramirez	6
20	Dalla Porta	6
21	Arbolino	5
22	Arenas	4
23	Baldassarri	4
24	Luthi	1

Constructor Points

1	Kalex	100
2	Boscoscuro	36
3	MV Agusta	4

Moto3

RACE DISTANCE: 22 laps, 60.463 miles/97.306km · **RACE WEATHER:** Dry (air 18°, humidity 54%, track 27°)

Pos.	Rider	Nat.	No.	Entrant	Machine	Laps	Time & Speed
1	Pedro Acosta	SPA	37	Red Bull KTM Ajo	KTM	22	39m 22.266s 92.1mph/148.2km/h
2	Romano Fenati	ITA	55	Sterilgarda Max Racing Team	Husqvarna	22	39m 22.683s
3	Jeremy Alcoba	SPA	52	Indonesian Racing Gresini Moto3	Honda	22	39m 22.793s
4	Andrea Migno	ITA	16	Rivacold Snipers Team	Honda	22	39m 22.814s
5	Ayumu Sasaki	JPN	71	Red Bull KTM Tech 3	KTM	22	39m 23.237s
6	Carlos Tatay	SPA	99	Avintia Esponsorama Moto3	KTM	22	39m 23.263s
7	Jason Dupasquier	SWI	50	CarXpert PruestelGP	KTM	22	39m 23.309s
8	Niccolo Antonelli	ITA	23	Avintia Esponsorama Moto3	KTM	22	39m 23.410s
9	Xavier Artigas	SPA	43	Leopard Racing	Honda	22	39m 23.649s
10	Ryusei Yamanaka	JPN	6	CarXpert PruestelGP	KTM	22	39m 23.862s
11	Izan Guevara	SPA	28	Solunion GASGAS Aspar Team	GASGAS	22	39m 26.252s
12	Filip Salac	CZE	12	Rivacold Snipers Team	Honda	22	39m 26.655s
13	Sergio Garcia	SPA	11	Solunion GASGAS Aspar Team	GASGAS	22	39m 27.457s
14	Yuki Kunii	JPN	92	Honda Team Asia	Honda	22	39m 29.470s
15	Stefano Nepa	ITA	82	BOE Owlride	KTM	22	39m 30.460s
16	Kaito Toba	JPN	27	CIP Green Power	KTM	22	39m 35.088s
17	Riccardo Rossi	ITA	54	BOE Owlride	KTM	22	39m 35.135s
18	Andi Farid Izdihar	INA	19	Honda Team Asia	Honda	22	39m 35.256s
19	Maximilian Kofler	AUT	73	CIP Green Power	KTM	22	39m 39.584s
20	Deniz Oncu	TUR	53	Red Bull KTM Tech 3	KTM	22	39m 40.428s
21	Jaume Masia	SPA	5	Red Bull KTM Ajo	KTM	22	39m 41.705s
22	Darryn Binder	RSA	40	Petronas Sprinta Racing	Honda	22	39m 47.603s
23	Lorenzo Fellon	FRA	20	SIC58 Squadra Corse	Honda	22	39m 54.589s
24	Adrian Fernandez	SPA	31	Sterilgarda Max Racing Team	Husqvarna	22	40m 08.494s
	Dennis Foggia	ITA	7	Leopard Racing	Honda	19	DNF-crash
	Tatsuki Suzuki	JPN	24	SIC58 Squadra Corse	Honda	12	DNF-crash
	Gabriel Rodrigo	ARG	2	Indonesian Racing Gresini Moto3	Honda	4	DNF-crash
	John McPhee	GBR	17	Petronas Sprinta Racing	Honda	0	DNF-crash

Fastest lap: Izan Guevara, on lap 3, 1m 46.158s, 93.1mph/149.9km/h.
Lap record: Jaume Masia, 1m 46.060s, 93.3mph/150.1km/h (2020).
Event maximum speed: Ayumu Sasaki, 136.4mph/219.5km/h (race).

Qualifying:
Weather: Dry
Air: 19° Track: 37°
Humidity: 38%

1	Suzuki	1m 45.807s
2	Alcoba	1m 45.932s
3	Migno	1m 46.007s
4	Rodrigo	1m 46.048s
5	Fenati	1m 46.166s
6	McPhee	1m 46.185s
7	Binder	1m 46.288s
8	Sasaki	1m 46.312s
9	Antonelli	1m 46.440s
10	Oncu	1m 46.449s
11	Guevara	1m 46.522s
12	Salac	1m 46.566s
13	Acosta	1m 46.667s
14	Dupasquier	1m 46.714s
15	Masia	1m 46.843s
16	Tatay	1m 47.060s
17	Artigas	1m 47.517s
18	Kunii	1m 47.686s
Q1		
19	Yamanaka	1m 46.579s
20	Izdihar	1m 46.737s
21	Garcia	1m 46.754s
22	Fernandez	1m 46.763s
23	Foggia	1m 46.777s
24	Rossi	1m 46.830s
25	Nepa	1m 46.839s
26	Toba	1m 46.867s
27	Kofler	1m 47.114s
28	Fellon	1m 47.686s

Fastest race laps

1	Guevara	1m 46.158s
2	Garcia	1m 46.164s
3	Oncu	1m 46.217s
4	Tatay	1m 46.221s
5	Artigas	1m 46.306s
6	Alcoba	1m 46.318s
7	Sasaki	1m 46.328s
8	Acosta	1m 46.341s
9	Migno	1m 46.344s
10	Dupasquier	1m 46.402s
11	Fenati	1m 46.409s
12	Masia	1m 46.427s
13	Yamanaka	1m 46.449s
14	Salac	1m 46.484s
15	Kunii	1m 46.536s
16	Nepa	1m 46.545s
17	Binder	1m 46.581s
18	Foggia	1m 46.621s
19	Rodrigo	1m 46.648s
20	Antonelli	1m 46.648s
21	Kofler	1m 46.694s
22	Suzuki	1m 46.701s
23	Toba	1m 46.729s
24	Rossi	1m 46.808s
25	Izdihar	1m 46.934s
26	Fellon	1m 47.225s
27	Fernandez	1m 47.638s

Championship Points

1	Acosta	95
2	Antonelli	44
3	Migno	42
4	Fenati	40
5	Masia	39
6	Binder	36
7	Sasaki	33
8	Rodrigo	25
9	Garcia	24
10	Guevara	24
11	Dupasquier	24
12	Yamanaka	22
13	Foggia	20
14	Alcoba	18
15	Toba	18
16	Tatay	14
17	Suzuki	12
18	Salac	10
19	Artigas	7
20	Nepa	6
21	Kunii	3
22	Kofler	3
23	Oncu	1

Constructor Points

1	KTM	100
2	Honda	72
3	Husqvarna	40
4	GASGAS	36

FIM WORLD CHAMPIONSHIP · ROUND 5
FRENCH GRAND PRIX
LE MANS CIRCUIT

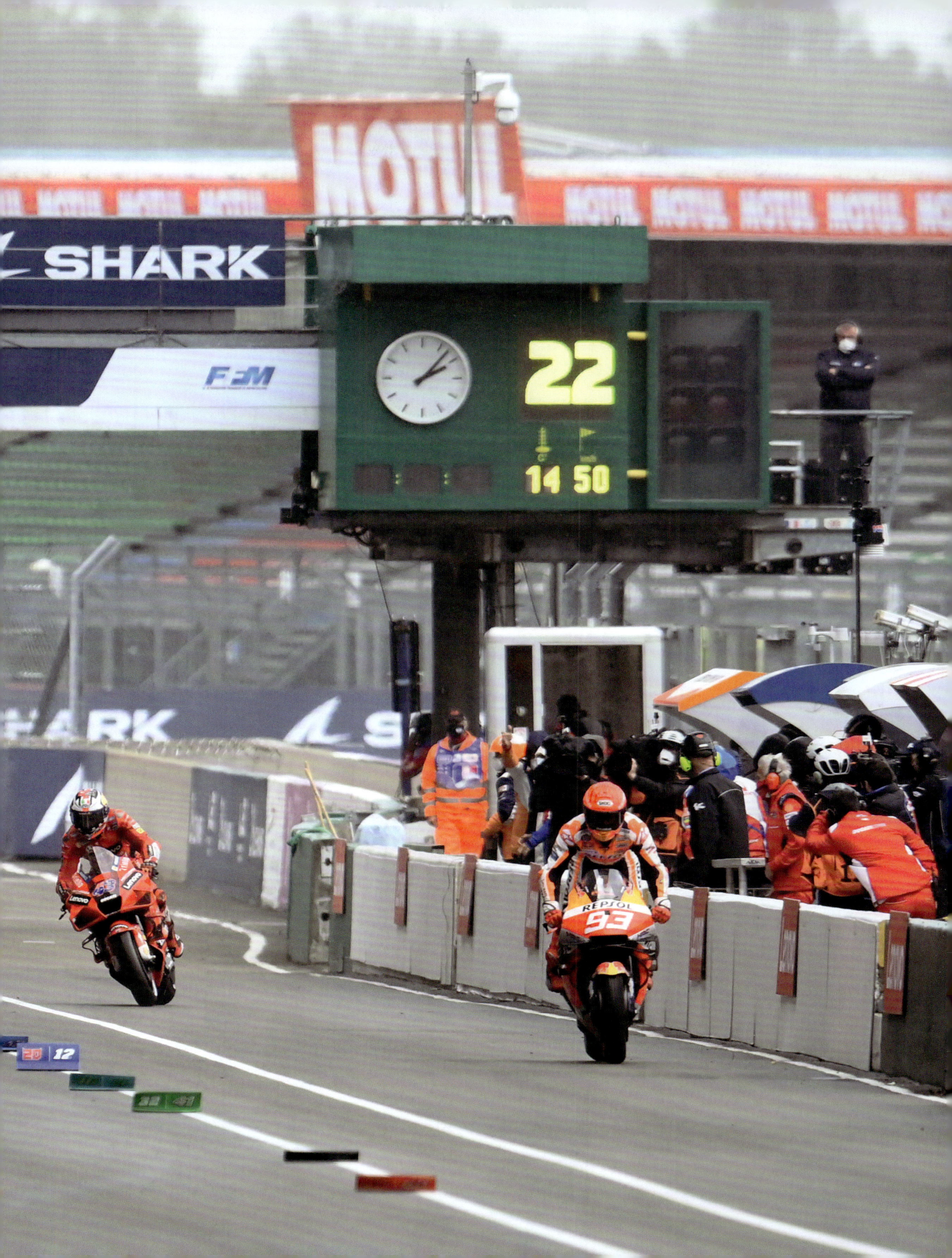
MOTUL
SHARK
22
14 50
REPSOL
93

Above row (from left): Crashing was all too easy. Marc Marquez fell four times on Saturday; Alex Rins twice in the race; Oliveira just once.
Photos: Gold & Goose

Top: First-chicane scramble. Miller leads Vinales, Quartararo (hidden), Marquez and Nakagami (30) away from the start.
Photo: Ducati Corse

Top right: With dark clouds looming, Zarco looks gloomy on the grid.
Photo: Pramac Racing

Right: The disrupted race gave Alex Marquez and Danilo Petrucci a chance for their best results so far in the season.

Opening spread: Marquez and Miller lead the charge into the pits to swap bikes on lap four.
Photos: Gold & Goose

SHOULD there be grand prix racing at Le Mans in early spring? There were 117 crashes over a weekend of cold and constantly changing conditions – too many for comfort. Rain hit MotoGP for the first flag-to-flag bike-change race since 2017, to the great benefit of the entertainment value, with another win for the always adventurous Jack Miller, in spite of a double long-lap penalty. But although having six non-finishers was perhaps not excessive, for many the price was too high, and the date of the French GP should be changed.

Said the ever volublе Aleix Espargaro: "I don't know if someone sees it as funny that we crash. Why don't we change the race to a normal situation? It's very difficult to predict what is going to happen. And the MotoGP allocation of the front – we have one tyre, which normally I don't even put on the wheels. It's super-soft, but even with this [we were] crashing. And Michelin have no other option."

He was one of several who argued that the race should be held later in the year, but even then rain is frequent and the track's unique problems would remain.

Other tracks have recorded higher numbers. Weather-hit Valencia in 2019 had 150 falls; at Misano in 2017, teeming rain and suspect resurfacing racked up 140. But these were in exceptional conditions. Le Mans numbers are consistently high: 109 in 2018 and 100 in 2020, when in fact the race was held in October.

As numbers on a list, when dubbed a "crash fest", and when there are no serious injuries, it's hard not to smile at some incidents. At opposite ends of the scale, Marc Marquez and Indonesian Moto3 rookie Andi Farid Izdihar each suffered four crashes over the weekend, Marquez twice in the race alone, one of them while he was leading. Alex Rins also crashed twice in the race; Maverick Vinales ridiculously fell at some 20km/h while leaving the pits.

Although they were spread around the track, 37 of them – more than 30 per cent – occurred at Turn Three, the left-hand first part of the chicane before the Dunlop Bridge.

Valentino Rossi explained: "Turn Three is a nightmare. Every lap you're very worried. First of all, it's the first left after two corners of right, a long straight and two more corners on the right, so with low temperatures the tyre is cold, there is not a lot of grip. The second thing is the banking is opposite. The negative camber is a disaster for a bike. The third factor is this track is used for car racing, the 24 Hours, and the parts that cars use have less grip. The asphalt is more old. When you make 24 hours with 70 cars, the track becomes old very early."

Marquez's crash from the lead ended a demonstration of his strength in mixed conditions, his ability to get front tyres up to temperature quicker than other riders, and his courage and determination. He hadn't expected to have the chance, at a clockwise track with mainly right-hand corners. In general, he said, his muscle strength was close to 80 per cent, "but some are 50 per cent. It depends on the movement. I'm struggling more, especially the back of the right shoulder." He was not fully recovered from surgery there two winters before, thanks to residual nerve damage, and it left him struggling in long right corners, "like Turn One, Five, Eight …

120 FRENCH GRAND PRIX

but then in the left corners, I'm feeling really good, normal." That created its own problems: "It's where I want to gain time, and I push too much. If you check, in Jerez and here, I crashed in a left corner, because it's where I feel the most confident and I try to take all the lap time." He would have to wait until the Sachsenring for an anti-clockwise circuit.

The first in-season test – just one day – had been held on the Monday after the race at Jerez, giving a rare chance to experiment without the pressure of qualifying and racing. Rossi took the benefit, with different forks and suspension settings that changed the balance, he said: "We tried also a different carbon swing-arm, which is good. All these things helped us, especially braking and entry. It can bring more speed in the corner without running wide, and I feel better on the bike." It seemed it might be the start of a recovery, with respectable pace in the dry and a good seventh in wet warm-up, a big improvement from Jerez. But 11th in the race remained below expectations, and his disappointing season continued.

Perhaps the distraction of setting up his MotoGP team had played a part. Reports from Italy were that Yamaha had offered him the satellite bikes at half the price paid by the Petronas squad.

There were more tests also for Andrea Dovizioso on the Aprilia, in private at Mugello. Again, they were spoiled by bad weather, prompting Aleix Espargaro – making a good fist on the new bike without any outside help – to say, "At the moment, there are no advantages from his tests."

The latest Covid effect was another calendar reshuffle. The proposed first Finnish GP since 1982, at the all-new KymiRing, was postponed for a second year. And in line for a second double-header in succession, Austria's Red Bull Ring stepped into the breach. The Finnish round had been scheduled for 11th July; the replacement Styrian GP would be on 8th August, a week before the Austrian GP. This created the longest ever mid-season break in modern GP racing: five summer weekends.

There was some dismay, however, because it was confirmed that the circuit in the foothills of the Styrian Alps would not be altered as riders had hoped. There had been two horrifying crashes there in 2020, with Rossi and Vinales narrowly escaping being struck by Franco Morbidelli's somersaulting bike at Turn Three, which cuts back across to the right after a very fast left-hand sweep, taken under braking. One rider who expressed concern was Miller. "I'd have preferred a chicane between Turns One and Three to slow it down a bit," he said.

MOTOGP RACE – 27 laps

France threw all sorts of weather into the weekend – wet; dry; wet, but drying; and dry with intermittent showers. The only constant was low temperature. Q1 was wet, and while Savadori and Marini made it through, that left Mir, Rins and Bagnaia on the fifth and sixth rows of the grid. Just ten minutes later, Q2 was dry, with the Yamahas of Quartararo and team-mate Vinales on the front row, Miller alongside. Lap times not far off the race record showed how quickly the track could recover.

It was clear that this would be a chaotic contest from the start as the dark clouds closed in. Miller led away on a dry track, Vinales and Quartararo close behind. Nakagami, Marquez and the fast-starting Rins made up a feisty fight for fourth, while a first-lap moment for Pol Espargaro caused Morbidelli to misjudge a move on the Spaniard at the following turn, taking himself down and pushing Rossi wide in the process.

And that was only the start. Rain began peppering the circuit on lap three. By lap four, it was a downpour. From leading, Vinales "was nowhere" after a mistake at Turn Nine; Miller ran off track at Turn 11, which dropped him to fourth; Mir crashed out at Turn 12 just as the field pitted for wet rubber at the close of that lap. Rins soon followed, falling at Turn Four as he exited the pit lane on wets, just behind the leaders.

By then, Marquez had gained the initiative, taking advantage of Quartararo napping in the pit lane to lead once the bike swap was complete. At the end of the seventh lap, he was 1.5 seconds clear, with Miller a further 3.9 seconds back in third.

Nakagami, Zarco and Alex Marquez were in another race, 13 seconds in arrears in a significantly revised top six.

For three laps at least, the race was poised to be remembered as Marc Marquez's rapid, glorious return to the top. From 2014 to 2017, he'd been all but untouchable in flag-to-flag races, triumphing in six out of seven contests. His fast reactions and ability to bring Michelin's super-stiff tyres quickly up to temperature on cold, damp asphalt, the magic formula, were in evidence again as he led a MotoGP race for the first time in 302 days.

But there would be no dream ending. Marquez lost the rear and was thrown at the final corner on lap eight. He rejoined in 18th and had charged to 11th, his speed in these conditions still unparalleled, when he crashed again, this time unable to continue, and angry at an opportunity lost.

His lap-eight dismount opened the door for Quartararo, apparently in control. Arm-pump and surgery 12 days before were forgotten. But he'd blundered in the bike swap, stopping in Vinales's pit instead of his own next door. This earned a long-lap, which he served on the 12th.

For Miller, there was no sense of a lucky break, as in Spain, for he had to serve a double long-lap penalty for speeding in the pit lane. "The old French speed traps get me all the time," he joked. Nothing daunted, his speed in the iffy conditions was devastating, not only carrying him past leader Quartararo, but also allowing him to control the gap over the late-charging Zarco in the final exchanges. A lead that, at one point, was better than seven seconds was still almost four at the flag. He was the first Australian to win back-to-back MotoGP races since Stoner in 2012. "Somebody needs to pinch me," he said.

Zarco's advantage lay in his choice of medium wet tyres front and rear, which paid him back in the drying final laps – Miller had medium/soft, Quartararo soft/medium.

Bagnaia was another later charger on medium/medium tyres. He'd been 19th early on and had also garnered a double long-lap for pit-lane speeding. He'd passed Petrucci (who had qualified last) with four laps to go and left him trailing.

Another two seconds away, Alex Marquez led a widely spaced Honda trio from Nakagami and Pol Espargaro, his best Honda finish so far. Lecuona was next, taking ninth off a tepid Vinales on the last lap, having done the same to 11th-placed Rossi on the lap before. It was still Rossi's best result of the year so far.

The remaining five finishers were spread out, with Rabat taking the last point well clear of the remounted Morbidelli.

As well as Marquez and the Suzukis, Oliveira crashed out; both Aprilias retired to the pits with technical issues.

MOTO2 RACE – 25 laps

Mixed conditions in qualifying brought a first pole for rising star Raul Fernandez, with a quarter-second lead in wet Q2 over Bezzecchi and Roberts, through from Q1 – the American always strong in the rain and at Le Mans, having been on pole there in 2020.

Canet put his Boscoscuro among the Kalexes at the head of row two, from Augusto Fernandez and Bendsneyder; Gardner headed row three.

Ogura, the other hot rookie – albeit overshadowed by Raul Fernandez – was down in 16th after also coming through from Q1.

The track had dried out after torrential morning rain, and riders had to navigate a dry, but patchy track on slick tyres in the early laps.

122 FRENCH GRAND PRIX

Raul Fernandez somehow maintained his cool in a frenzied opening, which claimed seven riders in the first seven laps. The list included a number of podium contenders, Canet, Augusto Fernandez and Roberts, in the first four laps. Garzo and Manzi also tumbled, the former's crash triggered by a wayward Di Giannantonio, who was given a long-lap penalty for it, then had to serve a second for short-cutting the first.

Also out in the initial scrimmage was early title leader Lowes, who took Vierge down with him at Turn Eight on lap four, added woe after his blazing start to the year continued to turn sour.

Bezzecchi had been out in front, but on lap five, Raul Fernandez moved past the Sky VR46 Kalex to seize the initiative. Only his Ajo Kalex team-mate, Gardner, could match his pace, but the Australian had been mired back in ninth after clashing with Vierge and Garzo the first time through the chicane.

Keeping out of trouble while he was promoted by the many crashes, Gardner then found himself engaged with another fast rookie, Arbolino, and Dutchman Bendsneyder. It took him until lap 16 to finally pass and get clear of them; then he took second off Bezzecchi three laps later.

That left Raul Fernandez to win by 1.4 seconds, the first rider in Moto2 history to win twice in his first five races in the class. Behind Gardner, Bezzecchi collected a second straight podium, and there were personal-best results for Arbolino and Bendsneyder, fading in fifth by the finish.

By then, Luthi had also crashed out, while Schrotter managed to get to the front of a fearsome gang all going for sixth. Ogura was on his back wheel, then came Di Giannantonio, Corsi, Navarro, Chantra, Dalla Porta and Bulega, sixth to 13th covered by 1.076 seconds. Chantra was dropped one place for exceeding track limits on the last lap, and Dalla Porta thus promoted, only for the Italian to be disqualified because the combined weight of his bike and rider was 1kg below the minimum limit of 117kg.

Beaubier had come from 23rd on the grid to fight through this group, and was at the front of it when he became the last name on the long crash list with five laps to go.

Dixon, 2020's hero, was never in the hunt, having started 25th and finished 19th.

MOTO3 RACE – 22 laps

All eyes were on title leader Acosta, for his first time at Le Mans and in mixed conditions. He qualified 21st, then lit up the contest by moving through to sixth after only two laps. But the new star proved susceptible to the treacherous Turn Three, sliding off where so many others had done all weekend.

Hastily remounted, he fought back to eighth from 27th. It made little difference to his title hopes, however, with main challengers Antonelli, Masia and Binder having crashed out on laps one, two and nine. Other fancied runners to fall early on included Suzuki, Alcoba and Rodrigo.

After four epic last-lap fights, this was an unusually subdued contest.

Migno was on pole, ahead of Rossi and Masia; McPhee led the second row from Rodrigo and Antonelli. But it was Salac who led lap one, from Rossi and fellow third-row qualifier Garcia, after Antonelli had crashed at Turn 12.

Garcia and Salac broke clear up front to play a cat-and-mouse chase. The Spaniard's mistake on lap 13 allowed the Czech by, but Salac's time at the front was fleeting. Garcia retook the lead a lap later and gradually increased his margin to better than two seconds at the flag.

Rossi stayed clear of a late attack from McPhee for third, a maiden podium for himself and Salac.

Sasaki was eight seconds back in fourth; rookie Adrian Fernandez (brother of Raul) narrowly beat Artigas for sixth. Acosta, Oncu and Fenati rounded out the top ten, the last named well clear of Migno.

Left: Flying the flag. Miller was the first Australian since Stoner to take back-to-back wins.
Photo: Ducati Corse

Below left: Moto2 rookie Tony Arbolino (14) was fourth, Bo Bendsneyder (64) a career-best fifth.

Bottom far left: Third in Moto3 was Riccardo Rossi's first podium.

Bottom centre: A second win for Raul Fernandez took him to within a point of team-mate Gardner in Moto2.

Below: Down, and up again. Moto3 star rookie Acosta slid off his KTM, but remounted to take eighth.

Bottom: Garcia, Salac and Rossi – 1-2-3 in Moto3.
Photos: Gold & Goose

FIM WORLD CHAMPIONSHIP: ROUND 5

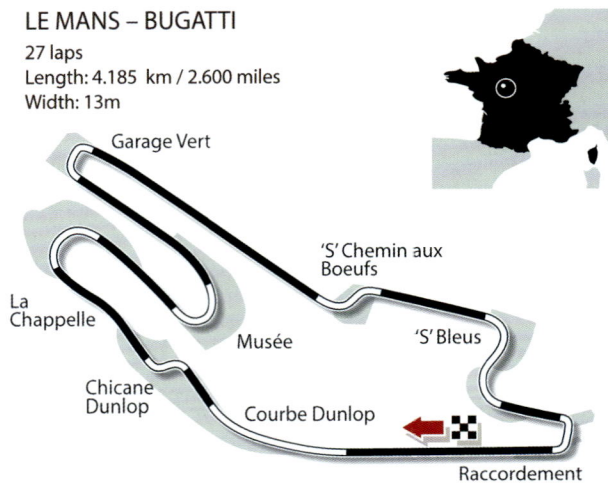

SHARK GRAND PRIX DE FRANCE

14–16 MAY, 2021

LE MANS – BUGATTI
27 laps
Length: 4.185 km / 2.600 miles
Width: 13m

MotoGP
RACE DISTANCE: 27 laps, 70.212 miles/112.995km · RACE WEATHER: Dry (air 17°, humidity 63%, track 31°)

Pos.	Rider	Nat.	No.	Entrant	Machine	Tyres	Race tyre choice	Laps	Time & speed
1	Jack Miller	AUS	43	Ducati Lenovo Team	Ducati Desmosedici	M	F: Soft/R: Soft	27	47m 25.473s 88.8mph/142.9km/h
2	Johann Zarco	FRA	5	Pramac Racing	Ducati Desmosedici	M	F: Soft/R: Soft	27	47m 29.443s
3	Fabio Quartararo	FRA	20	Monster Energy Yamaha MotoGP	Yamaha YZR-M1	M	F: Soft/R: Soft	27	47m 39.941s
4	Francesco Bagnaia	ITA	63	Ducati Lenovo Team	Ducati Desmosedici	M	F: Soft/R: Soft	27	47m 41.645s
5	Danilo Petrucci	ITA	9	Tech 3 KTM Factory Racing	KTM RC16	M	F: Soft/R: Soft	27	47m 46.903s
6	Alex Marquez	SPA	73	LCR Honda CASTROL	Honda RC213V	M	F: Soft/R: Soft	27	47m 48.982s
7	Takaaki Nakagami	JPN	30	LCR Honda IDEMITSU	Honda RC213V	M	F: Soft/R: Soft	27	47m 55.637s
8	Pol Espargaro	SPA	44	Repsol Honda Team	Honda RC213V	M	F: Soft/R: Soft	27	48m 00.694s
9	Iker Lecuona	SPA	27	Tech 3 KTM Factory Racing	KTM RC16	M	F: Soft/R: Soft	27	48m 05.905s
10	Maverick Vinales	SPA	12	Monster Energy Yamaha MotoGP	Yamaha YZR-M1	M	F: Soft/R: Soft	27	48m 06.050s
11	Valentino Rossi	ITA	46	Petronas Yamaha SRT	Yamaha YZR-M1	M	F: Soft/R: Soft	27	48m 07.671s
12	Luca Marini	ITA	10	SKY VR46 Avintia	Ducati Desmosedici	M	F: Soft/R: Soft	27	48m 17.881s
13	Brad Binder	RSA	33	Red Bull KTM Factory Racing	KTM RC16	M	F: Soft/R: Soft	27	48m 24.850s
14	Enea Bastianini	ITA	23	Avintia Esponsorama	Ducati Desmosedici	M	F: Soft/R: Soft	27	48m 27.697s
15	Tito Rabat	SPA	53	Pramac Racing	Ducati Desmosedici	M	F: Soft/R: Soft	27	48m 35.124s
16	Franco Morbidelli	ITA	21	Petronas Yamaha SRT	Yamaha YZR-M1	M	F: Soft/R: Soft	23	48m 45.192s
	Marc Marquez	SPA	93	Repsol Honda Team	Honda RC213V	M	F: Soft/R: Soft	17	DNF-crash
	Aleix Espargaro	SPA	41	Aprilia Racing Team Gresini	Aprilia RS-GP	M	F: Soft/R: Soft	15	DNF-technical
	Miguel Oliveira	POR	88	Red Bull KTM Factory Racing	KTM RC16	M	F: Soft/R: Soft	12	DNF-crash
	Alex Rins	SPA	42	Team SUZUKI ECSTAR	Suzuki GSX-RR	M	F: Soft/R: Soft	12	DNF-crash
	Lorenzo Savadori	ITA	32	Aprilia Racing Team Gresini	Aprilia RS-GP	M	F: Soft/R: Soft	11	DNF-technical
	Joan Mir	SPA	36	Team SUZUKI ECSTAR	Suzuki GSX-RR	M	F: Soft/R: Soft	4	DNF-crash

Fastest lap: Fabio Quartararo, on lap 2, 1m 33.048s, 100.6mph/161.9km/h.
Lap record: Maverick Vinales, 1m 32.309s, 101.4mph/163.2km/h (2017).
Event maximum speed: Alex Marquez, 201.1mph/323.7km/h (free practice).

Qualifying
Weather: Wet-Dry
Air Temp: 15° **Humidity:** 73%
Track Temp: 21°

1	Quartararo	1m 32.600s
2	Vinales	1m 32.681s
3	Miller	1m 32.704s
4	Morbidelli	1m 32.766s
5	Zarco	1m 32.877s
6	M. Marquez	1m 33.037s
7	Nakagami	1m 33.120s
8	P. Espargaro	1m 33.150s
9	Rossi	1m 33.391s
10	Oliveira	1m 33.867s
11	Savadori	1m 34.258s
12	Marini	1m 34.265s

Q1

13	A. Espargaro	1m 43.418s
14	Mir	1m 43.422s
15	Rins	1m 43.523s
16	Bagnaia	1m 43.530s
17	Petrucci	1m 43.857s
18	Lecuona	1m 44.324s
19	A. Marquez	1m 45.146s
20	Rabat	1m 45.590s
21	Binder	1m 45.911s
22	Bastianini	1m 46.123s

Fastest race laps

1	Quartararo	1m 33.048s
2	Vinales	1m 33.108s
3	Rins	1m 33.154s
4	M. Marquez	1m 33.427s
5	Nakagami	1m 33.506s
6	Miller	1m 33.609s
7	P. Espargaro	1m 33.643s
8	Zarco	1m 33.750s
9	Mir	1m 33.750s
10	Oliveira	1m 33.753s
11	Lecuona	1m 33.886s
12	Petrucci	1m 33.929s
13	A. Espargaro	1m 33.968s
14	Rossi	1m 34.077s
15	Marini	1m 34.506s
16	A. Marquez	1m 34.606s
17	Bastianini	1m 34.628s
18	Binder	1m 34.776s
19	Bagnaia	1m 34.809s
20	Savadori	1m 34.890s
21	Rabat	1m 35.507s
22	Morbidelli	1m 43.803s

Championship Points

1	Quartararo	80
2	Bagnaia	79
3	Zarco	68
4	Miller	64
5	Vinales	56
6	Mir	49
7	A. Espargaro	35
8	Morbidelli	33
9	Nakagami	28
10	P. Espargaro	25
11	Binder	24
12	Rins	23
13	Bastianini	20
14	A. Marquez	18
15	Martin	17
16	Petrucci	16
17	M. Marquez	16
18	Bradl	11
19	Rossi	9
20	Oliveira	9
21	Marini	9
22	Lecuona	8
23	Savadori	2
24	Rabat	1

Constructor Points

1	Ducati	110
2	Yamaha	107
3	Suzuki	53
4	Honda	43
5	KTM	38
6	Aprilia	35

21 Pit stop   21 Lapped rider

124 FRENCH GRAND PRIX

Moto2

RACE DISTANCE: 25 laps, 65.011 miles/104.625km · **RACE WEATHER:** Dry (air 16°, humidity 64%, track 25°)

Pos.	Rider	Nat.	No.	Entrant	Machine	Laps	Time & Speed
1	Raul Fernandez	SPA	25	Red Bull KTM Ajo	Kalex	25	40m 46.101s 95.6mph/153.9km/h
2	Remy Gardner	AUS	87	Red Bull KTM Ajo	Kalex	25	40m 47.591s
3	Marco Bezzecchi	ITA	72	SKY Racing Team VR46	Kalex	25	40m 50.700s
4	Tony Arbolino	ITA	14	Liqui Moly Intact GP	Kalex	25	40m 53.604s
5	Bo Bendsneyder	NED	64	Pertamina Mandalika SAG Team	Kalex	25	40m 57.988s
6	Marcel Schrotter	GER	23	Liqui Moly Intact GP	Kalex	25	41m 13.930s
7	Ai Ogura	JPN	79	IDEMITSU Honda Team Asia	Kalex	25	41m 14.076s
8	Fabio Di Giannantonio	ITA	21	Federal Oil Gresini Moto2	Kalex	25	41m 14.213s
9	Simone Corsi	ITA	24	MV Agusta Forward Racing	MV Agusta	25	41m 14.305s
10	Jorge Navarro	SPA	9	MB Conveyors Speed Up	Boscoscuro	25	41m 14.533s
11	Nicolo Bulega	ITA	11	Federal Oil Gresini Moto2	Kalex	25	41m 15.417s
12	Somkiat Chantra	THA	35	IDEMITSU Honda Team Asia	Kalex	25	41m 14.850s
13	Marcos Ramirez	SPA	42	American Racing	Kalex	25	41m 17.706s
14	Albert Arenas	SPA	75	Inde Aspar Team	Boscoscuro	25	41m 18.181s
15	Hafizh Syahrin	MAL	55	NTS RW Racing GP	NTS	25	41m 18.672s
16	Barry Baltus	BEL	70	NTS RW Racing GP	NTS	25	41m 19.410s
17	Lorenzo Baldassarri	ITA	7	MV Agusta Forward Racing	MV Agusta	25	41m 25.137s
18	Jake Dixon	GBR	96	Petronas Sprinta Racing	Kalex	25	41m 27.170s
19	Celestino Vietti	ITA	13	SKY Racing Team VR46	Kalex	25	41m 31.700s
20	Tommaso Marcon	ITA	10	MV Agusta Forward Racing	MV Agusta	25	42m 05.261s
	Cameron Beaubier	USA	6	American Racing	Kalex	20	DNF-crash
	Thomas Luthi	SWI	12	Pertamina Mandalika SAG Team	Kalex	14	DNF-crash
	Hector Garzo	SPA	40	Flexbox HP40	Kalex	6	DNF-crash
	Joe Roberts	USA	16	Italtrans Racing Team	Kalex	4	DNF-crash
	Xavi Vierge	SPA	97	Petronas Sprinta Racing	Kalex	3	DNF-crash
	Sam Lowes	GBR	22	Elf Marc VDS Racing Team	Kalex	3	DNF-crash
	Stefano Manzi	ITA	62	Flexbox HP40	Kalex	2	DNF-crash
	Alonso Lopez	SPA	2	MB Conveyors Speed Up	Boscoscuro	2	DNF-crash
	Augusto Fernandez	SPA	37	Elf Marc VDS Racing Team	Kalex	1	DNF-crash
	Aron Canet	SPA	44	Inde Aspar Team	Boscoscuro	0	DNF-crash
	Lorenzo Dalla Porta	ITA	19	Italtrans Racing Team	Kalex	-	DSQ

Fastest lap: Remy Gardner, on lap 18, 1m 36.893s, 96.6mph/155.4km/h.
Lap record: Jorge Navarro, 1m 36.764s, 96.7mph/155.6km/h (2019).
Event maximum speed: Somkiat Chantra, 169.8mph/273.2km/h (race).

Qualifying
Weather: Wet
Air: 15° Track: 18°
Humidity: 69%

1	R. Fernandez	1m 50.135s
2	Bezzecchi	1m 50.375s
3	Roberts	1m 50.514s
4	Canet	1m 50.782s
5	A. Fernandez	1m 50.796s
6	Bendsneyder	1m 51.132s
7	Gardner	1m 51.146s
8	Garzo	1m 51.215s
9	Manzi	1m 51.360s
10	Lowes	1m 52.031s
11	Bulega	1m 52.223s
12	Vierge	1m 52.273s
13	Baldassarri	1m 52.587s
14	Schrotter	1m 52.753s
15	Di Giannantonio	1m 53.398s
16	Ogura	1m 54.436s
17	Corsi	1m 55.409s
18	Navarro	1m 56.706s
Q1		
19	Arbolino	1m 37.154s
20	Chantra	1m 37.191s
21	Dalla Porta	1m 37.231s
22	Ramirez	1m 37.238s
23	Luthi	1m 37.286s
24	Beaubier	1m 37.511s
25	Arenas	1m 37.556s
26	Dixon	1m 37.564s
27	Syahrin	1m 37.676s
28	Vietti	1m 37.958s
29	Baltus	1m 38.150s
30	Marcon	1m 38.489s
31	Lopez	1m 39.154s

Fastest race laps

1	Gardner	1m 36.893s
2	R. Fernandez	1m 36.983s
3	Arbolino	1m 37.013s
4	Bezzecchi	1m 37.026s
5	Bendsneyder	1m 37.233s
6	Di Giannantonio	1m 37.568s
7	Navarro	1m 37.583s
8	Corsi	1m 37.653s
9	Beaubier	1m 37.729s
10	Arenas	1m 37.759s
11	Baldassarri	1m 37.792s
12	Chantra	1m 37.797s
13	Ramirez	1m 37.809s
14	Ogura	1m 37.814s
15	Baltus	1m 37.851s
16	Bulega	1m 37.892s
17	Syahrin	1m 37.987s
18	Dalla Porta	1m 38.015s
19	Schrotter	1m 38.037s
20	Roberts	1m 38.122s
21	Garzo	1m 38.137s
22	Luthi	1m 38.143s
23	Vietti	1m 38.312s
24	Dixon	1m 38.325s
25	Lowes	1m 38.341s
26	Vierge	1m 38.736s
27	Marcon	1m 39.243s
28	Manzi	1m 39.509s
29	Lopez	1m 40.826s

Championship Points

1	Gardner	89
2	R. Fernandez	88
3	Bezzecchi	72
4	Lowes	66
5	Di Giannantonio	60
6	Roberts	31
7	Canet	30
8	Schrotter	30
9	Ogura	29
10	Vierge	26
11	Bendsneyder	24
12	A. Fernandez	23
13	Navarro	19
14	Arbolino	18
15	Vietti	13
16	Beaubier	12
17	Manzi	11
18	Dixon	9
19	Ramirez	9
20	Garzo	8
21	Corsi	7
22	Dalla Porta	6
23	Arenas	6
24	Bulega	5
25	Chantra	4
26	Baldassarri	3
27	Syahrin	1
28	Luthi	1

Constructor Points

1	Kalex	100
2	Boscoscuro	36
3	MV Agusta	4
4	NTS	1

Moto3

RACE DISTANCE: 22 laps, 57.210 miles/92.070km · **RACE WEATHER:** Wet (air 13°, humidity 86%, track 17°)

Pos.	Rider	Nat.	No.	Entrant	Machine	Laps	Time & Speed
1	Sergio Garcia	SPA	11	Gaviota GASGAS Aspar Team	GASGAS	22	42m 21.172s 81.0mph/130.4km/h
2	Filip Salac	CZE	12	Rivacold Snipers Team	Honda	22	42m 23.521s
3	Riccardo Rossi	ITA	54	BOE Owlride	KTM	22	42m 26.761s
4	John McPhee	GBR	17	Petronas Sprinta Racing	Honda	22	42m 28.330s
5	Ayumu Sasaki	JPN	71	Red Bull KTM Tech 3	KTM	22	42m 36.054s
6	Adrian Fernandez	SPA	31	Sterilgarda Max Racing Team	Husqvarna	22	42m 48.451s
7	Xavier Artigas	SPA	43	Leopard Racing	Honda	22	42m 48.580s
8	Pedro Acosta	SPA	37	Red Bull KTM Ajo	KTM	22	42m 51.052s
9	Deniz Oncu	TUR	53	Red Bull KTM Tech 3	KTM	22	42m 56.270s
10	Romano Fenati	ITA	55	Sterilgarda Max Racing Team	Husqvarna	22	42m 57.788s
11	Andrea Migno	ITA	16	Rivacold Snipers Team	Honda	22	43m 03.519s
12	Ryusei Yamanaka	JPN	6	CarXpert PruestelGP	KTM	22	43m 03.911s
13	Jason Dupasquier	SWI	50	CarXpert PruestelGP	KTM	22	43m 03.928s
14	Izan Guevara	SPA	28	Gaviota GASGAS Aspar Team	GASGAS	22	43m 12.063s
15	Andi Farid Izdihar	INA	19	Honda Team Asia	Honda	22	43m 13.925s
16	Maximilian Kofler	AUT	73	CIP Green Power	KTM	22	43m 14.226s
17	Stefano Nepa	ITA	82	BOE Owlride	KTM	22	43m 14.740s
18	Dennis Foggia	ITA	7	Leopard Racing	Honda	22	43m 40.167s
19	Lorenzo Fellon	FRA	20	SIC58 Squadra Corse	Honda	22	43m 40.275s
20	Darryn Binder	RSA	40	Petronas Sprinta Racing	Honda	22	44m 15.296s
21	Kaito Toba	JPN	27	CIP Green Power	KTM	21	42m 44.595s
22	Jeremy Alcoba	SPA	52	Indonesian Racing Gresini Moto3	Honda	18	42m 35.147s
	Carlos Tatay	SPA	99	Avintia Esponsorama Moto3	KTM	14	DNF-ret in pit
	Takuma Matsuyama	JPN	32	Honda Team Asia	Honda	3	DNF-crash
	Gabriel Rodrigo	ARG	2	Indonesian Racing Gresini Moto3	Honda	2	DNF-crash
	Jaume Masia	SPA	5	Red Bull KTM Ajo	KTM	1	DNF-crash
	Tatsuki Suzuki	JPN	24	SIC58 Squadra Corse	Honda	1	DNF-crash
	Niccolo Antonelli	ITA	23	Avintia Esponsorama Moto3	Honda	1	DNF-crash

Fastest lap: Riccardo Rossi, on lap 22, 1m 50.822s, 84.4mph/135.9km/h.
Lap record: Celestino Vietti, 1m 41.690s, 92.0mph/148.1km/h (2020).
Event maximum speed: Kaito Toba, 141.1mph/227.1km/h (qualifying).

Qualifying:
Weather: Wet
Air: 15° Track: 18°
Humidity: 69%

1	Migno	1m 47.407s
2	Rossi	1m 49.408s
3	Masia	1m 49.611s
4	McPhee	1m 49.640s
5	Rodrigo	1m 49.684s
6	Antonelli	1m 49.894s
7	Salac	1m 50.594s
8	Garcia	1m 50.786s
9	Suzuki	1m 50.927s
10	Fenati	1m 50.962s
11	Nepa	1m 51.145s
12	Yamanaka	1m 51.303s
13	Oncu	1m 51.375s
14	Dupasquier	1m 51.510s
15	Sasaki	1m 52.332s
16	Binder	1m 52.511s
17	Alcoba	1m 54.034s
18	Foggia	1m 54.345s
Q1		
19	Toba	1m 43.290s
20	Tatay	1m 43.303s
21	Acosta	1m 43.376s
22	Kofler	1m 43.393s
23	Kunii	1m 43.636s
24	Izdihar	1m 43.663s
25	Matsuyama	1m 44.284s
26	Guevara	1m 44.435s
27	Fellon	1m 44.784s
28	Fernandez	1m 47.081s
	Artigas	No Time

Fastest race laps

1	Rossi	1m 50.822s
2	Oncu	1m 51.196s
3	McPhee	1m 51.204s
4	Guevara	1m 51.565s
5	Acosta	1m 51.830s
6	Fenati	1m 52.058s
7	Garcia	1m 52.193s
8	Artigas	1m 52.253s
9	Salac	1m 52.293s
10	Fernandez	1m 52.381s
11	Izdihar	1m 52.702s
12	Dupasquier	1m 52.896s
13	Yamanaka	1m 53.278s
14	Sasaki	1m 53.314s
15	Migno	1m 53.463s
16	Kofler	1m 53.790s
17	Nepa	1m 53.889s
18	Fellon	1m 54.483s
19	Foggia	1m 54.547s
20	Alcoba	1m 55.190s
21	Toba	1m 55.218s
22	Binder	1m 55.723s
23	Tatay	1m 57.109s
24	Rodrigo	1m 59.857s
25	Matsuyama	2m 00.348s

Championship Points

1	Acosta	103
2	Garcia	49
3	Migno	47
4	Fenati	46
5	Antonelli	44
6	Sasaki	44
7	Masia	39
8	Binder	36
9	Salac	30
10	Dupasquier	27
11	Guevara	26
12	Yamanaka	26
13	Rodrigo	25
14	Foggia	20
15	Alcoba	18
16	Toba	18
17	Rossi	16
18	Artigas	16
19	Tatay	14
20	McPhee	13
21	Suzuki	12
22	Fernandez	10
23	Oncu	8
24	Nepa	6
25	Kunii	3
26	Kofler	3
27	Izdihar	1

Constructor Points

1	KTM	116
2	Honda	92
3	GASGAS	61
4	Husqvarna	50

FRENCH GRAND PRIX 125

FIM WORLD CHAMPIONSHIP · ROUND 6
ITALIAN GRAND PRIX
MUGELLO CIRCUIT

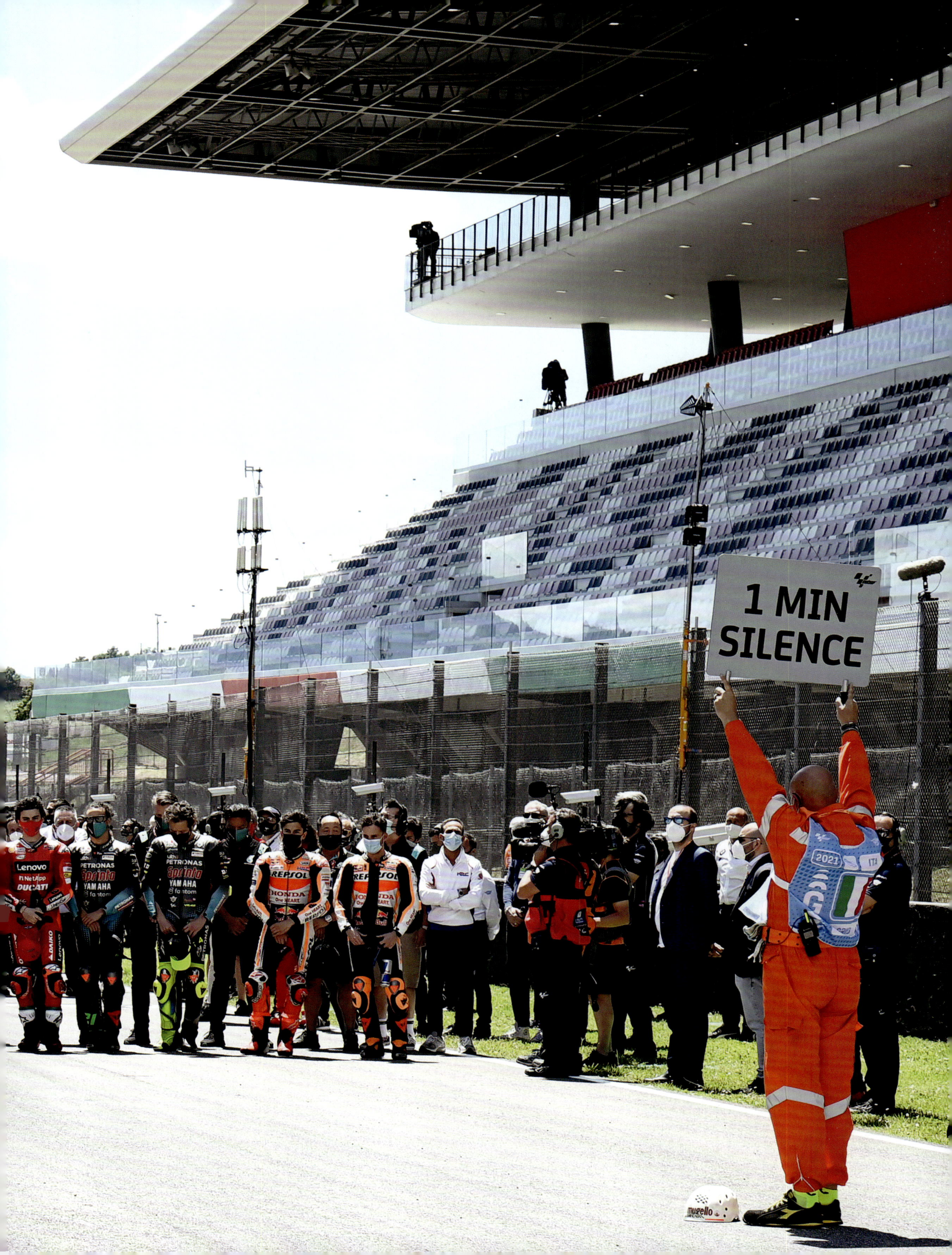
1 MIN
SILENCE

Above row (from left): **Bezzecchi and Roberts dispute third; fully focused, former Mugello winner Danilo Petrucci; top-speed tiger Brad Binder enjoyed the KTM upgrades.**

Above centre: **No spectators were allowed inside the circuit, but not to be denied, some peered over the perimeter anyway.**

Top: **Demoted, then restored, Miguel Oliveira savoured second place.**

Top right: **"Hey, you, get off my cloud." Vinales eyeballs the shadowing Marquez during Q1 qualifying.**

Right: **Mugello mirth from Rossi and his bovine helmet.**

Opening spread: **MotoGP riders front the paddock line-up for a minute's silence on the grid; Quartararo (*inset*) offers his trophy to the fallen Dupasquier.**

Photos: Gold & Goose

NATURALLY, the death of Swiss teenager Jason Dupasquier cast a pall over Sunday's racing. The confirmation, while not unexpected, was ill timed – shortly after noon, as the Moto2 grid was forming up for its 12:20pm start. There was little time to react, or for riders to process their emotions; only enough to arrange the customary minute of silence before the start of the MotoGP race at 2pm.

The Swiss rider's friend and mentor, Thomas Luthi, had already pulled out of the Moto2 race, to spend the teenager's last hours at his bedside with his family. His CarXpert Pruestel team also withdrew his team-mate, Ryusei Yamanaka. At least three riders – Pecco Bagnaia, Aleix Espargaro and Danilo Petrucci – felt that racing should have been cancelled, as had happened for mid-race MotoGP victim Marco Simoncelli in Malaysia in 2011. All three MotoGP podium finishers, however, defended the decision. Said winner Fabio Quartararo: "We know the difficult moments that can happen. Unfortunately, it's sad to say, but it's our job." Alongside him, Miguel Oliveira summed it up with customary clarity: "I wish this sport could not be so cruel ... but it is our passion."

Without exception, the podium finishers dedicated their races to his memory. The rising star had suffered random misfortune – straying off track slightly on the fast Arrabbiata 2 after Sergio Garcia had slipped past inside. Dupasquier lost control on the rumble strip before bike and rider crabbed back across the track instead of sliding outwards (the same quirk that had done for Simoncelli and, in 2010, Shoya Tomizawa). Two following riders, Ayumu Sasaki and Jeremy Alcoba, were unable to avoid him, and his multiple injuries included a fatal head injury. After lengthy treatment where he fell, he was flown to hospital in Florence, but was certified brain dead in the early hours of the following morning.

There was also some relief – thankfully, only three riders had been involved, only one succumbing. Dread had been accumulating in Moto3, with ever larger groups becoming increasingly closer every weekend, and reckless behaviour a particular focus. This accident had a different cause, but the dread would not go away.

The efforts of Race Direction and the stewards to impose 'sensible riding' had so far proved as effective as attempting to herd cats, but they were not discouraged. In fact, there was only one Moto3 sanction: a double long-lap for Xavier Artigas for cruising in Q1. The censorious action came in Moto2 and MotoGP, with post-race decisions after last-lap incidents in both classes triggering yet more debate.

In Moto2, Joe Roberts was demoted from third, which would have been a second career podium, after grazing the green on the exit of Turn Five.

The end of the MotoGP race verged on farce. A preposterous decision meant that initially Oliveira was demoted from second to third because he'd narrowly exceeded track limits on the final lap. But he was soon reinstated, as Joan Mir, briefly placed second, was judged to have done the same. But with Johann Zarco not far behind the pair, should he not have been promoted automatically? The rule states that a rider must drop a place if track limits are exceeded on the final lap and there is no clear disadvantage.

Pramac team boss Francesco Guidotti sought clarification from the stewards: "They told me that both riders, Oliveira and Mir, went on the green at Turn Five. In that sector, Zarco was 0.7 behind, so in that case, he was far enough not to apply the penalty. If it was less than half a second in the last sector, it would be a different interpretation, but 0.7 behind at Turn Five … when they went out 5–10cm. To be honest, for me, it's okay." There had been many other times, however, when riders had wished the stewards had shown the same level of sensible discretion.

Entertainment in qualifying came from Marc Marquez and Maverick Vinales, both of whom had been striving to graduate from Q1. Vinales had the speed, Marquez – who, team manager Alberto Puig revealed, had been contemplating withdrawing because of right-shoulder pain – did not. He decided to follow somebody: "We checked the list. The fastest guy was Vinales." He shadowed the Yamaha for much of the session, much to Vinales's chagrin, even following through the short cut into the pit lane after an aborted out-lap. As the minutes ticked down, Vinales had no other option but to push – and towed his adversary around to quickest time. Vinales then messed up the following lap as Bagnaia put in a flier. That meant Marquez went through to Q2 and he didn't. Maverick remained tight-lipped; Marquez tried to justify the move, and had apologised: "I know that it's not completely fair. I told him, 'You have a reason to be angry.' In the end, it's at the limit, but inside the rules." Except, of course, in Moto3, where slow riding in qualifying is always punished.

Yamaha riders had a reason to be happy: the advent of a front-end holeshot device after continual pleas. This arrangement locks the suspension down off the line to lower the centre of gravity, and the M1 had been the only bike on the grid not to be equipped with one. Now, all machines except the Suzuki could compress the front and rear suspension. Suzuki had only the front system.

Happier still, KTM's factory riders, whose prospects had been transformed by the arrival of an all-new chassis, first seen at the post-race tests at Jerez. Said motorsport chief Pit Beirer: "That test was a massive step for us. Really small changes to the chassis and small parts, swing-arm area and how we mount the engine… We still have both versions in the garage this weekend. The riders want to compare. But from what I saw with the lap time, it's quite clear."

Brad Binder praised the chassis upgrade: "The goal … was to help us line the bike up a bit better to get out of the corners better, and it seems to be working well." A switch from Elf to ECS fuel had also improved power. As a result, the factory RC16s could match the Ducatis for speed. Binder equalled Zarco's Losail record of 362.4km/h; Oliveira was sixth fastest, the pair sandwiching the Ducatis of Zarco, Enea Bastianini and Jack Miller, and the continuingly impressive Aleix Espargaro's Aprilia.

Two wins in a row meant that Miller's position at Ducati was equalised with his team-mate, and most of the rest of MotoGP. In place of the usual two-year contract, the Australian had been promoted to the factory squad for just one. Now that was extended to cover 2022 as well.

MOTOGP RACE – 23 laps

Top-speed deficit or not (it was, by the way, a touch more than 8mph), Quartararo claimed a fourth pole in a row, from the Ducatis of Bagnaia and Zarco. His advantage of 0.23 of a second was impressive, considering that the same time interval covered from second to Jack Miller in fifth. Aleix Espargaro's Aprilia led row two, in fourth; Binder and Oliveira's KTMs sixth and seventh; then the Suzukis, Rins ahead of Mir – five different makes on the front three rows.

The top Honda was Marquez, in the middle of the next row; Rossi – wearing a special cow-themed 'Moo-Gello' helmet to celebrate a track where he had claimed seven MotoGP wins – was a lowly 19th.

Did the pre-race silence unsettle some riders? One barely explicable incident came after the warm-up lap, when Bastianini smashed into the back of Zarco as the Frenchman was (as is usual) warming up his carbon brakes. The rookie ran to start on his spare from the pit lane, only to crash out on lap one.

Then, after a blazing start and in an impressive lead, Bagnaia crashed out on the entry to Arrabbiata 2 on the second lap. It had been, he said between tears, "one of the worst days of my life".

Zarco, concerned about the condition of his battered bike, led that lap over the line, using his significant top-speed advantage to surge past Quartararo – and again after passing the line on the following lap. But the Yamaha gave the points leader the equivalent ease of overtaking elsewhere on the fast corners, and after a pair of delicious moves – the first at Casanova-Savelli (Turns Six and Seven) on lap three, the second at Poggio Seco (Turn Four) a lap later – gave him a lead he could build upon.

A series of 1m 46s laps put him better than a second ahead on lap seven, two seconds on lap nine and better than three after the 13th. He was able to back off to win by 2.5 seconds, obliterating the previous race record by 15.7seconds for his third win of the year.

Jason Dupasquier, 2001–2021

SWISS teenager Jason Dupasquier, a rising star in Moto3, paid the ultimate price for a minor mistake when striving to improve his 11th-fastest qualifying time at Mugello, sustaining fatal injuries after falling into the path of following riders.

The 19-year-old was in his second GP season, riding a KTM for the German-based CarXpert PruestelGP team and making an impact. He had scored points in every race, with a best of seventh at the Spanish GP, just one second behind the winner.

From Bulle in Switzerland, he was the son of Philippe Dupasquier, a former podium finisher in the 125cc Motocross World Championship.

Jason had won national Supermoto titles before switching to circuit racing, winning the German Moto3 Championship in 2016.

A move to the Red Bull Rookies Cup in 2018 was thwarted by injury, but he became a top-ten regular in the 2019 series, placed eighth overall, up against current Moto3 contemporaries Pedro Acosta, Carlos Tatay, Yuki Kunii and Lorenzo Fellon.

He moved to the Moto3 World Championship with the Pruestel team in 2020, with a best finish of 17th. After a dedicated training programme in Spain over the winter, he returned in 2021 as a serious top-ten threat.

A bright future came to a premature close at Mugello.

Above: After Bagnaia crashed out on lap one, Quartararo took total control of proceedings.
Photo: Monster Energy Yamaha

Top right: Lowes piled the pressure on Gardner mid-race – but then crashed out.

Top far right: Dennis Foggia's first win of the year marked another high in his roller-coaster Moto3 season.

Above right: CEV Moto2 champion Fermin Aldeguer made a debut as a substitute for injured Yan Montella.

Above far right: Dirty dozen – the Moto3 lead riders crawl all over each other.

Right: Cameron Beaubier leads Syahrin (55), Garzo (40), Canet (44) and Bendsneyder (64) on his way to eighth place.

Below right: Mid-race, Foggia leads Rodrigo (2) and Acosta.
Photos: Gold & Goose

He held a Swiss flag aloft on the podium, where understandably celebrations were muted. "Every time you go through Turn Nine [where Dupasquier had crashed], there is only one thing going through your mind: for Jason and all his family."

Zarco's attentions soon turned to defending second, no easy task with the fast-starting Oliveira, Mir and Rins on his heels. The much-improved KTM matched the Ducati on the straight, and Oliveira moved into second on lap 16, with Mir and Rins soon following suit on laps 17 and 19. But Rins's challenge came apart when he crashed at Bucine on lap 19, his fourth consecutive DNF.

Notwithstanding the stewards' ridiculous on-again/off-again decision, the podium was set. "A fantastic weekend for us. I think we were quite discreet, but strong in every session," said Oliveira after KTM's first podium of 2021.

Zarco held on to fourth, clear of Binder, who encountered a strange early problem when a bump with Marc Marquez triggered the airbag in his leathers. When this had deflated, he had to pass first Aleix Espargaro, then on lap eight, Miller, who was troubled by the gusty winds. The South African was now close to Mir, but could make no further progress and was more than a second adrift at the end.

Miller and Espargaro were not far behind; then there was a big gap to Vinales, his prospects having been ruined by starting from 13th. He'd lost three more places after a poor getaway and took until almost half-distance to work through, then pass wild-card Michele Pirro for an eventual safe, but distant eighth.

Petrucci was another six seconds away, one place clear of Rossi, for whom tenth was the best he had achieved in the season so far.

Lecuona was hounding the old master; Pol Espargaro a second adrift on the best Honda, with Pirro's Ducati right behind after running wide and losing four places with three laps left. The final points went to Alex Marquez and Savadori.

Another six seconds away came the luckless Morbidelli, another victim of Marc Marquez, who had crashed out early on lap two and send the satellite Yamaha way out wide to rejoin in a distant last place.

Nakagami also crashed out, on lap 20, after climbing from 15th on the grid to a lonely eighth.

A return to his emphatic winning ways gave Quartararo almost a race's worth of breathing space in the championship, 24 points ahead of Zarco and the rest.

MOTO2 RACE – 21 laps

Raul Fernandez was on fine form, heading free practice and qualifying, his closest challenger Lowes. They were joined on the front row for the first time in the season by Navarro, the fast corners giving his Boscoscuro chassis the chance to challenge the Kalexes.

Gardner led the second row from Di Giannantonio and class rookie Arbolino, his best of the year.

Fernandez continued his strong showing, building a lead approaching 1.5 seconds over Gardner by lap nine.

Lowes had been slow away and finished lap one fifth, behind also Navarro and Arbolino. But now he'd managed to catch Gardner, and after a frenetic exchange through Turns One, Two and Four, finally he moved ahead. This allowed Fernandez to stretch his advantage to almost two seconds, but he was starting to suffer from front tyre wear.

Lowes started to close gradually, but remorselessly. By lap 13, the deficit was under a second, and he skimmed a further two-tenths off the following time around. But his effort came apart at Arrabbiata 1 on lap 16, when he slid off for a third crash in four races.

It was left to Gardner to take up the fight. Although slightly short of his team-mate's pace early on, "I stayed calm and preserved energy, because Mugello is a physical track. I could study Raul, planned my pass and made it happen."

He'd caught up with two laps remaining. Such was his speed through Arrabbiata 2 that his race-winning overtake at Scarperia looked nonchalant. From there, he just held on as they approached the line for a first win of 2021 by 0.014 of a second.

The others were in a different race. Eight seconds back, Roberts crossed the line third, narrowly holding off Bezzecchi – the pair had been exchanging blows for most of the race. Later, the American was demoted a place for exceeding track limits on the final lap.

It was a race of attrition for a number of top runners. Augusto Fernandez had crashed out on lap one (as had Dalla Porta); Baldassarri from near the back on lap three; Navarro on lap five, having fallen to eighth after his front-row start.

Next time around, Vierge crashed out of seventh; while Di Giannantonio held on to fourth, ahead of Bezzecchi and Roberts until lap 12, when he too slipped off.

That left Schrotter to a lonely fifth, with Ogura catching and passing Arbolino for sixth.

130 ITALIAN GRAND PRIX

More than ten seconds back, after another impressive climb through the field from 25th on the grid and 18th on lap one, Beaubier headed a pack of seven, from Syahrin, Manzi, Canet, Aldeguer, Garzo and Dixon, with Bendsneyder another five seconds down for the last point.

It was an impressive GP debut for Fermin Aldeguer, who had replaced Le Mans injury victim Yari Montella in the Boscoscuro team. The defending CEV Moto2 champion, also riding for the Aspar team in MotoE, had distinguished himself in topping Q1 and had qualified 15th.

MOTO3 RACE – 20 laps

Moto3's biggest winning margin at Mugello is 0.099 of a second, but somehow pole-starter Suzuki found an extra six-tenths ahead of Acosta and Rodrigo, the first two both through from Q1. Foggia's turquoise Leopard Honda led row two from Masia and Alcoba.

Binder was down in 16th, one place ahead of Migno. The former would join the typically huge 15-rider pack at the front; the Italian became the innocent victim of a four-bike first-lap tangle that also eliminated Oncu, Kofler and Tatay. Kofler suffered a spinal fracture, Tatay a broken ankle. Earlier on the lap, Fernandez and wild-card Alberto Serra had also fallen together.

Acosta led first over the line, Foggia the next nine times; Suzuki, Binder and Fenati each had at least one turn. But it was only notional, with a jostling swarm changing places into the first corner and almost everywhere else.

Foggia's early spell was the sign, and he took the win with a fine tactical display, underlining his erratic reputation, after two DNFs, two non-scoring finishes and one second place so far in the season.

He'd led the penultimate lap, slipstreamed into the first corner by Fenati. Crucially, he put space between himself and Masia and Acosta (fourth and eighth at Turn One).

Masia followed Rodrigo in picking off Fenati at Savelli-Arrabbiata 1 and dived inside the Argentinean at Scarperia. But by then, Foggia had gained just enough space to cling on by 0.036 of a second for his second GP win, thanks to his superior top speed.

Sasaki shrugged off his qualifying spill for a remarkable fourth, ahead of Binder, Fenati and McPhee, promoted to seventh when Acosta and Garcia exceeded track limits on the final lap.

FIM WORLD CHAMPIONSHIP: ROUND 6

GRAN PREMIO OAKLEY D'ITALIA

28–30 MAY, 2021

AUTODROMO INTERNAZIONALE DEL MUGELLO
23 laps
Length: 5.245 km / 3,259 miles
Width: 14m

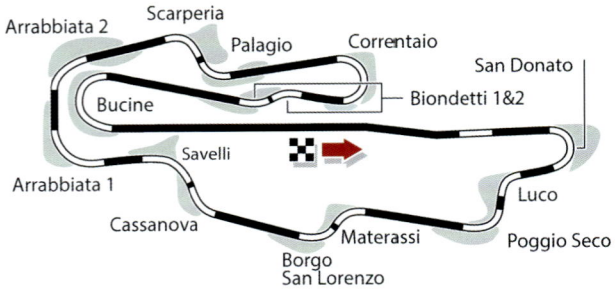

MotoGP

RACE DISTANCE: 23 laps, 74.959 miles/120.635km · RACE WEATHER: Dry (air 23°, humidity 30%, track 42°)

Pos.	Rider	Nat.	No.	Entrant	Machine	Tyres	Race tyre choice	Laps	Time & speed
1	Fabio Quartararo	FRA	20	Monster Energy Yamaha MotoGP	Yamaha YZR-M1	M	F: Medium/R: Medium	23	41m 16.344s 108.9mph/175.3km/h
2	Miguel Oliveira	POR	88	Red Bull KTM Factory Racing	KTM RC16	M	F: Hard/R: Medium	23	41m 18.936s
3	Joan Mir	SPA	36	Team SUZUKI ECSTAR	Suzuki GSX-RR	M	F: Medium/R: Medium	23	41m 19.344s
4	Johann Zarco	FRA	5	Pramac Racing	Ducati Desmosedici	M	F: Medium/R: Medium	23	41m 19.879s
5	Brad Binder	RSA	33	Red Bull KTM Factory Racing	KTM RC16	M	F: Medium/R: Medium	23	41m 21.247s
6	Jack Miller	AUS	43	Ducati Lenovo Team	Ducati Desmosedici	M	F: Medium/R: Medium	23	41m 22.577s
7	Aleix Espargaro	SPA	41	Aprilia Racing Team Gresini	Aprilia RS-GP	M	F: Hard/R: Medium	23	41m 24.374s
8	Maverick Vinales	SPA	12	Monster Energy Yamaha MotoGP	Yamaha YZR-M1	M	F: Medium/R: Medium	23	41m 33.583s
9	Danilo Petrucci	ITA	9	Tech 3 KTM Factory Racing	KTM RC16	M	F: Hard/R: Medium	23	41m 39.640s
10	Valentino Rossi	ITA	46	Petronas Yamaha SRT	Yamaha YZR-M1	M	F: Medium/R: Medium	23	41m 41.490s
11	Iker Lecuona	SPA	27	Tech 3 KTM Factory Racing	KTM RC16	M	F: Hard/R: Medium	23	41m 41.496s
12	Pol Espargaro	SPA	44	Repsol Honda Team	Honda RC213V	M	F: Medium/R: Soft	23	41m 42.403s
13	Michele Pirro	ITA	51	Pramac Racing	Ducati Desmosedici	M	F: Medium/R: Medium	23	41m 42.526s
14	Alex Marquez	SPA	73	LCR Honda CASTROL	Honda RC213V	M	F: Hard/R: Soft	23	41m 45.744s
15	Lorenzo Savadori	ITA	32	Aprilia Racing Team Gresini	Aprilia RS-GP	M	F: Medium/R: Medium	23	41m 48.722s
16	Franco Morbidelli	ITA	21	Petronas Yamaha SRT	Yamaha YZR-M1	M	F: Medium/R: Medium	23	41m 54.250s
17	Luca Marini	ITA	10	SKY VR46 Avintia	Ducati Desmosedici	M	F: Medium/R: Medium	23	42m 06.650s
	Takaaki Nakagami	JPN	30	LCR Honda IDEMITSU	Honda RC213V	M	F: Medium/R: Soft	19	DNF-crash
	Alex Rins	SPA	42	Team SUZUKI ECSTAR	Suzuki GSX-RR	M	F: Medium/R: Medium	18	DNF-crash
	Francesco Bagnaia	ITA	63	Ducati Lenovo Team	Ducati Desmosedici	M	F: Medium/R: Medium	1	DNF-crash
	Marc Marquez	SPA	93	Repsol Honda Team	Honda RC213V	M	F: Hard/R: Medium	1	DNF-crash
	Enea Bastianini	ITA	23	Avintia Esponsorama	Ducati Desmosedici	M	F: Medium/R: Medium	0	DNF-crash

Fastest lap: Johann Zarco, on lap 2, 1m 46.810s, 109.8mph/176.7km/h.
Lap record: Marc Marquez, 1m 47.639s, 109.0mph/175.4km/h (2013).
Event maximum speed: Brad Binder, 225.2mph/362.4km/h (free practice).

Qualifying

Weather: Dry
Air Temp: 25° Track Temp: 41°
Humidity: 37%

1	Quartararo	1m 45.187s
2	Bagnaia	1m 45.417s
3	Zarco	1m 45.432s
4	A. Espargaro	1m 45.538s
5	Miller	1m 45.598s
6	Binder	1m 45.743s
7	Oliveira	1m 45.745s
8	Rins	1m 45.996s
9	Mir	1m 46.076s
10	Morbidelli	1m 46.084s
11	M. Marquez	1m 46.125s
12	P. Espargaro	1m 46.393s

Q1

13	Vinales	1m 46.045s
14	Bastianini	1m 46.129s
15	Nakagami	1m 46.195s
16	Pirro	1m 46.302s
17	Marini	1m 46.481s
18	Petrucci	1m 46.548s
19	Rossi	1m 46.770s
20	Lecuona	1m 47.084s
21	Savadori	1m 47.146s
22	A. Marquez	1m 47.216s

Fastest race laps

1	Zarco	1m 46.810s
2	Quartararo	1m 46.836s
3	Oliveira	1m 46.917s
4	Binder	1m 46.993s
5	Mir	1m 47.028s
6	Rins	1m 47.104s
7	Miller	1m 47.139s
8	Nakagami	1m 47.191s
9	A. Espargaro	1m 47.331s
10	Lecuona	1m 47.443s
11	Vinales	1m 47.533s
12	Rossi	1m 47.659s
13	Petrucci	1m 47.664s
14	P. Espargaro	1m 47.741s
15	Pirro	1m 47.745s
16	Savadori	1m 47.983s
17	Morbidelli	1m 47.993s
18	A. Marquez	1m 48.056s
19	Marini	1m 48.727s

Championship Points

1	Quartararo	105
2	Zarco	81
3	Bagnaia	79
4	Miller	74
5	Mir	65
6	Vinales	64
7	A. Espargaro	44
8	Binder	35
9	Morbidelli	33
10	Oliveira	29
11	P. Espargaro	29
12	Nakagami	28
13	Rins	23
14	Petrucci	23
15	A. Marquez	20
16	Bastianini	20
17	Martin	17
18	M. Marquez	16
19	Rossi	15
20	Lecuona	13
21	Bradl	11
22	Marini	9
23	Pirro	3
24	Savadori	3
25	Rabat	1

Constructor Points

1	Yamaha	132
2	Ducati	123
3	Suzuki	69
4	KTM	58
5	Honda	47
6	Aprilia	44

Grid order

Grid order	1	2	3	4	5	6	7	8	9	10	11	12	13	14	15	16	17	18	19	20	21	22	23	
20 QUARTARARO	63	5	20	20	20	20	20	20	20	20	20	20	20	20	20	20	20	20	20	20	20	20	20	1
63 BAGNAIA	20	20	5	5	5	5	5	5	5	5	5	5	5	5	5	88	88	88	88	88	88	88	88	2
5 ZARCO	5	88	88	88	88	88	88	88	88	88	88	88	88	88	88	5	36	36	36	36	36	36	36	3
41 A. ESPARGARO	88	43	43	43	43	43	43	42	42	42	36	36	36	36	36	5	42	5	5	5	5	5	5	4
43 MILLER	43	42	42	42	36	42	42	36	36	36	42	42	42	42	42	42	5	33	33	33	33	33	33	5
33 BINDER	36	36	36	36	42	36	36	33	33	33	33	33	33	33	33	33	33	43	43	43	43	43	43	6
88 OLIVEIRA	42	41	41	41	33	33	33	43	43	43	43	43	43	43	43	43	43	41	41	41	41	41	41	7
42 RINS	33	33	33	33	41	41	41	41	41	41	41	41	41	41	41	41	41	30	12	12	12	12	12	8
36 MIR	41	30	51	51	51	51	51	30	30	30	30	30	30	30	30	30	30	12	51	9	9	9	9	9
21 MORBIDELLI	93	51	30	30	30	30	30	51	51	51	51	12	12	12	12	12	12	51	9	27	46	46	46	10
93 M. MARQUEZ	21	44	44	44	44	44	44	44	12	12	12	51	51	51	51	51	51	9	27	46	46	27	27	11
44 P. ESPARGARO	30	9	9	12	12	12	12	12	44	27	9	9	9	9	9	9	9	27	46	44	44	44	44	12
12 VINALES	51	12	12	27	27	27	27	27	9	9	27	27	27	27	27	27	27	46	44	51	51	51	51	13
23 BASTIANINI	44	27	27	9	9	9	9	9	9	44	44	44	44	44	44	44	44	44	46	44	73	73	73	73	14
30 NAKAGAMI	9	32	73	32	32	32	32	46	46	46	46	46	46	46	46	46	44	73	32	32	32	32	32	15
51 PIRRO	12	73	32	73	73	73	46	73	73	73	73	73	73	73	73	73	73	32	21	21	21	21		
10 MARINI	27	46	46	46	46	46	73	32	32	32	32	32	32	32	32	32	32	21	10	10	10	10		
9 PETRUCCI	73	10	10	10	10	10	10	21	21	21	21	21	21	21	21	21	21	10						
46 ROSSI	32	21	21	21	21	21	21	10	10	10	10	10	10	10	10	10	10							
27 LECUONA	46																							
32 SAVADORI	10																							
73 A. MARQUEZ																								

132 ITALIAN GRAND PRIX

Moto2
RACE DISTANCE: 21 laps, 68.441 miles/110.145km · RACE WEATHER: Dry (air 23°, humidity 39%, track 40°)

Pos.	Rider	Nat.	No.	Entrant	Machine	Laps	Time & Speed
1	Remy Gardner	AUS	87	Red Bull KTM Ajo	Kalex	21	39m 17.667s 104.5mph/168.1km/h
2	Raul Fernandez	SPA	25	Red Bull KTM Ajo	Kalex	21	39m 17.681s
3	Marco Bezzecchi	ITA	72	SKY Racing Team VR46	Kalex	21	39m 25.688s
4	Joe Roberts	USA	16	Italtrans Racing Team	Kalex	21	39m 25.671s
5	Marcel Schrotter	GER	23	Liqui Moly Intact GP	Kalex	21	39m 30.010s
6	Ai Ogura	JPN	79	IDEMITSU Honda Team Asia	Kalex	21	39m 40.837s
7	Tony Arbolino	ITA	14	Liqui Moly Intact GP	Kalex	21	39m 41.431s
8	Cameron Beaubier	USA	6	American Racing	Kalex	21	39m 52.492s
9	Hafizh Syahrin	MAL	55	NTS RW Racing GP	NTS	21	39m 52.516s
10	Stefano Manzi	ITA	62	Flexbox HP40	Kalex	21	39m 52.632s
11	Aron Canet	SPA	44	Kipin Energy Aspar Team	Boscoscuro	21	39m 52.917s
12	Fermin Aldeguer	SPA	54	MB Conveyors Speed Up	Boscoscuro	21	39m 52.967s
13	Hector Garzo	SPA	40	Flexbox HP40	Kalex	21	39m 53.117s
14	Jake Dixon	GBR	96	Petronas Sprinta Racing	Kalex	21	39m 53.828s
15	Bo Bendsneyder	NED	64	Pertamina Mandalika SAG Team	Kalex	21	39m 58.367s
16	Celestino Vietti	ITA	13	SKY Racing Team VR46	Kalex	21	40m 03.930s
17	Barry Baltus	BEL	70	NTS RW Racing GP	NTS	21	40m 04.070s
18	Somkiat Chantra	THA	35	IDEMITSU Honda Team Asia	Kalex	21	40m 06.233s
19	Tommaso Marcon	ITA	10	MV Agusta Forward Racing	MV Agusta	21	40m 33.880s
	Marcos Ramirez	SPA	42	American Racing	Kalex	18	DNF-crash
	Sam Lowes	GBR	22	Elf Marc VDS Racing Team	Kalex	15	DNF-crash
	Fabio Di Giannantonio	ITA	21	Federal Oil Gresini Moto2	Kalex	11	DNF-crash
	Simone Corsi	ITA	24	MV Agusta Forward Racing	MV Agusta	11	DNF-crash
	Albert Arenas	SPA	75	Kipin Energy Aspar Team	Boscoscuro	11	DNF-crash
	Xavi Vierge	SPA	97	Petronas Sprinta Racing	Kalex	5	DNF-crash
	Jorge Navarro	SPA	9	MB Conveyors Speed Up	Boscoscuro	4	DNF-crash
	Lorenzo Baldassarri	ITA	7	MV Agusta Forward Racing	MV Agusta	2	DNF-crash
	Lorenzo Dalla Porta	ITA	19	Italtrans Racing Team	Kalex	0	DNF-crash
	Augusto Fernandez	SPA	37	Elf Marc VDS Racing Team	Kalex	0	DNF-crash

Fastest lap: Sam Lowes, on lap 3, 1m 51.208s, 105.4mph/169.7km/h.
Lap record: Alex Marquez, 1m 51.881s, 104.8mph/168.7km/h (2019).
Event maximum speed: Somkiat Chantra, 169.8mph/273.2km/h (race).

Qualifying
Weather: Dry **Air:** 25° **Track:** 34° **Humidity:** 51%

1	R. Fernandez	1m 50.723s
2	Lowes	1m 50.990s
3	Navarro	1m 51.097s
4	Gardner	1m 51.306s
5	Di Giannantonio	1m 51.355s
6	Arbolino	1m 51.448s
7	Bezzecchi	1m 51.462s
8	Vierge	1m 51.497s
9	Schrotter	1m 51.504s
10	Roberts	1m 51.541s
11	Dalla Porta	1m 51.793s
12	Ogura	1m 51.884s
13	A. Fernandez	1m 51.917s
14	Ramirez	1m 52.066s
15	Aldeguer	1m 52.191s
16	Bendsneyder	1m 52.480s
17	Canet	1m 52.937s
18	Chantra	1m 53.527s

Q1
19	Garzo	1m 52.160s
20	Syahrin	1m 52.287s
21	Corsi	1m 52.303s
22	Dixon	1m 52.368s
23	Manzi	1m 52.382s
24	Bulega	1m 52.455s
25	Baldassarri	1m 52.863s
26	Beaubier	1m 53.008s
27	Vietti	1m 53.111s
28	Luthi	1m 53.130s
29	Baltus	1m 53.564s
30	Arenas	1m 54.566s
31	Marcon	1m 54.649s

Fastest race laps
1	Lowes	1m 51.208s
2	R. Fernandez	1m 51.281s
3	Gardner	1m 51.449s
4	Bezzecchi	1m 51.576s
5	Vierge	1m 51.607s
6	Di Giannantonio	1m 51.621s
7	Roberts	1m 51.698s
8	Navarro	1m 51.845s
9	Arbolino	1m 51.845s
10	Schrotter	1m 51.878s
11	Ogura	1m 52.049s
12	Ramirez	1m 52.162s
13	Chantra	1m 52.551s
14	Bendsneyder	1m 52.582s
15	Syahrin	1m 52.605s
16	Beaubier	1m 52.648s
17	Garzo	1m 52.712s
18	Corsi	1m 52.761s
19	Baldassarri	1m 52.835s
20	Manzi	1m 52.847s
21	Dixon	1m 52.911s
22	Canet	1m 52.949s
23	Aldeguer	1m 53.158s
24	Baltus	1m 53.270s
25	Vietti	1m 53.347s
26	Arenas	1m 53.416s
27	Marcon	1m 53.993s

Championship Points
	Rider	Pts
1	Gardner	114
2	R. Fernandez	108
3	Bezzecchi	88
4	Lowes	66
5	Di Giannantonio	60
6	Roberts	44
7	Schrotter	41
8	Ogura	39
9	Canet	35
10	Arbolino	27
11	Vierge	26
12	Bendsneyder	25
13	A. Fernandez	23
14	Beaubier	20
15	Navarro	19
16	Manzi	17
17	Vietti	13
18	Dixon	11
19	Garzo	11
20	Ramirez	9
21	Syahrin	8
22	Corsi	7
23	Dalla Porta	6
24	Arenas	6
25	Bulega	5
26	Chantra	4
27	Aldeguer	4
28	Baldassarri	3
29	Luthi	1

Constructor Points
1	Kalex	150
2	Boscoscuro	47
3	MV Agusta	10
4	NTS	8

Moto3
RACE DISTANCE: 20 laps, 65.182 miles/104.900km · RACE WEATHER: Dry (air 20°, humidity 41%, track 33°)

Pos.	Rider	Nat.	No.	Entrant	Machine	Laps	Time & Speed
1	Dennis Foggia	ITA	7	Leopard Racing	Honda	20	39m 37.497s 98.7mph/158.8km/h
2	Jaume Masia	SPA	5	Red Bull KTM Ajo	KTM	20	39m 37.533s
3	Gabriel Rodrigo	ARG	2	Indonesian Racing Gresini Moto3	Honda	20	39m 37.642s
4	Ayumu Sasaki	JPN	71	Red Bull KTM Tech 3	KTM	20	39m 37.737s
5	Darryn Binder	RSA	40	Petronas Sprinta Racing	Honda	20	39m 37.996s
6	Romano Fenati	ITA	55	Sterilgarda Max Racing Team	Husqvarna	20	39m 38.208s
7	John McPhee	GBR	17	Petronas Sprinta Racing	Honda	20	39m 38.415s
8	Pedro Acosta	SPA	37	Red Bull KTM Ajo	KTM	20	39m 38.242s
9	Sergio Garcia	SPA	11	Valresa GASGAS Aspar Team	GASGAS	20	39m 38.358s
10	Tatsuki Suzuki	JPN	24	SIC58 Squadra Corse	Honda	20	39m 38.460s
11	Filip Salac	CZE	12	Rivacold Snipers Team	Honda	20	39m 38.577s
12	Kaito Toba	JPN	27	CIP Green Power	KTM	20	39m 38.848s
13	Niccolo Antonelli	ITA	23	Avintia Esponsorama Moto3	KTM	20	39m 38.926s
14	Stefano Nepa	ITA	82	BOE Owlride	KTM	20	39m 41.969s
15	Jeremy Alcoba	SPA	52	Indonesian Racing Gresini Moto3	Honda	20	39m 49.988s
16	Xavier Artigas	SPA	43	Leopard Racing	Honda	20	40m 00.990s
17	Izan Guevara	SPA	28	Valresa GASGAS Aspar Team	GASGAS	20	40m 00.996s
18	Riccardo Rossi	ITA	54	BOE Owlride	KTM	20	40m 01.106s
19	Lorenzo Fellon	FRA	20	SIC58 Squadra Corse	Honda	20	40m 01.271s
20	Elia Bartolini	ITA	22	Team Bardahl VR46 Riders Academy	KTM	20	40m 17.456s
21	Andi Farid Izdihar	INA	19	Honda Team Asia	Honda	20	40m 17.520s
22	Takuma Matsuyama	JPN	32	Honda Team Asia	Honda	20	40m 17.532s
	Deniz Oncu	TUR	53	Red Bull KTM Tech 3	KTM	0	DNF-crash
	Andrea Migno	ITA	16	Rivacold Snipers Team	Honda	0	DNF-crash
	Alberto Surra	ITA	67	Team Bardahl VR46 Riders Academy	KTM	0	DNF-crash
	Adrian Fernandez	SPA	31	Sterilgarda Max Racing Team	Husqvarna	0	DNF-crash
	Carlos Tatay	SPA	99	Avintia Esponsorama Moto3	KTM	0	DNF-crash
	Maximilian Kofler	AUT	73	CIP Green Power	KTM	0	DNF-crash

Fastest lap: Sergio Garcia, on lap 2, 1m 57.188s, 100.1mph/161.1km/h.
Lap record: Fabio Di Giannantonio, 1m 56.628s, 100.5mph/161.8km/h (2018).
Event maximum speed: John McPhee, 153.5mph/247.1km/h (race).

Qualifying
Weather: Dry **Air:** 21° **Track:** 42° **Humidity:** 41%

1	Suzuki	1m 56.001s
2	Acosta	1m 56.597s
3	Rodrigo	1m 56.685s
4	Foggia	1m 56.980s
5	Masia	1m 56.985s
6	Alcoba	1m 57.107s
7	Fenati	1m 57.110s
8	Antonelli	1m 57.137s
9	McPhee	1m 57.152s
10	Sasaki	1m 57.206s
11	Dupasquier	1m 57.213s
12	Toba	1m 57.298s
13	Oncu	1m 57.574s
14	Nepa	1m 57.776s
15	Garcia	1m 58.456s
16	Binder	1m 58.472s
17	Migno	2m 01.176s
18	Salac	2m 01.325s

Q1
19	Surra	1m 57.698s
20	Artigas	1m 57.794s
21	Rossi	1m 57.832s
22	Izdihar	1m 57.964s
23	Bartolini	1m 57.977s
24	Fellon	1m 58.138s
25	Yamanaka	1m 58.280s
26	Fernandez	1m 58.290s
27	Tatay	1m 58.452s
28	Kofler	1m 59.219s
29	Guevara	2m 00.834s
	Matsuyama	No Time

Fastest race laps
1	Garcia	1m 57.188s
2	Toba	1m 57.342s
3	Artigas	1m 57.353s
4	Nepa	1m 57.405s
5	Masia	1m 57.490s
6	Salac	1m 57.563s
7	Rodrigo	1m 57.580s
8	Fenati	1m 57.605s
9	McPhee	1m 57.627s
10	Antonelli	1m 57.677s
11	Suzuki	1m 57.686s
12	Sasaki	1m 57.708s
13	Binder	1m 57.712s
14	Alcoba	1m 57.727s
15	Foggia	1m 57.766s
16	Acosta	1m 57.771s
17	Guevara	1m 58.469s
18	Fellon	1m 58.489s
19	Rossi	1m 58.506s
20	Izdihar	1m 59.369s
21	Matsuyama	1m 59.374s
22	Bartolini	1m 59.395s

Championship Points
	Rider	Pts
1	Acosta	111
2	Masia	59
3	Sasaki	57
4	Garcia	56
5	Fenati	56
6	Binder	47
7	Migno	47
8	Antonelli	47
9	Foggia	45
10	Rodrigo	41
11	Salac	35
12	Dupasquier	27
13	Guevara	26
14	Yamanaka	26
15	McPhee	22
16	Toba	22
17	Alcoba	19
18	Suzuki	18
19	Rossi	16
20	Artigas	16
21	Tatay	14
22	Fernandez	10
23	Oncu	8
24	Nepa	8
25	Kunii	3
26	Kofler	3
27	Izdihar	1

Constructor Points
1	KTM	136
2	Honda	117
3	GASGAS	68
4	Husqvarna	60

ITALIAN GRAND PRIX

FIM WORLD CHAMPIONSHIP · ROUND 7
CATALAN GRAND PRIX
BARCELONA-CATALUNYA CIRCUIT

MEO
SHARK
GIVES YOU WINGS
HYUNDAI
ENEOS
20
MONSTER
KTM
88
KTM

Above: 'Zipgate'. Quartararo's leathers are open to the waist as Miller follows closely.
Photo: Monster Energy Yamaha

Top right: Reasons to be cheerful? Rins's thumbs-up was the limit of his involvement, after his careless cycling accident.
Photo: Gold & Goose

Above right: Maverick Vinales's crew-chief switch improved neither his results nor his mood.
Photo: Monster Energy Yamaha

Right: Fans were back in the stands. At least some of them were.

Below right: Mir holds off Vinales on his way to fifth. Both would be promoted one place.
Photo: www.suzuki-racing.com

Opening spread: Modern MotoGP – close and noisy. Oliveira heads Quartararo, Zarco (hidden), Mir, Miller and the pursuit.
Photo: Gold & Goose

FROM tragedy in Italy to comedy in Catalonia, the circus continued. The jester was championship leader Fabio Quartararo, in sensational form at his favourite circuit, with a fifth consecutive pole. It all came undone, literally, in the final five laps. For reasons still unclear, he either unzipped his leathers or (less plausibly) the zip spontaneously undid itself, then flung away his chest protector at racing speed. Seemingly, it had worked its way up his chest, becoming uncomfortable and restricting his breathing, though he never confirmed this.

Struggling to reclothe himself, which he didn't manage until the slow-down lap, he ceded victory to Miguel Oliveira's reborn KTM before dropping further.

The farcical nature of the situation was compounded first by the rider's reluctance to provide any explanation (obliging Alpinestars to mount a full investigation, which confirmed no malfunction of their zip), and secondly by controversy surrounding Race Direction's response to a clear breach of the rules. Protective clothing "must be worn, correctly fastened, at all times during on-track activity". Race rivals Jack Miller and Pecco Bagnaia were backed by Casey Stoner in saying that Quartararo should have been black-flagged. Race director Mike Webb explained that they'd run out of time to act during the race, but that a retrospective three-second penalty reflected the time the stewards judged he would have lost, had he slowed to refasten his zip. The disparity between the two punishments prompted yet more heated debate.

It also overshadowed Oliveira's calm and confident first win of the year. Twenty-five points were fair compensation.

The track had been reprofiled again at Turn Ten, scene of many crashes, upping the speed and easing the braking at the end of the back straight. It also flowed better with the second apex and was universally liked.

KTM were in the news for contracts. Firstly, they'd extended Brad Binder's by an extra three years until the end of 2024, mirroring Honda's unusual arrangement with Marc Marquez. This reward, after against-the-odds finishes at Doha and Portimao in 2021, and 2020's first MotoGP win, reinforced the company's unique riders' ladder through the classes. Binder had won the Moto3 title in 2016 on a KTM and had been strong in Moto2. Said director Pit Beirer: "Sometimes, you find a racer with a mentality that really fits with your own philosophy, and the fact that Brad has come all the way to the top with us in a ten-year period is a very special story."

There was more, with confirmation that current Moto2 leader Remy Gardner would step up from the factory-backed Ajo team to MotoGP in 2022, with the Tech3 satellite squad. This latest son of a champion (his racing number '87' reflects the year Wayne won the 500 title) had matured a lot since his 2016 Moto2 debut, said Tech3 boss Herve Poncharal: "He's a much better rider, but also a much more stable person."

Warning signs at Yamaha, after Vinales's Mugello indignities. Long-term ally and crew chief Esteban Garcia brought in by Maverick midway through 2019, was abruptly replaced by veteran Silvano Galbusera, ex-Rossi and ex-test team. Yamaha's reasoning was not entirely clear, but the rider's erratic performance would not improve, and his relationship with the team even less so.

"Basically, from three or four races ago, I wasn't feeling good, I didn't feel the maximum potential. Sometimes it was difficult to find a good setting, a good balance, and for the last four races, I've been very fast n FP1 and then gone backwards all weekend," Vinales said. Hence this radical "new strategy". Worse was to follow, as his season continued to unravel.

At Suzuki, defending champion Joan Mir issued a rallying cry to improve the one-lap performance of his GSX-RR – he was on the fourth row of the grid again and had not qualified better than ninth all year. "I think that we can push a bit more [to develop the bike], honestly. A lot of manufacturers improved and we didn't," he said. "We have a good base, but I have the same bike as last year. I'm two-tenths faster than last year in qualifying, and I was eighth. Now I'm tenth. We need to have more material and test more things to improve."

At least he was racing. Team-mate Rins had already compounded his dire early season with an embarrassing and costly freak accident. Cycling the track on Thursday, he was using both hands to send a message on his smartphone. Thus distracted, he hit a service van parked on the outside of Turn One. Apart from a bang on the head, he landed heavily enough on his right wrist to fracture the radius bone, requiring screw-fix surgery at the conveniently nearby Dexeus University Hospital.

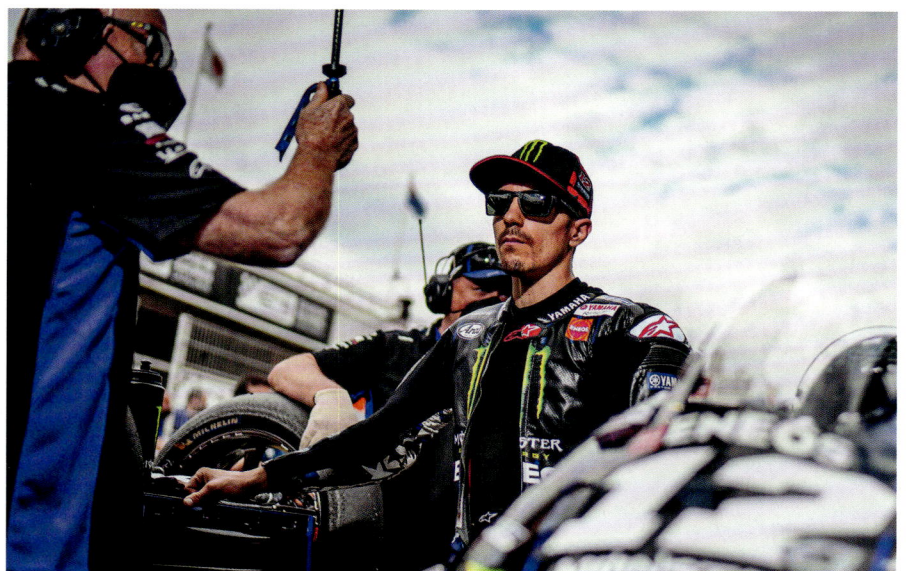

Marc Marquez laid on a second successive qualifying cameo, picking a rider to follow. At Mugello, he'd discombobulated Vinales. This time, he picked Miller, and as he prepared to tuck in behind, the Australian twiddled thumb and fingers to say, "How much will you pay?" It was a reference, Marquez revealed, to a joking conversation they'd had the previous day. "I said, 'Later, later, we will speak about it.'" This time, Marquez didn't make it out of Q2, but Miller did, and he remained good humoured: "If you go out there thinking only about the guy behind you, you've already lost."

It was another miserable weekend for Honda. Only Pol Espargaro managed to scrape into Q2; he and Marc Marquez crashed out of the race when riding over the limit. The LCR riders were at the bottom of the points. The problem was a chronic lack of rear grip, affecting corner entry and exit, said Marquez: "In acceleration, we cannot get the grip, and in the entry, we cannot stop the bike ... two different problems, in two different areas, but I think the solution is going in the same way. So we are braking late, and when you're braking with a lot of banking, these things happen. Like me and Pol today." All the same, risking a lot to fight among the top six had been "for me, the best seven laps of the year. I was riding like I want. Today was the day to take a risk, because just burning fuel and tyres riding for P12, P14 is not me."

MOTOGP RACE – 24 laps

Quartararo's fifth straight pole came with a new all-time lap record, but times were close, the top ten riders inside just over half a second, and Miller less than four-hundredths away. Zarco was alongside; Oliveira led row two from Morbidelli and Vinales. With Mir tenth, Rossi (for once straight into Q2) was 11th, and Pol Espargaro 12th, after crashing early in the session.

It took only two laps to show that this would be no Quartararo walkover. Miller and Oliveira got the jump, with the Frenchman third at Turn One, leading fast-away Mir and Aleix Espargaro. Then a mistake at Turn Seven allowed the pair through, with Zarco also breezing by on the straight to put the Yamaha sixth.

Quartararo rallied, soon past Zarco again. A mistake by Miller on lap seven dropped the Australian to fourth. On the same lap, Quartararo dived under Mir brilliantly at Turn Three. Only Oliveira was ahead.

Tyre degradation was critical with the long corners, and as a result, each of the leaders showed restraint early on, bunching the group together, so it was as well Quartararo had jumped back up the order. At times, it was chaotic behind. Marquez displayed glimmers of brilliance as he rose from 13th on the grid to join the leading train, picking off Vinales and Binder on lap three, Zarco on lap four to hint at a season-best result. Yet the Honda's limitations didn't take long to materialise, as he crashed out on lap eight. Teammate Espargaro had already fallen on lap five.

Marquez's battling allowed the lead quartet to break clear, and now Quartararo began working on Oliveira's lead. By lap 12, he was with the Portuguese rider, dipping in front with an expertly executed move at Turn Five. The trouble was that Mir, Miller and the recovering Zarco had come with him. Vinales, Bagnaia and Binder made up the second group, while Aleix Espargaro's Aprilia joined Marquez in the Turn Ten gravel on lap 11.

Oliveira was more than comfortable behind. "When he overtook me, I saw my chance to stay with him and maybe disturb him a little bit," recalled the Portuguese rider. He did more than that, confidently retaking the lead on lap 14.

Two laps later, Mir was struggling with worsening wheel-

Above: Zarco outpaced Miller to take second.

Top right: Gardner leads team-mate Fernandez to a third consecutive Red Bull KTM 1-2 finish.

Above right: Rossi's season continued to decline, after his second crash and fourth occasion lacking points in seven races.

Centre right: Winning riders Gardner and Garcia sported special T-shirts in memory of Jason Dupasquier.

Below right: A frenzied and controversial Moto3 race finally went to Garcia (11), then Alcoba (52), with Oncu (hidden) third. Masia (5) was next past the flag, then Binder (40), Rodrigo (2) and Acosta.

Photos: Gold & Goose

spin, lamenting his last-minute tyre decision of the medium front and rear (all those ahead had the hard rear). Zarco and Miller got by with the minimum of fuss, and the champion's attentions turned to fending off Vinales.

A grandstand finale was on the cards, with Oliveira and Quartararo covered by two-tenths after 20 laps. Then came controversy. Suddenly, Oliveira had more than nine-tenths in hand, while in a bizarre twist replays showed Quartararo with leathers open to the waist, throwing away his chest protector on the inside of Turn Three. "I just know that I had the leathers completely opened in the first corner, I think five laps to go, and I just tried to put [the zip] in a normal position again," he said. "I couldn't do it."

It got worse, as Zarco closed in and blew by on the straight with three laps left. Quartararo tried to fight back into Turn One, but ran wide, rejoining just behind the Ducati. He should have dropped one place, and the error earned a three-second penalty. Zarco, meanwhile, was closing on Oliveira, less than two-tenths adrift over the line.

Miller knew that he didn't need to pass Quartararo – the obvious penalty meant that he could be just behind for a podium return.

But there was more to come for the Frenchman. After much deliberation, a further three-second penalty for 'Zipgate' dropped him to sixth, behind Mir and Vinales.

A relatively sedate Bagnaia was seventh, after a tussle with Binder, a couple of tenths away; Morbidelli was out of touch behind.

Bastianini filled the top ten; satellite Honda riders Marquez and Nakagami sandwiched Marini in 11th and 13th. The Japanese had dropped to last with a long-lap penalty after a short cut, but came through to narrowly hold off Martin, who had recovered from a sighting-lap tumble for 14th. Savadori was 15th and last finisher.

Petrucci was an early faller; team-mate Lecuona tumbled from the top ten on lap 17. One lap earlier, Rossi had also crashed out, having dropped to 16th after a bad first lap, and up to 13th mainly because of falls ahead of him.

The penalties cut Quartararo's championship lead over Zarco to just 14 points.

MOTO2 RACE – 22 laps

A repeat performance from the Ajo Red Bull team. Fresh from his first win of the season, Gardner exuded confidence all weekend. Rookie team-mate Raul Fernandez shadowed him all the way.

The pair had led practice, Bendsreyder joining them on row one, ahead of Augusto Fernandez, Di Giannantonio and Vierge. Ogura led row three from Lowes; Bezzecchi the fourth. Canet and Navarro were the first non-Kalex chassis, 11th and 12th on the Boscoscuros.

Gardner led away and stayed in front from the first lap to the tenth. But he was unable to shake off his young team-mate, who finally outbraked him at the end of the straight 12 laps in.

Gardner didn't flinch: "In the beginning, I'd tried to break away, but I didn't want to burn up the rear, just being smooth. Raul came by, made a push, and I thought, 'Okay, I'll follow you.' I knew I had more in me and I had half the race to study him."

The attack came at Turn One with three laps to go, and from there Fernandez had no response. Gardner's second win in as many races was by almost two seconds.

Bendsneyder held third for the first 15 laps, but Vierge was never far away, and Bezzecchi also in the running. Vierge expertly picked off the Dutchman on lap 16, with Bezzecchi following him through a lap later.

Vierge managed to get marginally clear for his first podium since 2018.

Bezzecchi was left heading a close and hectic group of six, although the order didn't alter over the last five laps. The only change came when Ogura crashed out of seventh on the 20th lap. Augusto Fernandez was fifth (it was his Marc VDS team's 200th start), then Bendsneyder and Lowes. Third to seventh were over the line in just two seconds.

The next gang were another ten seconds away as the laps ticked down, second VDS rider Garzo holding Di Giannantonio at bay at the front of it. The pair tangled and fell on lap 20, leaving a safe eighth for long-term shadow Schrotter. Less than two seconds behind, Thai rider Chantra, who had

FIM WORLD CHAMPIONSHIP

qualified ninth, finished in the same position, equalling his career best.

Roberts narrowly held off Navarro to the flag; a couple of seconds back, rookies Arenas, Arbolino and Vietti finished ahead of veteran Luthi, taking the last point by seven-tenths from fellow old-timer Corsi.

Canet was an early faller from seventh. Ramirez and Dalla Porta also crashed out. Dixon's difficult season continued, with zero points for 18th.

Gardner extended his championship lead to 11 points over Fernandez, with Bezzecchi another 27 behind.

MOTO3 RACE – 21 laps

Tactics versus risk: the debate was ramped up at Catalunya and the Moto3 riders hauled up before Race Direction for a severe talking to.

The main villain was second-placed Alcoba, widely condemned for sitting up through the penultimate turn on the penultimate lap, refusing to lead on to the straight. Or was it another of the 15 riders who bunched up behind him, crossing the line to start the last lap inside seven-tenths of a second? Or even the nature of Moto3, where rules designed to make all machines as equal as possible had led to these massive ultra-close groups, ducking and weaving with frightening intensity?

The early laps had been bad enough: eight different leaders over the line, seldom still in front by the first corner, and one of them – McPhee – tumbling under the wheels of the followers, taking Migno and Suzuki down with him.

On the last lap, first Sasaki high-sided out of Turn Seven, taking Leopard Honda team-mates Foggia and Artigas down, breaking the pack apart and bringing out a red flag. Then rookie Guevara crashed at Turn Ten, narrowly avoiding a host of other riders.

Up front, Garcia just held off Alcoba by 0.015 of a second, for his second win in three races.

Masia crossed the line third, but was demoted a place for exceeding track limits on the final lap, putting Oncu on to a first podium. Binder, Rodrigo, Acosta, Antonelli, Toba and Nepa made up a top ten covered by 0.9 of a second; Fenati was a little behind in 11th. The remaining results were taken from the previous lap, because riders had not passed the red flag when it was first shown.

Complicated, thrilling, but uncomfortable viewing.

FIM WORLD CHAMPIONSHIP: ROUND 7

GRAN PREMI MONSTER ENERGY DE CATALUNYA

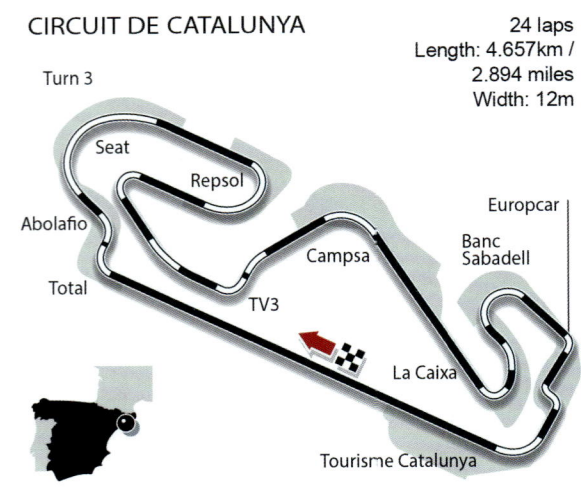

4-6 JUNE, 2021

CIRCUIT DE CATALUNYA
24 laps
Length: 4.657km / 2.894 miles
Width: 12m

MotoGP

RACE DISTANCE: 24 laps, 69.449 miles/111.768km · RACE WEATHER: Dry (air 25°, humidity 54%, track 41°)

Pos.	Rider	Nat.	No.	Entrant	Machine	Tyres	Race tyre choice	Laps	Time & speed
1	Miguel Oliveira	POR	88	Red Bull KTM Factory Racing	KTM RC16	M	F: Hard/R: Hard	24	40m 21.749s / 103.2mph / 166.1km/h
2	Johann Zarco	FRA	5	Pramac Racing	Ducati Desmosedici	M	F: Medium/R: Hard	24	40m 21.924s
3	Jack Miller	AUS	43	Ducati Lenovo Team	Ducati Desmosedici	M	F: Medium/R: Hard	24	40m 23.739s
4	Joan Mir	SPA	36	Team SUZUKI ECSTAR	Suzuki GSX-RR	M	F: Medium/R: Medium	24	40m 27.074s
5	Maverick Vinales	SPA	12	Monster Energy Yamaha MotoGP	Yamaha YZR-M1	M	F: Medium/R: Medium	24	40m 28.030s
6	Fabio Quartararo	FRA	20	Monster Energy Yamaha MotoGP	Yamaha YZR-M1	M	F: Medium/R: Hard	24	40m 29.564s
7	Francesco Bagnaia	ITA	63	Ducati Lenovo Team	Ducati Desmosedici	M	F: Medium/R: Medium	24	40m 29.924s
8	Brad Binder	RSA	33	Red Bull KTM Factory Racing	KTM RC16	M	F: Hard/R: Hard	24	40m 30.127s
9	Franco Morbidelli	ITA	21	Petronas Yamaha SRT	Yamaha YZR-M1	M	F: Medium/R: Medium	24	40m 37.401s
10	Enea Bastianini	ITA	23	Avintia Esponsorama	Ducati Desmosedici	M	F: Medium/R: Medium	24	40m 41.046s
11	Alex Marquez	SPA	73	LCR Honda CASTROL	Honda RC213V	M	F: Medium/R: Soft	24	40m 43.399s
12	Luca Marini	ITA	10	SKY VR46 Avintia	Ducati Desmosedici	M	F: Medium/R: Medium	24	40m 44.282s
13	Takaaki Nakagami	JPN	30	LCR Honda IDEMITSU	Honda RC213V	M	F: Hard/R: Medium	24	40m 49.582s
14	Jorge Martin	SPA	89	Pramac Racing	Ducati Desmosedici	M	F: Medium/R: Hard	24	40m 50.824s
15	Lorenzo Savadori	ITA	32	Aprilia Racing Team Gresini	Aprilia RS-GP	M	F: Medium/R: Medium	24	41m 02.040s
	Iker Lecuona	SPA	27	Tech 3 KTM Factory Racing	KTM RC16	M	F: Medium/R: Hard	16	DNF-crash
	Valentino Rossi	ITA	46	Petronas Yamaha SRT	Yamaha YZR-M1	M	F: Medium/R: Hard	15	DNF-crash
	Aleix Espargaro	SPA	41	Aprilia Racing Team Gresini	Aprilia RS-GP	M	F: Medium/R: Soft	10	DNF-crash
	Marc Marquez	SPA	93	Repsol Honda Team	Honda RC213V	M	F: Hard/R: Medium	7	DNF-crash
	Danilo Petrucci	ITA	9	Tech 3 KTM Factory Racing	KTM RC16	M	F: Hard/R: Hard	5	DNF-crash
	Pol Espargaro	SPA	44	Repsol Honda Team	Honda RC213V	M	F: Medium/R: Medium	4	DNF-crash

Fastest lap: Johann Zarco, on lap 8, 1m 39.939s, 104.2mph/167.7km/h.
Lap record: New layout.
Event maximum speed: Jack Miller, 220.7mph/355.2km/h (free practice).

Qualifying

Weather: Dry
Air Temp: 25° Track Temp: 40°
Humidity: 55%

1	Quartararo	1m 38.853s
2	Miller	1m 38.890s
3	Zarco	1m 39.049s
4	Oliveira	1m 39.099s
5	Morbidelli	1m 39.109s
6	Vinales	1m 39.157s
7	A. Espargaro	1m 39.218s
8	Binder	1m 39.343s
9	Bagnaia	1m 39.359s
10	Mir	1m 39.431s
11	Rossi	1m 39.605s
12	P. Espargaro	1m 41.791s

Q1

13	M. Marquez	1m 39.181s
14	Nakagami	1m 39.347s
15	Martin	1m 39.532s
16	Lecuona	1m 39.567s
17	Bastianini	1m 39.590s
18	Petrucci	1m 39.744s
19	Marini	1m 39.942s
20	A. Marquez	1m 40.009s
21	Savadori	1m 40.158s

Fastest race laps

1	Zarco	1m 39.939s
2	Quartararo	1m 40.109s
3	Oliveira	1m 40.204s
4	Mir	1m 40.228s
5	A. Espargaro	1m 40.234s
6	Vinales	1m 40.247s
7	Miller	1m 40.306s
8	M. Marquez	1m 40.379s
9	Binder	1m 40.406s
10	Bagnaia	1m 40.502s
11	Lecuona	1m 40.635s
12	Nakagami	1m 40.637s
13	P. Espargaro	1m 40.660s
14	Morbidelli	1m 40.702s
15	Bastianini	1m 40.831s
16	Rossi	1m 40.841s
17	A. Marquez	1m 40.896s
18	Martin	1m 40.926s
19	Savadori	1m 41.016s
20	Marini	1m 41.033s
21	Petrucci	1m 41.126s

Championship Points

1	Quartararo	115
2	Zarco	101
3	Miller	90
4	Bagnaia	88
5	Mir	78
6	Vinales	75
7	Oliveira	54
8	A. Espargaro	44
9	Binder	43
10	Morbidelli	40
11	Nakagami	31
12	P. Espargaro	29
13	Bastianini	26
14	A. Marquez	25
15	Rins	23
16	Petrucci	23
17	Martin	19
18	M. Marquez	16
19	Rossi	15
20	Lecuona	13
21	Marini	13
22	Bradl	11
23	Savadori	4
24	Pirro	3
25	Rabat	1

Constructor Points

1	Yamaha	143
2	Ducati	143
3	KTM	83
4	Suzuki	82
5	Honda	52
6	Aprilia	45

Grid order / Lap-by-lap

Grid	Rider	1	2	3	4	5	6	7	8	9	10	11	12	13	14	15	16	17	18	19	20	21	22	23	24
20	QUARTARARO	43	88	88	88	88	88	88	88	88	88	88	20	20	88	88	88	88	88	88	88	88	88	88	88
43	MILLER	88	43	43	43	43	36	20	20	20	20	20	88	88	20	20	20	20	20	20	20	5	5	5	
5	ZARCO	20	36	41	41	36	20	36	36	36	36	36	36	36	36	36	5	5	5	5	5	20	20	20	
88	OLIVEIRA	36	41	36	36	20	43	43	43	43	43	43	43	43	5	5	43	43	43	43	43	43	43	43	
21	MORBIDELLI	41	20	20	20	41	5	5	5	5	5	5	5	5	43	43	36	36	36	36	36	36	36	36	
12	VINALES	5	5	5	93	93	41	41	41	41	41	12	12	12	12	12	12	12	12	12	12	12	12	12	
41	A. ESPARGARO	12	12	93	5	5	93	93	12	12	12	33	63	63	63	63	63	63	63	63	33	33	63	63	
33	BINDER	33	33	12	12	12	12	12	33	33	33	63	33	33	33	33	33	33	33	33	63	63	33	33	
63	BAGNAIA	93	93	63	33	33	33	63	63	63	27	27	27	27	27	21	21	21	21	21	21	21	21	21	
36	MIR	21	63	33	63	63	63	27	27	27	21	21	21	21	21	23	23	23	23	23	23	23	23	23	
46	ROSSI	27	44	27	44	27	27	21	21	21	23	23	23	23	23	73	73	73	73	73	73	73	73	73	
44	P. ESPARGARO	63	27	44	27	21	21	30	30	23	73	73	73	73	73	10	10	10	10	10	10	10	10	10	
93	M. MARQUEZ	44	30	30	30	30	30	23	23	73	46	46	46	46	46	30	30	30	30	30	30	30	30	30	
30	NAKAGAMI	73	21	21	21	23	23	23	73	73	46	10	10	10	10	30	89	89	89	89	89	89	89	89	
89	MARTIN	30	23	23	23	73	73	73	46	46	30	32	89	89	89	89	32	32	32	32	32	32	32	32	
27	LECUONA	46	73	46	73	9	46	46	10	10	32	89	89	32	32	32	10								
23	BASTIANINI	23	46	73	46	46	10	10	32	32	89	30	30	30	30										
9	PETRUCCI	9	9	9	9	10	32	32	89	89	89														
10	MARINI	89	10	10	10	32	89	89																	
73	A. MARQUEZ	10	32	32	32	89																			
32	SAVADORI	32	89	89	89																				

140 CATALUNYA GRAND PRIX

Moto2

RACE DISTANCE: 22 laps, 63.662 miles/102.454km · **RACE WEATHER:** Dry (air 28°, humidity 42%, track 44°)

Pos.	Rider	Nat.	No.	Entrant	Machine	Laps	Time & Speed
1	Remy Gardner	AUS	87	Red Bull KTM Ajo	Kalex	22	38m 22.284s 99.5mph/160.2km/h
2	Raul Fernandez	SPA	25	Red Bull KTM Ajo	Kalex	22	38m 24.156s
3	Xavi Vierge	SPA	97	Petronas Sprinta Racing	Kalex	22	38m 25.150s
4	Marco Bezzecchi	ITA	72	SKY Racing Team VR46	Kalex	22	38m 25.491s
5	Augusto Fernandez	SPA	37	Elf Marc VDS Racing Team	Kalex	22	38m 26.183s
6	Bo Bendsneyder	NED	64	Pertamina Mandalika SAG Team	Kalex	22	38m 26.825s
7	Sam Lowes	GBR	22	Elf Marc VDS Racing Team	Kalex	22	38m 27.159s
8	Marcel Schrotter	GER	23	Liqui Moly Intact GP	Kalex	22	38m 38.257s
9	Somkiat Chantra	THA	35	IDEMITSU Honda Team Asia	Kalex	22	38m 39.799s
10	Joe Roberts	USA	16	Italtrans Racing Team	Kalex	22	38m 42.122s
11	Jorge Navarro	SPA	9	MB Conveyors Speed Up	Boscoscuro	22	38m 42.855s
12	Albert Arenas	SPA	75	Inde Aspar Team	Boscoscuro	22	38m 44.796s
13	Tony Arbolino	ITA	14	Liqui Moly Intact GP	Kalex	22	38m 44.842s
14	Celestino Vietti	ITA	13	SKY Racing Team VR46	Kalex	22	38m 45.522s
15	Thomas Luthi	SWI	12	Pertamina Mandalika SAG Team	Kalex	22	38m 46.242s
16	Simone Corsi	ITA	24	MV Agusta Forward Racing	MV Agusta	22	38m 47.383s
17	Nicolo Bulega	ITA	11	Federal Oil Gresini Moto2	Kalex	22	38m 53.628s
18	Jake Dixon	GBR	96	Petronas Sprinta Racing	Kalex	22	38m 59.413s
19	Cameron Beaubier	USA	6	American Racing	Kalex	22	39m 00.179s
20	Hafizh Syahrin	MAL	55	NTS RW Racing GP	NTS	22	39m 00.722s
21	Alonso Lopez	SPA	2	MB Conveyors Speed Up	Boscoscuro	22	39m 02.531s
22	Barry Baltus	BEL	70	NTS RW Racing GP	NTS	22	39m 02.958s
23	Lorenzo Baldassarri	ITA	7	MV Agusta Forward Racing	MV Agusta	22	39m 03.068s
24	Stefano Manzi	ITA	62	Flexbox HP40	Kalex	22	39m 10.872s
25	Piotr Biesiekirski	POL	74	Pertamina Mandalika SAG Euvic	Kalex	22	39m 11.924s
26	Keminth Kubo	THA	81	VR46 Master Camp Team	Kalex	22	39m 11.978s
	Hector Garzo	SPA	40	Flexbox HP40	Kalex	20	DNF-crash
	Fabio Di Giannantonio	ITA	21	Federal Oil Gresini Moto2	Kalex	20	DNF-crash
	Ai Ogura	JPN	79	IDEMITSU Honda Team Asia	Kalex	19	DNF-crash
	Lorenzo Dalla Porta	ITA	19	Italtrans Racing Team	Kalex	18	DNF-crash
	Marcos Ramirez	SPA	42	American Racing	Kalex	7	DNF-crash
	Aron Canet	SPA	44	Inde Aspar Team	Boscoscuro	6	DNF-crash

Fastest lap: Raul Fernandez, on lap 2, 1m 43.757s, 100.4mph/161.5km/h.
Lap record: New layout.
Event maximum speed: Marcos Ramirez, 185.4mph/298.3km/h (free practice).

Qualifying
Weather: Dry
Air: 25° **Track:** 40°
Humidity: 51%

1	Gardner	1m 42.977s
2	R. Fernandez	1m 43.135s
3	Bendsneyder	1m 43.400s
4	A. Fernandez	1m 43.501s
5	Di Giannantonio	1m 43.566s
6	Vierge	1m 43.567s
7	Ogura	1m 43.609s
8	Lowes	1m 43.693s
9	Chantra	1m 43.716s
10	Bezzecchi	1m 43.738s
11	Canet	1m 43.774s
12	Navarro	1m 43.904s
13	Schrotter	1m 44.031s
14	Arbolino	1m 44.063s
15	Dalla Porta	1m 44.102s
16	Bulega	1m 44.158s
17	Roberts	1m 44.346s
18	Ramirez	1m 44.498s
Q1		
19	Garzo	1m 43.926s
20	Syahrin	1m 43.934s
21	Arenas	1m 44.055s
22	Corsi	1m 44.076s
23	Luthi	1m 44.098s
24	Baldassarri	1m 44.321s
25	Vietti	1m 44.335s
26	Baltus	1m 44.409s
27	Manzi	1m 44.528s
28	Beaubier	1m 44.720s
29	Lopez	1m 45.463s
30	Kubo	1m 45.535s
31	Biesiekirski	1m 45.914s
32	Dixon	1m 50.609s

Fastest race laps

1	R. Fernandez	1m 43.757s
2	Gardner	1m 43.870s
3	Bendsneyder	1m 43.914s
4	Vierge	1m 44.009s
5	Bezzecchi	1m 44.122s
6	Lowes	1m 44.249s
7	A. Fernandez	1m 44.279s
8	Canet	1m 44.313s
9	Ogura	1m 44.340s
10	Garzo	1m 44.452s
11	Di Giannantonio	1m 44.575s
12	Navarro	1m 44.763s
13	Arbolino	1m 44.775s
14	Arenas	1m 44.789s
15	Schrotter	1m 44.792s
16	Dalla Porta	1m 44.833s
17	Chantra	1m 44.951s
18	Ramirez	1m 44.995s
19	Roberts	1m 44.999s
20	Luthi	1m 45.009s
21	Vietti	1m 45.045s
22	Corsi	1m 45.112s
23	Bulega	1m 45.255s
24	Syahrin	1m 45.260s
25	Dixon	1m 45.432s
26	Beaubier	1m 45.463s
27	Lopez	1m 45.548s
28	Baltus	1m 45.561s
29	Baldassarri	1m 45.563s
30	Kubo	1m 45.925s
31	Manzi	1m 45.966s
32	Biesiekirski	1m 46.122s

Championship Points

1	Gardner	139
2	R. Fernandez	128
3	Bezzecchi	101
4	Lowes	75
5	Di Giannantonio	60
6	Roberts	50
7	Schrotter	49
8	Vierge	42
9	Ogura	39
10	Canet	35
11	Bendsneyder	35
12	A. Fernandez	34
13	Arbolino	30
14	Navarro	24
15	Beaubier	20
16	Manzi	17
17	Vietti	15
18	Dixon	11
19	Garzo	11
20	Chantra	11
21	Arenas	10
22	Ramirez	9
23	Syahrin	8
24	Corsi	7
25	Dalla Porta	6
26	Bulega	5
27	Aldeguer	4
28	Baldassarri	3
29	Luthi	2

Constructor Points

1	Kalex	175
2	Boscoscuro	52
3	MV Agusta	10
4	NTS	8

Moto3

RACE DISTANCE: 21 laps, 60.768 miles/97.797km · **RACE WEATHER:** Dry (air 25°, humidity 53%, track 39°)

Pos.	Rider	Nat.	No.	Entrant	Machine	Laps	Time & Speed
1	Sergio Garcia	SPA	11	Solunion GASGAS Aspar Team	GASGAS	21	38m 33.760s 94.5mph/152.1km/h
2	Jeremy Alcoba	SPA	52	Indonesian Racing Gresini Moto3	Honda	21	38m 33.775s
3	Deniz Oncu	TUR	53	Red Bull KTM Tech 3	KTM	21	38m 33.878s
4	Jaume Masia	SPA	5	Red Bull KTM Ajo	KTM	21	38m 33.839s
5	Darryn Binder	RSA	40	Petronas Sprinta Racing	Honda	21	38m 33.964s
6	Gabriel Rodrigo	ARG	2	Indonesian Racing Gresini Moto3	Honda	21	38m 34.077s
7	Pedro Acosta	SPA	37	Red Bull KTM Ajo	KTM	21	38m 34.140s
8	Niccolo Antonelli	ITA	23	Avintia Esponsorama Moto3	KTM	21	38m 34.558s
9	Kaito Toba	JPN	27	CIP Green Power	KTM	21	38m 34.693s
10	Stefano Nepa	ITA	82	BOE Owlride	KTM	21	38m 34.743s
11	Romano Fenati	ITA	55	Sterilgarda Max Racing Team	Husqvarna	21	38m 37.094s
12	Yuki Kunii	JPN	92	Honda Team Asia	Honda	20	36m 56.601s
13	Elia Bartolini	ITA	22	Avintia Esponsorama Moto3	KTM	20	36m 56.644s
14	Ryusei Yamanaka	JPN	6	CarXpert PruestelGP	KTM	20	36m 56.850s
15	Daniel Holgado	SPA	96	CIP Green Power	KTM	20	36m 57.173s
16	Lorenzo Fellon	FRA	20	SIC58 Squadra Corse	Honda	20	36m 57.261s
17	Andi Farid Izdihar	INA	19	Honda Team Asia	Honda	20	36m 57.600s
18	Takuma Matsuyama	JPN	32	Honda Team Asia	Honda	20	37m 31.900s
	Izan Guevara	SPA	28	Solunion GASGAS Aspar Team	GASGAS	20	DNF-crash
	Ayumu Sasaki	JPN	71	Red Bull KTM Tech 3	KTM	20	DNF-crash
	Dennis Foggia	ITA	7	Leopard Racing	Honda	20	DNF-crash
	Xavier Artigas	SPA	43	Leopard Racing	Honda	20	DNF-crash
	Filip Salac	CZE	12	Rivacold Snipers Team	Honda	15	DNF-ret in pit
	Adrian Fernandez	SPA	31	Sterilgarda Max Racing Team	Husqvarna	11	DNF-crash
	John McPhee	GBR	17	Petronas Sprinta Racing	Honda	9	DNF-crash
	Andrea Migno	ITA	16	Rivacold Snipers Team	Honda	9	DNF-crash
	Tatsuki Suzuki	JPN	24	SIC58 Squadra Corse	Honda	9	DNF-crash
	Riccardo Rossi	ITA	54	BOE Owlride	KTM	0	DNS-crash

Fastest lap: Darryn Binder, on lap 5, 1m 48.209s, 96.3mph/154.9km/h.
Lap record: New layout.
Event maximum speed: Kaito Toba, 153.2mph/246.5km/h (race).

Qualifying:
Weather: Dry
Air: 27° **Track:** 42°
Humidity: 46%

1	Rodrigo	1m 47.597s
2	Alcoba	1m 47.914s
3	Antonelli	1m 47.958s
4	Nepa	1m 48.295s
5	Guevara	1m 48.318s
6	McPhee	1m 48.350s
7	Binder	1m 48.489s
8	Suzuki	1m 48.498s
9	Masia	1m 48.500s
10	Rossi	1m 48.552s
11	Fenati	1m 48.662s
12	Oncu	1m 48.717s
13	Toba	1m 48.860s
14	Sasaki	1m 48.957s
15	Fernandez	1m 48.984s
16	Foggia	1m 49.226s
17	Salac	1m 49.297s
18	Artigas	1m 49.421s
19	Garcia	1m 49.077s
20	Kunii	1m 49.198s
21	Migno	1m 49.482s
22	Yamanaka	1m 49.504s
23	Holgado	1m 49.645s
24	Fellon	1m 49.659s
25	Acosta	1m 49.743s
26	Izdihar	1m 49.812s
27	Matsuyama	1m 49.852s
28	Bartolini	1m 50.143s

Fastest race laps

1	Binder	1m 48.209s
2	Rodrigo	1m 48.340s
3	Guevara	1m 48.530s
4	Alcoba	1m 48.581s
5	McPhee	1m 48.593s
6	Migno	1m 48.665s
7	Masia	1m 48.704s
8	Artigas	1m 48.718s
9	Fenati	1m 48.737s
10	Acosta	1m 48.810s
11	Antonelli	1m 48.820s
12	Toba	1m 48.841s
13	Garcia	1m 48.852s
14	Sasaki	1m 48.872s
15	Nepa	1m 48.936s
16	Oncu	1m 48.966s
17	Suzuki	1m 48.989s
18	Holgado	1m 49.050s
19	Foggia	1m 49.217s
20	Kunii	1m 49.262s
21	Bartolini	1m 49.478s
22	Salac	1m 49.514s
23	Fellon	1m 49.546s
24	Yamanaka	1m 49.551s
25	Izdihar	1m 49.793s
26	Fernandez	1m 49.884s
27	Matsuyama	1m 50.366s

Championship Points

1	Acosta	120
2	Garcia	81
3	Masia	72
4	Fenati	61
5	Binder	58
6	Sasaki	57
7	Antonelli	55
8	Rodrigo	51
9	Migno	47
10	Foggia	45
11	Alcoba	39
12	Salac	35
13	Toba	29
14	Yamanaka	28
15	Dupasquier	27
16	Guevara	26
17	Oncu	24
18	McPhee	22
19	Suzuki	18
20	Rossi	16
21	Artigas	16
22	Tatay	14
23	Nepa	14
24	Fernandez	10
25	Kunii	7
26	Bartolini	3
27	Kofler	3
28	Izdihar	1
29	Holgado	1

Constructor Points

1	KTM	152
2	Honda	137
3	GASGAS	93
4	Husqvarna	65

CATALUNYA GRAND PRIX 141

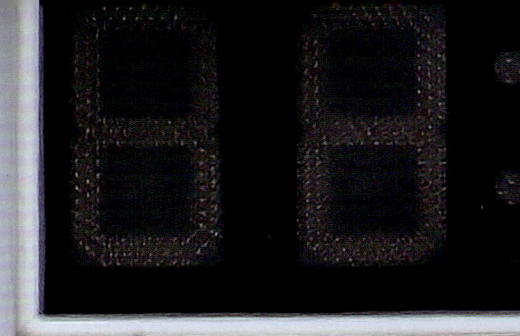

FIM WORLD CHAMPIONSHIP · ROUND 8
GERMAN GRAND PRIX
SACHSENRING CIRCUIT

TISSOT
SWISS WATCHES SINCE 1853

Above: Aleix Espargaro put the new improved Aprilia on the front row.
Photo: Gold & Goose

Top: Zarco took a first pole of the year, but a first MotoGP win remained elusive.
Photo: Pramac Racing

Above centre: Darryn Binder was deeply disgruntled as the stewards took aim at him again.
Photo: Gold & Goose

Above right: Maverick Vinales fights a losing battle with his Yamaha.
Photo: Monster Energy Yamaha

Right: Marquez pulls the trigger: "It was time to take the risk." Espargaro, Miller and the rest had no answer.

Opening spread: "Lawks a-mercy!" Marquez appears stricken with disbelief after his brilliant win. Miguel Oliveira could only watch in admiration.
Photo: Gold & Goose

IT took six races and 581 days for Marc Marquez to return to winning form. This ranks with great post-race comebacks by Barry Sheene and Mick Doohan, who – the Spaniard revealed in an emotional post-race briefing – had spoken to him at length and inspiringly about the difficulties of returning in a weakened state after his own botched surgery in 1992.

Marquez was sensational around the tight German layout, seizing the initiative mid-race during a brief shower, displaying all the brilliance and daring that had won him eight titles and legendary status. If this seems like hyperbole, Marquez provided context soon after: "In September, October and November, I was scared about more than not winning again. [At that time, his right humerus had been beset by infection after two failed surgeries.] Every time, I felt less power and worse feeling. I was thinking about my arm, my life, not about racing."

For his return, without any pre-season testing and two races into the campaign, he was fighting on two fronts. Firstly, to recover racing fitness while striving to regain comfort with a revised riding position, necessitated by pain in his right arm and shoulder; secondly, to reverse the fortunes of Honda, which had stagnated in his absence.

The Doohan factor came after the Mugello race: "I was 30 minutes on a phone call with him. I was just listening, he was speaking. He was explaining his situation [in 1993, weakened and still partially crippled], but it was like he was explaining my situation. He had exactly the same problems ... you don't understand the bike, you are not riding like you want, stupid mistakes, stupid crashes. Some races. you will be fast; some practices, you will be slow and you don't know why. All the problems I've had this year is what he had in the past. This conversation helped me a lot to keep pushing."

Marquez had won the previous ten races at the Sachsenring, where the predominant left-hand corners echoed his favoured anti-clockwise dirt-track training regime and now, more importantly, reduced the physical strain on his recovering right arm and shoulder.

In the spotlight even before the race, he took the opportunity for a casual swipe at Rossi, whose open enmity had been clear for several years, explaining how he could never imagine being in the multi-champion's current situation: "One of the motivations is because I like the taste of the podium and winning races. As soon as I feel I can't be fighting for top positions, it's time to consider ... I'm surprised by the way Valentino accepts this. It looks like he is enjoying, but I cannot imagine staying in this championship and not have the chance to be on the podium."

Rossi's weekend followed his form thus far in the season: qualified 16th, finished 14th. At least he did better than his former factory team-mate. Maverick Vinales took a step closer towards meltdown in an exasperating weekend. Qualified 21st, second from last, he finished last and vented his frustration. His sole job, he said gloomily, was "to collect data."

Yamaha catered only to Quartararo, he claimed, saying he'd been using his rivals' set-up for two years, with the team "teaching me to ride: 'Take the brake, let go of the brake ... he turns on the gas, turns off the gas.' But each rider has his style and has to take his set-up. I don't want to use Fabio's set-up because I don't ride like him. I want them to make a motorcycle for me."

In the race, he had effectively given up: "I spent 15 laps behind Marini and Bastianini. I could not pass them. Impossible. They had more power, they braked later. I spent ten laps there and I decided to go back, get fresh air and collect data to see how the bike is working alone." In this way, he'd cut his lap times, but lost positions, and done irrevocable damage to his relationship with the team.

At Aprilia, a bullish Aleix Espargaro secured the marque's first front-row start since 2000. "We are showing that Aprilia is getting a serious bike, closer to the top guys at every circuit," he said. Braking stability was a strong point, and a podium seemed possible, as he held second for the first nine laps. But problems with rear traction meant that eventually he dropped to seventh, albeit still within ten seconds of the winner – a standard he had achieved at every race so far.

In 2022, Aprilia would run the team directly, the factory having been granted its own entry. Confirmation came now that Gresini, which had run the squad since the 2015 return, would switch to Ducati, bringing to eight (with Rossi's new team) the number of Desmosedicis on the grid. Riders were named as Enea Bastianini and, promoted from Moto2, Fabio Di Giannantonio.

Bastianini was the only rider punished by the stewards for unseemly behaviour in MotoGP, where riders strayed far from setting an example for the mischievous tykes in Moto3. Bastianini's transgression had been "riding slow [sic] on line disturbing another rider" in Q1, and it earned a three-position grid penalty. In Q2, a pack of riders slowed almost to walking pace through the last corners. Miguel Oliveira, a prominent offender, got away with it, explaining, "On the second run, I was in front of many guys when I looked behind, and I was not going to push. I know from experience … you will always get a disadvantage if you are always in the front."

The sharp knives were reserved for Moto3, where Darryn Binder (again) was made an example, for a marginal racing incident. Anxious for one more lap late in Q1, which he was leading, he came out of the pit lane and promptly collided with 18-year-old Australian Joe Kelso, a GP first-timer replacing the injured Max Kofler in the CIP team. Only Binder crashed, awkwardly into the air-fence, but this was not thought punishment enough for causing "unnecessary danger", and he was disqualified from Q2, plus given a ride-through race penalty. He served this at the required 60km/h, tucked ironically into a full racing crouch.

It was announced on Friday that the late Jason Dupasquier's racing number '50' would be retired from the class.

MOTOGP RACE – 30 laps

Practice and qualifying took place in sweltering heat, but the weather turned on Sunday, with rain threatened for the afternoon. Marc Marquez relished the prospect. He'd served notice by leading FP1, but by the end had been consigned to fifth on a grid led by Zarco, Quartararo and Aleix Espargaro. Miller, heading row two, had also shown good pace; and Oliveira (in sixth) had sustained his strong form. Chances of an 11th straight win seemed slim.

But he promised to try anyway, and his intent was clear from the first corner, as he expertly squeezed out Quartararo to emerge second, behind Espargaro's Aprilia. By Turn 13, he was ahead, and though the Aprilia outbraked him at Turn 12 on the following lap, he immediately resumed control, and held it to the end.

That doesn't tell the full story. A procession formed behind them: Zarco third, then Quartararo, Miller, Oliveira and Binder (from 13th on the grid) all within reach. Quartararo appeared the least assured, and Miller took fourth from him at Turn One on lap three, with Oliveira following suit at Turn 13 a lap later.

Then came the changing conditions that favoured Marquez. Drops of rain started to fall on lap eight, with white flags out next time around. Marquez recalled, "When I saw some drops on my screen, I said, 'Now is my time. Time to take a risk.'" Risk it all, he did. As Miller and Oliveira jostled to breach the hesitant Espargaro, Marquez was at his dazzling best out front, gapping his pursuers to the tune of 1.2s on lap nine, and 1.7s next time. He had seized the moment.

Behind, it was all change. Miller finally deposed Espargaro at Turn One, with Oliveira muscling a way through at the following corner. Zarco began to fade, Quartararo demoting his countryman to fifth later on that lap. And Miller couldn't fend off Oliveira, gliding effortlessly inside at the final turn next

Above: Oliveira had to be content to be best of the rest.

Top right: Alex Marquez and Danilo Petrucci exchange insurance details after their early-race crash.

Above right: Remy Gardner sped past team-mate Fernandez to take a third straight Moto2 win…

Centre right: …and then the Spaniard fell in pursuit, extending his rival's championship lead.

Centre far right: A career-best Moto2 finish of second for Aron Canet and his Boscoscuro.

Below right: Eventual winner Acosta leads another unseemly Moto3 brawl from Foggia, Suzuki and the ever-shuffling pack.

Below far right: Kaito Toba acknowledges the plaudits after his last-gasp second place in Moto3.

Photos: Gold & Goose

time around. Now he had to work on that 1.9s of empty tarmac ahead.

In Oliveira's own words, it was "cat and mouse" across 18 laps full of tension and intrigue. The shower had passed, and Marquez and Oliveira began trading fastest laps. Marquez was superior in the track's tight first half, Oliveira was just as strong in sector three. By lap 18, the lead was down to 1.5s. On lap 22, it had been reduced to 1.1. And with six to go, it was under a second for the first time.

Would Marquez wilt? From a front-row seat, Oliveira had the growing impression that ultimately his efforts would prove futile. "I put the pressure on him," he explained, "but I didn't have the best situation to manage the tyre because I used a lot to try to get to him. I felt like he was in control the whole race. Three laps to the end, he pushed when I was completely empty."

Marquez's last effort was enough to stretch out a 1.6s advantage at the flag. Even in a career of superhuman feats, this ranked as one of his greatest triumphs. Oliveira could take heart from a third strong performance in three races. Nobody had ever made Marquez work here like he had.

Behind, Quartararo made the best of a tough situation, riding with maturity on a day when his Yamaha stablemates were a shambles – Rossi best in 14th, Morbidelli four places back and Vinales last. On lap 19, he reached the front of a six-rider fight for third, which included Miller, Aleix Espargaro, Binder, Zarco and Mir, through from 17th on the grid.

The Frenchman stayed there, but deteriorating rear grip and off-throttle slides hindered Miller. That helped Binder through to fourth, capping another fine day for KTM. And Bagnaia had ghosted through from 16th on lap four, nicking fifth off Miller at Turn Eight on the final lap for good measure.

Espargaro was frustrated with a close seventh, complaining of a similar lack of traction. Zarco faded to eighth, another couple of seconds adrift, but narrowly ahead of Mir, cursing another wretched qualifying. Pol Espargaro was alone and disconsolate in tenth.

Rins took 11th off Martin with two laps to go; Nakagami trailed in, then a loose-knit gang led by Rossi from half-brother Marini, Bastianini, Lecuona, Morbidelli and Vinales. Petrucci, Savadori and Alex Marquez were early fallers.

With his closest rivals all behind, third was good enough for Quartararo to extend his championship lead.

MOTO2 RACE – 28 laps

Remy Gardner's third successive win was a first for an Australian rider in the intermediate class. More than making history, however, was that he had extended his championship lead to a yawning 36 points, after team-mate Raul Fernandez had tumbled out for the first no-score of his rookie Moto2 campaign.

Fernandez had claimed his third consecutive pole, with Di Giannantonio second and Gardner completing the front row, ahead of Bezzecchi (through from Q1), Vierge and Navarro, the first rider not on a Kalex. Lowes led row three from Ogura and Bendsneyder, times unusually widely spaced on this technical track.

The Ajo team-mates were in a class apart, eight-tenths clear of the pack on the first lap, another second away after the second. The younger rider had led the first; Gardner eased past on the second, and they continued to pull clear.

Until the fifth lap. Fernandez lost the front in the looping Omega Curve and slid off at a tangent, unable to get going again. For Gardner, "I expected a hard battle today with Raul, but I knew he'd struggle with the front. I was fast at the start so I passed him, but I was being smooth. A few laps later, I saw '+4.5s'. Then it was just about not losing concentration."

It was his most dominant performance to date, managing the gap to win by better than six seconds on what felt like a pivotal day in the championship fight.

None of the pursuers could match the early rhythm. Vierge and Bezzecchi were in podium contention early on, until Canet on the Boscoscuro took over second on lap five. He was able to open an advantage and then hold on to repeat his career-best second of the Portuguese GP, almost a second clear of Bezzecchi, who had been striving to reel him in.

Di Giannantonio was a similar distance behind, survivor of a group that had included Ogura and Vierge until the last lap. The Japanese had taken fifth off the Spaniard a few laps earlier, and they crashed out separately. This handed fifth

146 GERMAN GRAND PRIX

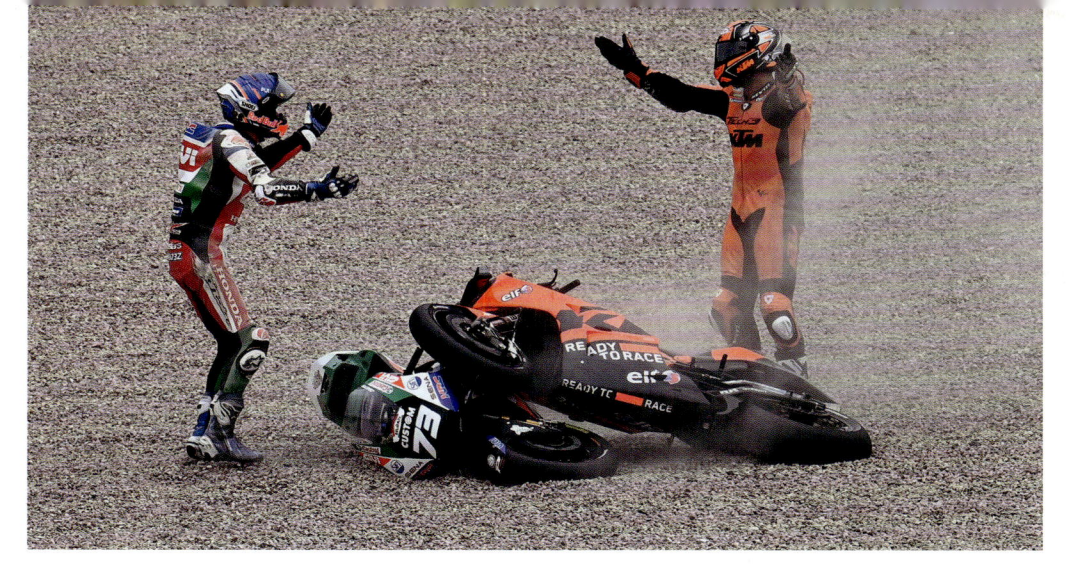

and sixth to Lowes and Schrotter, close spectators of the pair's downfall.

Navarro was a lone seventh. Roberts had also fallen on the last lap, after losing tenth to Arenas, promoted to a best-so-far eighth by the other crashes ahead of him, the rookie's first top-ten.

With Ramirez ninth, Beaubier led the next group for tenth, consigning Bulega to 11th, ahead of Lopez, Bendsnyder and Baltus. The American had qualified 25th and finished the first lap 21st.

A strong race for Dixon was spoiled, after he'd climbed from 15th on the grid to eighth, when he tangled with Augusto Fernandez at the penultimate corner. Fernandez fell, Dixon managed to stay on board in the gravel, rejoining last – only to be handed a long-lap penalty for the next race when the stewards blamed him for the incident. Roberts was handed the same penalty: he had crashed while "not respecting a yellow flag".

MOTO3 RACE – 27 laps

The Catalunya carpeting did not produce a more sedate contest – with three riders handed long-lap penalties and three of the lead group dropped one place apiece on the final lap.

Qualifying had already yielded a ride-through for Binder, and a career-first pole for Salac, who headed a trio of fellow Honda riders: Foggia, Suzuki and McPhee, with fifth-fastest Toba the top KTM.

Acosta, qualified 15th, took just six laps to reach the front, engaging in a race-long duel with Foggia, at the head of a pack that had been whittled down to nine strong after half-distance by a number of incidents, mainly at Turn One.

Fenati had knocked off Oncu and Fellon there; Masia crashed in the same place two laps later. Fenati received a long-lap penalty; Masia had already earned one for "irresponsible riding" (replacement rider Bartolini was the other so punished).

Toba and Suzuki each led briefly. On the penultimate lap, Acosta moved past Foggia, and the mercurial Italian's response into Turn Eight on the last lap sent him wide. That allowed Alcoba and Toba through, the latter grabbing second at Turn 12. Alcoba crossed the line third, but he had failed to lose one position for an earlier infringement, so Foggia was promoted.

Migno, Garcia, Suzuki, Antonelli and Artigas followed them home, with Antonelli promoted to sixth because both Garcia and Suzuki had exceeded track limits on the last lap. Six seconds away, Guevara led McPhee and Bartolini for tenth.

Acosta's fourth win after three races off the podium extended his lead once more over Catalunya winner Garcia to a massive 55 points.

GERMAN GRAND PRIX 147

FIM WORLD CHAMPIONSHIP: ROUND 8

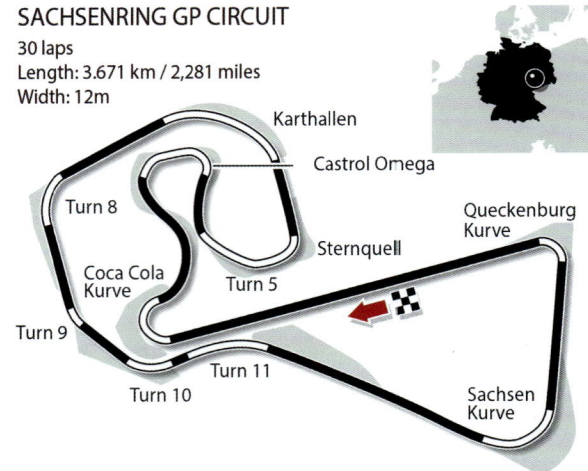

LIQUI MOLY MOTORRAD GRAND PRIX DEUTSCHLAND

18–20 JUNE, 2021

SACHSENRING GP CIRCUIT
30 laps
Length: 3.671 km / 2,281 miles
Width: 12m

MotoGP

RACE DISTANCE: 30 laps, 68.432 miles/110.130km · RACE WEATHER: Dry (air 28°, humidity 51%, track 39°)

Pos.	Rider	Nat.	No.	Entrant	Machine	Tyres	Race tyre choice	Laps	Time & speed
1	Marc Marquez	SPA	93	Repsol Honda Team	Honda RC213V	M	F: Hard/R: Medium	30	41m 07.243s / 99.8mph / 160.6km/h
2	Miguel Oliveira	POR	88	Red Bull KTM Factory Racing	KTM RC16	M	F: Hard/R: Medium	30	41m 08.853s
3	Fabio Quartararo	FRA	20	Monster Energy Yamaha MotoGP	Yamaha YZR-M1	M	F: Hardk/R: Medium	30	41m 14.015s
4	Brad Binder	RSA	33	Red Bull KTM Factory Racing	KTM RC16	M	F: Hard/R: Medium	30	41m 15.165s
5	Francesco Bagnaia	ITA	63	Ducati Lenovo Team	Ducati Desmosedici	M	F: Medium/R: Medium	30	41m 15.834s
6	Jack Miller	AUS	43	Ducati Lenovo Team	Ducati Desmosedici	M	F: Hard/R: Medium	30	41m 16.329s
7	Aleix Espargaro	SPA	41	Aprilia Racing Team Gresini	Aprilia RS-GP	M	F: Hard/R: Medium	30	41m 16.614s
8	Johann Zarco	FRA	5	Pramac Racing	Ducati Desmosedici	M	F: Hard/R: Medium	30	41m 18.682s
9	Joan Mir	SPA	36	Team SUZUKI ECSTAR	Suzuki GSX-RR	M	F: Hard/R: Medium	30	41m 18.868s
10	Pol Espargaro	SPA	44	Repsol Honda Team	Honda RC213V	M	F: Hard/R: Medium	30	41m 22.012s
11	Alex Rins	SPA	42	Team SUZUKI ECSTAR	Suzuki GSX-RR	M	F: Hard/R: Medium	30	41m 24.046s
12	Jorge Martin	SPA	89	Pramac Racing	Ducati Desmosedici	M	F: Medium/R: Medium	30	41m 24.158s
13	Takaaki Nakagami	JPN	30	LCR Honda IDEMITSU	Honda RC213V	M	F: Medium/R: Soft	30	41m 26.460s
14	Valentino Rossi	ITA	46	Petronas Yamaha SRT	Yamaha YZR-M1	M	F: Hard/R: Medium	30	41m 29.543s
15	Luca Marini	ITA	10	SKY VR46 Avintia	Ducati Desmosedici	M	F: Hard/R: Medium	30	41m 30.858s
16	Enea Bastianini	ITA	23	Avintia Esponsorama	Ducati Desmosedici	M	F: Hard/R: Medium	30	41m 30.981s
17	Iker Lecuona	SPA	27	Tech 3 KTM Factory Racing	KTM RC16	M	F: Hard/R: Medium	30	41m 31.189s
18	Franco Morbidelli	ITA	21	Petronas Yamaha SRT	Yamaha YZR-M1	M	F: Hard/R: Medium	30	41m 31.657s
19	Maverick Vinales	SPA	12	Monster Energy Yamaha MotoGP	Yamaha YZR-M1	M	F: Medium/R: Medium	30	41m 31.958s
	Lorenzo Savadori	ITA	32	Aprilia Racing Team Gresini	Aprilia RS-GP	M	F: Hard/R: Medium	5	DNF-crash
	Danilo Petrucci	ITA	9	Tech 3 KTM Factory Racing	KTM RC16	M	F: Hard/R: Medium	4	DNF-crash
	Alex Marquez	SPA	73	LCR Honda CASTROL	Honda RC213V	M	F: Hard/R: Medium	4	DNF-crash

Fastest lap: Miguel Oliveira, on lap 15, 1m 21.701s, 100.5mph/161.7km/h.
Lap record: Marc Marquez, 1m 21.228s, 101.0mph/162.6km/h (2019).
Event maximum speed: Jorge Martin, 187.4mph/301.6km/h (free practice).

Qualifying

Weather: Dry
Air Temp: 33° **Track Temp:** 48°
Humidity: 40%

1	Zarco	1m 20.236s
2	Quartararo	1m 20.247s
3	A. Espargaro	1m 20.447s
4	Miller	1m 20.508s
5	M. Marquez	1m 20.567s
6	Oliveira	1m 20.589s
7	Martin	1m 20.617s
8	P. Espargaro	1m 20.659s
9	Nakagami	1m 20.810s
10	Bagnaia	1m 20.811s
11	Rins	1m 20.949s
12	A. Marquez	1m 21.135s

Q1

13	Binder	1m 20.736s
14	Marini	1m 20.864s
15	Bastianini	1m 20.953s
16	Rossi	1m 20.972s
17	Mir	1m 21.014s
18	Morbidelli	1m 21.091s
19	Petrucci	1m 21.137s
20	Lecuona	1m 21.154s
21	Vinales	1m 21.165s
22	Savadori	1m 21.411s

Fastest race laps

1	Oliveira	1m 21.701s
2	M. Marquez	1m 21.772s
3	Bagnaia	1m 21.849s
4	A. Espargaro	1m 22.008s
5	Mir	1m 22.024s
6	Miller	1m 22.025s
7	Vinales	1m 22.045s
8	Rossi	1m 22.045s
9	P. Espargaro	1m 22.059s
10	Quartararo	1m 22.065s
11	Binder	1m 22.077s
12	Nakagami	1m 22.085s
13	Rins	1m 22.087s
14	Martin	1m 22.094s
15	Zarco	1m 22.104s
16	Lecuona	1m 22.211s
17	Morbidelli	1m 22.391s
18	Marini	1m 22.514s
19	Bastianini	1m 22.518s
20	A. Marquez	1m 22.530s
21	Savadori	1m 22.730s
22	Petrucci	1m 22.834s

Championship Points

1	Quartararo	131
2	Zarco	109
3	Miller	100
4	Bagnaia	99
5	Mir	85
6	Vinales	75
7	Oliveira	74
8	Binder	56
9	A. Espargaro	53
10	M. Marquez	41
11	Morbidelli	40
12	P. Espargaro	35
13	Nakagami	34
14	Rins	28
15	Bastianini	26
16	A. Marquez	25
17	Martin	23
18	Petrucci	23
19	Rossi	17
20	Marini	14
21	Lecuona	13
22	Bradl	11
23	Savadori	4
24	Pirro	3
25	Rabat	1

Constructor Points

1	Yamaha	159
2	Ducati	154
3	KTM	103
4	Suzuki	89
5	Honda	77
6	Aprilia	54

Grid Order

Grid Order	1	2	3	4	5	6	7	8	9	10	11	12	13	14	15	16	17	18	19	20	21	22	23	24	25	26	27	28	29	30	
5 ZARCO	93	93	93	93	93	93	93	93	93	93	93	93	93	93	93	93	93	93	93	93	93	93	93	93	93	93	93	93	93	93	1
20 QUARTARARO	41	41	41	41	41	41	41	41	41	43	88	88	88	88	88	88	88	88	88	88	88	88	88	88	88	88	88	88	88	88	2
41 A. ESPARGARO	5	5	5	5	5	5	43	43	88	88	43	43	43	43	43	43	43	20	20	20	20	20	20	20	20	20	20	20	20	20	3
43 MILLER	20	20	43	43	43	43	5	88	41	41	41	41	41	41	41	20	20	43	43	43	43	43	43	43	43	33	33	33	33	33	4
93 M. MARQUEZ	43	43	20	88	88	88	88	5	20	20	20	20	20	20	20	41	41	41	41	41	41	33	33	33	33	43	43	43	43	63	5
88 OLIVEIRA	88	88	88	20	20	20	20	20	5	5	5	5	5	5	5	5	5	33	33	33	33	41	41	41	41	41	41	41	63	43	6
89 MARTIN	33	33	33	33	33	33	33	33	33	33	33	33	33	33	33	33	33	5	5	5	5	5	5	63	63	63	63	63	41	41	7
44 P. ESPARGARO	89	42	42	42	42	42	42	42	42	36	36	36	36	36	36	36	36	36	36	36	36	36	36	5	5	5	5	5	5	5	8
30 NAKAGAMI	42	89	89	89	89	89	89	89	36	42	89	89	89	89	89	89	89	89	63	63	63	63	63	36	36	36	36	36	36	36	9
63 BAGNAIA	44	30	30	36	36	36	36	36	44	89	44	44	44	44	44	44	44	63	89	89	44	89	89	44	44	44	44	44	44	44	10
42 RINS	30	44	44	44	44	44	44	44	89	44	42	42	42	42	63	63	63	63	63	44	89	44	44	89	89	89	44	42	89	42	11
73 A. MARQUEZ	9	36	36	30	30	30	30	30	30	30	63	42	42	42	42	42	42	42	42	42	42	42	42	42	42	42	44	42	89	89	12
33 BINDER	36	9	27	27	27	27	27	27	27	63	30	30	30	30	30	30	30	30	30	30	30	30	30	30	30	30	30	30	30	30	13
10 MARINI	63	27	9	9	46	46	46	46	46	63	27	27	27	46	46	46	46	46	46	46	46	46	46	46	46	46	46	46	46	46	14
46 ROSSI	27	63	73	73	63	63	63	63	63	46	46	46	46	46	27	27	27	27	23	10	10	10	10	10	10	10	10	10	10	10	15
36 MIR	73	73	63	63	23	23	23	23	23	23	10	10	10	10	10	27	10	23	23	23	23	23	23	23	23	23	23	23	27	23	
21 MORBIDELLI	10	46	46	46	10	10	10	10	10	10	10	23	23	23	23	23	23	10	10	12	12	12	27	27	27	27	27	27	23	27	
23 BASTIANINI	23	10	10	10	32	21	21	21	21	21	21	21	21	21	21	21	21	21	21	27	27	27	12	12	12	12	12	12	12	21	
9 PETRUCCI	46	32	23	23	21	12	12	12	12	12	12	12	12	12	12	12	12	12	12	21	21	21	21	21	21	21	21	21	21	12	
27 LECUONA	32	23	32	32	12																										
12 VINALES	12	21	21	21																											
32 SAVADORI	21	12	12	12																											

148 GERMAN GRAND PRIX

Moto2
RACE DISTANCE: 28 laps, 63.870 miles/102.788km · **RACE WEATHER:** Dry (air 28°, humidity 51%, track 38°)

Pos.	Rider	Nat.	No.	Entrant	Machine	Laps	Time & Speed
1	Remy Gardner	AUS	87	Red Bull KTM Ajo	Kalex	28	39m 39.191s / 96.6mph / 155.5km/h
2	Aron Canet	SPA	44	Aspar Team Moto2	Boscoscuro	28	39m 45.349s
3	Marco Bezzecchi	ITA	72	SKY Racing Team VR46	Kalex	28	39m 46.221s
4	Fabio Di Giannantonio	ITA	21	Federal Oil Gresini Moto2	Kalex	28	39m 47.336s
5	Sam Lowes	GBR	22	Elf Marc VDS Racing Team	Kalex	28	39m 49.079s
6	Marcel Schrotter	GER	23	Liqui Moly Intact GP	Kalex	28	39m 49.713s
7	Jorge Navarro	SPA	9	+EGO Speed Up	Boscoscuro	28	39m 55.230s
8	Albert Arenas	SPA	75	Aspar Team Moto2	Boscoscuro	28	39m 58.585s
9	Marcos Ramirez	SPA	42	American Racing	Kalex	28	40m 00.909s
10	Cameron Beaubier	USA	6	American Racing	Kalex	28	40m 05.584s
11	Nicolo Bulega	ITA	11	Federal Oil Gresini Moto2	Kalex	28	40m 05.923s
12	Alonso Lopez	SPA	2	Flexbox HP40	Kalex	28	40m 06.026s
13	Bo Bendsneyder	NED	64	Pertamina Mandalika SAG Team	Kalex	28	40m 07.225s
14	Barry Baltus	BEL	70	NTS RW Racing GP	NTS	28	40m 08.175s
15	Celestino Vietti	ITA	13	SKY Racing Team VR46	Kalex	28	40m 10.605s
16	Tony Arbolino	ITA	14	Liqui Moly Intact GP	Kalex	28	40m 12.367s
17	Hafizh Syahrin	MAL	55	NTS RW Racing GP	NTS	28	40m 12.616s
18	Somkiat Chantra	THA	35	IDEMITSU Honda Team Asia	Kalex	28	40m 18.829s
19	Thomas Luthi	SWI	12	Pertamina Mandalika SAG Team	Kalex	28	40m 18.873s
20	Stefano Manzi	ITA	62	Flexbox HP40	Kalex	28	40m 23.804s
21	Jake Dixon	GBR	96	Petronas Sprinta Racing	Kalex	28	40m 26.607s
	Ai Ogura	JPN	79	IDEMITSU Honda Team Asia	Kalex	27	DNF-crash
	Xavi Vierge	SPA	97	Petronas Sprinta Racing	Kalex	27	DNF-crash
	Joe Roberts	USA	16	Italtrans Racing Team	Kalex	27	DNF-crash
	Lorenzo Dalla Porta	ITA	19	Italtrans Racing Team	Kalex	14	DNF-technical
	Augusto Fernandez	SPA	37	Elf Marc VDS Racing Team	Kalex	6	DNF-crash
	Lorenzo Baldassarri	ITA	7	MV Agusta Forward Racing	MV Agusta	6	DNF-crash
	Raul Fernandez	SPA	25	Red Bull KTM Ajo	Kalex	4	DNF-crash
	Fermin Aldeguer	SPA	54	+EGO Speed Up	Boscoscuro	3	DNF-crash
	Simone Corsi	ITA	24	MV Agusta Forward Racing	MV Agusta	0	DNF-crash

Fastest lap: Remy Gardner, on lap 3, 1m 23.767s, 98.0mph/157.7km/h.
Lap record: Alex Marquez, 1m 24.317s, 97.4mph/156.7km/h (2019).
Event maximum speed: Xavi Vierge, 159.0mph/255.9km/h (free practice).

Qualifying
Weather: Dry
Air Temp: 32° **Track Temp:** 46°
Humidity: 40%

1	R. Fernandez	1m 23.397s
2	Di Giannantonio	1m 23.744s
3	Gardner	1m 23.769s
4	Bezzecchi	1m 24.184s
5	Vierge	1m 24.296s
6	Navarro	1m 24.301s
7	Lowes	1m 24.416s
8	Ogura	1m 24.439s
9	Bendsneyder	1m 24.474s
10	Canet	1m 24.500s
11	Bulega	1m 24.503s
12	Roberts	1m 24.521s
13	Chantra	1m 24.594s
14	A. Fernandez	1m 24.600s
15	Dixon	1m 24.611s
16	Ramirez	1m 24.616s
17	Schrotter	1m 24.624s
18	Arenas	1m 24.807s
Q1		
19	Dalla Porta	1m 24.378s
20	Arbolino	1m 24.569s
21	Vietti	1m 24.604s
22	Lopez	1m 24.619s
23	Aldeguer	1m 24.667s
24	Baldassarri	1m 24.694s
25	Beaubier	1m 24.738s
26	Syahrin	1m 24.874s
27	Manzi	1m 24.946s
28	Luthi	1m 24.998s
29	Corsi	1m 25.407s
30	Baltus	1m 25.600s

Fastest race laps
1	Gardner	1m 23.767s
2	R. Fernandez	1m 23.883s
3	Dixon	1m 24.459s
4	Canet	1m 24.533s
5	Bezzecchi	1m 24.616s
6	Lowes	1m 24.635s
7	A. Fernandez	1m 24.713s
8	Ogura	1m 24.741s
9	Schrotter	1m 24.771s
10	Di Giannantonio	1m 24.808s
11	Bendsneyder	1m 24.838s
12	Vierge	1m 24.882s
13	Navarro	1m 24.896s
14	Ramirez	1m 25.040s
15	Dalla Porta	1m 25.082s
16	Arenas	1m 25.093s
17	Beaubier	1m 25.099s
18	Roberts	1m 25.179s
19	Arbolino	1m 25.287s
20	Chantra	1m 25.342s
21	Bulega	1m 25.348s
22	Lopez	1m 25.368s
23	Baltus	1m 25.413s
24	Aldeguer	1m 25.534s
25	Luthi	1m 25.558s
26	Syahrin	1m 25.590s
27	Vietti	1m 25.624s
28	Baldassarri	1m 25.654s
29	Manzi	1m 25.741s

Championship Points
1	Gardner	164
2	R. Fernandez	128
3	Bezzecchi	117
4	Lowes	86
5	Di Giannantonio	73
6	Schrotter	59
7	Canet	55
8	Roberts	50
9	Vierge	42
10	Ogura	39
11	Bendsneyder	38
12	A. Fernandez	34
13	Navarro	33
14	Arbolino	30
15	Beaubier	26
16	Arenas	18
17	Manzi	17
18	Vietti	16
19	Ramirez	16
20	Dixon	11
21	Garzo	11
22	Chantra	11
23	Bulega	10
24	Syahrin	8
25	Corsi	7
26	Dalla Porta	6
27	Lopez	4
28	Aldeguer	4
29	Baldassarri	3
30	Baltus	2
31	Luthi	2

Constructor Points
1	Kalex	200
2	Boscoscuro	72
3	MV Agusta	10
4	NTS	10

Moto3
RACE DISTANCE: 27 laps, 61.588 miles/99.117km · **RACE WEATHER:** Dry (air 28°, humidity 53%, track 33°)

Pos.	Rider	Nat.	No.	Entrant	Machine	Laps	Time & Speed
1	Pedro Acosta	SPA	37	Red Bull KTM Ajo	KTM	27	39m 38.791s / 93.2mph / 150.0km/h
2	Kaito Toba	JPN	27	CIP Green Power	KTM	27	39m 38.921s
3	Dennis Foggia	ITA	7	Leopard Racing	Honda	27	39m 39.050s
4	Jeremy Alcoba	SPA	52	Indonesian Racing Gresini Moto3	Honda	27	39m 38.997s
5	Andrea Migno	ITA	16	Rivacold Snipers Team	Honda	27	39m 39.250s
6	Niccolo Antonelli	ITA	23	Avintia Esponsorama Moto3	KTM	27	39m 39.519s
7	Sergio Garcia	SPA	11	Gaviota GASGAS Aspar Team	GASGAS	27	39m 39.328s
8	Tatsuki Suzuki	JPN	24	SIC58 Squadra Corse	Honda	27	39m 39.438s
9	Xavier Artigas	SPA	43	Leopard Racing	Honda	27	39m 39.655s
10	Izan Guevara	SPA	28	Gaviota GASGAS Aspar Team	GASGAS	27	39m 45.348s
11	John McPhee	GBR	17	Petronas Sprinta Racing	Honda	27	39m 46.303s
12	Elia Bartolini	ITA	22	Avintia Esponsorama Moto3	KTM	27	39m 46.367s
13	Romano Fenati	ITA	55	Sterilgarda Max Racing Team	Husqvarna	27	39m 59.693s
14	Darryn Binder	RSA	40	Petronas Sprinta Racing	Honda	27	40m 16.646s
15	Andi Farid Izdihar	INA	19	Honda Team Asia	Honda	27	40m 17.088s
16	Deniz Oncu	TUR	53	Red Bull KTM Tech 3	KTM	27	40m 33.505s
17	Joel Kelso	AUS	66	CIP Green Power	KTM	27	40m 37.214s
18	Ryusei Yamanaka	JPN	6	CarXpert PruestelGP	KTM	27	41m 05.861s
	Stefano Nepa	ITA	82	BOE Owlride	KTM	15	DNF-crash
	Jaume Masia	SPA	5	Red Bull KTM Ajo	KTM	14	DNF-crash
	Riccardo Rossi	ITA	54	BOE Owlride	KTM	14	DNF-crash
	Lorenzo Fellon	FRA	20	SIC58 Squadra Corse	Honda	12	DNF-crash
	Filip Salac	CZE	12	Rivacold Snipers Team	Honda	12	DNF-technical
	Gabriel Rodrigo	ARG	2	Indonesian Racing Gresini Moto3	Honda	10	DNF-crash
	Adrian Fernandez	SPA	31	Sterilgarda Max Racing Team	Husqvarna	7	DNF-crash
	Yuki Kunii	JPN	92	Honda Team Asia	Honda	3	DNF-crash

Fastest lap: Jaume Masia, on lap 3, 1m 27.033s, 94.3mph/151.8km/h.
Lap record: Can Oncu, 1m 26.714s, 94.7mph/152.4km/h (2019).
Event maximum speed: Deniz Oncu, 132.8mph/213.8km/h (race).

Qualifying:
Weather: Dry
Air Temp: 32° **Track Temp:** 49°
Humidity: 43%

1	Salac	1m 26.913s
2	Foggia	1m 27.096s
3	Suzuki	1m 27.127s
4	McPhee	1m 27.228s
5	Toba	1m 27.350s
6	Fellon	1m 27.392s
7	Antonelli	1m 27.398s
8	Fenati	1m 27.475s
9	Nepa	1m 27.522s
10	Migno	1m 27.629s
11	Oncu	1m 27.693s
12	Guevara	1m 27.899s
13	Acosta	1m 27.906s
14	Garcia	1m 27.919s
15	Artigas	1m 27.995s
16	Kunii	1m 28.365s
17	Masia	1m 28.393s
18	Binder	DSQ
Q1		
19	Rodrigo	1m 28.051s
20	Alcoba	1m 28.178s
21	Yamanaka	1m 28.183s
22	Rossi	1m 28.439s
23	Fernandez	1m 28.523s
24	Kelso	1m 28.713s
25	Bartolini	1m 28.756s
26	Izdihar	1m 29.041s

Fastest race laps
1	Masia	1m 27.033s
2	Rodrigo	1m 27.097s
3	Guevara	1m 27.138s
4	Yamanaka	1m 27.216s
5	Acosta	1m 27.281s
6	Oncu	1m 27.296s
7	Fenati	1m 27.316s
8	Alcoba	1m 27.331s
9	Antonelli	1m 27.347s
10	Artigas	1m 27.366s
11	Toba	1m 27.372s
12	Fellon	1m 27.385s
13	Nepa	1m 27.389s
14	Bartolini	1m 27.391s
15	Migno	1m 27.401s
16	Garcia	1m 27.415s
17	Suzuki	1m 27.415s
18	Foggia	1m 27.476s
19	McPhee	1m 27.509s
20	Kunii	1m 27.529s
21	Salac	1m 27.640s
22	Fernandez	1m 27.658s
23	Rossi	1m 27.862s
24	Izdihar	1m 28.098s
25	Binder	1m 28.434s
26	Kelso	1m 28.452s

Championship Points
1	Acosta	145
2	Garcia	90
3	Masia	72
4	Antonelli	65
5	Fenati	64
6	Foggia	61
7	Binder	60
8	Migno	58
9	Sasaki	57
10	Alcoba	52
11	Rodrigo	51
12	Toba	49
13	Salac	35
14	Guevara	32
15	Yamanaka	28
16	McPhee	27
17	Dupasquier	27
18	Suzuki	26
19	Oncu	24
20	Artigas	23
21	Rossi	16
22	Tatay	14
23	Nepa	14
24	Fernandez	10
25	Bartolini	7
26	Kunii	7
27	Kofler	3
28	Izdihar	2
29	Holgado	1

Constructor Points
1	KTM	177
2	Honda	153
3	GASGAS	102
4	Husqvarna	68

FIM WORLD CHAMPIONSHIP · ROUND 9
DUTCH TT
ASSEN CIRCUIT

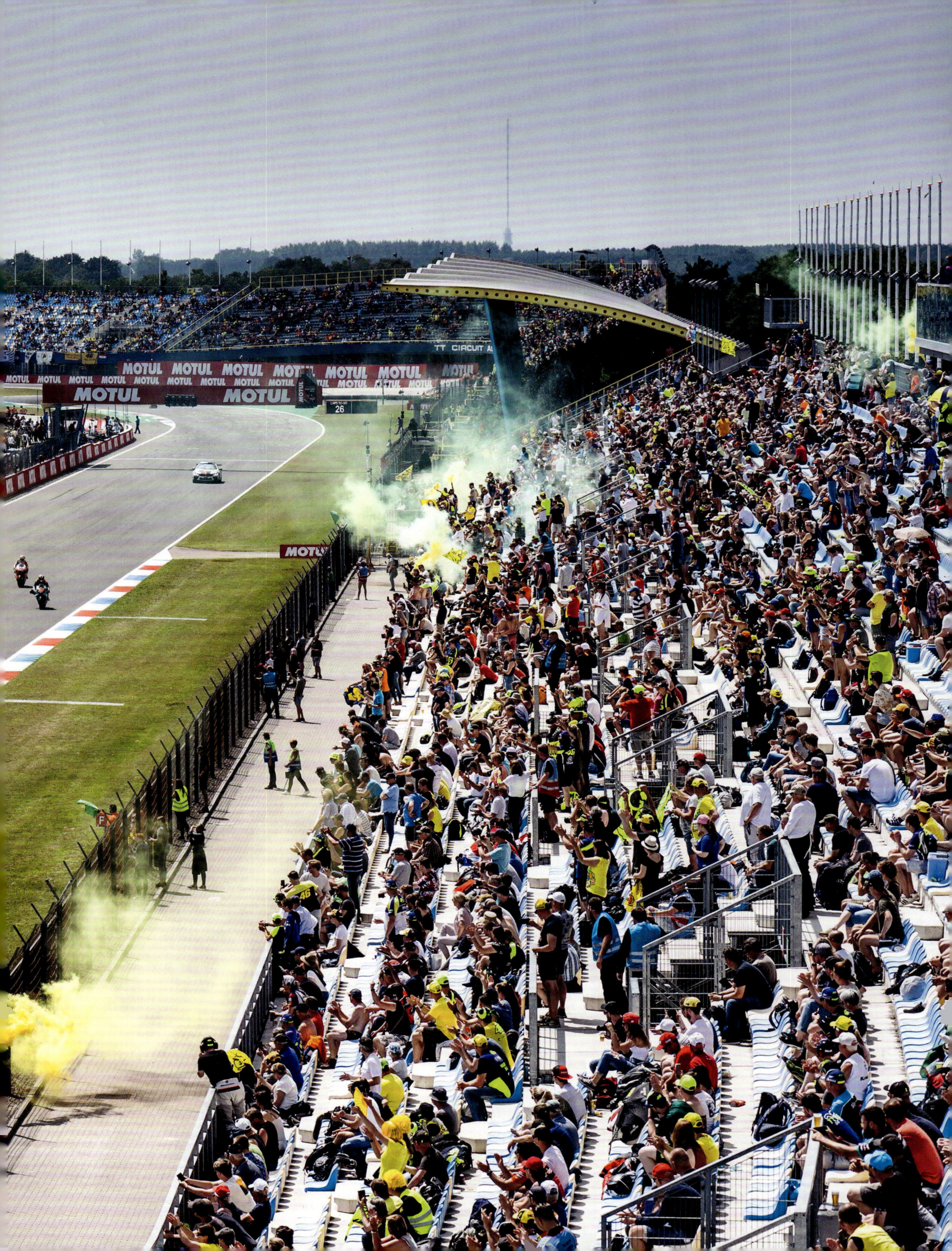

MOTUL
TT CIRCUIT
26

Above: Pole gave Vinales something to smile about in a glum weekend of high achievement and low spirits.
Photo: Monster Energy Yamaha

Top right: Marc Marquez was lucky to escape injury in a heavy FP2 high-side. He blamed wayward electronics.
Photo: Gold & Goose

Above right: Pecco Bagnaia gets the maximum angle from his Desmosedici.
Photo: Ducati Corse

Right: Yamaha's World Superbike rider Garrett Gerloff debriefs with crew chief Ramon Forcada.
Photo: Gold & Goose

Opening spread: Assen was back, albeit with restricted crowd numbers. Quartararo leads Bagnaia and Zarco away for the warm-up lap.
Photo: Monster Energy Yamaha

THE fourth race in five weekends preceded the longest ever summer break – five free weekends. A relief for most, and especially those unable to return home for even longer due to Covid travel restrictions, but an unwelcome lapse for many riders, who'd have been happier to keep racing, having got themselves into the groove.

By the end of the return to the classic Netherlands venue after a year's absence, Fabio Quartararo had drawn still further ahead of Johann Zarco in the title chase – by 34 points; while in the smaller classes, the points gap had shrunk. But only very slightly. Remy Gardner's buffer to team-mate Raul Fernandez in Moto2 was still more than one race win wide at 31; while Pedro Acosta's domination of Moto3 put him almost two wins clear of Sergio Garcia, at 48.

If the title leaders could take a sense of ease on holiday, others had serious concerns. None more so than Maverick Vinales, after yet another extraordinary weekend. Whereas in Germany, he had languished disastrously at the back, at Assen, he took pole and finished second – but his mood was even worse as he shrugged off the team's congratulations on the podium.

His frustration with Yamaha had finally reached resolution on Friday night, with agreement to divorce after five years together. His contract ran to the end of 2022, but now would be terminated a year early, thanks to rising tensions, including the forced replacement of his personally selected crew chief in June. Yamaha released a statement confirming that the split had come "following Maverick Vinales's request". Major sources of friction had been the success of new team-mate Quartararo, and his feeling that Yamaha, instead of developing the bike for his style, had insisted that he adapt to ride in a similar way to his team-mate.

Team boss Massimo Meregalli explained Yamaha's side: "To finish last [in Germany] is not his position. We also saw that during that race, he was the fastest Yamaha in terms of fastest lap. It's frustrating also for us to understand this kind of behaviour. From the Sachsenring to here, the bike was changed a bit, but not enough for this [fastest in FP1 and on pole position]."

Yamaha Racing CEO Lin Jarvis also expressed disappointment: "After the German GP, which was the most difficult weekend of our partnership, we had important discussions in Assen and came to the conclusion that it would be in the interest of both parties to go our separate ways in the future."

Aprilia was thought to be the Spanish star's future destination. Aprilia Racing CEO Massimo Rivola hedged: "We need to know if the rider is on the market. If he is available, then we will try our best to convince him."

There was discord of a different sort at Honda, where Marc Marquez had been very lucky to escape injury in a brutal FP2 high-side at the far right-hand corners on the old section of the track. He blamed an electronic issue that needed to be remedied urgently: "We cannot have these kinds of crashes. The electronics are there to avoid this. The thing is, only Honda riders have these kinds of high-sides. In Portimao, Alex [Marquez] and Pol [Espargaro] had similar crashes. Here, me. It was a similar crash in 2020 in Jerez. I checked the data if I did something wrong. I was riding in the same way as the previous lap, but the TC [traction control] didn't keep the slide."

On the positive side, Honda had brought an all-new chassis, after he had rejected the previous 2021 version. It was "the first item that more or less is different and works this year." He used it for the race.

The paddock's worst kept secret was verified on Thursday, when the VR46 team confirmed that it would use Ducatis in 2022. There was no indication of riders, however, and a line from Saudi Prince Abdulaziz bin Abdullah Al Saud, the figure behind Aramco's supposed sponsorship, read: "It would be fantastic for me if Valentino Rossi could compete in the next few years as a rider in our team together with his brother Luca Marini." This forced a comment from the rider, who said that he had yet to decide whether he would continue after a season that so far had been "not fantastic, I think it will be very difficult that I race next year." Marco Bezzecchi was tipped to join Marini in the new squad.

Franco Morbidelli's season went from bad to worse. He had re-injured the left knee that had troubled him since mid-

FIM WORLD CHAMPIONSHIP | 9

May. The problem had first come to light at Le Mans, where he had collapsed during a practice bike swap. Now a training accident had exacerbated the ligament damage, forcing him to undergo surgery on Friday, with an eight-week rehabilitation programme on the cards. He would not be ready for action when racing resumed in Austria in August; Cal Crutchlow was later signed to substitute. At Assen, that role went to Superbike rider Garrett Gerloff, who finished 17th in his second MotoGP appearance.

Moto3 revelation Acosta's luck was severely tested in a shocking crash at the end of FP3, with uncomfortable echoes of the Mugello catastrophe. It occurred at the exit of the final chicane and was his own error. Pushing hard to try to confirm passage directly to Q2 (lying 14th, he was on the brink), he fell on the exit at the head of a pack. Directly behind, Ricardo Rossi ran over him, with team-mate Stefano Nepa also down. None was able to run in qualifying; Acosta and Rossi were hospitalised overnight for observation. Both returned to race, with Acosta managing to run from 18th on the grid to fourth to help preserve his points advantage.

A Moto3 penalty with a difference came on Friday, to Max Racing Husqvarna team-mates Romano Fenati and Adrian Fernandez, with a double long-lap penalty apiece. The pair had clashed on track in FP1, squabbled again where they had stopped for a practice start, and then came to blows back in the pit, with Raul Fernandez also involved – though he insisted he had only gone in to rescue his younger brother. Fenati had form for blowing a fuse, having been sacked from Rossi's Moto3 team in 2015 after a tantrum in the pit, then suspended in 2018 after a notorious incident in Moto2, when he had reached over to squeeze a rival's front brake lever.

MOTOGP RACE – 26 laps

This should have been a Yamaha party, after pole position and a one-two result. Bitterness surrounding the Vinales split marred the celebrations.

On a track that had been resurfaced since the previous visit in 2019, Vinales took pole with a new track record, his first since two in a row at Misano, 2020. He had run first or second in every session. Quartararo had qualified next, then Bagnaia. The Ducati rider was through from Q1, along with Zarco, in the middle of row two, between top Honda Nakagami and top KTM Oliveira. Rins led row three; Rossi had made it straight into Q2, but was 12th, the battered Marc Marquez down in 20th.

A clutch problem off the start spoiled Maverick's getaway, and he finished the first lap fourth. It was Bagnaia in the lead after a frenetic exchange through Ruskenhoek and Stekkenwal, Turns Nine and Ten, from Quartararo and Nakagami; with Rins and Zarco right behind the second Yamaha.

On lap two, Zarco's ambitious dive inside at Mandeveen, Turn 12, did for Rins, who complained bitterly that an "idiotic movement" had destroyed his race. The Ducati's wing had caught his arm, and he'd had to pick up and run off the track, dropping to last place.

Bagnaia's red Ducati led over the line for the first four laps, but his attempts to block Quartararo became increasingly desperate. Crucially, the Yamaha had better corner speed, and the eventual outcome was inevitable. Their skirmishing allowed the pursuers to catch up, with Mir, Oliveira, Miller, Aleix Espargaro and Marc Marquez – having risen from the seventh row to ninth – tagging along behind the top four.

Quartararo had got by for a first time at the GT Chicane on lap three, only for the Ducati to sail by on the front straight. He tried again two laps later, only to be frustrated in the same fashion on the run to Turn One. Then, on lap five, he was able to use the Yamaha's agility to almost embarrassing effect through the old fast corners, riding around the outside at the 150mph Meeuwenmeer. It wasn't as easy as it might have looked. "I tried many times there and even hit the back of his bike once," the Frenchman said.

DUTCH TT 153

Above: Untouchable. Quartararo finished the first part of the season with a fourth win and an extended points lead.
Photo: Gold & Goose

Top right: Mir leads Oliveira in the fight for third place. The Suzuki rider made it.
Photo: www.suzuki-racing.com

Top far right: Gerloff was steady, but out of the points in his one-off ride on Morbidelli's Yamaha.

Above right: Raul Fernandez celebrates his third Moto2 win of the season.

Right: Leading mid-race, Augusto Fernandez holds off Sam Lowes, Raul Fernandez and Gardner.

Below right: Leopard Honda's Dennis Foggia celebrates his first Moto3 win of the year.
Photos: Gold & Goose

The title leader immediately set about breaking clear. Within a lap, he was eight-tenths ahead, and he smashed the race lap record by a full eight-tenths on lap eight. From that point, this race was going only one way.

Now we awaited Vinales's response, but he remained mired behind Nakagami, frustration growing, for too long to challenge. In the end, he was gifted a way into second. Bagnaia's stellar defence came at a price: having repeatedly exceeded track limits, he earned a long-lap penalty, which he served on lap 15, dropping to eighth. Meanwhile, Nakagami's attempts to get by the Ducati – he attacked twice at the final chicane, only to lose out on the straight – had burned up his rear tyre. Soon Vinales was by, with a daring move at the flat-out Hoge Heide on lap 14.

Quartararo was struggling with muscle cramp in his right arm, and Vinales slashed eight-tenths off his four-second lead on lap 18. But the Frenchman was able to respond and took the flag almost three seconds clear.

Behind the Yamahas, a series of mistakes had dropped Nakagami to the back of the leading group. Miller had crashed out of eighth on lap 15, leaving Zarco, Mir and Oliveira to contend for the final podium place. The Suzuki man earned it with a decisive move on the Ducati at the tight, looping Strubben, his favourite overtaking spot, on lap 19. Later, he apologised for his many block-passes there.

Zarco retained an impressive fourth at a historically bad track for Ducati; Oliveira was a couple of seconds shy by the end. Bagnaia had recovered to sixth, having held off a buoyant Marc Marquez and Aleix Espargaro on the final lap. Nakagami had faded to ninth, a place ahead of Pol Espargaro; Rins had recovered to 11th, Binder on his back wheel. Petrucci, Alex Marquez and Bastianini, spaced out evenly, wrapped up the points.

Any hopes of a Rossi revival at the scene of his last win, in 2017, were short lived when he crashed out of 17th place on lap eight, after a shocking start. Lecuona also crashed; Martin pitted to retire, as did the remounted Miller.

Quartararo's fourth win in nine races stretched the points gap over Zarco to 34, a commanding lead to take into the summer break. Bagnaia, Mir and Miller were still within 25 points of the runner-up.

MOTO2 RACE – 24 laps

The previous occasion when a class rookie had scored four pole positions in Moto2 had been in 2011. That had been Marc Marquez. His compatriot, Raul Fernandez, now took one less race to do the same, going to a fine third win, having recovered his composure after a second-lap error that had dropped him to ninth.

Team-mate Gardner had qualified alongside, with Lowes completing the all-Kalex front row, and Canet's Boscoscuro heading the second from Garzo and rookie Ogura. Canet and Garzo were both through from Q1; Di Giannantonio and Beaubier had not escaped, to start from 14th and a distant 24th, on row eight – both having been promoted one spot after Garzo withdrew following a positive Covid test.

Lowes, Canet and Gardner led the first lap from Raul Fernandez and Ogura. Next time around, the first three had swapped their order, Gardner in front, but Ogura was now fourth, from Augusto Fernandez, Schrotter, Vierge and Di Giannantonio, with Raul ninth.

It took him two laps to get to seventh, two more to displace Ogura and Canet. Now he was fourth, but more than a second adrift of an exciting three-way fight for the lead, between Lowes, the other Fernandez and Gardner.

By half-distance, he had joined the trio. Gardner and Lowes had no answer for him, and he picked them off on laps 14 and 16. And once he had outbraked his namesake with a fine move on lap 18, the race was as good as over. He set a new lap record next time around and came home one second clear.

Gardner salvaged second place – an eighth podium in nine races – with a brilliant late attack to pass Lowes on lap 23 and Augusto Fernandez on lap 24. The latter came home third for a first podium since September, 2019.

Lowes was now barely half a second adrift, and comfortably clear of Bezzecchi, who had picked his way forward after starting 16th and finishing the first lap 13th.

His last victim had been Di Giannantonio on lap 15, and his compatriot had crashed trying to retaliate on the following lap. Canet had also fallen, one place behind Ogura on lap 20. That left the Japanese rider unmolested in sixth.

Navarro's Boscoscuro, in seventh, was the first non-Kalex, a second clear of Vierge and Schrotter; with a lone Vietti completing the top ten; Chantra headed Arenas, Manzi and Luthi in the next gang. On the last lap, Bendsneyder finally managed to get back ahead of Beaubier to snitch the last point, after serving a double long-lap for jumping the start.

Dalla Porta and Arbolino had crashed out on lap one; Roberts out of 15th on lap 21, after taking the long-lap carried over from the previous race. Dixon had a similar hangover penalty, then another long-lap for exceeding track limits, which dropped him to 18th.

MOTO3 RACE – 22 laps

Moto3's top positions were decided largely by speed and riding, rather than pot luck in a mad melee. At least some were, although the stewards took a hand even before the start. There were six ride-through penalties for slow riding in practice, among the victims potential front-runner Masia.

Another post-race decision demoted perennially unlucky Binder from fourth to seventh for exceeding track limits twice on the last lap, triggering more general disquiet about this frequently apparently unfair punishment.

The question was whether championship leader Acosta would race, but both he and fellow overnight hospital inmate Rossi made it. The former charged through from 18th on the grid to join a lead group that also included McPhee, Binder, Suzuki and Artigas as well as frequent leader Foggia.

Fenati recovered brilliantly from his double long-lap to lead with four to go. But the top speed of Foggia's Honda was clear as he powered by his countryman on the run to Ramshoek. Despite Garcia's best efforts, he couldn't get close enough to try a move. Foggia held on by less than a tenth, with Fenati 1.3 seconds back. Binder was fourth, but demoted to seventh for exceeding track limits twice on the final lap. Acosta, McPhee and Suzuki each gained a position as a result.

Pole-starter Alcoba was tenth, having lost places from the outset. Migno and Antonelli crashed out together.

DUTCH TT 155

FIM WORLD CHAMPIONSHIP: ROUND 9

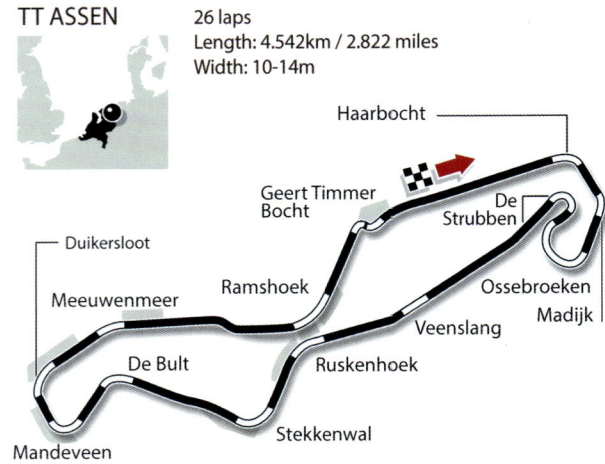

MOTUL TT ASSEN

TT ASSEN — 26 laps
Length: 4.542km / 2.822 miles
Width: 10-14m

25-27 JUNE, 2021

MotoGP
26 laps, 73.379 miles/118.092km · RACE WEATHER: Dry (air 24°, humidity 68%, track 34°)

Pos.	Rider	Nat.	No.	Entrant	Machine	Tyres	Race tyre choice	Laps	Time & speed
1	Fabio Quartararo	FRA	20	Monster Energy Yamaha MotoGP	Yamaha YZR-M1	M	F: Medium/R: Hard	26	40m 35.031s / 108.4mph / 174.5km/h
2	Maverick Vinales	SPA	12	Monster Energy Yamaha MotoGP	Yamaha YZR-M1	M	F: Soft/R: Hard	26	40m 37.788s
3	Joan Mir	SPA	36	Team SUZUKI ECSTAR	Suzuki GSX-RR	M	F: Medium/R: Hard	26	40m 40.791s
4	Johann Zarco	FRA	5	Pramac Racing	Ducati Desmosedici	M	F: Medium/R: Hard	26	40m 41.161s
5	Miguel Oliveira	POR	88	Red Bull KTM Factory Racing	KTM RC16	M	F: Medium/R: Hard	26	40m 43.433s
6	Francesco Bagnaia	ITA	63	Ducati Lenovo Team	Ducati Desmosedici	M	F: Medium/R: Hard	26	40m 45.066s
7	Marc Marquez	SPA	93	Repsol Honda Team	Honda RC213V	M	F: Medium/R: Soft	26	40m 45.141s
8	Aleix Espargaro	SPA	41	Aprilia Racing Team Gresini	Aprilia RS-GP	M	F: Medium/R: Hard	26	40m 45.377s
9	Takaaki Nakagami	JPN	30	LCR Honda IDEMITSU	Honda RC213V	M	F: Medium/R: Medium	26	40m 47.256s
10	Pol Espargaro	SPA	44	Repsol Honda Team	Honda RC213V	M	F: Medium/R: Soft	26	40m 53.596s
11	Alex Rins	SPA	42	Team SUZUKI ECSTAR	Suzuki GSX-RR	M	F: Medium/R: Hard	26	40m 56.403s
12	Brad Binder	RSA	33	Red Bull KTM Factory Racing	KTM RC16	M	F: Medium/R: Hard	26	40m 56.707s
13	Danilo Petrucci	ITA	9	Tech 3 KTM Factory Racing	KTM RC16	M	F: Medium/R: Hard	26	41m 02.814s
14	Alex Marquez	SPA	73	LCR Honda CASTROL	Honda RC213V	M	F: Medium/R: Soft	26	41m 04.803s
15	Enea Bastianini	ITA	23	Avintia Esponsorama	Ducati Desmosedici	M	F: Medium/R: Hard	26	41m 07.816s
16	Lorenzo Savadori	ITA	32	Aprilia Racing Team Gresini	Aprilia RS-GP	M	F: Medium/R: Medium	26	41m 12.604s
17	Garrett Gerloff	USA	31	Petronas Yamaha SRT	Yamaha YZR-M1	M	F: Medium/R: Hard	26	41m 28.244s
18	Luca Marini	ITA	10	SKY VR46 Avintia	Ducati Desmosedici	M	F: Medium/R: Medium	26	41m 41.822s
	Iker Lecuona	SPA	27	Tech 3 KTM Factory Racing	KTM RC16	M	F: Medium/R: Medium	18	DNF-crash
	Jack Miller	AUS	43	Ducati Lenovo Team	Ducati Desmosedici	M	F: Medium/R: Hard	18	DNF-ret in pit
	Jorge Martin	SPA	89	Pramac Racing	Ducati Desmosedici	M	F: Medium/R: Medium	14	DNF-crash
	Valentino Rossi	ITA	46	Petronas Yamaha SRT	Yamaha YZR-M1	M	F: Medium/R: Hard	7	DNF-crash

Fastest lap: Fabio Quartararo, on lap 8, 1m 32.869s, 109.4mph/176.0km/h.
Lap record: Marc Marquez, 1m 33.617s, 108.5mph/174.6km/h (2015).
Event maximum speed: Jorge Martin, 197.0mph/317.0km/h (qualifying).

Qualifying
Weather: Dry
Air Temp: 25° Track Temp: 34°
Humidity: 55%

1	Vinales	1m 31.814s
2	Quartararo	1m 31.885s
3	Bagnaia	1m 32.116s
4	Nakagami	1m 32.314s
5	Zarco	1m 32.394s
6	Oliveira	1m 32.450s
7	Rins	1m 32.597s
8	Miller	1m 32.609s
9	A. Espargaro	1m 32.666s
10	Mir	1m 32.748s
11	P. Espargaro	1m 32.830s
12	Rossi	1m 32.919s

Q1

13	Lecuona	1m 32.724s
14	Martin	1m 32.850s
15	Savadori	1m 33.258s
16	A. Marquez	1m 33.288s
17	Marini	1m 33.321s
18	Petrucci	1m 33.378s
19	Bastianini	1m 33.404s
20	M. Marquez	1m 33.477s
21	Binder	1m 33.597s
22	Gerloff	1m 33.739s

Fastest race laps

1	Quartararo	1m 32.869s
2	Vinales	1m 33.045s
3	M. Marquez	1m 33.172s
4	Bagnaia	1m 33.173s
5	Mir	1m 33.213s
6	Zarco	1m 33.234s
7	Miller	1m 33.316s
8	Oliveira	1m 33.377s
9	Nakagami	1m 33.381s
10	A. Espargaro	1m 33.385s
11	P. Espargaro	1m 33.419s
12	Rins	1m 33.514s
13	Binder	1m 33.610s
14	Lecuona	1m 33.699s
15	Petrucci	1m 33.768s
16	A. Marquez	1m 33.836s
17	Martin	1m 33.864s
18	Bastianini	1m 34.054s
19	Rossi	1m 34.257s
20	Savadori	1m 34.309s
21	Gerloff	1m 34.569s
22	Marini	1m 35.194s

Championship Points

1	Quartararo	156
2	Zarco	122
3	Bagnaia	109
4	Mir	101
5	Miller	100
6	Vinales	95
7	Oliveira	85
8	A. Espargaro	61
9	Binder	60
10	M. Marquez	50
11	Nakagami	41
12	P. Espargaro	41
13	Morbidelli	40
14	Rins	33
15	A. Marquez	27
16	Bastianini	27
17	Petrucci	26
18	Martin	23
19	Rossi	17
20	Marini	14
21	Lecuona	13
22	Bradl	11
23	Savadori	4
24	Pirro	3
25	Rabat	1

Constructor Points

1	Yamaha	184
2	Ducati	167
3	KTM	114
4	Suzuki	105
5	Honda	86
6	Aprilia	62

Grid order / Lap by lap

Grid order	1	2	3	4	5	6	7	8	9	10	11	12	13	14	15	16	17	18	19	20	21	22	23	24	25	26	
12 VINALES	63	63	63	63	20	20	20	20	20	20	20	20	20	20	20	20	20	20	20	20	20	20	20	20	20	20	1
20 QUARTARARO	20	20	20	20	63	63	63	63	63	63	63	63	63	12	12	12	12	12	12	12	12	12	12	12	12	12	2
63 BAGNAIA	30	30	30	30	30	30	30	30	30	30	30	30	63	36	5	5	5	5	36	36	36	36	36	36	36	36	3
30 NAKAGAMI	12	12	12	12	12	12	12	12	12	12	12	5	36	36	36	36	5	5	5	5	5	5	5	5	5	5	4
5 ZARCO	42	5	5	5	5	5	5	5	5	5	5	5	30	88	88	88	88	88	88	88	88	88	88	88	88	88	5
88 OLIVEIRA	5	43	43	36	36	36	36	36	36	36	36	36	36	30	41	63	63	63	63	63	63	63	63	63	63	63	6
42 RINS	43	36	36	88	88	88	88	88	88	88	88	88	88	41	63	41	41	93	93	93	93	93	41	93	93	93	7
43 MILLER	36	88	88	43	43	43	43	43	43	43	43	43	43	63	93	93	93	41	41	41	41	41	93	41	41	41	8
41 A. ESPARGARO	88	41	41	41	41	41	41	41	41	41	41	41	41	93	30	30	30	30	30	30	30	30	30	30	30	30	9
36 MIR	41	93	93	93	93	93	93	93	93	93	93	93	93	44	44	44	44	44	44	44	44	44	44	44	44	44	10
44 P. ESPARGARO	44	44	44	44	44	44	44	44	44	44	44	44	44	27	27	33	33	42	42	42	42	42	42	42	42	42	11
46 ROSSI	93	89	89	89	27	27	27	27	27	27	27	27	27	9	9	9	9	33	33	33	33	33	33	33	33	33	12
27 LECUONA	27	27	27	27	89	89	89	89	89	89	89	9	9	33	33	33	73	9	9	9	9	9	9	9	9	9	13
89 MARTIN	89	73	73	73	73	73	73	73	73	73	73	33	73	73	73	42	42	73	73	73	73	73	73	73	73	73	14
32 SAVADORI	73	23	23	9	33	33	33	33	33	33	9	89	33	42	42	73	23	23	23	23	23	23	23	23	23	23	15
73 A. MARQUEZ	23	33	33	23	9	9	9	9	9	9	33	73	89	42	23	23	23	32	32	32	32	32	32	32	32	32	
10 MARINI	9	9	9	33	23	46	46	23	23	42	42	42	42	23	32	32	32	31	31	31	31	31	31	31	31	31	
9 PETRUCCI	33	32	32	32	32	23	23	42	42	23	23	23	23	32	43	43	31	31	10	10	10	10	10	10	10	10	
23 BASTIANINI	10	46	46	46	32	32	32	32	32	32	32	32	32	89	10	31	10	10									
93 M. MARQUEZ	32	10	10	10	42	42	10	10	10	10	10	10	10	31	10	10	43										
33 BINDER	46	31	31	31	42	10	10	31	31	31	31	31	31														
31 GERLOFF	31	42	42	42	31	31	31																				

89 Pit stop

156 DUTCH TT

Moto2

RACE DISTANCE: 24 laps, 67.734 miles/109.008km · **RACE WEATHER:** Dry (air 23°, humidity 70%, track 31°)

Pos.	Rider	Nat.	No.	Entrant	Machine	Laps	Time & Speed
1	Raul Fernandez	SPA	25	Red Bull KTM Ajo	Kalex	24	39m 01.832s 104.1mph/167.5km/h
2	Remy Gardner	AUS	87	Red Bull KTM Ajo	Kalex	24	39m 02.898s
3	Augusto Fernandez	SPA	37	Elf Marc VDS Racing Team	Kalex	24	39m 03.097s
4	Sam Lowes	GBR	22	Elf Marc VDS Racing Team	Kalex	24	39m 03.711s
5	Marco Bezzecchi	ITA	72	SKY Racing Team VR46	Kalex	24	39m 10.161s
6	Ai Ogura	JPN	79	IDEMITSU Honda Team Asia	Kalex	24	39m 12.792s
7	Jorge Navarro	SPA	9	+EGO Speed Up	Boscoscuro	24	39m 15.825s
8	Xavi Vierge	SPA	97	Petronas Sprinta Racing	Kalex	24	39m 17.884s
9	Marcel Schrotter	GER	23	Liqui Moly Intact GP	Kalex	24	39m 17.926s
10	Celestino Vietti	ITA	13	SKY Racing Team VR46	Kalex	24	39m 19.417s
11	Somkiat Chantra	THA	35	IDEMITSU Honda Team Asia	Kalex	24	39m 20.118s
12	Albert Arenas	SPA	75	Aspar Team Moto2	Boscoscuro	24	39m 20.644s
13	Stefano Manzi	ITA	62	Flexbox HP40	Kalex	24	39m 21.105s
14	Thomas Luthi	SWI	12	Pertamina Mandalika SAG Team	Kalex	24	39m 21.481s
15	Bo Bendsneyder	NED	64	Pertamina Mandalika SAG Team	Kalex	24	39m 23.994s
16	Cameron Beaubier	USA	6	American Racing	Kalex	24	39m 24.055s
17	Alonso Lopez	SPA	2	+EGO Speed Up	Boscoscuro	24	39m 27.401s
18	Jake Dixon	GBR	96	Petronas Sprinta Racing	Kalex	24	39m 28.077s
19	Nicolo Bulega	ITA	11	Federal Oil Gresini Moto2	Kalex	24	39m 29.155s
20	Marcos Ramirez	SPA	42	American Racing	Kalex	24	39m 29.295s
21	Simone Corsi	ITA	24	MV Agusta Forward Racing	MV Agusta	24	39m 29.470s
22	Manuel Gonzalez	SPA	18	MV Agusta Forward Racing	MV Agusta	24	39m 37.740s
23	Hafizh Syahrin	MAL	55	NTS RW Racing GP	NTS	24	39m 40.349s
24	Barry Baltus	BEL	70	NTS RW Racing GP	NTS	24	39m 48.560s
	Aron Canet	SPA	44	Aspar Team Moto2	Boscoscuro	19	DNF-crash
	Fabio Di Giannantonio	ITA	21	Federal Oil Gresini Moto2	Kalex	15	DNF-crash
	Joe Roberts	USA	16	Italtrans Racing Team	Kalex	7	DNF-crash
	Lorenzo Dalla Porta	ITA	19	Italtrans Racing Team	Kalex	0	DNF-crash
	Tony Arbolino	ITA	14	Liqui Moly Intact GP	Kalex	0	DNF-crash

Fastest lap: Raul Fernandez, on lap 21, 1m 36.690s, 105.1mph/169.1km/h.
Lap record: Augusto Fernandez, 1m 37.323s, 104.4mph/168.0km/h (2019).
Event maximum speed: Celestino Vietti, 163.9mph/263.7km/h (race).

Qualifying:
Weather: Dry
Air Temp: 26° Track Temp: 37°
Humidity: 56%

1	R. Fernandez	1m 36.356s
2	Gardner	1m 36.542s
3	Lowes	1m 36.686s
4	Canet	1m 36.765s
5	Garzo	1m 36.802s
6	Ogura	1m 36.804s
7	Navarro	1m 36.816s
8	A. Fernandez	1m 36.884s
9	Dalla Porta	1m 36.951s
10	Arbolino	1m 37.007s
11	Vietti	1m 37.023s
12	Luthi	1m 37.079s
13	Bendsneyder	1m 37.118s
14	Schrotter	1m 37.147s
15	Di Giannantonio	1m 37.230s
16	Arenas	1m 37.235s
17	Bezzecchi	1m 37.249s
18	Chantra	1m 37.373s
Q1		
19	Roberts	1m 37.041s
20	Ramirez	1m 37.054s
21	Corsi	1m 37.063s
22	Dixon	1m 37.171s
23	Manzi	1m 37.181s
24	Vierge	1m 37.236s
25	Beaubier	1m 37.261s
26	Bulega	1m 37.281s
27	Lopez	1m 37.299s
28	Baltus	1m 37.926s
29	Gonzalez	1m 38.141s
30	Syahrin	1m 38.515s

Fastest race laps

1	R. Fernandez	1m 36.690s
2	Lowes	1m 37.009s
3	Gardner	1m 37.023s
4	A. Fernandez	1m 37.044s
5	Ogura	1m 37.165s
6	Bezzecchi	1m 37.184s
7	Di Giannantonio	1m 37.269s
8	Navarro	1m 37.301s
9	Vierge	1m 37.302s
10	Vietti	1m 37.336s
11	Chantra	1m 37.404s
12	Bendsneyder	1m 37.507s
13	Manzi	1m 37.514s
14	Arenas	1m 37.521s
15	Beaubier	1m 37.534s
16	Dixon	1m 37.544s
17	Luthi	1m 37.547s
18	Canet	1m 37.549s
19	Schrotter	1m 37.580s
20	Ramirez	1m 37.647s
21	Corsi	1m 37.755s
22	Bulega	1m 37.786s
23	Lopez	1m 37.867s
24	Roberts	1m 37.922s
25	Gonzalez	1m 37.928s
26	Syahrin	1m 38.262s
27	Baltus	1m 38.357s

Championship Points

1	Gardner	184
2	R. Fernandez	153
3	Bezzecchi	128
4	Lowes	99
5	Di Giannantonio	73
6	Schrotter	66
7	Canet	55
8	A. Fernandez	50
9	Vierge	50
10	Roberts	50
11	Ogura	49
12	Navarro	42
13	Bendsneyder	39
14	Arbolino	30
15	Beaubier	26
16	Vietti	22
17	Arenas	22
18	Manzi	20
19	Chantra	16
20	Ramirez	16
21	Dixon	11
22	Garzo	11
23	Bulega	10
24	Syahrin	8
25	Corsi	7
26	Dalla Porta	6
27	Lopez	4
28	Aldeguer	4
29	Luthi	4
30	Baldassarri	3
31	Baltus	2

Constructor Points

1	Kalex	225
2	Boscoscuro	81
3	MV Agusta	10
4	NTS	10

Moto3

RACE DISTANCE: 22 laps, 62.090 miles/99.924km · **RACE WEATHER:** Dry (air 23°, humidity 70%, track 31°)

Pos.	Rider	Nat.	No.	Entrant	Machine	Laps	Time & Speed
1	Dennis Foggia	ITA	7	Leopard Racing	Honda	22	37m 35.287s 99.1mph/159.5km/h
2	Sergio Garcia	SPA	11	Gaviota GASGAS Aspar Team	GASGAS	22	37m 35.365s
3	Romano Fenati	ITA	55	Sterilgarda Max Racing Team	Husqvarna	22	37m 35.494s
4	Pedro Acosta	SPA	37	Red Bull KTM Ajo	KTM	22	37m 36.639s
5	Tatsuki Suzuki	JPN	24	SIC58 Squadra Corse	Honda	22	37m 36.732s
6	John McPhee	GBR	17	Petronas Sprinta Racing	Honda	22	37m 36.797s
7	Darryn Binder	RSA	40	Petronas Sprinta Racing	Honda	22	37m 36.625s
8	Gabriel Rodrigo	ARG	2	Indonesian Racing Gresini Moto3	Honda	22	37m 44.382s
9	Xavier Artigas	SPA	43	Leopard Racing	Honda	22	37m 44.427s
10	Jeremy Alcoba	SPA	52	Indonesian Racing Gresini Moto3	Honda	22	37m 45.670s
11	Stefano Nepa	ITA	82	BOE Owlride	KTM	22	37m 48.790s
12	Izan Guevara	SPA	28	Gaviota GASGAS Aspar Team	GASGAS	22	37m 48.842s
13	Kaito Toba	JPN	27	CIP Green Power	KTM	22	37m 56.344s
14	Niccolo Antonelli	ITA	23	Avintia Esponsorama Moto3	KTM	22	37m 57.377s
15	Deniz Oncu	TUR	53	Red Bull KTM Tech 3	KTM	22	38m 02.323s
16	Elia Bartolini	ITA	22	Avintia Esponsorama Moto3	KTM	22	38m 11.032s
17	Ryusei Yamanaka	JPN	6	CarXpert PruestelGP	KTM	22	38m 11.088s
18	Riccardo Rossi	ITA	54	BOE Owlride	KTM	22	38m 11.098s
19	Alberto Surra	ITA	67	Rivacold Snipers Team	Honda	22	38m 11.166s
20	Jaume Masia	SPA	5	Red Bull KTM Ajo	KTM	22	38m 20.957s
21	Lorenzo Fellon	FRA	20	SIC58 Squadra Corse	Honda	22	38m 38.779s
22	Joel Kelso	AUS	66	CIP Green Power	KTM	22	38m 38.839s
23	Yuki Kunii	JPN	92	Honda Team Asia	Honda	22	38m 39.056s
24	Andi Farid Izdihar	INA	19	Honda Team Asia	Honda	22	38m 39.266s
25	Takuma Matsuyama	JPN	32	Honda Team Asia	Honda	22	38m 39.424s
	Adrian Fernandez	SPA	31	Sterilgarda Max Racing Team	Husqvarna	13	DNF-crash
	Andrea Migno	ITA	16	Rivacold Snipers Team	Honda	10	DNF-crash

Fastest lap: Pedro Acosta, on lap 16, 1m 41.618s, 100.0mph/160.9km/h.
Lap record: Aron Canet, 1m 42.007s, 99.5mph/160.2km/h (2018).
Event maximum speed: John McPhee, 137.3mph/220.9km/h (race).

Qualifying:
Weather: Dry
Air Temp: 26° Track Temp: 35°
Humidity: 52%

1	Alcoba	1m 41.194s
2	Fenati	1m 41.406s
3	Foggia	1m 41.472s
4	Garcia	1m 41.473s
5	Toba	1m 41.479s
6	Rodrigo	1m 41.534s
7	Antonelli	1m 41.667s
8	Binder	1m 41.755s
9	Artigas	1m 41.878s
10	Masia	1m 42.003s
11	McPhee	1m 42.043s
12	Suzuki	1m 42.056s
13	Guevara	1m 42.194s
14	Fellon	1m 42.388s
15	Oncu	1m 42.392s
16	Bartolini	1m 42.526s
17	Migno	1m 42.539s
18	Acosta	No Time
Q1		
19	Kelso	1m 42.941s
20	Kunii	1m 43.011s
21	Fernandez	1m 43.162s
22	Yamanaka	1m 43.186s
23	Matsuyama	1m 43.258s
24	Izdihar	1m 44.320s
	Rossi	No Time
	Surra	No Time
	Nepa	No Time

Fastest race laps

1	Acosta	1m 41.618s
2	Nepa	1m 41.632s
3	Fenati	1m 41.660s
4	McPhee	1m 41.664s
5	Garcia	1m 41.694s
6	Binder	1m 41.727s
7	Suzuki	1m 41.733s
8	Foggia	1m 41.759s
9	Rodrigo	1m 41.885s
10	Artigas	1m 41.949s
11	Antonelli	1m 42.002s
12	Migno	1m 42.028s
13	Guevara	1m 42.104s
14	Toba	1m 42.112s
15	Alcoba	1m 42.276s
16	Oncu	1m 42.410s
17	Fernandez	1m 42.655s
18	Surra	1m 42.683s
19	Rossi	1m 42.814s
20	Matsuyama	1m 42.903s
21	Masia	1m 42.916s
22	Bartolini	1m 43.054s
23	Yamanaka	1m 43.116s
24	Izdihar	1m 43.119s
25	Kunii	1m 43.526s
26	Kelso	1m 43.580s
27	Fellon	1m 43.645s

Championship Points

1	Acosta	158
2	Garcia	110
3	Foggia	86
4	Fenati	80
5	Masia	72
6	Binder	69
7	Antonelli	67
8	Rodrigo	59
9	Alcoba	58
10	Migno	58
11	Sasaki	57
12	Toba	52
13	McPhee	37
14	Suzuki	37
15	Guevara	36
16	Salac	35
17	Artigas	30
18	Yamanaka	28
19	Dupasquier	27
20	Oncu	25
21	Nepa	19
22	Rossi	16
23	Tatay	14
24	Fernandez	10
25	Bartolini	7
26	Kunii	7
27	Kofler	3
28	Izdihar	2
29	Holgado	1

Constructor Points

1	KTM	190
2	Honda	178
3	GASGAS	122
4	Husqvarna	84

DUTCH TT 157

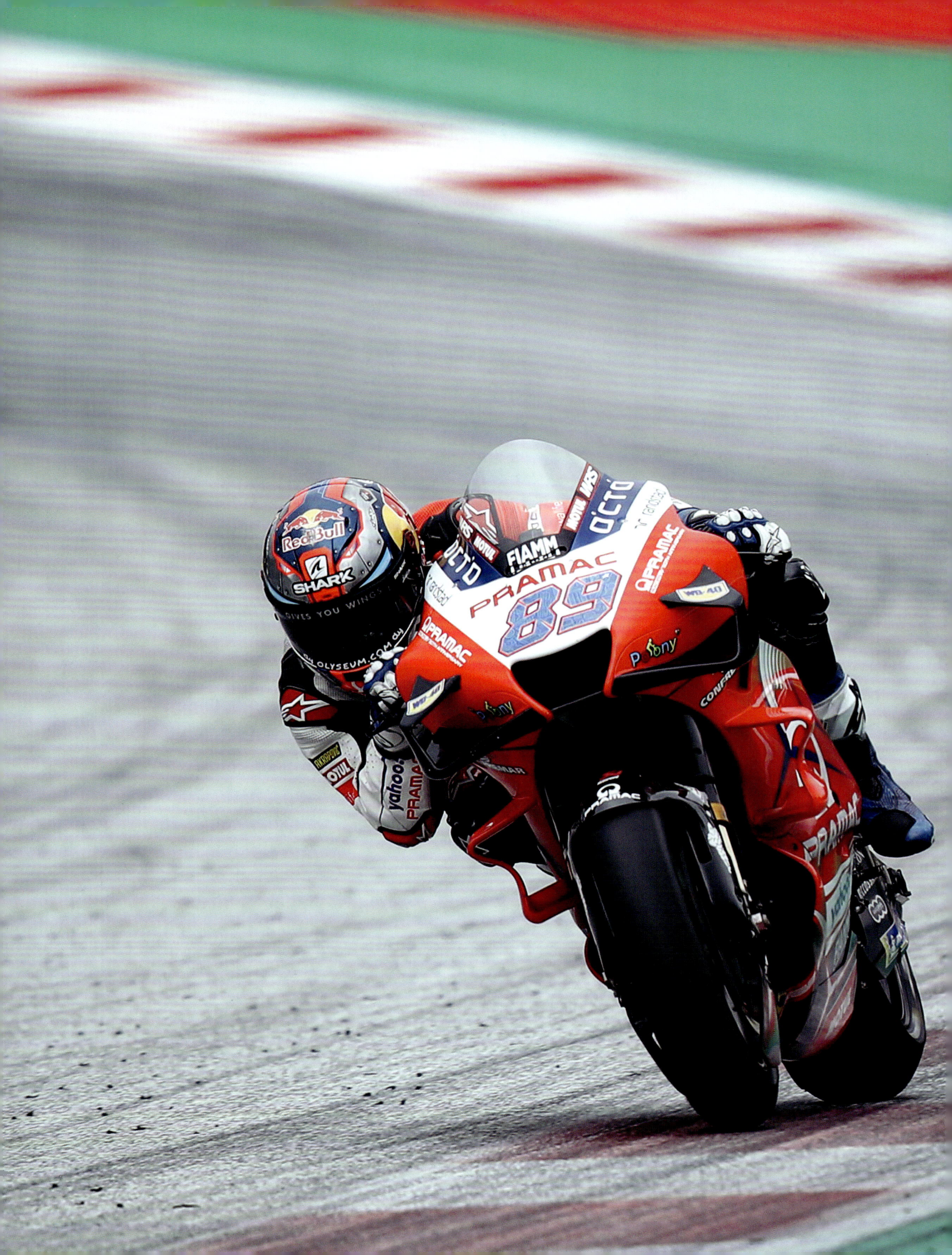

Red Bull
SHARK
FIAMM
PRAMAC
89

FIM WORLD CHAMPIONSHIP · ROUND 10

STYRIAN GRAND PRIX

RED BULL RING

Above: Burnt offerings. Marshals tackle the blazing remains of Savadori and Pedrosa's bikes.

Top right: Weather check – Jack Miller apprehensive on the grid.

Above right: Pedrosa looks on in dismay at the aftermath of the race-stopping crash.

Right: Smiling through, Rossi surprised nobody by announcing his retirement, but disappointed many hundreds of thousands.

Opening spread: Pramac Ducati rookie Jorge Martin held off defending champion Mir's revived Suzuki.
Photos: Gold & Goose

Opening spread, inset: The first-timer maintained Ducati's perfect record in Austria.
Photo: Pramac Racing

THE weekend began with an "exceptional press conference", called by Valentino Rossi on Thursday. Though it was not hard to surmise the reason – to announce his retirement – it was not certain. He had kept it secret from everybody except (newly pregnant) girlfriend Francesca Sofia Novello and his mother – and he had told her only the previous evening.

It came a year earlier than he'd hoped. At the start of the 2021 season, "I want to continue [for two years], but I needed to understand if I was fast enough." He wasn't. In his worst season of twenty-five-and-a-half, just a single top-ten was proof enough. Any temptation to ride a Ducati for his own new VR46 team, encouraged by earnest entreaties from the Saudi sponsor/fixer, had been denied. Interesting, he said, for two or three years, but for one year, "possibly dangerous".

Racing cars would help fill the void: he would miss being an athlete, working with his team, and the butterflies of race morning, but "number one, I will miss riding the MotoGP bike. It's always a great emotion."

It goes without saying that he will be much missed. Tributes poured in not only from former and current deadly rivals (Biaggi, Stoner and Marquez), but also from across the panoply of motor sports and beyond; while a massive tribute flag dangled from a helicopter on race day.

Trepidation doubtless stalked the corridors of Dorna and IRTA: Rossi's global popularity, reaching far beyond niche-sport boundaries, had made the single greatest contribution to their coffers during his carefully curated tenure. The question "What will happen when Rossi goes?" had been lurking for a decade or more.

Well, racing will go on, as it did on this weekend, back after an unprecedented five-weekend break. And to prove that there will be plenty of talent, 23-year-old class rookie Jorge Martin's first win reinforced talk of the changing of the guard. He was the sixth first-time winner in 13 months.

MotoGP's fastest track remained controversial, with safety called into question again. Riders were disappointed that requests for a chicane before Turn Three (scene of 2020's horrendous near disaster, when Rossi and Maverick Vinales had been missed by inches by the somersaulting motorbikes of Franco Morbidelli and Johann Zarco) had fallen on deaf ears. This time, problems on the exit from that corner brought out red flags after Dani Pedrosa slipped off early in the race and an unsighted Lorenzo Savadori ploughed into the fallen bike. The result was a spectacular fireball that required a lengthy clean up, while Savadori fractured a bone in his ankle.

This was the third red-flagged MotoGP race in succession at the circuit, and while Jack Miller insisted that such an incident could happen at any track, Aleix Espargaro had stronger words: "This track ... is not designed for motorbike races. We've been very lucky three times, but what about number four? What if today Lorenzo hit Dani instead of the fuel tank of the KTM?"

Pedrosa's appearance as a wild-card might have alleviated some of Rossi's brewing nostalgia, more than two years after his retirement. Snapped up as a test rider for KTM, the former Honda rider had played a major role in the marque's rapid progress from beginners to winners. Back on track with old rival Valentino, he outqualified and outraced him.

Also back in the saddle was Cal Crutchlow, riding the recuperating Morbidelli's two-year-old Yamaha in the Petronas SRT team, a cautious approach for a solid weekend two places out of the points. And news came that Morbidelli would finally be rewarded for his strong 2020 performance with promotion to the factory team, where at last he would get an up-to-date, full-factory-spec bike.

The summer break brought a long-requested rear ride-

160 STYRIAN GRAND PRIX

FIM WORLD CHAMPIONSHIP | 10

height system for Suzuki, the last MotoGP bike not to offer the ability to squat the rear on corner exit, lowering the centre of gravity to limit wheelies. It arrived only at the last minute and was fitted for the first time on Saturday, leaving Joan Mir and Alex Rins scant time to set it up. It proved beneficial immediately, for while Rins struggled again with poor qualifying, Mir finished a close second, his best of the year so far. "Without it, we were always at a disadvantage. Finally, it works – we gain acceleration. We need to work a bit more on it, but they made a great job," he said.

Rumours about Moto2 sensation Raul Fernandez's future had been circulating before the summer break. Now they came to an abrupt head, midway through Saturday's FP4. He would move from Moto2 to MotoGP for 2022, riding alongside current team-mate Remy Gardner in the satellite Tech3 squad,

The timing caught Tech3 off guard, completely blind-siding current riders Danilo Petrucci and Iker Lecuona, but there was a reason for this apparent lapse in diplomacy and good manners. A report that Jordi Arilla, one of Fernandez's representatives, had dined with Petronas SRT Yamaha boss Razlan Razali on Thursday infuriated KTM bosses, who hastily brought the decision forward, stressing their dismay at the attempted poaching of a prized occupant of their fabled riders' ladder through the classes.

Motorsports director Pit Beirer explained: "I actually got a little bit mad finding out that other manufacturers were talking to Raul, ripping his shirt. I was not so happy about it because he was quite happy to stay in Moto2. This was his wish; we were not pushing him in one direction or the other. If he wanted to go to MotoGP, of course, he would have had the chance on our side. So that's why I wanted to make everything quickly." Asked by a Spanish broadcaster whether he would be racing where he wanted to be in 2022, Fernandez's reply was a simple "No".

Vinales might have offered a different response, although protocol prevented him from confirming Italian media reports that he would definitely be joining Aprilia in 2022. This was officially confirmed two weeks later, but by then a whole new controversy had emerged. He had qualified ninth, and he made a strong start on Sunday, only for the race to be red-flagged. It went badly wrong on the restart, and he finished the first lap in last place. The coming laps yielded little improvement, and he pulled into the pits on the last lap, although he was classified as a finisher because his garage was beyond the finish line,

We would have to wait until the following week before full details of what had happened, and the dire consequences, were revealed. At this stage, unbeknown to all, this would be his last race for Yamaha.

MOTOGP RACE – 27 laps (shortened)

Out with the old, in with the new. Twenty-three-year-old Pramac Ducati rookie Jorge Martin's second pole of the year set a new track record, with fellow youngsters alongside – Bagnaia (24) and Quartararo (22) – on the front row. On the second: Miller (26) and Mir (23) came before the first older rider, 31-year-old Zarco.

Aleix Espargaro (32) led row three, but other old-timers were trailing: Pedrosa (35) was 14th, Pol Espargaro (30) alongside; Rossi (42) was 17th, Crutchlow (35) 23rd and last. Marc Marquez (28), qualified eighth, might have had pause for thought…

The odds were skewed in favour of one Ducati rider or another, Desmosedicis having won five of the previous six races at this track.

The first start was hectic, Marc Marquez's first-corner lunge on Aleix Espargaro a harbinger of things to come. Bagnaia led Martin, Mir and an all-action fight for fourth, Marquez and the Yamahas of Quartararo and Vinales. Quartararo's two-in-one move on Marquez and Mir at Turn Six on the second lap was a particular highlight.

STYRIAN GRAND PRIX 161

The Pedrosa/Savadori crash, three laps in, brought out the red flags as the track was engulfed in flames. Forty-one minutes late came the restart, the race cut by one lap.

As they lined up, Vinales stalled on the grid, forcing a pit-lane start; and it was clear that two other previous front-runners would play no part up front. Not long after Marquez had pushed Espargaro wide at the first turn for the second time in 40 minutes, the Repsol Honda went wide there again, dropping him from tenth to 14th. He would struggle for rear grip throughout. The same issue affected Bagnaia, who dropped away from sixth on lap one to a frustrated ninth, then fell to 11th with a three-second penalty in lieu of a long-lap. Others infringing track limits, very easily done here, took the penalty: Vinales, Bastianini, Lecuona and Pol Espargaro.

Miller made the early pace, Martin, Mir, Quartararo and Zarco in hot pursuit; the LCR Hondas of Alex Marquez and Nakagami ahead of Bagnaia on lap two.

A small, but costly mistake by Miller out of Turn One gave Martin the chance to lead for the first time. By Turn Six, Mir was also past the Australian, setting up a clash with old Rookies Cup and Moto3 rival Martin.

Miller and Quartararo behind were engaged in their own duel: on lap seven, they exchanged places three times, the Frenchman gaining the upper hand.

Ahead, Mir stalked his countryman for ten laps, never more than two-tenths behind. But the Ducati's acceleration from Turns One and Three was clear, and by lap 15 the defending champion was struggling. By lap 19, the deficit was seven-tenths; on the 22nd, the deciding moment came when Mir ran into Turn Three too hot. Suddenly, the rookie had 1.2 seconds in hand, and the race was won.

Mir remained pleased with second, after Suzuki's productive summer break, with eight races remaining. "To be fighting for the victory is a really great reward," he said.

By half-distance, Quartararo had been more than 2.5 seconds away, keeping a persistent Miller behind. By lap 17, the Australian appeared close enough to attack, only to tuck the front at Turn Seven a lap later. From there, the Frenchman could coast to third, a massive boost considering Yamaha's woes at the track in 2020. "More than my victories, the difference from last year is about the three third positions at Sachsenring, Le Mans and here," he said, having further extended his points lead.

Title rival Zarco had sat fourth since Miller's demise, but had been powerless as Nakagami and Binder caught up with one lap to go. As before, the South African was ferocious on tired tyres. Outbraking moves on Zarco (Turn Four) and Nakagami (Turn Nine) resulted in a surprise fourth, after starting 16th and struggling with front grip.

Rins, seventh, counted the cost of poor qualifying, with Marc Marquez frustrated in eighth, ahead of brother Alex and Pedrosa, in his first race in two years and nine months.

With Bagnaia demoted to 11th and Bastianini another four seconds away, Rossi was close; Marini and Lecuona taking the last points, a final-lap run-off costing Petrucci 15th. Pol Espargaro was 16th, blaming a lack of grip on a tyre that had already been through one heat cycle, all that was left to him for the restart.

Both Aleix Espargaro and Oliveira retired, the latter with his front tyre chunking. Vinales didn't bother to finish.

MOTO2 RACE – 25 laps

For once, at the sponsor's home track, the Red Bull duo didn't even make the podium, in a race made more fraught than usual by not only very close qualifying times – 16 inside the same second – but also iffy conditions. The track had dried enough for slicks, but early crashes for Roberts, Corsi and Baltus, plus a Turn Nine mistake by Raul Fernandez, which dropped him from fourth to ninth, showed how tricky it was.

Gardner was back on pole for the first time in three races, with Raul Fernandez directly behind, leading row two. Along-

Above: On the gas, Bezzecchi, Canet and Ogura dispute Moto2 honours.

Top: Too close for comfort in the first-corner shuffle in MotoGP. Bagnaia has the advantage, Quartararo and Miller (half hidden) are on the inside, but Marquez is forcing Espargaro to head for the run-off area.
Photos: Gold & Goose

Top right: This close. A long-awaited suspension upgrade returned the smile to second-placed Joan Mir.
Photo: www.suzuki-racing.com

Above right: At last, Bezzecchi could celebrate a first win of 2021.

Right: Garcia (11) leads Acosta, Fenati follows. The front pair ran away, far enough for Garcia to fall, remount and still finish second.
Photos: Gold & Goose

side the Australian for a career-first front row, the other notable rookie, Ogura, with Bezzecchi third.

Canet and Augusto Fernandez completed row two; Lowes led the third from Dalla Porta and Ogura's Honda Team Asia team-mate, Chantra. But the hopes of the team, run by the last ever 250 champion, Hiroshi Aoyama, would be thwarted somewhat by the dreaded intervention of the stewards.

Bezzecchi got the jump off the line, from Raul Fernandez, Gardner, Canet and Ogura. By lap six, the first four were a second ahead of the Japanese rider, all skirting the damp patches. Then Fernandez fell foul of one of them next time around and dropped out of the lead group.

On the same lap, a shuffle up front resulted in Canet leading briefly, while Gardner moved to second, then into the lead at Turn Nine. Now he had the initiative, with Canet and Bezzecchi pushing to keep up, and Ogura gaining speed to make a quartet.

Bezzecchi reeled in Gardner, moving ahead on lap 19. Then the Australian made an uncustomary mistake at Turn Four, running off track, to rejoin in fifth, which left Ogura to take the fight to Bezzecchi, Canet still in close attendance.

Misfortune awaited the Japanese youngster, as he strayed over the white line once too often. A long-lap penalty was awarded, and he dropped from second to fifth on lap 22. He held the position behind Gardner, crossing the line a tenth adrift. But he had strayed again in the run through the penalty lane and, with no time to serve another long-lap, would be docked three seconds at the end. Fortunately, he didn't lose another position.

Canet pushed again, but Bezzecchi had enough to get clear by better than a second, his first win of the year.

Augusto Fernandez took advantage of the chaos ahead to come through steadily for a second straight third, with Gardner and Ogura next. Vietti had moved up impressively from 18th on lap one to nab sixth from Raul Fernandez at the flag.

Chantra was a career-best eighth, having held Vierge and Schrotter at bay. Dixon came through for 11th, from Dalla Porta and Di Giannantonio, with Lowes right behind. The Englishman had run as high as sixth after half-distance, but a couple of slips had dropped him back.

MOTO3 RACE – 23 laps

Acosta's championship charge showed no signs of slowing after he beat Garcia in a straight last-lap duel. In fact, the latter slipped off in the last corners, but the pair were so far ahead that he was able to remount without losing second.

Conditions were especially fraught: heavy morning rain had left the track wet, but clear skies and dry patches began forming on the sighting lap. Eight riders gambled on slicks, including Binder and Oncu, who left the switch too late and had to start from the back of the grid, losing any advantage he might have gained from his career-first pole position.

That left Garcia and Fenati up front; Acosta, Guevara and Foggia on row two.

Garcia and Acosta immediately showed why they led the championship, and by half-distance they had a seven-second lead over a three-rider fight for third – Fenati, Masia and Sasaki. Garcia led the most, but Acosta rode with swagger behind, studying his compatriot.

On the last lap, Garcia took them both wide at Turn Three to seize the lead. Acosta's response into Turn Nine took them wide again, Garcia finding a wet patch to slip off. He remounted to finish 14 seconds away, but still one clear of Fenati and Masia, with Sasaki a little behind.

The slick gamble didn't quite pay off for Binder, the race just a couple of laps too short as he charged through in the later stages, setting fastest lap. He was less than two seconds behind Sasaki in sixth.

The next best rider on slicks was McPhee in 13th; Oncu, and fellow gamblers Rodrigo and Alcoba were left trailing well out of the points.

STYRIAN GRAND PRIX 163

FIM WORLD CHAMPIONSHIP: ROUND 10

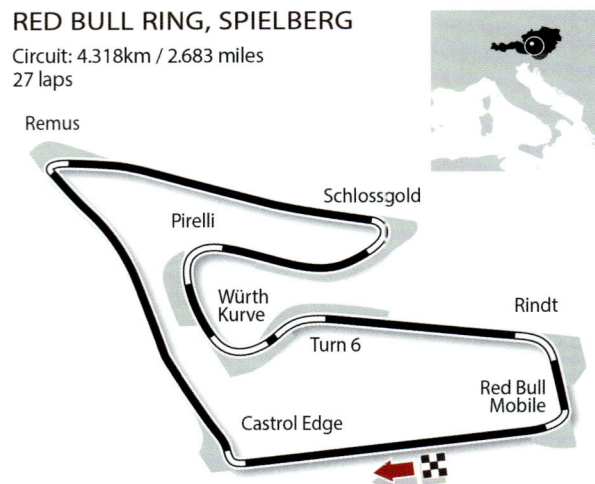

MICHELIN GRAND PRIX OF STYRIA
6–8 AUGUST, 2021

RED BULL RING, SPIELBERG
Circuit: 4.318km / 2.683 miles
27 laps

MotoGP
RACE DISTANCE: 27 laps, 72.443 miles / 116.586km · RACE WEATHER: Dry (air 19°, humidity 67%, track 19°)

Pos.	Rider	Nat.	No.	Entrant	Machine	Race tyre choice	Laps	Time & speed
1	Jorge Martin	SPA	89	Pramac Racing	Ducati Desmosedici	F: Medium / R: Medium	27	38m 07.879s 114.0mph/183.4km/h
2	Joan Mir	SPA	36	Team SUZUKI ECSTAR	Suzuki GSX-RR	F: Medium/R: Medium	27	38m 09.427s
3	Fabio Quartararo	FRA	20	Monster Energy Yamaha MotoGP	Yamaha YZR-M1	F: Medium/R: Medium	27	38m 17.511s
4	Brad Binder	RSA	33	Red Bull KTM Factory Racing	KTM RC16	F: Hard/R: Medium	27	38m 20.650s
5	Takaaki Nakagami	JPN	30	LCR Honda IDEMITSU	Honda RC213V	F: Medium/R: Medium	27	38m 20.802s
6	Johann Zarco	FRA	5	Pramac Racing	Ducati Desmosedici	F: Medium/R: Soft	27	38m 20.910s
7	Alex Rins	SPA	42	Team SUZUKI ECSTAR	Suzuki GSX-RR	F: Hard/R: Medium	27	38m 22.718s
8	Marc Marquez	SPA	93	Repsol Honda Team	Honda RC213V	F: Hard/R: Medium	27	38m 25.832s
9	Alex Marquez	SPA	73	LCR Honda CASTROL	Honda RC213V	F: Medium/R: Medium	27	38m 26.938s
10	Dani Pedrosa	SPA	26	Red Bull KTM Factory Racing	KTM RC16	F: Medium/R: Medium	27	38m 27.268s
11	Francesco Bagnaia	ITA	63	Ducati Lenovo Team	Ducati Desmosedici	F: Medium/R: Medium	27	38m 29.546s
12	Enea Bastianini	ITA	23	Avintia Esponsorama	Ducati Desmosedici	F: Medium/R: Medium	27	38m 33.146s
13	Valentino Rossi	ITA	46	Petronas Yamaha SRT	Yamaha YZR-M1	F: Medium/R: Soft	27	38m 34.161s
14	Luca Marini	ITA	10	SKY VR46 Avintia	Ducati Desmosedici	F: Medium/R: Medium	27	38m 35.371s
15	Iker Lecuona	SPA	27	Tech 3 KTM Factory Racing	KTM RC16	F: Hard/R: Medium	27	38m 38.955s
16	Pol Espargaro	SPA	44	Repsol Honda Team	Honda RC213V	F: Medium/R: Medium	27	38m 39.029s
17	Cal Crutchlow	GBR	35	Petronas Yamaha SRT	Yamaha YZR-M1	F: Medium/R: Medium	27	38m 48.287s
18	Danilo Petrucci	ITA	9	Tech 3 KTM Factory Racing	KTM RC16	F: Medium/R: Medium	27	38m 55.993s
	Maverick Vinales	SPA	12	Monster Energy Yamaha MotoGP	Yamaha YZR-M1	F: Medium/R: Medium	27	39m 11.028s
	Jack Miller	AUS	43	Ducati Lenovo Team	Ducati Desmosedici	F: Medium/R: Medium	18	DNF-crash
	Miguel Oliveira	POR	88	Red Bull KTM Factory Racing	KTM RC16	F: Hard/R: Medium	14	DNF-tyre
	Aleix Espargaro	SPA	41	Aprilia Racing Team Gresini	Aprilia RS-GP	F: Hard/R: Medium	4	DNF-technical
	Lorenzo Savadori	ITA	32	Aprilia Racing Team Gresini	Aprilia RS-GP	F: Medium/R: Soft	–	DNS-injured

Fastest lap: Joan Mir, on lap 7, 1m 24.209s, 114.6mph/184.5km/h.
Lap record: Andrea Dovizioso, 1m 23.827s, 115.2mph/185.4km/h (2019).
Event maximum speed: Francesco Bagnaia, 199.7mph/321.4km/h (race).

Qualifying
Weather: Dry
Air Temp: 25° **Track Temp:** 32°
Humidity: 50%

1	Martin	1m 22.994s
2	Bagnaia	1m 23.038s
3	Quartararo	1m 23.075s
4	Miller	1m 23.300s
5	Mir	1m 23.322s
6	Zarco	1m 23.376s
7	A. Espargaro	1m 23.448s
8	M. Marquez	1m 23.489s
9	Vinales	1m 23.508s
10	Nakagami	1m 23.536s
11	A. Marquez	1m 23.841s
12	Oliveira	1m 23.944s

Q1

13	Rins	1m 23.585s
14	Pedrosa	1m 23.730s
15	P. Espargaro	1m 23.971s
16	Binder	1m 24.050s
17	Rossi	1m 24.097s
18	Marini	1m 24.115s
19	Lecuona	1m 24.141s
20	Bastianini	1m 24.245s
21	Savadori	1m 24.405s
22	Petrucci	1m 24.465s
23	Crutchlow	1m 24.513s

Fastest race laps

1	Mir	1m 24.209s
2	Martin	1m 24.232s
3	Zarco	1m 24.302s
4	Quartararo	1m 24.347s
5	Miller	1m 24.477s
6	Binder	1m 24.509s
7	Rins	1m 24.555s
8	Nakagami	1m 24.592s
9	Vinales	1m 24.619s
10	A. Marquez	1m 24.630s
11	Oliveira	1m 24.630s
12	Bagnaia	1m 24.731s
13	M. Marquez	1m 24.759s
14	Pedrosa	1m 24.854s
15	Bastianini	1m 24.918s
16	Lecuona	1m 24.922s
17	Marini	1m 24.996s
18	P. Espargaro	1m 25.025s
19	Rossi	1m 25.119s
20	Petrucci	1m 25.120s
21	A. Espargaro	1m 25.147s
22	Crutchlow	1m 25.533s

Championship Points

1	Quartararo	172
2	Zarco	132
3	Mir	121
4	Bagnaia	114
5	Miller	100
6	Vinales	95
7	Oliveira	85
8	Binder	73
9	A. Espargaro	61
10	M. Marquez	58
11	Nakagami	52
12	Martin	48
13	Rins	42
14	P. Espargaro	41
15	Morbidelli	40
16	A. Marquez	34
17	Bastianini	31
18	Petrucci	26
19	Rossi	20
20	Marini	16
21	Lecuona	14
22	Bradl	11
23	Pedrosa	6
24	Savadori	4
25	Pirro	3
26	Rabat	1

Constructor Points

1	Yamaha	200
2	Ducati	192
3	KTM	127
4	Suzuki	125
5	Honda	97
6	Aprilia	62

Grid order / Lap-by-lap leaders

Grid order	1	2	3	4	5	6	7	8	9	10	11	12	13	14	15	16	17	18	19	20	21	22	23	24	25	26	27	
89 MARTIN	43	43	43	89	89	89	89	89	89	89	89	89	89	89	89	89	89	89	89	89	89	89	89	89	89	89	89	1
63 BAGNAIA	89	36	89	36	36	36	36	36	36	36	36	36	36	36	36	36	36	36	36	36	36	36	36	36	36	36	36	2
20 QUARTARARO	36	89	36	43	43	43	20	20	20	20	20	20	20	20	20	20	20	20	20	20	20	20	20	20	20	20	20	3
43 MILLER	20	20	20	20	20	20	43	43	43	43	43	43	43	43	43	43	5	5	5	5	5	5	5	5	5	5	33	4
36 MIR	5	5	5	5	5	5	5	5	5	5	5	5	5	5	5	5	30	30	30	30	30	30	30	30	30	30	30	5
5 ZARCO	63	73	73	73	73	73	30	73	30	30	30	30	30	30	30	30	42	42	42	42	42	33	33	33	33	5	5	6
41 A. ESPARGARO	73	30	30	30	30	30	73	30	73	73	73	73	73	73	73	42	33	33	33	33	33	42	42	42	42	42	42	7
93 M. MARQUEZ	42	63	63	33	33	33	42	42	42	42	42	42	42	42	42	73	33	93	93	93	93	93	93	93	93	93	93	8
12 VINALES	30	42	33	42	42	42	33	33	33	33	33	33	33	33	33	33	73	73	73	73	73	73	73	73	73	73	73	9
30 NAKAGAMI	93	33	42	88	88	88	88	88	88	88	88	93	93	93	93	93	63	63	63	63	63	63	63	63	63	63	63	10
73 A. MARQUEZ	33	27	88	63	63	63	63	63	63	93	93	88	63	63	63	63	26	26	26	26	26	26	26	26	26	26	26	11
88 OLIVEIRA	88	88	27	27	93	93	93	93	63	63	63	63	23	23	23	26	27	27	27	27	27	27	23	23	23	23	23	12
42 RINS	27	44	93	93	27	27	27	27	27	27	23	23	26	26	27	27	44	44	46	23	23	23	46	46	46	46	46	13
26 PEDROSA	44	93	44	44	44	26	26	26	26	23	26	26	27	27	44	44	46	46	23	46	46	46	10	10	10	10	10	14
44 P. ESPARGARO	26	26	26	26	26	23	23	23	26	27	27	27	44	44	46	46	23	23	9	9	9	9	10	10	9	9	27	15
33 BINDER	23	41	41	41	23	44	44	44	44	44	46	44	44	46	9	23	9	10	10	10	10	10	9	9	27	27	44	
46 ROSSI	41	23	23	23	46	46	46	46	46	46	44	46	46	9	9	23	10	10	44	44	44	44	44	44	44	44	35	
10 MARINI	9	46	46	9	9	9	9	9	9	9	10	10	10	10	10	12	12	12	12	12	12	12	12	12	35	35	9	
27 LECUONA	46	46	9	9	10	10	10	10	10	12	12	12	12	12	35	35	35	35	35	35	35	35	35	12	12	12	12	
23 BASTIANINI	10	10	10	10	35	35	35	35	12	10	10	35	12	12	12	35	43											
9 PETRUCCI	35	35	35	35	12	12	12	12	35	35	35	12	88				88 Pit stop											
35 CRUTCHLOW	12	12	12	12																								

164 STYRIAN GRAND PRIX

Moto2

RACE DISTANCE: 25 laps, 67.077 miles/107.950km · **RACE WEATHER:** Dry (air 18°, humidity 81%, track 18°)

Pos.	Rider	Nat.	No.	Entrant	Machine	Laps	Time & Speed
1	Marco Bezzecchi	ITA	72	SKY Racing Team VR46	Kalex	25	37m 29.460s 107.3mph/ 172.7KM/h
2	Aron Canet	SPA	44	Aspar Team Moto2	Boscoscuro	25	37m 30.631s
3	Augusto Fernandez	SPA	37	Elf Marc VDS Racing Team	Kalex	25	37m 32.720s
4	Remy Gardner	AUS	87	Red Bull KTM Ajo	Kalex	25	37m 33.316s
5	Ai Ogura	JPN	79	IDEMITSU Honda Team Asia	Kalex	25	37m 36.382s
6	Celestino Vietti	ITA	13	SKY Racing Team VR46	Kalex	25	37m 38.850s
7	Raul Fernandez	SPA	25	Red Bull KTM Ajo	Kalex	25	37m 39.050s
8	Somkiat Chantra	THA	35	IDEMITSU Honda Team Asia	Kalex	25	37m 41.677s
9	Xavi Vierge	SPA	97	Petronas Sprinta Racing	Kalex	25	37m 42.207s
10	Marcel Schrotter	GER	23	Liqui Moly Intact GP	Kalex	25	37m 42.334s
11	Jake Dixon	GBR	96	Petronas Sprinta Racing	Kalex	25	37m 42.992s
12	Lorenzo Dalla Porta	ITA	19	Italtrans Racing Team	Kalex	25	37m 43.531s
13	Fabio Di Giannantonio	ITA	21	Federal Oil Gresini Moto2	Kalex	25	37m 43.657s
14	Sam Lowes	GBR	22	Elf Marc VDS Racing Team	Kalex	25	37m 43.996s
15	Albert Arenas	SPA	75	Aspar Team Moto2	Boscoscuro	25	37m 48.076s
16	Thomas Luthi	SWI	12	Pertamina Mandalika SAG Team	Kalex	25	37m 48.838s
17	Tony Arbolino	ITA	14	Liqui Moly Intact GP	Kalex	25	37m 49.120s
18	Stefano Manzi	ITA	62	Flexbox HP40	Kalex	25	37m 51.927s
19	Marcos Ramirez	SPA	42	American Racing	Kalex	25	37m 52.222s
20	Jorge Navarro	SPA	9	Lightech Speed Up	Boscoscuro	25	37m 54.727s
21	Lorenzo Baldassarri	ITA	7	MV Agusta Forward Racing	MV Agusta	25	37m 59.581s
22	Nicolo Bulega	ITA	11	Federal Oil Gresini Moto2	Kalex	25	38m 07.004s
23	Bo Bendsneyder	NED	64	Pertamina Mandalika SAG Team	Kalex	25	38m 07.555s
24	Yari Montella	ITA	5	Lightech Speed Up	Boscoscuro	25	38m 08.467s
25	Simone Corsi	ITA	24	MV Agusta Forward Racing	MV Agusta	23	37m 56.606s
	Cameron Beaubier	USA	6	American Racing	Kalex	19	DNF-crash
	Hector Garzo	SPA	40	Flexbox HP40	Kalex	17	DNF-crash
	Hafizh Syahrin	MAL	55	NTS RW Racing GP	NTS	9	DNF-crash
	Joe Roberts	USA	16	Italtrans Racing Team	Kalex	9	DNF-crash
	Barry Baltus	BEL	70	NTS RW Racing GP	NTS	1	DNF-crash

Fastest lap: Ai Ogura, on lap 25, 1m 28.922s, 108.6mph/174.8km/h.
Lap record: Marco Bezzecchi, 1m 28.687s, 108.9mph/175.2km/h (2020).
Event maximum speed: Hector Garzo, 164.5mph/264.7km/h (race).

Qualifying
Weather: Dry
Air Temp: 26° **Track Temp:** 32°
Humidity: 48%

1	Gardner	1m 28.668s
2	Ogura	1m 28.789s
3	Bezzecchi	1m 28.811s
4	R. Fernandez	1m 28.978s
5	Canet	1m 29.004s
6	A. Fernandez	1m 29.005s
7	Lowes	1m 29.138s
8	Dalla Porta	1m 29.220s
9	Chantra	1m 29.223s
10	Schrotter	1m 29.238s
11	Vierge	1m 29.275s
12	Di Giannantonio	1m 29.334s
13	Luthi	1m 29.361s
14	Garzo	1m 29.385s
15	Arenas	1m 29.416s
16	Ramirez	1m 29.572s
17	Manzi	1m 29.778s
18	Arbolino	1m 29.929s

Q1
19	Vietti	1m 29.494s
20	Roberts	1m 29.531s
21	Dixon	1m 29.565s
22	Bendsneyder	1m 29.719s
23	Bulega	1m 29.739s
24	Beaubier	1m 29.747s
25	Navarro	1m 29.785s
26	Baldassarri	1m 29.832s
27	Syahrin	1m 29.911s
28	Corsi	1m 29.979s
29	Baltus	1m 30.032s
30	Montella	1m 30.354s

Fastest race laps

1	Ogura	1m 28.922s
2	Bezzecchi	1m 29.048s
3	Gardner	1m 29.053s
4	Vietti	1m 29.203s
5	Canet	1m 29.261s
6	A. Fernandez	1m 29.286s
7	Navarro	1m 29.420s
8	R. Fernandez	1m 29.439s
9	Beaubier	1m 29.498s
10	Schrotter	1m 29.507s
11	Vierge	1m 29.534s
12	Arbolino	1m 29.540s
13	Dalla Porta	1m 29.569s
14	Lowes	1m 29.601s
15	Garzo	1m 29.601s
16	Di Giannantonio	1m 29.604s
17	Dixon	1m 29.611s
18	Chantra	1m 29.635s
19	Manzi	1m 29.664s
20	Arenas	1m 29.731s
21	Luthi	1m 29.756s
22	Ramirez	1m 29.789s
23	Bendsneyder	1m 30.026s
24	Bulega	1m 30.115s
25	Montella	1m 30.128s
26	Syahrin	1m 30.188s
27	Baldassarri	1m 30.233s
28	Corsi	1m 30.359s
29	Roberts	1m 31.884s

Championship Points

1	Gardner	197
2	R. Fernandez	162
3	Bezzecchi	153
4	Lowes	101
5	Di Giannantonio	76
6	Canet	75
7	Schrotter	72
8	A. Fernandez	66
9	Ogura	60
10	Vierge	57
11	Roberts	50
12	Navarro	42
13	Bendsneyder	39
14	Vietti	32
15	Arbolino	30
16	Beaubier	26
17	Chantra	24
18	Arenas	23
19	Manzi	20
20	Dixon	16
21	Ramirez	16
22	Garzo	11
23	Bulega	10
24	Dalla Porta	10
25	Syahrin	8
26	Corsi	7
27	Lopez	4
28	Aldeguer	4
29	Luthi	4
30	Baldassarri	3
31	Baltus	2

Constructor Points

1	Kalex	250
2	Boscoscuro	101
3	MV Agusta	10
4	NTS	10

Moto3

RACE DISTANCE: 23 laps, 61.711 miles/99.314km · **RACE WEATHER:** Wet (air 17°, humidity 87%, track 17°)

Pos.	Rider	Nat.	No.	Entrant	Machine	Laps	Time & Speed
1	Pedro Acosta	SPA	37	Red Bull KTM Ajo	KTM	23	39m 45.869s 93.1mph/ 149.8km/h
2	Sergio Garcia	SPA	11	SANTANDER Consumer GASGAS	GASGAS	23	40m 00.300s
3	Romano Fenati	ITA	55	Sterilgarda Max Racing Team	Husqvarna	23	40m 01.279s
4	Jaume Masia	SPA	5	Red Bull KTM Ajo	KTM	23	40m 01.379s
5	Ayumu Sasaki	JPN	71	Red Bull KTM Tech 3	KTM	23	40m 04.716s
6	Darryn Binder	RSA	40	Petronas Sprinta Racing	Honda	23	40m 06.403s
7	Ryusei Yamanaka	JPN	6	CarXpert PruestelGP	KTM	23	40m 15.949s
8	Yuki Kunii	JPN	92	Honda Team Asia	Honda	23	40m 16.043s
9	Maximilian Kofler	AUT	73	CIP Green Power	KTM	23	40m 16.114s
10	Adrian Fernandez	SPA	31	Sterilgarda Max Racing Team	Husqvarna	23	40m 22.224s
11	Filip Salac	CZE	12	CarXpert PruestelGP	KTM	23	40m 22.306s
12	Kaito Toba	JPN	27	CIP Green Power	KTM	23	40m 22.528s
13	John McPhee	GBR	17	Petronas Sprinta Racing	Honda	23	40m 22.534s
14	Izan Guevara	SPA	28	SANTANDER Consumer GASGAS	GASGAS	23	40m 23.383s
15	Tatsuki Suzuki	JPN	24	SIC58 Squadra Corse	Honda	23	40m 23.787s
16	Lorenzo Fellon	FRA	20	SIC58 Squadra Corse	Honda	23	40m 33.514s
17	Andrea Migno	ITA	16	Rivacold Snipers Team	Honda	23	40m 38.746s
18	Jeremy Alcoba	SPA	52	Indonesian Racing Gresini Moto3	Honda	23	40m 38.875s
19	Stefano Nepa	ITA	82	BOE Owlride	KTM	23	40m 41.813s
20	Gabriel Rodrigo	ARG	2	Indonesian Racing Gresini Moto3	Honda	23	40m 52.409s
21	Deniz Oncu	TUR	53	Red Bull KTM Tech 3	KTM	23	40m 58.160s
22	Dennis Foggia	ITA	7	Leopard Racing	Honda	23	41m 08.507s
23	Riccardo Rossi	ITA	54	BOE Owlride	KTM	23	41m 17.357s
	David Salvador	SPA	38	Rivacold Snipers Team	Honda	14	DNF-crash
	Andi Farid Izdihar	INA	19	Honda Team Asia	Honda	12	DNF-crash
	Carlos Tatay	SPA	99	Avintia Esponsorama Moto3	KTM	-	DNS

Fastest lap: Darryn Binder, on lap 22, 1m 40.659s, 95.9mph/154.4km/h.
Lap record: Ayumu Sasaki, 1m 36.103s, 100.5mph/161.7km/h (2020).
Event maximum speed: Izan Guevara, 137.8mph/221.7km/h (free practice).

Qualifying
Weather: Dry
Air Temp: 27° **Track Temp:** 37°
Humidity: 47%

1	Oncu	1m 36.453s
2	Garcia	1m 36.477s
3	Fenati	1m 36.506s
4	Acosta	1m 36.575s
5	Guevara	1m 36.635s
6	Foggia	1m 36.637s
7	Masia	1m 36.637s
8	Binder	1m 36.657s
9	Alcoba	1m 36.716s
10	Rodrigo	1m 36.720s
11	Antonelli	1m 36.728s
12	McPhee	1m 36.743s
13	Rossi	1m 36.807s
14	Suzuki	1m 36.819s
15	Sasaki	1m 37.116s
16	Migno	1m 37.296s
17	Nepa	1m 37.513s
18	Salac	No Time

Q1
19	Artigas	1m 36.742s
20	Tatay	1m 36.818s
21	Yamanaka	1m 36.872s
22	Kunii	1m 36.882s
23	Fellon	1m 36.953s
24	Kofler	1m 36.970s
25	Toba	1m 37.317s
26	Salvador	1m 37.366s
27	Fernandez	1m 37.538s
28	Izdihar	1m 37.713s

Fastest race laps

1	Binder	1m 40.659s
2	Oncu	1m 41.155s
3	McPhee	1m 41.267s
4	Migno	1m 41.350s
5	Rossi	1m 41.696s
6	Garcia	1m 41.790s
7	Acosta	1m 41.801s
8	Sasaki	1m 42.007s
9	Rodrigo	1m 42.090s
10	Guevara	1m 42.182s
11	Fenati	1m 42.299s
12	Masia	1m 42.492s
13	Salac	1m 42.958s
14	Fernandez	1m 42.975s
15	Toba	1m 43.265s
16	Suzuki	1m 43.406s
17	Yamanaka	1m 43.424s
18	Kofler	1m 43.531s
19	Kunii	1m 43.546s
20	Fellon	1m 43.717s
21	Alcoba	1m 43.954s
22	Nepa	1m 43.991s
23	Salvador	1m 44.714s
24	Foggia	1m 45.660s
25	Izdihar	1m 46.437s

Championship Points

1	Acosta	183
2	Garcia	130
3	Fenati	96
4	Foggia	86
5	Masia	85
6	Binder	79
7	Sasaki	68
8	Antonelli	67
9	Rodrigo	59
10	Alcoba	58
11	Migno	58
12	Toba	56
13	Salac	40
14	McPhee	40
15	Suzuki	38
16	Guevara	38
17	Yamanaka	37
18	Artigas	30
19	Dupasquier	27
20	Oncu	25
21	Nepa	19
22	Rossi	16
23	Fernandez	16
24	Kunii	15
25	Tatay	14
26	Kofler	10
27	Bartolini	7
28	Izdihar	2
29	Holgado	1

Constructor Points

1	KTM	215
2	Honda	188
3	GASGAS	142
4	Husqvarna	100

STYRIAN GRAND PRIX

0 Laps

FIM WORLD CHAMPIONSHIP · ROUND 11

AUSTRIAN GRAND PRIX

RED BULL RING

Above: Not racing, "it was surviving". Binder was happy to have survived.

Inset, top: Naked bike. Bastianini's promising race was ruined after his Ducati shed half its fairing.

Inset, top right: Sorry is the hardest word. Vinales was on hand to apologise to Yamaha.

Inset, above right: Marquez switched to wets, but fell anyway. He restarted to claim one point.
Photos: Gold & Goose

Right: Feels like rain? The impending deluge ended a fascinating three-way battle between Bagnaia, Marquez and Quartararo.
Photo: Ducati Corse

Opening spread: Fortune favours the brave. Binder creeps over the line, but still almost 13 seconds ahead of his more prudent rivals.
Photo: Gold & Goose

SOMETHING different for the second weekend in Austria – 86,000 fans. They were rewarded with an extraordinary race, culminating in a final few laps that would have seemed almost nonsensical, had they not been so exciting.

In that time span, a full weekend or more of teamwork, preparation and science was blown away. In their place, guesswork, gambling and blind courage. And a victory for the ages (and by well over ten seconds) for a truly heroic Brad Binder.

The KTM rider's last lap had been a full 14 seconds slower than that of the next fastest, by Pecco Bagnaia, and an astonishing 25.870 seconds slower than Fabio Quartararo's earlier fastest race lap. One more lap, and Binder would have been consumed – had he even survived it. Already, riding on slick tyres on a sodden surface that felt like ice, his carbon brakes cooled to the point of uselessness, he was peering over the precipice, only thin air beneath.

On such fine distinctions heroes are made.

The rain had been threatening throughout, and when it hit, almost all the front-runners dived into the pits in a group for various athletic versions of the bike swap. Binder, sitting a close sixth after coming through from tenth, had in his mind the words of his brother, Darryn – whose own slick-tyre gamble the week before in Moto3 had come close to success – that "this track has good grip for slicks when it's wet". That and a cussed streak. "I saw them all pull in and decided I had to try. The first lap was good." But there were still three more to go, and on the last of them, he ran off the track twice. "The only thing working was my rear brake. I touched it and the thing was sideways, and touched the steering lock. This wasn't racing, it was surviving."

His rivals were not only envious, but also impressed. Bagnaia said, "It's a choice only Jack [Miller] could do, and now also Brad. It was not easy. With slicks, already the lap before, Turn Three was very slippery, also Turn Four. He did something incredible today." Or, as Bagnaia's team boss, Davide Tardozzi, put it, "Brad showed two big balls. He deserved this win."

The weekend had started with the Maverick Vinales surprise. On race eve, a communique from Yamaha explained that his entry had been withdrawn and the rider suspended, "due to the unexplained irregular operation of the motorcycle ... which could have caused serious risks to the rider and possibly a danger to other riders". They cited "in-depth analysis of telemetry and data", but the "unexplained" element didn't last long, after footage emerged of him revving the engine hard on the final laps, apparently trying to blow it up. Cal Crutchlow, close to him on track, watched in puzzlement as he ran fast laps, slowed down, speeded up to whizz past again, then slowed once more, obviously distressed.

Vinales was present at the track and ready for a humble apology. Accepting the verdict, he explained, "It was a moment of great frustration. The first race was perfect, and I had started strong, but then everything went wrong [including a back-of-the-grid start after stalling before the warm-up lap, followed by a long-lap penalty]. It was an explosion of frustration that I did not know how to channel in the best way, and that is why I have to make excuses for Yamaha. But the frustration was so great that I did not know how to manage it."

His contrition was plain to see, but it was not enough. In the ensuing week's break before the British GP, Yamaha cut the ties. The unhappy marriage was over.

The loss of a race-winning rider would clearly have a potentially damaging impact on the chances of winning the triple crown. Yamaha had started the weekend 40 points clear in the riders' championship, and 53 ahead of Ducati Lenovo in the teams', but just eight ahead of Ducati in the constructors'. They left Austria with the numbers changed to 47, 37 – and minus three respectively, with Ducati taking over as leading constructor.

168 AUSTRIAN GRAND PRIX

FIM WORLD CHAMPIONSHIP

There were more problems for Yamaha, with the news that Petronas had decided to withdraw its sponsorship from the Sepang Racing Team (SRT) from the end of the year. The immediate effect was on the lesser classes, where SRT had first entered the series in 2015, with both Moto2 and Moto3 teams due to be disbanded at the end of the current season.

Nothing was certain for MotoGP except that, having built a successful effort over the past two years, team management – led by principal Razlan Razali and director Johan Stigefelt – had no intention of abandoning the role of Yamaha satellite team.

Nothing was certain either for most of their riders, let alone crews – those in the lesser classes likely to be cut adrift, though with talk of a possible MotoGP role for Moto2 rider Dixon, and a leapfrog promotion to the top class for Darryn Binder, following in Jack Miller's footsteps. Franco Morbidelli would definitely be switching to the factory squad, and Rossi retiring, leaving two vacancies in the SRT team. Attempts elsewhere had already failed: with Raul Fernandez handcuffed to KTM, and Toprak Razgatlioglu having elected to stay in WorldSBK.

Another hangover from the previous weekend stemmed from the chunking failure of Miguel Oliveira's mixed-compound front tyre, which had brought his race to a premature end. Michelin had withdrawn the tyre from the allocation to ensure no repeat.

A freak occurrence did the same this weekend to Enea Bastianini, poised for a best MotoGP result, having climbed from 15th to tenth in the first three laps. Then the left side of the Ducati's fairing came loose spectacularly as he made the high-speed climb up to Turn Three, grazing his arm and flying over the trackside barrier on the fifth lap. "Another unlucky day," he shrugged.

Danilo Petrucci, displaced by Fernandez for 2022 in the Tech3 team, revealed that he was considering an offer from the KTM factory – to switch disciplines and race the Dakar rally. The proposal had come from CEO Stefan Pierer on the Saturday night, Petrucci said: "I thought he was joking, but he was not." The factory planned to allow a year for training and to do some races, before making a serious assault on the big rally in 2023.

MOTOGP RACE – 28 laps

A second pole in succession put Martin (through after heading Q1) three-hundredths clear of Quartararo and Bagnaia; Zarco headed row two from Marc Marquez and Miller. Mir led the third.

Had the clouds steered clear, this would have been a classic finale of a different kind. For 22 laps, Bagnaia, Marquez and Quartararo ran together, occasionally trading paint at around 200mph, in a thrilling contest, Martin and Mir unable to keep up.

Marquez had looked likely to spoil Ducati's domination, but neither he nor Quartararo finished where they might have expected after their pit stops. Marquez crashed out on the penultimate lap, his wet front tyre not yet up to temperature; Quartararo failed to cut quickly enough through those who, like Binder, had continued on slicks. For the first time, he later revealed, his thoughts had turned to protecting the championship lead.

Bagnaia led all but one of the race's opening 24 laps, chased at first by Martin, who was passed on lap two by Zarco and Marquez after a tangle with Quartararo,

Marquez bared his teeth on lap three to take second, while Quartararo disposed of Miller, then Zarco in quick succession for fourth. On lap six, Marquez and Martin again went at it, swapping second place twice before Martin's failed lunge on Bagnaia pushed him back to third, then fourth as Quartararo pounced two corners later.

The fighting was constant, and on lap eight, Quartararo

Above: Last-lap redemption for Quartararo as he slices past the slick-shod Rossi (46), Alex Marquez (73) and Aleix Espargaro (41).

Top: Marquez and Mir exit the pits after their bike swap.
Photos: Gold & Goose

Top right: Martin and Bagnaia were happy to have made the podium.
Photo: Ducati Corse

Top far right: Raul Fernandez won Moto2 from a pressing Ai Ogura and Augusto Fernandez.

Above right: Foggia plays caboose to the Moto3 express, headed by Oncu from Acosta, Garcia, Masia and Fenati.

Right: Garcia celebrates his win, Oncu his first podium.
Photos: Gold & Goose

took the lead for one lap with a daring around-the-outside move. This was shaping up to be a classic.

Then nature made its first intervention. Rain flags were shown around the track on lap eight, then withdrawn three laps on. Around that point, slow-starting Mir came to life as he dropped Binder, then the fading Miller to place sixth, gradually closing a gap of a second on the leaders.

Soon it was Zarco's turn to fade, dropping back into the Suzuki man's grasp before crashing at Turn Nine 18 laps in. Mir was now fifth.

Martin's chances were slipping away, with Bagnaia, Quartararo and Marquez eking out the tenths. On lap 20, Marquez showed Quartararo a front wheel on the exit of Turn One, causing the Frenchman to outbrake himself into Three. Two laps on, a neat switchback took him by Bagnaia on the exit of Turn Three, only for the Ducati to respond into the following turn.

But now the madness began. The rain flags reappeared with six laps to go.

Miller and Rins were the first to take the plunge, pitting for a bike swap on lap 23. Miller's crew was taken by surprise, and he exited last. But the track wasn't yet wet enough to give them any advantage. By lap 25, it most certainly was. The pace had slowed, bunching Martin, Mir and Binder together with the lead trio.

Marquez led them all into the pit lane to switch to spare bikes fitted with wets. All except Binder, of course.

Martin's bike swap was particularly dramatic: arriving at his mark with the rear wheel well up in the air and leaping off before it had hit the ground.

Likewise, the race was turned on its head. Aleix Espargaro stayed out on slicks, as did Rossi, Lecuona and Marini, making the unlikeliest of top fives, as well as Alex Marquez, Petrucci and Nakagami. From behind, the wet-shod riders were closing rapidly. Oliveira had already crashed out of eighth on lap 23; Pol Espargaro pitted for wet tyres on the penultimate lap, much too late.

Marquez's unravelling came on the penultimate lap at Turn One. At the start of the last, the rain had intensified, slowing the leaders' pace to a crawl. That led to barely believable scenes as Bagnaia, Martin and Mir – their wets now working well – sliced through the top ten with ease, Bagnaia rescuing second ahead of Martin and Mir.

But Binder was the star, still 12 seconds clear as he passed the flag at what looked like walking pace. The FIM stewards penalised him three seconds for exceeding track limits on the final lap, a decision lacking any form of reason or understanding. Perhaps in recognition of such, the penalty was later withdrawn. But it didn't matter.

Mir grabbed fourth, with Marini a career-best fifth, Lecuona likewise in sixth. Quartararo extended his title advantage with seventh, and Rossi was a season-best eighth. Alex Marquez and Aleix Espargaro were still close; Miller salvaged 11th, having narrowly passed Petrucci and Nakagami on the last lap. Rins and a remounted Marc Marquez wrapped up the points, Pol Espargaro and Crutchlow trailing behind.

Quartararo was the fortnight's big winner, stretching his lead over new second-placer Bagnaia, with Zarco now fourth overall behind Mir.

MOTO2 RACE – 25 laps

The race was processional, but the margins close, the tension high, the effect on the championship interesting – and the deferred arrival on the podium of a second fast class rookie adding a fresh pinch of spice.

Lowes was back on pole, his fourth of the year, but first since the opening three rounds; alongside him the new kids – Raul Fernandez and Ogura, a repeat front row for the Japanese rider.

The previous weekend had been Fernandez's most subdued showing of the year. Now he would make amends.

Lowes claimed the early lead from the young Spaniard, Ogura and the other Fernandez. By lap three, however, Raul had taken control at the usual passing point, Turn Three, with Lowes shuffled back to fourth.

The leading quartet was never more than 2.2 seconds apart until lap 21, when Marc VDS team-mates Augusto Fernandez and Lowes started to fade. That left Ogura to carry the fight to his fellow rookie.

On lap 23, Fernandez upped the pace by two-tenths. Ogura followed suit, but only for one lap, and Fernandez had eked out an advantage of eight-tenths by the flag.

Augusto Fernandez and Lowes followed in. Behind, another rookie – Vietti – was fifth over the line, only to be dropped a place for exceeding track limits on the last lap, promoting Chantra to a career-best fifth.

Gardner was another five seconds away after a recovery ride. He'd been pushed well wide at the first corner, finishing the first lap tenth. He blamed Canet for the move. "If I hadn't picked up, I'd have been on the floor," he said.

Stricken also with an overheating front tyre in the pack, it had taken him much of the race to get past Canet, in eighth, with the previous week's winner, Bezzecchi, adrift in tenth, behind Luthi (a small revival for the veteran), after qualifying a lowly 16th.

Dixon led a close trio for 11th, from Di Giannantonio and Arbolino; a distant Vierge and Garzo wrapped up the points.

Both Manzi and Navarro went out early after a Turn One crash triggered by Beaubier, later given a long-lap penalty as a consequence, to finish 20th. Fellow American Roberts was also entangled, but escaped censure. He finished one place, but almost four seconds, out of the points.

Schrotter had been with the lead pack in the early laps, but crashed out of fifth on lap nine. After rejoining at the back, he was given a long-lap penalty for exceeding track limits and finished second-last.

MOTO3 RACE – 23 laps

Acosta was not Spain's only Moto3 diamond rookie. Garcia was another gem, and his last-lap masterclass was further evidence, while he – just – kept the title race alive.

Fenati was on pole from Suzuki and Alcoba, with Masia, Oncu and Sasaki on the second row, and Acosta heading the third. Fenati led away, with Oncu heading the pursuit and taking over to lead 17 laps altogether. Acosta, Masia, Garcia and Foggia were able to hold on. The gap to Binder, leading the rest of the field, stretched towards half-distance, then closed again as he brought team-mate McPhee with him to swell the lead group.

Come the final lap, and Oncu and Acosta had edged clear by three-tenths, with Garcia forced to defend from a late surge by Foggia. It looked like another Acosta show, but for once the title leader's last-lap composure deserted him

He ran wide at Turn Three after a failed passing move on Oncu. Garcia seized his chance, taking second on the run down to Turn Four. Then an expert move at Turn Nine, where he had fallen on the last lap a week before, was enough to claim a third win of the year, Oncu was mere hundredths behind, Foggia, Acosta and Fenati past the flag within less than half a second of the leader.

Masia was just three-tenths adrift, but half a second clear of McPhee, from late-coming Guevara, who actually lost two places on the last lap; then the ultimately fading Binder.

The pursuit was unusually widely spaced.

The win warmed Garcia's distant title threat, and he closed to within 41 points of Acosta.

FIM WORLD CHAMPIONSHIP: ROUND 11

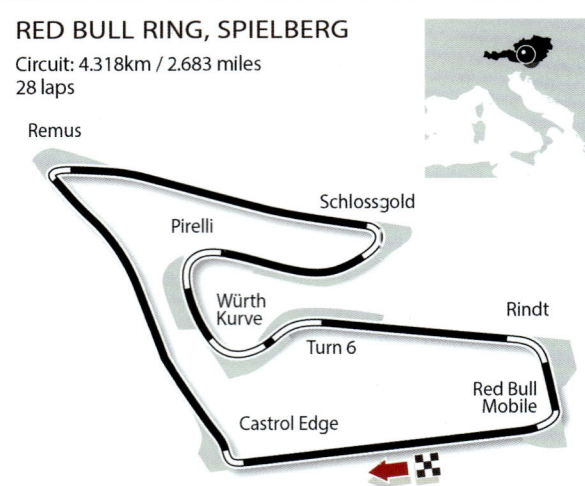

BITCI MOTORRAD GRAND PRIX VON ÖSTERREICH

RED BULL RING, SPIELBERG
Circuit: 4.318km / 2.683 miles
28 laps

13–15 AUGUST, 2021

MotoGP

RACE DISTANCE: 28 laps, 75.126 miles/120.904km · RACE WEATHER: Dry-Wet (air 31°, humidity 44%, track 41°)

Pos.	Rider	Nat.	No.	Entrant	Machine	Race tyre choice	Laps	Time & speed
1	Brad Binder	RSA	33	Red Bull KTM Factory Racing	KTM RC16	F: Hard/R: Medium	28	40m 43.928s / 110.6mph / 178.0km/h
2	Francesco Bagnaia	ITA	63	Ducati Lenovo Team	Ducati Desmosedici	F: Hard/R: Medium	28	40m 56.919s
3	Jorge Martin	SPA	89	Pramac Racing	Ducati Desmosedici	F: Hard/R: Medium	28	40m 58.498s
4	Joan Mir	SPA	36	Team SUZUKI ECSTAR	Suzuki GSX-RR	F: Medium/R: Medium	28	40m 59.551s
5	Luca Marini	ITA	10	SKY VR46 Avintia	Ducati Desmosedici	F: Hard/R: Medium	28	41m 01.759s
6	Iker Lecuona	SPA	27	Tech 3 KTM Factory Racing	KTM RC16	F: Hard/R: Medium	28	41m 01.880s
7	Fabio Quartararo	FRA	20	Monster Energy Yamaha MotoGP	Yamaha YZR-M1	F: Hard/R: Medium	28	41m 03.578s
8	Valentino Rossi	ITA	46	Petronas Yamaha SRT	Yamaha YZR-M1	F: Hard/R: Medium	28	41m 04.078s
9	Alex Marquez	SPA	73	LCR Honda CASTROL	Honda RC213V	F: Medium/R: Medium	28	41m 04.620s
10	Aleix Espargaro	SPA	41	Aprilia Racing Team Gresini	Aprilia RS-GP	F: Hard/R: Medium	28	41m 05.198s
11	Jack Miller	AUS	43	Ducati Lenovo Team	Ducati Desmosedici	F: Hard/R: Medium	28	41m 12.072s
12	Danilo Petrucci	ITA	9	Tech 3 KTM Factory Racing	KTM RC16	F: Hard/R: Medium	28	41m 12.121s
13	Takaaki Nakagami	JPN	30	LCR Honda IDEMITSU	Honda RC213V	F: Hard/R: Medium	28	41m 12.531s
14	Alex Rins	SPA	42	Team SUZUKI ECSTAR	Suzuki GSX-RR	F: Medium/R: Medium	28	41m 17.570s
15	Marc Marquez	SPA	93	Repsol Honda Team	Honda RC213V	F: Hard/R: Soft	28	41m 22.387s
16	Pol Espargaro	SPA	44	Repsol Honda Team	Honda RC213V	F: Hard/R: Medium	28	41m 27.312s
17	Cal Crutchlow	GBR	35	Petronas Yamaha SRT	Yamaha YZR-M1	F: Hard/R: Medium	28	41m 39.878s
	Miguel Oliveira	POR	88	Red Bull KTM Factory Racing	KTM RC16	F: Hard/R: Medium	22	DNF-crash
	Johann Zarco	FRA	5	Pramac Racing	Ducati Desmosedici	F: Hard/R: Medium	18	DNF-crash
	Enea Bastianini	ITA	23	Avintia Esponsorama	Ducati Desmosedici	F: Hard/R: Medium	6	DNF-technical

Fastest lap: Fabio Quartararo, on lap 12, 1m 24.451s, 114.3mph/184.0km/h.
Lap record: Andrea Dovizioso, 1m 23.827s, 115.2mph/185.4km/h (2019).
Event maximum speed: Francesco Bagnaia, 197.9mph/318.5km/h (free practice).

Qualifying

Weather: Dry
Air Temp: 30° Track Temp: 38°
Humidity: 47%

1	Martin	1m 22.643s
2	Quartararo	1m 22.677s
3	Bagnaia	1m 23.063s
4	Zarco	1m 23.120s
5	M. Marquez	1m 23.227s
6	Miller	1m 23.320s
7	Mir	1m 23.378s
8	A. Espargaro	1m 23.423s
9	Oliveira	1m 23.499s
10	Binder	1m 23.568s
11	P. Espargaro	1m 23.738s
12	Nakagami	1m 23.990s
Q1		
13	Rins	1m 23.470s
14	A. Marquez	1m 23.535s
15	Bastianini	1m 23.790s
16	Lecuona	1m 23.825s
17	Marini	1m 23.834s
18	Rossi	1m 23.939s
19	Petrucci	1m 24.405s
20	Crutchlow	1m 24.509s

Fastest race laps

1	Quartararo	1m 24.451s
2	M. Marquez	1m 24.474s
3	Bagnaia	1m 24.479s
4	Martin	1m 24.502s
5	A. Espargaro	1m 24.529s
6	Zarco	1m 24.543s
7	Rins	1m 24.552s
8	Mir	1m 24.573s
9	Oliveira	1m 24.612s
10	Binder	1m 24.655s
11	Miller	1m 24.723s
12	Bastianini	1m 24.758s
13	Lecuona	1m 24.810s
14	Nakagami	1m 24.814s
15	Marini	1m 24.919s
16	A. Marquez	1m 24.924s
17	P. Espargaro	1m 24.946s
18	Rossi	1m 24.987s
19	Petrucci	1m 25.332s
20	Crutchlow	1m 25.430s

Championship Points

1	Quartararo	181
2	Bagnaia	134
3	Mir	134
4	Zarco	132
5	Miller	105
6	Binder	98
7	Vinales	95
8	Oliveira	85
9	A. Espargaro	67
10	Martin	64
11	M. Marquez	59
12	Nakagami	55
13	Rins	44
14	A. Marquez	41
15	P. Espargaro	41
16	Morbidelli	40
17	Bastianini	31
18	Petrucci	30
19	Rossi	28
20	Marini	27
21	Lecuona	24
22	Bradl	11
23	Pedrosa	6
24	Savadori	4
25	Pirro	3
26	Rabat	1

Constructor Points

1	Ducati	212
2	Yamaha	209
3	KTM	152
4	Suzuki	138
5	Honda	104
6	Aprilia	68

Lap-by-lap grid order

Grid order	1	2	3	4	5	6	7	8	9	10	11	12	13	14	15	16	17	18	19	20	21	22	23	24	25	26	27	28	*
89 MARTIN	63	63	63	63	63	63	63	20	63	63	63	63	63	63	63	63	63	63	63	63	63	63	63	63	33	33	33	33	1
20 QUARTARARO	89	5	93	89	89	93	20	63	20	20	20	20	20	20	20	20	20	20	93	93	93	93	93	93	41	41	41	63	2
63 BAGNAIA	5	93	5	93	93	20	93	93	93	93	93	93	93	93	93	93	93	93	20	20	20	20	20	20	93	46	27	89	3
5 ZARCO	93	89	89	5	20	89	89	89	89	89	89	89	89	89	89	89	89	89	89	89	89	89	89	89	63	27	10	36	4
93 M. MARQUEZ	20	43	20	20	5	5	5	5	5	5	5	5	5	5	5	5	36	36	36	36	36	36	36	36	89	10	46	10	5
43 MILLER	43	20	43	43	43	43	43	43	43	43	43	36	36	36	36	36	5	5	33	33	33	33	33	33	20	30	73	27	6
36 MIR	36	36	36	36	36	33	36	36	36	36	36	43	43	43	43	43	33	33	41	41	41	41	41	41	36	73	30	20	7
41 A. ESPARGARO	41	27	27	33	33	36	33	33	33	33	33	33	33	33	33	33	41	41	43	43	88	43	27	30	44	44*	46		8
88 OLIVEIRA	33	33	33	27	88	88	88	88	88	88	88	88	88	88	88	41	41	41	88	88	43	27	30	27	9	9	73		9
33 BINDER	88	41	23	23	41	41	41	41	41	41	41	41	41	41	41	88	88	88	42	42	42	42	42	46	46	93*	63	41	10
44 P. ESPARGARO	27	23	88	88	27	27	27	42	42	42	42	42	42	42	42	42	27	30	30	30	30	30	46	42	10	10	63*	89	43	11
30 NAKAGAMI	23	88	41	41	73	42	42	42	27	27	27	27	27	27	27	27	30	27	27	27	27	27	9	73	73	89*	36	9	12
42 RINS	73	42	42	42	42	73	73	73	73	73	73	30	30	30	30	30	46	10	10	10	46	44	44	36*	30	20			13
73 A. MARQUEZ	30	30	30	30	30	30	30	30	30	30	73	10	10	10	10	46	46	46	46	46	10	73		9	9	20*	43	42	14
23 BASTIANINI	44	10	73	73	10	10	10	10	10	10	10	73	73	44	44	44	44	73	44	35	35*	43	42	93					15
27 LECUONA	42	73	10	10	10	44	44	44	44	44	44	44	44	46	46	73	73	73	73	44	9	42*	43	42	93	44			
10 MARINI	10	44	44	44	44	46	46	46	46	46	46	46	46	73	73	9	9	9	9	9	35	43*	42	35	35	35			
46 ROSSI	9	46	46	46	46	9	9	9	9	9	9	9	9	9	9	35	35	35	35	35									
9 PETRUCCI	35	9	9	9	9	35	35	35	35	35	35	35	35	35	35	5													
35 CRUTCHLOW	46	35	35	35	35	23																							

5 Lapped rider (retired at pits) 23 Pit stop – * bike swap

172 AUSTRIAN GRAND PRIX

Moto2
RACE DISTANCE: 25 laps, 67.077 miles/107.950km · RACE WEATHER: Dry (air 30°, humidity 44%, track 39°)

Pos.	Rider	Nat.	No.	Entrant	Machine	Laps	Time & Speed
1	Raul Fernandez	SPA	25	Red Bull KTM Ajo	Kalex	25	37m 19.890s 107.7mph/173.4km/h
2	Ai Ogura	JPN	79	IDEMITSU Honda Team Asia	Kalex	25	37m 20.735s
3	Augusto Fernandez	SPA	37	Elf Marc VDS Racing Team	Kalex	25	37m 22.637s
4	Sam Lowes	GBR	22	Elf Marc VDS Racing Team	Kalex	25	37m 24.302s
5	Somkiat Chantra	THA	35	IDEMITSU Honda Team Asia	Kalex	25	37m 28.740s
6	Celestino Vietti	ITA	13	SKY Racing Team VR46	Kalex	25	37m 28.672s
7	Remy Gardner	AUS	87	Red Bull KTM Ajo	Kalex	25	37m 33.547s
8	Aron Canet	SPA	44	Aspar Team Moto2	Boscoscuro	25	37m 36.389s
9	Thomas Luthi	SWI	12	Pertamina Mandalika SAG Team	Kalex	25	37m 36.998s
10	Marco Bezzecchi	ITA	72	SKY Racing Team VR46	Kalex	25	37m 39.478s
11	Jake Dixon	GBR	96	Petronas Sprinta Racing	Kalex	25	37m 41.173s
12	Fabio Di Giannantonio	ITA	21	Federal Oil Gresini Moto2	Kalex	25	37m 41.593s
13	Tony Arbolino	ITA	14	Liqui Moly Intact GP	Kalex	25	37m 41.756s
14	Xavi Vierge	SPA	97	Petronas Sprinta Racing	Kalex	25	37m 47.036s
15	Hector Garzo	SPA	40	Flexbox HP40	Kalex	25	37m 49.018s
16	Joe Roberts	USA	16	Italtrans Racing Team	Kalex	25	37m 52.948s
17	Bo Bendsneyder	NED	64	Pertamina Mandalika SAG Team	Kalex	25	37m 58.125s
18	Hafizh Syahrin	MAL	55	NTS RW Racing GP	NTS	25	37m 58.247s
19	Simone Corsi	ITA	24	MV Agusta Forward Racing	MV Agusta	25	37m 58.533s
20	Cameron Beaubier	USA	6	American Racing	Kalex	25	38m 04.234s
21	Taiga Hada	JPN	29	Pertamina Mandalika SAG Teluru	Kalex	25	38m 06.380s
22	Nicolo Bulega	ITA	11	Federal Oil Gresini Moto2	Kalex	25	38m 07.450s
23	Marcel Schrotter	GER	23	Liqui Moly Intact GP	Kalex	25	38m 25.474s
24	Stefano Manzi	ITA	62	Flexbox HP40	Kalex	25	38m 29.326s
	Yari Montella	ITA	5	Lightech Speed Up	Boscoscuro	15	DNF-crash
	Marcos Ramirez	SPA	42	American Racing	Kalex	13	DNF-crash
	Barry Baltus	BEL	70	NTS RW Racing GP	NTS	10	DNF-crash
	Lorenzo Dalla Porta	ITA	19	Italtrans Racing Team	Kalex	5	DNF-crash
	Albert Arenas	SPA	75	Aspar Team Moto2	Boscoscuro	1	DNF-technical
	Jorge Navarro	SPA	9	Lightech Speed Up	Boscoscuro	0	DNF-crash

Fastest lap: Somkiat Chantra, on lap 5, 1m 29.193s, 108.2mph/174.2km/h.
Lap record: Marco Bezzecchi, 1m 28.687s, 108.9mph/175.2km/h (2020).
Event maximum speed: Hector Garzo, 164.0mph/264.0km/h (free practice).

Qualifying: Weather: Dry, Air Temp: 32°, Track Temp: 39°, Humidity: 45%

1	Lowes	1m 28.659s
2	R. Fernandez	1m 28.727s
3	Ogura	1m 28.802s
4	A. Fernandez	1m 28.811s
5	Gardner	1m 28.961s
6	Canet	1m 29.015s
7	Chantra	1m 29.059s
8	Vietti	1m 29.199s
9	Dalla Porta	1m 29.220s
10	Luthi	1m 29.283s
11	Schrotter	1m 29.333s
12	Ramirez	1m 29.355s
13	Dixon	1m 29.359s
14	Navarro	1m 29.380s
15	Di Giannantonio	1m 29.450s
16	Bezzecchi	1m 29.488s
17	Manzi	1m 29.563s
18	Bulega	1m 29.624s

Q1
19	Arenas	1m 29.375s
20	Vierge	1m 29.393s
21	Roberts	1m 29.409s
22	Garzo	1m 29.457s
23	Arbolino	1m 29.470s
24	Syahrin	1m 29.483s
25	Beaubier	1m 29.504s
26	Bendsneyder	1m 29.507s
27	Corsi	1m 29.694s
28	Montella	1m 29.786s
29	Baldassarri	1m 29.815s
30	Baltus	1m 29.841s
31	Hada	1m 30.327s

Fastest race laps

1	Chantra	1m 29.193s
2	R. Fernandez	1m 29.204s
3	Vietti	1m 29.210s
4	Ogura	1m 29.218s
5	A. Fernandez	1m 29.265s
6	Gardner	1m 29.327s
7	Lowes	1m 29.333s
8	Schrotter	1m 29.356s
9	Luthi	1m 29.584s
10	Bezzecchi	1m 29.638s
11	Canet	1m 29.731s
12	Arbolino	1m 29.812s
13	Dixon	1m 29.812s
14	Vierge	1m 29.825s
15	Di Giannantonio	1m 29.862s
16	Ramirez	1m 29.899s
17	Roberts	1m 29.945s
18	Garzo	1m 30.075s
19	Beaubier	1m 30.100s
20	Syahrin	1m 30.310s
21	Manzi	1m 30.412s
22	Bendsneyder	1m 30.440s
23	Bulega	1m 30.466s
24	Baltus	1m 30.548s
25	Corsi	1m 30.569s
26	Dalla Porta	1m 30.580s
27	Hada	1m 30.619s
28	Montella	1m 30.657s

Championship Points

1	Gardner	206
2	R. Fernandez	187
3	Bezzecchi	159
4	Lowes	114
5	Canet	83
6	A. Fernandez	82
7	Di Giannantonio	80
8	Ogura	80
9	Schrotter	72
10	Vierge	59
11	Roberts	50
12	Vietti	42
13	Navarro	42
14	Bendsneyder	39
15	Chantra	35
16	Arbolino	33
17	Beaubier	26
18	Arenas	23
19	Dixon	21
20	Manzi	20
21	Ramirez	16
22	Garzo	12
23	Luthi	11
24	Bulega	10
25	Dalla Porta	10
26	Syahrin	8
27	Corsi	7
28	Lopez	4
29	Aldeguer	4
30	Baldassarri	3
31	Baltus	2

Constructor Points

1	Kalex	275
2	Boscoscuro	109
3	MV Agusta	10
4	NTS	10

Moto3
RACE DISTANCE: 23 laps, 61.711 miles/99.314km · RACE WEATHER: Dry (air 27°, humidity 62%, track 34°)

Pos.	Rider	Nat.	No.	Entrant	Machine	Laps	Time & Speed
1	Sergio Garcia	SPA	11	SANTANDER Consumer GASGAS	GASGAS	23	37m 10.345s (mph/km/h) 99.6/160.3
2	Deniz Oncu	TUR	53	Red Bull KTM Tech 3	KTM	23	37m 10.372s
3	Dennis Foggia	ITA	7	Leopard Racing	Honda	23	37m 10.691s
4	Pedro Acosta	SPA	37	Red Bull KTM Ajo	KTM	23	37m 10.739s
5	Romano Fenati	ITA	55	Sterilgarda Max Racing Team	Husqvarna	23	37m 10.807s
6	Jaume Masia	SPA	5	Red Bull KTM Ajo	KTM	23	37m 11.139s
7	John McPhee	GBR	17	Petronas Sprinta Racing	Honda	23	37m 11.676s
8	Izan Guevara	SPA	28	SANTANDER Consumer GASGAS	GASGAS	23	37m 11.785s
9	Darryn Binder	RSA	40	Petronas Sprinta Racing	Honda	23	37m 12.744s
10	Kaito Toba	JPN	27	CIP Green Power	KTM	23	37m 16.480s
11	Tatsuki Suzuki	JPN	24	SIC58 Squadra Corse	Honda	23	37m 16.947s
12	Filip Salac	CZE	12	CarXpert PruestelGP	KTM	23	37m 25.061s
13	Stefano Nepa	ITA	82	BOE Owlride	KTM	23	37m 25.265s
14	Jeremy Alcoba	SPA	52	Indonesian Racing Gresini Moto3	Honda	23	37m 32.013s
15	Andi Farid Izdihar	INA	19	Honda Team Asia	Honda	23	37m 32.321s
16	Carlos Tatay	SPA	99	Avintia Esponsorama Moto3	KTM	23	37m 32.492s
17	Lorenzo Fellon	FRA	20	SIC58 Squadra Corse	Honda	23	37m 32.506s
18	Yuki Kunii	JPN	92	Honda Team Asia	Honda	23	37m 32.543s
19	Riccardo Rossi	ITA	54	BOE Owlride	KTM	23	37m 32.708s
20	Gabriel Rodrigo	ARG	2	Indonesian Racing Gresini Moto3	Honda	23	37m 34.799s
21	David Salvador	SPA	38	Rivacold Snipers Team	Honda	23	37m 35.051s
22	Maximilian Kofler	AUT	73	CIP Green Power	KTM	23	37m 35.474s
23	Elia Bartolini	ITA	22	Avintia VR46	KTM	23	37m 44.865s
	Adrian Fernandez	SPA	31	Sterilgarda Max Racing Team	Husqvarna	11	DNF-technical
	Ayumu Sasaki	JPN	71	Red Bull KTM Tech 3	KTM	5	DNF-crash
	Andrea Migno	ITA	16	Rivacold Snipers Team	Honda	0	DNF-crash

Fastest lap: Izan Guevara, on lap 19, 1m 36.058s, 100.5mph/161.8km/h.
Lap record: Ayumu Sasaki, 1m 36.103s, 100.5mph/161.7km/h (2020).
Event maximum speed: Deniz Oncu, 138.6mph/223.1km/h (race).

Qualifying: Weather: Dry, Air Temp: 29°, Track Temp: 37°, Humidity: 51%

1	Fenati	1m 35.850s
2	Suzuki	1m 35.921s
3	Alcoba	1m 36.060s
4	Masia	1m 36.093s
5	Oncu	1m 36.104s
6	Sasaki	1m 36.169s
7	Acosta	1m 36.207s
8	Rodrigo	1m 36.224s
9	Foggia	1m 36.233s
10	Nepa	1m 36.241s
11	Guevara	1m 36.354s
12	Rossi	1m 36.369s
13	Toba	1m 36.398s
14	Garcia	1m 36.409s
15	McPhee	1m 36.455s
16	Tatay	1m 36.482s
17	Salac	1m 36.603s
18	Binder	1m 36.722s

Q1
19	Salvador	1m 36.627s
20	Kunii	1m 36.792s
21	Migno	1m 36.837s
22	Fernandez	1m 36.892s
23	Fellon	1m 37.121s
24	Kofler	1m 37.359s
25	Izdihar	1m 37.411s
26	Bartolini	1m 37.760s

Fastest race laps

1	Guevara	1m 36.058s
2	Masia	1m 36.074s
3	Garcia	1m 36.281s
4	Binder	1m 36.318s
5	Oncu	1m 36.387s
6	McPhee	1m 36.388s
7	Salac	1m 36.395s
8	Foggia	1m 36.409s
9	Acosta	1m 36.462s
10	Fenati	1m 36.471s
11	Toba	1m 36.537s
12	Suzuki	1m 36.663s
13	Sasaki	1m 36.714s
14	Alcoba	1m 36.800s
15	Nepa	1m 36.822s
16	Rodrigo	1m 36.862s
17	Kunii	1m 36.972s
18	Tatay	1m 36.995s
19	Izdihar	1m 37.003s
20	Salvador	1m 37.030s
21	Rossi	1m 37.032s
22	Fernandez	1m 37.092s
23	Bartolini	1m 37.153s
24	Fellon	1m 37.194s
25	Kofler	1m 37.238s

Championship Points

1	Acosta	196
2	Garcia	155
3	Fenati	107
4	Foggia	102
5	Masia	95
6	Binder	86
7	Sasaki	68
8	Antonelli	67
9	Toba	62
10	Alcoba	60
11	Rodrigo	59
12	Migno	58
13	McPhee	49
14	Guevara	46
15	Oncu	45
16	Salac	44
17	Suzuki	43
18	Yamanaka	37
19	Artigas	30
20	Dupasquier	27
21	Nepa	22
22	Rossi	16
23	Fernandez	16
24	Kunii	15
25	Tatay	14
26	Kofler	10
27	Bartolini	7
28	Izdihar	3
29	Holgado	1

Constructor Points

1	KTM	235
2	Honda	204
3	GASGAS	167
4	Husqvarna	111

AUSTRIAN GRAND PRIX 173

FIM WORLD CHAMPIONSHIP · ROUND 12

BRITISH GRAND PRIX

SILVERSTONE CIRCUIT

Main: Quartararo and the Yamaha were unbeatable at Silverstone.
Photo: Monster Energy Yamaha
Insets, from top: Happy faces – Quartararo shouts with glee; Rins glows with his first top-three of 2021; Espargaro proud of Aprilia's first MotoGP podium.

Above: Long lap, fast corners. Aleix Espargaro spreads the Aprilia's wings at Woodcote.
Photo: Gold & Goose

Top right: Breakthrough! Pol Espargaro celebrates his first pole on the hitherto hard-to-handle Honda.
Photo: Repsol Honda

Above right: Iker Lecuona impressed with a strong ride from 18th to seventh.
Photo: KTM Tech3

Right: "Ciao" from Valentino to his British fans in his last UK race.
Photo: Monster Energy

Far right, top: Substitute promotion for Yamaha test rider Cal Crutchlow, in for Vinales on the factory team.
Photo: Monster Energy

Far right, bottom: Ditto for fellow Briton Jake Dixon, up from the SRT Moto2 team to MotoGP to replace Crutchlow on Morbidelli's Yamaha.
Photo: Gold & Goose

THE longest lap of the year, mainly fast corners and admirably short of stop-and-go sections, finally yielded the result that Aleix Espargaro had been waiting for ever since his all-new Aprilia had showed its equally all-new turn of speed at pre-season tests. In a fine performance that threatened to overshadow winner Fabio Quartararo's indomitability, he gave the marque its first podium finish in the four-stroke era.

He did it with a fighting last lap, bullying his way back past Jack Miller's Ducati. Since the bike's weakness later in races had made him wait for this result, the Italian squad were more than hopeful that this would prove to be the final step towards full competitive potential.

The progress had been promising – consistent top-ten finishes and briefly the lead at the German GP; and Espargaro's average gap to the leader – just 8.6 seconds – showed the degree of improvement. The same figure in 2020 had been 17.2, and 25.9 the previous year.

The factory had been largely on the rise since the end of 2018, when it had hired CEO Massimo Rivola, formerly of Ferrari in Formula 1. That had lightened the load of Romano Albesiano, the technical brains behind the RS-GP, by freeing him from the burden of logistical and man-management duties. Further canny recruitment had followed, Aprilia taking on engineers from Suzuki's MotoGP project, as well as Mercedes and Ferrari in Formula 1.

Crucial was an engine redesign: a 90-degree V4 had arrived in 2020 to replace the 70-degree V4. A year of refinement was coupled with radically improved aerodynamics, making the RS-GP a genuine force. "This is another bike, completely another story," said Espargaro of the '21 incarnation of the RS-GP. "The stability is a lot higher. You can brake a lot harder without collapsing the front tyre, which was my problem last year. In the acceleration phase, you see how big are the wings, so the downforce helps me have more power with less wheelie. Also, the engine performance is much stronger. The future looks good for us,"

A further boost was coming, as the fast-moving Yamaha/Vinales break-up sprang another surprise. Yamaha had confirmed that the split was final on the Friday before the British GP, freeing Maverick from his contract with immediate effect. By then, Aprilia had also confirmed that he would be joining the team in 2022, but now there was no need for further delay, and the Noale factory revealed that he would be testing the bike at Misano in the week after the British GP. Another week later, he was racing it…

More surprises followed directly.

Yamaha had filled the gap in the factory team by promoting test rider Cal Crutchlow from his replacement role at Petronas. In turn, Petronas Moto2 rider Jake Dixon was booted up for an unexpected MotoGP debut in the satellite team – a 'deep-end' experience that he carried off with maturity, if not dazzlingly.

More surprising, however, were plans for the future. Franco Morbidelli was expected back from his recuperation for the Misano race in three weekends, and he would be put straight into the factory team, answering at last his desire for a 2021 bike to replace his two-year-old M1. And though Dixon would race again, next time out in Aragon, thereafter erstwhile Aprilia hopeful and former Ducati star Andrea Dovizioso would take over. Not just for the rest of the season, but for 2022 as well. The veteran, currently on sabbatical, would lead the rebranded ex-Petronas SRT team, running under the same management with new sponsorship from Italian energy company WithU. Darryn Binder remained favourite to take the second seat.

This was a second race in a row with fans present, although numbers were limited to 70,000 by the circuit, due to limited parking and other facilities rather than Covid: 140,000 had been catered for a month before at the Formula 1 race.

Many had come to bid farewell to Valentino Rossi, by the evidence of long queues at the VR46 merchandise stands and the swathes of yellow. He qualified eighth, second best of his final year, but there was no further glory for his last Silverstone outing. Stricken with familiar grip issues, he dropped to 18th on Sunday.

The early departure of two podium contenders helped Aprilia's cause. Marc Marquez and Jorge Martin had collided on the first lap. Marquez took responsibility, admitting an excess of optimism: they'd already had a bump earlier that lap, but his dive inside a few corners later put them both on the floor. Martin made a telling comment: "I hope Marc can learn from this and improve for the future."

It was Marquez's second crash of the weekend, bringing his total for his abbreviated season so far to 16 – the most of any rider (team-mate Pol Espargaro was next on 15). He had been very lucky to escape injury in the first, a 170mph flier in FP1, after touching the kerb, then losing the front on the way into Maggotts, the second corner. His bike continued back across the entrance to Becketts, bringing out the red flags to cut the session short. The multi-champion walked away with nothing worse than grit in one eye, although that required a hospital visit that evening.

A three-year extension to Triumph's supply of engines to Moto2 was welcomed, after the success of the first two-and-a-half years of the melodious 765cc triple. In that time, 34 new lap records had attested to the performance boost compared with the more basic 600cc Hondas they had replaced; while rookie MotoGP success by Brad Binder and Jorge Martin appeared to reinforce a feeling that the extra power, more sophisticated electronics and adjustable gearing were better preparation for the big class. More would follow, said Triumph chief product officer Steve Sargent, who revealed that further refinements were planned for 2022, with closer-ratio gearing and more peak power.

MOTOGP RACE – 20 laps

Cool conditions improved grip and finally gave Pol Espargaro the chance to use his hard braking style to get the best out of his Honda. Pole position was by far his best qualifying of the season – he'd been eighth in Germany and France, but unable to escape Q1 on four other occasions.

Bagnaia and Quartararo were alongside, while Martin headed the second row from Marc Marquez and a hopeful Aleix Espargaro.

Quartararo had survived an awkward crash on Friday, when his leg had been trapped under the bike in a low-side slip-off at Vale. Fears of a fractured ankle were allayed at the medical centre – it was merely sprained, and he returned to set fastest time of the day in the afternoon. That was a harbinger of a weekend when everything went right for him, and the other way for his increasingly distant title rivals. He would claim a resounding win, while Mir and Bagnaia were ninth and 14th, complaining of tyre defects, and a subdued Zarco was an anonymous 11th.

Pol Espargaro was the only top rider to use the soft Michelin rear, and he led away confidently, from Bagnaia, brother Aleix and Quartararo.

Close behind, Marquez and Martin tangled. With them gone, Miller and Suzuki riders Mir and Rins joined the lead group, passing Rossi, who was only ever briefly in touch. Ahead, for two laps, it was an all-Espargaro fight, Aleix nibbling at Pol for the first time on lap three at Stowe, only to run wide. But their time up front was short-lived: Quartararo soon began moving forward. He took third off Bagnaia on lap three, the Aprilia a lap later, his attacks coming at Village and The Loop. On lap five, he moved under the leading Honda at Farm.

Now he was in full flow: seven-tenths quicker than anyone on lap six, quickly establishing a lead of better than a second, then stretching it to almost four by lap 15. "The massive improvement from last year was the front feeling. The overtake on Pol, you need confidence to do that," he said.

Above: Best of the year for Alex Rins, second after a troubled season.
Photo: www.suzuki-racing.com

Top: Best so far also for LCR/s Alex Marquez, en route to eighth.

Above right: And the same for Aleix Espargaro as he guns the Aprilia past the flag for third, ahead of Miller's Ducati.

Right: Remy Gardner holds the lead from Navarro, Di Giannantonio, Raul Fernandez, Augusto Fernandez and Aron Canet.

Below right: Second-placed Bezzecchi hounded Gardner to the line.

Below centre right: Romano Fenati was a dominant Moto3 winner.

Below far right: Niccolo Antonelli overcame injury to place second in an all-Italian Moto3 top three.
Photos: Gold & Goose

Victory was now a formality, and he eased off later on for a comfortable 2.8-second win.

The action was behind. Aleix finally passed Pol neatly at Vale on lap six, heading what was now a six-bike fight for second, the factory Suzukis and Ducatis still close, until split by the advancing Rins on lap eight. At the same time, Bagnaia's challenge hit the rocks as his tyre mysteriously lost grip, and likewise Mir's, although with less severity. After half-distance, Bagnaia was dropping back radically through the pack, his lap times by the finish almost three seconds slower than at the beginning.

Earlier, a mistake at Copse on lap six had dropped Miller to seventh, but he was past the troubled pair without problems to rejoin the fight for second. By then, Rins had pounced on a slip-up by Aleix at Stowe to head the battle, but he was never able to get more than four-tenths clear.

On lap 15, Miller took advantage of Pol's slowing pace, the Honda rider paying the price for choosing a soft rear tyre.

That set up the finale. With Rins clear in second, Miller closed on the Aprilia for a last-lap assault. Pushing hard, he pounced at Village and hung on through the change of direction. But Espargaro wasn't for giving up his first podium since 2014 and retaliated at The Loop, hanging on to third to the end.

Pol had lost touch, but fifth was his best result yet on a Honda. "The right side of the tyre was completely dead after half-distance," he said. "It was impossible to make fast corner entries."

Binder produced a trademark late surge to nab sixth after a tough weekend, having passed Bagnaia, Mir and Alex Marquez in the last five laps; Lecuona underlined a good recovery for KTM after a difficult round, taking seventh off Alex Marquez on the last lap for his best dry finish. Mir was ninth, all but ready to concede the title and complaining about a faulty front tyre. Petrucci snitched tenth from an off-form Zarco on the last lap; Bastianini did the same to Nakagami, with Bagnaia narrowly saving the last point ahead of Marini.

Then came the other three Yamahas, part-timers Crutchlow and Dixon sandwiching Rossi, a sharp contrast to winner Quartararo, who now stood 65 points clear of Mir.

MOTO2 RACE – 18 laps

By Sunday evening, there was a feeling that Raul Fernandez might have been regretting talking up his chances on Friday. Fresh from victory in Austria, on top in FP2, he had declaimed, "Now I have the belief I can win the title."

Instead, the weekend was a reversal for the rookie, and confirmation for team-mate Gardner, after arguably the Australian's best performance to date. He had taken his fourth win after a high-stakes battle with Bezzecchi, while the younger Fernandez had buckled, crashing out of seventh on lap 15.

Bezzecchi had qualified on pole, his first of the year. Navarro, rejuvenated later in the season, was second, then Lowes at home. Gardner led row two from his team-mate and Di Giannantonio.

Unusually the last race of the day, Moto2 also laid on an unusually lively battle to celebrate the renewal of the Triumph engine supply.

Bezzecchi led away, but Lowes took over for the first lap. By the fourth, however, first Bezzecchi then Gardner had dropped him to third. Navarro and Di Giannantonio were close behind, swapping several times, with the Spaniard gaining control by half-distance and closing again on the leading trio.

Up front, Gardner and Bezzecchi exchanged the lead on several occasions, but by lap 16, Gardner had edged away by four-tenths. Bezzecchi wouldn't let up, but the Australian was faultless, maintaining that gap to the flag for a crucial maximum-points score.

With four laps to go, Navarro's late surge was enough to push Lowes off the podium and interpose a Boscoscuro chassis in the Kalex domination, on the weekend that the German chassis manufacturer secured the constructors' title for the ninth year in succession.

Raul Fernandez had been dropped by the lead group by lap four and fell into the clutches of Augusto Fernandez, eventually succumbing to his namesake before half-distance and dropping away as the latter closed on the front-runners. Now he came under pressure from Canet until slipping off on lap 15.

Augusto went on to depose Di Giannantonio from fifth, only to lose the position again on the final lap.

Canet was a couple of seconds clear of Vierge and Ogura, the Japanese rider's final assault having been fought off by mere hundredths of a second. Close behind, Roberts made a return to the top ten after four races with zero points.

Then came Luthi, comfortably clear of Vietti, who had made his way through from 20th on lap one in familiar style. Schrotter, Bulega and Bendsneyder wrapped up the points; impressive rookie Aldeguer missed points by three seconds on his first visit to Silverstone – the CEV and European champion elect moonlighting in place of the injured Montella in the Boscoscuro squad for a third time.

Garzo, Manzi and Beaubier crashed out, the last named again in the points before he fell.

MOTO3 RACE – 17 laps

Fenati, rampant, topped every session, then showed how intelligence – a virtue not often ascribed to him nor to Moto3 – can trump bravery and risk.

There were two races. One was between three leading Italians, as Antonelli and Migno followed Fenati's early lead, until the perennially misfortunate Migno sputtered to a stop on lap six. The second was an absorbing fight for tenth, including title leaders Acosta and Garcia, for their toughest weekend so far.

For 14 laps, Antonelli stuck with Fenati, bravely ignoring the pain and weakness of two broken bones in his right hand, sustained in practice for the Styrian GP, which had forced him out of both Red Bull Ring rounds. Thereafter, the gap stretched, and the Italian had to defend second from the rapidly advancing Foggia and Guevara, the former finally getting the better of the Spanish rookie after a lively exchange on the last lap.

Suzuki prevailed over Masia and Binder in the fight for fifth; Oncu and Rossi finished almost side by side for eighth and ninth.

Then came the usual big gang, tenth to 18th covered by two seconds. Acosta was promoted to tenth ahead of McPhee after the latter was dropped one place for a last-lap track-limits excursion, during a lunge from 16th to tenth over the line. Garcia missed the points by less than three-tenths.

Acosta's championship lead narrowly stretched again, 201 to Garcia's 155, but Fenati had closed to within 23 points of second place, and Foggia's late-season form was bringing him into the picture as well.

FIM WORLD CHAMPIONSHIP: ROUND 12

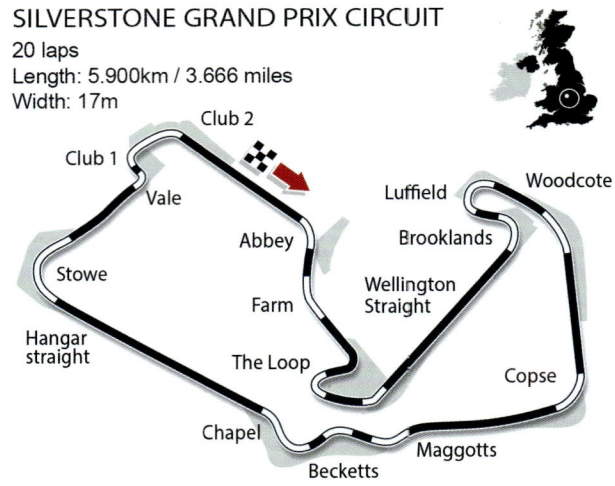

MONSTER ENERGY BRITISH GRAND PRIX
27–29 AUGUST, 2021

SILVERSTONE GRAND PRIX CIRCUIT
20 laps
Length: 5.900km / 3.666 miles
Width: 17m

MotoGP
RACE DISTANCE: 20 laps, 73.322 miles/118.000km · RACE WEATHER: Dry (air 17°, humidity 66%, track 24°)

Pos.	Rider	Nat.	No.	Entrant	Machine	Race tyre choice	Laps	Time & speed
1	Fabio Quartararo	FRA	20	Monster Energy Yamaha MotoGP	Yamaha YZR-M1	F: Soft/R: Medium	20	40m 20.579s / 109.0mph / 175.4km/h
2	Alex Rins	SPA	42	Team SUZUKI ECSTAR	Suzuki GSX-RR	F: Medium/R: Medium	20	40m 23.242s
3	Aleix Espargaro	SPA	41	Aprilia Racing Team Gresini	Aprilia RS-GP	F: Medium/R: Medium	20	40m 24.684s
4	Jack Miller	AUS	43	Ducati Lenovo Team	Ducati Desmosedici	F: Medium/R: Medium	20	40m 24.833s
5	Pol Espargaro	SPA	44	Repsol Honda Team	Honda RC213V	F: Medium/R: Soft	20	40m 29.041s
6	Brad Binder	RSA	33	Red Bull KTM Factory Racing	KTM RC16	F: Medium/R: Medium	20	40m 32.768s
7	Iker Lecuona	SPA	27	Tech 3 KTM Factory Racing	KTM RC16	F: Medium/R: Medium	20	40m 34.139s
8	Alex Marquez	SPA	73	LCR Honda CASTROL	Honda RC213V	F: Medium/R: Soft	20	40m 34.623s
9	Joan Mir	SPA	36	Team SUZUKI ECSTAR	Suzuki GSX-RR	F: Soft/R: Medium	20	40m 36.805s
10	Danilo Petrucci	ITA	9	Tech 3 KTM Factory Racing	KTM RC16	F: Medium/R: Medium	20	40m 36.866s
11	Johann Zarco	FRA	5	Pramac Racing	Ducati Desmosedici	F: Medium/R: Medium	20	40m 36.918s
12	Enea Bastianini	ITA	23	Avintia Esponsorama	Ducati Desmosedici	F: Medium/R: Soft	20	40m 38.275s
13	Takaaki Nakagami	JPN	30	LCR Honda IDEMITSU	Honda RC213V	F: Soft/R: Soft	20	40m 38.864s
14	Francesco Bagnaia	ITA	63	Ducati Lenovo Team	Ducati Desmosedici	F: Soft/R: Medium	20	40m 41.492s
15	Luca Marini	ITA	10	SKY VR46 Avintia	Ducati Desmosedici	F: Medium/R: Medium	20	40m 41.597s
16	Miguel Oliveira	POR	88	Red Bull KTM Factory Racing	KTM RC16	F: Medium/R: Medium	20	40m 42.601s
17	Cal Crutchlow	GBR	35	Monster Energy Yamaha MotoGP	Yamaha YZR-M1	F: Medium/R: Medium	20	40m 43.811s
18	Valentino Rossi	ITA	46	Petronas Yamaha SRT	Yamaha YZR-M1	F: Medium/R: Medium	20	40m 50.337s
19	Jake Dixon	GBR	96	Petronas Yamaha SRT	Yamaha YZR-M1	F: Soft/R: Medium	20	41m 11.424s
	Jorge Martin	SPA	89	Pramac Racing	Ducati Desmosedici	F: Medium/R: Medium	1	DNF-crash
	Marc Marquez	SPA	93	Repsol Honda Team	Honda RC213V	F: Medium/R: Soft	0	DNF-crash

Fastest lap: Fabio Quartararo, on lap 6, 2m 0.098s, 109.9mph/176.8km/h.
Lap record: Marc Marquez, 1m 59.936s, 110.0mph/177.0km/h (2019).
Event maximum speed: Jack Miller, 211.0mph/339.6km/h (race).

Qualifying
Weather: Dry
Air Temp: 19° **Track Temp:** 26°
Humidity: 59%

1	P. Espargaro	1m 58.889s
2	Bagnaia	1m 58.911s
3	Quartararo	1m 58.925s
4	Martin	1m 59.074s
5	M. Marquez	1m 59.086s
6	A. Espargaro	1m 59.273s
7	Miller	1m 59.368s
8	Rossi	1m 59.531s
9	Zarco	1m 59.579s
10	Rins	1m 59.639s
11	Mir	1m 59.763s
12	Binder	1m 59.977s
Q1		
13	Bastianini	1m 59.553s
14	Marini	1m 59.764s
15	Nakagami	1m 59.881s
16	Petrucci	1m 59.997s
17	A. Marquez	2m 00.117s
18	Lecuona	2m 00.131s
19	Crutchlow	2m 00.217s
20	Oliveira	2m 00.391s
21	Dixon	2m 00.869s

Fastest race laps
1	Quartararo	2m 00.098s
2	Miller	2m 00.442s
3	Rins	2m 00.502s
4	A. Espargaro	2m 00.579s
5	P. Espargaro	2m 00.600s
6	Mir	2m 00.647s
7	Nakagami	2m 00.703s
8	Zarco	2m 00.708s
9	A. Marquez	2m 00.760s
10	Binder	2m 00.776s
11	Lecuona	2m 00.778s
12	Bagnaia	2m 00.840s
13	Rossi	2m 00.949s
14	Petrucci	2m 00.970s
15	Marini	2m 01.042s
16	Bastianini	2m 01.080s
17	Crutchlow	2m 01.226s
18	Oliveira	2m 01.237s
19	Dixon	2m 02.752s

Championship Points
1	Quartararo	206
2	Mir	141
3	Zarco	137
4	Bagnaia	136
5	Miller	118
6	Binder	108
7	Vinales	95
8	Oliveira	85
9	A. Espargaro	83
10	Martin	64
11	Rins	64
12	M. Marquez	59
13	Nakagami	58
14	P. Espargaro	52
15	A. Marquez	49
16	Morbidelli	40
17	Petrucci	36
18	Bastianini	35
19	Lecuona	33
20	Marini	28
21	Rossi	28
22	Bradl	11
23	Pedrosa	6
24	Savadori	4
25	Pirro	3
26	Rabat	1

Constructor Points
1	Yamaha	234
2	Ducati	225
3	KTM	162
4	Suzuki	158
5	Honda	115
6	Aprilia	84

Grid order / Lap chart

Grid order	1	2	3	4	5	6	7	8	9	10	11	12	13	14	15	16	17	18	19	20
44 P. ESPARGARO	44	44	44	44	20	20	20	20	20	20	20	20	20	20	20	20	20	20	20	20
63 BAGNAIA	41	41	41	20	44	41	41	41	41	41	42	42	42	42	42	42	42	42	42	42
20 QUARTARARO	63	63	20	63	41	44	44	42	42	42	42	41	41	41	41	41	41	41	41	41
89 MARTIN	20	20	63	41	63	63	42	44	44	44	44	44	44	43	43	43	43	43	43	43
93 M. MARQUEZ	43	43	43	43	43	36	36	36	36	36	36	43	43	43	44	44	44	44	44	44
41 A. ESPARGARO	46	36	36	36	36	42	63	63	43	43	43	36	36	36	36	36	33	33	33	33
43 MILLER	36	46	42	42	42	43	43	43	63	63	63	73	73	73	73	36	73	36	27	27
46 ROSSI	42	42	46	46	46	46	73	73	73	73	73	63	63	33	33	73	27	27	73	73
5 ZARCO	30	5	5	73	73	73	46	46	46	46	30	30	30	30	27	27	27	73	36	36
42 RINS	5	30	30	5	30	30	30	30	30	46	33	33	33	27	30	63	5	5	5	9
36 MIR	73	73	73	30	5	33	33	33	33	33	46	5	27	63	5	5	9	9	9	5
33 BINDER	27	33	33	33	33	5	5	5	5	5	27	27	5	5	9	30	30	30	23	23
23 BASTIANINI	33	27	27	27	27	27	27	27	27	27	9	9	9	9	30	23	23	23	30	30
10 MARINI	9	9	23	23	9	9	9	9	9	9	46	46	46	10	10	10	10	63	63	63
30 NAKAGAMI	10	23	9	9	23	23	10	10	23	23	23	10	10	23	23	9	63	10	10	10
9 PETRUCCI	23	10	10	10	10	10	23	10	10	10	10	23	23	46	46	35	88	88		
73 A. MARQUEZ	35	35	35	35	35	35	35	35	35	35	35	35	35	88	35	35				
27 LECUONA	96	88	88	88	88	88	88	88	88	88	88	88	88	88	46	46	46			
35 CRUTCHLOW	88	96	96	96	96	96	96	96	96	96	96	96	96	96	96	96	96	96		
88 OLIVEIRA	89																			
96 DIXON																				

89 Pit stop

180 BRITISH GRAND PRIX

Moto2

RACE DISTANCE: 18 laps, 65.990 miles/106.200km · **RACE WEATHER:** Dry (air 17°, humidity 69%, track 24°)

Pos.	Rider	Nat.	No.	Entrant	Machine	Laps	Time & Speed
1	Remy Gardner	AUS	87	Red Bull KTM Ajo	Kalex	18	37m 31.642s 105.4mph/169.4km/h
2	Marco Bezzecchi	ITA	72	SKY Racing Team VR46	Kalex	18	37m 32.123s
3	Jorge Navarro	SPA	9	Lightech Speed Up	Boscoscuro	18	37m 33.572s
4	Sam Lowes	GBR	22	Elf Marc VDS Racing Team	Kalex	18	37m 33.926s
5	Fabio Di Giannantonio	ITA	21	Federal Oil Gresini Moto2	Kalex	18	37m 38.594s
6	Augusto Fernandez	SPA	37	Elf Marc VDS Racing Team	Kalex	18	37m 38.701s
7	Aron Canet	SPA	44	Kipin Energy Aspar Team	Boscoscuro	18	37m 42.348s
8	Xavi Vierge	SPA	97	Petronas Sprinta Racing	Kalex	18	37m 44.484s
9	Ai Ogura	JPN	79	IDEMITSU Honda Team Asia	Kalex	18	37m 44.519s
10	Joe Roberts	USA	16	Italtrans Racing Team	Kalex	18	37m 45.986s
11	Thomas Luthi	SWI	12	Pertamina Mandalika SAG Team	Kalex	18	37m 51.754s
12	Celestino Vietti	ITA	13	SKY Racing Team VR46	Kalex	18	37m 54.013s
13	Marcel Schrotter	GER	23	Liqui Moly Intact GP	Kalex	18	37m 54.167s
14	Nicolo Bulega	ITA	11	Federal Oil Gresini Moto2	Kalex	18	37m 55.314s
15	Bo Bendsneyder	NED	64	Pertamina Mandalika SAG Team	Kalex	18	37m 55.758s
16	Fermin Aldeguer	SPA	54	Lightech Speed Up	Boscoscuro	18	37m 58.489s
17	Somkiat Chantra	THA	35	IDEMITSU Honda Team Asia	Kalex	18	37m 58.638s
18	Tony Arbolino	ITA	14	Liqui Moly Intact GP	Kalex	18	37m 58.848s
19	Albert Arenas	SPA	75	Kipin Energy Aspar Team	Boscoscuro	18	37m 59.056s
20	Marcos Ramirez	SPA	42	American Racing	Kalex	18	38m 04.010s
21	Hafizh Syahrin	MAL	55	NTS RW Racing GP	NTS	18	38m 10.256s
22	Simone Corsi	ITA	24	MV Agusta Forward Racing	MV Agusta	18	38m 10.716s
23	Barry Baltus	BEL	70	NTS RW Racing GP	NTS	18	38m 10.759s
	Raul Fernandez	SPA	25	Red Bull KTM Ajo	Kalex	14	DNF-crash
	Cameron Beaubier	USA	6	American Racing	Kalex	13	DNF-crash
	Adam Norrodin	MAL	77	Petronas Sprinta Racing	Kalex	12	DNF-physical
	Stefano Manzi	ITA	62	Flexbox HP40	Kalex	9	DNF-crash
	Hector Garzo	SPA	40	Flexbox HP40	Kalex	5	DNF-crash
	Lorenzo Baldassarri	ITA	7	MV Agusta Forward Racing	MV Agusta	3	DNF-technical

Fastest lap: Jorge Navarro, on lap 17, 2m 4.312s, 106.1mph/170.8km/h.
Lap record: Augusto Fernandez, 2m 4.835s, 105.7mph/170.1km/h (2019).
Event maximum speed: Marcos Ramirez, 176.6mph/284.2km/h (race).

Qualifying
Weather: Dry
Air Temp: 19° Track Temp: 26°
Humidity: 50%

1	Bezzecchi	2m 03.988s
2	Navarro	2m 04.061s
3	Lowes	2m 04.069s
4	Gardner	2m 04.195s
5	R. Fernandez	2m 04.209s
6	Di Giannantonio	2m 04.372s
7	A. Fernandez	2m 04.588s
8	Canet	2m 04.636s
9	Vierge	2m 04.815s
10	Roberts	2m 05.036s
11	Bulega	2m 05.057s
12	Manzi	2m 05.123s
13	Bendsneyder	2m 05.132s
14	Ogura	2m 05.199s
15	Schrotter	2m 05.255s
16	Aldeguer	2m 05.504s
17	Luthi	2m 05.754s
18	Chantra	2m 05.880s
Q1		
19	Beaubier	2m 05.272s
20	Garzo	2m 05.613s
21	Arenas	2m 05.640s
22	Arbolino	2m 05.657s
23	Vietti	2m 05.788s
24	Corsi	2m 05.838s
25	Baldassarri	2m 05.841s
26	Syahrin	2m 05.879s
27	Ramirez	2m 05.885s
28	Baltus	2m 05.925s
29	Norrodin	2m 07.967s
	Dalla Porta	No Time

Fastest race laps

1	Navarro	2m 04.312s
2	Bezzecchi	2m 04.326s
3	Gardner	2m 04.340s
4	Lowes	2m 04.414s
5	A. Fernandez	2m 04.804s
6	Di Giannantonio	2m 04.852s
7	Canet	2m 05.085s
8	Ogura	2m 05.134s
9	R. Fernandez	2m 05.156s
10	Vierge	2m 05.182s
11	Bendsneyder	2m 05.349s
12	Roberts	2m 05.351s
13	Schrotter	2m 05.381s
14	Luthi	2m 05.521s
15	Vietti	2m 05.584s
16	Beaubier	2m 05.590s
17	Manzi	2m 05.619s
18	Garzo	2m 05.728s
19	Aldeguer	2m 05.769s
20	Arenas	2m 05.818s
21	Chantra	2m 05.827s
22	Bulega	2m 05.839s
23	Arbolino	2m 05.864s
24	Syahrin	2m 06.120s
25	Ramirez	2m 06.130s
26	Corsi	2m 06.165s
27	Baltus	2m 06.204s
28	Norrodin	2m 06.788s
29	Baldassarri	2m 07.650s

Championship Points

1	Gardner	231
2	R. Fernandez	187
3	Bezzecchi	179
4	Lowes	127
5	Canet	92
6	A. Fernandez	92
7	Di Giannantonio	91
8	Ogura	87
9	Schrotter	75
10	Vierge	67
11	Navarro	58
12	Roberts	56
13	Vietti	46
14	Bendsneyder	40
15	Chantra	35
16	Arbolino	33
17	Beaubier	26
18	Arenas	23
19	Dixon	21
20	Manzi	20
21	Ramirez	16
22	Luthi	16
23	Garzo	12
24	Bulega	12
25	From	10
26	Syahrin	8
27	Courses	7
28	Aldeguer	4
29	Lopez	4
30	Baldassarri	3
31	Baltus	2

Constructor Points

1	Kalex	275
2	Boscoscuro	109
3	MV Agusta	10
4	NTS	10

Moto3

RACE DISTANCE: 17 laps, 62.324 miles/100.300km · **RACE WEATHER:** Dry (air 16°, humidity 68%, track 22°)

Pos.	Rider	Nat.	No.	Entrant	Machine	Laps	Time & Speed
1	Romano Fenati	ITA	55	Sterilgarda Max Racing Team	Husqvarna	17	37m 26.974s 99.8mph/160.6km/h
2	Niccolo Antonelli	ITA	23	Avintia VR46	KTM	17	37m 28.653s
3	Dennis Foggia	ITA	7	Leopard Racing	Honda	17	37m 29.081s
4	Izan Guevara	SPA	28	Valresa GASGAS Aspar Team	GASGAS	17	37m 29.128s
5	Tatsuki Suzuki	JPN	24	SIC58 Squadra Corse	Honda	17	37m 34.449s
6	Jaume Masia	SPA	5	Red Bull KTM Ajo	KTM	17	37m 34.515s
7	Darryn Binder	RSA	40	Petronas Sprinta Racing	Honda	17	37m 34.533s
8	Deniz Oncu	TUR	53	Red Bull KTM Tech 3	KTM	17	37m 41.497s
9	Riccardo Rossi	ITA	54	BOE Owlride	KTM	17	37m 41.515s
10	Carlos Tatay	SPA	99	Avintia Esponsorama Moto3	KTM	17	37m 47.477s
11	Pedro Acosta	SPA	37	Red Bull KTM Ajo	KTM	17	37m 48.872s
12	John McPhee	GBR	17	Petronas Sprinta Racing	Honda	17	37m 48.833s
13	Ayumu Sasaki	JPN	71	Red Bull KTM Tech 3	KTM	17	37m 49.002s
14	Filip Salac	CZE	12	CarXpert PruestelGP	KTM	17	37m 49.081s
15	Gabriel Rodrigo	ARG	2	Indonesian Racing Gresini Moto3	Honda	17	37m 49.131s
16	Sergio Garcia	SPA	11	Valresa GASGAS Aspar Team	GASGAS	17	37m 49.418s
17	Stefano Nepa	ITA	82	BOE Owlride	KTM	17	37m 49.305s
18	Xavier Artigas	SPA	43	Leopard Racing	Honda	17	37m 49.554s
19	Adrian Fernandez	SPA	31	Sterilgarda Max Racing Team	Husqvarna	17	37m 52.189s
20	Alberto Surra	ITA	67	Rivacold Snipers Team	Honda	17	37m 54.492s
21	Jeremy Alcoba	SPA	52	Indonesian Racing Gresini Moto3	Honda	17	37m 59.795s
22	Lorenzo Fellon	FRA	20	SIC58 Squadra Corse	Honda	17	37m 59.989s
23	Ryusei Yamanaka	JPN	6	CarXpert PruestelGP	KTM	17	38m 00.284s
24	Yuki Kunii	JPN	92	Honda Team Asia	Honda	17	38m 19.794s
25	Maximilian Kofler	AUT	73	CIP Green Power	KTM	17	38m 19.832s
	Andrea Migno	ITA	16	Rivacold Snipers Team	Honda	5	DNF-technical
	Kaito Toba	JPN	27	CIP Green Power	KTM	3	DNF-crash

Fastest lap: Izan Guevara, on lap 3, 2m 11.347s, 100.5mph/161.7km/h.
Lap record: Tatsuki Suzuki, 2m 12.140s, 99.9mph/160.7km/h (2019).
Event maximum speed: Xavier Artigas, 150.1mph/241.6km/h (race).

Qualifying:
Weather: Dry
Air Temp: 18° Track Temp: 26°
Humidity: 64%

1	Fenati	2m 11.325s
2	Rodrigo	2m 11.368s
3	Rossi	2m 11.522s
4	Migno	2m 11.590s
5	Antonelli	2m 11.715s
6	Salac	2m 11.803s
7	Alcoba	2m 11.850s
8	Foggia	2m 11.885s
9	Oncu	2m 12.391s
10	Masia	2m 12.512s
11	Guevara	2m 12.535s
12	Nepa	2m 12.591s
13	Suzuki	2m 12.705s
14	Tatay	2m 12.927s
15	McPhee	2m 13.074s
16	Binder	2m 13.643s
17	Sasaki	2m 14.265s
18	Fellon	No Time
Q1		
19	Fernandez	2m 12.439s
20	Yamanaka	2m 12.625s
21	Surra	2m 12.695s
22	Acosta	2m 12.708s
23	Kunii	2m 12.921s
24	Garcia	2m 13.017s
25	Artigas	2m 13.186s
26	Toba	2m 13.236s
27	Kofler	2m 13.952

Fastest race laps

1	Guevara	2m 11.347s
2	McPhee	2m 11.350s
3	Binder	2m 11.363s
4	Suzuki	2m 11.426s
5	Antonelli	2m 11.428s
6	Fenati	2m 11.430s
7	Toba	2m 11.437s
8	Foggia	2m 11.458s
9	Masia	2m 11.494s
10	Oncu	2m 11.530s
11	Migno	2m 11.534s
12	Rossi	2m 11.685s
13	Nepa	2m 11.761s
14	Acosta	2m 11.776s
15	Artigas	2m 11.960s
16	Garcia	2m 12.071s
17	Tatay	2m 12.172s
18	Surra	2m 12.235s
19	Fernandez	2m 12.259s
20	Salac	2m 12.267s
21	Alcoba	2m 12.270s
22	Fellon	2m 12.307s
23	Sasaki	2m 12.331s
24	Rodrigo	2m 12.352s
25	Yamanaka	2m 12.773s
26	Kofler	2m 13.434s
27	Kunii	2m 14.317s

Championship Points

1	Acosta	201
2	Garcia	155
3	Fenati	132
4	Foggia	118
5	Masia	105
6	Binder	95
7	Antonelli	87
8	Sasaki	71
9	Toba	62
10	Alcoba	60
11	Rodrigo	60
12	Guevara	59
13	Migno	58
14	Suzuki	54
15	Oncu	53
16	McPhee	53
17	Salac	46
18	Yamanaka	37
19	Artigas	30
20	Dupasquier	27
21	Rossi	23
22	Nepa	22
23	Tatay	20
24	Fernandez	16
25	Kunii	15
26	Kofler	10
27	Bartolini	7
28	Izdihar	3
29	Holgado	1

Constructor Points

1	KTM	255
2	Honda	220
3	GASGAS	180
4	Husqvarna	136

FIM WORLD CHAMPIONSHIP · ROUND 13
ARAGON GRAND PRIX
ARAGON CIRCUIT

TISSOT
SUOMY
ADVANCE
randstad
63
FRECCIAROSSA
Lenovo
DUCATI

Above: Master versus apprentice. Marc Marquez shadowed Bagnaia relentlessly.
Photo: Repsol Honda

Top right: The spoils of victory for Ducati's Luigi Dall'Igna and Pecco Bagnaia.
Photo: Ducati Corse

Above right: Remy Gardner helped Red Bull KTM Ajo clinch the team championship early.

Centre right: Miller and Zarco discuss matters Ducati.

Centre far right: Another rookie on the rise – Enea Bastianini was gaining confidence and speed.

Right: Same number, different paint. Maverick Vinales was back in action for Aprilia.

Opening spread: Seven times lucky. Bagnaia repulsed that many attacks after a compelling race-long duel.
Photos: Gold & Goose

THE confrontation was both fascinating and potentially very portentous: rising star coming of age against old master scrabbling to hold on.

Not that Marc Marquez, at 28, was ageing, but as he explained, the lingering effects of his injury continued to hamper his riding ability, particularly robbing him of the upper-body strength he needs to perform his miracle rescues – picking up a crashing bike on knee and elbow. "The word 'save' is not in my dictionary any more," he said. With his competitive strength further compromised by an intractable RC213V, he was obliged to work harder than ever while not being any more effective.

Pecco Bagnaia, by contrast, was much on the upward curve. Frequently producing potential race-winning pace, hitherto he had displayed a tendency to make mistakes under pressure. For example, crashing out while leading at Misano in 2020 and Mugello in 2021, qualifying poorly in Portugal. Technical gremlins had further undermined his chances in Styria and at Silverstone.

That changed at Aragon. The pressure was fearsome: race-long shadowing culminating in no fewer than seven attacking overtakes in the final laps; Bagnaia's composure was complete. Each time Marquez pushed past into one of his favoured left-handers, he went straight back in front again.

His first victory came by less than a second. Would it open the floodgates? With Fabio Quartararo a downbeat and fading eighth, after slipping back with a problem tyre, it injected at least a morsel of doubt into his title charge, which was augmented a week later. For Bagnaia, considering his struggles at the track a year before – crashing out of 16th and 18th in the two races – it was all the more impressive. One difference was milder conditions – it had been very cold later in the year in 2020; another was how bike and rider had grown together, "in a direction that he loves", according to Ducati team manager Davide Tardozzi.

After two races away, Maverick Vinales was back, in new Aprilia colours and fresh from a promising two-day familiarisation test at Misano, where he had been two-tenths off the lap record. Leaving Yamaha had been "a release for me," he said. "I was in a 'blocked' moment." His enthusiasm had been immediately restored.

There was much to learn, with his focus clearly on 2022. The RS-GP's 90-degree V4 demanded different riding techniques compared with the inline Suzukis and Yamahas he had ridden hitherto: "The acceleration is very good and I can control well the slide. But I need to get used to the braking area, because it is different." He came home 18th, almost half a minute behind the race winner.

Honda continued chassis experiments, Marc Marquez trying a third different spec in five races. The first had proved promising at Assen, and in Austria and England, with better stability in fast corners, though giving something away in slow corners. "Now we need to understand which way to follow for the future," he said. "The other Honda riders are using another chassis and are going in another way. But when they try my way, sometimes they like, sometimes no. Still we are a little bit confused."

Team-mate Pol Espargaro concurred: "We are trying to improve the low grip on the edge, floating on entry, spinning with the bike straight ... trying to get more grip or applying force on the rear tyre in a different way." His search was clearly less successful than that of Marquez.

The slump in erstwhile title challenger Johann Zarco's results continued, 11th at Silverstone being followed by a zero-points 17th, and he confirmed that arm-pump was largely to blame, and that he was contemplating following compatriot Quartararo's example of mid-season surgery. Having ridden his old-school 1981 Ducati 900SS from his South of France home more than 900km to Aragon, he explained, "I often say if I feel good on the bike, I won't have arm-pump. But this problem it seems is now part of our sport. It is coming with all the bikes, because we have better acceleration and can brake very hard. If you do it so relaxed, you don't bring the bike anywhere."

Much belated, the 2021 calendar was finally confirmed,

FIM WORLD CHAMPIONSHIP

with the Malaysian GP joining the Japanese, Australian and Thai rounds on the cancelled list, being replaced by a second event at Misano, after the US round, for a repeat of 2020's Emilia Romagna GP. Hopes of a late visit to Argentina, long on the provisional calendar with a TBC date, were also dashed.

The Red Bull Ajo pair of Remy Gardner and Raul Fernandez took a fifth one-two result in Moto2, the rookie in front for a third time. The maximum 45 points secured the teams' championship with five races to spare. One reward had already been announced: they would get a taste of their 2022 MotoGP tasks in the two-day tests after the Misano race the following weekend, with a first ride on the KTM RC16 machine. Pedro Acosta was impressively faster, though.

Also on the KTM after the Misano race, Dani Pedrosa, whose role as full-time test rider for the Austrian factory was credited with much of the marque's improvement. But a planned wild-card run in the race itself was cancelled. "We just stopped it. I don't think we are going to see him racing again," said race department chief Pit Beirer. Pedrosa's earlier wild-card ride had resulted in him being involved in a scary crash, which brought out the red flags, before racing to a creditable tenth place.

MOTOGP RACE – 23 laps

Warmer conditions freed up tyre choice and set records tumbling. Bagnaia's second pole of the season cut three-tenths off Marc Marquez's 2015 all-time record. That's the difference conferred by an air temperature of 27°C rather than 20, and a track at 45°C rather than 28.

It was Ducati's 50th pole, and team-mate Miller was alongside for the marque's first one-two in three years, three-tenths down; then Quartararo, preserving his remarkable front-row record.

Much was expected of Marc Marquez on the anti-clockwise layout, as he had won five times in the previous seven visits to the track. He fell twice working on his speed in FP2 and FP3, but was rewarded by the lead of the second row, ahead of Martin and Aleix Espargaro, whose new Aprilia team-mate, Vinales, was 18th, some nine-tenths slower.

The track temperature approached 50 degrees on race day, and all the riders started with Michelin's softest rear tyre. Warnings to be cautious in the early laps made no difference to Bagnaia, who scorched away in the lead. Miller followed, only to be displaced by Marc Marquez into the second corner. Aleix Espargaro, Mir, Quartararo and Martin slotted in behind, the last pair having exchanged places by the end of the first lap.

In the early laps, Miller had the speed to chase the leading pair. Then the two ahead went faster still. By one-third-distance, it was a two-man fight.

Miller, Aleix Espargaro, Mir and Martin ran in a procession; the early interest lay in the obvious struggles of Quartararo at his bogey track. Hopes of a top-three faded fast as he dropped back quickly. By lap nine, he was ninth, with the KTMs of Lecuona and Binder ahead of him. He blamed Michelin for an "iffy" rear tyre.

Come lap 11, Miller began to struggle with his gear lever, which caused several mistakes as he downshifted, including running off while braking from 211mph at Turn 16, rejoining behind Espargaro and Mir. A lap on, and the reigning world champion was neatly past the Aprilia at Turn Four. From there, third, fourth and fifth were set.

Behind, Martin started to drop, Binder and Lecuona both ahead by lap 16, although the latter promptly ran wide and lost several places.

Further back, Quartararo had fallen into the hands of Bastianini and Nakagami in an interesting, if unexpected, battle for ninth. All three swapped places on lap 14, with Nakagami getting in Bastianini's way, allowing Quartararo brief respite. It was temporary, however, the Italian rookie clearly being the fastest.

ARAGON GRAND PRIX 185

Above: Espargaro in pursuit, but he had to cede the final podium place to Mir.
Photo: www.suzuki-racing.com

Top right: On the road to nowhere, Crutchlow, Vinales and Rossi failed to score points.
Photo: Monster Energy Yamaha

Above right: The defining moment: Marquez runs wide after seven fruitless overtakes.

Centre right: Domination. The KTM Red Bull team-mates, Fernandez and Gardner, took a fifth one-two finish of the year.

Below right: Third-placed Sasaki fends off Guevara (28), Migno (hidden), Binder (40) and the rest.

Below far right: On a roll. Leopard's Dennis Foggia celebrates his third win of the year.
Photos: Gold & Goose

The action was up front. Until lap 21, Marc Marquez had been content to sit behind Bagnaia, studying for a late attack. "I tried to analyse his weak points, but there were no weak points. He was braking later than me, stopping better and accelerating better. Fighting against Ducati is much more difficult than other bikes," he said.

He tried anyway – with seven separate overtakes in the last two laps, each immediately reversed on corner exit. A dream finally come true for Bagnaia, whose understatement was masterful: "To win against one of the riders with more titles in MotoGP is always nice."

Not far short in brilliance was Mir's third. He had ditched his ride-height device, still unhappy with the feeling in braking when it disengaged. He was disgruntled about time lost in the early laps, struggling to overtake Miller and Aleix Espargaro. Once past, "my pace was really similar to the leaders. But then they were too far."

Espargaro was another five seconds behind, pleased with the Aprilia's fourth top-six of the year; Miller frustrated in fifth, blaming puzzling gear-shifting problems: "I had to use my whole leg to change gear."

Bastianini's final flourish took him past Binder on the last lap. Quartararo blamed tyres for a lack of grip, traction and stopping performance, but managed to hold off a swarm of riders at the end for eighth, narrowly ahead of Martin, Nakagami and Lecuona, whose lap-17 mistake had dropped him four places.

Rins was close, paying the price for a wretched qualifying in 20th. At least he had passed and eventually dropped Pol Espargaro's Repsol Honda, another to complain of unexpected tyre problems.

Oliveira trailed in, then Petrucci, followed by Crutchlow, the Italian snitching the final point. Zarco and Vinales were close behind; Rossi and Marini not so. Alex Marquez crashed out on the first lap; Dixon's second MotoGP ride ended the same way a lap later.

With his lead trimmed to 53 points, did Quartararo have much to worry about? He would find out more in a week's time at Misano.

MOTO2 RACE – 21 laps

Another remarkable chapter in the story of super-rookie Raul Fernandez began when he fell off his bicycle on the Friday after the British GP. While virtually stationary, his foot had been caught in the pedal clip. It was undignified and injurious: he broke the fifth metacarpal of his right hand. It was straight to Dr Mir's surgery for a quick fix, and the promise that he would race at Aragon if able.

"Able" proved an understatement. Ice-packing the injury between sessions and avoiding long runs, Fernandez was on top of the pile by the end of FP3. He qualified on the front row and went on to dominate the race completely.

An on-form Lowes took pole position, three-tenths clear of Gardner and Fernandez; Garzo headed the second row from Ogura and Arenas, best so far for the reigning Moto3 champion.

Lowes jumped to an early advantage, blazing away to put better than half a second on the two Ajo riders. But by lap four, Fernandez was in the lead; while Gardner was already out of touch, scrapping and for two laps behind Ogura and briefly also Garzo, until the Spaniard obligingly crashed out on lap five.

It soon became clear that not even Lowes could live with Fernandez, and by lap seven, he was better than a second clear. And a few tenths more when Lowes crashed out for a fourth time in a difficult season.

Fernandez was clear to cruise home. His fifth win was by 5.4 seconds, and only in *parc fermé* did it become obvious just how painful the effort had been.

Gardner had managed to regain and retain second from lap five; while Ogura came under serious pressure from Boscoscuro riders Navarro and Canet, who had closed from behind after disposing of Vierge and Arenas, both of whom fell.

They were joined before half-distance by Bezzecchi, from 11th on the first lap, and all three were ahead of Ogura by lap seven.

Then it was Bezzecchi's turn to fall in a race of many crashes; while Augusto Fernandez was about to join the

FIM WORLD CHAMPIONSHIP 13

group, having gained speed and positions steadily from 15th on lap two, Di Giannantonio with him.

Augusto's pace was strong enough to break up the scrap. Only Navarro was able to hold him back, until with three laps to go, the Kalex rider was through, for his fourth podium in five races.

Canet was now out of touch, and Di Giannantonio a further five seconds away.

Another impressive ride came from probably the next Spanish sensation, substitute Boscoscuro rider Aldeguer. The teenager passed both Schrotter and then Ogura on the last lap for seventh, in only his fourth grand prix. Qualified 17th, he had dropped to 19th in the first three laps, then picked off more experienced riders with aplomb.

Ogura retained eighth, narrowly ahead of Arbolino, another rookie to impress, after starting 23rd. Three seconds back, Corsi was ahead of Schrotter, who had ruined his final lap.

Americans Roberts and Beaubier made the points; Luthi, Dalla Porta and Chantra added to a long crash list.

MOTO3 RACE – 19 laps

For one title contender to crash out is unfortunate. To lose two must be judged careless.

A frantic eight-rider scrap was 16 laps old when points leader Acosta, qualified only ninth, made his first big mistake of the year, slipping off and taking fellow rookie Artigas down with him at Turn Five.

A golden chance for title rival Garcia to cut away at Acosta's 46-point lead. With two laps to go, he was third, behind Foggia and Oncu. But if he had hoped for any support from Aspar GasGas team-mate Guevara, it would have been in vain. On the last lap, the pair rubbed fairings three times.

That gave Foggia and Oncu the chance to edge away, even while exchanging the lead twice on the final lap. Garcia gave furious chase – too furious, as he slipped off at Turn 12. His big chance was gone.

Oncu seemed poised for a long awaited first win, but the reliably fast Leopard Honda outpaced him on the long back straight. Foggia's third win of the year moved him to third overall, just 12 points off Garcia and overtaking an off-form Fenati, out of the points after a lap-six run-off.

In the last-lap scramble, Sasaki snatched third from a gutted Guevara, deprived of a debut podium for a second successive race. Antonelli and Migno were next, the top six past the flag in a fraction over a second.

Pole-starter Binder, a second back, led the remnants of the front group, Nepa and Suzuki; Masia completed the top ten. Second qualifier Rodrigo had led the first two laps, dropped back and then fallen for the fourth time in 2021.

ARAGON GRAND PRIX 187

FIM WORLD CHAMPIONSHIP: ROUND 13

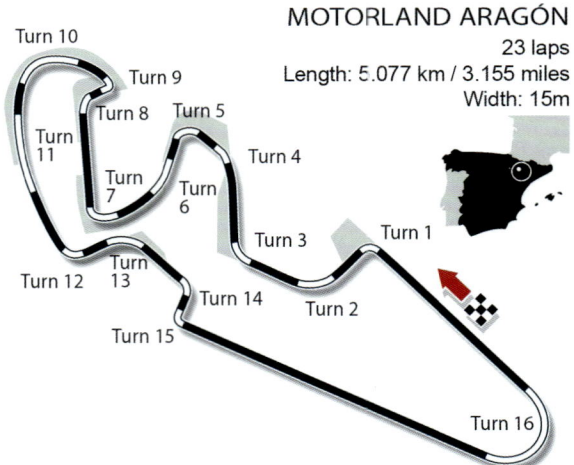

GRAN PREMIO TISSOT DE ARAGÓN

10-12 SEPTEMBER, 2021

MOTORLAND ARAGÓN
23 laps
Length: 5.077 km / 3.155 miles
Width: 15m

MotoGP

RACE DISTANCE: 23 laps, 72.558 miles/116.771km · RACE WEATHER: Dry (air 30°, humidity 40%, track 48°)

Pos.	Rider	Nat.	No.	Entrant	Machine	Race tyre choice	Laps	Time & speed
1	Francesco Bagnaia	ITA	63	Ducati Lenovo Team	Ducati Desmosedici	F: Hard/R: Soft	23	41m 44.422s 104.3mph/167.8km/h
2	Marc Marquez	SPA	93	Repsol Honda Team	Honda RC213V	F: Hard/R: Sof	23	41m 45.095s
3	Joan Mir	SPA	36	Team SUZUKI ECSTAR	Suzuki GSX-RR	F: Hard/R: Soft	23	41m 48.333s
4	Aleix Espargaro	SPA	41	Aprilia Racing Team Gresini	Aprilia RS-GP	F: Hard/R: Soft	23	41m 53.691s
5	Jack Miller	AUS	43	Ducati Lenovo Team	Ducati Desmosedici	F: Hard/R: Soft	23	41m 56.350s
6	Enea Bastianini	ITA	23	Avintia Esponsorama	Ducati Desmosedici	F: Hard/R: Soft	23	41m 58.179s
7	Brad Binder	RSA	33	Red Bull KTM Factory Racing	KTM RC16	F: Hard/R: Soft	23	41m 58.486s
8	Fabio Quartararo	FRA	20	Monster Energy Yamaha MotoGP	Yamaha YZR-M1	F: Hard/R: Soft	23	42m 00.997s
9	Jorge Martin	SPA	89	Pramac Racing	Ducati Desmosedici	F: Hard/R: Soft	23	42m 01.037s
10	Takaaki Nakagami	JPN	30	LCR Honda IDEMITSU	Honda RC213V	F: Hard/R: Soft	23	42m 01.326s
11	Iker Lecuona	SPA	27	Tech 3 KTM Factory Racing	KTM RC16	F: Hard/R: Soft	23	42m 01.546s
12	Alex Rins	SPA	42	Team SUZUKI ECSTAR	Suzuki GSX-RR	F: Hard/R: Soft	23	42m 02.132s
13	Pol Espargaro	SPA	44	Repsol Honda Team	Honda RC213V	F: Hard/R: Soft	23	42m 04.102s
14	Miguel Oliveira	POR	88	Red Bull KTM Factory Racing	KTM RC16	F: Hard/R: Soft	23	42m 07.125s
15	Danilo Petrucci	ITA	9	Tech 3 KTM Factory Racing	KTM RC16	F: Hard/R: Soft	23	42m 10.145s
16	Cal Crutchlow	GBR	35	Monster Energy Yamaha MotoGP	Yamaha YZR-M1	F: Hard/R: Soft	23	42m 10.835s
17	Johann Zarco	FRA	5	Pramac Racing	Ducati Desmosedici	F: Medium/R: Soft	23	42m 11.042s
18	Maverick Vinales	SPA	12	Aprilia Racing Team Gresini	Aprilia RS-GP	F: Hard/R: Soft	23	42m 11.550s
19	Valentino Rossi	ITA	46	Petronas Yamaha SRT	Yamaha YZR-M1	F: Hard/R: Soft	23	42m 16.939s
20	Luca Marini	ITA	10	SKY VR46 Avintia	Ducati Desmosedici	F: Hard/R: Soft	23	42m 23.495s
	Jake Dixon	GBR	96	Petronas Yamaha SRT	Yamaha YZR-M1	F: Hard/R: Soft	1	DNF-crash
	Alex Marquez	SPA	73	LCR Honda CASTROL	Honda RC213V	F: Hard/R: Soft	0	DNF-crash

Fastest lap: Marc Marquez, on lap 6, 1m 48.139s, 105.0mph/169.0km/h.
Lap record: Franco Morbidelli, 1m 48.089s, 105.0mph/169.0km/h (2020).
Event maximum speed: Brad Binder, 217.2mph/349.5km/h (free practice).

Qualifying

Weather: Dry
Air Temp: 27° **Track Temp:** 45°
Humidity: 47%

1	Bagnaia	1m 46.322s
2	Miller	1m 46.688s
3	Quartararo	1m 46.719s
4	M. Marquez	1m 46.736s
5	Martin	1m 46.878s
6	A. Espargaro	1m 46.883s
7	Mir	1m 47.162s
8	P. Espargaro	1m 47.194s
9	Bastianini	1m 47.278s
10	Zarco	1m 47.288s
11	Nakagami	1m 47.366s
12	Binder	1m 47.932s

Q1

13	Lecuona	1m 47.508s
14	A. Marquez	1m 47.542s
15	Crutchlow	1m 47.613s
16	Petrucci	1m 47.708s
17	Marini	1m 47.741s
18	Oliveira	1m 47.750s
19	Vinales	1m 47.764s
20	Rins	1m 47.790s
21	Rossi	1m 47.863s
22	Dixon	1m 48.146s

Fastest race laps

1	M. Marquez	1m 48.139s
2	Bagnaia	1m 48.333s
3	Miller	1m 48.349s
4	A. Espargaro	1m 48.440s
5	Mir	1m 48.492s
6	Martin	1m 48.515s
7	Lecuona	1m 48.566s
8	Quartararo	1m 48.625s
9	Nakagami	1m 48.667s
10	Binder	1m 48.753s
11	Bastianini	1m 48.827s
12	Rins	1m 48.837s
13	Oliveira	1m 49.022s
14	Zarco	1m 49.072s
15	Crutchlow	1m 49.095s
16	Petrucci	1m 49.098s
17	P. Espargaro	1m 49.136s
18	Vinales	1m 49.215s
19	Marini	1m 49.570s
20	Rossi	1m 49.587s

Championship Points

1	Quartararo	214
2	Bagnaia	161
3	Mir	157
4	Zarco	137
5	Miller	129
6	Binder	117
7	A. Espargaro	96
8	Vinales	95
9	Oliveira	87
10	M. Marquez	79
11	Martin	71
12	Rins	68
13	Nakagami	64
14	P. Espargaro	55
15	A. Marquez	49
16	Bastianini	45
17	Morbidelli	40
18	Lecuona	38
19	Petrucci	37
20	Marini	28
21	Rossi	28
22	Bradl	11
23	Pedrosa	6
24	Savadori	4
25	Pirro	3
26	Rabat	1

Constructor Points

1	Yamaha	234
2	Ducati	225
3	KTM	162
4	Suzuki	158
5	Honda	115
6	Aprilia	84

Grid order / Lap-by-lap

Grid order	1	2	3	4	5	6	7	8	9	10	11	12	13	14	15	16	17	18	19	20	21	22	23
63 BAGNAIA	63	63	63	63	63	63	63	63	63	63	63	63	63	63	63	63	63	63	63	63	63	63	63
43 MILLER	93	93	93	93	93	93	93	93	93	93	93	93	93	93	93	93	93	93	93	93	93	93	93
20 QUARTARARO	43	43	43	43	43	43	43	43	43	43	41	36	36	36	36	36	36	36	36	36	36	36	36
93 M. MARQUEZ	41	41	41	41	41	41	41	41	41	41	36	41	41	41	41	41	41	41	41	41	41	41	41
89 MARTIN	36	36	36	36	36	36	36	36	36	36	43	43	43	43	43	43	43	43	43	43	43	43	43
41 A. ESPARGARO	89	89	89	89	89	89	89	89	89	89	89	89	89	33	33	33	33	33	33	33	33	23	23
36 MIR	20	20	20	20	20	27	27	27	27	27	27	27	27	89	27	89	89	89	89	23	23	33	33
44 P. ESPARGARO	44	33	27	27	27	20	20	33	33	33	33	33	33	27	89	20	20	20	23	89	89	20	20
23 BASTIANINI	33	27	33	33	33	33	33	20	20	20	20	20	23	20	20	20	23	23	23	20	20	20	89
5 ZARCO	27	23	23	23	23	23	23	23	23	23	23	20	30	23	23	27	30	30	30	30	30	30	30
30 NAKAGAMI	23	44	30	30	30	30	30	30	30	30	30	23	20	30	30	27	27	27	27	27	27	27	27
33 BINDER	30	30	44	42	42	42	42	42	42	42	42	42	42	42	42	42	42	42	42	42	42	42	42
27 LECUONA	5	5	42	44	44	44	44	44	44	44	44	44	44	44	44	44	44	44	44	44	44	44	44
73 A. MARQUEZ	88	42	5	5	88	88	88	88	88	88	88	88	88	88	88	88	88	88	88	88	88	88	88
35 CRUTCHLOW	42	88	88	88	5	5	5	5	5	5	5	5	9	9	9	9	9	9	9	9	9	9	9
9 PETRUCCI	9	9	9	9	9	9	9	9	9	9	9	35	5	35	5	35	5	35	5	35	5	35	35
10 MARINI	10	10	35	35	35	35	35	35	35	35	35	5	35	5	35	5	35	5	35	5	35	5	5
88 OLIVEIRA	12	35	10	10	10	10	10	10	10	10	12	12	12	12	12	12	12	12	12	12	12	12	12
12 VINALES	35	12	12	12	12	12	12	46	46	46	46	46	46	46	46	46	46	46	46	46	46	46	46
42 RINS	96	46	46	46	46	46	46	10	10	10	10	10	10	10	10	10	10	10	10	10	10	10	10
46 ROSSI	46																						
96 DIXON																							

188 ARAGON GRAND PRIX

Moto2

RACE DISTANCE: 21 laps, 66.249 miles/106.617km · **RACE WEATHER:** Dry (air 27°, humidity 54%, track 41°)

Pos.	Rider	Nat.	No.	Entrant	Machine	Laps	Time & Speed
1	Raul Fernandez	SPA	25	Red Bull KTM Ajo	Kalex	21	39m 49.990s 99.7mph/ 160.5 km/h
2	Remy Gardner	AUS	87	Red Bull KTM Ajo	Kalex	21	39m 55.398s
3	Augusto Fernandez	SPA	37	Elf Marc VDS Racing Team	Kalex	21	39m 56.814s
4	Jorge Navarro	SPA	9	+EGO Speed Up	Boscoscuro	21	39m 57.041s
5	Aron Canet	SPA	44	Kipin Energy Aspar Team	Boscoscuro	21	40m 00.685s
6	Fabio Di Giannantonio	ITA	21	Federal Oil Gresini Moto2	Kalex	21	40m 05.150s
7	Fermin Aldeguer	SPA	54	+EGO Speed Up	Boscoscuro	21	40m 06.720s
8	Ai Ogura	JPN	79	IDEMITSU Honda Team Asia	Kalex	21	40m 07.075s
9	Tony Arbolino	ITA	14	Liqui Moly Intact GP	Kalex	21	40m 07.694s
10	Simone Corsi	ITA	24	MV Agusta Forward Racing	MV Agusta	21	40m 10.111s
11	Marcel Schrotter	GER	23	Liqui Moly Intact GP	Kalex	21	40m 10.842s
12	Marcos Ramirez	SPA	42	American Racing	Kalex	21	40m 14.592s
13	Joe Roberts	USA	16	Italtrans Racing Team	Kalex	21	40m 16.076s
14	Cameron Beaubier	USA	6	American Racing	Kalex	21	40m 19.091s
15	Celestino Vietti	ITA	13	SKY Racing Team VR46	Kalex	21	40m 20.291s
16	Barry Baltus	BEL	70	NTS RW Racing GP	NTS	21	40m 20.410s
17	Manuel Gonzalez	SPA	81	MV Agusta Forward Racing	MV Agusta	21	40m 24.967s
18	Stefano Manzi	ITA	62	Flexbox HP40	Kalex	21	40m 25.779s
19	Hafizh Syahrin	MAL	55	NTS RW Racing GP	NTS	21	40m 26.026s
20	John McPhee	GBR	17	Petronas Sprinta Racing	Kalex	21	40m 37.746s
21	Xavi Cardelus	AND	18	Cerba Promoracing Team	Kalex	21	40m 37.824s
	Somkiat Chantra	THA	35	IDEMITSU Honda Team Asia	Kalex	17	DNF-crash
	Nicolo Bulega	ITA	11	Federal Oil Gresini Moto2	Kalex	16	DNF-technical
	Sam Lowes	GBR	22	Elf Marc VDS Racing Team	Kalex	13	DNF-crash
	Bo Bendsneyder	NED	64	Pertamina Mandalika SAG Team	Kalex	12	DNF-crash
	Marco Bezzecchi	ITA	72	SKY Racing Team VR46	Kalex	12	DNF-crash
	Lorenzo Dalla Porta	ITA	19	Italtrans Racing Team	Kalex	7	DNF-crash
	Albert Arenas	SPA	75	Kipin Energy Aspar Team	Boscoscuro	5	DNF-crash
	Hector Garzo	SPA	40	Flexbox HP40	Kalex	4	DNF-crash
	Xavi Vierge	SPA	97	Petronas Sprinta Racing	Kalex	3	DNF-crash
	Thomas Luthi	SWI	12	Pertamina Mandalika SAG Team	Kalex	3	DNF-crash
	Piotr Biesiekirski	POL	74	Pertamina Mandalika SAG Euvic	Kalex	2	DNF-crash

Fastest lap: Raul Fernandez, on lap 2, 1m 52.206s, 101.2mph/162.8km/h.
Lap record: Sam Lowes, 1m 51.730s, 101.6mph/163.5km/h (2020).
Event maximum speed: Hector Garzo, 180.9mph/291.2km/h (free practice).

Qualifying
Weather: Dry Air Temp: 27° Track Temp: 41° Humidity: 47%

1	Lowes	1m 51.778s
2	Gardner	1m 52.057s
3	R. Fernandez	1m 52.084s
4	Garzo	1m 52.107s
5	Ogura	1m 52.148s
6	Arenas	1m 52.170s
7	Navarro	1m 52.197s
8	Di Giannantonio	1m 52.387s
9	Bezzecchi	1m 52.391s
10	Ramirez	1m 52.400s
11	Canet	1m 52.478s
12	A. Fernandez	1m 52.494s
13	Vierge	1m 52.528s
14	Bulega	1m 52.626s
15	Schrotter	1m 52.856s
16	Luthi	1m 52.879s
17	Aldeguer	1m 52.947s
18	Roberts	1m 53.310s

Q1
19	Beaubier	1m 52.784s
20	Corsi	1m 52.830s
21	Dalla Porta	1m 52.846s
22	Baltus	1m 52.929s
23	Arbolino	1m 52.993s
24	Manzi	1m 53.005s
25	Syahrin	1m 53.114s
26	Vietti	1m 53.259s
27	Chantra	1m 53.264s
28	Bendsneyder	1m 53.416s
29	McPhee	1m 53.475s
30	Gonzalez	1m 53.589s
31	Cardelus	1m 54.477s
32	Biesiekirski	1m 54.502s

Fastest race laps
1	R. Fernandez	1m 52.206s
2	Ogura	1m 52.498s
3	Lowes	1m 52.517s
4	Garzo	1m 52.534s
5	Gardner	1m 52.548s
6	Bezzecchi	1m 52.610s
7	Navarro	1m 52.753s
8	Di Giannantonio	1m 52.819s
9	Canet	1m 52.864s
10	Arenas	1m 53.006s
11	Vierge	1m 53.103s
12	A. Fernandez	1m 53.290s
13	Bulega	1m 53.512s
14	Corsi	1m 53.593s
15	Ramirez	1m 53.593s
16	Schrotter	1m 53.616s
17	Roberts	1m 53.620s
18	Baltus	1m 53.710s
19	Beaubier	1m 53.732s
20	Arbolino	1m 53.790s
21	Aldeguer	1m 53.821s
22	Vietti	1m 53.930s
23	Gonzalez	1m 54.045s
24	Dalla Porta	1m 54.208s
25	Chantra	1m 54.246s
26	Luthi	1m 54.273s
27	Syahrin	1m 54.312s
28	Manzi	1m 54.409s
29	Cardelus	1m 54.820s
30	McPhee	1m 54.822s
31	Bendsneyder	1m 55.803s

Championship Points
1	Gardner	251
2	R. Fernandez	212
3	Bezzecchi	179
4	Lowes	127
5	A. Fernandez	108
6	Canet	103
7	Di Giannantonio	101
8	Ogura	95
9	Schrotter	80
10	Navarro	71
11	Vierge	67
12	Roberts	59
13	Vietti	47
14	Arbolino	40
15	Bendsneyder	40
16	Chantra	35
17	Beaubier	28
18	Arenas	23
19	Dixon	21
20	Manzi	20
21	Ramirez	20
22	Luthi	16
23	Aldeguer	13
24	Corsi	13
25	Garzo	12
26	Bulega	12
27	Dalla Porta	10
28	Syahrin	8
29	Lopez	4
30	Baldassarri	3
31	Baltus	2

Constructor Points
1	Kalex	325
2	Boscoscuro	138
3	MV Agusta	16
4	NTS	10

Moto3

RACE DISTANCE: 19 laps, 59.939 miles/96.463km · **RACE WEATHER:** Dry (air 22°, humidity 82%, track 33°)

Pos.	Rider	Nat.	No.	Entrant	Machine	Laps	Time & Speed
1	Dennis Foggia	ITA	7	Leopard Racing	Honda	19	37m 53.710s 94.9mph/ 152.7km/h
2	Deniz Oncu	TUR	53	Red Bull KTM Tech 3	KTM	19	37m 53.751s
3	Ayumu Sasaki	JPN	71	Red Bull KTM Tech 3	KTM	19	37m 54.354s
4	Izan Guevara	SPA	28	GAVIOTA GASGAS Aspar Team	GASGAS	19	37m 54.418s
5	Niccolo Antonelli	ITA	23	Avintia VR46	KTM	19	37m 54.588s
6	Andrea Migno	ITA	16	Rivacold Snipers Team	Honda	19	37m 54.890s
7	Darryn Binder	RSA	40	Petronas Sprinta Racing	Honda	19	37m 55.843s
8	Stefano Nepa	ITA	82	BOE Owlride	KTM	19	37m 56.395s
9	Tatsuki Suzuki	JPN	24	SIC58 Squadra Corse	Honda	19	37m 56.496s
10	Jaume Masia	SPA	5	Red Bull KTM Ajo	KTM	19	37m 58.424s
11	Ryusei Yamanaka	JPN	6	CarXpert PruestelGP	KTM	19	38m 01.985s
12	Adrian Fernandez	SPA	31	Sterilgarda Max Racing Team	Husqvarna	19	38m 03.209s
13	Syarifuddin Azman	MAL	63	Petronas Sprinta Racing	Honda	19	38m 03.355s
14	Romano Fenati	ITA	55	Sterilgarda Max Racing Team	Husqvarna	19	38m 08.507s
15	Riccardo Rossi	ITA	54	BOE Owlride	KTM	19	38m 12.590s
16	Kaito Toba	JPN	27	CIP Green Power	KTM	19	38m 12.604s
17	Yuki Kunii	JPN	92	Honda Team Asia	Honda	19	38m 12.982s
18	Sergio Garcia	SPA	11	GAVIOTA GASGAS Aspar Team	GASGAS	19	38m 13.598s
19	Maximilian Kofler	AUT	73	CIP Green Power	KTM	19	38m 13.643s
20	Andi Farid Izdihar	INA	19	Honda Team Asia	Honda	19	38m 32.350s
21	Alberto Surra	ITA	67	Rivacold Snipers Team	Honda	19	38m 32.454s
	Jeremy Alcoba	SPA	52	Indonesian Racing Gresini Moto3	Honda	18	DNF-crash
	Lorenzo Fellon	FRA	20	SIC58 Squadra Corse	Honda	18	DNF-crash
	Xavier Artigas	SPA	43	Leopard Racing	Honda	15	DNF-crash
	Pedro Acosta	SPA	37	Red Bull KTM Ajo	KTM	15	DNF-crash
	Carlos Tatay	SPA	99	Avintia Esponsorama Moto3	KTM	12	DNF-crash
	Gabriel Rodrigo	ARG	2	Indonesian Racing Gresini Moto3	Honda	5	DNF-crash
	Filip Salac	CZE	12	CarXpert PruestelGP	KTM	2	DNF-crash

Fastest lap: Izan Guevara, on lap 7, 1m 58.589s, 95.8mph/154.1km/h.
Lap record: Sergio Garcia, 1m 57.976s, 96.3mph/154.9km/h (2020).
Event maximum speed: Niccolo Antonelli, 151.6mph/244.0km/h (race).

Qualifying:
Weather: Dry Air Temp: 26° Track Temp: 43° Humidity: 46%

1	Binder	1m 57.724s
2	Rodrigo	1m 57.905s
3	Suzuki	1m 57.976s
4	Garcia	1m 58.069s
5	Migno	1m 58.103s
6	Oncu	1m 58.314s
7	Alcoba	1m 58.362s
8	Antonelli	1m 58.381s
9	Acosta	1m 58.434s
10	Fellon	1m 58.463s
11	Salac	1m 58.475s
12	Artigas	1m 58.490s
13	Guevara	1m 58.613s
14	Foggia	1m 58.646s
15	Masia	1m 58.830s
16	Sasaki	1m 58.893s
17	Fenati	1m 58.953s
18	Toba	1m 59.039s

Q1
19	Nepa	1m 59.411s
20	Tatay	1m 59.455s
21	Azman	1m 59.725s
22	Fernandez	1m 59.741s
23	Rossi	1m 59.760s
24	Kofler	1m 59.931s
25	Kunii	1m 59.937s
26	Izdihar	2m 00.209s
27	Yamanaka	2m 00.522s
28	Surra	2m 00.761s

Fastest race laps
1	Guevara	1m 58.589s
2	Artigas	1m 58.822s
3	Sasaki	1m 58.862s
4	Yamanaka	1m 58.902s
5	Fenati	1m 59.002s
6	Acosta	1m 59.022s
7	Nepa	1m 59.037s
8	Garcia	1m 59.046s
9	Masia	1m 59.077s
10	Rodrigo	1m 59.082s
11	Öncü	1m 59.089s
12	Antonelli	1m 59.091s
13	Suzuki	1m 59.099s
14	Fellon	1m 59.132s
15	Migno	1m 59.160s
16	Foggia	1m 59.167s
17	Alcoba	1m 59.176s
18	Salac	1m 59.230s
19	Azman	1m 59.230s
20	Binder	1m 59.258s
21	Tatay	1m 59.325s
22	Fernandez	1m 59.376s
23	Kofler	1m 59.405s
24	Toba	1m 59.411s
25	Rossi	1m 59.475s
26	Kunii	1m 59.524s
27	Izdihar	1m 59.854s
28	Surra	2m 00.580s

Championship Points
1	Acosta	201
2	Garcia	155
3	Foggia	143
4	Fenati	134
5	Masia	111
6	Binder	104
7	Antonelli	98
8	Sasaki	87
9	Oncu	73
10	Guevara	72
11	Migno	68
12	Toba	62
13	Suzuki	61
14	Alcoba	60
15	Rodrigo	60
16	McPhee	53
17	Salac	46
18	Yamanaka	42
19	Artigas	30
20	Nepa	30
21	Dupasquier	27
22	Rossi	24
23	Tatay	20
24	Fernandez	20
25	Kunii	15
26	Kofler	10
27	Bartolini	7
28	Azman	3
29	Izdihar	3
30	Holgado	1

Constructor Points
1	KTM	275
2	Honda	245
3	GASGAS	193
4	Husqvarna	140

ARAGON GRAND PRIX

Audi Sport
aruba.it
Lenovo
UnipolSai
FLEX-BOX
riello ups
FLEX-BOX
Lenovo
alpinestars
Lenovo

FIM WORLD CHAMPIONSHIP · ROUND 14

SAN MARINO GRAND PRIX

MISANO WORLD CIRCUIT MARCO SIMONCELLI

GRAN PREMIO OCTO DI SAN MARINO E DELLA RIVIERA DI RIMINI

Misano World Circuit Marco Simoncelli | 2021

Above: Two wins in a row gave Bagnaia the possibility of upending the championship.

Right: Brilliant Bastianini on a two-year-old Ducati outpaced and impressed Marc Marquez.
Photos: Gold & Goose

Opening spread: Renaissance in red. Ducati's Bagnaia prepares for action under threatening skies.
Photo: Ducati Corse

ROOKIE surprises were not over. Now it was Enea Bastianini's turn to rock the establishment with a debut-season podium that almost, though not quite, overshadowed Pecco Bagnaia's second straight defeat of Quartararo – Ducati's first back-to-back wins since 2018.

Bastianini first. The reigning Moto2 champion had impressed with a steady improvement on his two-year-old Desmosedici, most recently sixth at Aragon. At his home circuit, he excelled with a ride of strength and maturity to third from 12th on the grid (his second time in Q2 in two races), passing all but the top two and setting lap times that more than matched the leaders, with a new record on the 17th of 24 laps. Along the way, he impressed no less than Marc Marquez: "When he overtook me, I was following him, and we were catching Quartararo and the top guys. But then I saw that I was over my limit, and I said, 'Okay, cool down, let him go.' But he was riding very good, he was understanding a lot the way to ride the Ducati. He was braking so late, and exiting of the corner with a lot of torque and a lot of grip."

To the victor the spoils, however, and that was Bagnaia, in a second successive display of late-race determination, as a three-second advantage over Quartararo was slashed to just a tenth with one lap remaining. Victory at Aragon, he explained, "gave me a lot of motivation, a lot more trust in myself. Arriving here, I was more prepared to win." He held off the late attack by 0.364 of a second and in the process established himself as at least a mathematically credible title challenger.

The opposite happened to defending champion Joan Mir, who crossed the line fifth, but was demoted to sixth for having exceeded track limits on the last lap. Although still in contention numerically, he conceded that his title defence was over. He was scuppered by a wrong choice of front tyre – medium instead of hard. But over the year, he had been undermined by a lack of progress by Suzuki relative to their rivals and a slow response to his increasingly frantic demands to improve the bike's one-lap potential. He had been able to race strongly, but not qualify well – only once on even the second row, and 11th for this race.

"I'm a bit angry because I knew my potential this year," said Mir. "I'm making less mistakes and I'm a better rider. And I will not get the championship. It's difficult to understand. It's not I made a mistake. It's just I wasn't competitive as everyone expected. That's why I'm disappointed. I expected more. It's a difficult day for me."

Franco Morbidelli was back, his first appearance at a MotoGP race since June after sitting out five races due to a complex knee injury that required surgery. During that time, in answer to his early complaints about his two-year-old motorcycle, he had been promoted to Yamaha's factory team until the end of the year, and signed up to stay there until the end of 2023. This was thanks to the untimely departure of Maverick Vinales, and the Italian inherited crew chief Silvano Galbusera and the rest of the Vinales pit.

Did the upgrade meet expectations? "Just jumping on the bike after so much time, it basically just feels like a spaceship," he said. "So I cannot give any feedback or anything about the difference between the two bikes."

Part two of the Yamaha reshuffle was at least as intriguing: the return from self-imposed exile of Andrea Dovizioso. Having stepped down from Ducati, possibly before being dispensed with, Dovi had been testing the Aprilia, and for a while he had been tipped to join the team full-time, before Vinales had taken that role. The Italian had other ambitions, however, and now they happened to coincide with Yamaha's. Not only was he shoehorned into the satellite team to replace Morbidelli, but also on race eve at Misano, it was confirmed that he would race a factory-spec Yamaha for the team in 2022.

"I was feeling good at home, I was doing what I liked, my passion [motocross], and I was more relaxed, 100 per cent. Especially my girlfriend 'explained' that to me," Dovi said.

192 SAN MARINO GRAND PRIX

"But when that door opened, I couldn't say no. After 2012 [when he had raced for Tech3 Yamaha], my dream was always to race a factory Yamaha, and that didn't happen. So that remained in my mind."

Dovi joined Morbidelli's former crew chief, Ramon Forcada, with old rival Rossi as team-mate. Now 35, that brought their combined age to 77, with the team originally trumpeted as a place to nurture young talent fielding the two oldest riders on the grid (Ducati wild-card Michele Pirro being some three months younger than Dovi).

A run of wretched results that had dropped Johann Zarco out of championship contention, and pre-race confirmation of compartment-syndrome problems, convinced the French rider to schedule arm-pump surgery on the Wednesday after the race, with the surgeon who had operated on Quartararo for the same problem earlier in the season.

Official actions raised questions at Misano, the first concerning MotoGP's concussion protocol, after Moto3 runner Deniz Oncu was passed fit to ride in Sunday's race after suffering a horrendous high-side on Saturday morning. FP3 was red-flagged as medics rushed to Oncu's assistance, and the 18-year-old later tweeted, "After that horrible accident, I woke up in the medical centre." If he was unconscious for the best part of half an hour, it is highly likely that the Turk would have suffered some form of concussion, but team chief Herve Poncharal contradicted the tweet, denying that Oncu had been knocked unconscious. There were no such doubts for other Moto3 injury victims on Saturday. Surra missed qualifying, while Gabriel Rodrigo withdrew, his Aragon injuries effectively ending his season.

Due diligence was fulfilled, however, and some thought exceeded, after Race Direction and the FIM stewards handed out their strongest penalty yet. Japanese Moto3 rider Yuki Kunii was disqualified after he let up on the entry to Curvone during the closing moments of FP3, causing Surra to hit his rear tyre, and crash at 130mph.

MOTOGP RACE – 27 laps

Bagnaia led free practice and qualifying for a second successive pole, his third of the year. Team-mate Miller was alongside, then Quartararo. Ducatis looked strong, with Pramac pair Martin and Zarco heading row two from Pol Espargaro, best of the Hondas. Marc Marquez led row three; Vinales – fastest in FP1 – was tenth, one row behind Aprilia team-mate Aleix Espargaro.

Bagnaia led into the tight first-corner complex, from Miller and Quartararo, and again demonstrated his improving ability to gain an early advantage. At the end of the first lap, he was better than a second clear, an impressive gap that had doubled on lap eight after Miller made a small slip and ran wide at Turn 12.

First, Quartararo had to shake off a persistent Martin on laps two and three, with two quick ripostes to passes at Turns Four and Ten. Then the rookie's afternoon went sour as he tucked the front at Turn 14, remounting only to retire. But the Frenchman failed to profit from Miller's slip, making the same error.

Soon Miller would feel the onset of a vibration generated by rear tyre wear, and when Quartararo got by cleanly on lap 14, he started to drop away.

At this point, Bagnaia's lead was 2.7 seconds. While he and Miller had chosen the soft Michelin rear, Quartararo was on the medium. "Our calculations said that with ten laps to go, the soft [rear] should drop," explained Yamaha team boss Massimo Meregalli. His rider was tasked with slowly building rhythm before launching a late attack.

After half-distance, the Yamaha rider had really found his groove. He posted his personal best time on lap 19, then nearly matched it the following time around. With his long-time lead diminishing, Bagnaia's small mistake on lap 23 allowed his rival to gain further ground.

Memories of 2020, when he had crashed out of a comfortable lead, were still fresh: "I was terrorised at the thought. I was thinking, 'Don't crash!'" said the Italian. By lap 26, Quartararo was just a tenth back, setting up a breathless finale. Bagnaia admitted that the pressure had told. "There were two or three laps where I struggled, seeing his pace," he said. "So I took a breath and tried to be consistent to have more tyre in the last two laps."

It worked. Just when Quartararo was close enough to attack, Bagnaia responded. "I wanted to overtake in Turn Six, but I was too far and I had quite a lot of spin," said the Frenchman. As the Italian glided through the three fast rights at the end of the back straight, it was clear that the race was his. "The lean angle he had on Turn 12, I said, 'It's the moment to keep calm.'" said Quartararo. Bagnaia's final lap gave him three-tenths in hand at the flag.

Behind, Marc Marquez had led a high-speed train, including Aleix Espargaro (in front a couple of times early on), then Pol Espargaro, Rins, Bastianini and Mir, recovering from his trademark poor qualifying in 11th.

Bastianini, 12th on the grid, made sensational progress through the brawl. He gained three places on lap one, and passed Rins, Pol and then Aleix to lie fifth on lap five. A lap later, he was past Marquez as well.

Fourth would have been good enough, but Miller's mysterious rear-tyre vibration made him a sitting duck. The rookie reeled off a pair of record laps on the 16th and 17th, to take third on lap 19. Rins had crashed out at Turn One a lap earlier trying to keep up.

Miller was still fourth with a lap to go, but Mir's block pass on the Australian at Turn 14 gave Marquez an opening, which he snatched. Mir crossed the line a frustrated fifth in his 100th GP start, but he was demoted to sixth, behind Miller, for exceeding track limits on the exit of T15 – some measure of comfort for the dispossessed Australian.

Pol was the first Espargaro brother, in seventh, with Aleix eighth. Brad Binder was through to ninth from 17th on the grid, best of the KTMs in a tough weekend for the marque – Petrucci was 16th, out of the points, the detuned Oliveira 20th, while Lecuona had crashed out.

Nakagami was tenth; then came wild-card Pirro from the off-form Zarco, who narrowly held off Vinales. Bradl and Alex Marquez wrapped up the points.

MOTO2 RACE – 25 laps

Moto2 lost the first day of practice to rain; on Saturday, Raul Fernandez was in control, taking his fifth pole ahead of Lowes and namesake Augusto, continuing his late-season strong showing. Gardner led row two from the Boscoscuro chassis of Canet and Navarro; Bezzecchi was in the middle of row three between Vierge and Di Giannantonio.

Lowes led away, chased for the first two laps by Raul before Canet took over the pursuit on lap eight, thanks to a slip by Lowes. Raul also got ahead into second, but the English rider closed up again, and it remained a three-way fight as they passed half-distance.

By then, Gardner was firmly in fourth, although still almost a second adrift. It had taken him until lap six to get there, after having to skirmish his way past Bezzecchi and then a determined Vierge.

It took the younger Fernandez until lap 15 before he had disposed of Canet to get to the front, and from there on, his consistency was unerring. He posted consecutive fastest laps – short of a new record – on laps 18 and 19 to eke out a gap of four-tenths.

Gardner had also been at work. He passed Lowes on lap 16, then purposefully tailed Canet, making a successful attack on the 23rd lap.

Now he could close on his team-mate. With Fernandez showing possible signs of fatigue, the Australian smelt blood, taking a quarter of a second out of the lead on the penultimate lap, another three-tenths in the first half of the last.

A move was coming at Turn 14, the last and slowest of the four rights late in the lap. But it never happened. Instead, at Curvone, the first and fastest of them, taken at around 160mph, Gardner was obliged to save a massive slide: "A little hairy. It's just instinct at that point." Now he had to focus on defending from Canet, still right up close and less than two-tenths behind past the flag.

Fernandez won by four-tenths, Lowes was still only a second behind, the top four covered by 1.5 seconds.

Front-row starter Augusto Fernandez had been unable to make progress in the early stages and complained of poor rear grip throughout, but by the finish, he had closed to within half a second of Bezzecchi in fifth.

Above: A maiden podium and lap record for Bastianini.

Top: Raul Fernandez leads the Moto2 pack at the start. In pursuit, Bulega (11), Canet (44), Gardner (87), Vierge (97), Ogura (79) and Schrotter (23).

Top right: Zarco leads Nakagami, Binder, Marini. Lecuona and Vinales in their early midfield scrap.
Photos: Gold & Goose

Above centre right: Morbidelli was back, promoted to the factory team.
Photo: Monster Energy Yamaha

Above right: Bewigged Migno took a second Moto3 podium of the year.

Right: Foggia leads the front pack, from Garcia (11), Masia (5), Migno (16), Binder (40) and Antonelli (23).
Photos: Gold & Goose

194 SAN MARINO GRAND PRIX

FIM WORLD CHAMPIONSHIP | 14

A late charge from Ogura scored seventh, after passing Vierge with four laps to go. The Spaniard only narrowly managed to hold Di Giannantonio at bay over the line.

Rookie Celestino Vietti had yet another impressive run through the field, from 20th on lap one to tenth at the flag, having passed and easily outpaced Luthi and Schrotter.

Navarro made a bad start, then on lap three tangled with 34-year-old veteran Corsi. The Italian crashed, and Navarro was given a long-lap penalty. Back to 22nd on lap seven, he had worked through to a lonely 13th by the end, with Ramirez and Arbolino scrapping over the last points.

Baltus, Chantra and Dalla Porta crashed out, the last named aggravating a shoulder injury and retiring from the rest of the season for corrective surgery.

Gardner's title lead had now shrunk to 34 points, with Bezzecchi dropping further out of touch.

MOTO3 RACE – 23 laps

For 14 laps, one of those rarest of things in Moto3 was on the cards: a second runaway victory in three races. At a track where he had twice previously won, Romano Fenati followed the strategy that had served him so well at Silverstone three weeks before – push from the start and build an insurmountable lead.

Starting from pole and setting a new record on lap five, he made it look effortless. This was deceptive, as proved on lap 14. At Turn 15, a treacherous first left after four right-handers, he lost the front. The potential race win, and any faint title hopes, vanished.

From that point, Foggia took control. He'd qualified second and built up a half-second lead as Garcia, Migno, Masia and third front-row starter Antonelli scrabbled behind him. However, it remained a strangely processional duel by Moto3 standards.

Eventually, Antonelli recovered from a mistake on lap ten to take second, with Migno eight-tenths behind. Garcia was next, ahead of Masia and Binder. The South African had come through to an erstwhile fourth from 14th on the grid, but the effort had cost him tyre grip, and he was off the back of the group at the end.

Another two seconds away, Acosta was next after another tough day. A lack of confidence in braking had spoiled his pace, but he still performed a late rescue mission, clinching seventh in a tight fight with Tatay, Nepa, Sasaki and Rossi.

Foggia's second straight win, his fourth podium in a row, closed him to within 42 points, now equal with the less-threatening Garcia.

FIM WORLD CHAMPIONSHIP: ROUND 14

GRAN PREMIO OCTO DI SAN MARINO E DELLA RIVIERA DI RIMINI

17-19 SEPTEMBER, 2021

MISANO WORLD CIRCUIT
27 laps
Length: 4.226 km / 2.626 miles
Width: 14m

MotoGP

RACE DISTANCE: 27 laps, 70.900 miles/114.102km · RACE WEATHER: Dry (air 26°, humidity 52%, track 29°)

Pos.	Rider	Nat.	No.	Entrant	Machine	Race tyre choice	Laps	Time & speed
1	Francesco Bagnaia	ITA	63	Ducati Lenovo Team	Ducati Desmosedici	F: Hard/R: Soft	27	41m 48.305s / 101.7mph/ 163.7km/h
2	Fabio Quartararo	FRA	20	Monster Energy Yamaha MotoGP	Yamaha YZR-M1	F: Hard/R: Medium	27	41m 48.669s
3	Enea Bastianini	ITA	23	Avintia Esponsorama	Ducati Desmosedici	F: Hard/R: Soft	27	41m 53.094s
4	Marc Marquez	SPA	93	Repsol Honda Team	Honda RC213V	F: Hard/R: Soft	27	41m 58.550s
5	Jack Miller	AUS	43	Ducati Lenovo Team	Ducati Desmosedici	F: Hard/R: Soft	27	41m 58.774s
6	Joan Mir	SPA	36	Team SUZUKI ECSTAR	Suzuki GSX-RR	F: Hard/R: Medium	27	41m 58.630s
7	Pol Espargaro	SPA	44	Repsol Honda Team	Honda RC213V	F: Hard/R: Medium	27	42m 01.539s
8	Aleix Espargaro	SPA	41	Aprilia Racing Team Gresini	Aprilia RS-GP	F: Medium/R: Medium	27	42m 04.003s
9	Brad Binder	RSA	33	Red Bull KTM Factory Racing	KTM RC16	F: Hard/R: Medium	27	42m 04.434s
10	Takaaki Nakagami	JPN	30	LCR Honda IDEMITSU	Honda RC213V	F: Medium/R: Soft	27	42m 06.824s
11	Michele Pirro	ITA	51	Ducati Lenovo Team	Ducati Desmosedici	F: Medium/R: Soft	27	42m 08.678s
12	Johann Zarco	FRA	5	Pramac Racing	Ducati Desmosedici	F: Hard/R: Soft	27	42m 09.371s
13	Maverick Vinales	SPA	12	Aprilia Racing Team Gresini	Aprilia RS-GP	F: Medium/R: Medium	27	42m 09.563s
14	Stefan Bradl	GER	6	Team Honda HRC	Honda RC213V	F: Medium/R: Medium	27	42m 16.447s
15	Alex Marquez	SPA	73	LCR Honda CASTROL	Honda RC213V	F: Hard/R: Soft	27	42m 18.991s
16	Danilo Petrucci	ITA	9	Tech 3 KTM Factory Racing	KTM RC16	F: Hard/R: Medium	27	42m 20.959s
17	Valentino Rossi	ITA	46	Petronas Yamaha SRT	Yamaha YZR-M1	F: Medium/R: Medium	27	42m 22.158s
18	Franco Morbidelli	ITA	21	Monster Energy Yamaha MotoGP	Yamaha YZR-M1	F: Medium/R: Medium	27	42m 24.577s
19	Luca Marini	ITA	10	SKY VR46 Avintia	Ducati Desmosedici	F: Hard/R: Soft	27	42m 25.144s
20	Miguel Oliveira	POR	88	Red Bull KTM Factory Racing	KTM RC16	F: Hard/R: Soft	27	42m 25.507s
21	Andrea Dovizioso	ITA	4	Petronas Yamaha SRT	Yamaha YZR-M1	F: Medium/R: Medium	27	42m 30.892s
	Alex Rins	SPA	42	Team SUZUKI ECSTAR	Suzuki GSX-RR	F: Medium/R: Medium	17	DNF-crash
	Iker Lecuona	SPA	27	Tech 3 KTM Factory Racing	KTM RC16	F: Hard/R: Soft	14	DNF-crash
	Jorge Martin	SPA	89	Pramac Racing	Ducati Desmosedici	F: Medium/R: Soft	10	DNF-crash

Fastest lap: Enea Bastianini, on lap 17, 1m 32.242s, 102.5mph/164.9km/h.
Lap record: Francesco Bagnaia, 1m 32.319s, 102.3mph/164.7km/h (2020).
Event maximum speed: Johann Zarco, 188.0mph/302.5km/h (race).

Qualifying

Weather: Dry
Air Temp: 28° **Track Temp:** 37°
Humidity: 56%

1	Bagnaia	1m 31.065s
2	Miller	1m 31.314s
3	Quartararo	1m 31.367s
4	Martin	1m 31.663s
5	Zarco	1m 31.836s
6	P. Espargaro	1m 31.923s
7	M. Marquez	1m 31.935s
8	A. Espargaro	1m 31.937s
9	Rins	1m 32.017s
10	Vinales	1m 32.121s
11	Mir	1m 32.426s
12	Bastianini	1m 32.461s

Q1

13	Nakagami	1m 32.210s
14	Pirro	1m 32.287s
15	Marini	1m 32.289s
16	Morbidelli	1m 32.296s
17	Binder	1m 32.427s
18	Bradl	1m 32.439s
19	A. Marquez	1m 32.476s
20	Lecuona	1m 32.481s
21	Oliveira	1m 32.821s
22	Petrucci	1m 32.891s
23	Rossi	1m 32.967s
24	Dovizioso	1m 33.098s

Fastest race laps

1	Bastianini	1m 32.242s
2	Quartararo	1m 32.336s
3	Miller	1m 32.390s
4	A. Espargaro	1m 32.400s
5	Bagnaia	1m 32.422s
6	Rins	1m 32.466s
7	Mir	1m 32.508s
8	M. Marquez	1m 32.545s
9	Zarco	1m 32.710s
10	Martin	1m 32.731s
11	P. Espargaro	1m 32.739s
12	Binder	1m 32.764s
13	Nakagami	1m 32.856s
14	Vinales	1m 32.900s
15	Pirro	1m 32.920s
16	Bradl	1m 32.984s
17	Lecuona	1m 33.023s
18	A. Marquez	1m 33.209s
19	Marini	1m 33.220s
20	Petrucci	1m 33.277s
21	Rossi	1m 33.305s
22	Oliveira	1m 33.377s
23	Dovizioso	1m 33.493s
24	Morbidelli	1m 33.500s

Championship Points

1	Quartararo	234
2	Bagnaia	186
3	Mir	167
4	Zarco	141
5	Miller	140
6	Binder	124
7	A. Espargaro	104
8	Vinales	98
9	M. Marquez	92
10	Oliveira	87
11	Martin	71
12	Nakagami	70
13	Rins	68
14	P. Espargaro	64
15	Bastianini	61
16	A. Marquez	50
17	Morbidelli	40
18	Lecuona	38
19	Petrucci	37
20	Marini	28
21	Rossi	28
22	Bradl	13
23	Pirro	8
24	Pedrosa	6
25	Savadori	4
26	Rabat	1

Constructor Points

1	Ducati	275
2	Yamaha	262
3	Suzuki	184
4	KTM	178
5	Honda	148
6	Aprilia	105

Grid order / Lap chart

Grid order	1	2	3	4	5	6	7	8	9	10	11	12	13	14	15	16	17	18	19	20	21	22	23	24	25	26	27	
63 BAGNAIA	63	63	63	63	63	63	63	63	63	63	63	63	63	63	63	63	63	63	63	63	63	63	63	63	63	63	63	1
43 MILLER	43	43	43	43	43	43	43	43	43	43	43	43	43	20	20	20	20	20	20	20	20	20	20	20	20	20	20	2
20 QUARTARARO	20	89	20	20	20	20	20	20	20	20	20	20	20	43	43	43	43	23	23	23	23	23	23	23	23	23	23	3
89 MARTIN	93	20	41	41	93	23	23	23	23	23	23	23	23	23	23	23	23	43	43	43	43	43	43	43	43	93	93	4
5 ZARCO	89	41	93	93	23	93	93	93	93	93	93	93	93	42	42	42	42	41	93	93	93	93	93	93	93	36	36	5
44 P. ESPARGARO	41	93	44	23	41	42	42	42	42	42	42	42	42	93	93	93	93	93	41	41	41	41	41	36	36	36	43	6
93 M. MARQUEZ	44	44	23	42	42	41	41	41	41	41	41	41	41	41	41	41	41	36	36	36	36	36	36	41	41	44	44	7
41 A. ESPARGARO	42	42	42	44	44	44	36	36	36	36	36	36	36	36	36	36	36	44	44	44	44	44	44	44	44	41	41	8
42 RINS	23	23	36	36	36	36	44	44	44	44	44	44	44	44	44	44	44	30	30	30	33	33	33	33	33	33	33	9
12 VINALES	36	36	51	51	51	51	51	51	51	51	51	51	51	51	51	51	30	33	33	33	30	30	30	30	30	30	30	10
36 MIR	30	51	30	5	5	5	30	30	30	30	30	30	30	30	30	30	33	51	51	51	51	51	51	51	51	51	51	11
23 BASTIANINI	5	30	5	30	30	30	33	33	33	33	33	33	33	33	33	33	51	5	5	5	5	5	5	5	5	5	5	12
30 NAKAGAMI	51	5	33	33	33	33	27	27	27	5	5	5	5	5	5	5	12	12	12	12	12	12	12	12	12	12	12	13
51 PIRRO	33	33	10	10	10	27	5	5	5	12	12	12	12	12	12	12	73	73	73	73	73	73	73	73	73	73	73	14
10 MARINI	10	10	27	27	27	10	10	12	12	12	27	27	27	27	73	73	73	6	6	73	73	73	73	73	73	73	73	15
21 MORBIDELLI	27	27	12	12	12	12	12	10	10	73	73	73	73	73	6	6	6	9	9	9	9	9	9	9	9	9	9	
33 BINDER	12	73	73	73	73	73	73	73	73	10	6	6	6	6	9	9	9	46	46	46	46	46	46	46	46	46	46	
6 BRADL	73	12	6	6	6	6	6	6	6	9	9	9	9	9	21	21	46	21	21	21	21	21	21	10	10	10	21	
73 A. MARQUEZ	21	6	21	21	21	9	9	9	9	21	21	21	21	21	46	46	21	10	10	10	10	21	21	21	21	21	10	
27 LECUONA	6	21	9	9	9	21	21	21	21	46	46	46	46	46	10	10	10	88	88	88	88	88	88	88	88	88	88	
88 OLIVEIRA	9	9	88	88	88	88	88	88	46	46	10	10	10	10	88	88	88	4	4	4	4	4	4	4	4	4	4	
9 PETRUCCI	88	88	46	46	46	46	46	46	88	88	88	88	88	88	4	4	4											
46 ROSSI	4	4	4	4	4	4	4	4	4	4	4	4	4	4				89 Pit stop										
4 DOVIZIOSO	46	46	89	89	89	89	89	89	89	89																		

196 SAN MARINO GRAND PRIX

Moto2
RACE DISTANCE: 25 laps, 65.648 miles/105.650km · RACE WEATHER: Dry (air 27°, humidity 48%, track 30°)

Pos.	Rider	Nat.	No.	Entrant	Machine	Laps	Time & Speed
1	Raul Fernandez	SPA	25	Red Bull KTM Ajo	Kalex	25	40m 40.563s 96.8mph/155.8km/h
2	Remy Gardner	AUS	87	Red Bull KTM Ajo	Kalex	25	40m 40.965s
3	Aron Canet	SPA	44	Inde Aspar Team	Boscoscuro	25	40m 41.132s
4	Sam Lowes	GBR	22	Elf Marc VDS Racing Team	Kalex	25	40m 42.141s
5	Marco Bezzecchi	ITA	72	SKY Racing Team VR46	Kalex	25	40m 45.483s
6	Augusto Fernandez	SPA	37	Elf Marc VDS Racing Team	Kalex	25	40m 45.924s
7	Ai Ogura	JPN	79	IDEMITSU Honda Team Asia	Kalex	25	40m 46.799s
8	Xavi Vierge	SPA	97	Petronas Sprinta Racing	Kalex	25	40m 48.031s
9	Fabio Di Giannantonio	ITA	21	Federal Oil Gresini Moto2	Kalex	25	40m 48.125s
10	Celestino Vietti	ITA	13	SKY Racing Team VR46	Kalex	25	40m 53.793s
11	Thomas Luthi	SWI	12	Pertamina Mandalika SAG Team	Kalex	25	40m 56.159s
12	Marcel Schrotter	GER	23	Liqui Moly Intact GP	Kalex	25	40m 56.735s
13	Jorge Navarro	SPA	9	+EGO Speed Up	Boscoscuro	25	41m 00.797s
14	Marcos Ramirez	SPA	42	American Racing	Kalex	25	41m 03.382s
15	Tony Arbolino	ITA	14	Liqui Moly Intact GP	Kalex	25	41m 03.578s
16	Stefano Manzi	ITA	62	Flexbox HP40	Kalex	25	41m 06.715s
17	Nicolo Bulega	ITA	11	Federal Oil Gresini Moto2	Kalex	25	41m 07.550s
18	Hafizh Syahrin	MAL	55	NTS RW Racing GP	NTS	25	41m 07.794s
19	Jake Dixon	GBR	96	Petronas Sprinta Racing	Kalex	25	41m 08.713s
20	Hector Garzo	SPA	40	Flexbox HP40	Kalex	25	41m 09.089s
21	Cameron Beaubier	USA	6	American Racing	Kalex	25	41m 10.427s
22	Albert Arenas	SPA	75	Inde Aspar Team	Boscoscuro	25	41m 13.703s
23	Joe Roberts	USA	16	Italtrans Racing Team	Kalex	25	41m 16.661s
24	Lorenzo Baldassarri	ITA	7	MV Agusta Forward Racing	MV Agusta	25	41m 24.424s
25	Bo Bendsneyder	NED	64	Pertamina Mandalika SAG Team	Kalex	25	41m 27.892s
	Somkiat Chantra	THA	35	IDEMITSU Honda Team Asia	Kalex	22	DNF-crash
	Lorenzo Dalla Porta	ITA	19	Italtrans Racing Team	Kalex	19	DNF-crash
	Barry Baltus	BEL	70	NTS RW Racing GP	NTS	12	DNF-crash
	Yari Montella	ITA	5	+EGO Speed Up	Boscoscuro	12	DNF-crash
	Simone Corsi	ITA	24	MV Agusta Forward Racing	MV Agusta	2	DNF-crash

Fastest lap: Raul Fernandez, on lap 19, 1m 36.938s, 97.5mph/156.9km/h.
Lap record: Sam Lowes, 1m 36.195s, 98.2mph/158.1km/h (2020).
Event maximum speed: Hector Garzo, 156.4mph/251.7km/h (race).

Qualifying: Weather: Dry, Air Temp: 26° Track Temp: 32° Humidity: 69%

1	R. Fernandez	1m 36.264s
2	Lowes	1m 36.615s
3	A. Fernandez	1m 36.788s
4	Gardner	1m 36.861s
5	Canet	1m 36.869s
6	Navarro	1m 36.928s
7	Vierge	1m 36.928s
8	Bezzecchi	1m 37.021s
9	Di Giannantonio	1m 37.171s
10	Dalla Porta	1m 37.192s
11	Bulega	1m 37.232s
12	Ogura	1m 37.312s
13	Schrotter	1m 37.345s
14	Luthi	1m 37.388s
15	Roberts	1m 37.432s
16	Manzi	1m 37.474s
17	Vietti	1m 37.617s
18	Chantra	1m 37.669s
Q1		
19	Syahrin	1m 38.717s
20	Dixon	1m 38.769s
21	Garzo	1m 38.793s
22	Arbolino	1m 38.815s
23	Ramirez	1m 38.998s
24	Montella	1m 39.017s
25	Corsi	1m 39.132s
26	Arenas	1m 39.144s
27	Bendsneyder	1m 39.227s
28	Beaubier	1m 39.251s
29	Baldassarri	1m 39.496s
30	Baltus	1m 39.563s

Fastest race laps

1	R. Fernandez	1m 36.938s
2	Canet	1m 36.995s
3	Gardner	1m 37.000s
4	Lowes	1m 37.054s
5	Ogura	1m 37.067s
6	Vietti	1m 37.117s
7	Bezzecchi	1m 37.135s
8	A. Fernandez	1m 37.163s
9	Vierge	1m 37.219s
10	Schrotter	1m 37.286s
11	Navarro	1m 37.308s
12	Di Giannantonio	1m 37.336s
13	Luthi	1m 37.472s
14	Dalla Porta	1m 37.503s
15	Chantra	1m 37.562s
16	Arbolino	1m 37.576s
17	Beaubier	1m 37.577s
18	Ramirez	1m 37.656s
19	Bulega	1m 37.709s
20	Dixon	1m 37.753s
21	Manzi	1m 37.795s
22	Garzo	1m 37.805s
23	Syahrin	1m 37.929s
24	Arenas	1m 37.989s
25	Montella	1m 38.214s
26	Roberts	1m 38.217s
27	Baltus	1m 38.232s
28	Baldassarri	1m 38.324s
29	Bendsneyder	1m 38.495s
30	Corsi	1m 38.844s

Championship Points

1	Gardner	271
2	R. Fernandez	237
3	Bezzecchi	190
4	Lowes	140
5	Canet	119
6	A. Fernandez	118
7	Di Giannantonio	108
8	Ogura	104
9	Schrotter	84
10	Vierge	75
11	Navarro	74
12	Roberts	59
13	Vietti	53
14	Arbolino	41
15	Bendsneyder	40
16	Chantra	35
17	Beaubier	28
18	Arenas	23
19	Ramirez	22
20	Dixon	21
21	Luthi	21
22	Manzi	20
23	Aldeguer	13
24	Corsi	13
25	Garzo	12
26	Bulega	12
27	Dalla Porta	10
28	Syahrin	8
29	Lopez	4
30	Baldassarri	3
31	Baltus	2

Constructor Points

1	Kalex	350
2	Boscoscuro	154
3	MV Agusta	16
4	NTS	10

Moto3
23 laps, 60.396 miles/97.198km · RACE WEATHER: Dry (air 26°, humidity 55%, track 28°)

Pos.	Rider	Nat.	No.	Entrant	Machine	Laps	Time & Speed
1	Dennis Foggia	ITA	7	Leopard Racing	Honda	23	39m 17.002s 92.2mph/148.4km/h
2	Niccolo Antonelli	ITA	23	Avintia VR46	KTM	23	39m 17.567s
3	Andrea Migno	ITA	16	Rivacold Snipers Team	Honda	23	39m 17.819s
4	Sergio Garcia	SPA	11	GAVIOTA GASGAS Aspar Team	GASGAS	23	39m 19.142s
5	Jaume Masia	SPA	5	Red Bull KTM Ajo	KTM	23	39m 20.100s
6	Darryn Binder	RSA	40	Petronas Sprinta Racing	Honda	23	39m 24.635s
7	Pedro Acosta	SPA	37	Red Bull KTM Ajo	KTM	23	39m 26.993s
8	Carlos Tatay	SPA	99	Avintia Esponsorama Moto3	KTM	23	39m 27.186s
9	Stefano Nepa	ITA	82	BOE Owlride	KTM	23	39m 27.343s
10	Ayumu Sasaki	JPN	71	Red Bull KTM Tech 3	KTM	23	39m 27.346s
11	Riccardo Rossi	ITA	54	BOE Owlride	KTM	23	39m 27.362s
12	Izan Guevara	SPA	28	GAVIOTA GASGAS Aspar Team	GASGAS	23	39m 31.628s
13	John McPhee	GBR	17	Petronas Sprinta Racing	Honda	23	39m 31.900s
14	Kaito Toba	JPN	27	CIP Green Power	KTM	23	39m 32.021s
15	Tatsuki Suzuki	JPN	24	SIC58 Squadra Corse	Honda	23	39m 32.074s
16	Jeremy Alcoba	SPA	52	Indonesian Racing Gresini Moto3	Honda	23	39m 35.861s
17	Ryusei Yamanaka	JPN	6	CarXpert PruestelGP	KTM	23	39m 35.876s
18	Matteo Bertelle	ITA	18	Bardahl VR46 Riders Academy	KTM	23	39m 35.923s
19	Lorenzo Fellon	FRA	20	SIC58 Squadra Corse	Honda	23	39m 36.305s
20	Adrian Fernandez	SPA	31	Sterilgarda Max Racing Team	Husqvarna	23	39m 38.365s
21	Deniz Oncu	TUR	53	Red Bull KTM Tech 3	KTM	23	39m 43.964s
22	Maximilian Kofler	AUT	73	CIP Green Power	KTM	23	39m 47.468s
23	Alberto Surra	ITA	67	Rivacold Snipers Team	Honda	23	40m 03.658s
24	Andi Farid Izdihar	INA	19	Honda Team Asia	Honda	23	40m 10.472s
	Filip Salac	CZE	12	CarXpert PruestelGP	KTM	17	DNF-technical
	Xavier Artigas	SPA	43	Leopard Racing	Honda	14	DNF-injured
	Romano Fenati	ITA	55	Sterilgarda Max Racing Team	Husqvarna	13	DNF-crash
	Elia Bartolini	ITA	22	Bardahl VR46 Riders Academy	KTM	1	DNF-crash

Fastest lap: Romano Fenati, on lap 5, 1m 41.648s, 93.0mph/149.6km/h.
Lap record: Gabriel Rodrigo, 1m 41.988s, 92.6mph/149.1km/h (2020).
Event maximum speed: Niccolo Antonelli, 132.6mph/213.4km/h (race).

Qualifying: Weather: Dry, Air Temp: 29° Track Temp: 38° Humidity: 49%

1	Fenati	1m 41.756s
2	Foggia	1m 42.013s
3	Antonelli	1m 42.020s
4	Migno	1m 42.099s
5	Masia	1m 42.111s
6	Artigas	1m 42.271s
7	Rossi	1m 42.276s
8	Bartolini	1m 42.552s
9	Acosta	1m 42.558s
10	Tatay	1m 42.566s
11	Nepa	1m 42.619s
12	Garcia	1m 42.687s
13	Sasaki	1m 42.729s
14	Binder	1m 42.752s
15	Bertelle	1m 42.796s
16	Yamanaka	1m 43.021s
17	Guevara	1m 43.033s
18	Toba	1m 43.107s
Q1		
19	McPhee	1m 43.351s
20	Izdihar	1m 43.433s
21	Fernandez	1m 43.459s
22	Kofler	1m 43.474s
23	Fellon	1m 43.493s
24	Kunii	1m 43.784s
25	Alcoba	1m 44.037s
26	Salac	1m 44.488s
	Rodrigo	No Time
	Suzuki	No Time
	Oncu	No Time
	Surra	No Time

Fastest race laps

1	Fenati	1m 41.648s
2	Garcia	1m 41.735s
3	Foggia	1m 41.753s
4	Migno	1m 41.805s
5	Antonelli	1m 41.809s
6	Masia	1m 41.871s
7	Binder	1m 41.879s
8	Artigas	1m 41.976s
9	Suzuki	1m 42.017s
10	Guevara	1m 42.044s
11	Nepa	1m 42.050s
12	Sasaki	1m 42.074s
13	Acosta	1m 42.083s
14	Rossi	1m 42.142s
15	Salac	1m 42.156s
16	Tatay	1m 42.201s
17	McPhee	1m 42.292s
18	Bertelle	1m 42.312s
19	Alcoba	1m 42.345s
20	Toba	1m 42.374s
21	Fernandez	1m 42.392s
22	Yamanaka	1m 42.430s
23	Oncu	1m 42.498s
24	Fellon	1m 42.610s
25	Kofler	1m 42.689s
26	Surra	1m 42.778s
27	Izdihar	1m 43.751s

Championship Points

1	Acosta	210
2	Foggia	168
3	Garcia	168
4	Fenati	134
5	Masia	122
6	Antonelli	118
7	Binder	114
8	Sasaki	93
9	Migno	84
10	Guevara	76
11	Oncu	73
12	Toba	64
13	Suzuki	62
14	Alcoba	60
15	Rodrigo	60
16	McPhee	56
17	Salac	46
18	Yamanaka	42
19	Nepa	37
20	Artigas	30
21	Rossi	29
22	Tatay	28
23	Dupasquier	27
24	Fernandez	20
25	Kunii	15
26	Kofler	10
27	Bartolini	7
28	Azman	3
29	Izdihar	3
30	Holgado	1

Constructor Points

1	KTM	295
2	Honda	270
3	GASGAS	206
4	Husqvarna	140

SAN MARINO GRAND PRIX 197

PETRONAS
04
41
9
PETRONAS
46
27
23
21
MONSTER
73
63
Lenovo
PRAMAC
89
REPSOL
93

FIM WORLD CHAMPIONSHIP · ROUND 15

GRAND PRIX OF THE AMERICAS

CIRCUIT OF THE AMERICAS

Above: Turning left. Marquez could use his full lopsided body strength to maximum effect at CoTA.
Photo: Whit Bazemore

Top right: Jeremy Alcoba and Deniz Oncu close up before their terrifying collision.

Above centre right: Struggling to regain control, Sergio Garcia heads for the barrier.
Photos: Gold & Goose

Above right: Garcia suffered a bruised kidney, and his title hopes were over.
Photo: Whit Bazemore

Right: Yet another silent tribute for a dead teenage racer.

Opening spread: Twenty-one-strong thunder is unleashed as Marc Marquez leads the pack up the hill.
Photos: Gold & Goose

IN his pomp, it had often been said that Marc Marquez could win at CoTA riding with one arm. And while it might have been an exaggeration to suggest that he had done as much on his return to the track after a year's absence, the champion dominated the Grand Prix of The Americas with an ease reminiscent of years gone by, even though the after-effects of his right arm injury were still keenly felt.

These he explained in yet more detail: "At Aragon, I was struggling with a lot of pain in the shoulder." A modification to his leathers, making them roomier at the right shoulder, had brought relief, but "still from the brake point to going in, I don't feel comfortable. I can't slide the bike and turn … one of my strong points. Now I go in like the others. In left corners, I can push with the left, but in right corners, I have understeering. For this reason, I crash many times about the front, and I cannot save with the elbow."

CoTA's anti-clockwise layout favoured him, and unlike some of the other riders, he found the ever worsening bumps at least manageable. Others were vocal, with serious issues at Turns Two, Three, Four and especially Ten, where the bikes were visibly thrown around at high speed. Quartararo called it a joke, Aleix Espargaro, a nightmare, and Rossi, very dangerous. Parts of the back straight and the entire final sector had been resurfaced since 2019, so the surface was a mishmash of three different types of asphalt. By Friday evening, the riders had issued an ultimatum: resurface the tarmac between Turns Two and Ten before the 2022 event, scheduled for April, or MotoGP won't return.

The pressure from the riders' Safety Commission bore fruit, with a promise of a full resurfacing before the 2022 GP.

Jack Miller had a different complaint, about inconsistent tyre performance. He had topped the combined first three timed practice sessions and also FP4, which is more about race pace. Then followed a puzzling lack of grip in an underwhelming qualifying attack, which led to a disappointing tenth position. "It's happened a few times, and I am getting effing sick of it," he fumed. On this occasion, Michelin blamed a slow out-lap for the sub-optimal performance.

Safety was high on the agenda, following a third fatal accident involving a teenage racer within four months, after 18-year-old Jason Dupasquier at Mugello and 14-year-old Spaniard Hugo Millan at a European Talent Cup race at Aragon. The latest victim, Dean Berta Vinales (15), had died in the World Supersport 300 race at Jerez the previous week.

The name, of course, was familiar – he was a cousin of Maverick, and Dean had been racing for Maverick's father's team. One immediate effect was the withdrawal of the new Aprilia rider. Maverick had arrived in Texas planning to race "for my cousin, but my emotions are too deep and it makes it difficult to remain focused," he wrote on Instagram.

This fresh tragedy triggered a period of introspection. Most riders acknowledged that there are no easy answers, although some offered explanations. "It's happening more than some years ago just because there are more young kids racing," said Aleix Espargaro. Parity of equipment was also a factor. "The talent of these young guys is amazing and they reach the level of these small bikes with these small engines very quick, so the difference between them is so small," he continued. Miller struck a common note, saying, "I'm getting sick and tired of going to these minutes of silence for kids that were so, so young. That can't continue."

Response from the GP Commission came within the month: on 22nd October, a statement announcing upgrades to safety regulations outlined the raising of minimum age limits for grand prix feeder series, as well as a lower limit for grid numbers. For 2023, all MotoGP classes would match the current premier class's minimum age limit of 18 – Motos 2 and 3 presently stood at 16; while airbag leathers would be compulsory in all FIM circuit championships. (see 'State of Racing' on page 14 for further details.)

It added piquancy to the FIM stewards' harshest penalty yet, after a terrifying multi-bike collision that took down three

200 GRAND PRIX OF THE AMERICAS

riders in the Moto3 race, with providential escapes for both Andrea Migno and championship leader Pedro Acosta.

The race had already been stopped once, after Filip Salac and Niccolo Antonelli had fallen, the former in a dangerous position. The restart was for a hectic five-lap sprint, and hectic was the word, with the full pack all locked together, the only tactic being for a rider to elbow himself forwards.

It had been triggered by Deniz Oncu, who had moved across on the long straight. Inches behind, the hapless Jeremy Alcoba's front wheel had made contact with his rear, and the Honda rider fell awkwardly. At top speed, Migno and Acosta had no chance to avoid the fallen bike, though by a miracle the rider wasn't hit. The pair were sent somersaulting terrifyingly through the air. Unlikely as it seemed at the time, all three were able to walk away.

Hours later, Oncu was notified that he had been suspended from the next two races for causing the incident. The MotoGP field largely agreed with the penalty. "The movement of one rider that created all these things," said Marc Marquez. "It's a very strong penalty. Of course, it was not the intention of Oncu, but in the end, they must go in that way if they want to stop these movements [on the straight]."

Valentino Rossi was adamant in agreement: "He has to stay home for two races minimum. They have to do something serious because the situation is completely out of control, for me." The five-lap restart was already a mistake, he continued. "It's too dangerous … like Russian Roulette. Oncu moved on the straight when he knew he had another rider on the side and caused a crash that potentially could be more than a crash. They are very, very lucky that nothing happened."

Oncu's camp protested the unfairness, because he was far from the only rider to have acted in this way – ironically, Alcoba was not exactly innocent in this respect. But in the prevailing atmosphere, making an example of him was understandable.

MOTOGP RACE – 20 laps

Bagnaia, on a roll, claimed a third pole in a row, with Quartararo second. More significantly, as it transpired, Marc Marquez was third on the grid – his first time on the front row since his return.

Martin, Nakagami and Zarco were behind; then Suzuki pair Rins and Mir joined by Marini, his third time through to Q2.

In a way, Marquez's second win of the year was something of a non-event. He led every turn of every lap, victory never in doubt from the sixth, after a two-lap blitz that had broken the back of Quartararo's challenge. The Catalan crossed the finish line with the biggest winning margin of the year and appeared barely to have broken sweat.

Off the start, Quartararo had put himself ahead of Rins, Bagnaia, Martin, Mir and Nakagami. There was little in it during those early exchanges, although even the moderate pace was too much for Nakagami on the second lap, when he crashed out on the bumps into Turn 12.

Miller, earmarked by Marquez as a potential contender from tenth on the grid, made up two places early on to sit eighth, behind Bastianini, another fast starter, from 16th on the grid.

With the bumps pushing riders into all kinds of added exertion, Marquez was wary of his own physical condition in the closing laps, so it was imperative for him to make an early gap. By lap seven, it was a comfortable 1.5 seconds, which he gradually extended to 4.6 seconds by the chequered flag. The only scare was a front slide at Turn Six three laps from home. Even then, Marquez only lost a tenth to his pursuer. "Lucky for me, all the strong brake points are on the left side, so I can manage it in a good way," he said.

Quartararo was a solid second throughout, and since his main title rival, Bagnaia, was not threatening, he saw no point in risking it up front. "The best second place of my

Above: Quartararo overcame pre-race nerves to claim a solid and valuable second.

Top right: Bagnaia secured third as Martin served his long-lap penalty.

Above right: Ride 'em cowboy! Marc Marquez's domination of CoTA continued.

Right: Cameron Beaubier, heading the hidden Augusto Fernandez and Tony Arbolino, was a year's-best fifth at his only familiar track of the year.

Below right: Remy Gardner's crash opened up the Moto2 championship.

Below centre right: Raul Fernandez's win took him to within nine points of his fallen team-mate.

Below far right: With results from the original race reinstated, Ivan Guevera went from broken down to his first Moto3 win.

Photos: Gold & Goose

career," the Frenchman called it, after suffering from a bout of pre-race nerves. "Before the start, I was feeling stressed, to be honest. But from the first corner, the stress was off." Now he faced a first match point next time out.

Bagnaia had lost places in the early laps to Martin, who then took third off Rins and briefly threatened Quartararo. On lap five, Miller also passed his team-mate. Rins dropped to the back of the group at half-distance, at which point Miller, his front tyre losing grip, waved his team-mate through, demonstrating the voluntary support he had already promised.

Bagnaia took no time in reeling in Martin, initially two seconds ahead, but tiring, a bicep tendon issue still niggling after his Portuguese fall in April, and he nearly high-sided at Turn Four and ran off track. Importantly, he didn't give up the position when rejoining, so the FIM stewards handed him a long-lap penalty, which he served on the final lap. That eased Ducati nerves, for Martin had no plan to give up the final podium place to Bagnaia.

Rins inherited fourth, courtesy of Martin's penalty and Miller losing speed with his tyre issue; behind Martin, Bastianini claimed sixth after a last-lap skirmish with Mir. As at the previous race, he lunged at Miller at Turn 14, and the move sat both men up, allowing the rookie through.

Mir earned a one-place penalty, which dropped him to eighth, behind Miller, and also a stern ticking off from the Australian after their fourth run-in of the year. Said Miller later, "Every time I race with the guy, he runs into the side of me. In Misano, I went from fourth to sixth, here from sixth to eighth. It doesn't even make sense because he jams himself wide as well, and that allows the next guy through. I think there are better ways you can go about the situation." For the Spaniard: "I don't understand, because if all the races are like this, you don't overtake. It's better not to try. Racing will lose its essence."

In another underwhelming weekend for KTM, Binder was the best of them in ninth, with Pol Espargaro fighting a lack of front-end feel in tenth. Then a lone Oliveira, with 12th-placed Alex Marquez narrowly ahead of Dovizioso, after passing him in the latter half. Marini and Rossi wrapped up the points; Zarco and Aleix Espargaro crashed out. It was the hapless Spaniard's fifth tumble of the weekend.

MOTO2 RACE – 18 laps

The championship fight was blown wide open in Austin. Raul Fernandez dominated all weekend, while points leader Remy Gardner suffered a first non-score of the season. A still-comfortable lead of 34 points before the trip Stateside was slashed to just nine. With three races remaining, every one would be crucial.

The younger Red Bull Ajo team-mate was on blazing form, his hand injury now forgotten, and he led every free practice and qualified on pole. Gardner was second, and he might have been able to plan another race of damage control. Events during the opening laps dictated otherwise, and multiple US champion Cameron Beaubier was the catalyst.

At a familiar track and fired with patriotic fervour, Beaubier qualified his best yet on the middle of the second row, behind Fernandez, Gardner and Di Giannantonio, and between Bezzecchi and Augusto Fernandez.

The home rider made a perfect start and led into Turn One, albeit briefly. Crucially, Raul Fernandez got the American on the cut back and started to edge clear. Gardner got through, too, but Beaubier was back at Turn One the following lap, taking second and bringing Di Giannantonio through as well.

Knowing he had both the pace and the need to go with Fernandez, for once Gardner was discomposed. He regained second on the third lap and set about reeling in his team-mate, 1.3 seconds ahead. But a crucial mistake braking for Turn 15 on the fifth lap took him down, his first race crash in 23 starts.

The crash happened "between where the two asphalts connect together. There is a little crease. I was 10cm to the right, got the crease and the thing folded. Nothing's over yet, there are still three races to go. We need to change our plan. Maybe less defending, more attacking," he explained.

Despite some brief pressure from Di Giannantonio, Fernandez was seldom made to work from there, coming home not far short of two seconds ahead for his seventh win of the season – equalling Marc Marquez's ten-year-old record for the number of wins by a rookie in the class. Di Giannantonio's first podium since May was comfortable enough, with

FIM WORLD CHAMPIONSHIP | 15

Bezzecchi more than a second behind in a processional end to the race.

Augusto Fernandez had risen to fourth after a cautious first lap, just ahead of Beaubier, with his best result to date. Fellow rookie Arbolino was sixth, all alone for his third top-ten, after a rare strong qualifying had put him on the third row.

Another rookie, Ogura, had finally got the better of a fading Vierge for seventh. Ramirez was a second behind, and a couple of tenths clear of Dixon, tenth the Englishman's best result since the opening round.

An off-form Canet led the next group, where Navarro, Corsi, Chantra and Bendsneyder wrapped up the points. Returned Tetsuta Nagashima, subbing for shoulder-injury victim Dalla Porta, was 16th.

Luthi, Arenas and Vietti crashed out; Schrotter retired, as did Lowes when a misfire ended a difficult outing.

MOTO3 RACE – 7 laps (red-flagged)

Masia took his first pole in 13 races, with the last remaining title challenger, Foggia, second, and Alcoba alongside on the front row. Points leader Acosta was down in 15th.

Artigas came from row two to lead the first lap, but had jumped the start and was given a double long-lap penalty. Spanish rookie Guevara took over.

At first, Masia was second, but on lap five, Foggia came through to take up the pursuit, with Alcoba slotting in behind Masia. But the pack was still close and positions shifting constantly. Among those pushing through was McPhee, into third on lap six.

On lap seven came Salac's high-side at Turn 11, which left the rider prone at the trackside, and the red flags came out.

The finishing order at the end of seven laps determined the grid positions for a five-lap shootout 22 minutes later.

Guevara led the first lap, but at the end of the straight next time around, he ran wide, then cruised back to his pit, visibly furious. The others would not complete another lap, after tragedy was miraculously avoided.

Ten riders were contesting the lead when Alcoba was thrown off after hitting the swerving Oncu. Migno and Acosta were launched over his bike with sickening violence. Acosta was a particular concern after flying close to 40m before thudding against the trackside barrier.

It was incomprehensible that there were no injuries.

The rulebook (article 1.26.6) provided for results to be declared from the first running, with full points. That restored Guevara to a first victory – from chair kicking to champagne spraying within minutes – and promoted Foggia to second from the fourth place he had occupied in the restart. In the same way, a disgruntled McPhee had been leading the restart, but was dropped to third. Masia was fourth, Oncu fifth, Alcoba sixth.

Acosta's eventual eighth trimmed his points lead over Foggia to 30. Garcia had been injured (bruised kidney) in a Friday fall, effectively ending his title chances.

GRAND PRIX OF THE AMERICAS 203

FIM WORLD CHAMPIONSHIP: ROUND 15

RED BULL GRAND PRIX OF THE AMERICAS

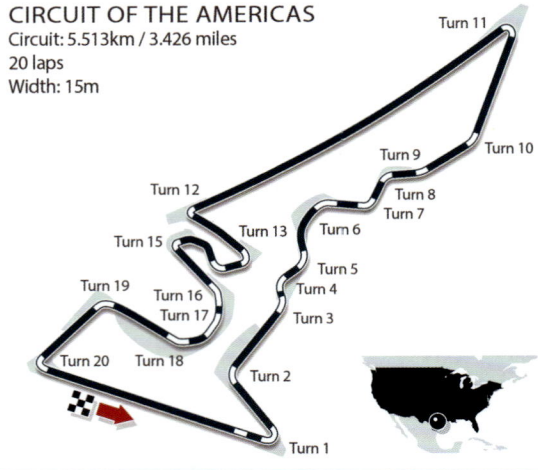

1–3 OCTOBER, 2021

CIRCUIT OF THE AMERICAS
Circuit: 5.513km / 3.426 miles
20 laps
Width: 15m

MotoGP

RACE DISTANCE: 20 laps, 68.512 miles/110.260km · RACE WEATHER: Dry (air 32°, humidity 46%, track 41°)

Pos.	Rider	Nat.	No.	Entrant	Machine	Race tyre choice	Laps	Time & speed
1	Marc Marquez	SPA	93	Repsol Honda Team	Honda RC213V	F: Hard/R: Soft	20	41m 41.435s 98.5mph/ 158.6km/h
2	Fabio Quartararo	FRA	20	Monster Energy Yamaha MotoGP	Yamaha YZR-M1	F: Hard/R: Soft	20	41m 46.114s
3	Francesco Bagnaia	ITA	63	Ducati Lenovo Team	Ducati Desmosedici	F: Hard/R: Soft	20	41m 49.982s
4	Alex Rins	SPA	42	Team SUZUKI ECSTAR	Suzuki GSX-RR	F: Hard/R: Soft	20	41m 52.533s
5	Jorge Martin	SPA	89	Pramac Racing	Ducati Desmosedici	F: Hard/R: Soft	20	41m 53.187s
6	Enea Bastianini	ITA	23	Avintia Esponsorama	Ducati Desmosedici	F: Hard/R: Soft	20	41m 54.704s
7	Jack Miller	AUS	43	Ducati Lenovo Team	Ducati Desmosedici	F: Hard/R: Hard	20	41m 56.157s
8	Joan Mir	SPA	36	Team SUZUKI ECSTAR	Suzuki GSX-RR	F: Hard/R: Soft	20	41m 54.841s
9	Brad Binder	RSA	33	Red Bull KTM Factory Racing	KTM RC16	F: Hard/R: Soft	20	41m 57.267s
10	Pol Espargaro	SPA	44	Repsol Honda Team	Honda RC213V	F: Hard/R: Soft	20	42m 01.700s
11	Miguel Oliveira	POR	88	Red Bull KTM Factory Racing	KTM RC16	F: Hard/R: Soft	20	42m 04.490s
12	Alex Marquez	SPA	73	LCR Honda CASTROL	Honda RC213V	F: Hard/R: Soft	20	42m 06.178s
13	Andrea Dovizioso	ITA	4	Petronas Yamaha SRT	Yamaha YZR-M1	F: Hard/R: Soft	20	42m 06.742s
14	Luca Marini	ITA	10	SKY VR46 Avintia	Ducati Desmosedici	F: Hard/R: Medium	20	42m 08.288s
15	Valentino Rossi	ITA	46	Petronas Yamaha SRT	Yamaha YZR-M1	F: Hard/R: Medium	20	42m 09.490s
16	Iker Lecuona	SPA	27	Tech 3 KTM Factory Racing	KTM RC16	F: Hard/R: Soft	20	42m 12.424s
17	Takaaki Nakagami	JPN	30	LCR Honda IDEMITSU	Honda RC213V	F: Hard/R: Soft	20	42m 16.686s
18	Danilo Petrucci	ITA	9	Tech 3 KTM Factory Racing	KTM RC16	F: Hard/R: Soft	20	42m 23.674s
19	Franco Morbidelli	ITA	21	Monster Energy Yamaha MotoGP	Yamaha YZR-M1	F: Hard/R: Soft	20	42m 31.289s
	Aleix Espargaro	SPA	41	Aprilia Racing Team Gresini	Aprilia RS-GP	F: Hard/R: Soft	8	DNF-crash
	Johann Zarco	FRA	5	Pramac Racing	Ducati Desmosedici	F: Hard/R: Soft	5	DNF-crash

Fastest lap: Marc Marquez, on lap 7, 2m 4.368s, 99.1mph/159.5km/h.
Lap record: Marc Marquez, 2m 2.135s, 100.9mph/162.4km/h (2015).
Event maximum speed: Jack Miller, 219.3mph/352.9km/h (race).

Qualifying

Weather: Dry
Air Temp: 31° **Track Temp:** 41°
Humidity: 54%

1	Bagnaia	2m 02.781s
2	Quartararo	2m 03.129s
3	M. Marquez	2m 03.209s
4	Martin	2m 03.278s
5	Nakagami	2m 03.292s
6	Zarco	2m 03.379s
7	Rins	2m 03.453s
8	Mir	2m 03.528s
9	Marini	2m 03.546s
10	Miller	2m 03.720s
11	Binder	2m 03.781s
12	P. Espargaro	2m 03.875s

Q1

13	Morbidelli	2m 03.872s
14	Dovizioso	2m 04.044s
15	A. Marquez	2m 04.100s
16	Bastianini	2m 04.118s
17	Lecuona	2m 04.324s
18	Oliveira	2m 04.392s
19	A. Espargaro	2m 04.419s
20	Rossi	2m 04.699s
21	Petrucci	2m 04.829s

Fastest race laps

1	M. Marquez	2m 04.368s
2	Nakagami	2m 04.499s
3	Miller	2m 04.631s
4	Quartararo	2m 04.761s
5	Martin	2m 04.821s
6	Rins	2m 04.940s
7	Bagnaia	2m 04.955s
8	P. Espargaro	2m 04.957s
9	Oliveira	2m 05.012s
10	Zarco	2m 05.060s
11	Binder	2m 05.070s
12	Bastianini	2m 05.093s
13	Mir	2m 05.103s
14	Dovizioso	2m 05.386s
15	Lecuona	2m 05.460s
16	A. Marquez	2m 05.519s
17	Marini	2m 05.627s
18	A. Espargaro	2m 05.691s
19	Morbidelli	2m 05.854s
20	Rossi	2m 05.914s
21	Petrucci	2m 06.157s

Championship Points

1	Quartararo	254
2	Bagnaia	202
3	Mir	175
4	Miller	149
5	Zarco	141
6	Binder	131
7	M. Marquez	117
8	A. Espargaro	104
9	Vinales	98
10	Oliveira	92
11	Martin	82
12	Rins	81
13	Bastianini	71
14	Nakagami	70
15	P. Espargaro	70
16	A. Marquez	54
17	Morbidelli	40
18	Lecuona	38
19	Petrucci	37
20	Marini	30
21	Rossi	29
22	Bradl	13
23	Pirro	8
24	Pedrosa	6
25	Savadori	4
26	Dovizioso	3
27	Rabat	1

Constructor Points

1	Ducati	291
2	Yamaha	282
3	Suzuki	197
4	KTM	185
5	Honda	173
6	Aprilia	105

Grid order / Lap-by-lap

Grid order	1	2	3	4	5	6	7	8	9	10	11	12	13	14	15	16	17	18	19	20
63 BAGNAIA	93	93	93	93	93	93	93	93	93	93	93	93	93	93	93	93	93	93	93	93
20 QUARTARARO	20	20	20	20	20	20	20	20	20	20	20	20	20	20	20	20	20	20	20	20
93 M. MARQUEZ	42	42	42	89	89	89	89	89	89	89	89	89	89	89	89	89	89	63	63	63
89 MARTIN	63	89	89	42	42	43	43	43	43	43	43	43	63	63	63	63	63	89	89	42
30 NAKAGAMI	89	63	63	63	63	42	42	42	42	63	63	63	43	43	42	42	42	42	42	89
5 ZARCO	30	36	43	43	43	63	63	63	63	42	42	42	42	42	43	43	43	43	43	23
42 RINS	36	33	36	36	36	33	33	33	36	36	36	36	36	36	36	36	36	36	36	36
36 MIR	33	43	33	33	33	36	36	36	33	33	33	33	33	33	23	23	23	23	23	43
10 MARINI	43	5	5	5	44	44	44	23	23	23	23	23	23	23	33	33	33	33	33	33
43 MILLER	5	44	44	44	23	23	23	44	44	44	44	44	44	44	44	44	44	44	44	44
33 BINDER	44	73	23	23	73	88	88	88	88	88	88	88	88	88	88	88	88	88	88	88
44 P. ESPARGARO	73	23	73	73	88	73	73	41	4	4	4	4	73	73	73	73	73	73	73	73
21 MORBIDELLI	23	88	88	88	10	4	41	4	73	73	73	73	4	4	4	4	4	4	4	4
4 DOVIZIOSO	10	10	10	10	4	10	4	73	10	10	10	10	10	10	10	10	10	10	10	10
73 A. MARQUEZ	21	21	21	4	41	41	10	10	27	27	46	46	46	46	46	46	46	46	46	46
23 BASTIANINI	88	4	4	21	21	21	21	46	46	21	27	27	27	27	27	27	27	27	27	27
27 LECUONA	4	41	41	41	27	27	27	21	21	46	21	21	9	9	9	9	9	30	30	30
88 OLIVEIRA	41	9	27	27	9	46	46	46	9	9	9	21	21	21	21	30	30	9	9	9
41 A. ESPARGARO	27	27	9	9	46	9	9	9	30	30	30	30	30	30	30	21	21	21	21	21
46 ROSSI	9	46	46	46	30	30	30													
9 PETRUCCI	46	30	30	30	5															

5 Pit stop

204 GRAND PRIX OF THE AMERICAS

Moto2
18 laps, 61.661 miles/99.234km · RACE WEATHER: Dry (air 30°, humidity 54%, track 39°)

Pos.	Rider	Nat.	No.	Entrant	Machine	Laps	Time & Speed
1	Raul Fernandez	SPA	25	Red Bull KTM Ajo	Kalex	18	39m 10.521s 94.4mph/151.9km/h
2	Fabio Di Giannantonio	ITA	21	Federal Oil Gresini Moto2	Kalex	18	39m 12.255s
3	Marco Bezzecchi	ITA	72	SKY Racing Team VR46	Kalex	18	39m 13.621s
4	Augusto Fernandez	SPA	37	Elf Marc VDS Racing Team	Kalex	18	39m 14.582s
5	Cameron Beaubier	USA	6	American Racing	Kalex	18	39m 15.902s
6	Tony Arbolino	ITA	14	Liqui Moly Intact GP	Kalex	18	39m 18.098s
7	Ai Ogura	JPN	79	IDEMITSU Honda Team Asia	Kalex	18	39m 21.608s
8	Xavi Vierge	SPA	97	Petronas Sprinta Racing	Kalex	18	39m 25.470s
9	Marcos Ramirez	SPA	42	American Racing	Kalex	18	39m 26.572s
10	Jake Dixon	GBR	96	Petronas Sprinta Racing	Kalex	18	39m 28.799s
11	Aron Canet	SPA	44	Inde Aspar Team	Boscoscuro	18	39m 31.200s
12	Jorge Navarro	SPA	9	MB Conveyors Speed Up	Boscoscuro	18	39m 33.259s
13	Simone Corsi	ITA	24	MV Agusta Forward Racing	MV Agusta	18	39m 33.434s
14	Somkiat Chantra	THA	35	IDEMITSU Honda Team Asia	Kalex	18	39m 33.768s
15	Bo Bendsneyder	NED	64	Pertamina Mandalika SAG Team	Kalex	18	39m 33.629s
16	Tetsuta Nagashima	JPN	45	Italtrans Racing Team	Kalex	18	39m 37.527s
17	Barry Baltus	BEL	70	NTS RW Racing GP	NTS	18	39m 38.607s
18	Joe Roberts	USA	16	Italtrans Racing Team	Kalex	18	39m 43.240s
19	Stefano Manzi	ITA	62	Flexbox HP40	Kalex	18	39m 48.063s
20	Hafizh Syahrin	MAL	55	NTS RW Racing GP	NTS	18	39m 50.179s
21	Fermin Aldeguer	SPA	54	MB Conveyors Speed Up	Boscoscuro	18	39m 51.206s
22	Lorenzo Baldassarri	ITA	7	MV Agusta Forward Racing	MV Agusta	18	39m 57.689s
	Celestino Vietti	ITA	13	SKY Racing Team VR46	Kalex	14	DNF-crash
	Marcel Schrotter	GER	23	Liqui Moly Intact GP	Kalex	13	DNF-technical
	Albert Arenas	SPA	75	Inde Aspar Team	Boscoscuro	11	DNF-crash
	Hector Garzo	SPA	40	Flexbox HP40	Kalex	10	DNF-physical
	Sam Lowes	GBR	22	Elf Marc VDS Racing Team	Kalex	9	DNF-technical
	Remy Gardner	AUS	87	Red Bull KTM Ajo	Kalex	5	DNF-crash
	Thomas Luthi	SWI	12	Pertamina Mandalika SAG Team	Kalex	2	DNF-crash

Fastest lap: Raul Fernandez, on lap 2, 2m 9.794s, 95.0mph/152.9km/h.
Lap record: Alex Rins, 2m 8.850s, 95.7mph/154.0km/h (2016).
Event maximum speed: Marcos Ramirez, 180.9mph/291.1km/h (free practice).

Qualifying
Weather: Dry
Air Temp: 31° Track Temp: 40°
Humidity: 54%

1	R. Fernandez	2m 08.979s
2	Gardner	2m 09.299s
3	Di Giannantonio	2m 09.457s
4	Bezzecchi	2m 09.557s
5	Beaubier	2m 09.584s
6	A. Fernandez	2m 09.638s
7	Arbolino	2m 09.745s
8	Ogura	2m 09.803s
9	Arenas	2m 09.825s
10	Vietti	2m 09.829s
11	Ramirez	2m 09.886s
12	Vierge	2m 09.942s
13	Dixon	2m 10.047s
14	Canet	2m 10.272s
15	Chantra	2m 10.502s
16	Lowes	2m 15.903s
17	Navarro	2m 16.506s
18	Corsi	2m 21.579s
Q1		
19	Schrotter	2m 10.111s
20	Garzo	2m 10.217s
21	Nagashima	2m 10.347s
22	Manzi	2m 10.456s
23	Bendsneyder	2m 10.497s
24	Baltus	2m 10.503s
25	Aldeguer	2m 10.567s
26	Roberts	2m 10.672s
27	Syahrin	2m 10.846s
28	Luthi	2m 11.209s
29	Baldassarri	2m 11.605s

Fastest race laps

1	R. Fernandez	2m 09.794s
2	Beaubier	2m 09.806s
3	Gardner	2m 09.952s
4	Arbolino	2m 10.036s
5	Di Giannantonio	2m 10.050s
6	Bezzecchi	2m 10.225s
7	Ramirez	2m 10.236s
8	A. Fernandez	2m 10.242s
9	Vierge	2m 10.304s
10	Ogura	2m 10.340s
11	Canet	2m 10.581s
12	Chantra	2m 10.582s
13	Arenas	2m 10.646s
14	Vietti	2m 10.671s
15	Navarro	2m 10.674s
16	Garzo	2m 10.688s
17	Dixon	2m 10.695s
18	Corsi	2m 10.729s
19	Schrotter	2m 10.832s
20	Nagashima	2m 10.871s
21	Lowes	2m 10.935s
22	Bendsneyder	2m 10.951s
23	Manzi	2m 10.991s
24	Baltus	2m 11.073s
25	Roberts	2m 11.232s
26	Syahrin	2m 11.545s
27	Luthi	2m 11.685s
28	Aldeguer	2m 11.720s
29	Baldassarri	2m 11.773s

Championship Points

1	Gardner	271
2	R. Fernandez	262
3	Bezzecchi	206
4	Lowes	140
5	A. Fernandez	131
6	Di Giannantonio	128
7	Canet	124
8	Ogura	113
9	Schrotter	84
10	Vierge	83
11	Navarro	78
12	Roberts	59
13	Vietti	53
14	Arbolino	51
15	Bendsneyder	41
16	Beaubier	39
17	Chantra	37
18	Ramirez	29
19	Dixon	27
20	Arenas	23
21	Luthi	21
22	Manzi	20
23	Corsi	16
24	Aldeguer	13
25	Garzo	12
26	Bulega	12
27	Dalla Porta	10
28	Syahrin	8
29	Lopez	4
30	Baldassarri	3
31	Baltus	2

Constructor Points

1	Kalex	375
2	Boscoscuro	159
3	MV Agusta	19
4	NTS	10

Moto3
RACE DISTANCE: 7 laps, 23.979 miles/38.591km · RACE WEATHER: Dry (air 29°, humidity 61%, track 36°)

Pos.	Rider	Nat.	No.	Entrant	Machine	Laps	Time & Speed
1	Izan Guevara	SPA	28	Solunion GASGAS Aspar Team	GASGAS	7	15m 57.747s 90.1mph/145.0km/h
2	Dennis Foggia	ITA	7	Leopard Racing	Honda	7	15m 58.132s
3	John McPhee	GBR	17	Petronas Sprinta Racing	Honda	7	15m 58.246s
4	Jaume Masia	SPA	5	Red Bull KTM Ajo	KTM	7	15m 58.453s
5	Deniz Oncu	TUR	53	Red Bull KTM Tech 3	KTM	7	15m 59.013s
6	Jeremy Alcoba	SPA	52	Indonesian Racing Gresini Moto3	Honda	7	15m 59.018s
7	Darryn Binder	RSA	40	Petronas Sprinta Racing	Honda	7	15m 59.138s
8	Pedro Acosta	SPA	37	Red Bull KTM Ajo	KTM	7	15m 59.290s
9	Tatsuki Suzuki	JPN	24	SIC58 Squadra Corse	Honda	7	15m 59.567s
10	Andrea Migno	ITA	16	Rivacold Snipers Team	Honda	7	16m 00.227s
11	Stefano Nepa	ITA	82	BOE Owlride	KTM	7	16m 00.430s
12	Romano Fenati	ITA	55	Sterilgarda Max Racing Team	Husqvarna	7	16m 01.004s
13	Ayumu Sasaki	JPN	71	Red Bull KTM Tech 3	KTM	7	16m 01.239s
14	Xavier Artigas	SPA	43	Leopard Racing	Honda	7	16m 01.399s
15	Niccolo Antonelli	ITA	23	Avintia VR46	KTM	7	16m 03.833s
16	Lorenzo Fellon	FRA	20	SIC58 Squadra Corse	Honda	7	16m 06.691s
17	Maximilian Kofler	AUT	73	CIP Green Power	KTM	7	16m 07.276s
18	Carlos Tatay	SPA	99	Avintia Esponsorama Moto3	KTM	7	16m 07.724s
19	Alberto Surra	ITA	67	Rivacold Snipers Team	Honda	7	16m 07.877s
20	Riccardo Rossi	ITA	54	BOE Owlride	KTM	7	16m 08.283s
21	Adrian Fernandez	SPA	31	Sterilgarda Max Racing Team	Husqvarna	7	16m 11.854s
22	Ryusei Yamanaka	JPN	6	CarXpert PruestelGP	KTM	7	16m 11.975s
23	Kaito Toba	JPN	27	CIP Green Power	KTM	7	16m 12.384s
24	Andi Farid Izdihar	INA	19	Honda Team Asia	Honda	7	16m 12.541s
25	Yuki Kunii	JPN	92	Honda Team Asia	Honda	7	16m 12.715s
	Filip Salac	CZE	12	CarXpert PruestelGP	KTM	6	DNF-crash

Fastest lap: Tatsuki Suzuki, on lap 7, 2m 16.172s, 90.5mph/145.7km/h.
Lap record: Aron Canet, 2m 14.644s, 91.6mph/147.4km/h (2017).
Event maximum speed: Ayumu Sasaki, 149.1mph/240.0km/h (race).

Qualifying:
Weather: Dry
Air Temp: 29° Track Temp: 39°
Humidity: 62%

1	Masia	2m 15.986s
2	Foggia	2m 16.179s
3	Alcoba	2m 16.182s
4	Guevara	2m 16.311s
5	Artigas	2m 16.334s
6	Suzuki	2m 16.356s
7	Salac	2m 16.445s
8	Migno	2m 16.506s
9	Oncu	2m 16.510s
10	McPhee	2m 16.592s
11	Fenati	2m 16.613s
12	Nepa	2m 16.642s
13	Antonelli	2m 16.701s
14	Sasaki	2m 16.712s
15	Acosta	2m 16.766s
16	Fellon	2m 16.861s
17	Binder	2m 17.092s
18	Surra	2m 17.407s
Q1		
19	Tatay	2m 18.053s
20	Rossi	2m 18.068s
21	Kofler	2m 18.071s
22	Fernandez	2m 18.098s
23	Yamanaka	2m 18.136s
24	Kunii	2m 18.247s
25	Izdihar	2m 18.452s
26	Toba	2m 19.172s

Fastest race laps

1	Suzuki	2m 16.172s
2	McPhee	2m 16.174s
3	Artigas	2m 16.195s
4	Acosta	2m 16.309s
5	Masia	2m 16.350s
6	Nepa	2m 16.391s
7	Foggia	2m 16.439s
8	Sasaki	2m 16.463s
9	Binder	2m 16.498s
10	Fenati	2m 16.527s
11	Alcoba	2m 16.557s
12	Migno	2m 16.567s
13	Guevara	2m 16.588s
14	Oncu	2m 16.634s
15	Antonelli	2m 16.706s
16	Kofler	2m 16.746s
17	Salac	2m 16.873s
18	Fellon	2m 17.105s
19	Tatay	2m 17.365s
20	Fernandez	2m 17.421s
21	Surra	2m 17.466s
22	Rossi	2m 17.504s
23	Izdihar	2m 17.863s
24	Yamanaka	2m 17.888s
25	Kunii	2m 17.888s
26	Toba	2m 18.006s

Championship Points

1	Acosta	218
2	Foggia	188
3	Garcia	168
4	Fenati	138
5	Masia	135
6	Binder	123
7	Antonelli	119
8	Guevara	101
9	Sasaki	96
10	Migno	90
11	Oncu	84
12	McPhee	72
13	Alcoba	70
14	Suzuki	69
15	Toba	64
16	Rodrigo	60
17	Salac	46
18	Yamanaka	42
19	Nepa	42
20	Artigas	32
21	Rossi	29
22	Tatay	28
23	Dupasquier	27
24	Fernandez	20
25	Kunii	15
26	Kofler	10
27	Bartolini	7
28	Azman	3
29	Izdihar	3
30	Holgado	1

Constructor Points

1	KTM	308
2	Honda	290
3	GASGAS	231
4	Husqvarna	144

GRAND PRIX OF THE AMERICAS 205

2021
MOTOGP
WORLD
CHAMPION
MONSTER
ENERGY
ENEOS
YAMAHA
alpinestars
withu

FIM WORLD CHAMPIONSHIP · ROUND 16

EMILIA ROMAGNA GRAND PRIX

MISANO WORLD CIRCUIT MARCO SIMONCELLI

Main and inset, above: Winners. Quartararo (*left*) shouts his triumph; Marquez and Espargaro (*above*) beam their first one-two together.
Photos: Gold & Goose

Inset, top: Losers. Ducati's Jack Miller consoles fellow faller Bagnaia.
Photo: Ducati Corse

Above: Down and out. Bagnaia's tyre gamble left him undone.
Photo: Ducati Corse

Top right: Much mixed conditions helped Luca Marini to a first front-row start.

Above right: Friday practice. Alex Marquez leaps from his Honda, Petrucci takes avoiding action.

Right: Local hero. Rossi soaks up the applause in his final appearance on home soil.
Photos: Gold & Goose

BY this stage of the season, it was clearly meant to be. The return to Misano produced all sorts of obstacles to the first French premier-class champion in 73 years of the World Championships. In the end, none of them counted a damn.

There was adversity from unpleasant and unpredictable weather. Rain on both practice days put Fabio Quartararo in his worst ever MotoGP grid position of 15th.

There was the increasingly imperious challenge of late-season rival Pecco Bagnaia, who had swept to a fourth consecutive pole position and then led convincingly on a finally sunny Sunday.

And there was every chance that the hitherto calm and collected Quartararo would succumb to the temperament that had spoiled his challenge the year before.

But his newfound maturity did not desert him, and he faced his first ever match point much as he had dealt with adversity all year, keeping his cool as he scythed through the field, overtaking ten riders with well-contained aggression. It made him a barely believing MotoGP world champion at 22 years and 187 days, the sixth youngest in history.

The key, he explained, was Yamaha's ability to find a setting that had allowed him to brake late and turn quickly in his preferred manner. "Last year, we fought to have the factory bike, but the '19 bike was better," said Quartararo. "But with the '21, I felt much better. The feeling on the front is what helped me win. We know that the power is something that we need to work on, but the feeling I have on braking to overtake has been much higher than '19 and '20."

New fellow Yamaha rider Andrea Dovizioso underlined the point: "He brakes very late, but it's easy to brake late. It's difficult to brake late and turn the bike like him. And he's doing it easily."

And in the Yamaha pit, team manager Massimo Meregalli was full of admiration for the ambience he had brought with him, along with crew chief Diego Gubellini and data technician Pablo Guilliem. "He brought some happiness in the garage," said Meregalli. "He has always been humble, happy and polite. He created a group and he is able to get 100 per cent from the people that are working with him. I only saw this quality in Valentino before."

And how did Bagnaia's challenge falter? Well, he picked a bad time to crash out of the lead, for the third time in four consecutive home races. Falling temperatures that undermined his hard-tyre gamble were to blame, but he felt his strong end to the season had prepared him for a better challenge in 2022: "This year was a year not to win the championship, but to learn. I learned a lot. In the last five races, always at the top fighting for the win. This is an incredible step in front that we did at the start of the season. We lost the championship in Mugello, when I crashed when I was in front. In Austria 1, when I took this tyre that was not working, in Silverstone, when I took another tyre that was not working. But it's not correct to think this way. With this step forward we did, I'm sure we will arrive more prepared."

Echoing similar optimism for 2022, a jubilant factory Repsol Honda team and riders. Strong qualifying by both Marc Marquez and Pol Espargaro was followed by steadfast rides. Again with the help of Bagnaia and Ducati team-mate Miller, who also crashed out ahead of the pair, they achieved a long awaited and much heartening one-two finish – the first for the factory team since 2017. "It feels like we have been able to break this wall," said Espargaro.

This was the culmination of a busy weekend, marked by Rossi's last home race, with the yellow army of fans even more enthusiastic than usual, and (with 35,000 allowed in on race day) thankfully saved from the preceding days' cold and rain. Riders in his VR46 teams in MotoGP and Moto2 appeared with their bikes painted dazzling yellow, with the legend '*GRAZIE VALE*', but the omens for the departing hero had not been promising. He had qualified only 23rd, equalling his worst of the year, at the same track two races before, but race day was more encouraging, with a top-ten finish that equalled his second best in his final year. The emotions

208 EMILIA ROMAGNA GRAND PRIX

were mixed, he said, not least because of a ceremony honouring his close friend and first true protégé Marco Simoncelli. It was ten years to the day since his fatal accident, and Vale joined his parents at the planting of a memorial oak tree at the eponymous circuit's Quercia (oak) corner.

There was much else to exercise the mind at Misano, not least the announcement of a provisional 2022 calendar with a record 21 races, including two new tracks – Mandalika in Indonesia and the on-again/off-again Kymi Ring in Finland. Reactions were mixed. The return to countries like Indonesia would, said Vinales, "help the championship grow", but some felt it had already grown enough. Marc Marquez thought that 21 was too many. "Dorna has to cap the number," he said. Some established races would have to give way. The obvious targets would be one or two of the four scheduled in Spain.

The long awaited confirmation of Yamaha's fourth rider for 2022 finally laid to rest rumours that the company was waiting to see if Razgatlioglu might win the Superbike title, then be persuaded to change his mind about staying there. If this was ever on the cards, it was now too late, and the other rumour turned out to be true. The second seat at the renamed ex-Petronas satellite squad, alongside Dovizioso, would go to current Petronas Moto3 rider Darryn Binder, the South African thus following Jack Miller in bypassing Moto2. "A dream come true" was his inevitable response, while older brother Brad added a warning to his heartfelt welcome: "If you start beating me, you have to move out of my house."

MOTOGP RACE – 27 laps

Cold and rain spoiled free practice; dry qualifying sessions offered 15-minute windows to test dry settings while also going for all-important grid positions.

Bagnaia had the benefit of both, fastest in Q1 to make the Q2 cut, which he also won. Miller was second, Marini a surprise third, his first front row, and the first Ducati front-row lockout. Pol Espargaro timed it well for fourth.

Mired midfield, champion-elect Quartararo, third-fastest in Q1 (behind Lecuona), was 13th on the grid. Even worse off, defending champion Mir, a disillusioned 19th.

Warm-up was only just drying, exacerbating set-up issues. Aleix Espargaro summed it up: "There are a lot of doubts for all riders. Should make a fun race." For those who guessed best, it did.

Postponement of Quartararo's match point looked likely after the start, as Bagnaia led Miller, Marquez (up from seventh in a lively opening), Oliveira, Pol Espargaro, Morbidelli and Marini at the close of lap one. Quartararo, meanwhile, was 14th after losing ground at the first chicane.

The deciding factor was already in play, however. Bagnaia and Miller alone had chosen Michelin's hard front compound. The medium was too soft and liable to collapse during braking, according to the Italian. The decision, described as "left field" by Miller, dismayed Rossi, Bagnaia's mentor. He was "a little angry with him." Ultimately, the challenge of maintaining heat on the left side proved impossible.

The first indication of treacherous grip came on lap three, when Mir folded the front at Turn Two, taking Petrucci down to cap a miserable weekend. A lap later, Miller – riding within himself in second to protect Bagnaia's lead – did the same, this time at Turn 15, the track's first left after 40 seconds. It wasn't quite warm enough for the tyre gamble to work.

With Espargaro and Oliveira outpaced, Bagnaia just had to fend off Marquez to claim his third win in four races. Judged by September's outing at the same track, that should have been simple. But Marquez was buoyed by his Austin win, and crucially he had felt fresh on Sunday morning, thanks to the less strenuous wet running all weekend. "That gave me the chance to arrive to Sunday with energy," he said. No matter how hard Bagnaia pushed, he just couldn't shake off the Honda.

That wasn't Bagnaia's only concern. Hopes of big inroads into Quartararo's championship lead were fading as the

Above: Breaking the wall: a first one-two for Repsol Honda since 2017.

Top right: A lowly 18th on the grid, Bastianini pushed his secondhand Duke to a second home podium.

Above right: Sam Lowes outpaced Canet to return to victory at last.

Right: Vietti took his lurid VR46 Kalex to a best-yet fourth.

Below right: Masia and Acosta celebrate Red Bull KTM Ajo's Moto3 team championship.

Below far right: Moto3 winner Foggia leads Binder, Acosta and Antonelli as Migno slides down and out.

Photos: Gold & Goose

Frenchman launched a resolute recovery, joining Aleix Espargaro, Morbidelli, Marini and Rins on lap 13 in a lively fight for fifth, Zarco just behind. The Yamaha rider was past them all within six laps, with a series of clean and clear overtakes exploiting his braking skills.

Up front, Marquez was still hovering in second, posting his personal best time 20 laps in. But Bagnaia finally put some distance on his pursuer with a burst of late-race aggression. By lap 22, he had finally gained some breathing space, with Marquez now seven-tenths behind. The win appeared a formality. Until on lap 23, he suffered a carbon copy of Miller's Turn 15 crash, the front tucking at speed. Team boss Davide Tardozzi dropped to his knees. The title fight was over.

Bagnaia explained the fine margins of the hard front: "You needed to push like hell every single lap to keep the tyre hot. On this lap, maybe I braked a little earlier in Turn Eight."

Marquez was clear to win his third race of 2021 by 4.8 seconds, his first at a clockwise track in more than two years.

Pol Espargaro inherited a safe second, while Bagnaia's crash had rendered Quartararo's position meaningless – he was already champion. Still, he found himself third after Oliveira fell at Turn 14 on lap 23. But that wouldn't last, with Bastianini nabbing the final podium place three turns from the chequered flag, having followed Quartararo's lead, ghosting through the pack after ending the first lap 18th. A repeat home podium had looked impossible after he had crashed three times in qualifying, leaving him 16th on the grid.

Zarco came through to fifth, ahead of Rins; Aleix Espargaro dropped to seventh and was nearly caught by team-mate Vinales. Marini's ninth was two seconds ahead of half-brother Rossi, whose final home flourish had been to pass Binder on the last lap, the South African having rejoined ahead of the veteran after a long-lap penalty for exceeding track limits. Wild-card Pirro was a couple of tenths behind.

With only 15 finishers, there were points for all: Dovizioso a lone 13th after his own long-lap, then Morbidelli – another track-limits transgressor – and 40 seconds down, Nakagami, fastest in morning warm-up, who had fallen and remounted.

Lecuona and Martin crashed out; Alex Marquez retired following an alarm on his Honda's dash.

MOTO2 RACE – 25 laps

The finely balanced title fight took another lurch in Misano, offering slight relief for narrow leader Gardner.

Moto2 faced similar weather issues to MotoGP, and damp qualifying was difficult for all, including the title contenders, with a spate of crashes and yellow flags causing several lap times to be cancelled. Lowes, Navarro and Augusto Fernandez completed the front row; Canet, Vietti and Ramirez the second. Raul Fernandez was a second off the pace in ninth, and Gardner in the thick of the midfield in 14th.

Lowes got the jump, from Augusto Fernandez and Canet, but the last named was in front by the end of the first lap, and he stayed there for the next two, while Navarro pushed briefly into second and then into the lead at slow Turn 14. In the process, he put himself and Canet wide, allowing the English rider to take over again. He held on up front until lap 13, by which time Raul Fernandez, having made his way through quickly from seventh on lap one, had been pushing and probing with increasing intensity.

The outlook for his title rival was grim. After making up early ground, the Australian's progress had stalled in seventh, a position he had gained with a forceful move on fast qualifier Chantra at Turn 14. As Gardner pushed inside, the Thai rider was taken by surprise and forced to lift suddenly. He ran off to crash, shaking his fist.

The verdict was marginal, but on the wrong side for the rider. After four laps, the stewards decided that Gardner deserved a long-lap penalty. At least by now, the midfield was sufficiently spaced that he lost only one position, to Augusto Fernandez, who had also served a long-lap on lap two for irresponsible riding in qualifying.

Then fortune played the joker.

One lap after taking the lead, at the same corner where he had done so, Raul locked the front while braking, still upright, and was down. Gardner was reprieved.

Lowes and Canet fought for the lead, and a superb Turn Two pass three laps from the flag flipped the contest in Lowes's favour for his third win of 2021.

Canet looked safe in second, but on the exit of the final

FIM WORLD CHAMPIONSHIP

corner, he slowed suddenly, allowing Augusto Fernandez past after a tremendous comeback. Canet gestured angrily, then stuttered to a stop on the slow-down lap. He was out of fuel.

Vietti capitalised on a career-first second row for a career-best fourth; Navarro stayed clear of Manzi. Nine seconds away, Gardner was seventh, with an 18-point breathing space in the championship.

Other fancied runners had mixed fortunes. Di Giannantonio came through from 20th to eighth, less than two seconds from Gardner, but comfortably clear of the next trio, where Ogura (18th on the grid) rescued ninth from Ramirez and Arenas. Bendsneyder, Dixon, Luthi and Schrotter wrapped up the points, fast rookie Aldeguer missing out by just over a second after his own long-lap.

Bezzecchi was one of several to crash, with three laps to go after pushing through to seventh from 24th on the grid. Beaubier, Vierge, Garzo and Arbolino also fell.

MOTO3 RACE – 23 laps

Wet qualifying similarly shuffled Moto3, with Antonelli joined by Salac and Rossi on the front row; Guevara, Acosta and Masia were on row two. Foggia, no fan of wet surfaces, languished in 14th.

The first race of Sunday was dry although still patchy, and Foggia's outlook darker as he was shuffled back to 16th in the opening exchanges.

Antonelli led, interrupted for two laps by Nepa, with Masia, Guevara, Acosta, Salac and soon also Binder in the mix.

Seemingly out of touch, Foggia remained unflustered and found his rhythm.

His comeback was exhilarating. By lap six, he was tenth and at the head of the second group. Seven laps on, and he was third, crucially passing Acosta. Then he got by Masia on lap 15 to lead for the first time. With Antonelli now at the back of the group, only the Spaniard could stay with him as they edged clear of Binder in third, with Acosta struggling to keep Nepa behind.

Starting the final lap just a tenth ahead, Foggia eked out an unbridgeable gap midway around. Masia had no answer. A last-lap error by Binder allowed Acosta to grab third, with Nepa a close fifth.

Antonelli was sixth, Fenati through to seventh from 20th on the first lap; Ayumu Sasaki eighth, Artigas having wrested ninth from Salac, Yamanaka a lone 11th, well ahead of Guevara, who had slipped off and remounted. Rossi, McPhee, Suzuki and the perennially luckless Migno crashed out, and at the end also Kunii.

Foggia's fifth win closed him to within 21 tantalising points of Acosta.

EMILIA ROMAGNA GRAND PRIX 211

FIM WORLD CHAMPIONSHIP: ROUND 16

GP NOLAN DEL MADE IN ITALY E DELL'EMILIA-ROMAGNA

22-24 OCTOBER, 2021

MISANO WORLD CIRCUIT
27 laps
Length: 4.226 km / 2.626 miles
Width: 14m

MotoGP

RACE DISTANCE: 27 laps, 70.900 miles/114.102km · RACE WEATHER: Dry (air 18°, humidity 55%, track 23°)

Pos.	Rider	Nat.	No.	Entrant	Machine	Race tyre choice	Laps	Time & speed
1	Marc Marquez	SPA	93	Repsol Honda Team	Honda RC213V	F: Medium/R: Soft	27	41m 52.830s / 101.5mph / 163.4km/h
2	Pol Espargaro	SPA	44	Repsol Honda Team	Honda RC213V	F: Medium /R: Soft	27	41m 57.689s
3	Enea Bastianini	ITA	23	Avintia Esponsorama	Ducati Desmosedici	F: Medium /R: Soft	27	42m 04.843s
4	Fabio Quartararo	FRA	20	Monster Energy Yamaha MotoGP	Yamaha YZR-M1	F: Medium /R: Medium	27	42m 05.605s
5	Johann Zarco	FRA	5	Pramac Racing	Ducati Desmosedici	F: Medium/R: Medium	27	42m 09.288s
6	Alex Rins	SPA	42	Team SUZUKI ECSTAR	Suzuki GSX-RR	F: Medium/R: Soft	27	42m 10.499s
7	Aleix Espargaro	SPA	41	Aprilia Racing Team Gresini	Aprilia RS-GP	F: Medium/R: Soft	27	42m 11.298s
8	Maverick Vinales	SPA	12	Aprilia Racing Team Gresini	Aprilia RS-GP	F: Medium/R: Soft	27	42m 11.437s
9	Luca Marini	ITA	10	SKY VR46 Avintia	Ducati Desmosedici	F: Medium/R: Soft	27	42m 18.247s
10	Valentino Rossi	ITA	46	Petronas Yamaha SRT	Yamaha YZR-M1	F: Medium/R: Soft	27	42m 20.565s
11	Brad Binder	RSA	33	Red Bull KTM Factory Racing	KTM RC16	F: Medium/R: Soft	27	42m 20.709s
12	Michele Pirro	ITA	51	Ducati Lenovo Team	Ducati Desmosedici	F: Medium/R: Soft	27	42m 20.967s
13	Andrea Dovizioso	ITA	4	Petronas Yamaha SRT	Yamaha YZR-M1	F: Medium/R: Soft	27	42m 34.243s
14	Franco Morbidelli	ITA	21	Monster Energy Yamaha MotoGP	Yamaha YZR-M1	F: Medium/R: Soft	27	42m 35.660s
15	Takaaki Nakagami	JPN	30	LCR Honda IDEMITSU	Honda RC213V	F: Medium/R: Soft	27	43m 15.292s
	Francesco Bagnaia	ITA	63	Ducati Lenovo Team	Ducati Desmosedici	F: Hard/R: Soft	22	DNF-crash
	Miguel Oliveira	POR	88	Red Bull KTM Factory Racing	KTM RC16	F: Medium/R: Soft	22	DNF-crash
	Jorge Martin	SPA	89	Pramac Racing	Ducati Desmosedici	F: Medium/R: Soft	12	DNF-crash
	Iker Lecuona	SPA	27	Tech 3 KTM Factory Racing	KTM RC16	F: Medium/R: Soft	10	DNF-crash
	Alex Marquez	SPA	73	LCR Honda CASTROL	Honda RC213V	F: Medium/R: Soft	9	DNF-technical
	Jack Miller	AUS	43	Ducati Lenovo Team	Ducati Desmosedici	F: Hard/R: Medium	3	DNF-crash
	Danilo Petrucci	ITA	9	Tech 3 KTM Factory Racing	KTM RC16	F: Medium/R: Soft	2	DNF-crash
	Joan Mir	SPA	36	Team SUZUKI ECSTAR	Suzuki GSX-RR	F: Medium/R: Soft	2	DNF-crash
	Lorenzo Savadori	ITA	32	Aprilia Racing Team Gresini	Aprilia RS-GP	-	-	DNS-injured

Fastest lap: Francesco Bagnaia, on lap 16, 1m 32.171s, 102.5mph/165.0km/h.
Lap record: Enea Bastianini, 1m 32.242s, 102.5mph/164.9km/h (2021).
Event maximum speed: Johann Zarco, 189.5mph/305.0km/h (race).

Qualifying

Weather: Dry
Air Temp: 17° Track Temp: 17°
Humidity: 86%

1	Bagnaia	1m 33.045s
2	Miller	1m 33.070s
3	Marini	1m 33.130s
4	P. Espargaro	1m 33.313s
5	Oliveira	1m 33.439s
6	Morbidelli	1m 33.526s
7	M. Marquez	1m 33.850s
8	Lecuona	1m 33.893s
9	Petrucci	1m 34.140s
10	Zarco	1m 34.687s
11	A. Espargaro	1m 34.963s
12	Martin	2m 24.631s
	Q1	
13	Rins	1m 34.418s
14	A. Marquez	1m 34.454s
15	Quartararo	1m 34.476s
16	Bastianini	1m 35.236s
17	Nakagami	1m 35.641s
18	Mir	1m 35.683s
19	Vinales	1m 35.835s
20	Binder	1m 36.478s
21	Dovizioso	1m 36.639s
22	Pirro	1m 37.880s
23	Rossi	1m 38.261s
	Savadori	No Time

Fastest race laps

1	Bagnaia	1m 32.171s
2	Bastianini	1m 32.244s
3	M. Marquez	1m 32.256s
4	Vinales	1m 32.533s
5	P. Espargaro	1m 32.577s
6	Oliveira	1m 32.694s
7	Quartararo	1m 32.718s
8	A. Espargaro	1m 32.791s
9	Rins	1m 32.819s
10	Miller	1m 32.840s
11	Martin	1m 32.927s
12	Nakagami	1m 32.973s
13	Morbidelli	1m 32.990s
14	Marini	1m 33.044s
15	Zarco	1m 33.049s
16	Binder	1m 33.083s
17	Rossi	1m 33.083s
18	A. Marquez	1m 33.203s
19	Pirro	1m 33.210s
20	Lecuona	1m 33.293s
21	Dovizioso	1m 33.339s
22	Mir	1m 35.551s
23	Petrucci	1m 36.021s

Championship Points

1	Quartararo	267
2	Bagnaia	202
3	Mir	175
4	Zarco	152
5	Miller	149
6	M. Marquez	142
7	Binder	136
8	A. Espargaro	113
9	Vinales	106
10	Oliveira	92
11	Rins	91
12	P. Espargaro	90
13	Bastianini	87
14	Martin	82
15	Nakagami	71
16	A. Marquez	54
17	Morbidelli	42
18	Lecuona	38
19	Petrucci	37
20	Marini	37
21	Rossi	35
22	Bradl	13
23	Pirro	12
24	Pedrosa	6
25	Dovizioso	6
26	Savadori	4
27	Rabat	1

Constructor Points

1	Ducati	307
2	Yamaha	295
3	Suzuki	207
4	Honda	198
5	KTM	190
6	Aprilia	114

Grid order / lap chart

Grid order	Rider
63	BAGNAIA
43	MILLER
10	MARINI
44	P. ESPARGARO
88	OLIVEIRA
21	MORBIDELLI
93	M. MARQUEZ
27	LECUONA
9	PETRUCCI
5	ZARCO
41	A. ESPARGARO
89	MARTIN
42	RINS
73	A. MARQUEZ
20	QUARTARARO
23	BASTIANINI
30	NAKAGAMI
36	MIR
12	VINALES
33	BINDER
4	DOVIZIOSO
51	PIRRO
46	ROSSI

EMILIA-ROMAGNA GRAND PRIX

Moto2

RACE DISTANCE: 25 laps, 65.648 miles/105.650km · **RACE WEATHER:** Dry (air 19°, humidity 52%, track 22°)

Pos.	Rider	Nat.	No.	Entrant	Machine	Laps	Time & Speed
1	Sam Lowes	GBR	22	Elf Marc VDS Racing Team	Kalex	25	40m 25.180s 97.4mph/156.8km/h
2	Augusto Fernandez	SPA	37	Elf Marc VDS Racing Team	Kalex	25	40m 26.413s
3	Aron Canet	SPA	44	Aspar Team Moto2	Boscoscuro	25	40m 26.580s
4	Celestino Vietti	ITA	13	SKY Racing Team VR46	Kalex	25	40m 27.734s
5	Jorge Navarro	SPA	9	+EGO Speed Up	Boscoscuro	25	40m 29.423s
6	Stefano Manzi	ITA	62	Flexbox HP40	Kalex	25	40m 30.378s
7	Remy Gardner	AUS	87	Red Bull KTM Ajo	Kalex	25	40m 39.441s
8	Fabio Di Giannantonio	ITA	21	Federal Oil Gresini Moto2	Kalex	25	40m 41.048s
9	Ai Ogura	JPN	79	IDEMITSU Honda Team Asia	Kalex	25	40m 44.085s
10	Marcos Ramirez	SPA	42	American Racing	Kalex	25	40m 44.249s
11	Albert Arenas	SPA	75	Aspar Team Moto2	Boscoscuro	25	40m 44.855s
12	Bo Bendsneyder	NED	64	Pertamina Mandalika SAG Team	Kalex	25	40m 49.489s
13	Jake Dixon	GBR	96	Petronas Sprinta Racing	Kalex	25	40m 51.957s
14	Thomas Luthi	SWI	12	Pertamina Mandalika SAG Team	Kalex	25	40m 59.879s
15	Marcel Schrotter	GER	23	Liqui Moly Intact GP	Kalex	25	41m 01.420s
16	Fermin Aldeguer	SPA	54	+EGO Speed Up	Boscoscuro	25	41m 02.770s
17	Barry Baltus	BEL	70	NTS RW Racing GP	NTS	25	41m 03.079s
18	Nicolo Bulega	ITA	11	Federal Oil Gresini Moto2	Kalex	25	41m 03.146s
19	Simone Corsi	ITA	24	MV Agusta Forward Racing	MV Agusta	25	41m 15.967s
20	Lorenzo Baldassarri	ITA	7	MV Agusta Forward Racing	MV Agusta	25	41m 28.154s
	Marco Bezzecchi	ITA	72	SKY Racing Team VR46	Kalex	22	DNF-crash
	Xavi Vierge	SPA	97	Petronas Sprinta Racing	Kalex	16	DNF-crash
	Tony Arbolino	ITA	14	Liqui Moly Intact GP	Kalex	16	DNF-crash
	Mattia Casadei	ITA	27	Italtrans Racing Team	Kalex	15	DNF-ret in pit
	Raul Fernandez	SPA	25	Red Bull KTM Ajo	Kalex	14	DNF-crash
	Hector Garzo	SPA	40	Flexbox HP40	Kalex	12	DNF-crash
	Tommaso Marcon	ITA	10	NTS RW Racing GP	NTS	9	DNF-injured
	Cameron Beaubier	USA	6	American Racing	Kalex	8	DNF-crash
	Somkiat Chantra	THA	35	IDEMITSU Honda Team Asia	Kalex	6	DNF-crash

Fastest lap: Augusto Fernandez, on lap 20, 1m 36.182s, 98.2mph/158.1km/h.
Lap record: Sam Lowes, 1m 36.195s, 98.2mph/158.1km/h (2020).
Event maximum speed: Marco Bezzecchi, 157.9mph/254.1km/h (race).

Qualifying
Weather: Dry
Air Temp: 17° **Track Temp:** 17°
Humidity: 88%

1	Lowes	1m 36.510s
2	Navarro	1m 36.555s
3	A. Fernandez	1m 36.744s
4	Canet	1m 36.950s
5	Vietti	1m 37.100s
6	Ramirez	1m 37.300s
7	Manzi	1m 37.511s
8	Arenas	1m 37.558s
9	R. Fernandez	1m 37.602s
10	Chantra	1m 37.686s
11	Luthi	1m 37.695s
12	Bendsneyder	1m 37.767s
13	Aldeguer	1m 37.780s
14	Gardner	1m 37.825s
15	Garzo	1m 37.904s
16	Vierge	1m 38.482s
17	Dixon	1m 38.556s
18	Ogura	1m 39.683s

Q1

19	Beaubier	1m 38.097s
20	Di Giannantonio	1m 38.122s
21	Schrotter	1m 38.366s
22	Baldassarri	1m 38.748s
23	Baltus	1m 39.543s
24	Bezzecchi	1m 40.068s
25	Marcon	1m 43.096s
	Bulega	No Time
	Arbolino	No Time
	Roberts	No Time
	Corsi	No Time
	Casadei	No Time

Fastest race laps

1	A. Fernandez	1m 36.182s
2	Lowes	1m 36.236s
3	Canet	1m 36.265s
4	Vietti	1m 36.286s
5	R. Fernandez	1m 36.333s
6	Navarro	1m 36.436s
7	Bezzecchi	1m 36.480s
8	Manzi	1m 36.534s
9	Gardner	1m 36.565s
10	Di Giannantonio	1m 36.625s
11	Vierge	1m 36.643s
12	Arenas	1m 36.732s
13	Ogura	1m 36.804s
14	Chantra	1m 37.012s
15	Garzo	1m 37.013s
16	Ramirez	1m 37.081s
17	Dixon	1m 37.096s
18	Arbolino	1m 37.114s
19	Beaubier	1m 37.117s
20	Bendsneyder	1m 37.117s
21	Aldeguer	1m 37.151s
22	Bulega	1m 37.319s
23	Luthi	1m 37.373s
24	Schrotter	1m 37.488s
25	Baltus	1m 37.685s
26	Corsi	1m 37.937s
27	Baldassarri	1m 38.629s
28	Casadei	1m 39.714s
29	Marcon	1m 40.930s

Championship Points

1	Gardner	280
2	R. Fernandez	262
3	Bezzecchi	206
4	Lowes	165
5	A. Fernandez	151
6	Canet	140
7	Di Giannantonio	136
8	Ogura	120
9	Navarro	89
10	Schrotter	85
11	Vierge	83
12	Vietti	66
13	Roberts	59
14	Arbolino	51
15	Bendsneyder	45
16	Beaubier	39
17	Chantra	37
18	Ramirez	35
19	Manzi	30
20	Dixon	30
21	Arenas	28
22	Luthi	23
23	Corsi	16
24	Aldeguer	13
25	Garzo	12
26	Bulega	12
27	Dalla Porta	10
28	Syahrin	8
29	Lopez	4
30	Baldassarri	3
31	Baltus	2

Constructor Points

1	Kalex	400
2	Boscoscuro	175
3	MV Agusta	19
4	NTS	10

Moto3

RACE DISTANCE: 23 laps, 60.396 miles/97.198km · **RACE WEATHER:** Dry (air 18°, humicity 56%, track 16°)

Pos.	Rider	Nat.	No.	Entrant	Machine	Laps	Time & Speed
1	Dennis Foggia	ITA	7	Leopard Racing	Honda	23	39m 33.170s 91.6mph/147.4/h
2	Jaume Masia	SPA	5	Red Bull KTM Ajo	KTM	23	39m 33.462s
3	Pedro Acosta	SPA	37	Red Bull KTM Ajo	KTM	23	39m 37.856s
4	Darryn Binder	RSA	40	Petronas Sprinta Racing	Honda	23	39m 37.967s
5	Stefano Nepa	ITA	82	BOE Owlride	KTM	23	39m 38.023s
6	Niccolo Antonelli	ITA	23	Avintia VR46	KTM	23	39m 38.222s
7	Romano Fenati	ITA	55	Sterilgarda Max Racing Team	Husqvarna	23	39m 38.505s
8	Ayumu Sasaki	JPN	71	Red Bull KTM Tech 3	KTM	23	39m 39.812s
9	Xavier Artigas	SPA	43	Leopard Racing	Honda	23	39m 39.906s
10	Filip Salac	CZE	12	CarXpert PruestelGP	KTM	23	39m 39.970s
11	Ryusei Yamanaka	JPN	6	CarXpert PruestelGP	KTM	23	39m 43.705s
12	Izan Guevara	SPA	28	GAVIOTA GASGAS Aspar Team	GASGAS	23	39m 50.981s
13	Adrian Fernandez	SPA	31	Sterilgarda Max Racing Team	Husqvarna	23	39m 51.220s
14	Jeremy Alcoba	SPA	52	Indonesian Racing Gresini Moto3	Honda	23	39m 51.430s
15	Andi Farid Izdihar	INA	19	Honda Team Asia	Honda	23	39m 52.434s
16	Alberto Surra	ITA	67	Rivacold Snipers Team	Honda	23	39m 53.387s
17	Kaito Toba	JPN	27	CIP Green Power	KTM	23	39m 57.874s
18	Maximilian Kofler	AUT	73	CIP Green Power	KTM	23	39m 58.072s
19	Lorenzo Fellon	FRA	20	SIC58 Squadra Corse	Honda	23	39m 58.146s
20	Daniel Holgado	SPA	96	Red Bull KTM Tech 3	KTM	23	39m 58.493s
21	Mario Aji	INA	64	Honda Team Asia	Honda	23	40m 19.665s
22	David Alonso	COL	80	GAVIOTA GASGAS Aspar Team	GASGAS	23	40m 58.377s
	Yuki Kunii	JPN	92	Honda Team Asia	Honda	20	DNF-crash
	Andrea Migno	ITA	16	Rivacold Snipers Team	Honda	12	DNF-crash
	Carlos Tatay	SPA	99	Avintia Esponsorama Moto3	KTM	12	DNF-injured
	Tatsuki Suzuki	JPN	24	SIC58 Squadra Corse	Honda	10	DNF-crash
	John McPhee	GBR	17	Petronas Sprinta Racing	Honda	8	DNF-crash
	Riccardo Rossi	ITA	54	BOE Owlride	KTM	5	DNF-crash

Fastest lap: Andrea Migno, on lap 8, 1m 42.284s, 92.4mph/148.7km/h.
Lap record: Romano Fenati, 1m 41.648s, 93.0mph/149.6km/h (2021).
Event maximum speed: Izan Guevara, 132.8mph/213.8km/h (race).

Qualifying:
Weather: Wet
Air Temp: 16° **Track Temp:** 16°
Humidity: 90%

1	Antonelli	1m 48.563s
2	Salac	1m 49.174s
3	Rossi	1m 49.280s
4	Guevara	1m 49.495s
5	Acosta	1m 49.582s
6	Masia	1m 49.633s
7	Surra	1m 49.677s
8	Nepa	1m 49.697s
9	Artigas	1m 50.211s
10	Sasaki	1m 50.352s
11	Fernandez	1m 50.609s
12	McPhee	1m 50.695s
13	Kunii	1m 50.746s
14	Foggia	1m 50.988s
15	Izdihar	1m 51.004s
16	Binder	1m 51.025s
17	Fellon	1m 51.349s
18	Holgado	1m 51.726s

Q1

19	Fenati	1m 50.522s
20	Yamanaka	1m 50.590s
21	Tatay	1m 50.662s
22	Migno	1m 50.819s
23	Aji	1m 51.163s
24	Suzuki	1m 51.280s
25	Alonso	1m 52.013s
26	Alcoba	1m 52.084s
27	Toba	1m 52.230s
28	Kofler	1m 53.602s

Fastest race laps

1	Migno	1m 42.284s
2	Foggia	1m 42.293s
3	Guevara	1m 42.358s
4	Masia	1m 42.363s
5	Artigas	1m 42.375s
6	Binder	1m 42.379s
7	Fenati	1m 42.486s
8	Yamanaka	1m 42.537s
9	Salac	1m 42.557s
10	Acosta	1m 42.573s
11	Nepa	1m 42.609s
12	Antonelli	1m 42.615s
13	Sasaki	1m 42.615s
14	Alcoba	1m 42.693s
15	Izdihar	1m 43.055s
16	Fernandez	1m 43.071s
17	Surra	1m 43.164s
18	Holgado	1m 43.217s
19	Fellon	1m 43.239s
20	Kunii	1m 43.256s
21	McPhee	1m 43.270s
22	Kofler	1m 43.270s
23	Toba	1m 43.352s
24	Suzuki	1m 43.416s
25	Aji	1m 43.596s
26	Tatay	1m 43.737s
27	Rossi	1m 43.949s
28	Alonso	1m 45.018s

Championship Points

1	Acosta	234
2	Foggia	213
3	Garcia	168
4	Masia	155
5	Fenati	147
6	Binder	136
7	Antonelli	129
8	Guevara	105
9	Sasaki	104
10	Migno	90
11	Oncu	84
12	Alcoba	72
13	McPhee	72
14	Suzuki	69
15	Toba	64
16	Rodrigo	60
17	Nepa	53
18	Salac	52
19	Yamanaka	47
20	Artigas	39
21	Rossi	29
22	Tatay	28
23	Dupasquier	27
24	Fernandez	23
25	Kunii	15
26	Kofler	10
27	Bartolini	7
28	Izdihar	4
29	Azman	3
30	Holgado	1

Constructor Points

1	KTM	328
2	Honda	315
3	GASGAS	235
4	Husqvarna	153

FIM WORLD CHAMPIONSHIP · ROUND 17
ALGARVE GRAND PRIX
ALGARVE INTERNATIONAL CIRCUIT

Main: Home and away – Gardner stretches the lead for a vital victory. Tyre choice proved crucial.

Inset: Sporting spirit. The vanquished Fernandez congratulates his team-mate.
Photos: Gold & Goose

Above: The moment the Moto3 championship was decided. Darryn Binder meets the unexpectedly slowed Dennis Foggia.

Top right: Iker Lecuona brings down luckless home hero Miguel Oliveira, triggering the red flags.

Above right: When the shark bites, with his teeth dear – *El Tiburon de Mazarrón* takes his lap of honour.
Photos: Gold & Goose

Right: Francesco Bagnaia and Ducati were in complete control.
Photo: Ducati Corse

THE biggest news on the second 2021 visit to Portimao's scenic swoops came by stealth – the absence of Marc Marquez was attributed by Repsol Honda to a simple "precautionary measure", after the winner the previous time out had suffered "a slight concussion" in a training accident the previous Saturday.

He'd been riding with Enduro world champion Josep Garcia. Now, after "a few days rest at home", assessed by doctors, he'd withdrawn from the race. Further details were sparse, much as in 2020 when his right arm hadn't been healing. This prompted speculation from, among others, Aleix Espargaro: "If it's a head concussion, it must be hard. If it wasn't, Marc would be here racing for sure. I don't know if concussion is the right word. I think it's something bigger."

He turned out to be correct, confirmed a week later when Marc missed the final race as well, and the important tests the following week. It emerged that the fall had triggered a return of the double vision (diplopia) that had come close to ending his career in 2011. That had been solved with delicate and difficult microsurgery. The same would be required again, with no guarantee of success.

Non-Spanish speakers (there remained a handful in the fraternity) learned another new phrase in 2021: *Tiburon de Mazarrón*, nickname for the precociously talented Pedro Acosta. The talented teenager hails from Puerto de Mazarrón, in Murcia on the Mediterranean coast. 'Tiburon' means shark.

His first ever race at Portimao in April had been rewarded with the finest of victories, just 0.051s ahead of Dennis Foggia's Honda. Then he surged ahead in the championship, winning five of the first ten races to lead nearest rival Sergio Garcia by 53 points, and fourth-placed Foggia by 97.

There had been no more wins, however, while Foggia's purple patch had featured three wins, a second and two thirds in the six races since then. The Italian (Shark of Rome?) arrived at Portimao 21 points adrift, with a small, but real chance of overturning the championship.

It was resolved with high drama. Foggia led most of the race and seemed able to repulse the rookie. When Acosta seized the lead on the final lap with a block pass at Turn Four, Foggia slowed on entry, planning an exit attack.

Right behind, Darryn Binder cut inside for his own victory bid, only to find Foggia in his path. They collided. Foggia fell off. End of championship.

It was a significant triumph for Acosta, who had impressed all season with his talent and maturity, one day short (at 17 years and 166 days) of 1990's youngest ever champion, Loris Capirossi.

And opprobrium for Binder, so recently luxuriating in confirmation of a move to MotoGP. At least, that is how some observers took it, including the FIM stewards, who disqualified him forthwith from fourth. Some MotoGP riders, including Foggia's compatriot, Bagnaia, eagerly joined the condemnation, suggesting a super-licence for riders before graduating to MotoGP: "We have seen a lot of crashes like this from him. Next year, [he] will be with us, and with MotoGP we are faster. I hope that will not happen."

Jack Miller, who also had leapfrogged Moto2 and understood from first-hand experience the pressure of going from Moto3 to MotoGP, was more understanding: "Darryn is a bit wild … but this is racing. Accidents like that can happen." It was a welcome dose of rationality when feelings were running so high that when Binder went to Foggia's pit after the race to explain, he was angrily shooed out.

Ironically, a week later, Foggia knocked Acosta down with a much more cynical move, but received only a derisory three-second penalty.

That left only Moto2 to be decided, and by comparison, progress in the middle class was serene, after the teammate protagonists had each blundered in the past two rounds. Gardner profited from a wiser tyre choice, took over the lead halfway to take the flag three seconds clear and stretched his 18-point margin to a slightly more comfortable 23. In contrast to the ill feeling in Moto3, Fernandez was one of the first riders to congratulate Gardner on the slow-down lap.

Present at the track, for the first time since 2018, was a former superstar who was no stranger to psychological warfare. Casey Stoner spent time spotting for Ducati out on track, prompting Antipodean compatriot Miller to propose that he be employed more often in that capacity, his advice having been most helpful in putting the factory bikes first and second on the grid, and first and third past the chequered flag, securing the constructors' championship for the Bologna firm.

Stoner spoke of health issues over recent years, blamed on chronic fatigue syndrome: "I couldn't get off the couch for basically five months. I've had to learn to walk everywhere, which I hate, I always used to jog just about everywhere." He also met old arch-rival and sometimes nemesis Valentino Rossi, and paid a typically carefully-wrought tribute: "One thing that was fantastic about racing Valentino, and it's what I got to learn from him, whether on track or off the track: with his media, he was always very savvy and very clever, very cunning. I think also my achievements were validated all the more having raced against him in his era."

In the top satellite Ducati team, rookie sensation Jorge Martin admitted to being a little scared when returning to the scene of a horrific crash that had occurred in practice in April. Eight fractures had been enough to make him fear that his career was over: "When I knew we were coming back to Portimao, I was a bit scared because at the end of day, it changed my life. After this crash, I didn't know if I could be back on the bike again."

A strange sight on Friday: red tail-lights on the MotoGP bikes, in dazzling sun. Usually, they are only used in the wet or low visibility, but this trial was to check visibility in full daylight (Race Control can send signals to turn the lights on when the bikes are on track) as a potential extra safety measure to warn riders of an incident ahead, after several lethal on-track collisions.

MOTOGP RACE – 23 laps (shortened)

For the second time in the season, and in two consecutive races, Quartararo was off the front row. Fastest on Friday, he ended up leading row three. Up front, Bagnaia finally got ahead of Miller with a new circuit best lap. Alongside, amazingly his first time ever qualified in the top three, defending champion Mir.

Martin and Zarco led row two from Pol Espargaro. The next best Honda was Alex Marquez's, in a career-best eighth, between Quartararo and Morbidelli.

Miller got the jump off the line, Bagnaia took over on the exit of Turn Four, and by the end of the lap, Mir was also ahead. The pair established an early lead over the Australian, who was left to defend third from Martin, Marquez and Quartararo. At the same time, Zarco, Lecuona and Pol Espargaro were not far behind.

Unlike Alex Marquez, past Martin at Turn Four, Quartararo remained stuck behind the rookie's faster Ducati: "Even if he was riding one second slower, I couldn't overtake." Desperation, and mistakes, began to set in,

Mir stuck with Bagnaia in the early laps, but any hopes of ending Suzuki's year-long victory duck started to fade on lap nine, when the Ducati began to stretch ahead by two-tenths per lap. By lap 11, the lead surpassed one second, and Bagnaia could cruise to his third victory in five races, having set fastest lap on the fifth, short of the record, and 2.4 seconds clear at the end. "Everything was coming better and better every lap," he said.

Mir had a similarly lonely ride behind, but there was more jeopardy in the fight for third.

An inspired Marquez was more than making up for his older brother's absence, leaving Martin behind as he closed in on old Moto3 foe Miller. He cut past on lap 12 into the first corner. Miller stayed calm and held firm, saving his rear tyre for a final push. By lap 19, it was time to attack, and he duplicated the Turn One outbraking move, only to run mar-

Above: The World Champion folds his arms for impact – it was his first non-finish of the season.
Photo: Gold & Goose

Above right: Second place and his fifth podium returned the smile to ex-champion Joan Mir's face.
Photo: www.suxuki-racing.com

Above far right: Little brother at play. Fourth was easily Alex Marquez's best race of the year.

Right: Moto3 mayhem, with Pedro Acosta pursued by Garcia (11), Foggia (7), Binder(40) and Migno (16).

Below right: Marco Bezzecchi's soft rear tyre is starting to fade as Gardner begins to reel him in.
Photos: Gold & Goose

ginally wide on the exit and cede the place again. But on lap 21, another chance arose when the Honda ran slightly wide. Miller was back in third, and it was Marquez's turn to watch and wait. In vain, as it transpired.

Quartararo's difficult afternoon was compounded by a massive front-end slide at Turn 13 on the 11th lap. He lost sixth place to Zarco. At the same time, Pol Espargaro was closing threateningly.

Battle raged, and on lap 18, Quartararo was briefly ahead of Zarco. Next next time around, Zarco was ahead and then promptly also past Martin. Quartararo aimed to follow him through, and did nip inside the Spaniard, only to slide off a couple of corners later, once again the victim of rising front-tyre temperature when stuck in a group of faster bikes. It was his first non-finish of the year.

Rins had been running alone in eighth, but now he had a sniff of the fading Martin and closed to within just over a second on lap 22. A couple of seconds behind, a fearsome foursome were at each other: Bastianini finally ahead of Oliveira, with two more KTM riders, Binder and Lecuona, exchanging blows.

On lap 23, Lecuona made a desperate lunge on Oliveira, sliding off in the process and knocking the Portuguese rider flying. Red flags were shown the following lap as Oliveira (winded, but not seriously hurt) was stretchered away, and results were declared at the end of lap 23.

That put Miller third, and added to Quartararo's misfortune, Ducati sealed the constructors' title for the second straight year. Marquez was a season-best fourth, with Zarco's solid fifth place enough to secure him the title of the year's top Independent rider.

Espargaro was a muted sixth at the end of a weekend that had promised more; Martin lucky to hold on to seventh from Rins, who had finished lap one 13th.

Bastianini and Binder were narrowly ahead of Nakagami, whose run through from the back of the grid, after a crash in qualifying, might have yielded better than 11th in a full-length race.

Marini was just ahead of Rossi for 12th, the next quartet still close, inside two seconds, but only Dovizioso and Bradl in the points. Vinales and Morbidelli missed out.

Petrucci was squeezed off and crashed out on the first lap; Aleix Espargaro suffered the same fate from 15th eight laps later.

The top championship positions were now set, but Miller's podium put him past Zarco again for fourth; Binder closed to equal points with the absent Marc Marquez for sixth.

MOTO2 RACE – 23 laps

The first match point ensured maximum tension in the Red Bull Ajo team pit. With an 18-point lead and one more mistake from his team-mate, Gardner could tie it up. Equally, put things the other way around, and Fernandez could prolong the agony. Each had crashed out in the previous two races, so nothing was certain.

Gardner led FP1, Fernandez FP2 – when the stakes were raised when the former crashed after running into the back wheel of an unexpectedly slow Marcos Ramirez. He walked away, keeping it secret that he had suffered left-side rib fractures from the bruising high-speed fall.

Fernandez took pole, his seventh; Gardner was second, with Di Giannantonio completing row one. Canet, Augusto Fernandez and Beaubier were behind, the American equalling his second row at CoTA at a familiar circuit.

The race would be decided by rubber. Dunlop had brought a softer rear compared with the April visit, but on Friday, a spokesman asserted that it would not last race distance. That was until Raul did a consistent long run in FP3 on it, which convinced him to use it for the race, and turned other riders' heads, including that of Bezzecchi.

Gardner stuck with the hard rear, and he slotted in behind when Raul got the jump. Nor was it surprising when Bezzecchi took second off him on lap three.

The grippier tyre had flattered to deceive. Nine laps in, Gardner retook second from the Italian and set about closing a nine-tenths gap. Within four laps, he was in front, and despite Fernandez's efforts, sitting half a second behind, it was clear by lap 20 that his grip levels were diminishing.

Gardner could ease off to secure this most important race by three seconds.

Fernandez was now forced to look over his shoulder, with Lowes closing to within less than a second over the line.

The Englishman had broken free from a pursuit group where, in the early stages, Canet and Beaubier had disputed control, with Vierge in close attendance, plus Di Giannantonio and Ogura. The Japanese slipped off on lap 11, and a foot fracture ended a worthwhile rookie season early. Vierge also crashed out of the group.

On lap seven, Lowes had taken over and moved away, and

by lap 17, he had caught and passed Bezzecchi, who carried on losing places as his tyre choice played him foul.

Beaubier and Canet continued to dispute fourth, the American ahead until the last lap, when the Spaniard seized the initiative, just five-thousandths of a second ahead over the line. Fifth still equalled Beaubier's best finish.

Vietti made another trademark run through from 15th on lap one to sixth, getting there with three laps to go. His last victim had been fading team-mate Bezzecchi, who then succumbed to Navarro with two laps to go, the Boscoscuro rider less than a second behind Vietti.

Augusto Fernandez was ninth at the head of the next trio, from Schrotter and Di Giannantonio. Garzo, Manzi and Ramirez finished off the points. Chantra, Arenas and Dixon swelled the crash list.

MOTO3 RACE – 23 laps

Pedro Acosta might have qualified 14th, ten places behind title rival Foggia, but he was confident that he could still clinch the title with a race to spare, as evidenced by his cheeky wave and then wheel bump to his adversary at the end of warm-up on Sunday morning.

That niggle set the scene for a glorious contest that settled this slow-burner title fight. As per recent form, it was no surprise to see Foggia hitting the front as early as lap two. But this time, he didn't have the speed to pull clear. Soon, Acosta was cutting through the pack.

By the third lap, Foggia led Binder, Artigas and Acosta; five laps later, Masia, Migno, Antonelli and Garcia had swelled the group. But even in the crowd, Acosta wouldn't be denied. He led once more with three laps to go, only to lose out to Foggia the following lap.

This was set to go to the flag, until Acosta's last-lap pass at Turn Four lifted Foggia up. As the Italian lost speed midturn, Binder clattered in from behind, taking him down along with Garcia.

Acosta held off Migno by three-tenths; Antonelli, Alcoba, Guevara, Sasaki and Artigas taking third to eighth inside 1.5 seconds. Binder had been fourth, but was disqualified.

Suzuki was still close; Salac completed the top ten; Masia crashed out, as did McPhee. Australian Joel Kelso, subbing for a third time for an ailing Koffler, took two points for 14th.

Acosta and Foggia were now unassailable in the championship; Garcia, in third, under threat from Fenati and Masia.

ALGARVE GRAND PRIX 219

FIM WORLD CHAMPIONSHIP: ROUND 17

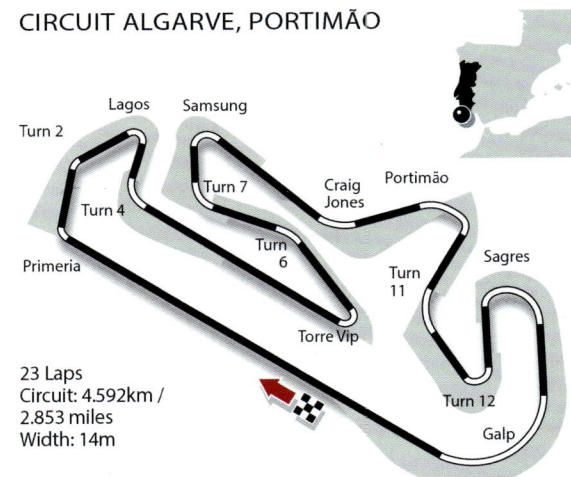

GRANDE PRÉMIO BREMBO DO ALGARVE

5-7 NOVEMBER, 2021

CIRCUIT ALGARVE, PORTIMÃO

23 Laps
Circuit: 4.592km / 2.853 miles
Width: 14m

MotoGP

RACE DISTANCE: 23 laps, 65.627 miles/105.616km · RACE WEATHER: Dry (air 21°, humidity 21%, track 29°)

Pos.	Rider	Nat.	No.	Entrant	Machine	Tyres	Race tyre choice	Laps	Time & speed
1	Francesco Bagnaia	ITA	63	Ducati Lenovo Team	Ducati Desmosedici	M	F: Medium/R: Medium	23	38m 17.720s 102.8mph/ 165.4km/h
2	Joan Mir	SPA	36	Team SUZUKI ECSTAR	Suzuki GSX-RR	M	F: Medium/R: Medium	23	38m 20.198s
3	Jack Miller	AUS	43	Ducati Lenovo Team	Ducati Desmosedici	M	F: Medium/R: Medium	23	38m 24.122s
4	Alex Marquez	SPA	73	LCR Honda CASTROL	Honda RC213V	M	F: Medium/R: Hard	23	38m 24.173s
5	Johann Zarco	FRA	5	Pramac Racing	Ducati Desmosedici	M	F: Medium/R: Hard	23	38m 25.602s
6	Pol Espargaro	SPA	44	Repsol Honda Team	Honda RC213V	M	F: Medium/R: Hard	23	38m 27.293s
7	Jorge Martin	SPA	89	Pramac Racing	Ducati Desmosedici	M	F: Medium/R: Medium	23	38m 27.864s
8	Alex Rins	SPA	42	Team SUZUKI ECSTAR	Suzuki GSX-RR	M	F: Medium/R: Medium	23	38m 28.462s
9	Enea Bastianini	ITA	23	Avintia Esponsorama	Ducati Desmosedici	M	F: Medium/R: Medium	23	38m 31.560s
10	Brad Binder	RSA	33	Red Bull KTM Factory Racing	KTM RC16	M	F: Medium/R: Hard	23	38m 32.207s
11	Takaaki Nakagami	JPN	30	LCR Honda IDEMITSU	Honda RC213V	M	F: Medium/R: Hard	23	38m 38.632s
12	Luca Marini	ITA	10	SKY VR46 Avintia	Ducati Desmosedici	M	F: Medium/R: Medium	23	38m 40.170s
13	Valentino Rossi	ITA	46	Petronas Yamaha SRT	Yamaha YZR-M1	M	F: Medium/R: Medium	23	38m 40.472s
14	Andrea Dovizioso	ITA	4	Petronas Yamaha SRT	Yamaha YZR-M1	M	F: Medium/R: Hard	23	38m 43.927s
15	Stefan Bradl	GER	6	Repsol Honda Team	Honda RC213V	M	F: Medium/R: Medium	23	38m 44.004s
16	Maverick Vinales	SPA	12	Aprilia Racing Team Gresini	Aprilia RS-GP	M	F: Medium/R: Medium	23	38m 44.548s
17	Franco Morbidelli	ITA	21	Monster Energy Yamaha MotoGP	Yamaha YZR-M1	M	F: Medium/R: Hard	23	38m 45.583s
	Miguel Oliveira	POR	88	Red Bull KTM Factory Racing	KTM RC16	M	F: Medium/R: Hard	22	DNF-crash
	Iker Lecuona	SPA	27	Tech 3 KTM Factory Racing	KTM RC16	M	F: Medium/R: Hard	22	DNF-crash
	Fabio Quartararo	FRA	20	Monster Energy Yamaha MotoGP	Yamaha YZR-M1	M	F: Medium/R: Medium	20	DNF-crash
	Aleix Espargaro	SPA	41	Aprilia Racing Team Gresini	Aprilia RS-GP	M	F: Medium/R: Medium	7	DNF-crash
	Danilo Petrucci	ITA	9	Tech 3 KTM Factory Racing	KTM RC16	M	F: Medium/R: Hard	0	DNF-crash

Fastest lap: Francesco Bagnaia, on lap 5, 1m 39.467s, 103.2mph/166.1km/h.
Lap record: Francesco Bagnaia, 1m 38.725s, 104.0mph/167.4km/h (2021).
Event maximum speed: Johann Zarco, 218.5mph/351.7km/h (race).

Qualifying

Weather: Dry
Air Temp: 19° **Humidity:** 27%
Track Temp: 27°

1	Bagnaia	1m 38.725s
2	Miller	1m 38.829s
3	Mir	1m 38.893s
4	Martin	1m 38.916s
5	Zarco	1m 38.918s
6	P. Espargaro	1m 39.058s
7	Quartararo	1m 39.131s
8	A. Marquez	1m 39.191s
9	Morbidelli	1m 39.321s
10	Lecuona	1m 39.387s
11	Rins	1m 39.649s
12	Marini	1m 39.828s

Q1

13	Bastianini	1m 39.283s
14	A. Espargaro	1m 39.389s
15	Petrucci	1m 39.595s
16	Rossi	1m 39.604s
17	Oliveira	1m 39.624s
18	Vinales	1m 39.738s
19	Binder	1m 39.859s
20	Bradl	1m 39.907s
21	Dovizioso	1m 39.918s
22	Nakagami	1m 40.009s

Fastest race laps

1	Bagnaia	1m 39.467s
2	Zarco	1m 39.484s
3	Miller	1m 39.539s
4	Martin	1m 39.549s
5	Mir	1m 39.572s
6	Quartararo	1m 39.574s
7	P. Espargaro	1m 39.580s
8	A. Marquez	1m 39.618s
9	Rins	1m 39.657s
10	Lecuona	1m 39.705s
11	Binder	1m 39.806s
12	Bastianini	1m 39.846s
13	Oliveira	1m 39.850s
14	Nakagami	1m 39.985s
15	A. Espargaro	1m 40.140s
16	Vinales	1m 40.153s
17	Rossi	1m 40.231s
18	Bradl	1m 40.275s
19	Morbidelli	1m 40.280s
20	Marini	1m 40.293s
21	Dovizioso	1m 40.371s

Championship Points

1	Quartararo	267
2	Bagnaia	227
3	Mir	195
4	Miller	165
5	Zarco	163
6	M. Marquez	142
7	Binder	142
8	A. Espargaro	113
9	Vinales	106
10	P. Espargaro	100
11	Rins	99
12	Bastianini	94
13	Oliveira	92
14	Martin	91
15	Nakagami	76
16	A. Marquez	67
17	Morbidelli	42
18	Marini	41
19	Lecuona	38
20	Rossi	38
21	Petrucci	37
22	Bradl	14
23	Pirro	12
24	Dovizioso	8
25	Pedrosa	6
26	Savadori	4
27	Rabat	1

Constructor Points

1	Ducati	332
2	Yamaha	298
3	Suzuki	227
4	Honda	211
5	KTM	196
6	Aprilia	114

Grid order / Lap leaders

Grid	Rider	1	2	3	4	5	6	7	8	9	10	11	12	13	14	15	16	17	18	19	20	21	22	23
63	BAGNAIA	63	63	63	63	63	63	63	63	63	63	63	63	63	63	63	63	63	63	63	63	63	63	63
43	MILLER	36	36	36	36	36	36	36	36	36	36	36	36	36	36	36	36	36	36	36	36	36	36	36
36	MIR	43	43	43	43	43	43	43	43	43	43	73	73	73	73	73	73	73	73	43	43	43	43	43
89	MARTIN	89	89	89	73	73	73	73	73	73	73	43	43	43	43	43	43	43	43	73	73	73	73	73
5	ZARCO	73	73	73	89	89	89	89	89	89	89	89	89	89	89	89	89	89	89	5	5	5	5	5
44	P. ESPARGARO	44	20	20	20	20	20	20	20	20	20	5	5	5	5	5	5	5	20	20	5	89	44	44
20	QUARTARARO	27	27	27	5	5	5	5	5	5	5	20	20	20	20	20	20	20	5	5	20	44	89	89
73	A. MARQUEZ	20	5	5	27	27	27	44	44	44	44	44	44	44	44	44	44	44	44	44	44	42	42	42
21	MORBIDELLI	5	44	44	44	44	44	88	88	42	42	42	42	42	42	42	42	42	42	42	42	23	23	23
27	LECUONA	41	88	88	88	88	88	42	42	88	88	88	88	88	88	88	88	88	88	88	27	88	33	
42	RINS	21	21	42	42	42	42	23	23	23	23	23	23	23	23	23	23	23	23	88	33	30		
10	MARINI	88	23	23	23	23	23	27	27	27	33	33	33	33	33	27	27	27	27	33	27	10		
23	BASTIANINI	42	42	21	21	21	21	33	33	33	33	33	33	33	33	33	33	33	33	30	30	46		
41	A. ESPARGARO	23	33	33	21	21	21	21	21	21	30	30	30	30	30	30	30	30	30	10	10	4		
9	PETRUCCI	33	46	46	46	46	41	41	30	30	30	21	21	10	10	10	10	10	10	46	46	6		
46	ROSSI	46	41	41	41	41	46	30	46	46	46	46	46	10	21	46	46	46	46	46	4	4	12	
88	OLIVEIRA	10	10	10	10	10	30	46	10	10	10	10	46	46	6	6	6	6	4	6	6	21		
12	VINALES	6	30	30	30	30	10	10	6	6	6	6	6	6	4	4	4	4	6	21	12			
33	BINDER	30	6	6	6	6	6	6	4	4	4	4	4	4	12	12	21	21	21	4	21			
6	BRADL	4	4	4	4	4	4	12	12	12	12	12	12	12	21	21	12	12	12					
4	DOVIZIOSO	12	12	12	12	12	12																	
30	NAKAGAMI																							

220 ALGARVE GRAND PRIX

Moto2

RACE DISTANCE: 23 laps, 65.627 miles/105.616km · **RACE WEATHER:** Dry (air 21°, humidity 22%, track 27°)

Pos.	Rider	Nat.	No.	Entrant	Machine	Laps	Time & Speed
1	Remy Gardner	AUS	87	Red Bull KTM Ajo	Kalex	23	39m 36.275s 99.4mph/160.0km/h
2	Raul Fernandez	SPA	25	Red Bull KTM Ajo	Kalex	23	39m 39.289s
3	Sam Lowes	GBR	22	Elf Marc VDS Racing Team	Kalex	23	39m 40.174s
4	Aron Canet	SPA	44	QuieroCorredor Aspar Team	Boscoscuro	23	39m 43.891s
5	Cameron Beaubier	USA	6	American Racing	Kalex	23	39m 43.896s
6	Celestino Vietti	ITA	13	SKY Racing Team VR46	Kalex	23	39m 46.296s
7	Jorge Navarro	SPA	9	Termozeta Speed Up	Boscoscuro	23	39m 47.183s
8	Marco Bezzecchi	ITA	72	SKY Racing Team VR46	Kalex	23	39m 47.861s
9	Augusto Fernandez	SPA	37	Elf Marc VDS Racing Team	Kalex	23	39m 49.396s
10	Marcel Schrotter	GER	23	Liqui Moly Intact GP	Kalex	23	39m 49.561s
11	Fabio Di Giannantonio	ITA	21	Federal Oil Gresini Moto2	Kalex	23	39m 50.889s
12	Hector Garzo	SPA	40	Flexbox HP40	Kalex	23	40m 01.813s
13	Stefano Manzi	ITA	62	Flexbox HP40	Kalex	23	40m 02.786s
14	Marcos Ramirez	SPA	42	American Racing	Kalex	23	40m 03.500s
15	Bo Bendsneyder	NED	64	Pertamina Mandalika SAG Team	Kalex	23	40m 04.620s
16	Fermin Aldeguer	SPA	54	Termozeta Speed Up	Boscoscuro	23	40m 04.687s
17	Simone Corsi	ITA	24	MV Agusta Forward Racing	MV Agusta	23	40m 08.557s
18	Hafizh Syahrin	MAL	55	NTS RW Racing GP	NTS	23	40m 11.662s
19	Thomas Luthi	SWI	12	Pertamina Mandalika SAG Team	Kalex	23	40m 15.459s
20	Tony Arbolino	ITA	14	Liqui Moly Intact GP	Kalex	23	40m 20.078s
21	Tetsuta Nagashima	JPN	45	Italtrans Racing Team	Kalex	23	40m 19.707s
22	Nicolo Bulega	ITA	11	Federal Oil Gresini Moto2	Kalex	23	40m 19.766s
23	Barry Baltus	BEL	70	NTS RW Racing GP	NTS	23	40m 22.122s
24	Joe Roberts	USA	16	Italtrans Racing Team	Kalex	23	40m 30.625s
25	Piotr Biesiekirski	POL	74	Pertamina Mandalika SAG Euvic	Kalex	23	40m 44.894s
	Lorenzo Baldassarri	ITA	7	MV Agusta Forward Racing	MV Agusta	14	DNF-ret in pit
	Xavi Vierge	SPA	97	Petronas Sprinta Racing	Kalex	10	DNF-crash
	Jake Dixon	GBR	96	Petronas Sprinta Racing	Kalex	9	DNF-crash
	Ai Ogura	JPN	79	IDEMITSU Honda Team Asia	Kalex	2	DNF-crash
	Albert Arenas	SPA	75	QuieroCorredor Aspar Team	Boscoscuro	1	DNF-crash
	Somkiat Chantra	THA	35	IDEMITSU Honda Team Asia	Kalex	-	DSQ

Fastest lap: Cameron Beaubier, on lap 12, 1m 42.671s, 100.0mph/161.0km/h.
Lap record: Raul Fernandez, 1m 42.101s, 100.6mph/161.9km/h (2021).
Event maximum speed: Fermin Aldeguer, 183.3mph/295.0km/h (race).

Qualifying: Weather: Dry, Air: 17°, Track: 25°, Humidity: 31%

1	R. Fernandez	1m 42.101s
2	Gardner	1m 42.370s
3	Di Giannantonio	1m 42.506s
4	Canet	1m 42.511s
5	A. Fernandez	1m 42.616s
6	Beaubier	1m 42.620s
7	Bezzecchi	1m 42.697s
8	Lowes	1m 42.701s
9	Ogura	1m 42.783s
10	Navarro	1m 42.822s
11	Vierge	1m 42.829s
12	Garzo	1m 42.980s
13	Ramirez	1m 43.023s
14	Vietti	1m 43.034s
15	Schrotter	1m 43.078s
16	Syahrin	1m 43.178s
17	Manzi	1m 43.353s
18	Arenas	1m 43.367s

Q1
19	Chantra	1m 43.288s
20	Dixon	1m 43.545s
21	Corsi	1m 43.554s
22	Roberts	1m 43.554s
23	Arbolino	1m 43.605s
24	Luthi	1m 43.617s
25	Nagashima	1m 43.642s
26	Baltus	1m 43.781s
27	Bulega	1m 43.895s
28	Aldeguer	1m 43.979s
29	Bendsneyder	1m 44.014s
30	Baldassarri	1m 44.691s
31	Biesiekirski	1m 45.819s

Fastest race laps

1	Beaubier	1m 42.671s
2	Bezzecchi	1m 42.685s
3	R. Fernandez	1m 42.714s
4	Gardner	1m 42.782s
5	Vietti	1m 42.971s
6	Lowes	1m 42.989s
7	Canet	1m 43.007s
8	Navarro	1m 43.013s
9	Vierge	1m 43.061s
10	Di Giannantonio	1m 43.113s
11	A. Fernandez	1m 43.162s
12	Ramirez	1m 43.200s
13	Schrotter	1m 43.212s
14	Manzi	1m 43.270s
15	Dixon	1m 43.331s
16	Garzo	1m 43.364s
17	Ogura	1m 43.516s
18	Aldeguer	1m 43.623s
19	Luthi	1m 43.674s
20	Syahrin	1m 43.694s
21	Bendsneyder	1m 43.733s
22	Roberts	1m 43.785s
23	Nagashima	1m 43.811s
24	Corsi	1m 43.929s
25	Bulega	1m 44.128s
26	Baltus	1m 44.330s
27	Arbolino	1m 44.451s
28	Baldassarri	1m 45.050s
29	Biesiekirski	1m 45.357s

Championship Points

1	Gardner	305
2	R. Fernandez	282
3	Bezzecchi	214
4	Lowes	181
5	A. Fernandez	158
6	Canet	153
7	Di Giannantonio	141
8	Ogura	120
9	Navarro	98
10	Schrotter	91
11	Vierge	83
12	Vietti	76
13	Roberts	59
14	Arbolino	51
15	Beaubier	50
16	Bendsneyder	46
17	Chantra	37
18	Ramirez	37
19	Manzi	33
20	Dixon	30
21	Arenas	28
22	Luthi	23
23	Garzo	16
24	Corsi	16
25	Aldeguer	13
26	Bulega	12
27	Dalla Porta	10
28	Syahrin	8
29	Lopez	4
30	Baldassarri	3
31	Baltus	2

Constructor Points

1	Kalex	425
2	Boscoscuro	188
3	MV Agusta	19
4	NTS	10

Moto3

RACE DISTANCE: 21 laps, 59.920 miles/96.432km · **RACE WEATHER:** Dry (air 19°, humidity 24%, track 26°)

Pos.	Rider	Nat.	No.	Entrant	Machine	Laps	Time & Speed
1	Pedro Acosta	SPA	37	Red Bull KTM Ajo	KTM	21	38m 04.339s 94.4mph/151.9km/h
2	Andrea Migno	ITA	16	Rivacold Snipers Team	Honda	21	38m 04.693s
3	Niccolo Antonelli	ITA	23	Avintia VR46	KTM	21	38m 05.219s
4	Jeremy Alcoba	SPA	52	Indonesian Racing Gresini Moto3	Honda	21	38m 06.107s
5	Izan Guevara	SPA	28	MuchoNeumatico GASGAS Aspar Team	GASGAS	21	38m 06.178s
6	Ayumu Sasaki	JPN	71	Red Bull KTM Tech 3	KTM	21	38m 06.213s
7	Romano Fenati	ITA	55	Sterilgarda Max Racing Team	Husqvarna	21	38m 06.311s
8	Xavier Artigas	SPA	43	Leopard Racing	Honda	21	38m 06.672s
9	Tatsuki Suzuki	JPN	24	SIC58 Squadra Corse	Honda	21	38m 07.762s
10	Filip Salac	CZE	12	CarXpert PruestelGP	KTM	21	38m 10.930s
11	Adrian Fernandez	SPA	31	Sterilgarda Max Racing Team	Husqvarna	21	38m 11.279s
12	Carlos Tatay	SPA	99	Avintia Esponsorama Moto3	KTM	21	38m 13.731s
13	Daniel Holgado	SPA	96	Red Bull KTM Tech 3	KTM	21	38m 14.269s
14	Joel Kelso	AUS	66	CIP Green Power	KTM	21	38m 14.335s
15	Alberto Surra	ITA	67	Rivacold Snipers Team	Honda	21	38m 14.755s
16	Stefano Nepa	ITA	82	BOE Owlride	KTM	21	38m 15.989s
17	Lorenzo Fellon	FRA	20	SIC58 Squadra Corse	Honda	21	38m 16.034s
18	Riccardo Rossi	ITA	54	BOE Owlride	KTM	21	38m 16.075s
19	Jaume Masia	SPA	5	Red Bull KTM Ajo	KTM	21	38m 17.955s
20	Yuki Kunii	JPN	92	Honda Team Asia	Honda	21	38m 34.340s
21	Ryusei Yamanaka	JPN	6	CarXpert PruestelGP	KTM	21	38m 34.522s
22	Andi Farid Izdihar	INA	19	Honda Team Asia	Honda	21	38m 34.588s
	Kaito Toba	JPN	27	CIP Green Power	KTM	13	Not classified
	Dennis Foggia	ITA	7	Leopard Racing	Honda	20	DNF-crash
	Sergio Garcia	SPA	11	MuchoNeumatico GASGAS Aspar Team	GASGAS	20	DNF-crash
	John McPhee	GBR	17	Petronas Sprinta Racing	Honda	4	DNF-crash
	Darryn Binder	RSA	40	Petronas Sprinta Racing	Honda	-	DSQ

Fastest lap: Jaume Masia, on lap 8, 1m 47.666s, 95.4mph/153.5km/h.
Lap record: Sergio Garcia, 1m 47.274s, 95.8mph/154.1km/h (2021).
Event maximum speed: Lorenzo Fellon, 155.7mph/250.5km/h (race).

Qualifying: Weather: Dry, Air: 18°, Track: 28°, Humidity: 30%

1	Garcia	1m 47.274s
2	McPhee	1m 47.291s
3	Fernandez	1m 47.404s
4	Foggia	1m 47.517s
5	Masia	1m 47.570s
6	Artigas	1m 47.586s
7	Binder	1m 47.712s
8	Antonelli	1m 47.774s
9	Salac	1m 47.811s
10	Sasaki	1m 47.817s
11	Alcoba	1m 47.829s
12	Guevara	1m 47.835s
13	Fenati	1m 47.900s
14	Acosta	1m 47.986s
15	Surra	1m 48.096s
16	Migno	1m 48.270s
17	Kunii	1m 48.682s
18	Suzuki	No Time

Q1
19	Kelso	1m 48.990s
20	Rossi	1m 49.042s
21	Holgado	1m 49.074s
22	Nepa	1m 49.085s
23	Fellon	1m 49.127s
24	Yamanaka	1m 49.179s
25	Izdihar	1m 49.192s
26	Tatay	1m 49.213s
27	Toba	1m 50.196s

Fastest race laps

1	Masia	1m 47.666s
2	Fenati	1m 47.675s
3	Alcoba	1m 47.724s
4	Sasaki	1m 47.737s
5	Migno	1m 47.783s
6	Artigas	1m 47.816s
7	Antonelli	1m 47.856s
8	Garcia	1m 47.868s
9	Rossi	1m 47.879s
10	Acosta	1m 47.904s
11	Fernandez	1m 47.917s
12	Salac	1m 47.960s
13	Binder	1m 47.986s
14	Guevara	1m 48.012s
15	Holgado	1m 48.032s
16	Suzuki	1m 48.069s
17	Foggia	1m 48.129s
18	Kelso	1m 48.224s
19	Nepa	1m 48.251s
20	Surra	1m 48.313s
21	McPhee	1m 48.350s
22	Kunii	1m 48.351s
23	Fellon	1m 48.366s
24	Yamanaka	1m 48.495s
25	Tatay	1m 48.548s
26	Izdihar	1m 49.147s
27	Toba	1m 50.891s

Championship Points

1	Acosta	259
2	Foggia	213
3	Garcia	168
4	Fenati	156
5	Masia	155
6	Antonelli	145
7	Binder	136
8	Guevara	116
9	Sasaki	114
10	Migno	110
11	Alcoba	85
12	Oncu	84
13	Suzuki	76
14	McPhee	72
15	Toba	64
16	Rodrigo	60
17	Salac	58
18	Nepa	53
19	Artigas	47
20	Yamanaka	47
21	Tatay	32
22	Rossi	29
23	Fernandez	28
24	Dupasquier	27
25	Kunii	15
26	Kofler	10
27	Bartolini	7
28	Holgado	4
29	Izdihar	4
30	Azman	3
31	Kelso	2
32	Surra	1

Constructor Points

1	KTM	353
2	Honda	335
3	GASGAS	246
4	Husqvarna	162

Above: "After you, Signor." Pupil Franco Morbidelli escorted Rossi home to complete "my best race of the season."
Photo: Gold & Goose

Top: Twenty-six years, and 'The Doctor' remained irrepressible.
Photo: MotoGP.com/Gold & Goose

Right: Covid restrictions suspended, massed fans came to bid farewell.
Photo: Gold & Goose

VALENCIA GRAND PRIX

FIM WORLD CHAMPIONSHIP · ROUND 18

RICARDO TORMO CIRCUIT

Above: While the winners celebrated on the podium, the Rossi gang partied in his pit. Protégés Migno and Bezzecchi acted as cheerleaders.
Photo: MotoGP.com /Gold & Goose

Top right: After more than 300 races, former 125 champion Tom Luthi also brought the curtain down.
Photo: Gold & Goose

Above right: Bagnaia and Martin were in total command for Ducati.
Photo: Ducati Corse

Right: Popular Danilo Petrucci bowed out of MotoGP. Next stop, the Dakar Rally in 2022.
Photo: Tech3 KTM

THE Valentino Rossi farewell tour reached its climax at Valencia, and the veteran went out on a high. Qualifying and finishing tenth was an upgrade in itself. More important, the fanfare of love and support. Several old rivals, including Casey Stoner, Jorge Lorenzo and Max Biaggi, were present, as was a capacity crowd of 75,000 fans, and the intensity of the media spotlight. Rossi did well to find the relevant focus for his final bow.

The 42-year-old was determined to end his two-wheeled racing career on a high: "In the last races, we improved a lot the bike and we worked well together with … all the team. They give to me a fantastic support because the season was long and not easy.

"After the Algarve GP [where he finished 13th], we speak together, and I said, 'In Valencia, we have to give the maximum, because it's the last race. That track is the worst for me, and I don't want to arrive last.' So to finish in the top ten today, I think this is the best race of my season. I enjoyed very much."

The day closed, after fireworks and fiestas, with Rossi's admission to the MotoGP Hall of Fame, when he was officially inducted and named a Legend.

As if nobody knew that already.

Any regrets? "That it's finished," he said.

Not present to share the moment, the next great legend, Marc Marquez. Repsol team manager Alberto Puig had no further news of his worrying condition: "It's not a bone – it's something more complicated, more delicate. You have to be calm and see how it goes … the doctor was positive, but we have to be patient. Marc will take this with calm."

Marquez faced a fourth successive winter of uncertainty and rehabilitation in a row, after 2019 (left shoulder injury), 2020 (right shoulder injury) and 2021 (upper right arm injury). Honda faced an anxious wait to see if its star would be ready once pre-season testing resumes in February.

And that anxiety was made the more acute on Saturday morning, when their sole remaining rider, Pol Espargaro, suffered a mighty crash at the fastest corner of the tight little track. In good form after finishing Friday second fastest, Pol was looking to improve on a cool, but sunny FP3, opening the throttle on the left-hander, a favourite spot for paddock aficionados and photographers to catch the angle of slide at high speed. The Honda slewed sideways and flung him spinning through the air, to a hard landing.

Mercifully, nothing was broken after an accident that observers thought the bike's electronics should have prevented (as with Marquez at Assen), but he had received a heavy impact and was taken to hospital for examination, which revealed no fractures. "But I have a lot of pain from around my ribs when I breathe," he said. Clearly, he was out of the race, but he was able to join the crucial first 2022 tests on the ensuing Thursday and Friday at Jerez – a last chance to test engine upgrades that had been frozen for two years.

It was the first time with no factory Honda on the grid since the 1992 Dutch TT, when both Mick Doohan and Wayne Gardner had crashed in practice, and a wretched end to a complicated year for the beleaguered marque.

Rossi wasn't the only MotoGP rider to say goodbye to the paddock. Iker Lecuona departed for WorldSBK, where a factory Honda team ride was some compensation after a spasmodically impressive season on the satellite KTM, albeit distinguished with the most crashes in the class, 26. He claimed a final point, finishing 15th.

Also leaving, popular double GP winner Danilo Petrucci, given a fitting send-off with a round of applause from all of the pit lane that had him in tears before the race had even started. Post-race, the self-effacing Italian asserted that he would be the last 'normal' rider to have success in the premier class: "When I started this adventure in 2012 [on the lowly Ioda CRT bike], I don't know if I was lost. Until 2014, for many races, I was last in practice, last in qualifying and last in the race. But I never quit.

224 VALENCIA GRAND PRIX

"Maybe, I'm one of the last ... that a normal person can make it without being a phenomenon, something ultra-natural. When I was young, I was just a good rider. I was fast, but there were people faster than me. But I never stopped believing."

Hardly had the dust settled than thoughts turned to 2022, with MotoGP teams variously smug or concerned about the late-season domination of Ducati. In the former group, a pack of eight riders, with Miller gloating that although the bike was already at the highest level, "for sure they'll find more improvements." He and factory team-mate Bagnaia, as well as both Pramac riders, Zarco and Martin, plus VR46 rider Luca Marini would have new GP22 bikes; second VR46 rider Bezzecchi, a GP21 for his rookie season. Also on the 2021 bike, Gresini riders Bastianini and rookie Fabio Di Giannantonio.

Yamaha factory riders Quartararo and Morbidelli, and satellite rider Dovizioso would have new M1s; rookie Darryn Binder, a 2021 bike. And both KTM rookies, Remy Gardner and Raul Fernandez, would have 2022 bikes, in line with the company's policy of equal machines for all.

Entry lists were released early the following week, with some surprises. For example, the Aramco sponsorship for Rossi's new MotoGP team, present on the earlier provisional list, had gone missing, fuelling further speculation about the truth behind the claimed Saudi backing.

In Moto2, Kalex had gained ground, with Japanese chassis manufacturer NTS withdrawing after four undistinguished years, and just two Boscoscuro riders, Romano Fenati and rookie Fermin Aldeguer in the factory SpeedUp team. With two MV Agustas, the rest would be on Kalexes, although two would be renamed GASGAS.

Renaming expanded in Moto3, with KTM further reducing its constructor-title chances with two bikes now named for Chinese manufacturer CFMoto, joining Husqvarna and GASGAS as rebadged clones. Good news for British fans: the arrival of Michael Laverty's new Vision track team with rookie riders Joshua Whatley and Scott Ogden.

MOTOGP RACE – 27 laps

Ducati's show of superiority, verging on cruelty, began with the second front-row lockout of the year. Pole went to Pramac rider Martin, his fourth of an amazing rookie season, after snitching it from Bagnaia, who shortly before had deposed Miller.

Mir led row two, a rare strong qualifying reinforcing hopes of repeating his 2020 victory here. Alongside him, Zarco, and then Suzuki team-mate Rins, through from Q1. Likewise Binder, ahead of eighth-fastest Quartararo, the South African's second best grid position of the year.

Rossi was tenth, after Bagnaia had twice waited to show him the way. The veteran displayed his old, inimitable aggression off the start as he jostled for position with Quartararo around the outside of the first turn.

Up front, Martin led away and Mir took second, between Miller and Bagnaia. Binder, Rins, Quartararo and Aleix Espargaro followed, with Rossi squeezed back to tenth at Turn Two.

The Suzukis enjoyed a spirited opening. Mir pounced on a vulnerable Miller on lap two with an expertly crafted move at Turn Four. A lap later, and both Bagnaia and Rins had relegated the Australian to fifth, at Turns One and Two respectively. But Suzuki's task of overhauling all the Ducatis would be impossible. The ease with which Bagnaia drafted past Mir on the start-finish straight when starting lap four was a case in point.

Behind, Miller was in all sorts of trouble while trying to conserve his rear tyre. "Like a deer in the headlights," he later admitted, after facing a barrage of attacks. Now Quartararo pounced on the final turn on lap four, only to run wide. And there was an immediate retaliation to the Ducati's superior straight-line top speed four corners into the next lap. This bickering gave the leading quartet room to draw ahead of the pack, a phase Miller would later regret.

Above: Ducati's first ever podium lockout, and test rider Michele Pirro joined Martin, Bagnaia and Miller in *parc fermé*, overlooked by a giant one-off Rossi mural.
Photo: Ducati Corse

Top right: Better to burn out than fade out. Departing Tech3 KTM riders Petrucci and Lecuona make smoke.

Top far right: A first grand prix win for Leopard Racing's Xavier Artigas.

Above right: Rins slid out in his efforts to keep pace with Martin and Bagnaia.

Centre right: Veteran Simone Corsi claimed the Moto2 pole, but missed the race.

Right: Tenth was sufficient for Remy Gardner to claim the Moto2 crown.

Far right: Flying the Australian flag, Gardner followed in his father's footsteps. His number '87' reflects Wayne Gardner's 1987 500cc title.
Photos: Gold & Goose

The narrow Ricardo Tormo Circuit is an unforgiving layout. An early mistake by Binder at Turn Seven dropped him to seventh, and a Turn Six crash for FP4 pace-setter Nakagami demonstrated the perils of missing a braking marker by a fraction. Sadly, Rins followed suit on lap 11. Having made short work of team-mate Mir at Turn Six, he had been hovering behind Martin and Bagnaia when he tucked the front at the same place – a disheartening sixth crash from a possible podium battle in the season.

From there, it was a two-way fight for honours. Martin led admirably considering that he was suffering a bout of food poisoning from Saturday. "From 10pm to 5am, I wasn't sleeping, just vomiting," he said. "I thought I couldn't make the race." But the past five races had shown that Bagnaia was in formidable form. By lap 15, he was putting the rookie under pressure, attempting a move at Turn Six before diving clinically under the Spaniard into the final turn. The pace went up immediately, with Bagnaia posting the race's fastest lap on the next circuit, a new record.

Enfeebled be damned, Martin wouldn't relent as he set his own personal best on lap 17 to hold station just behind the leader. This burst was well timed, as Miller had found his second wind, after repassing Quartararo on lap 11. As Mir faded, fuming at his Suzuki's shortcomings, the Australian passed him for third on lap 18 to make it a Ducati one, two, three. The gap to the leaders was 1.2s, and Miller made a sturdy attempt at closing it. Then an error on the last lap – failing to engage his ride-height device – cost him the chance to attack. The three red bikes crossed the line 0.8 of a second apart, offering a nice symmetry to the year after Ducatis had swarmed the field at the first turn of the first race.

Mir was four seconds adrift at the flag, having narrowly held off Quartararo's late challenge. He had been pursued by Espargaro, but the Aprilia rider wilted at the end, succumbing not only to a late charge by Zarco, but also Binder (fastest on track in the closing laps) and Bastianini who, in typical style, had picked his way through from 17th on the first lap. Eighth was not enough by nine points to beat Martin to Rookie of the Year.

Rossi was tenth, less than a second behind Espargaro, accompanied by loyal protégé Morbidelli, happy to follow him home. On the slow-down lap, al the riders pulled up at Turn Two with Valentino to pay a final tribute, echoed by the packed stands.

Dovizioso narrowly led Marquez; then the KTMs of Oliveira and Lecuona tied up the last points, Vinales missing out by half a second. In the championship, Binder overtook Marquez for sixth; Martin passed Vinales for ninth.

MOTO2 RACE – 16 laps (shortened)

The situation was simple. Raul Fernandez must win. Then, if Gardner placed 14th or worse, he would be champion in his rookie year – something not even Marquez had achieved.

The circumstances were complex, however, in a race that lasted not even a single lap at the first attempt, bringing double jeopardy to the Australian points leader.

Still nursing two broken ribs, Gardner had qualified eighth, a precarious position with an uncomfortably strong chance at this very tight track of becoming mixed up in somebody else's mistakes.

Fernandez was only one row better off, qualified fifth. On pole, 34-year-old veteran Simone Corsi on the MV Agusta. It was only his second pole in the class – the first had been at Aragon in 2012. Rookie Vietti was alongside, his first front row; then Augusto Fernandez, with Di Giannantonio and retiring veteran Tom Luthi bracketing Raul on row two.

Di Giannantonio led away, but on only the second corner, Bezzecchi and Vierge came together and fell mid-pack, with Baldassarri unable to avoid the debris and crashing a little further around. Nobody was hurt, but oil had been spilled, and the red flags came out directly for a 25-minute delay.

Vierge and Bezzecchi lined up again, Baldassarri, without a ride for 2022, did not make the restart of potentially his last GP. Nor did the luckless Corsi, who had slowed and then pitted from the warm-up lap with an electronic glitch.

Augusto Fernandez led away, but his namesake, Raul, took just a lap-and-a-half to get out front, with Di Giannan-

226 VALENCIA GRAND PRIX

FIM WORLD CHAMPIONSHIP

tonio and Canet just behind. Then the leader attempted to slow the pace, repeatedly exchanging places with Augusto. This packed the pursuers together, leaving Gardner – a nervy ninth on the third lap – precarious with a gaggle behind.

Di Giannantonio saved his day, seizing the lead on lap four and upping the pace by over a second. Raul had no option but to chase him, Augusto in tow, and the pack stretched out, much to Gardner's relief. He found breathing space in tenth, a place he held until the flag to become Australia's first intermediate-class champion since Kel Carruthers had won the 250cc crown in 1969.

Raul did what he had to, retaking the lead with three laps to play and holding on for his eighth win of the campaign by 0.5 of a second. Di Giannantonio and Augusto Fernandez completed the podium; Vietti was a strong fourth, ahead of Canet, Vierge and Sam Lowes.

Ahead of Gardner, Schrotter in a lone ninth; close behind him, former team-mate and friend Tetsuta Nagashima, who had tried a pass earlier on, but then held station, narrowly ahead of Luthi. In a tight threesome, Manzi, Ramirez and Syahrin (also in his last GP) secured the final points.

Bezzecchi, whose delayed bike repair meant that he had to start from the pit lane, finished 20th. Garzo and Dimas Ekky Pratama crashed out.

Just four points separated Gardner and Fernandez, with no position changes in the top ten, Bezzecchi already unassailable in third. Ai Ogura missed the race after suffering a foot fracture in Portugal, but he retained eighth ahead of Navarro, as second-best rookie.

MOTO3 RACE – 23 laps

Fittingly, the final Moto3 contest of 2021 came down to a duel between the two standout names of the class. Between them, Acosta and Foggia had won 11 of the 17 races so far. Now they were face to face in a juicy last lap.

Until then, Acosta – emboldened by his first ever pole position – was riding with a champion's swagger and meaning to win, as witnessed by his treatment of Garcia, whom he barged out of the lead at Turn Two on lap 13, and of Deniz Oncu, who was further disadvantaged, along with another erstwhile leader, Filip Salac, by being given a long-lap penalty for exceeding track limits.

Foggia, tenth on lap 12, made stealthy progress towards the front and led the penultimate lap. Acosta got him back at Turn One; into Turn Two, Foggia dived inside, but braked too late, taking his rival down and relegating himself to fifth.

It was an ironic and seemingly more deliberate replay of the crash that had taken him out a week before in Portugal.

In their absence, Artigas stole a maiden win from Garcia at the final corner, with Masia resisting Oncu's all-or-nothing attack for third. Salac was fourth, ahead of Oncu. Foggia was a preliminary sixth, but was handed a three-second penalty for the clash, which dropped him to 13th.

That moved Nepa to sixth, with Guevara almost alongside, and Tatay, Antonelli and Sasaki together right behind.

There was no change to the championship top three, with Garcia safe in third, but Masia took fourth from 12th-placed earlier title challenger Fenati.

VALENCIA GRAND PRIX 227

FIM WORLD CHAMPIONSHIP: ROUND 18 MOTOGP

GRAN PREMIO MOTUL DE LA COMUNITAT VALENCIANA

12–14 NOVEMBER, 2021

CIRCUITO DE LA COMUNITAT VALENCIANA
27 laps
Length: 4.005 km / 2.489 miles
Width: 12m

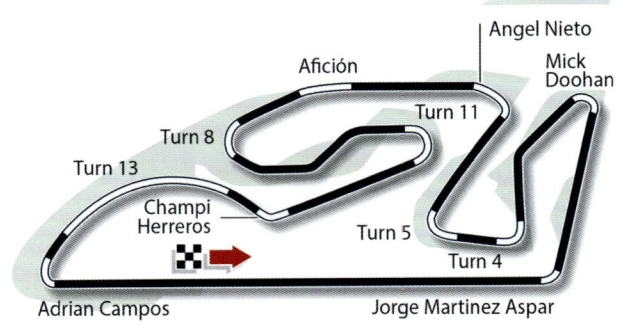

MotoGP

RACE DISTANCE: 27 laps, 67.192 miles/108.135km · RACE WEATHER: Dry (air 21°, humidity 21%, track 29°)

Pos.	Rider	Nat.	No.	Entrant	Machine	Tyres	Race tyre choice	Laps	Time & speed
1	Francesco Bagnaia	ITA	63	Ducati Lenovo Team	Ducati Desmosedici	M	F: Hard/R: Medium	27	41m 15.481s 97.7mph/157.2km/h
2	Jorge Martin	SPA	89	Pramac Racing	Ducati Desmosedici	M	F: Hard/R: Medium	27	41m 15.970s
3	Jack Miller	AUS	43	Ducati Lenovo Team	Ducati Desmosedici	M	F: Hard/R: Medium	27	41m 16.304s
4	Joan Mir	SPA	36	Team SUZUKI ECSTAR	Suzuki GSX-RR	M	F: Hard/R: Medium	27	41m 20.695s
5	Fabio Quartararo	FRA	20	Monster Energy Yamaha MotoGP	Yamaha YZR-M1	M	F: Hard/R: Medium	27	41m 20.920s
6	Johann Zarco	FRA	5	Pramac Racing	Ducati Desmosedici	M	F: Hard/R: Medium	27	41m 22.474s
7	Brad Binder	RSA	33	Red Bull KTM Factory Racing	KTM RC16	M	F: Hard/R: Medium	27	41m 23.918s
8	Enea Bastianini	ITA	23	Avintia Esponsorama	Ducati Desmosedici	M	F: Hard/R: Medium	27	41m 26.414s
9	Aleix Espargaro	SPA	41	Aprilia Racing Team Gresini	Aprilia RS-GP	M	F: Hard/R: Medium	27	41m 28.132s
10	Valentino Rossi	ITA	46	Petronas Yamaha SRT	Yamaha YZR-M1	M	F: Hard/R: Medium	27	41m 28.949s
11	Franco Morbidelli	ITA	21	Monster Energy Yamaha MotoGP	Yamaha YZR-M1	M	F: Hard/R: Medium	27	41m 29.566s
12	Andrea Dovizioso	ITA	4	Petronas Yamaha SRT	Yamaha YZR-M1	M	F: Hard/R: Medium	27	41m 32.015s
13	Alex Marquez	SPA	73	LCR Honda CASTROL	Honda RC213V	M	F: Hard/R: Medium	27	41m 32.540s
14	Miguel Oliveira	POR	88	Red Bull KTM Factory Racing	KTM RC16	M	F: Hard/R: Medium	27	41m 33.702s
15	Iker Lecuona	SPA	27	Tech 3 KTM Factory Racing	KTM RC16	M	F: Hard/R: Medium	27	41m 34.714s
16	Maverick Vinales	SPA	12	Aprilia Racing Team Gresini	Aprilia RS-GP	M	F: Hard/R: Medium	27	41m 35.296s
17	Luca Marini	ITA	10	SKY VR46 Avintia	Ducati Desmosedici	M	F: Hard/R: Medium	27	41m 44.341s
18	Danilo Petrucci	ITA	9	Tech 3 KTM Factory Racing	KTM RC16	M	F: Hard/R: Medium	27	41m 47.650s
	Alex Rins	SPA	42	Team SUZUKI ECSTAR	Suzuki GSX-RR	M	F: Hard/R: Medium	10	DNF-crash
	Takaaki Nakagami	JPN	30	LCR Honda IDEMITSU	Honda RC213V	M	F: Hard/R: Medium	4	DNF-crash
	Pol Espargaro	SPA	44	Repsol Honda Team	Honda RC213V	M	-	-	DNS-injured

Fastest lap: Francesco Bagnaia, on lap 5, 1m 39.467s, 103.2mph/166.1km/h.
Lap record: Marc Marquez, 1m 31.116s, 98.3mph/158.2km/h (2019).
Event maximum speed: Johann Zarco, 209.4mph/337.0km/h (race).

Qualifying
Weather: Dry
Air Temp: 21° Track Temp: 24°
Humidity: 50%

1	Martin	1m 29.936s
2	Bagnaia	1m 30.000s
3	Miller	1m 30.325s
4	Mir	1m 30.395s
5	Zarco	1m 30.418s
6	Rins	1m 30.475s
7	Binder	1m 30.509s
8	Quartararo	1m 30.620s
9	Nakagami	1m 30.644s
10	Rossi	1m 30.746s
11	Morbidelli	1m 30.781s
12	A. Espargaro	1m 31.024s

Q1

13	Dovizioso	1m 30.859s
14	Vinales	1m 30.991s
15	Lecuona	1m 30.994s
16	Petrucci	1m 31.045s
17	Marini	1m 31.073s
18	Bastianini	1m 31.185s
19	A. Marquez	1m 31.251s
20	Oliveira	1m 31.319s

Fastest race laps

1	Bagnaia	1m 31.042s
2	Martin	1m 31.141s
3	Miller	1m 31.170s
4	Mir	1m 31.203s
5	Rins	1m 31.261s
6	Binder	1m 31.292s
7	Zarco	1m 31.350s
8	Bastianini	1m 31.437s
9	Quartararo	1m 31.475s
10	A. Espargaro	1m 31.500s
11	Vinales	1m 31.674s
12	Rossi	1m 31.701s
13	Morbidelli	1m 31.714s
14	A. Marquez	1m 31.781s
15	Oliveira	1m 31.799s
16	Dovizioso	1m 31.800s
17	Lecuona	1m 31.856s
18	Nakagami	1m 31.894s
19	Petrucci	1m 32.140s
20	Marini	1m 32.143s

Championship Points

1	Quartararo	278
2	Bagnaia	252
3	Mir	208
4	Miller	181
5	Zarco	173
6	Binder	151
7	M. Marquez	142
8	A. Espargaro	120
9	Martin	111
10	Vinales	106
11	Bastianini	102
12	P. Espargaro	100
13	Rins	99
14	Oliveira	94
15	Nakagami	76
16	A. Marquez	70
17	Morbidelli	47
18	Rossi	44
19	Marini	41
20	Lecuona	39
21	Petrucci	37
22	Bradl	14
23	Pirro	12
24	Dovizioso	12
25	Pedrosa	6
26	Savadori	4
27	Rabat	1

Constructor Points

1	Ducati	357
2	Yamaha	309
3	Suzuki	240
4	Honda	214
5	KTM	205
6	Aprilia	121

Grid order

Grid order	1	2	3	4	5	6	7	8	9	10	11	12	13	14	15	16	17	18	19	20	21	22	23	24	25	26	27	
89 MARTIN	89	89	89	89	89	89	89	89	89	89	89	89	89	89	63	63	63	63	63	63	63	63	63	63	63	63	63	1
63 BAGNAIA	43	36	36	63	63	63	63	63	63	63	63	63	63	63	89	89	89	89	89	89	89	89	89	89	89	89	89	2
43 MILLER	36	63	63	42	42	42	42	42	42	42	36	36	36	36	36	36	36	43	43	43	43	43	43	43	43	43	43	3
36 MIR	63	43	42	36	36	36	36	36	36	36	43	43	43	43	43	43	43	36	36	36	36	36	36	36	36	36	36	4
5 ZARCO	42	42	43	43	20	20	20	20	43	43	20	20	20	20	20	20	20	20	20	20	20	20	20	20	20	20	20	5
42 RINS	20	20	20	20	43	43	43	43	20	20	41	41	41	41	41	41	41	41	5	5	5	5	5	5	5	5	5	6
33 BINDER	41	41	41	41	41	41	41	41	41	33	33	33	33	5	5	5	5	5	41	41	41	33	33	33	33	33	33	7
20 QUARTARARO	33	33	33	33	33	33	33	33	33	5	5	5	5	33	33	33	33	33	33	33	33	41	41	23	23	23	23	8
30 NAKAGAMI	46	46	46	5	5	5	5	5	23	23	23	23	23	23	23	23	23	23	23	23	23	23	23	41	41	41	41	9
46 ROSSI	5	5	5	46	46	46	46	23	23	46	46	46	46	46	46	46	46	46	46	46	46	46	46	46	46	46	46	10
21 MORBIDELLI	30	30	30	23	23	23	46	46	21	21	21	21	21	21	21	21	21	21	21	21	21	21	21	21	21	21	21	11
41 A. ESPARGARO	4	4	4	21	21	21	21	21	21	21	4	4	4	4	4	4	4	4	4	4	4	4	4	4	4	4	4	12
4 DOVIZIOSO	21	21	21	4	4	4	4	4	4	4	73	73	73	73	73	73	73	73	73	73	73	73	73	73	73	73	73	13
12 VINALES	12	12	23	23	73	73	73	73	73	73	88	88	88	88	88	88	88	88	88	88	88	88	88	88	88	88	88	14
27 LECUONA	88	23	73	73	88	88	88	88	88	88	27	27	27	27	27	27	27	27	27	27	27	27	27	27	27	27	27	15
9 PETRUCCI	73	88	88	88	27	27	27	27	27	27	12	12	12	12	12	12	12	12	12	12	12	12	12	12	12	12	12	
10 MARINI	23	73	12	27	9	9	9	9	12	9	9	9	9	9	9	9	9	9	10	10	10	10	10	10	10	10	10	
23 BASTIANINI	27	27	27	9	12	10	10	10	10	10	10	10	10	10	10	10	10	10	9	9	9	9	9	9	9	9	9	
73 A. MARQUEZ	9	9	9	12	10	12	12	12	9																			
88 OLIVEIRA	10	10	10	10																								

Moto2

RACE DISTANCE: 16 laps, 39.817 miles/64.080km · **RACE WEATHER:** Dry (air 20°, humidity 50%, track 22°)

Pos.	Rider	Nat.	No.	Entrant	Machine	Laps	Time & Speed
1	Raul Fernandez	SPA	25	Red Bull KTM Ajo	Kalex	16	25m 38.612s 93.1mph/149.9km/h
2	Fabio Di Giannantonio	ITA	21	Federal Oil Gresini Moto2	Kalex	16	25m 39.129s
3	Augusto Fernandez	SPA	37	Elf Marc VDS Racing Team	Kalex	16	25m 39.398s
4	Celestino Vietti	ITA	13	SKY Racing Team VR46	Kalex	16	25m 41.005s
5	Aron Canet	SPA	44	Inde Aspar Team	Boscoscuro	16	25m 43.590s
6	Xavi Vierge	SPA	97	Petronas Sprinta Racing	Kalex	16	25m 43.703s
7	Sam Lowes	GBR	22	Elf Marc VDS Racing Team	Kalex	16	25m 44.027s
8	Jorge Navarro	SPA	9	Termozeta Speed Up	Boscoscuro	16	25m 44.420s
9	Marcel Schrotter	GER	23	Liqui Moly Intact GP	Kalex	16	25m 46.553s
10	Remy Gardner	AUS	87	Red Bull KTM Ajo	Kalex	16	25m 47.724s
11	Tetsuta Nagashima	JPN	45	Italtrans Racing Team	Kalex	16	25m 48.032s
12	Thomas Luthi	SWI	12	Pertamina Mandalika SAG Team	Kalex	16	25m 48.967s
13	Stefano Manzi	ITA	62	Flexbox HP40	Kalex	16	25m 50.510s
14	Marcos Ramirez	SPA	42	American Racing	Kalex	16	25m 50.700s
15	Hafizh Syahrin	MAL	55	NTS RW Racing GP	NTS	16	25m 50.973s
16	Jake Dixon	GBR	96	Petronas Sprinta Racing	Kalex	16	25m 52.594s
17	Fermin Aldeguer	SPA	54	Termozeta Speed Up	Boscoscuro	16	25m 52.634s
18	Barry Baltus	BEL	70	NTS RW Racing GP	NTS	16	25m 52.757s
19	Somkiat Chantra	THA	35	IDEMITSU Honda Team Asia	Kalex	16	25m 55.723s
20	Marco Bezzecchi	ITA	72	SKY Racing Team VR46	Kalex	16	25m 57.885s
21	Cameron Beaubier	USA	6	American Racing	Kalex	16	25m 58.038s
22	Albert Arenas	SPA	75	Inde Aspar Team	Boscoscuro	16	25m 58.220s
23	Tony Arbolino	ITA	14	Liqui Moly Intact GP	Kalex	16	25m 58.598s
24	Nicolo Bulega	ITA	11	Federal Oil Gresini Moto2	Kalex	16	26m 02.417s
25	Bo Bendsneyder	NED	64	Pertamina Mandalika SAG Team	Kalex	16	26m 10.171s
	Hector Garzo	SPA	40	Flexbox HP40	Kalex	11	DNF-crash
	Dimas Ekky Pratama	INA	20	Pertamina Mandalika SAG Team	Kalex	2	DNF-crash
	Simone Corsi	ITA	24	MV Agusta Forward Racing	MV Agusta	0	DNS-technical
	Lorenzo Baldassarri	ITA	7	MV Agusta Forward Racing	MV Agusta	0	DNS-crash

Fastest lap: Raul Fernandez, on lap 16, 1m 35.356s, 94.0mph/151.2km/h.
Lap record: Thomas Luthi, 1m 34.820s, 94.4mph/152.0km/h (2019).
Event maximum speed: Hector Garzo, 172.9mph/278.3km/h (race).

Qualifying

Weather: Dry
Air Temp: 21° **Track Temp:** 24°
Humidity: 48%

1	Corsi	1m 34.956s
2	Vietti	1m 35.005s
3	A. Fernandez	1m 35.026s
4	Di Giannantonio	1m 35.034s
5	R. Fernandez	1m 35.036s
6	Luthi	1m 35.091s
7	Canet	1m 35.103s
8	Gardner	1m 35.117s
9	Navarro	1m 35.153s
10	Lowes	1m 35.179s
11	Bezzecchi	1m 35.232s
12	Vierge	1m 35.242s
13	Schrotter	1m 35.244s
14	Syahrin	1m 35.410s
15	Nagashima	1m 35.496s
16	Ramirez	1m 35.575s
17	Roberts	1m 35.620s
18	Beaubier	1m 35.961s
Q1		
19	Garzo	1m 35.368s
20	Manzi	1m 35.468s
21	Aldeguer	1m 35.477s
22	Bendsneyder	1m 35.508s
23	Dixon	1m 35.528s
24	Bulega	1m 35.620s
25	Chantra	1m 35.818s
26	Arenas	1m 35.916s
27	Arbolino	1m 36.218s
28	Baldassarri	1m 36.418s
29	Pratama	1m 37.476s
	Baltus	No Time

Fastest race laps

1	R. Fernandez	1m 35.356s
2	Vietti	1m 35.408s
3	Di Giannantonio	1m 35.500s
4	Lowes	1m 35.500s
5	A. Fernandez	1m 35.517s
6	Vierge	1m 35.546s
7	Canet	1m 35.600s
8	Navarro	1m 35.744s
9	Schrotter	1m 35.829s
10	Nagashima	1m 35.846s
11	Gardner	1m 35.850s
12	Manzi	1m 35.859s
13	Garzo	1m 35.914s
14	Beaubier	1m 35.995s
15	Aldeguer	1m 36.009s
16	Luthi	1m 36.014s
17	Ramirez	1m 36.041s
18	Dixon	1m 36.094s
19	Syahrin	1m 36.144s
20	Baltus	1m 36.145s
21	Chantra	1m 36.182s
22	Arbolino	1m 36.292s
23	Arenas	1m 36.340s
24	Bezzecchi	1m 36.341s
25	Bulega	1m 36.690s
26	Bendsneyder	1m 37.239s
27	Pratama	1m 38.477s

Championship Points

1	Gardner	311
2	R. Fernandez	307
3	Bezzecchi	214
4	Lowes	190
5	A. Fernandez	174
6	Canet	164
7	Di Giannantonio	161
8	Ogura	120
9	Navarro	106
10	Schrotter	98
11	Vierge	93
12	Vietti	89
13	Roberts	59
14	Arbolino	51
15	Beaubier	50
16	Bendsneyder	46
17	Ramirez	39
18	Chantra	37
19	Manzi	36
20	Dixon	30
21	Arenas	28
22	Luthi	27
23	Garzo	16
24	Corsi	16
25	Aldeguer	13
26	Bulega	12
27	Dalla Porta	10
28	Syahrin	9
29	Nagashima	5
30	Lopez	4
31	Baldassarri	3
32	Baltus	2

Constructor Points

1	Kalex	450
2	Boscoscuro	199
3	MV Agusta	19
4	NTS	11

Moto3

RACE DISTANCE: 23 laps, 57.238 miles/92.115km · **RACE WEATHER:** Dry (air 19°, humidity 53%, track 19°)

Pos.	Rider	Nat.	No.	Entrant	Machine	Laps	Time & Speed
1	Xavier Artigas	SPA	43	Leopard Racing	Honda	23	38m 30.302s 89.2mph/143.5km/h
2	Sergio Garcia	SPA	11	Valresa GASGAS Aspar Team	GASGAS	23	38m 30.345s
3	Jaume Masia	SPA	5	Red Bull KTM Ajo	KTM	23	38m 30.534s
4	Filip Salac	CZE	12	CarXpert PruestelGP	KTM	23	38m 30.745s
5	Deniz Oncu	TUR	53	Red Bull KTM Tech 3	KTM	23	38m 30.842s
6	Stefano Nepa	ITA	82	BOE Owlride	KTM	23	38m 31.458s
7	Izan Guevara	SPA	28	Valresa GASGAS Aspar Team	GASGAS	23	38m 31.511s
8	Carlos Tatay	SPA	99	Avintia Esponsorama Moto3	KTM	23	38m 32.411s
9	Niccolo Antonelli	ITA	23	Avintia VR46	KTM	23	38m 32.487s
10	Ayumu Sasaki	JPN	71	Red Bull KTM Tech 3	KTM	23	38m 32.624s
11	John McPhee	GBR	17	Petronas Sprinta Racing	Honda	23	38m 33.093s
12	Romano Fenati	ITA	55	Sterilgarda Max Racing Team	Husqvarna	23	38m 32.763s
13	Dennis Foggia	ITA	7	Leopard Racing	Honda	23	38m 34.121s
14	Adrian Fernandez	SPA	31	Sterilgarda Max Racing Team	Husqvarna	23	38m 43.600s
15	Jeremy Alcoba	SPA	52	Indonesian Racing Gresini Moto3	Honda	23	38m 43.650s
16	Riccardo Rossi	ITA	54	BOE Owlride	KTM	23	38m 43.671s
17	Kaito Toba	JPN	27	CIP Green Power	KTM	23	38m 47.551s
18	Andrea Migno	ITA	16	Rivacold Snipers Team	Honda	23	39m 15.883s
19	Ryusei Yamanaka	JPN	6	CarXpert PruestelGP	KTM	23	39m 04.058s
	Pedro Acosta	SPA	37	Red Bull KTM Ajo	KTM	22	DNF-crash
	Alberto Surra	ITA	67	Rivacold Snipers Team	Honda	20	DNF-crash
	Tatsuki Suzuki	JPN	24	SIC58 Squadra Corse	Honda	17	DNF-crash
	Yuki Kunii	JPN	92	Honda Team Asia	Honda	12	DNF-crash
	Joel Kelso	AUS	66	CIP Green Power	KTM	4	DNF-crash
	Jose Antonio Rueda	SPA	95	Indonesian Racing Gresini Moto3	Honda	4	DNF-crash
	Lorenzo Fellon	FRA	20	SIC58 Squadra Corse	Honda	0	DNF-crash
	Darryn Binder	RSA	40	Petronas Sprinta Racing	Honda	0	DNF-crash

Fastest lap: Xavier Artigas, on lap 2, 1m 39.287s, 90.2mph/145.2km/h.
Lap record: Sergio Garcia, 1m 38.858s, 90.6mph/145.8km/h (2020).
Event maximum speed: Izan Guevara, 146.3mph/235.4km/h (race).

Qualifying

Weather: Dry
Air Temp: 20° **Track Temp:** 23°
Humidity: 48%

1	Acosta	1m 38.668s
2	Suzuki	1m 38.978s
3	Guevara	1m 39.053s
4	Migno	1m 39.060s
5	Salac	1m 39.092s
6	Fellon	1m 39.133s
7	Foggia	1m 39.134s
8	Fenati	1m 39.143s
9	Antonelli	1m 39.149s
10	Garcia	1m 39.309s
11	Tatay	1m 39.317s
12	Alcoba	1m 39.370s
13	Oncu	1m 39.493s
14	Nepa	1m 39.562s
15	McPhee	1m 39.666s
16	Binder	1m 39.810s
17	Artigas	1m 39.970s
18	Kelso	1m 40.109s
Q1		
19	Fernandez	1m 39.428s
20	Kunii	1m 39.604s
21	Antonio Rueda	1m 39.617s
22	Yamanaka	1m 39.873s
23	Masia	1m 39.980s
24	Toba	1m 40.162s
25	Surra	1m 40.202s
26	Sasaki	1m 40.339s
	Rossi	No Time

Fastest race laps

1	Artigas	1m 39.287s
2	Oncu	1m 39.411s
3	Salac	1m 39.441s
4	Masia	1m 39.465s
5	Nepa	1m 39.471s
6	Foggia	1m 39.481s
7	Acosta	1m 39.537s
8	Fenati	1m 39.565s
9	Guevara	1m 39.630s
10	Sasaki	1m 39.669s
11	Suzuki	1m 39.677s
12	Garcia	1m 39.680s
13	Kunii	1m 39.693s
14	Migno	1m 39.705s
15	McPhee	1m 39.724s
16	Kelso	1m 39.727s
17	Antonio	1m 39.748s
18	Rossi	1m 39.756s
19	Fernandez	1m 39.761s
20	Toba	1m 39.786s
21	Antonelli	1m 39.856s
22	Tatay	1m 39.871s
23	Alcoba	1m 39.876s
24	Surra	1m 40.155s
25	Yamanaka	1m 40.410s

Championship Points

1	Acosta	259
2	Foggia	216
3	Garcia	188
4	Masia	171
5	Fenati	160
6	Antonelli	152
7	Binder	136
8	Guevara	125
9	Sasaki	120
10	Migno	110
11	Oncu	95
12	Alcoba	86
13	McPhee	77
14	Suzuki	76
15	Artigas	72
16	Salac	71
17	Toba	64
18	Nepa	63
19	Rodrigo	60
20	Yamanaka	47
21	Tatay	40
22	Fernandez	30
23	Rossi	29
24	Dupasquier	27
25	Kunii	15
26	Kofler	10
27	Bartolini	7
28	Holgado	4
29	Izdihar	4
30	Azman	3
31	Kelso	2
32	Surra	1

Constructor Points

1	KTM	369
2	Honda	360
3	GASGAS	266
4	Husqvarna	166

VALENCIA GRAND PRIX

2021 FIM MotoGP™ WORLD CHAMPIONS

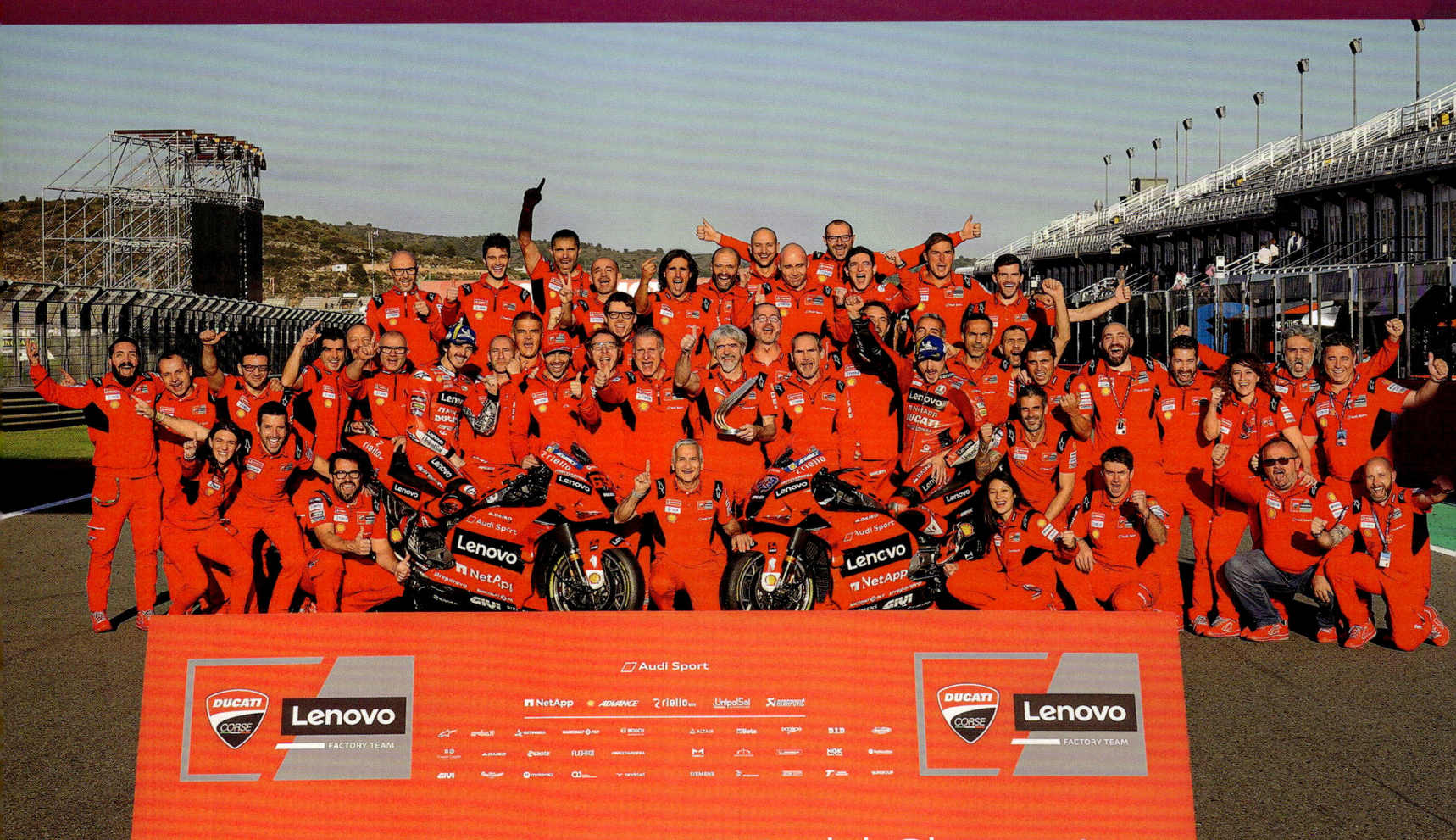

2021 MotoGP Team World Champion

WORLD CHAMPIONSHIP POINTS 2021
Compiled by PETER McLAREN

MotoGP – Riders

Position	Rider	Nationality	Machine	Qatar	Doha	Portugal	Spain	France	Italy	Catalunya	Germany	Netherlands	Styria	Austria	Great Britain	Aragon	San Marino	United States	Emilio-Romagna	Algarve	Valencia	Points total
1	Fabio Quartararo	FRA	Yamaha	11	25	25	3	16	25	10	16	25	16	9	25	8	20	20	13	-	11	278
2	Francesco Bagnaia	ITA	Ducati	16	10	20	20	13	-	9	11	10	5	20	2	25	25	16	-	25	25	252
3	Joan Mir	SPA	Suzuki	13	9	16	11	-	16	13	7	16	20	13	7	16	10	8	-	20	13	208
4	Jack Miller	AUS	Ducati	7	7	-	25	25	10	16	10	-	-	5	13	11	11	9	-	16	16	181
5	Johann Zarco	FRA	Ducati	20	20	-	8	20	13	20	8	13	10	-	5	0	4	-	11	11	10	173
6	Brad Binder	RSA	KTM	2	8	11	-	3	11	8	13	4	13	25	10	9	7	7	5	6	9	151
7	Marc Marquez	SPA	Honda	-	-	9	7	-	-	-	25	9	8	1	-	20	13	25	25	-	-	142
8	Aleix Espargaro	SPA	Aprilia	9	6	10	10	-	9	-	9	8	-	6	16	13	8	-	9	-	7	120
9	Jorge Martin	SPA	Ducati	1	16	-	-	-	-	2	4	-	25	16	-	7	-	11	-	9	20	111
10	Maverick Vinales	SPA	Yamaha/Aprilia	25	11	5	9	6	8	11	0	20	-	-	-	0	3	-	8	0	0	106
11	Enea Bastianini	ITA	Ducati	6	5	7	-	2	-	6	0	1	4	-	4	10	16	10	16	7	8	102
12	Pol Espargaro	SPA	Honda	8	3	-	6	8	4	-	6	6	0	0	11	3	9	6	20	10	-	100
13	Alex Rins	SPA	Suzuki	10	13	-	0	-	-	-	5	5	9	2	20	4	-	13	10	8	-	99
14	Miguel Oliveira	POR	KTM	3	1	0	5	-	20	25	20	11	-	-	0	2	0	5	-	-	2	94
15	Takaaki Nakagami	JPN	Honda	-	0	6	13	9	-	3	3	7	11	3	3	6	6	0	1	5	-	76
16	Alex Marquez	SPA	Honda	-	-	8	-	10	2	5	-	2	7	7	8	-	1	4	-	13	3	70
17	Franco Morbidelli	ITA	Yamaha	0	4	13	16	0	0	7	0	-	-	-	-	-	0	0	2	0	5	47
18	Valentino Rossi	ITA	Yamaha	4	0	-	0	5	6	-	2	-	3	8	0	0	0	1	6	3	6	44
19	Luca Marini	ITA	Ducati	0	0	4	1	4	0	4	1	0	2	11	1	0	0	2	7	4	0	41
20	Iker Lecuona	SPA	KTM	0	-	1	0	7	5	-	0	-	1	10	9	5	-	0	-	-	1	39
21	Danilo Petrucci	ITA	KTM	-	0	3	2	11	7	-	-	3	0	4	6	1	0	0	-	-	0	37
22	Stefan Bradl	GER	Honda	5	2	-	4	-	-	-	-	-	-	-	-	-	-	2	-	1	-	14
23	Michele Pirro	ITA	Ducati	-	-	-	-	-	3	-	-	-	-	-	-	-	5	-	4	-	-	12
24	Andrea Dovizioso	ITA	Yamaha	-	-	-	-	-	-	-	-	-	-	-	-	-	0	3	3	2	4	12
25	Dani Pedrosa	SPA	KTM	-	-	-	-	-	-	-	-	-	6	-	-	-	-	-	-	-	-	6
26	Lorenzo Savadori	ITA	Aprilia	0	0	2	0	-	1	1	-	0	-	-	-	-	-	-	-	-	-	4
27	Tito Rabat	SPA	Ducati	-	-	-	-	0	1	-	-	-	-	-	-	-	-	-	-	-	-	1
28	Cal Crutchlow	GBR	Yamaha	-	-	-	-	-	-	-	-	-	-	0	0	0	0	-	-	-	-	0
29	Garrett Gerloff	USA	Yamaha	-	-	-	-	-	-	-	-	0	-	-	-	-	-	-	-	-	-	0
30	Jake Dixon	GBR	Yamaha	-	-	-	-	-	-	-	-	-	-	-	-	0	-	-	-	-	-	0

MotoGP - Teams

Position	Team	Qatar	Doha	Portugal	Spain	France	Italy	Catalunya	Germany	Netherlands	Styria	Austria	Great Britain	Aragon	San Marino	United States	Emilio-Romagna	Algarve	Valencia	Points total
1	Ducati Lenovo Team	23	17	20	45	38	10	25	21	10	5	25	15	36	36	25	-	41	41	433
2	Monster Energy Yamaha MotoGP	36	36	30	12	22	33	21	16	45	16	9	25	8	20	20	15	-	16	380
3	Team SUZUKI ECSTAR	23	22	16	11	-	16	13	12	21	29	15	27	20	10	21	10	28	13	307
4	Pramac Racing	21	36	-	8	21	16	22	12	13	35	16	5	7	4	11	11	20	30	288
5	Repsol Honda Team	13	5	9	13	8	4	-	31	15	8	1	11	23	22	31	45	11	-	250
6	Red Bull KTM Factory Racing	5	9	11	5	3	31	33	33	15	13	25	10	11	7	12	5	6	11	245
7	LCR Honda	-	-	14	13	19	2	8	3	9	18	10	11	6	7	4	1	18	3	146
8	Esponsorama Racing	6	5	11	1	6	-	10	1	1	6	11	5	10	16	12	23	11	8	143
9	Aprilia Racing Team Gresini	9	6	12	10	-	10	1	9	8	-	6	16	13	11	-	17	-	7	135
10	Petronas Yamaha SRT	4	4	13	16	5	6	7	2	-	3	8	-	-	-	4	9	5	10	96
11	Tech3 KTM Factory Racing	-	-	4	2	18	12	-	-	3	1	14	15	6	-	-	-	-	1	76

Moto2

Position	Rider	Nationality	Machine	Qatar	Doha	Portugal	Spain	France	Italy	Catalunya	Germany	Netherlands	Styria	Austria	Great Britain	Aragon	San Marino	United States	Emilio-Romagna	Algarve	Valencia	Points total
1	Remy Gardner	AUS	Kalex	20	20	16	13	20	25	25	25	20	13	9	25	20	20	-	9	25	6	**311**
2	Raul Fernandez	SPA	Kalex	11	16	25	11	25	20	20	-	25	9	25	-	25	25	25	-	20	25	**307**
3	Marco Bezzecchi	ITA	Kalex	13	13	10	20	16	16	13	16	11	25	6	20	-	11	16	-	8	0	**214**
4	Sam Lowes	GBR	Kalex	25	25	-	16	-	-	9	11	13	2	13	13	-	13	-	25	16	9	**190**
5	Augusto Fernandez	SPA	Kalex	2	10	11	-	-	11	-	16	16	16	10	16	10	13	20	7	16		**174**
6	Aron Canet	SPA	Boscoscuro	3	-	20	7	-	5	-	20	-	20	8	9	11	16	5	16	13	11	**164**
7	Fabio Di Giannantonio	ITA	Kalex	16	6	5	25	8	-	13	-	3	4	11	10	7	20	8	5	20		**161**
8	Ai Ogura	JPN	Kalex	0	11	-	9	9	10	-	10	11	20	7	8	9	9	7	-	-		**120**
9	Jorge Navarro	SPA	Boscoscuro	6	3	0	4	6	-	5	9	9	0	-	16	13	3	4	11	9	8	**106**
10	Marcel Schrotter	GER	Kalex	8	-	6	6	10	11	8	10	7	6	0	3	5	4	-	1	6	7	**98**
11	Xavi Vierge	SPA	Kalex	-	7	9	10	-	-	16	-	8	7	2	8	-	8	8	-	-	10	**93**
12	Celestino Vietti	ITA	Kalex	4	9	-	0	0	0	2	1	6	10	10	4	1	6	-	13	10	13	**89**
13	Joe Roberts	USA	Kalex	10	-	13	8	-	13	6	-	-	-	0	6	3	0	0	-	0	-	**59**
14	Tony Arbolino	ITA	Kalex	0	5	0	0	13	9	3	0	-	0	3	0	7	1	10	-	0	0	**51**
15	Cameron Beaubier	USA	Kalex	5	-	7	-	-	8	0	6	0	-	0	-	-	2	0	11	-	11	0	**50**
16	Bo Bendsneyder	NED	Kalex	7	4	-	2	11	1	10	3	1	0	0	1	-	0	1	4	1	0	**46**
17	Marcos Ramirez	SPA	Kalex	-	-	1	5	3	-	-	7	0	0	-	0	4	2	7	6	2	2	**39**
18	Somkiat Chantra	THA	Kalex	-	0	0	-	4	0	7	0	5	8	11	0	-	-	2	-	-	0	**37**
19	Stefano Manzi	ITA	Kalex	0	8	-	3	-	6	0	-	3	0	0	-	0	0	0	10	3	3	**36**
20	Jake Dixon	GBR	Kalex	9	-	-	-	-	0	2	0	0	0	5	5	-	0	6	3	-	0	**30**
21	Albert Arenas	SPA	Boscoscuro	0	1	3	-	2	-	4	8	4	1	-	0	-	0	-	5	-	0	**28**
22	Thomas Luthi	SWI	Kalex	1	-	0	0	-	-	1	0	2	0	7	5	-	5	-	2	0	4	**27**
23	Hector Garzo	SPA	Kalex	-	0	8	-	-	3	-	-	-	-	-	1	-	0	-	-	4	-	**16**
24	Simone Corsi	ITA	MV Agusta	-	-	-	-	7	-	0	-	0	-	0	0	6	-	3	0	0	-	**16**
25	Fermin Aldeguer	SPA	Boscoscuro	-	-	-	-	-	4	-	-	-	-	-	-	0	9	-	0	0	0	**13**
26	Nicolo Bulega	ITA	Kalex	0	0	-	-	5	-	0	5	0	0	0	2	-	0	-	0	0	0	**12**
27	Lorenzo Dalla Porta	ITA	Kalex	0	2	4	0	-	-	-	-	-	-	4	-	-	-	-	-	-	-	**10**
28	Hafizh Syahrin	MAL	NTS	-	0	0	0	1	7	0	0	-	0	0	0	0	0	-	0	-	1	**9**
29	Tetsuta Nagashima	JPN	Kalex	-	-	-	-	-	-	-	-	-	-	-	-	-	0	-	0	5	-	**5**
30	Alonso Lopez	SPA	Boscoscuro/Kalex	-	-	-	-	-	0	4	0	-	-	-	-	-	-	-	-	-	-	**4**
31	Lorenzo Baldassarri	ITA	MV Agusta	-	-	0	2	1	0	-	-	-	0	-	-	-	0	0	0	-	-	**3**
32	Barry Baltus	BEL	NTS	-	-	-	-	0	0	0	2	0	-	-	0	-	0	-	0	0	0	**2**
33	Manuel Gonzalez	SPA	MV Agusta	-	-	-	-	-	-	-	-	0	-	-	-	0	-	-	-	-	-	**0**
34	Yari Montella	ITA	Boscoscuro	0	0	-	0	-	-	-	-	-	0	-	-	-	-	-	-	-	-	**0**
35	Tommaso Marcon	ITA	MV Agusta/NTS	-	-	-	0	0	0	-	-	-	-	-	-	-	-	-	-	-	-	**0**
36	Miquel Pons	SPA	MV Agusta	-	-	-	0	-	-	-	-	-	-	-	-	-	-	-	-	-	-	**0**
37	John McPhee	GBR	Kalex	-	-	-	-	-	-	-	-	-	-	-	-	0	-	-	-	-	-	**0**
38	Fraser Rogers	GBR	NTS	-	-	0	-	-	-	-	-	-	-	-	-	-	-	-	-	-	-	**0**
39	Taiga Hada	JPN	NTS/Kalex	-	-	-	-	0	-	-	-	-	0	-	-	-	-	-	-	-	-	**0**
40	Xavi Cardelus	AND	Kalex	-	-	-	-	-	-	-	-	-	-	-	-	-	0	-	-	-	-	**0**
41	Piotr Biesiekirski	POL	Kalex	-	-	-	-	-	-	0	-	-	-	-	-	-	-	-	-	0	-	**0**
42	Keminth Kubo	THA	Kalex	-	-	-	-	-	0	-	-	-	-	-	-	-	-	-	-	-	-	**0**

Moto3

Position	Rider	Nationality	Machine	Argentina	United States	Spain	France	Italy	Catalunya	Netherlands	Germany	Czech Republic	Austria	Great Britain	San Marino	Aragon	Thailand	Japan	Australia	Malaysia	Valencia	Points total
1	Pedro Acosta	SPA	KTM	20	25	25	25	8	8	9	25	13	25	13	5	-	9	8	16	25	-	**259**
2	Dennis Foggia	ITA	Honda	-	0	20	-	0	25	-	16	25	0	16	16	25	25	20	25	-	3	**216**
3	Sergio Garcia	SPA	GASGAS	13	0	8	3	25	7	25	9	20	20	25	0	0	13	-	-	-	20	**188**
4	Jaume Masia	SPA	KTM	25	7	7	0	-	20	13	-	0	13	10	10	6	11	13	20	0	16	**171**
5	Romano Fenati	ITA	Husqvarna	5	6	9	20	6	10	5	3	16	16	11	25	2	-	4	9	9	4	**160**
6	Niccolo Antonelli	ITA	KTM	10	16	10	8	-	3	8	10	2	-	-	20	11	20	1	10	16	7	**152**
7	Darryn Binder	RSA	Honda	16	20	0	0	0	11	11	2	9	10	7	9	9	10	9	13	-	-	**136**
8	Izan Guevara	SPA	GASGAS	9	10	0	5	2	0	-	6	4	2	8	13	13	4	25	4	11	9	**125**
9	Ayumu Sasaki	JPN	KTM	-	9	13	11	11	13	-	-	-	11	-	3	16	6	3	8	10	6	**120**
10	Andrea Migno	ITA	Honda	-	13	16	13	5	-	-	11	-	0	-	-	10	16	6	-	20	0	**110**
11	Deniz Oncu	TUR	KTM	0	0	1	0	7	-	16	0	1	0	20	8	20	0	11	-	-	11	**95**
12	Jeremy Alcoba	SPA	Honda	-	-	2	16	0	1	20	13	6	0	2	0	-	0	10	2	13	1	**86**
13	John Mcphee	GBR	Honda	-	-	0	-	13	9	-	5	10	3	9	4	-	3	16	-	-	5	**77**
14	Tatsuki Suzuki	JPN	Honda	8	4	-	-	-	6	-	8	11	1	5	11	7	1	7	-	7	-	**76**
15	Xavier Artigas	SPA	Honda	-	-	-	7	9	0	-	7	7	-	-	-	0	-	-	2	7	8	25	**72**
16	Filip Salac	CZE	Honda/KTM	3	-	3	4	20	5	-	-	-	5	4	2	-	-	-	6	6	13	**71**
17	Kaito Toba	JPN	KTM	7	11	-	0	0	4	7	20	3	4	6	-	0	2	0	0	-	0	**64**
18	Stefano Nepa	ITA	KTM	0	0	5	1	0	2	6	-	5	0	3	0	8	7	5	11	0	10	**63**
19	Gabriel Rodrigo	ARG	Honda	11	3	11	-	-	16	10	-	8	0	0	1	-	-	-	-	-	-	**60**
20	Ryusei Yamanaka	JPN	KTM	2	8	6	6	4	-	2	0	0	9	-	0	5	0	0	5	0	0	**47**
21	Carlos Tatay	SPA	KTM	4	0	0	10	-	-	-	-	-	-	0	6	-	8	0	-	4	8	**40**
22	Adrian Fernandez	SPA	Husqvarna	0	-	-	0	10	-	-	-	-	6	-	0	4	0	-	3	5	2	**30**
23	Riccardo Rossi	ITA	KTM	-	0	0	0	16	0	-	-	0	0	0	7	1	5	0	-	0	0	**29**
24	Jason Dupasquier	SWI	KTM	6	5	4	9	3	-	-	-	-	-	-	-	-	-	-	-	-	-	**27**
25	Yuki Kunii	JPN	Honda	0	1	0	2	-	-	4	-	0	8	0	0	0	-	0	-	0	-	**15**
26	Maximilian Kofler	AUT	KTM	1	2	0	0	0	-	-	-	-	7	0	0	0	0	0	0	-	-	**10**
27	Elia Bartolini	ITA	KTM	-	-	-	-	-	0	3	4	0	-	0	-	-	-	-	-	-	-	**7**
28	Daniel Holgado	SPA	KTM	-	-	-	-	-	-	-	-	1	-	-	-	-	-	-	0	3	-	**4**
29	Andi Farid Izdihar	INA	Honda	0	0	0	0	1	0	0	-	0	-	1	0	-	0	0	1	0	-	**4**
30	Syarifuddin Azman	MAL	Honda	-	-	-	-	-	-	-	-	-	-	-	-	3	-	-	-	-	-	**3**
31	Joel Kelso	AUS	KTM	-	-	-	-	-	-	-	0	0	-	-	-	-	-	-	2	-	-	**2**
32	Alberto Surra	ITA	KTM/Honda	-	-	-	-	-	-	-	-	0	-	0	0	0	0	0	1	-	-	**1**
33	Lorenzo Fellon	FRA	Honda	0	0	0	0	0	0	0	-	0	0	0	0	-	0	0	0	0	-	**0**
34	Takuma Matsuyama	JPN	Honda	-	-	-	-	-	0	0	-	0	-	-	-	-	-	-	-	-	-	**0**
35	Matteo Bertelle	ITA	KTM	-	-	-	-	-	-	-	-	-	-	-	-	-	-	-	0	-	-	**0**
36	Mario Aji	INA	Honda	-	-	-	-	-	-	-	-	-	-	-	-	-	-	-	0	-	-	**0**
37	David Salvador	SPA	Honda	-	-	-	-	-	-	-	-	-	-	-	0	-	-	-	-	-	-	**0**
38	David Alonso	COL	GASGAS	-	-	-	-	-	-	-	-	-	-	-	-	-	-	-	0	-	-	**0**

Photos: Gold & Goose

MOTOE REVIEW
TORRES TAKES CHARGE

The 2021 FIM Enel MotoE World Cup went down to the wire, in dramatic fashion – with a post-final intervention by the stewards turning triumph to dismay, and vice versa. OLIVER BARSTOW tells all...

THE intensity of the battle between Jordi Torres and Dominique Aegerter for the 2021 MotoE title was such that the showdown went down to the final lap of the final race, and then beyond...

Unseen officials determining penalties that alter the overall classification after the chequered flag is certainly not the way most want to see a championship decided. Nevertheless, it was required after the duel became physical within sight of the finish line.

Eleven riders began the Misano double-header with a mathematical shot at the crown, but ultimately the battle was between two Spanish and Swiss rivals with three corners remaining. Sensing the slimmest of margins to squeeze his Energica Ego up the inside of his rival, Aegerter came from too far back to get his bike stopped cleanly. As a result, he straight-lined the apex and kicked out a rear wheel. The pair made contact, and Torres couldn't save the ensuing thump to the asphalt.

Aegerter remained upright, his win versus Torres's remounted 13th more than enough to overhaul the erstwhile eight-point deficit – at least until the stewards ruled the Swiss guilty of irresponsible riding and duly slapped him with a 38-second penalty, which sent him right back down to 12th, reversing the standings.

Contentious though it may have been, the final act of an engrossing season should do nothing to take away from the Spaniard's achievements. His 2021 success duly doubled up with his 2020 title triumph, also with Pons Racing 40.

Until the final, the third iteration of the all-electric MotoE World Cup was as open as ever, with no single rider taking command of the compact, European-based, six-event, seven-race season.

Fewer recovery opportunities meant that errors and DNFs were punished, and it's telling that the top three in the standings – with Matteo Ferrari in third – were the only riders to finish each race in the upper echelons, despite clinching just two race wins between them.

With the mix of youth and experience enticed from domestic ranks, plucked from the GP classes or lured from the WorldSSP paddock, the 18-strong MotoE grid had a fresh overhaul for 2021, with nine rookies joining familiar faces.

Beyond Torres on the Pons bike, inaugural 2019 MotoE World Cup winner Matteo Ferrari entered his third season with Indonesian E-Racing Gresini MotoE, while Aegerter, dovetailing commitments in the WorldSSP championship that he'd go on to win, was also back with Dynavolt Intact GP. Other notable returnees included Eric Granado, now with the Malaysian-flagged One Energy Racing, Mattia Casadei on the Ongetta SIC58 Squadracorse, and Lukas Tulovic, once more with Tech3 E-Racing. Fresh faces included WorldSSP converts Hikari Okubo on the Avant Ajo MotoE and Corentin Perolari on the second of the Tech3 bikes, plus ex-MotoGP rider Yonny Hernandez with Octo Pramac MotoE.

Once again, a field of fully-charged Energica Ego Corsa sports-bikes awaited the riders, MotoE continuing to operate at odds with its three prototype-based weekend counterparts by sticking to a production-ready ethos. This will change from 2023, when Energica will be replaced by Ducati, under a fresh deal to supply the grid with all-new prototype racing motorcycles.

The Jerez curtain-raiser set the tone for the year ahead with plenty of action, even if some of the edgier braking passes and acrobatic backed-in slides perhaps had more to do with hard-charging racers pushing their somewhat leaden machinery to the limit. Regardless, it made for great action, with Jerez delivering a first-time winner in Alessandro Zaccone, the Octo Pramac rider in his second season. He had some good fortune when Eric Granado threw away victory from pole when he slid off unassisted while leading comfortably. But that's not to take away from Zaccone, who kept it tidy once in front to fend off Aegerter and Torres.

A rider who had evidently developed an affinity with his Energica Ego over the previous seasons, Granado went on to prove his pre-season status as one of the title favourites with a spectacular last-gasp victory in round two at Le Mans.

The race could have gone any number of ways, as the French venue's tricky camber changes invited different racing lines and subsequent bumps on meeting at the apex. It led to a seven-strong lead group crossing the line covered by just a single second.

Granado prevailed from one of his four consecutive E-Pole positions, however. He timed his attack to perfection in a breathless final-lap duel with Zaccone, who led until his rival launched up the inside at the penultimate corner. Undeterred Zaccone struck back through the final right-hander, but his wide exit allowed Granado and the closely-following Casadei to outdrag the Pramac man to the chequered flag.

A maiden visit to the Circuit de Barcelona-Catalunya presented perhaps the biggest test yet for the Energica package, namely the vast full-throttle home straight, which, at times, had MotoE looking more like Moto3 as riders sought a slipstream tow.

With timing in the bubble as critical as raw speed, on this occasion youth prevailed over experience, LCR rookie Miquel Pons breaking away to win in only his third start, capitalising on intimate circuit knowledge gleaned from competing in the Spanish domestic ranks. He led Aegerter and Torres home, each landing a second podium of the season, while Zaccone, in fourth, retained his overall lead.

The season's second half began with round four at another new venue, Assen. There, Granado's already roller-coaster season achieved another ascent, his second victory helping to negate the slumps of his crashes in Jerez and Catalunya.

With a fourth consecutive pole, the Brazilian was

Left: Winner and loser. Aegerter's joy was short-lived at Misano.

Centre left: Torres was awarded the championship only after the race.

Far left: Torres leads the pack in Barcelona.

Below left: Aegerter, 2021 World Supersport champion, just missed out on his double title bid.

Below: Matteo Ferrari finished third in the rankings, just ahead of Granado, Zaccone and Casadei.

Photos: Gold & Goose

made to work hard for victory, tussling with Tulovic initially before fighting off an inspired Zaccone. Eventually, he broke clear, leading home the ever-consistent Torres, who got the better of Zaccone on the final lap. Nevertheless, with Aegerter failing to score after hitting the deck at the final corner on lap one, Zaccone swelled his overall advantage over Torres to seven points.

Round five took MotoE back to the verdant hillside Red Bull Ring in Austria, where another first-time winner emerged. Tech3's Tulovic grabbed the lead at Turn One and never looked back.

A thrilling three-way tussle for second went down to the wire, Granado – who had charged from 13th on the grid – and Aegerter eventually filling the remaining podium spots after denying rookie and pole-man Fermin Aldeguer his first podium. With Zaccone and Torres only sixth and seventh, it condensed things at the sharp end of the standings ahead of the Misano double-header finale, leaving 11 riders with a mathematical chance of claiming the crown.

Realistically, it was hard to look beyond a top four separated by a mere 11 points. Zaccone still held firm at the summit, seven points clear of a rejuvenated Granado, who was eight ahead of Torres, with Aegerter still in close contention.

The tension told just moments into race one, when Zaccone's title hopes came to an abrupt and painful end with a high-side on the exit of Turn Three. Worse still, he was subsequently struck by the bike of unsighted Okubo, a heavy impact that resulted in a pelvic fracture, which ruled him out of the final race. He had led the championship from round one.

Now there were three, and Granado, Aegerter and Torres embarked on thrilling racing that made the live championship table flicker like a railway-station ticker board. However, just as it appeared that Aegerter would hold on for his first win of the year, a hard-charging Granado felt compelled to throw everything at a last-gasp pass into the last corner of the last lap. Instead, he threw his folding Energica into the scenery, his title dreams disappearing amid a hail of gravel.

Aegerter was fortunate not to trip over the Brazilian as he came skating across his bow, but the loss of momentum allowed a fortuitous Torres to capitalise, outdragging him to snatch victory, and with it the championship lead heading into the final race.

Thus, with Zaccone out of action and Granado needing a miracle to overhaul the 24-point margin to the top, it was down to Torres and Aegerter to duke it out, eight points splitting the pair.

Despite having a cushion that perhaps should have encouraged Torres to play it safe, the Spaniard seemed determined to clinch it in style, bolting into a sizeable early lead. However, a determined Aegerter closed up, latching on to Torres's tail going into the closing laps. Curiously, though Torres could have afforded to allow his rival through and still clinch the title, he upped the intensity by going toe to toe for the win.

It prompted a duel that bristled with tight overtakes and edgy near misses. Ultimately, though, it ended in the disaster of their last-lap tangle, a situation made all the more awkward by watching the moment that Aegerter and Intact GP had their celebrations abruptly stopped, as tears of despair became tears of joy at Pons Racing when Torres learned of the reversed results.

Elsewhere, fine margins of error throughout the field meant that the final classification bore little resemblance to that of the overall table going into Misano. Having capitalised on the drama ahead to inherit victory in the finale, Ferrari soared up the leaderboard to end the year third overall, his ascent coming at the expense of Granado in fourth, while the hapless Zaccone slid down to fifth.

Behind them, Casadei concluded the year in sixth, ahead of race winners Pons and Tulovic, while rookies Aldeguer and Hernandez completed the top ten.

TRANSFORMATION TIME

IN three seasons on the MotoGP support programme, MotoE has slowly but surely become part of the furniture, with good competitive racing and the general curiosity about its green agenda offering entertainment value that counteracted the doubts of traditional racing purists.

Energica will continue to supply the class for one more season, before the series undergoes an overhaul with the arrival of Ducati, which shocked the paddock in 2021 by confirming that it had secured a four-year tender to the end of 2026.

In a sharp change in philosophy for one of motorcycling's thoroughbred firms, Ducati's previously *laissez-faire* attitude to electric power will be transformed when it develops a prototype racer that is intended to be lighter and more powerful, and have greater range. It should mean longer races and allow for a more conventional qualifying format.

In 2022, Energica will finish what had started as a historic watershed moment for motorcycle racing in response to concerns about climate change. They developed a professional and conscientious statement that racing is racing, even over short distances, no matter the fuel.

MotoE has come a long way in three short years, but as Ducati waits in the wings to assume the baton in 2023, there is little doubt that even bolder, cleverer and more versatile solutions await the next stage of electric motorcycle racing.

MOTOE REVIEW 235

RED BULL ROOKIES CUP
ALONSO ALL THE WAY

The 2021 Rookies Cup was close-fought almost to the last. In the thick of it throughout, Colombian David Alonso finally claimed the title. PETER CLIFFORD tells the story...

Above: Alonso takes charge on the Algarve. The young Colombian won both opening rounds.

Top right: Socially-distanced rookies are briefed at the Sachsenring.

Above right: Japan's Taiyo Furusato made a sensational debut, winning first time out at Mugello.

Above far right: Italian youngster Matteo Bertelle tasted victory in Germany.

Right: Hunkered down, title runner-up David Munoz posted early-season race wins in Spain and Italy.

Photos: Red Bull Content Pool/Gold & Goose

IT was another thrilling Red Bull MotoGP Rookies Cup season. Not only did race positions change at every turn (that's a given in Rookies racing), but also the points lead was wrestled over until the home stretch. Only then did David Alonso manage to distance himself from the opposition and claim the 15th Cup.

The 15-year-old was the first Colombian Rookies winner, and he took the title in fine style, unquestionably the rider of the year after a strong 2020 debut, when he had claimed one win and eight top-four finishes after battling head to head with Pedro Acosta, finishing fourth overall. With only Acosta missing from the top five in 2021, he was one of the favourites.

The series visited Portimao for the first time, starting with the pre-season test. Alonso, always clear about his errors and limitations in 2020, had a good perspective: "I feel we really improved the bike from last year. I think I have also improved myself. I worked hard through the winter."

Covid-19 had made running the traditional Selection Event impossible, so new riders had been chosen according to established form. Rider coach Gustl Auinger was pleased to see the test go well: "Especially good because this year getting the newcomers without having a Selection Event, I was not really sure how it would work out. But these new guys fit perfectly into our Rookies Cup. After just three sessions, it was not possible to see the difference between the newcomers and the ones in the second or even the third year."

Good practice then for the first race weekend of the season at the same venue a week later, when Brazilian newcomer Diogo Moreira took pole ahead of Spaniards Alex Millan, David Munoz and Marcos Uriarte.

Alonso, on row two, was unfazed and broke free brilliantly from an intense lead battle to dominate the opening race. The chasing pack of six blasted across the line together, with Moreira getting the verdict over Uriarte and fellow Spaniard Daniel Holgado.

The race had gone according to plan for Alonso: "I think I rode well, and I also had a lot of fun. At the beginning, we had some fights. I did well in the fight, so tomorrow if we have to fight again, we are strong. For tomorrow, depending on the wind, we might change the gearing. Today, there was a lot of wind, but I ran near the wall on the straight where there was less wind."

He went into race two planning another breakaway, but this time he couldn't get clear from a fantastic battle, nine KTMs scrapping at every turn. Holgado led out of the last corner, but Alonso was perfectly positioned and stole the win out of the slipstream, with 16-year-old Millan on their tail in third.

The series remained on the Iberian peninsula for the second round in Jerez, where there had been no Cup races in 2020, and Alonso continued his great form. Fast all Friday, he found that little extra late in qualifying to secure pole.

Holgado, who had turned 16 on the preceding Tuesday, took second just ahead of Moreira, who had celebrated his 17th birthday the previous week. The trio appeared to be the class of the field, joined in the final session by 16-year-old Italian Filippo Farioli, fourth fastest.

Race one produced a great ride by Holgado, who appeared so well controlled. Despite being under incredible pressure and being passed several times, he seemed to have the answers as David Munoz and Ortola snapped at his heels. Moreira was equally determined, while Alonso seemed content just to be in a good top six, ready to make a play in the final laps.

As usual at Jerez, it did come down to the final corner, ten riders elbowing and lunging for the lead, with David Munoz doing the best job and Holgado going from first to fourth.

Ortola grabbed second ahead of Moreira, while Holgado went wide at the crucial last corner. Alonso was seventh after being in the heart of the front battle; he retained the points lead.

Underlining the high level of the Cup, 2020 Rookies winner Pedro Acosta scored his third Moto3 Grand Prix win in a row on Sunday morning in Jerez, extending his championship lead.

A few hours later, in Rookies Cup race two, Holgado con-

236 RED BULL ROOKIES CUP

tinued Saturday's great form in a stunning battle from the start. Again, a lead group of ten traded places throughout, and Holgado did most of the leading once more, this time managing to break away slightly in the second half of the race. He was chased by Moreira, but in the process, the Brazilian exceeded track limits too many times.

He took his long-lap penalty with six laps to go and, incredibly, fought back, making a lunge for the win on the final lap. That didn't work, but he was in the lead group at the line and claimed second when Alonso and Saturday winner David Munoz failed to take their late penalties and were each given a three-second post-race punishment.

That dropped Alonso to 8th and cost him enough points to give Holgado the title lead by four. The Spaniard was thrilled: "This race was incredible for me. Difficult, but I am happy for me and my team. Today, the difference was the last corner. Yesterday, it was very difficult for me, but today, much better."

Four weeks later, in qualifying through the Tuscan hills at Mugello, the quickest laps came early in the session. Holgado laid down the gauntlet, to be bettered 12 seconds later by Ortola, and a lap later by Uriarte. No one could quite match those early times, but they pushed hard, and a second covered the top 14.

The rain clouds had moved in before race one on Saturday, and spitting rain contributed to a very difficult situation.

Japanese Taiyo Furusato had only ridden a KTM for the first time on Friday, having been brought into the Cup as a replacement for the injured Gabin Planques. The 15-year-old had never seen Mugello before either. Qualified 18th, he set off from row six, yet he got the best of a 17-rider battle that had started in light rain and ended with a cavalry charge to the line, Furusato just clinging on to the lead.

Another thrilling battle had featured major position changes all the way. Noah Dettwiler, the 16-year-old Swiss, had climbed from the back of the pack to lead a Rookies race for the first time. Pole-man Uriarte had dropped to the back, and the 16-year-old Spaniard finished 12th. Collin Veijer was brilliant at the front in the tricky early laps, but the 16-year-old Dutchman was 11th at the flag.

Exciting exploits all the way, but Furusato's victory stood out. Taking the lead on lap four was sensation enough, and he smoothly held the advantage for a few laps before the slipstreaming pack demoted him. When he hit the front again in the final laps, he was even more certain and composed, eking out enough of an advantage that he could not be passed on the slipstreaming run to the line.

Moreira crossed the stripe second ahead of David Munoz, but he had exceeded track limits on the final circuit and was dropped one position.

After such an incredible debut, Furusato lined up as a likely race-two favourite. But nothing is predictable in the Cup, and though he was at the heart of the 17-rider lead pack, he had a big moment halfway around the last lap and split the group, finishing 14th.

Erstwhile points leader Holgado had a handy advantage out of the last corner, but was swamped and crossed the line fourth, after David Munoz had snatched the race win and the overall lead at the last moment, six KTMs within just a couple of square metres. Alonso was second as they flashed across the line, ahead of Ivan Ortola. Pole-man Uriarte was fifth; Matteo Bertelle, who had led the penultimate lap, took sixth, just 0.173 of a second behind the winner.

Veijer led the second group home, small consolation after having been a strong front-runner earlier on.

The Cup moved from Italy to Germany, and Bertelle continued his impressive performance gains to take pole at the Sachsenring. A second covered the top 13.

The race was a 14-rider fight almost throughout. Bertelle went down at the first corner on the last lap, along with Furusato and Daniel Munoz; Alonso charged across the finish line with the slightest advantage over Uriarte and David Munoz. His third win put him back on top on points, but only

RED BULL ROOKIES CUP 237

Above: The Rookies Express. Ivan Ortola leads David Alonso, Daniel Holgado, Daniel Munoz, Tatchakorn Buasri, Marcos Uriarte, Matteo Bertelle and Alex Millan at Red Bull Ring.

Top right: Six wins from 14 starts made David Alonso a worthy successor to Pedro Acosta.

Above right: Daniel Munoz took a first win in Austria.

Centre right: Faces of the future – Daniel Holgado (*left*), Tatchakorn Buasri (*centre*) and Daniel Munoz all featured up front.

Right: Holgado, David Munoz and Alonso fight it out for last-race honours at Aragon.

Photos: Red Bull Content Pool/Gold & Goose

by six from David Munoz, who did a fantastic job of recovering from a long-lap penalty.

Holgado, third in the title chase, was in the lead battle, but he was just off the podium thanks to that last-lap, first-corner mess.

The same circumstances dictated the result of race two, in even more dramatic fashion after another increasingly intense battle. Saturday winner Alonso seemed the most comfortable in the lead, although under great pressure from Holgado, David Munoz, Uriarte, Ortola and Bertelle.

The six funnelled into the first turn and simply didn't fit. Bertelle managed to back out of it, but the other five ended up in the gravel, fortunately without serious injury.

After a solitary last lap, Bertelle crossed the line more than two seconds ahead of Daniel Munoz. with Thailand's Tatchakorn Buasri granted third after Moreira was penalised a place for a last-lap track-limits infraction.

Then to Austria for a double-header at the Red Bull Ring. An intense qualifying session for the Grand Prix of Styria resulted in David Munoz being fastest by just 0.026 of a second over points leader Alonso. The latter was on pole, however, after Munoz was penalised as the cause of the Sachsenring's last-lap multiple crash, being given a back-row start plus a long-lap penalty.

Continuing his good form, Bertelle was third fastest, while Uriarte completed the front row.

Race one was a scorcher, and Daniel Munoz took a first win in fabulous style after an incredible race-long lead battle of eight. The 15-year-old Spaniard put in a perfect last lap to hold off Ortola and Alonso.

David Munoz had a superb ride from the back of the grid. His opening laps were sensational, and he quickly cut through to the front group, while arch-rival Alonso did most of the leading. Munoz also had the long-lap penalty to serve, however, and that dropped him out of the pack. Then Alonso received a long-lap penalty for exceeding track limits, so now they were together. They fought back into the lead group for the last two laps, Munoz finally fourth, 0.234 of a second behind Alonso.

Thus Alonso extended his points advantage, while Munoz was frustrated. Race two didn't help, as Alonso ramped it up a notch with a perfect effort to take victory by 4.7 seconds, ahead of a battle of eight KTMs, Buasri grabbing second over David Munoz.

All the front-runners, including the leader, had risked long-lap penalties for exceeding track limits, and Holgado was given a three-second post-race penalty again, which dropped him to seventh. After ninth on Saturday, the weekend severely dented his title challenge.

Mugello winner Furusato was another to be given a three-second penalty, dropping to eighth, which left Ortola fourth. Saturday winner Daniel Munoz had already served a long-lap penalty and finished fifth.

A week later, the Austrian GP was held at the same venue, but this time it was Barcelona's Millan who found form and grabbed pole from early in qualifying, and he kept getting quicker. David Munoz was second, boosting his Cup hopes, as a frustrated Alonso would start from the second row. Furusato completed the front row.

There was nothing frustrating about Alonso's race though, as he replicated his very cool and classy race-two victory from the previous weekend, winning by 3.8 seconds over David Munoz and Buasri.

After a fierce early battle, Alonso put the pressure on. Once he got away, the chasing pack could do nothing, and for the last handful of laps it came down to a five-rider chase group, with David Munoz and Buasri swapping places with Furusato, Holgado and Bertelle. On the penultimate lap, Holgado bumped Furusato wide, leaving Buasri and Munoz, the Spaniard taking second ahead of the 20-year-old Thai.

In Sunday's race, Alonso staked a strong claim to the title with his third Austrian win in a row. Right on his tail all the way was Buasri, with Ortola heading the chasing pack after a 13-rider lead battle for most of the race.

Alonso couldn't break away this time. Arch-rival David Munoz was particularly determined to hold on, but then nearly crashed. His big save gave Alonso and Buasri breathing space, and he finally crossed the line sixth to stand 38 points adrift with two races and 50 points still to be claimed at Motorland Aragon.

The last two races would decide the Cup between Alonso and David Munoz. The others just wanted to win.

Holgado staked an early claim with a blistering early lap, taking pole by over half a second, with Alonso on the other side of the grid in third. Moreira split the two, while David Munoz qualified seventh.

Race one was an intense decider, won by Holgado ahead of David Munoz and Alonso, who had done enough to claim the title with a race to spare. "It was a difficult race," he said, "maybe because of the pressure. I managed as best as I can and I could win the championship. Tomorrow I can enjoy the race."

The Colombian had fought for the race win all the way, but Holgado had the edge on the final lap. Moreira and Bertelle completed the top five, with just 0.409 of a second covering them all at the line. David Munoz locked out second place in the title chase, a repeat of 2020; Holgado secured third – he had been fifth in 2020.

The title had been decided, but the final race on Sunday was still a belter that went down to the line, with Ortola snatching the lead from pole-man and Saturday winner Holgado into the final corner. Out on to the finish straight, Alonso was right alongside in a seven-bike mass finish.

Ortola's winning margin was just 0.006 of a second over fellow Spaniard Holgado. Alonso was 0.050 behind and 0.108 ahead of David Munoz. Less than half a second covered the top seven, with Daniel Munoz fifth ahead of Moreira and Bertelle.

There is no doubt that David Alonso is a worthy Red Bull MotoGP Rookies Cup winner. He is already looking to the future and wondering if he can match Pedro Acosta's stunning achievement, going from 2020 Cup champion to 2021 Moto3 world champion.

SUPERBIKE WORLD CHAMPIONSHIP REVIEW OF 2021

By GORDON RITCHIE

SHOEI
YAMAHA
BRIXX.com
PATA
54
BMP TAPPI
YAMAHA
PATA
BMP TAPPI
YAMAHA

INTRODUCTION
NEW CHAMPION, NEW STRENGTH

By GORDON RITCHIE

Above: Champion and stuntman, Toprak Razgatlioglu was a crowd-pleaser in both roles.

Top right: Welshman Chaz Davies retired after a 22-year racing career.

Right: The final bow. Chaz on the grid in Indonesia.

Opening spread: The fight between Razgatlioglu and Rea defined the 2021 season, as the six-times champion fought in vain.
Photos: Gold & Goose

WE had all hoped that the pandemic would have been a distant memory by the time the 2021 season got going, but humanity didn't get that lucky. On the narrow, but passionate motorsport scene, that meant continuing travel restrictions, and testing, testing, testing… For WorldSBK, it actually meant far greater regulatory interference, admin, and sheer spend on Covid paperwork and clearances than in the relatively free season of 2020.

With a 13-round season scheduled at one time from Australia in the early part of the year to two flyaways in Argentina and Indonesia at the end, it was going to be busy again by WorldSBK standards.

Further regulatory conditions resulted in the season start being delayed and rejigged several times, before the action finally got going in late May. You would have been a brave optimist to predict that we would get all 13 rounds in, including the two tricky long-hauls at the end.

But we made it through, thanks to the collective will of the core Dorna personnel and the desire of the two long-haul rounds to hold their events. Argentina and Indonesia really did not want to leave it for another year.

In the end, WorldSBK got all the way back to base with 13 rounds and almost all the planned races being completed. Only human tragedy at Jerez and bad weather in Indonesia prevented us from completing a full 39 individual races.

The racing was as good as any in the previous 30-odd years, with five different winners, 13 podium finishers and four of the five competing manufacturers with at least one victory. Only Honda missed out, but they did score podiums.

WorldSBK's prestige, positive public attention and general feel-good factor expanded exponentially in 2021, as the groundhog days of six-times champion Jonathan Rea looked seriously under threat, and not just from 2020 rival Scott Redding and Ducati.

Toprak Razgatlioglu's ability to ride his Yamaha R1 to its very limits went from immense to extraordinary in almost every single race. Consistency and drama, ebullience and total control, his one-race-win-at-a-time approach made him champion.

Kawasaki not being given their expected 500 or so extra peak revs made a real difference to Rea, as the ageing long-stroke engine made life hard on corner entry and exit. Inertia was a problem for him and the other Ninja riders. Even the six-timer could not overcome this disadvantage when the free-riding Razgatlioglu was putting him under pressure almost every weekend.

DAVIES BOWS OUT

WELSHMAN Chaz Davies almost retired in 2020, but remained in the paddock he had called his racing home since 2009 for just one more year, in the well-supported Ducati GoEleven Independent team. He scored a final podium at Estoril before a mixture of injury and reality prompted him to officially announce his retirement at the Jerez round, at the age of 34.

Having been racing since the age of 12, in 2002, Davies graduated to the 125cc World Championship – at 15, the youngest rider ever. He competed in the GP junior classes, had a short spell in AMA racing and took part in three Ducati MotoGP races in 2007.

Swapping codes, he rode in WorldSSP for Triumph and Yamaha, then won WorldSBK races for Aprilia, BMW and Ducati. In all, he won 32 WorldSBK races, stood on 99 podiums and eventually recorded seven Superpole 'wins'.

Davies was a title runner-up on three occasions, in 2015, 2017 and 2018. Without Rea and the Kawasaki steamroller, there is no doubt that greater things would have been within the popular rider's reach.

Those who think he is one of the best WorldSBK riders never to have won a title are both right and wrong. He never was champion in the biggest production class, but he was a full FIM Supersport World Champion in 2009, with Yamaha.

The on-track action was often tactile, with different shades of paint and tyre marks joining sponsors' logos on fairings, elbows and knees.

Yamaha plus Razgatlioglu beat Kawasaki plus Rea; beat them straight up.

The champion from Turkey was the first at this level from a Muslim culture, a true product of WorldSBK's nursery classes, plus a stoppie and stunt king. The new WorldSBK riding boss and his pugilistic peers made every weekend an audio-visual thrill ride.

That forced WorldSBK back under the awestruck gazes of even those who normally would have shown little interest. Every weekend was a box of delights in 2021, and we never knew what we were going to get.

Many of the old guard, such as Chaz Davies, Leon Haslam and Tom Sykes, reached the end of their WorldSBK careers in 2021, while newer, younger, talents, like Michael Ruben Rinaldi and Axel Bassani, grew in stature.

A reverse-osmosis talent experiment by HRC will result in two MotoGP chargers, Iker Lecuona and Xavi Vierge, racing in WorldSBK in 2022, so the prospects seem good. Add in Redding and Alvaro Bautista changing factory teams, and we look set for anything but a season of foreseeable outcomes.

INTRODUCTION 243

Red Bull
YAMAHA RACING
YAMAHA Revs Your Heart
bLU CRU
AKRAPOVIČ
SHOEI
BMP TAPPI
YAMALUBE
GYTR
SNACK PATA

CHAMPION PROFILE: TOPRAK RAZGATLIOGLU

TOP OF THE TRACKS

By GORDON RITCHIE

IT was always going to take somebody special to dethrone the most successful WorldSBK racer of all time. The fact that Jonathan Rea got to within 13 points of the final winning total of Toprak Razgatlioglu shows that, although the man from Antalya was a clear and deserving FIM Superbike World Championship winner, he had to give his best every time to beat the best ever over a full year.

Of course, a closer examination of the season reminds us that Razgatlioglu lost three points scores due to no fault of his own. One because of a crash at Assen caused by another rider; then an electrical problem at Catalunya when he was leading; and finally crashing and no-scoring again when a faulty front fender mount came off and went under his front wheel at Portimao, leaving another raft of points stranded on the trackside sand dunes.

Many in the immediate aftermath of Yamaha's delirious winning celebrations said that he had made no mistakes at all in 2021, but that is not completely true. He wandered marginally on to the track-limits paint on the final lap of one Assen and one Magny-Cours race, losing a few points each time. Hardly hanging offences, but self-inflicted losses all the same.

In all other regards, Razgatlioglu was able to unleash his incredible bike control and judgement on to a very suspecting WorldSBK paddock, and make them work better than even Rea could.

Everybody within WorldSBK knows the level of Razgatlioglu's talent, and has known it for years, since the first time he stepped on to a Superbike for his former Kawasaki Puccetti Racing team in testing in 2018. Factory rider Rea towed him along and was happy to do so. But even then, he said that Razgatlioglu was fast, and he knew that the tall Turkish rider would be trouble one day.

That day is now.

The occasional spats between Yamaha, Kawasaki and even Redding in Ducati through 2021 added some spice to the Toprak mix, but the calm, collected and fundamentally shy rider just absorbed it all, and then went out and rode faster. That proved to be the correct approach, and it won him the championship.

At 25 years of age, Razgatlioglu is not some precocious young kid, but he does ride like one. Except that he almost never falls off through his own mistakes, and he made his unique approach work at every circuit, even the ones that did not suit his riding style or his machine's capabilities. He constantly surprised, after a steady start in Motorland and Estoril. There were very few non-Yamaha/non-Toprak venues during the season, as Razgatlioglu simply made up for any small disadvantages. With Yamaha riders winning all over, the R1 clearly had become the rounded package it had threatened to be, with enough of everything good and no obvious gaps in its capabilities.

The son of a stunt rider, who always told his boy he would be a world champion one day, Razgatlioglu rode to commemorate his father, who was killed on a motorcycle four years ago. His father is the clear inspiration for all the crowd-pleasing stoppies and other stunts he enjoys doing – and has the mental and talent spectrum to do – without them affecting his ability to concentrate on his racing.

Now some people say that the 2015 European Superstock champion should move up to MotoGP. That shows a fundamental misunderstanding of the man and the culture he comes from.

He is a Superbike guy by naturalisation and inclination. He simply doesn't want to go to MotoGP yet, maybe ever, because he didn't like it when he was in the Rookies Cup. He likes going home to Turkey at every opportunity. In MotoGP, with ever more races and tests to go to…

Of course, it's quite possible that he will go there one day, but that will be when he wants, and not before. And if no more GP offers come? Well, he can stay in WorldSBK, the hottest property right now and a champion at 25. Not my viewpoint, his stated viewpoint.

And what is he like?

Hard to know in some ways, as much because of the language barrier as anything, but he is his own man, polite, humble, but with vast reservoirs of skill and quiet determination to succeed. He only shows off and becomes aggressive on the bike.

There has never been a world champion like Toprak, as a rider or as a person.

SUPERBIKE WORLD CHAMPIONSHIP
2021 TEAMS & RIDERS

By GORDON RITCHIE

BMW

BMW Motorrad WorldSBK Team
British rider **Tom Sykes** (36) was joined in 2021 by Dutchman **Michael van der Mark** (28) in the official BMW team. It was an Anglo-German effort again, Shaun Muir leading the SMR side of the operation. Another Dutchman, Marc Bongers, was in charge of the overall BMW race project once more.

An important new step for the season was the replacement of the S1000RR with the M1000RR. **Eugene Laverty** (35) also raced for the factory team in some of the later rounds, as a replacement for the injured Tom Sykes.

Bonovo MGM Racing
Jonas Folger (28) made the leap to WorldSBK full time, but despite showing some flashes of pace in Michael Galinski's team, injury and other realities prevented him from showing the kind of pace needed to get into the top half of the WorldSBK yearbook.

RC Squadra Corse
Eugene Laverty (35) found himself in a one-rider effort that did not last the course. So, 2021 was yet another tough season for the one-time championship runner-up.

B-MAX Racing Team
The M1000RR-equipped privateer team brought CIV rider **Gabriele Ruiu** (21) to Portimao.

DUCATI

Aruba.it Racing – Ducati World Superbike Team
Scott Redding (28) had a new team-mate in **Michael Ruben Rinaldi** (25), in a potent Ducati line-up, and both riders duly won races, as factory riders must.

Once again, Feel Racing was responsible for many logistical aspects of the red army, in a team that was managed by Serafino Foti, but largely financed and controlled by Aruba.it, whose role was more than that of a major sponsor. Stefano Cecconi was in charge of the Aruba element.

As always, the technical aspects were overseen by Ducati Corse, with Marco Zambenedetti in charge for the Bolognese manufacturer.

A second year for Redding had much the same elements as his rookie year: brilliance and disappointment. The first factory season for Rinaldi was also up and down, but two home wins at Misano were a particular highlight.

Consistency of winning performance was still the elusive quality for Ducati's official team, but it was required more than ever.

Barni Racing Team Ducati
Tito Rabat (32) began the season as a WorldSBK debutant with high hopes. Barni is a team with a proven podium heritage, looking over the MotoGP hedge to get back into the leading mix. Results did not play out the way they expected, however, and Rabat ended up leaving halfway through.

Samuele Cavalieri (24) took over the ride, having left the TPR Kawasaki team. Another discordant symphony of musical saddles for some teams in 2021.

Team GO Eleven Ducati
Chaz Davies (34), one of the few to have really taken the fight to Jonathan Rea over several seasons, decided to stay in WorldSBK, despite having lost his factory slot. With some fiscal and technical support from the official sources, he was fleetingly fast when uninjured.

Loris Baz (28) was drafted in for a couple of rounds and played podium-sized hands of speed poker after his season-long MotoAmerica adventure had finished.

MotoCorsa Racing Ducati
Axel Bassani (22) and his fellow Italians showed what was possible even for a small WorldSBK effort on a modest budget – if you know what you are doing on and off track. They brought a real feel-good factor to the whole year, and they all grew in stature.

HONDA

Team HRC Honda
The second year of life for the official factory effort looked a lot like the first, with occasional high points, but an overall air of something being not quite right.

Alvaro Bautista (35) and **Leon Haslam** (38) were the most seasoned campaigners imaginable. The bike's engine was fast, but set-up and feel fickle.

Recent top WorldSBK rider Leon Camier came in as team manager, with an early brief to maximise performance by interpreting rider feedback, then communicating it effectively to Japan. Overall, it was another difficult year.

MIE Racing Honda Team
Leandro Mercado (29) scored points in 2021, but this was a truly challenging season for all. He withdrew at one point to return home and regroup, and there were some improvements towards the end of the season.

Alessandro Delbianco (24) rode for Midori Moriwaki's team at Most, but had little luck.

KAWASAKI

Kawasaki Racing Team
Northern Irish superstar **Jonathan Rea** (34) showed his class and quality once again by trading blows throughout with anybody who threatened his championship crown. He tore some chapters of the record books asunder yet again.

Alex Lowes (31) had almost no good fortune at all, with a shoulder injury and then a damaged throttle hand preventing him from producing more than occasional podium finishes.

Guim Roda headed the Provec Racing side of the KRT effort.

Kawasaki Puccetti Racing
Again a single-rider effort in 2021, the semi-supported Italians, led by Manuel Puccetti, featured French hard charger **Lucas Mahias** (32). There might have been too many hard charges from the full-season rookie as, while occasionally fast, he was too frequently injured to see the season out. A best result of seventh at Donington was his personal highpoint.

Tito Rabat replaced him in the final few rounds.

Outdo Kawasaki TPR
Back to a two-rider configuration, Lucio Pedercini's team started out with **Loris Cresson** (22) in a full-time slot, joined by **Samuele Cavalieri** (24). Youth over experience, as a deliberate policy. Cresson rode almost all season before injury, but only **Oliver Konig** (19) went to the final round, for his first WorldSBK race.

Over the season, Pedercini also ran **Luke Mossey** (29), **Luciano Ribodino** (27), **Jayson Uribe** (22), **Marco Solorza** (34) and **Lachlan Epis** (21).

Orelac Racing VerdNatura Kawasaki
Isaac Vinales (28) embarked on his first season in WorldSBK and found it tough on a private Kawasaki, despite producing some strong individual showings at season's end.

Vince 64
Andrea Mantovani (27) brought flair and expansive hair as a wild-card at Assen and Jerez while running inside the overall Puccetti technical tent.

SUZUKI

JEG Racing
Yes, a Suzuki, ridden at Navarra by **Naomichi Uramoto**. He just missed out on a point in race one.

YAMAHA

Pata Yamaha With Brixx WorldSBK Team
In a year when the Yamaha backroom efforts started to really pay off, **Toprak Razgatlioglu** (25) became the polished article. His consistency was almost perfect, his bike's a bit less so at times.

Andrea Locatelli (25) made the giant leap from WorldSSP to WorldSBK look straightforward, taking podium finishes in the process.

Crescent Racing faced new challenges, its United Kingdom location providing Paul Denning and his staff with a complicated season. Andrea Dosoli was responsible for the Yamaha tech and strategy side from HQ in Italy.

GRT Yamaha WorldSBK
Garrett Gerloff (26) had a tough second year in WorldSBK, and within GRT. Too many high-profile incidents with other riders appeared to inhibit him later in the campaign.

Kohta Nozane (26) had a challenging first year in such a strong field, but started to get the hang of it, via his radical hanging-off style, towards the end of the year.

Alstare/GIL Racing
This had started out as a collaboration between Francis Batta's Alstare organisation and GIL Racing, until health reasons forced Batta to remain at home. **Christophe Ponsson** (25) managed to score modest points almost regularly from the middle of the season onwards.

IXS-YART
Endurance excellence made for positive showings at Most and Jerez from **Marvin Fritz** (25), and at Most only for **Karel Hanika** (25).

Toprak Razgatlioglu	Jonathan Rea	Scott Redding
Andrea Locatelli	Michael Ruben Rinaldi	Michael van der Mark
Garrett Gerloff	Alex Lowes	Axel Bassani	Tom Sykes
Alvaro Bautista	Leon Haslam	Chaz Davies	Kohta Nozane
Tito Rabat	Isaac Vinales	Lucas Mahias	Eugene Laverty

2021 TEAMS AND RIDERS 247

SUPERBIKE WORLD CHAMPIONSHIP
THE SUPERBIKES OF 2021

By GORDON RITCHIE

DUCATI PANIGALE V4R

BMW M1000RR

YAMAHA YZF-R1

BMW M1000RR

FROM 'S' to 'M' in its nomenclature, BMW hoped its latest WorldSBK contender would go forward not backward through the alphabet of overall performance. The 'M' is an important symbol for BMW, gracing its performance cars, and there was enough difference between the old bike and the new one, inside and out, for the FIM to grant it a new homologation.

With a higher-revving stock bike engine, the official M's peak revs were limited to 15,500rpm, up 600 from the previous model. That was still 100 short of the Honda's maximum revs, and 600 short of the Ducati's. The uprated BMW engine gave around 4–5 per cent more power and torque. A different flywheel came as a concession part.

The existing 80 x 49.7mm bore-and-stroke ratio was retained for the M, which remained a 999cc transverse in-line four-cylinder design, with finger valve followers and 'shift cam' variable valve timing system. This arrangement changes the set of cam lobes that contacts the valves, via a solenoid, in one camshaft revolution. Lighter internal components reduced vibration.

The M version had different porting to the S, even as a stock bike, which made a better base for further tuning. Akrapovic supplied the all-new low-level exhaust.

A new clutch was employed, based on the standard M road bike, but with racing modifications.

Bosch/BMW's BMMS electronics were retained, with the stock ECU as its base. There was a completely new custom wiring loom for 2021, to improve the run of the cables and add reliability. It even included redundancy elements in case anything went wrong.

RVP25/30 front forks and RVP50 rear shocks were used again, the standard Öhlins suspension package. A new swing-arm appeared, manufactured by Suter, and one update followed. The new bike had the 2020 yokes and other front-end chassis parts. Bonamici supplied other ancillary elements of the rolling chassis.

PVM supplied the wheels, which were new for 2021.

Nissin supplied two different designs of front brake caliper, and BMW used them both, one for Sykes and another for van der Mark, in accordance with each rider's preference. New developments were made in this area, and at the most extreme braking tracks front brake air ducts, which had been designed and made in house on a 3D printer, appeared. There were two choices of diameter for the Yutaka brake rotors, and different thickness options, too.

The bike was not quite on the 168kg weight limit.

And those big front wings? They were said to deliver 16kg of downforce at 300km/h.

DUCATI PANIGALE V4R

THERE was nothing radical on the Ducati again, with no new homologation for 2021, but it was still upgraded in a few areas.

In general, with lots of privateers again in WorldSBK and other classes, and in an effort to keep costs down, Ducati tried to use as many stock parts as possible while maintaining on-track performance.

More work was done on fuel storage to reduce changes in the centre of gravity as laps counted down. The basic starting balance of Michael Ruben Rinaldi's bike was moved a couple of times in the season, to move it closer to Redding's overall setting.

A new rear linkage for the Öhlins RSP50 rear shock appeared. There were lots of small changes, but as Ducati said, the bike was an evolution, not a revolution. The lower part of the Öhlins 46mm RVP2530 front forks was modified to reduce the unsprung weight and improve rider feel. An FIM request that the front fender design be closer to stock was taken on board.

The latest Brembo radial P4X30-34 calipers gripped the front discs, which were available in a new 338.5mm size, although the 336mm versions were used at tracks that were less critical for brake performance. Vented forms of the new discs were also available, with multiple cooling fins protruding from the inside of the rotor. The new front calipers were also heavily vented on the front face to catch any cooling air. In addition, Ducati employed cooling air ducts for the front brakes.

Marchesini alloy wheels were fitted, front and rear.

It was still the highest-revving bike out there, with a mandated 16,100rpm ceiling. At 16,000rpm, it made more than 235bhp at the crankshaft. A slightly wider-diameter Akrapovic 4–2 exhaust was used. Work was also done over the winter to improve the STM dry clutch, which became lighter and more reliable, according to Ducati.

The 90-degree V4 contra-rotating desmodromic engine, with bore and stroke of 81 x 48.4mm, was fed by ride-by-wire elliptical throttle bodies, equivalent to a 56mm round intake.

There was no change of flywheel weight for 2021, although it is allowed under the latest rules, and Ducati had a modification ready to go.

YAMAHA YZF-R1

IN 2021, the Yamaha R1 became the bike it always had threatened to be, delivering consistency of high-level performance seemingly more than any of its peers. It expanded into every edge of its operating window, maximising performance, and the result was evident on track for all to see.

Few of these improvements came from radically different hardware, more an accumulation of good work from previous years and their latest testing programme.

The biggest improvement was in understanding how the tyres worked, and how to get the best from them, which allowed use of the softest tyres more often than most others. The bike could be set up to suit different weather conditions more easily, too. Testing at tracks where they had struggled was another step forward.

The 998cc in-line four-cylinder, with its cross-plane crankshaft beating out a 270–180–90–180-degree rhythm, was fast enough and controllable enough going into the corners. Straddling the gap between the most- and least-radical motors, the 79 x 50.9mm bore-and-stroke engine architecture could compete in a form that had really come to new life in 2020, with a host of new technical steps to help the R1 in race trim.

Yamaha teams in the championship ran the latest specification of machine.

The unique engine featured the now-common finger-style cam followers. The 45mm throttle butterflies were deliberately close to the intake port, while the Bosch injectors sat above the intake trumpets, not below.

There was a new Akrapovic exhaust, again a 4–2–1, said to be an update as part of the regular tuning developments. The maximum revs for the Yamaha remained stuck at the 2020 level of 14,950rpm.

Marelli's WorldSBK MLE electronics system, almost ubiquitous in WorldSBK, except for BMW's custom system, was chosen again. On the chassis side, a slightly new swing-arm was used by all, and there was unity of front fork yoke design. Rear links were a personal and set-up choice.

Lots of work was done in the winter to improve the aerodynamic performance, to help Yamaha's generally tall riders cut through the air better. Strict limits are in place for this kind of development, but a small improvement was made. Just like all the other small things that Yamaha said combined to make a big difference.

HONDA CBR1000RR-R SP

A VERY specially-made, but otherwise completely conventional across-the-frame four-cylinder machine, in its second year, had another tough winter of development, with so many restrictions on travel again for some key staff.

More podiums were earned, and in terms of outright engine performance, the Honda was in the top echelon once more.

Again, the radical 81 x 48.5mm bore-and-stroke motor was fed by four 52mm throttle bodies mounted very tightly to the inlet valve area. Improved throttle response, and increased combustion efficiency and chamber filling were all needed on the stock bike to allow the WorldSBK version to be fast enough in 2021. The engine featured titanium conrods and finger-follower valve actuation, while Akrapovic provided the 4–1 exhaust system.

In simple terms, the Honda was as fast an anything in a straight line – with Bautista on it at least.

The WorldSBK standard 46mm-diameter Öhlins RVP front forks and RVP rear shock provided suspension, as there was no new Öhlins WorldSBK-wide front fork for 2021. OZ wheels graced the bike front and rear.

Quite how much the internal winglets influenced downforce is still open to debate, but like all the others, they had to be the same as the road bike in shape and design.

Lots of small details were said to be the key to an uptick in performance on some weekends, but feel and feedback were still not quite there, consistency at high speed elusive at times.

KAWASAKI NINJA ZX-10RR

THERE was a new bike for 2021, according to Kawasaki, but there were not enough changes for the FIM to declare it a new model and grant a new homologation. Much to Kawasaki's disappointment. The oldest bike design on the grid had received regular homologations to allow it to remain competitive, but not this time.

The main internal change was a lower-friction piston, but it was not allowed to sing to its full extent. Kawasaki had tested all winter with their planned free-revving engine. They had expected to be granted 500 or 600 more revs at the top end, but the same limit of 14,600rpm was what they were given all year.

In general, the bike's performance in hot conditions was also not as strong as it had been in the cool of winter testing.

The Kawasaki ran the least radical basic engine design of all. The 76 x 55mm bore-and-stroke figures were way behind its rivals, giving it a different nature to ride, and especially different inertia characteristics entering corners. In some ways, it won by being more rideable in other areas of the racetrack, with the new pistons also making the engine power more linear.

Another drawback of not having the extra revs they had expected was that other bikes had better corner exit acceleration, which also compromised top speed.

Akrapovic provided the exhaust again; a Magneti Marelli MLE spec ECU controlled the engine.

There were upgrades for Showa's biggest WorldSBK partner, inside the front forks, which featured lighter internals. With a sturdy 48mm slider diameter, the Showas were visibly different from the Öhlins used by most other top teams.

Uniquely, the rear suspension unit was almost laid flat from the swing-arm link to the top mounting point, slightly to one side of the bike's centre-line. A new rear link was available, but it made only a small difference to fine-tune the set-up. Lowes and Rea chose different swing-arm designs with slightly altered rigidity.

Brembo provided their latest Superbike-approved and cost-capped calipers, with different fins and piston diameters, for the Kawasaki. The bigger-diameter discs with the fins on the inside were used only very sparingly. Marchesini wheels were the same as in 2020.

Outwardly, the new bike featured small internal front wings and pressure-balancing/airflow holes in the tail unit as parts of an almost completely new styling and aerodynamic package.

One main problem for even Rea was all that engine inertia pushing the bike into corners, and he tried to ride around it, sometimes too hard. Even with slipper-clutch and electronics-setting interventions, the inertia issue was still evident.

Another problem that the Kawasaki faced in 2021 was not being able to use the softest tyre most of the time, while some other machines could make more use of grippier rubber.

REV LIMITS 2021
There were no mid-season adjustments under the balancing rules
BMW – 15,500
Ducati – 16,100
Honda – 15,600
Kawasaki – 14,600
Suzuki – 14,900
Yamaha – 14,950

SUPERBIKE WORLD CHAMPIONSHIP
ARAGON
ROUND 1 · SPAIN

Above: Bautista tails Razgatlioglu in the sprint race.

Top: The Kawasakis of Rea and Lowes sandwich Redding's Ducati as they lead away for the first race of the year.

Above right: Tom Sykes qualified his new BMW on the front row.

Right: Michael van der Mark essayed intermediates to fifth in race two, but was overhauled by Lowes (22) and Sykes (66).
Photos: Gold & Goose

250 WORLD SUPERBIKE REVIEW

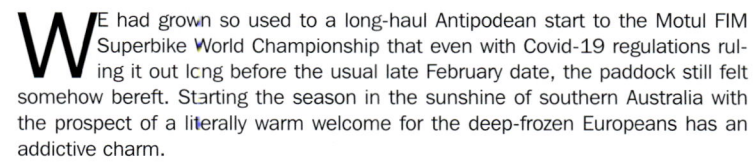

WE had grown so used to a long-haul Antipodean start to the Motul FIM Superbike World Championship that even with Covid-19 regulations ruling it out long before the usual late February date, the paddock still felt somehow bereft. Starting the season in the sunshine of southern Australia with the prospect of a literally warm welcome for the deep-frozen Europeans has an addictive charm.

So while there was no Phillip Island starter course for the 2021 feast, at least we kicked off at another circuit that had been built on a grand scale, albeit not until late May. And in Spain.

The new season's rider and team line-up, largely the same as 2020's, had only one Aragon-based round to contend with, but there were three individual races in which to flex their muscles for the first time in seven months.

A 1m 45.518s new track best from Jonathan Rea won him Tissot Superpole; Scott Redding and Tom Sykes joined him on the front row. With Alex Lowes fourth and Chaz Davies fifth, there was an all-UK top-five grid lockout for the first time since 1988. And with at least one rider from the five competing manufacturers inside the top seven places, everything looked set for a strong season, even before any racing had taken place.

When it did get under way, with Saturday's 18-lap race one, KRT riders Rea and Lowes immediately set about gapping everybody else by over a second.

With a struggling Redding losing early pace, a few of the challengers behind him were held up, and Rea made a great escape. Lowes was finally caught by the determined Toprak Razgatlioglu's Yamaha, but the fight continued to a last-lap crescendo of high-velocity belligerence.

Lowes fought back well, with some aggressive and effective riding securing second, the Yamaha rider spinning up his rear tyre out of the last corner. Redding repassed Davies for fourth.

Rea, on a 'new' Kawasaki, had found a new frontier of his own – an epoch-defining 100th career race win.

Sunday morning, with the now-traditional ten-lap Tissot Superpole Race, dawned wet and a bit miserable. On a drying track, the new season became more competitive than it had been on Saturday. Intermediates were the best choice, but almost nobody had ever used them. Rea and many others finally did, on the strong advice of single-make tyre supplier Pirelli.

Redding went for wets, however, and it proved the wrong option. As the track dried, his hopes evaporated, and he dropped to eighth as Rea and Lowes went one, two.

On the 'sprint' race podium in third, Garrett Gerloff notched up one for the Independent riders early in the year. Davies was fourth, while Michael van der Mark – on slicks, no less – had gone from 15th to fifth.

The track was still not completely dry for race two, and the first of a few early-season controversies involved Gerloff. He had tried to probe for a pass on Rea into the downhill chicane, but only succeeded in hitting him and falling. Run off the track after the contact, Rea battled back to an inspired second.

Up front, Redding's choice of dry tyres proved his redemption. He won with ease, with Lowes third behind Rea.

Some great tussles for podium potential had both official new BMWs in the thick of it: Sykes fourth and van der Mark fifth. While dry tyres had ruled, once again intermediates showed valid podium ability.

Above: Scott Redding opted for slicks for race two and reaped the rewards.
Photo: Ducati Corse

Left: Redding's slick after the race.

Top: Gerloff and Rea collide in race two. Rea fought back to second.

Below: Kawasaki mechanics fettle Lowes's bike for the sprint race.

Below right: Another milestone – Rea celebrates his 100th win.
Photos: Gold & Goose

ROUND 1 · ARAGON 251

SUPERBIKE WORLD CHAMPIONSHIP
ESTORIL
ROUND 2 · PORTUGAL

Above: Razgatlioglu takes the long-lap as Redding and Rea set the pace in race two.

Right: Pirelli SC0 tyres – a talking point all year.

Above right: Razgatlioglu and Davies tackle the language barrier after race two.
Photos: Gold & Goose

Top: The Ducatis of Redding and Rinaldi show the way through Estoril's uphill chicane.
Photo: Ducati Corse

252 WORLD SUPERBIKE REVIEW

ONE of the old-school WorldSBK circuits provided us with a second Superpole qualifying contest of the year and the second pre-race 'win' for Jonathan Rea. That, and a whole lot of controversy that would lead to a mid-season rule change.

Tito Rabat had run off at Turn One on his Barni Ducati, but not crashed, very close to the end of the always frantic Superpole session. Yellow flags meant that every other rider on a fast lap lost their single chance to earn a grid position using their rear qualifying tyre. Soon after this round, two qualifying tyres were issued per Superpole session.

Rea's pole advantage was overturned immediately in race one by both Redding and Razgatlioglu. Shortly after, Michael Ruben Rinaldi also eased past for a spell. With Redding and Razgatlioglu doing all the front running, the Ducati rider held his advantage all the way to his second win of the year. Razgatlioglu only just kept Rea behind, and the top three crossed the line within 0.915 of a second.

Having given the relatively new generation of super-soft SCX tyres a hard time in a very public and vocal way at the previous round, saying that only the smallest riders could use them for the longer races, Redding duly went out and won on an SCX rear at Portugal. Over 21 laps. Rea's Kawasaki had to use the harder SCO, which was almost always the case in 2021.

Behind the podium trio, the rest were chasing phantoms, with Gerloff almost ten seconds behind the winner, in fourth.

In a thrilling ten-lap Superpole race on Sunday, the top three protagonists were at it again, until Redding made an error that dropped him to fourth, where he remained until three laps from the end.

Counterintuitively, Rea used the SCO rear to win the short ten-lap race, from a closely following Razgatlioglu. The SCX should have been better. Redding was third, Gerloff fourth and Rinaldi fifth. For a single-make tyre supplier, Pirelli's habit of offering real options to demand different set-up decisions was a talking point all season.

The weekend clicked into full drama mode in race two, as both Redding and Razgatlioglu jumped the lights, earning the latter a double long-lap penalty. Early leader Redding penalised himself, and more harshly.

Rea was almost taken out by an early inside pass from the determined Rinaldi who, in turn, succumbed to another outbraking error from Gerloff at Turn Six on the second lap; both riders crashed out.

Rea inherited second when Razgatlioglu took his first long-lap penalty. Once he had closed on Redding, they had their own private battle, only ended when the latter slid out while shadow-boxing his rival's tail unit at Turn Four.

He would finally be ranked 16th, just missing the points.

With Rea's most immediate danger gone, Chaz Davies claimed a popular second on his Independent GoEleven Ducati. Only two rounds in, that result seemed to vindicate his decision to carry on after his factory career had been ended in 2020. He'd won an emotional final Estoril race for Aruba and Ducati the previous season, of course.

Razgatlioglu was almost ten seconds (a little more than two long-laps' worth) behind Rea in third, with Lowes fourth and rookie Andrea Locatelli, from the official Pata Yamaha with Brixx team, fifth.

Michael van der Mark claimed sixth, from outside the top ten, with the new BMW M1000RR.

In the sunshine of a Portuguese weekend, the future of the championship fight was confirmed as a three-way contest, between Rea, Razgatlioglu and Redding. The list of leading men would become a little longer, however, and very soon.

Above: A pair of top-tens for Eugene Laverty on the BMW.

Above centre: Rea leads Razgatlioglu, Gerloff and Redding on his way to the Superpole win.

Top: Chaz Davies claimed a welcome second and top Independent honours in race two.

Left: Rea takes the flag and extends his points lead with the race-two win.

Right: Garrett Gerloff was twice just off the podium.

Photos: Gold & Goose

ROUND 2 · ESTORIL 253

SUPERBIKE WORLD CHAMPIONSHIP
MISANO
ROUND 3 · ITALY

Above: Heavy company. Rinaldi leads Razgatlioglu, Rea and Redding.
Photo: Ducati Corse

Right: Two race wins and a second made a sweet home weekend for the young Italian.

Top right: Fast Friday. Razgatlioglu heads out for qualifying.
Photos: Gold & Goose

Above centre right: Not one podium for a glum Scott Redding.
Photo: Ducati Corse

Above centre far right: Keeping his cool – youngest rider Axel Bassani made an impression.

Above right: Michael van der Mark slithers out of the Superpole race.

Below right: Bassani took his Moto-corsa Racing Ducati into the top six in the Superpole race.

Below far right: Fans were back. Well, some of them, anyway.
Photos: Gold & Goose

254 WORLD SUPERBIKE REVIEW

THE paddock's rainbow of nationalities had been looking forward to a return to Italy. At times, the summer weather on the first trip to the seaside circuit since 2019 was too hot for some; while the signs of a happy local outcome were there from the opening day, when Michael Ruben Rinaldi topped the Friday time sheets.

With a tech snag causing Rea to miss valuable track time in FP1, and Rinaldi's fellow factory Ducati rider, Redding, losing the first part of FP2 in the pit lane, a sanction for not stopping for a black flag in FP1, it was hardly a normal Friday.

With Rea winning Superpole on Saturday at a new best pace, more normal service was resumed. After Razgatlioglu went second and Redding third, the soothsayers were even more convinced that there would be a great tussle later that day. Race pace, however, perennially buried in the details of the data, was in fourth-place qualifier Rinaldi's favour. His subsequent race-one win was not quite a career first, after his Motorland privateer victory in 2020, but a stuttering start to his full factory era was smoothed over by a victory of rare quality.

It was still rough-hewn stuff in the first few corners as he passed Rea and Razgatlioglu while demonstrating more vulgarity than finesse. The immediate squabbles and passes behind helped the Italian's cause.

Rea was most eager not to let the lead become too long, but he was never quite able to get into Rinaldi's slipstream. Then, with 12 laps to go, he lost the front, yet saved a crash, at Turn One, running off track and dropping behind Razgatlioglu.

The top three remained Rinaldi, Razgatlioglu and Rea to the flag, with Redding taking fourth.

Only 5,000 fans were allowed in, but they were the first anywhere in the season, and they were given what they wanted – a home win for bike and rider. Rinaldi lives 20 minutes from Misano.

In the ten-lap Sunday Superpole race, Razgatlioglu led until just over halfway, when Rinaldi passed him on the inside at the super-fast Turn 11, drawing gasps even from his own team as his audacity paid off; he won by 0.485 of a second.

Again, Razgatlioglu was second, Rea third, Redding fourth and Lowes fifth. The youngest rider in the field, Axel Bassani, was sixth for the first time on his Moto-Corsa V4R.

The Superpole results shuffled the first few grid spots of race two. Rinaldi started from pole, making the most of it to lead and surviving an early challenge from Razgatlioglu. Then Rea moved up from third to first as the final long race got into its stride.

In search of a *tripla*, Rinaldi retook the lead into the Quercia left-hander on lap two, until a very small, but completely flat-out, mistake into T11 allowed Rea past again. The weekend's action seemingly built into a crescendo of tension and action – except that it didn't. Race two was by far the least unpredictable and most metronomic for the leading riders.

Razgatlioglu was the main mover, taking the lead with 14 laps to go. But from then on, it was a largely evenly spaced fight to the finish.

Toprak took his first win of 2021, Rinaldi secured second and Rea inhabited one of his famous safe podium places, for a trio of third places.

Overall, the round was far from predictable. The prior expectation had been for a Rea-vs-Redding battle, but there were no wins for Rea, while three fourth-place finishes meant that Redding failed to score a single podium for the first time ever in a WorldSBK weekend.

ROUND 3 · MISANO 255

SUPERBIKE WORLD CHAMPIONSHIP
DONINGTON
ROUND 4 · GREAT BRITAIN

Above: Fenced in. Covid restrictions kept the public out of the paddock.

Above right: Plenty of space on the grass for spectators to enjoy a sunny Sunday finale.

Top: Backing it in, Razgatlioglu was clear of Rea at the Melbourne hairpin in race one.
Photos: Gold & Goose

Right: Leon Haslam fends off Gerloff for fourth in the sprint race.
Photo: HRC

Centre right: Wild-card Luke Mossey scored points in race one on the Bournemouth Kawasaki.
Photo: Gold & Goose

256 WORLD SUPERBIKE REVIEW

THIS being a race weekend in the UK, the weather was a talking point, and not just for the locals. Some epic rainfall, occasional sunshine and track conditions that careened from monsoon to midsummer – it was British racing weather at its foulest and finest.

Superpole was wet enough for Rea to claim his first ever pole at Donington, and the grand old lady of British racing became the 14th track where he had achieved this.

Championship challenger Razgatlioglu was only 13th on the grid, but in the tricky conditions, the new BMW M took Michael van der Mark to second, with team-mate Tom Sykes third.

On a wet, but drying surface, Rea led race one thanks to huge levels of confidence, but with an even more impressive early starter just behind. Razgatlioglu had gone from row five to second overall after only eight corners. Potential winner Redding had fallen at Hollywood, with just one lap completed.

With Rea sliding and slithering on his slick rear tyre, Razgatlioglu soon took the lead. The former almost suffered a high-side at the same Hollywood corner that had claimed Redding as he tried to keep up, running all the way down the grass to the left of Craner Curves like the old motocrosser he is.

He lost places, but soon got them back to regain second.

That was the best he was going to get, however, Razgatlioglu being the clear winner. Lowes was a home-town third, one-time almost unbeatable Donington force Sykes, fourth. Gerloff had fallen from a podium place in third, after returning from his one-off MotoGP ride at Assen. He recovered for seventh.

In a final comedic moment, after all that drama, Razgatlioglu almost ran out of fuel before the flag, and was helped home into the winner's circle by a push from Lowes's Kawasaki on the slow-down lap.

The Superpole race was held in conditions that prompted most to put their trust in intermediate tyres, but Redding went for full wets, spoiling his chances of an immediate recovery from his Saturday fall.

Lowes had tucked in behind Rea for an early KRT one, two, but fell on lap two at the Old Hairpin. As the track dried, that left Sykes and Michael van der Mark free to score second and third respectively, another big step forward for the German manufacturer.

Leon Haslam was fourth at very much his home track, an uptick in a second HRC season plagued by disappointment.

Sunshine came back into play at Donington for the final race of the weekend, with Rea leading Razgatlioglu into the first run down Craner Curves. The latter was on the ascent as he passed his rival into Coppice, then Rea almost clattered into him under braking into the Foggy Esses, with 18 laps to go.

Clearly Rea's bike was having issues with being pushed into corners under braking, but an error from Razgatlioglu allowed the former to pounce for the lead with 14 laps to run. Just one lap later, Rea fell entering Coppice, trail-braking on entry and washing out comprehensively as Razgatlioglu swept into the lead. Rea remounted and finished a pointless 20th.

Gerloff placed second – on the Fourth of July, no less – and Sykes secured a dry-weather third.

After a great start and very strong middle to his home weekend, Rea suffered a tough ending. The damage was maximised by the clear and present danger to his title, Razgatlioglu. With two race wins when it counted, the Turkish star took the championship lead, but more importantly he had snatched the initiative from Rea. Clearly, he was not going to ease away as usual, because Razgatlioglu's pace came with consistency baked in.

Above: Michael van der Mark prepares for the Superpole race, with a podium to come.

Left: Out of gas. New championship leader Razgatlioglu just made it across the line to win race one.

Top: Garrett Gerloff was second in Sunday's race two – his best result of the year.

Below: Happy Donington for BMW's Sykes, with two podiums.
Photos: Gold & Goose

SUPERBIKE WORLD CHAMPIONSHIP
ASSEN
ROUND 5 · NETHERLANDS

258 WORLD SUPERBIKE REVIEW

Above: It was all hands to the pumps as the fire brigade cleared the flooded track.

Left: Podium first-timer Locatelli shares the joy.

Far left: WorldSBK came back to Assen – both bikes and fans.

Below left: Razgatlioglu is skittled by team-mate Gerloff at race two's first corner.

Below far left: Italian youngster Andrea Mantovani was a lap down, but grabbed a couple of points in a depleted first race.
Photos: Gold & Goose

Bottom far left: Scott Redding wrestles with his Ducati to keep it off the green.
Photo: Ducati Corse

Below: Triple race winner Rea holds off Locatelli in race two.

Below right: "What's he got that I haven't?" Second-placed Redding checks out the winner's bike after race one.
Photos: Gold & Goose

THE return to 'The Cathedral' was cause for relief. Nothing else is quite like Assen, even in its endlessly modified form. It is one of WorldSBK's most visited venues for good reason.

Rea topped Friday's practice times, then put in a 1m 33.842s to make it five Superpoles in succession. Championship leader Razgatlioglu crashed in Superpole, but got going again to end up second fastest, with Scott Redding finally third.

In a dry first race of the weekend, Alex Lowes and Michael Ruben Rinaldi quickly fell from their top-five placings, leaving the championship's only *de facto* contenders to steal each other's slipstreams and corner entries for the first few minutes.

After those early flurries, Rea's unrivalled consistency, at a pace nobody else could match, allowed him to ease his way into a race-winning lead. His 13th Assen win was a record because nobody had scored quite so many victories at a single track in WorldSBK before. It was all over two laps early, as a fast crash for rookie Bonovo BMW rider Jonas Folger left him concussed and immobile at the side of the track, causing the race to be red-flagged.

Redding had finally outmatched Razgatlioglu for second, but in fourth place, the new BMW M was working well at home for Michael van der Mark.

A portent of things to come was Andrea Locatelli in a lonely, but assured fifth on the other factory Yamaha.

Truly epic overnight rains eventually cleared in time for the racing to start on Sunday, but the local fire service had to be called in to help the circuit organisers clear up the mess. Warm-up sessions were delayed, and even the short Superpole race started ten minutes late.

The sprint featured drama during and after its ten-lap duration. Rea was boxed in on the first few turns, followed soon after by a fast crash for van der Mark, then another for Alvaro Bautista.

Rinaldi led until Rea went past early on. Just when it looked likely that a podium for the Italian rider might be signed and sealed, first Razgatlioglu and then his countryman, rookie Locatelli, squeezed past for a first podium, no less. Or was it?

Rea's win was unchallenged, but when WorldSBK's version of VAR was called on, it was determined that both Razgatlioglu and Locatelli had marginally strayed on to the track-limit paint. Both had to lose a place. The final podium was Rea, Rinaldi and Razgatlioglu.

Thus race two started in a tense atmosphere for some, especially as Razgatlioglu had just lost even more championship ground to Rea. The final race was over for the former almost before it had started, as Garrett Gerloff tried one of his overambitious early moves for apex supremacy and cleaned out the Turkish rider's front wheel, tumbling the leading R1 rider into the dirt at Turn One of lap one.

The self-harming Yama-calamity left us with a very wide spread of unusual pieces on the board. Locatelli led, Rinaldi was second, Lowes third, Redding fourth and Rea only fifth.

Eventually, Rea lifted and separated himself from his team-mate and the double Ducati pairing to hunt down Locatelli and win a hat trick, a remarkable 15th victory at his favourite circuit. With three laps to go, Redding also passed Locatelli for second, but the rookie Yamaha rider finally got the podium he craved. Rea regained a title lead of 37 points, over 20 of them for free.

SUPERBIKE WORLD CHAMPIONSHIP
MOST
ROUND 6 · CZECH REPUBLIC

Above: Rea crashes out of race one.

Left: Fifth in race one for Bassani, top Independent rider.

Below left: American Jason Uribe had a tough weekend on the Pedercini Ducati.
Photos: Gold & Goose

Far left: Redding leads Lowes, Locatelli, Bassani and the rest.
Photo: Ducati Corse

Below far left: Perfect symmetry from Haslam and Gerloff.

Below centre left: Germany's Marvin Fritz took tenth in race one.

Bottom left: Chaos on the opening lap of race two as Axel Bassani falls in the pack. Karel Hanika (98) is about to join him, but the rest survived to race on.

Below: Pata Yamaha's double podium in race one was something to celebrate.

Below right: "Will you marry me?" Scott Redding proposes to girlfriend Jayce on the podium. Jonathan Rea appears to approve.
Photos: Gold & Goose

THE realities of modern WorldSBK racing in the time of Covid-19 dictated that we pulled back quite an old Iron Curtain and headed to a racetrack conceived and originally executed in darker times.

The track barriers were too close in a number of corners at Most, even in some of the faster places. The hillside layout was pleasingly flowing for the most part, however, with an impressive medieval castle perched high at one end and an unsightly industrial area (thankfully just out of shot) further down the hill.

With every area of the paddock on a different level from every other, because of its narrow and strung-out layout, it was reminiscent of Imola, if in this way only. For the racers, the tarmac had been resurfaced in some areas or was breaking up in others.

Good and bad was the general verdict. Importantly, it had character sprouting from every hectare. It just needed some extra acres of run-off, or for the layout to be remodelled.

Had it rained heavily at the wrong times, we probably would not have raced. Indeed, some riders simply sat out the wet periods on Friday anyway, but the occasionally wild weather played nice at just about the right times.

Once again, the racing was simply blistering, partly because of the nature of the 4.212km circuit. There were an impressive 21 distinct corners, with hairpins and chicanes punctuating the flow, including a T1/T2 chicane of bewilderingly tight severity. The crowds in the twin grandstands got to see a lot of action, and no small degree of controversy.

Superpole was topped by Rea (six from six so far), with Razgatlioglu second. In third, however, Redding was unavoidably penalised under the yellow-flag rules.

He finally got away from the other two big beasts of 2021 in the opening race – for a time – with Razgatlioglu managing to keep Rea behind. The latter's battle against his bike pushing him into corners finally took its toll, as he fell entering Turn One. He got going again to try for some points, but then fell once more, fast and hard, into T20.

With Rea no longer hassling him, Razgatlioglu had worked his way right back to Redding with a few laps to go, attempting a pass on the final lap. It was rebuffed by the Englishman, but not quite comprehensively enough.

Cue a final ambitious overtake into Turn 20 from Toprak. The surprised Ducati rider lifted, effectively allowing Razgatlioglu through for the race-one win, by just 0.040 of a second. Redding was furious at what he considered an unfair pass, although others didn't see it that way.

Behind the top two, Locatelli posted another podium.

In the Superpole race, the final one, two, three of Razgatlioglu, Redding and Rea did not quite tell the full story, as Rea had run wide entering T1, letting Redding back into his orbit after a trip down the slip road. The Ducati man took second on the penultimate lap, as Rea's machine or set-up could not quite match the pace of the top two again. However, it was his 200th career WorldSBK podium.

In the final race, the three top protagonists of 2021 were on the podium again, but all had had very different races after the close first few laps. Redding had gradually eased his way beyond the range of Razgatlioglu's potential attack to enjoy a margin of victory of over 3.5 seconds.

The Turkish rider was a very comfortable second, but Rea had been forced to spend too much time behind Locatelli to really challenge for anything better than third, some 12.460 seconds from the lead.

Having won again, Scott finally got to propose to his girlfriend, Jayce, on top of the podium. She said yes.

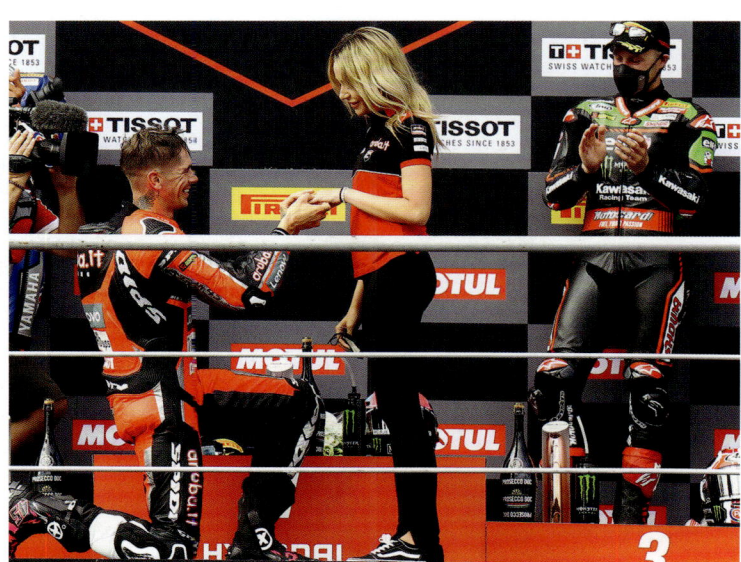

ROUND 6 · MOST 261

SUPERBIKE WORLD CHAMPIONSHIP
NAVARRA
ROUND 7 · SPAIN

Above: Redding had the measure of Rea in the first two races.
Photo: Ducati Corse

Top right: Razgatlioglu was back on top in race two, to draw level again on points.

Above right: With no SS300s competing, the Navarra paddock was adequate. Just.

Right: Locatelli leads Lowes, Sykes, Davies and Gerloff during the Superpole race.

Far right: Naomichi Uramoto was still looking to take his first points of the season.
Photos: Gold & Goose

AFTER Most, another new WorldSBK circuit – much newer in terms of build date and design features. Not quite as busy in terms of corners per kilometre, but instantly the slowest track on the calendar, despite a vast main straight and full-pace Turn One right-hander. Located in truly rural northern Spain, Navarra was a positive addition to a series that was always going to struggle for full MotoGP-scale venues with limited crowds during the pandemic.

No WorldSSP300s this weekend, but the Navarra paddock footprint is not exactly vast.

All in all, it turned out to be a good mid-size circuit with all the modern facilities needed, but with the usual teething problems with this level of event, including power supply dips and slips. The main issue was that the track surface was very bumpy in places. Blurry-vision bumpy. Being picky, the overall layout is a bit too busy and tight to be ideal for 230bhp-plus Superbikes.

None of these considerations affected the competitiveness of the series, however. The top riders took as much glee in attacking the lap times and occasionally each other as usual.

In Superpole, Rea took his seventh 'win' in succession, with Redding and Sykes alongside on row one. You had to scan down to eighth, and the third row, to find the name Razgatlioglu.

Redding had shocked the paddock by confirming on Thursday that he was leaving Ducati for BMW in 2022. Then he went out and won the first ever Navarra WorldSBK race on Saturday.

Rea had made a hard push to the front, clearing out Redding's line and filling in the Ducati rider's holeshot with his Kawasaki at Turn Six. The man in green led for five laps.

Redding made a brave, top-speed-assisted pass into the full-on Turn One kink, and eventually held off Rea by a clear 2.529 seconds. The latter had to perform one of his now regular 'mini-Marquez' front-end saves, at Turn Nine, trying to hold on to the leading pace. Another less dramatic outbraking moment ended his winning ambitions.

Razgatlioglu got himself out of potential trouble in the early laps and ended his day in third, with Locatelli fourth.

Bash Street Kids Rea and Redding played so rough in the early laps of the Superpole race that Razgatlioglu caught up with them both very early – again from eighth on the grid.

Rea mechanically muscled his way past Redding to lead, but a mistake let Redding through again, only for Rea to make another aggressive pass. That particular manoeuvre let Razgatlioglu into second, as Redding had to run wide. Then the Turkish rider attacked Rea inside at Turn One, but he dived back inside and they collided going into the next corner.

Rea was passed again by Redding's twin peaks of slipstreaming and engine performance, producing another Redding/Rea/Razgatlioglu podium.

It was all change in the early laps of race two at least, as Rea was pushed down to fifth, with Locatelli challenging Redding for the lead. Razgatlioglu used the fight between 'Loka' and Scott to hit the front.

As Rea moved up and Locatelli dropped back, the number-one Kawasaki rider used his favourite slow left-hander to get past Redding.

The top three rode inside their own personal aura of pace, but once again Rea had to produce a front-end save, which nearly allowed Redding to make a pass into his favoured Turn One. Yet another front-end tuck finally let him through to claim second.

Razgatlioglu and Rea left Spain tied on 311 points each, while Redding was just 38 adrift.

ROUND 7 · NAVARRA 263

SUPERBIKE WORLD CHAMPIONSHIP
MAGNY-COURS
ROUND 8 · FRANCE

Above: Locatelli and Razgatlioglu book-ended the podium in race one.

Right: Locatelli and Davies chase the podium in race two.

Far right: No holds barred. Razgatlioglu and Rea fought it out again in race two.

Below: Rea takes charge at the start of the Superpole race.
Photos: Gold & Goose

Above: Two wins in France put Toprak seven points clear.

Left: France's Christophe Ponsson kept up his unobtrusive accumulation of points at home.

Bottom: Rea was awarded the Superpole win after the event.

Below right: Just a single podium for Redding, whose championship challenge was waning.

Photos: Gold & Goose

BEFORE the real racing got under way in France, the big question was: could Rea extend his successive pole run to a new absolute record of eight? The answer came loud and clear – yes! He also took Kawasaki's 100th pole position with a new track best of 1m 35.683s.

Razgatlioglu had better race pace, however, despite starting from second on the grid. It was about to show, and how.

In race one, Rea and team-mate Lowes eased Razgatlioglu wide, with Rinaldi moving into the podium places soon after. But Rea's planned escape was short-lived, as Razgatlioglu made a lap-four pass that was tough enough to generate cheers from the crowd at Turn Five as they nudged.

Redding was down the order after a difficult Superpole, and eventually would crash, restarting to finish only 12th. Lowes also crashed after just a handful of laps, losing his podium place and unable to restart.

Razgatlioglu finally just motored away from Rea to win at his favourite circuit. With a five-second margin of victory, he celebrated with one of his trademark long stoppies – right over the finish line – underlining his showman's credentials.

Behind the leading pair, Locatelli claimed a podium, while Rinaldi took fourth place.

In Sunday's Superpole race, the sun was still shining, but it was initial gloom for Rea, as his great start and determined pace were soon matched by Razgatlioglu, who used the Turn Five hairpin to make his move into the lead.

The championship duo competed throughout, with Rea lucky not to tag Razgatlioglu under braking into T5 with two laps to go, running wide on the exit. He made up his lost time and made a move at the fast Turn 11 on the last lap, only for Razgatlioglu to respond into the final Lycee complex.

Rea had one final go, but again it was Razgatlioglu who took the winner's trophy. On track at least, he had definitely won. He had ridden on the track-limits green paint at Turn Ten, however, immediately before Rea had made his bold passing move. Kawasaki protested and – eventually – the result was overturned, Rea being declared winner. Unfortunately, that news was only made official after the end of race two later in the day.

The talk among the media and TV companies, therefore, was all about Toprak's first official triple winning weekend – because he was unbeatable again in race two – but that bubble of post-race satisfaction was finally burst by the regulations.

Much bad blood ensued, the green team being seen in a bad light by many, even though Razgatlioglu had indeed touched the green paint on the final lap. But his second 'line-fault' of the year had to be brought to the attention of the organisers by his rivals, unlike Assen's more visible error.

Race two itself had been another dose of pure leading entertainment, as Rea passed Razgatlioglu on lap four, with Redding their early shadow.

Michael van der Mark suffered a big scare when his front brake jammed on as he and Locatelli jostled for the same line on to the main straight. They touched, a vast plume of tyre smoke appeared like an evil genie, and van der Mark veered to the left, almost hitting the pit boards held out for the riders.

Up front, there was even more contact. At Turn Five, Razgatlioglu passed Rea, who held his line as the Turk went for the same point in space, all under the close scrutiny of Redding.

Pass and attempted pass characterised another wonderful contest up front, but Razgatlioglu had the Turn Five braking advantage all worked out again. Finally, he managed to ease away from Rea, with Redding third.

The spice of rivalry became a tad toxic after this round, at least for a time.

ROUND 8 · MAGNY-COURS 265

SUPERBIKE WORLD CHAMPIONSHIP
CATALUNYA
ROUND 9 · SPAIN

Above: Ducati's double – Rinaldi, Redding and pit staff enjoy the moment.

Above right: A concussed Sykes lies motionless while a worried Mahias goes to his aid.

Top: Razgatlioglu had nothing for runaway Rinaldi in race two.

Right: Rea and Razgatlioglu dispute the sprint-race win; Bautista brings the Honda home a close third.

Photos: Gold & Goose

266 WORLD SUPERBIKE REVIEW

Above: Bassani's Ducati heads Razgatlioglu's white-liveried Yamaha in race one.

Left: At last. Bautista hugs his factory Honda after taking a first podium of the season.

Below: A first podium also for rising star Bassani.

Below right: A late charge from Redding took him to the race-one win.

Photos: Gold & Goose

RACING on Dorna's doorstep at the Barcelona-Catalunya circuit was still weird for a few, even after almost a decade of Dorna rights ownership and the debut WorldSBK race weekend there in 2020.

Superpole on Saturday delivered hyperbole for Tom Sykes and he duly took a first leading grid position for the new M1000RR BMW. He was the first man to dethrone the latest would-be Superpole king, Jonathan Rea, in 2021. It had taken nine rounds to do it. It also extended Sykes's all-time pole tally to 51.

The first race came later that day in wet conditions. You could make out the Pata Yamahas particularly well through the spray and gloom, running a special 60th Grand Prix anniversary colour scheme, predominantly white with red speed blocks.

Rea had been down in tenth early on, despite his strong second place in qualifying, but soon he was fighting with early leader Razgatlioglu in a one-off white-vs-green contest. He got clear for a while, but surprise privateer Axel Bassani had come through to the podium places.

With nine laps remaining, Razgatlioglu had caught up to Rea again, then passed him. So too did Bassani as the rain waxed and waned.

Then, another splinter in Razgatlioglu's trophy cabinet as suddenly he slowed, an electronics issue ending his day early. The curse of the special liveries had struck again.

Once more, the top places shuffled as Rinaldi came through on Rea. Then, the fastest man of all, Redding, was past Rea with five to go.

Redding eased out to win from instant superstar Bassani, with Rinaldi third. Rea took a disappointing fourth place, albeit reclaiming the championship lead by six points, with one more day and two more races to go in Catalunya.

Even half of Sunday's race card suffered enough dry-weather incidents, accidents and clashes to fill a whole weekend, and the first attempt at a Superpole race only lasted five laps.

Van der Mark had skittled team-mate Sykes off track on lap one, with both out. Then Lucas Mahias and Chaz Davies collided, bringing out the red flag for a five-lap restart. Davies was out for the next two races.

Rea and Razgatlioglu clashed as they launched off the start line, and they would get physical again more than once. A Turn Nine touch ran Razgatlioglu wide, inviting an inside pass from Alvaro Bautista's Honda. Locatelli clipped the back of Lowes's machine and fell, scooping up Kohta Nozane, a blue reflection of the earlier BMW internecine incident.

Rea was just able to hold off Razgatlioglu, despite the Turkish rider's new lap record on the final lap. Nine points ahead for Rea.

With everyone expecting a Rea-Razgatlioglu dust-up in the final race, initial attention turned to Lowes and Christophe Ponsson as they touched. Lowes crashed and, after being missed by many, was finally met by the toppling Kawasaki of new stand-in Pedercini rider Lachlan Epis. The clout would affect Lowes's already injury-riven season for the next few rounds.

Another Catalunya race didn't make full distance, after a serious fall and head knock for Sykes, the result of a collision with Lucas Mahias.

In the final 19-lap race, Rea and Razgatliolgu were messing up each other out front, allowing Rinaldi to join the leading fight. As he upped his pace, Rea lost his, soon dropping into the clutches of Locatelli, Redding and Bautista. He ran off track to end up sixth, behind a top-five finishing order of Rinaldi, Razgatlioglu, Redding, Bautista and Locatelli. Razgatliolgu retook the title lead – by a single point.

Rinaldi's third win of the season showed that the Ducati was a very strong force, even if the Yamaha and Kawasaki were more consistent.

ROUND 9 · CATALUNYA 267

SUPERBIKE WORLD CHAMPIONSHIP
JEREZ
ROUND 10 · SPAIN

Above: Razgatlioglu squeaks it, heading Redding past the flag in race two.

Right: Chaz Davies called a press conference to announce his retirement.

Centre right: Loris Baz was drafted in to sub for the injured Welshman.

Below right: A full house as Chaz's peers gather to pay tribute.

Facing page:
Top: Rea and Razgatlioglu, at each other again in race one.

Centre: After Catalunya's sprint-race success, another podium delighted Bautista in the full-length race two.

Bottom: Bautista's Honda was finding its feet after a hard year so far.

Bottom right: Dean Berta Vinales is remembered by his team on the Jerez grid.
Photos: Gold & Goose

268 WORLD SUPERBIKE REVIEW

FROM Catalunya, the teams raced each other again on the impeccable Spanish highways from the extreme northeast to the very southwest, to get to the next contest of a busy autumn in Iberia with plenty of time to spare.

Even before the Jerez weekend had started, the still-injured Chaz Davies had arrived in the paddock, but he was not there to ride his GO Eleven Ducati. Instead, there was a press conference to announce his retirement. It was an emotional and well-attended event, with all his main rivals in the front two rows, and we came away thinking that we had just witnessed the most introspective, joyful and yet slightly sad moment of the weekend.

After the death of 15-year-old Dean Berta Vinales in the first WorldSSP300 race on Saturday, however, the full meaning of 'sad' struck home, in a terrible year for fatalities to young riders.

Racing was suspended on Saturday. Before the tragedy, Superpole had delivered another new 2021 pre-race supremo, after Razgatlioglu had held off the fast Kawasaki duo of Lowes and Rea.

Thus there were two full-distance WorldSBK races on Sunday, just like the old days, if for horribly different reasons.

Despite a subdued paddock, the race action was back to its best out front, with Rea and Rinaldi attacking each other from the very beginning. Several passes and even some less-than-tender bodywork kisses ensued, but Razgatlioglu finally worked his way into a lead that he would hold until the flag, just 1.225 seconds clear of Rea.

Redding had caught and passed Locatelli in a clean last-lap move just in time to claim the last podium place.

With 'Loka' fourth, Alvaro Bautista took his recently podium-capable Honda to fifth, but special mention had to be made of Davies's last-minute replacement, Loris Baz. A proven WorldSBK race winner of years gone by, he took a formidable sixth place in his first weekend back, after having to ride in MotoAmerica for 2021.

In the second race, the old Rea/Raz routine was played out again, but this time the former's inability to overcome his bike's wayward nature entering corners was holding him up – and messing him up. He often ran wide while trying to get stopped under braking, allowing Rinaldi and then Redding past.

Out of the podium places, Rea was simply being assaulted by other riders' pace and better-behaved riding packages, losing out so many times into Turn One. He was even hit by the following Bassani, into the back of the Kawasaki at the Turn One corner apex, just after Bautista had passed him.

At the end of a weekend when the racing results were somewhat secondary, Rea eventually managed to salvage fifth, keeping Bassani behind by calling on his vast experience.

Up at the front, Razgatlioglu maintained his lead from Redding to take victory again, both flashing under the shade of the 'flying saucer' VIP suite that dominates the sky above the finish line. The Ducati man was just 0.113 of a second behind the Yamaha.

Third went to Bautista, another strong result after his Catalunya podium. By now, Locatelli was becoming mightily annoyed at 'only' finishing fourth, seemingly all the time.

The result of the tenth round of the championship was that Razgatlioglu's 20-point advantage over Rea was the biggest he had ever had, and everybody was looking forward to the next race, the following weekend at Portimao.

Four race weekends in five weeks was an unusual schedule for WorldSBK, but it was the last thing on anybody's mind after Saturday's accident had put everything else that is the challenge of racing into proper perspective.

ROUND 10 · JEREZ 269

SUPERBIKE WORLD CHAMPIONSHIP
PORTIMAO
ROUND 11 · PORTUGAL

Above: Razgatlioglu, Redding and van der Mark lead away at the start of race two.

Right: Lucky escape – sequence shows Jonathan Rea's dramatic race-one crash, the rider mercifully free from the bike.

Centre right: Razgatlioglu and Redding in race two, before the former's Yamaha tipped him off at high speed.

Top right: Back from MotoAmerica, substitute rider Baz took two thirds and a fourth at Portimao.

Above right: Michael van der Mark's wet Superpole race win was BMW's first since 2013.

Far right: Third in Superpole qualifying helped Leon Haslam to fifth in race one, his best points all season.

Photos: Gold & Goose

270 WORLD SUPERBIKE REVIEW

ALMOST everything that could happen did happen at Portimao, as the excellent 2021 season bored even deeper into the collective memory at a peerlessly undulating circuit with a long main straight..

On a new surface, Razgatlioglu topped Superpole with a new track best of 1m 40.219s. Rea was second, more than three-tenths slower, but he claimed the overall Tissot-Superpole award for the season. Leon Haslam was a happy third.

In warm conditions, Razgatlioglu took the holeshot in race one, but in one of the best races of the season, he and Rea swapped the lead and some paint, while Redding took advantage on the main straight to join the leading fight, then head it.

Rea seized a chance to pass when Redding made an error with 16 laps to go, but then pushed too hard to get away and suffered a serious high-speed crash entering the final fast right. His bike spiralled high above, but thankfully behind him as he almost reached the trackside barriers.

The fight for the final podium place was all action, with Rinaldi, Baz (back in for Davies), Bautista, Haslam and Locatelli going all in, sometimes three abreast into the Turn One braking zone.

Up front, a late passing attempt from Redding was rebuffed, and Razgatlioglu scored the victory and full points – with Rea on zero points for the day.

Eventually, Locatelli would tag the back of the upwardly mobile van der Mark, taking both of them out. The Dutchman shoved Locatelli hard from behind as they ran to collect their horizontal bikes.

Bautista lost his chance of third with a last-corner crash that was similar to Rea's, which allowed Baz to score a remarkable privateer podium.

Memories of the infamous Magny-Cours track-limits protest were rekindled as Razgatlioglu stopped on the trackside to 'clean' some of the green paint with a long-handled broom. Ouch! He was 45 points ahead of Rea on Saturday night.

After Saturday's sunbathing, it was an early steam bath on Sunday as a wet track led to another amazing race. Razgatlioglu pulled another holeshot in the Superpole sprint, but Rea was soon into a leading position, until he lost the front under braking. Another DNF at his (former) best ever track.

The onrushing van der Mark would eventually win it, from Redding and the extraordinary Baz again, 'Magic Michael' giving BMW its first win since 2013, and the new M model its first win of all.

Razgatlioglu was sixth, behind off-podium finishers Locatelli and Bautista, but he still moved 49 points ahead of Rea.

Surely the more-or-less dry race two could not produce any more drama, or even deeper contrasting emotions, could it?

Rea made many of his team cry when eventually he won the last European race of the season, but it was his rival Razgatlioglu's team who should have been in tears, after he crashed out of the lead when his front fender broke with ten laps to run. It shattered and was dragged under his front tyre. And to give spectators even more reason to catch their breath, it happened at that hyper-fast final-corner approach again.

Rea gritted his teeth and pushed his bike to the limit to win. Redding was a very close second, but the final drama was reserved for the ding-dong between Baz and Bautista. With two laps to go, Baz passed Bautista on the inside – on the trackside paint – at Turn Five. On exit, they clashed and Bautista crashed. Baz would eventually lose his third place after Race Direction intervened and handed it to Locatelli.

Rea found the piece of green asphalt that Razgatlioglu had brushed clean on Saturday – and did a burnout on top. Ouch squared!

Only 24 points separated the top two.

ROUND 11 · PORTIMAO 271

SUPERBIKE WORLD CHAMPIONSHIP
VILLICUM
ROUND 12 · ARGENTINA

Above: Razgatlioglu leads Rea on the wide open spaces of the San Juan track in race one.

Right: Dust my broom. Toprak busies himself amid the sandstorm.

Centre right: Proceedings were delayed until the dust settled.

Below right: Samuele Cavalieri grabbed minor race-one points on the Barni Racing Team Ducati.

Below centre right: Alex Lowes took Kawasaki's red-and-black Ninja livery to fourth in race one.

Facing page:
From top: Rea's Kawasaki wore retro green on Saturday; Redding and Razgatlioglu fight it out ahead of Rea in race two; Redding took a clear and happy race-two win.
Photos: Gold & Goose and Ducati Corse

Bottom right: Rinaldi heels his Ducati to third in race one.
Photo: Ducati Corse

272 WORLD SUPERBIKE REVIEW

To the amazement of almost everyone, WorldSBK returned to Argentina and the brilliant, but sometimes flawed Circuito San Juan Villicum, with only a few paddock figures being caught out by Covid or other visa-related regulations. A small miracle of organisation and sheer will.

Even a serious pre-weekend sandstorm did not stop the practice sessions or the races. Tech issues with track-to-pit-lane communications did delay the start, but compared to previous years, it was solid.

Redding took Superpole (aided a little by yellow flags at the wrong time for the others), with Razgatlioglu second and Bassani a confident third. The Englishman deserved it, as he had never seen the place before. Rea was only fifth on the grid.

As Yamaha had done to mark their GP birthday in Catalunya, Kawasaki celebrated their company centenary with special liveries: retro ZXR750 green-and-white paintwork for Rea and 'Top Gun' Ninja red-and-black bodywork for Lowes, from Saturday and for the races only.

At the very start of race one, a slippery patch caught out Redding, the pole-man falling out of Turn One, which allowed Razgatlioglu to take an early lead over Rea. Scott restarted from last to finish ninth.

Rea chased hard in second, but to no greater result. Lowes's otherwise strong pace was hampered again by his hand injury. Bassani had moved into third, only to be overhauled by eventual podium rider Rinaldi.

Razgatlioglu didn't realise he had won the opening race, so did another lap just in case. With Rea a clear second, the potential curse of special bodywork was kept at bay. Lowes repassed Bassani for fourth.

In the usual crazy ten-lap Superpole race, Razgatlioglu and Redding finally fought it out for the win, with the Turk only 0.046 of a second ahead across the line, after some last-lap heroics from the Ducati rider. Rea was third, Bassani a brilliant fourth.

In the final race of an Argentinean weekend we had all thought would never happen, the top riders took the entertainment up yet another notch, as much through occasional errors during the early laps as their overheated competitiveness.

Rea was clearly outgunned on the back straight, as both Razgatlioglu and Redding passed him in one manoeuvre. Bassani was right there with the top three regulars, showing no fear and major skills in equal measure. He was also enjoying the big Ducati rev limit.

Eventually, Redding overcame his occasional early slip-ups and motored away to a masterclass win, but with six laps to go, nobody could call the fight between Rea and Razgatlioglu.

Rea, the clever battler, used his experience and determination as much as his outright talent to keep Razgatlioglu behind, shuffling the usual pack of top three kings again.

Having played the easy-going joker all year, rookie Bassani added gravitas to his reputation by narrowly beating Rinaldi to fourth.

Van der Mark was sixth, just over eight seconds from the race-winning pace of 2022 team-mate Redding.

Chaz Davies made a welcome racing return, but was a best of ninth in race two.

In the all-important championship fight, Razgatlioglu left South America with a 30-point lead. Redding's exuberant race-two celebrations had to compensate for him being out of the title fight now, with only a maximum of 62 points left and a deficit of 66.

So, was it worth all the testing, special flights, sandstorms, expense and endless hassle to put 'World' back into WorldSBK in Argentina? In every sense, yes, if only to show that those in charge really do mean global business, regardless of what is going on in Dorna's blue-riband MotoGP category.

ROUND 12 · VILLICUM 273

SUPERBIKE WORLD CHAMPIONSHIP
MANDALIKA
ROUND 13 · INDONESIA

Above: Tropical heat and two races on a Sunday in Indonesia. Rea leads the pack into the first corner of race one.

Left: Monsoon time, and the paddock was awash.
Photos: Gold & Goose

Below left: Bautista abandons the grid. Saturday's race was also abandoned, with the track flooded.
Photo: HRC Honda

Right: The rain-threatened race two was delayed and shortened.

Facing page:
From top: Michael van der Mark took third for BMW in the final race of the season; Rea and Razgatlioglu embrace after a compelling year-long battle; last race for the self-effacing Chaz Davies.

Bottom right: Paul Denning and the Pata Yamaha crew celebrate Razgatlioglu's second in race one – enough to secure the title.
Photos: Gold & Goose

MANDALIKA by the sea was the latest pretty ribbon of new tarmac to join the WorldSBK schedule, and the boys in leathers really liked it. Even though it started off as dirty and grimy as the building site it so recently had been, and some small stones came away from the track surface at Turn One on day one, the latest venue provided an exotic charm all its own.

The interesting and largely flowing layout was not yet matched by a polished – or even fully finished – exterior, but it was a miracle, just a month before Christmas, that everybody got there to race at all. There were enthusiastic fans, there were aerobatic displays, there were challenges in even just racing in the heat and extreme humidity, but we had a superb season finale.

In Superpole, Razgatlioglu, who had been fastest by miles on Friday in the 'blind' FP1 and 2 sessions, took the top spot away from Rea by more than 0.3 of a second. He appeared set to hold on to his 30-point advantage, even with 62 points available for the Ulsterman if he won all three of the races. Until suddenly it came down to 50 available points when the first full-distance race on Saturday never happened.

It was the rainy season in Indonesia, and we found out what that meant just as race one was about to start at 3pm. With everybody having been sent back to their boxes, the water became so deep that racing would have been impossible.

Time passed, decisions were finally made, and without the teams or riders having been consulted, the first race was pushed into Sunday morning and the ten-lap Superpole race cancelled.

The track drained well after the worst of the rain had stopped, and there might have been a chance to race before the sun went down, but we'll never know now.

Thus the riders had to wait until Sunday for the championship to be decided. It only took one race to make Toprak Razgatlioglu champion, but what a race it was. Once it got going…

Rain – spots, but enough spots to make it sketchy – caused a slight delay, and then we got off 15 minutes late, with all on slick tyres. And for 20 laps, not 21.

The damp sheen on the surface did not prevent the top riders from attacking each other at every opportunity. Rea, Razgatlioglu and Redding led at the start, but Axel Bassani came through to pass Razgatlioglu and lead very briefly.

The Turkish rider led again, then had a moment as he ran wide. Rea pounced, with Redding taking over second place.

That finishing result would have been enough to save Rea for a few hours, but Razgatlioglu combined a cool head and extravagant riding style to win a great battle with Redding for second, and then start the hunt for Rea.

He never quite caught him, but second was just enough to make him champion. After changing his helmet, leathers and top fairing colours to gold out on track, he did rolling burnouts down the pit lane to celebrate his title win, limiting Rea's unbroken run to six.

Redding was third in the opening race, the fast-advancing Locatelli fourth and Bassani fifth.

The final race nearly went the way of the first. But after consultations, delays, an easing of the rain and finally a trim to 12 laps, the surprisingly grippy wet track surface delivered a ferocious wet-weather street fight.

Bassani was knocked off when Michael van der Mark came through to an eventual third, one up on Razgatlioglu. Rea won an elbowing match with Redding in the final complex to match Razgatlioglu's win total of 13 for the year, while the Turk finally claimed the title by just 13 points.

As finales go, Mandalika had everything but the planned three races.

ROUND 13 · MANDALIKA 275

2021 WORLD SUPERBIKE CHAMPIONSHIP RESULTS

Compiled by Peter McLaren

Round 1 — ARAGON, Spain · 21–23 May, 2021 · 3.155-mile/5.077km circuit

Race 1: 18 laps, 56.785 miles/91.386km
Weather: Dry · Track 38°C · Air 20°C
Time of race: 33m 24.225s
Average speed: 101.997mph/164.148km/h

Pos.	Rider	Nat.	No.	Entrant	Machine	Time & Gap	Laps
1	Jonathan Rea	GBR	1	Kawasaki Racing Team WorldSBK	Kawasaki ZX-10RR		18
2	Alex Lowes	GBR	22	Kawasaki Racing Team WorldSBK	Kawasaki ZX-10RR	3.965s	18
3	Toprak Razgatlioglu	TUR	54	Pata Yamaha with BRIXX WorldSBK	Yamaha YZF R1	4.008s	18
4	Scott Redding	GBR	45	Aruba.it Racing - Ducati	Ducati Panigale V4 R	4.242s	18
5	Chaz Davies	GBR	7	Team GoEleven	Ducati Panigale V4 R	4.615s	18
6	Tom Sykes	GBR	66	BMW Motorrad WorldSBK Team	BMW M 1000 RR	6.784s	18
7	Michael Rinaldi	ITA	21	Aruba.it Racing - Ducati	Ducati Panigale V4 R	8.345s	18
8	Leon Haslam	GBR	91	Team HRC	Honda CBR1000 RR-R	10.187s	18
9	Garrett Gerloff	USA	31	GRT Yamaha WorldSBK Team	Yamaha YZF R1	10.326s	18
10	Andrea Locatelli	ITA	55	Pata Yamaha with BRIXX WorldSBK	Yamaha YZF R1	17.693s	18
11	Michael van der Mark	NED	60	BMW Motorrad WorldSBK Team	BMW M 1000 RR	21.154s	18
12	Axel Bassani	ITA	47	Motocorsa Racing	Ducati Panigale V4 R	27.523s	18
13	Isaac Vinales	ESP	32	Orelac Racing VerdNatura	Kawasaki ZX-10RR	30.963s	18
14	Kohta Nozane	JPN	3	GRT Yamaha WorldSBK Team	Yamaha YZF R1	36.769s	18
15	Lucas Mahias	FRA	44	Kawasaki Puccetti Racing	Kawasaki ZX-10RR	39.334s	18
16	Jonas Folger	GER	94	Bonovo MGM Racing	BMW M 1000 RR	41.544s	18
17	Christophe Ponsson	FRA	23	Alstare Yamaha	Yamaha YZF R1	43.179s	18
18	Loris Cresson	BEL	84	TPR Team Pedercini Racing	Kawasaki ZX-10RR	1m 21.460s	18
	Alvaro Bautista	ESP	19	Team HRC	Honda CBR1000 RR-R	DNF	
	Eugene Laverty	IRL	50	RC Squadra Corse	BMW M 1000 RR	DNF	13
	Samuele Cavalieri	ITA	76	TPR Team Pedercini Racing	Kawasaki ZX-10RR	DNF	9
	Leandro Mercado	ARG	36	MIE Racing Honda Racing	Honda CBR1000 RR-R	DNF	7
	Tito Rabat	ESP	53	Barni Racing Team	Ducati Panigale V4 R	DNF	2

Fastest race lap: Rea on lap 2, 1m 50.04s, 103.21mph/166.10km/h.
Lap record: Rea, 1m 49.62s, 103.60mph/166.73km/h (2020).

Superpole: 10 laps, 31.547 miles/50.770km
Weather: Wet · Track 18°C · Air 12°C
Time of race: 19m 47.979s
Average speed: 95.599mph/153.851km/h

Pos.	Rider	Time & Gap	Laps
1	Jonathan Rea		10
2	Alex Lowes	3.506s	10
3	Garrett Gerloff	5.051s	10
4	Chaz Davies	8.908s	10
5	Michael van der Mark	10.175s	10
6	Toprak Razgatlioglu	29.342s	10
7	Alvaro Bautista	29.565s	10
8	Scott Redding	33.361s	10
9	Kohta Nozane	33.675s	10
10	Leon Haslam	34.771s	10
11	Michael Rinaldi	36.451s	10
12	Andrea Locatelli	38.709s	10
13	Jonas Folger	41.188s	10
14	Tito Rabat	51.975s	10
15	Isaac Vinales	52.644s	10
16	Eugene Laverty	52.912s	10
17	Axel Bassani	1m 07.329s	10
18	Leandro Mercado	1m 15.604s	10
19	Christophe Ponsson	1m 16.459s	10
20	Loris Cresson	1m 17.105s	10
	Tom Sykes	DNF	7
	Samuele Cavalieri	DNF	3
	Lucas Mahias	DNF	2

Fastest race lap: van der Mark on lap 10, 1m 56.261s, 97.69mph/157.21km/h.

Race 2: 18 laps, 56.785 miles/91.386km
Weather: Wet · Track 19°C · Air 11°C
Time of race: 34m 19.394s
Average speed: 99.265mph/159.751km/h

Pos.	Rider	Time & Gap	Laps
1	Scott Redding		18
2	Jonathan Rea	9.856s	18
3	Alex Lowes	10.434s	18
4	Tom Sykes	12.094s	18
5	Michael van der Mark	16.234s	18
6	Toprak Razgatlioglu	20.191s	18
7	Garrett Gerloff	20.427s	18
8	Jonas Folger	20.587s	18
9	Andrea Locatelli	25.026s	18
10	Lucas Mahias	28.855s	18
11	Alvaro Bautista	35.644s	18
12	Kohta Nozane	38.275s	18
13	Isaac Vinales	41.585s	18
14	Axel Bassani	44.922s	18
15	Christophe Ponsson	46.022s	18
16	Michael Rinaldi	1m 08.072s	18
17	Eugene Laverty	1m 13.998s	18
18	Leandro Mercado	1m 14.859s	18
19	Chaz Davies	1 Lap	17
20	Loris Cresson	2 Laps	16
21	Samuele Cavalieri	3 Laps	15
	Tito Rabat	DNF	14
	Leon Haslam	DNF	4

Fastest race lap: Davies on lap 11, 1m 52.717s, 100.76mph/162.15km/h.

Superpole
1, Rea 1m 48.458s; 2, Redding 1m 48.733s; 3, Sykes 1m 48.840s; 4, Lowes 1m 48.890s; 5, Davies 1m 49.069s; 6, Gerloff 1m 49.185s; 7, Haslam 1m 49.246s; 8, Bautista 1m 49.338s; 9, Rinaldi 1m 49.516s; 10, Razgatlioglu 1m 49.704s; 11, Rabat 1m 49.761s; 12, Laverty 1m 49.767s; 13, Mahias 1m 49.951s; 14, Locatelli 1m 49.962s; 15, van der Mark 1m 50.189s; 16, Nozane 1m 50.435s; 17, Ponsson 1m 50.489s; 18, Folger 1m 50.628s; 19, Vinales 1m 50.672s; 20, Bassani 1m 51.107s; 21, Cavalieri 1m 52.717s; 22, Mercado 1m 53.120s; 23, Cresson 1m 53.649s.

Points
1, Rea 57; 2, Lowes 45; 3, Redding 40; 4, Razgatlioglu 30; 5, Sykes 23; 6, Gerloff 23; 7, van der Mark 21; 8, Davies 17; 9, Locatelli 13; 10, Rinaldi 9; 11, Folger 8; 12, Haslam 8; 13, Bautista 8; 14, Mahias 7; 15, Nozane 7; 16, Bassani 6; 17, Vinales 6; 18, Ponsson 1.

Round 2 — ESTORIL, Portugal · 28–30 May, 2021 · 2.599-mile/4.182km circuit

Race 1: 21 laps, 54.570 miles/87.822km
Weather: Dry · Track 39°C · Air 19°C
Time of race: 34m 8.039s
Average speed: 95.922mph/154.372km/h

Pos.	Rider	Nat.	No.	Entrant	Machine	Time & Gap	Laps
1	Scott Redding	GBR	45	Aruba.it Racing - Ducati	Ducati Panigale V4 R		21
2	Toprak Razgatlioglu	TUR	54	Pata Yamaha with BRIXX WorldSBK	Yamaha YZF R1	0.877s	21
3	Jonathan Rea	GBR	1	Kawasaki Racing Team WorldSBK	Kawasaki ZX-10RR	0.915s	21
4	Garrett Gerloff	USA	31	GRT Yamaha WorldSBK Team	Yamaha YZF R1	9.518s	21
5	Michael Rinaldi	ITA	21	Aruba.it Racing - Ducati	Ducati Panigale V4 R	13.636s	21
6	Chaz Davies	GBR	7	Team GoEleven	Ducati Panigale V4 R	17.177s	21
7	Michael van der Mark	NED	60	BMW Motorrad WorldSBK Team	BMW M 1000 RR	19.316s	21
8	Alvaro Bautista	ESP	19	Team HRC	Honda CBR1000 RR-R	20.185s	21
9	Tito Rabat	ESP	53	Barni Racing Team	Ducati Panigale V4 R	25.625s	21
10	Andrea Locatelli	ITA	55	Pata Yamaha with BRIXX WorldSBK	Yamaha YZF R1	27.772s	21
11	Axel Bassani	ITA	47	Motocorsa Racing	Ducati Panigale V4 R	30.349s	21
12	Leon Haslam	GBR	91	Team HRC	Honda CBR1000 RR-R	35.722s	21
13	Lucas Mahias	FRA	44	Kawasaki Puccetti Racing	Kawasaki ZX-10RR	35.885s	21
14	Tom Sykes	GBR	66	BMW Motorrad WorldSBK Team	BMW M 1000 RR	36.887s	21
15	Kohta Nozane	JPN	3	GRT Yamaha WorldSBK Team	Yamaha YZF R1	45.434s	21
16	Jonas Folger	GER	94	Bonovo MGM Racing	BMW M 1000 RR	46.472s	21
17	Isaac Vinales	ESP	32	Orelac Racing VerdNatura	Kawasaki ZX-10RR	51.132s	21
18	Eugene Laverty	IRL	50	RC Squadra Corse	BMW M 1000 RR	1m 09.888s	21
19	Alex Lowes	GBR	22	Kawasaki Racing Team WorldSBK	Kawasaki ZX-10RR	1m 09.903s	21
20	Loris Cresson	BEL	84	TPR Team Pedercini Racing	Kawasaki ZX-10RR	1m 26.686s	21
	Christophe Ponsson	FRA	23	Alstare Yamaha	Yamaha YZF R1	DNF	15
	Samuele Cavalieri	ITA	76	TPR Team Pedercini Racing	Kawasaki ZX-10RR	DNF	7

Fastest race lap: Razgatlioglu on lap 2, 1m 36.877s, 96.57mph/155.41km/h.
Lap record: Razgatlioglu, 1m 36.594s, 96.85mph/155.86km/h (2020).

Superpole: 10 laps, 25.986 miles/41.820km
Weather: Dry · Track 31°C · Air 19°C
Time of race: 16m 13.053s
Average speed: 96.139mph/154.721km/h

Pos.	Rider	Time & Gap	Laps
1	Jonathan Rea		10
2	Toprak Razgatlioglu	0.690s	10
3	Scott Redding	1.180s	10
4	Garrett Gerloff	2.059s	10
5	Michael Rinaldi	3.583s	10
6	Alex Lowes	3.623s	10
7	Tom Sykes	7.062s	10
8	Eugene Laverty	7.831s	10
9	Chaz Davies	8.969s	10
10	Alvaro Bautista	9.581s	10
11	Andrea Locatelli	10.013s	10
12	Tito Rabat	10.850s	10
13	Michael van der Mark	11.419s	10
14	Axel Bassani	15.703s	10
15	Kohta Nozane	16.678s	10
16	Leon Haslam	16.810s	10
17	Isaac Vinales	20.194s	10
18	Jonas Folger	22.250s	10
19	Loris Cresson	39.192s	10
20	Christophe Ponsson	1m 01.246s	10
	Samuele Cavalieri	DNF	8
	Lucas Mahias	DNF	1

Fastest race lap: Rea on lap 8, 1m 36.67s, 96.77mph/155.74km/h.

Race 2: 21 laps, 54.570 miles/87.822km
Weather: Dry · Track 43°C · Air 24°C
Time of race: 34m 13.197s
Average speed: 95.681mph/153.984km/h

Pos.	Rider	Time & Gap	Laps
1	Jonathan Rea		18
2	Chaz Davies	2.787s	18
3	Toprak Razgatlioglu	9.484s	18
4	Alex Lowes	12.401s	18
5	Andrea Locatelli	14.011s	18
6	Michael van der Mark	15.189s	18
7	Alvaro Bautista	15.899s	18
8	Tom Sykes	21.628s	18
9	Eugene Laverty	23.257s	18
10	Tito Rabat	25.344s	18
11	Axel Bassani	26.525s	18
12	Leon Haslam	28.227s	18
13	Kohta Nozane	29.878s	18
14	Lucas Mahias	38.911s	18
15	Isaac Vinales	39.128s	18
16	Scott Redding	44.162s	18
17	Christophe Ponsson	1m 03.983s	18
18	Loris Cresson	1m 07.458s	18
	Samuele Cavalieri	DNF	17
	Jonas Folger	DNF	2
	Michael Rinaldi	DNF	1
	Garrett Gerloff	DNF	1

Fastest race lap: Rea on lap 11, 1m 37.19s, 96.25mph/154.90km/h.

Superpole
1, Rea 1m 35.876s; 2, Redding 1m 36.047s; 3, Razgatlioglu 1m 36.164s; 4, Gerloff 1m 36.350s; 5, Sykes 1m 36.369s; 6, Rinaldi 1m 36.532s; 7, Mahias 1m 36.863s; 8, Rabat 1m 36.892s; 9, Locatelli 1m 37.031s; 10, Lowes 1m 37.049s; 11, Folger 1m 37.128s; 12, van der Mark 1m 37.193s; 13, Laverty 1m 37.266s; 14, Haslam 1m 37.399s; 15, Davies 1m 37.422s; 16, Nozane 1m 37.611s; 17, Bassani 1m 37.657s; 18, Bautista 1m 37.731s; 19, Vinales 1m 38.512s; 20, Ponsson 1m 38.854s; 21, Cresson 1m 40.008s; 22, Cavalieri 1m 40.288s.

Points
1, Rea 110; 2, Razgatlioglu 75; 3, Redding 72; 4, Lowes 62; 5, Davies 48; 6, Gerloff 42; 7, van der Mark 40; 8, Sykes 36; 9, Locatelli 30; 10, Rinaldi 25; 11, Bautista 25; 12, Haslam 16; 13, Bassani 16; 14, Rabat 13; 15, Mahias 12; 16, Nozane 11; 17, Laverty 9; 18, Folger 8; 19, Vinales 7; 20, Ponsson 1.

Round 3 — MISANO, Italy · 11–13 June, 2021 · 2.626-mile/4.226km circuit

Race 1: 21 laps, 55.144 miles/88.746km
Weather: Dry · Track 48°C · Air 29°C
Time of race: 33m 23.457s
Average speed: 99.088mph/159.467km/h

Pos.	Rider	Nat.	No.	Entrant	Machine	Time & Gap	Laps
1	Michael Rinaldi	ITA	21	Aruba.it Racing - Ducati	Ducati Panigale V4 R		21
2	Toprak Razgatlioglu	TUR	54	Pata Yamaha with BRIXX WorldSBK	Yamaha YZF R1	3.657s	21
3	Jonathan Rea	GBR	1	Kawasaki Racing Team WorldSBK	Kawasaki ZX-10RR	5.104s	21
4	Scott Redding	GBR	45	Aruba.it Racing - Ducati	Ducati Panigale V4 R	10.247s	21
5	Alex Lowes	GBR	22	Kawasaki Racing Team WorldSBK	Kawasaki ZX-10RR	13.474s	21
6	Alvaro Bautista	ESP	19	Team HRC	Honda CBR1000 RR-R	14.766s	21
7	Axel Bassani	ITA	47	Motocorsa Racing	Ducati Panigale V4 R	15.587s	21
8	Tom Sykes	GBR	66	BMW Motorrad WorldSBK Team	BMW M 1000 RR	16.694s	21
9	Andrea Locatelli	ITA	55	Pata Yamaha with BRIXX WorldSBK	Yamaha YZF R1	23.612s	21
10	Michael van der Mark	NED	60	BMW Motorrad WorldSBK Team	BMW M 1000 RR	28.364s	21
11	Lucas Mahias	FRA	44	Kawasaki Puccetti Racing	Kawasaki ZX-10RR	28.699s	21
12	Garrett Gerloff	USA	31	GRT Yamaha WorldSBK Team	Yamaha YZF R1	31.757s	21
13	Kohta Nozane	JPN	3	GRT Yamaha WorldSBK Team	Yamaha YZF R1	35.395s	21
14	Leon Haslam	GBR	91	Team HRC	Honda CBR1000 RR-R	35.603s	21
15	Tito Rabat	ESP	53	Barni Racing Team	Ducati Panigale V4 R	38.211s	21
16	Jonas Folger	GER	94	Bonovo MGM Racing	BMW M 1000 RR	38.372s	21
17	Isaac Vinales	ESP	32	Orelac Racing VerdNatura	Kawasaki ZX-10RR	47.720s	21
18	Christophe Ponsson	FRA	23	Alstare Yamaha	Yamaha YZF R1	1m 06.736s	21
19	Samuele Cavalieri	ITA	76	TPR Team Pedercini Racing	Kawasaki ZX-10RR	1m 11.668s	21
20	Loris Cresson	BEL	84	TPR Team Pedercini Racing	Kawasaki ZX-10RR	1m 14.491s	21
	Chaz Davies	GBR	7	Team GoEleven	Ducati Panigale V4 R	DNF	14
	Eugene Laverty	IRL	50	RC Squadra Corse	BMW M 1000 RR	DNS	-

Fastest race lap: Rea on lap 2, 1m 34.476s, 100.06mph/161.03km/h.
Lap record: Rea, 1m 34.72s, 99.80mph/160.62km/h (2015).

Superpole: 10 laps, 26.259 miles/42.260km
Weather: Dry · Track 41°C · Air 30°C
Time of race: 15m 50.711s
Average speed: 99.434mph/160.023km/h

Pos.	Rider	Time & Gap	Laps
1	Michael Rinaldi		10
2	Toprak Razgatlioglu	0.485s	10
3	Jonathan Rea	1.865s	10
4	Scott Redding	2.419s	10
5	Alex Lowes	5.671s	10
6	Axel Bassani	7.448s	10
7	Tom Sykes	10.560s	10
8	Garrett Gerloff	13.102s	10
9	Andrea Locatelli	13.110s	10
10	Alvaro Bautista	16.348s	10
11	Leon Haslam	18.585s	10
12	Kohta Nozane	20.167s	10
13	Eugene Laverty	20.796s	10
14	Tito Rabat	21.207s	10
15	Isaac Vinales	27.728s	10
16	Christophe Ponsson	30.205s	10
17	Samuele Cavalieri	35.374s	10
18	Loris Cresson	35.643s	10
19	Jonas Folger	37.066s	10
	Lucas Mahias	DNF	8
	Michael van der Mark	DNF	5
	Chaz Davies	DNF	0

Fastest race lap: Rinaldi on lap 2, 1m 34.356s, 100.19mph/161.24km/h.

Race 2: 21 laps, 55.144 miles/88.746km
Weather: Dry · Track 49°C · Air 31°C
Time of race: 33m 24.487s
Average speed: 99.037mph/159.385km

Pos.	Rider	Time & Gap	Laps
1	Toprak Razgatlioglu		21
2	Michael Rinaldi	1.286s	21
3	Jonathan Rea	2.987s	21
4	Scott Redding	9.102s	21
5	Garrett Gerloff	10.695s	21
6	Alex Lowes	13.117s	21
7	Axel Bassani	17.621s	21
8	Alvaro Bautista	17.893s	21
9	Andrea Locatelli	22.458s	21
10	Michael van der Mark	25.118s	21
11	Lucas Mahias	27.107s	21
12	Tom Sykes	28.353s	21
13	Kohta Nozane	33.391s	21
14	Tito Rabat	38.817s	21
15	Eugene Laverty	41.262s	21
16	Jonas Folger	43.046s	21
17	Isaac Vinales	53.844s	21
18	Christophe Ponsson	1'00.109s	21
19	Samuele Cavalieri	1'11.934s	21
20	Loris Cresson	1'23.648s	21
	Chaz Davies	DNF	4
	Leon Haslam	DNF	3

Fastest race lap: Razgatlioglu on lap 7, 1m 34.852s, 99.66mph/160.39km/h.

Superpole
1, Rea 1m 33.416s; 2, Razgatlioglu 1m 33.515s; 3, Redding 1m 33.534s; 4, Rinaldi 1m 33.678s; 5, Sykes 1m 33.860s; 6, Lowes 1m 33.897s; 7, Mahias 1m 33.924s; 8, Bassani 1m 34.012s; 9, Bautista 1m 34.217s; 10, Davies 1m 34.453s; 11, Locatelli 1m 34.464s; 12, Haslam 1m 34.520s; 13, van der Mark 1m 34.674s; 14, Nozane 1m 34.677s; 15, Folger 1m 34.892s; 16, Rabat 1m 35.156s; 17, Vinales 1m 35.622s; 18, Ponsson 1m 35.909s; 19, Cavalieri 1m 36.465s; 20, Cresson 1m 38.365s; 21, Gerloff No Time; 22, Laverty No Time.

Points
1, Rea 149; 2, Razgatlioglu 129; 3, Redding 104; 4, Lowes 88; 5, Rinaldi 82; 6, Gerloff 59; 7, van der Mark 52; 8, Sykes 51; 9, Davies 48; 10, Locatelli 45; 11, Bautista 43; 12, Bassani 38; 13, Mahias 22; 14, Haslam 18; 15, Nozane 17; 16, Rabat 16; 17, Laverty 10; 18, Folger 8; 19, Vinales 7; 20, Ponsson 1.

CHAMPIONSHIP RESULTS 277

Round 4 — DONINGTON PARK, Great Britain · 2–4 July, 2021 · 2.500-mile/4.023km circuit

Race 1: 23 laps, 57.495 miles/92.529km
Weather: Wet · Track 26°C · Air 19°C
Time of race: 34m 36.377s
Average speed: 99.684mph/160.426km/h

Pos.	Rider	Nat.	No.	Entrant	Machine	Time & Gap	Laps
1	Toprak Razgatlioglu	TUR	54	Pata Yamaha with BRIXX WorldSBK	Yamaha YZF R1		23
2	Jonathan Rea	GBR	1	Kawasaki Racing Team WorldSBK	Kawasaki ZX-10RR	2.419s	23
3	Alex Lowes	GBR	22	Kawasaki Racing Team WorldSBK	Kawasaki ZX-10RR	12.261s	23
4	Tom Sykes	GBR	66	BMW Motorrad WorldSBK Team	BMW M 1000 RR	14.625s	23
5	Michael van der Mark	NED	60	BMW Motorrad WorldSBK Team	BMW M 1000 RR	16.447s	23
6	Leon Haslam	GBR	91	Team HRC	Honda CBR1000 RR-R	17.028s	23
7	Garrett Gerloff	USA	31	GRT Yamaha WorldSBK Team	Yamaha YZF R1	33.345s	23
8	Alvaro Bautista	ESP	19	Team HRC	Honda CBR1000 RR-R	37.385s	23
9	Lucas Mahias	FRA	44	Kawasaki Puccetti Racing	Kawasaki ZX-10RR	43.566s	23
10	Axel Bassani	ITA	47	Motocorsa Racing	Ducati Panigale V4 R	43.836s	23
11	Chaz Davies	GBR	7	Team GoEleven	Ducati Panigale V4 R	48.102s	23
12	Michael Rinaldi	ITA	21	Aruba.it Racing - Ducati	Ducati Panigale V4 R	56.538s	23
13	Eugene Laverty	IRL	50	RC Squadra Corse	BMW M 1000 RR	59.392s	23
14	Luke Mossey	GBR	12	OUTDO TPR Team Pedercini Racing	Kawasaki ZX-10RR	1m 01.922s	23
15	Isaac Vinales	ESP	32	Orelac Racing VerdNatura	Kawasaki ZX-10RR	1m 22.275s	23
16	Loris Cresson	BEL	84	OUTDO TPR Team Pedercini Racing	Kawasaki ZX-10RR	1 Lap	22
	Jonas Folger	GER	94	Bonovo MGM Racing	BMW M 1000 RR	DNF	21
	Tito Rabat	ESP	53	Barni Racing Team	Ducati Panigale V4 R	DNF	13
	Andrea Locatelli	ITA	55	Pata Yamaha with BRIXX WorldSBK	Yamaha YZF R1	DNF	6
	Scott Redding	GBR	45	Aruba.it Racing - Ducati	Ducati Panigale V4 R	DNF	1
	Christophe Ponsson	FRA	23	Alstare Yamaha	Yamaha YZF R1	DNF	1

Fastest race lap: Razgatlioglu on lap 14, 1m 28.571s, 101.61mph/163.52km/h.
Lap record: Rea, 1m 27.166s, 103.24mph/166.15km/h (2019).

Superpole: 10 laps, 24.998 miles/40.230km
Weather: Wet · Track 24°C · Air 19°C
Time of race: 15m 17.958s
Average speed: 98.035mph/157.772km/h

Pos.	Rider	Time & Gap	Laps
1	Jonathan Rea		10
2	Tom Sykes	2.531s	10
3	Michael van der Mark	3.409s	10
4	Leon Haslam	3.955s	10
5	Garrett Gerloff	4.067s	10
6	Toprak Razgatlioglu	5.011s	10
7	Lucas Mahias	6.461s	10
8	Chaz Davies	11.599s	10
9	Andrea Locatelli	20.284s	10
10	Michael Rinaldi	24.865s	10
11	Axel Bassani	25.318s	10
12	Eugene Laverty	25.584s	10
13	Isaac Vinales	40.885s	10
14	Alex Lowes	1m 09.188s	10
15	Alvaro Bautista	1m 16.976s	10
16	Jonas Folger	1m 24.717s	10
17	Luke Mossey	1m 33.316s	10
18	Scott Redding	1m 37.702s	10
	Loris Cresson	DNF	7
	Christophe Ponsson	DNF	5
	Tito Rabat	DNF	1

Fastest race lap: Razgatlioglu on lap 7, 1m 30.196s, 99.77mph/160.57km/h.

Race 2: 23 laps, 57.495 miles/92.529km
Weather: Dry · Track 36°C · Air 22°C
Time of race: 34m 1.226s
Average speed: 101.400mph/163.188km/h

Pos.	Rider	Time & Gap	Laps
1	Toprak Razgatlioglu		23
2	Garrett Gerloff	2.243s	23
3	Tom Sykes	4.522s	23
4	Scott Redding	5.151s	23
5	Michael van der Mark	13.315s	23
6	Alex Lowes	14.444s	23
7	Chaz Davies	16.684s	23
8	Michael Rinaldi	18.757s	23
9	Leon Haslam	20.783s	23
10	Alvaro Bautista	22.938s	23
11	Andrea Locatelli	23.194s	23
12	Lucas Mahias	25.442s	23
13	Axel Bassani	32.898s	23
14	Tito Rabat	38.370s	23
15	Eugene Laverty	39.776s	23
16	Luke Mossey	43.182s	23
17	Isaac Vinales	56.811s	23
18	Christophe Ponsson	57.073s	23
19	Loris Cresson	1m 13.148s	23
20	Jonathan Rea	1m 14.103s	23
	Jonas Folger	DNF	6

Fastest race lap: Rea on lap 8, 1m 28.078s, 102.17mph/164.43km/h.

Superpole
1, Rea 1m 40.101s; 2, van der Mark 1m 40.626s; 3, Sykes 1m 40.763s; 4, Lowes 1m 41.351s; 5, Gerloff 1m 41.393s; 6, Redding 1m 42.067s; 7, Haslam 1m 42.206s; 8, Rinaldi 1m 42.587s; 9, Davies 1m 42.630s; 10, Mahias 1m 42.658s; 11, Locatelli 1m 42.683s; 12, Bassani 1m 42.801s; 13, Razgatlioglu 1m 42.840s; 14, Mossey 1m 43.212s; 15, Laverty 1m 43.345s; 16, Bautista 1m 43.625s; 17, Vinales 1m 44.630s; 18, Rabat 1m 44.703s; 19, Ponsson 1m 46.568s; 20, Folger 1m 46.660s; 21, Cresson 1m 46.775s.

Points
1, Razgatlioglu 183; 2, Rea 181; 3, Redding 117; 4, Lowes 114; 5, Rinaldi 94; 6, Gerloff 93; 7, Sykes 89; 8, van der Mark 81; 9, Davies 64; 10, Bautista 57; 11, Locatelli 51; 12, Bassani 47; 13, Haslam 41; 14, Mahias 36; 15, Rabat 18; 16, Nozane 17; 17, Laverty 14; 18, Folger 8; 19, Vinales 8; 20, Mossey 2; 21, Ponsson 1.

Round 5 — ASSEN, The Netherlands · 23–25 July, 2021 · 2.822-mile/4.542km circuit

Race 1: 19 laps, 6.884 miles/11.0789km
Weather: Dry · Track 37°C · Air 25°C
Time of race: 30m 48.682s
Average speed: 134.056mph/215.743km/h

Pos.	Rider	Nat.	No.	Entrant	Machine	Time & Gap	Laps
1	Jonathan Rea	GBR	1	Kawasaki Racing Team WorldSBK	Kawasaki ZX-10RR		19
2	Scott Redding	GBR	45	Aruba.it Racing - Ducati	Ducati Panigale V4 R	3.312s	19
3	Toprak Razgatlioglu	TUR	54	Pata Yamaha with BRIXX WorldSBK	Yamaha YZF R1	1 Sector	19
4	Michael van der Mark	NED	60	BMW Motorrad WorldSBK Team	BMW M 1000 RR	1 Sector	19
5	Andrea Locatelli	ITA	55	Pata Yamaha with BRIXX WorldSBK	Yamaha YZF R1	1 Sector	19
6	Garrett Gerloff	USA	31	GRT Yamaha WorldSBK Team	Yamaha YZF R1	1 Sector	19
7	Tom Sykes	GBR	66	BMW Motorrad WorldSBK Team	BMW M 1000 RR	1 Sector	19
8	Leon Haslam	GBR	91	Team HRC	Honda CBR1000 RR-R	1 Sector	19
9	Chaz Davies	GBR	7	Team GoEleven	Ducati Panigale V4 R	1 Sector	19
10	Axel Bassani	ITA	47	Motocorsa Racing	Ducati Panigale V4 R	1 Sector	19
11	Isaac Vinales	ESP	32	Orelac Racing VerdNatura	Kawasaki ZX-10RR	2 Sectors	19
12	Leandro Mercado	ARG	36	MIE Racing Honda Racing	Honda CBR1000 RR-R	2 Sectors	19
13	Loris Cresson	BEL	84	OUTDO TPR Team Pedercini Racing	Kawasaki ZX-10RR	1 Lap	18
14	Andrea Mantovani	ITA	9	Vince64	Kawasaki ZX-10RR	1 Lap	18
	Jonas Folger	GER	94	Bonovo MGM Racing	BMW M 1000 RR	DNF	18
	Tito Rabat	ESP	53	Barni Racing Team	Ducati Panigale V4 R	DNF	16
	Kohta Nozane	JPN	3	GRT Yamaha WorldSBK Team	Yamaha YZF R1	DNF	12
	Lucas Mahias	FRA	44	Kawasaki Puccetti Racing	Kawasaki ZX-10RR	DNF	12
	Michael Rinaldi	ITA	21	Aruba.it Racing - Ducati	Ducati Panigale V4 R	DNF	2
	Alex Lowes	GBR	22	Kawasaki Racing Team WorldSBK	Kawasaki ZX-10RR	DNF	2
	Alvaro Bautista	ESP	19	Team HRC	Honda CBR1000 RR-R	DNF	1

Fastest race lap: Redding on lap 2, 1m 34.654s, 107.34mph/172.75km/h.
Lap record: Bautista, 1m 34.564s, 107.44mph/172.91km/h (2019).

Superpole: 10 laps, 28.223 miles/45.420km
Weather: Dry · Track 30°C · Air 22°C
Time of race: 15m 54.593s
Average speed: 106.435mph/171.290km/h

Pos.	Rider	Time & Gap	Laps
1	Jonathan Rea		10
2	Michael Rinaldi	3.542s	10
3	Toprak Razgatlioglu	3.600s	10
4	Andrea Locatelli	4.343s	10
5	Scott Redding	4.501s	10
6	Alex Lowes	5.215s	10
7	Tom Sykes	8.010s	10
8	Garrett Gerloff	9.126s	10
9	Chaz Davies	11.891s	10
10	Axel Bassani	12.103s	10
11	Tito Rabat	13.553s	10
12	Leon Haslam	15.585s	10
13	Isaac Vinales	20.175s	10
14	Leandro Mercado	23.075s	10
15	Kohta Nozane	23.130s	10
16	Andrea Mantovani	28.596s	10
17	Loris Cresson	43.204s	10
18	Alvaro Bautista	1m 08.267s	10
	Michael van der Mark	DNF	0

Fastest race lap: Rea on lap 6, 1m 34.634s, 107.36mph/172.78km/h.

Race 2: 21 laps, 59.268 miles/95.382km
Weather: Dry · Track 31°C · Air 22°C
Time of race: 33m 27.685s
Average speed: 106.273mph/171.030km/h

Pos.	Rider	Time & Gap	Laps
1	Jonathan Rea		21
2	Scott Redding	1.605s	21
3	Andrea Locatelli	3.431s	21
4	Chaz Davies	8.695s	21
5	Alvaro Bautista	9.584s	21
6	Michael van der Mark	12.691s	21
7	Alex Lowes	12.992s	21
8	Michael Rinaldi	13.752s	21
9	Axel Bassani	19.087s	21
10	Leon Haslam	19.629s	21
11	Tito Rabat	20.974s	21
12	Kohta Nozane	34.615s	21
13	Leandro Mercado	35.640s	21
14	Isaac Vinales	38.917s	21
15	Tom Sykes	47.840s	21
16	Andrea Mantovani	56.387s	21
17	Loris Cresson	1m 09.598s	21
	Garrett Gerloff	DNF	12
	Toprak Razgatlioglu	DNF	0

Fastest race lap: Rea on lap 6, 1m 34.689s, 107.30mph/172.68km/h.

Superpole
1, Rea 1m 33.842s; 2, Razgatlioglu 1m 34.028s; 3, Redding 1m 34.053s; 4, Rinaldi 1m 34.067s; 5, Lowes 1m 34.252s; 6, Folger 1m 34.336s; 7, Locatelli 1m 34.375s; 8, Haslam 1m 34.467s; 9, van der Mark 1m 34.786s; 10, Bautista 1m 34.791s; 11, Rabat 1m 34.944s; 12, Bassani 1m 34.944s; 13, Davies 1m 35.002s; 14, Vinales 1m 35.251s; 15, Mahias 1m 35.335s; 16, Mercado 1m 35.558s; 17, Mantovani 1m 36.059s; 18, Nozane 1m 36.076s; 19, Cresson 1m 37.156s; 20, Sykes No Time; 21, Gerloff No Time.

Points
1, Rea 243; 2, Razgatlioglu 206; 3, Redding 162; 4, Lowes 127; 5, Rinaldi 111; 6, Gerloff 105; 7, van der Mark 104; 8, Sykes 102; 9, Davies 85; 10, Locatelli 84; 11, Bautista 68; 12, Bassani 60; 13, Haslam 55; 14, Mahias 36; 15, Rabat 23; 16, Nozane 21; 17, Vinales 15; 18, Laverty 14; 19, Folger 8; 20, Mercado 7; 21, Cresson 3; 22, Mantovani 2; 23, Mossey 2; 24, Ponsson 1.

Round 6 — MOST, Czech Republic · 6–8 August, 2021 · 2.617-mile/4.212km circuit

Race 1: 22 laps, 57.579 miles/92.664km
Weather: Dry · Track 39°C · Air 27°C
Time of race: 34m 14.370s
Average speed: 100.899mph/162.381km/h

Pos.	Rider	Nat.	No.	Entrant	Machine	Time & Gap	Laps
1	Toprak Razgatlioglu	TUR	54	Pata Yamaha with BRIXX WorldSBK	Yamaha YZF R1		22
2	Scott Redding	GBR	45	Aruba.it Racing - Ducati	Ducati Panigale V4 R	0.040s	22
3	Andrea Locatelli	ITA	55	Pata Yamaha with BRIXX WorldSBK	Yamaha YZF R1	13.838s	22
4	Michael Rinaldi	ITA	21	Aruba.it Racing - Ducati	Ducati Panigale V4 R	16.650s	22
5	Axel Bassani	ITA	47	Motocorsa Racing	Ducati Panigale V4 R	16.935s	22
6	Garrett Gerloff	USA	31	GRT Yamaha WorldSBK Team	Yamaha YZF R1	17.099s	22
7	Alvaro Bautista	ESP	19	Team HRC	Honda CBR1000 RR-R	22.590s	22
8	Leon Haslam	GBR	91	Team HRC	Honda CBR1000 RR-R	24.728s	22
9	Tom Sykes	GBR	66	BMW Motorrad WorldSBK Team	BMW M 1000 RR	26.924s	22
10	Marvin Fritz	GER	17	IXS-YART Yamaha	Yamaha YZF R1	39.559s	22
11	Christophe Ponsson	FRA	23	Gil Motor Sport-Yamaha	Yamaha YZF R1	58.991s	22
12	Isaac Vinales	ESP	32	Orelac Racing VerdNatura	Kawasaki ZX-10RR	59.105s	22
13	Alex Lowes	GBR	22	Kawasaki Racing Team WorldSBK	Kawasaki ZX-10RR	1m 21.929s	22
14	Kohta Nozane	JPN	3	GRT Yamaha WorldSBK Team	Yamaha YZF R1	1 Lap	21
	Jonathan Rea	GBR	1	Kawasaki Racing Team WorldSBK	Kawasaki ZX-10RR	DNF	17
	Michael van der Mark	NED	60	BMW Motorrad WorldSBK Team	BMW M 1000 RRP	DNF	13
	Loris Cresson	BEL	84	OUTDO TPR Team Pedercini Racing	Kawasaki ZX-10RR	DNF	10
	Tito Rabat	ESP	53	Barni Racing Team	Ducati Panigale V4 R	DNF	9
	Jonas Folger	GER	94	Bonovo MGM Racing	BMW M 1000 RR	DNF	6
	Chaz Davies	GBR	7	Team GoEleven	Ducati Panigale V4 R	DNF	5
	Karel Hanika	CZE	98	IXS-YART Yamaha	Yamaha YZF R1	DNF	3
	Jayson Uribe	USA	14	OUTDO TPR Team Pedercini Racing	Kawasaki ZX-10RR	DNF	3
	Alessandro Delbianco	ITA	52	MIE Racing Honda Racing	Honda CBR1000 RR-R	DNF	2

Fastest race lap: Razgatlioglu on lap 15, 1m 32.697s, 101.64mph/163.58km/h.
Lap record: New circuit.

Superpole: 10 laps, 26.172 miles/42.120km
Weather: Dry · Track 33°C · Air 21°C
Time of race: 15m 28.861s
Average speed: 101.436mph/163.245km/h

Pos.	Rider	Time & Gap	Laps
1	Toprak Razgatlioglu		10
2	Scott Redding	0.496s	10
3	Jonathan Rea	1.384s	10
4	Andrea Locatelli	5.765s	10
5	Tom Sykes	8.694s	10
6	Garrett Gerloff	9.306s	10
7	Alex Lowes	10.152s	10
8	Axel Bassani	11.216s	10
9	Alvaro Bautista	11.514s	10
10	Michael Rinaldi	12.344s	10
11	Michael van der Mark	12.518s	10
12	Marvin Fritz	14.342s	10
13	Leon Haslam	15.591s	10
14	Chaz Davies	22.917s	10
15	Kohta Nozane	24.924s	10
16	Christophe Ponsson	30.155s	10
17	Isaac Vinales	30.249s	10
18	Jonas Folger	30.804s	10
19	Loris Cresson	37.768s	10
20	Jayson Uribe	52.907s	10
	Alessandro Delbianco	DNF	8
	Tito Rabat	DNF	8
	Karel Hanika	DNF	3

Fastest race lap: Rea on lap 3, 1m 31.99€s, 102.41mph/164.82km/h.

Race 2: 22 laps, 57.579 miles/92.664km
Weather: Dry · Track 37°C · Air 24°C
Time of race: 34m 6.298s
Average speed: 101.297mph/163.021km/h

Pos.	Rider	Time & Gap	Laps
1	Scott Redding		22
2	Toprak Razgatlioglu	3.587s	22
3	Jonathan Rea	12.460s	22
4	Andrea Locatelli	15.206s	22
5	Michael Rinaldi	19.479s	22
6	Alex Lowes	19.901s	22
7	Michael van der Mark	20.034s	22
8	Garrett Gerloff	20.250s	22
9	Tom Sykes	24.043s	22
10	Alvaro Bautista	25.257s	22
11	Leon Haslam	29.203s	22
12	Chaz Davies	38.396s	22
13	Tito Rabat	41.674s	22
14	Kohta Nozane	45.843s	22
15	Christophe Ponsson	54.144s	22
16	Jonas Folger	54.354s	22
17	Isaac Vinales	1m 05.085s	22
18	Karel Hanika	1m 08.662s	22
19	Marvin Fritz	1m 12.286s	22
20	Loris Cresson	1m 12.374s	22
21	Jayson Uribe	1 Lap	21
	Axel Bassani	DNF	0
	Alessandro Delbianco	DNF	0

Fastest race lap: Redding on lap 10, 1m 32.415s, 101.95mph/164.08km/h.

Superpole

1, Rea 1m 31.684s; 2, Razgatlioglu 1m 31.751s; 3, Redding 1m 32.158s; 4, Sykes 1m 32.173s; 5, Gerloff 1m 32.238s; 6, Locatelli 1m 32.335s; 7, Haslam 1m 32.352s; 8, Rinaldi 1m 32.530s; 9, Lowes 1m 32.559s; 10, Bassani 1m 32.911s; 11, Bautista 1m 32.928s; 12, Fritz 1m 33.164s; 13, Hanika 1m 33.249s; 14, Delbianco 1m 33.434s; 15, Rabat 1m 33.470s; 16, Davies 1m 33.607s; 17, van der Mark 1m 33.994s; 18, Nozane 1m 34.167s; 19, Vinales 1m 34.280s; 20, Ponsson 1m 34.444s; 21, Folger 1m 34.499s; 22, Cresson 1m 35.936s; 23, Uribe 1m 36.118s...

Points

1, Rea 266; 2, Razgatlioglu 263; 3, Redding 216; 4, Lowes 143; 5, Rinaldi 135; 6, Gerloff 127; 7, Sykes 121; 8, Locatelli 119; 9, van der Mark 113; 10, Davies 89; 11, Bautista 84; 12, Bassani 73; 13, Haslam 68; 14, Mahias 36; 15, Rabat 26; 16, Nozane 25; 17, Vinales 19; 18, Laverty 14; 19, Folger 8; 20, Ponsson 7; 21, Mercado 7; 22, Fritz 6; 23, Cresson 3; 24, Mantovani 2; 25, Mossey 2.

Round 7 — NAVARRA, Spain · 20–22 August, 2021 · 2.444-mile/3.933km circuit

Race 1: 23 laps, 56.209 miles/90.459km
Weather: Dry · Track 45°C · Air 30°C
Time of race: 37m 50.793s
Average speed: 89.110mph/143.409km/h

Pos.	Rider	Nat.	No.	Entrant	Machine	Time & Gap	Laps
1	Scott Redding	GBR	45	Aruba.it Racing - Ducati	Ducati Panigale V4 R		23
2	Jonathan Rea	GBR	1	Kawasaki Racing Team WorldSBK	Kawasaki ZX-10RR	2.519s	23
3	Toprak Razgatlioglu	TUR	54	Pata Yamaha with Brixx WorldSBK	Yamaha YZF R1	5.894s	23
4	Andrea Locatelli	ITA	55	Pata Yamaha with Brixx WorldSBK	Yamaha YZF R1	9.405s	23
5	Alex Lowes	GBR	22	Kawasaki Racing Team WorldSBK	Kawasaki ZX-10RR	16.219s	23
6	Tom Sykes	GBR	66	BMW Motorrad WorldSBK Team	BMW M 1000 RR	20.600s	23
7	Michael van der Mark	NED	60	BMW Motorrad WorldSBK Team	BMW M 1000 RR	24.158s	23
8	Axel Bassani	ITA	47	Motocorsa Racing	Ducati Panigale V4 R	26.497s	23
9	Garrett Gerloff	USA	31	GRT Yamaha WorldSBK Team	Yamaha YZF R1	26.718s	23
10	Michael Rinaldi	ITA	21	Aruba.it Racing - Ducati	Ducati Panigale V4 R	29.602s	23
11	Kohta Nozane	JPN	3	GRT Yamaha WorldSBK Team	Yamaha YZF R1	39.387s	23
12	Tito Rabat	ESP	53	Barni Racing Team	Ducati Panigale V4 R	41.316s	23
13	Leon Haslam	GBR	91	Team HRC	Honda CBR1000 RR	44.338s	23
14	Jonas Folger	GER	94	Bonovo MGM Racing	BMW M 1000 RR-R	48.470s	23
15	Christophe Ponsson	FRA	23	Gil Motor Sport-Yamaha	Yamaha YZF R1	1m 21.773s	23
16	Naomichi Uramoto	JPN	6	JEG Racing	Suzuki GSX-R1000R	1m 21.956s	23
17	Loris Cresson	BEL	84	OUTDO TPR Team Pedercini Racing	Kawasaki ZX-10RR	1m 30.006s	23
18	Jayson Uribe	USA	14	OUTDO TPR Team Pedercini Racing	Kawasaki ZX-10RR	1 Lap	22
	Chaz Davies	GBR	7	Team GoEleven	Ducati Panigale V4 R	DNF	6
	Alvaro Bautista	ESP	19	Team HRC	Honda CBR1000 RR-R	DNF	6
	Lucas Mahias	FRA	44	Kawasaki Puccetti Racing	Kawasaki ZX-10RR	DNF	3
	Leandro Mercado	ARG	36	MIE Racing Honda Racing	Honda CBR1000 RR-R	DNF	3

Fastest race lap: Rea on lap 2, 1m 37.351s, 90.37mph/145.44km/h.
Lap record: New circuit.

Superpole: 10 laps, 24.439 miles/39.330km
Weather: Dry · Track 31°C · Air 23°C
Time of race: 16m 20.247s
Average speed: 89.751mph/144.441km/hh

Pos.	Rider	Time & Gap	Laps
1	Scott Redding		10
2	Jonathan Rea	0.631s	10
3	Toprak Razgatlioglu	3.040s	10
4	Andrea Locatelli	3.845s	10
5	Alex Lowes	4.501s	10
6	Tom Sykes	6.302s	10
7	Chaz Davies	7.203s	10
8	Michael van der Mark	10.054s	10
9	Garrett Gerloff	10.620s	10
10	Alvaro Bautista	16.297s	10
11	Kohta Nozane	16.791s	10
12	Axel Bassani	17.321s	10
13	Michael Rinaldi	17.353s	10
14	Leon Haslam	18.531s	10
15	Lucas Mahias	18.578s	10
16	Jonas Folger	20.506s	10
17	Christophe Ponsson	23.206s	10
18	Leandro Mercado	23.308s	10
19	Naomichi Uramoto	28.254s	10
20	Loris Cresson	40.060s	10
	Jayson Uribe	DNF	10
	Tito Rabat	DNF	6

Fastest race lap: Redding on lap 5, 1m 37.065s, 90.64mph/145.87km/h.

Race 2: 22 laps, 53.765 miles/86.526km
Weather: Dry · Track 41°C · Air 28°C
Time of race: 36m 9.492s
Average speed: 89.216mph/143.579km/hh

Pos.	Rider	Time & Gap	Laps
1	Toprak Razgatlioglu		22
2	Scott Redding	1.105s	22
3	Jonathan Rea	3.715s	22
4	Andrea Locatelli	10.758s	22
5	Tom Sykes	14.437s	22
6	Alex Lowes	15.151s	22
7	Michael Rinaldi	16.875s	22
8	Alvaro Bautista	18.272s	22
9	Michael van der Mark	18.991s	22
10	Axel Bassani	29.430s	22
11	Tito Rabat	31.834s	22
12	Jonas Folger	40.104s	22
13	Christophe Ponsson	49.695s	22
14	Lucas Mahias	1m 12.388s	22
15	Leandro Mercado	1m 14.472s	22
16	Jayson Uribe	1m 25.210s	22
17	Loris Cresson	1m 30.578s	22
	Kohta Nozane	DNF	21
	Leon Haslam	DNF	13
	Naomichi Uramoto	DNF	7
	Chaz Davies	DNF	0

Fastest race lap: Rea on lap 3, 1m 37.609s, 90.14mph/145.06km/h.

Superpole

1, Rea 1m 36.122s; 2, Redding 1m 36.215s; 3, Sykes 1m 36.546s; 4, Locatelli 1m 36.580s; 5, Davies 1m 36.693s; 6, Mahias 1m 36.729s; 7, Lowes 1m 36.744s; 8, Razgatlioglu 1m 36.752s; 9, Gerloff 1m 36.858s; 10, van der Mark 1m 36.895s; 11, Bassani 1m 37.240s; 12, Bautista 1m 37.412s; 13, Rinaldi 1m 37.468s; 14, Folger 1m 37.661s; 15, Nozane 1m 37.664s; 16, Mercado 1m 37.794s; 17, Haslam 1m 38.012s; 18, Rabat 1m 38.446s; 19, Ponsson 1m 38.948s; 20, Uramoto 1m 38.973s; 21, Uribe 1m 40.094s; 22, Cresson 1m 40.255s.

Points

1, Razgatlioglu 311; 2, Rea 311; 3, Redding 273; 4, Lowes 169; 5, Locatelli 151; 6, Rinaldi 150; 7, Sykes 146; 8, Gerloff 135; 9, van der Mark 131; 10, Davies 92; 11, Bautista 92; 12, Bassani 87; 13, Haslam 71; 14, Mahias 38; 15, Rabat 35; 16, Nozane 30; 17, Vinales 19; 18, Folger 14; 19, Laverty 14; 20, Ponsson 11; 21, Mercado 8; 22, Fritz 6; 23, Cresson 3; 24, Mantovani 2; 25, Mossey 2.

Round 8 — MAGNY-COURS, France · 3–5 September, 2021 · 2.741-mile/4.411km circuit

Race 1: 21 laps, 57.558 miles/92.631km
Weather: Dry · Track 40°C · Air 26°C
Time of race: 34m 6.037s
Average speed: 101.274mph/162.984km/h

Pos.	Rider	Nat.	No.	Entrant	Machine	Time & Gap	Laps
1	Toprak Razgatlioglu	TUR	54	Pata Yamaha with Brixx WorldSBK	Yamaha YZF R1		21
2	Jonathan Rea	GBR	1	Kawasaki Racing Team WorldSBK	Kawasaki ZX-10RR	4.467s	21
3	Andrea Locatelli	ITA	55	Pata Yamaha with Brixx WorldSBK	Yamaha YZF R1	10.285s	21
4	Michael Rinaldi	ITA	21	Aruba.it Racing - Ducati	Ducati Panigale V4 R	13.283s	21
5	Michael van der Mark	NED	60	BMW Motorrad WorldSBK Team	BMW M 1000 RR	15.535s	21
6	Alvaro Bautista	ESP	19	Team HRC	Honda CBR1000 RR-R	17.824s	21
7	Chaz Davies	GBR	7	Team GoEleven	Ducati Panigale V4 R	20.067s	21
8	Axel Bassani	ITA	47	Motocorsa Racing	Ducati Panigale V4 R	20.127s	21
9	Tom Sykes	GBR	66	BMW Motorrad WorldSBK Team	BMW M 1000 RR	20.150s	21
10	Leon Haslam	GBR	91	Team HRC	Honda CBR1000 RR-R	23.763s	21
11	Garrett Gerloff	USA	31	GRT Yamaha WorldSBK Team	Yamaha YZF R1	23.977s	21
12	Scott Redding	GBR	45	Aruba.it Racing - Ducati	Ducati Panigale V4 R	38.551s	21
13	Christophe Ponsson	FRA	23	Gil Motor Sport-Yamaha	Yamaha YZF R1	44.742s	21
14	Tito Rabat	ESP	53	Barni Racing Team	Ducati Panigale V4 R	45.494s	21
15	Isaac Vinales	ESP	32	Orelac Racing VerdNatura	Kawasaki ZX-10RR	45.612s	21
16	Jonas Folger	GER	94	Bonovo MGM Racing	BMW M 1000 RR	55.985s	21
17	Kohta Nozane	JPN	3	GRT Yamaha WorldSBK Team	Yamaha YZF R1	59.560s	21
18	Loris Cresson	BEL	84	OUTDO TPR Team Pedercini Racing	Kawasaki ZX-10RR	59.642s	21
	Alex Lowes	GBR	22	Kawasaki Racing Team WorldSBK	Kawasaki ZX-10RR	DNF	16
	Leandro Mercado	ARG	36	MIE Racing Honda Racing	Honda CBR1000 RR-R	DNF	7

Fastest race lap: Razgatlioglu on lap 7, 1m 36.937s, 101.79mph/163.81km/h.
Lap record: Razgatlioglu, 1m 37.018s, 101.71mph/163.68km/h (2019).

Superpole: 10 laps, 27.409 miles/44.110km
Weather: Dry · Track 32°C · Air 24°C
Time of race: 16m 7.436s
Average speed: 101.992mph/164.141km/h

Pos.	Rider	Time & Gap	Laps
1	Jonathan Rea		10
2	Toprak Razgatlioglu	0.148s	10
3	Alex Lowes	5.282s	10
4	Andrea Locatelli	6.643s	10
5	Scott Redding	7.384s	10
6	Michael van der Mark	8.119s	10
7	Alvaro Bautista	9.515s	10
8	Chaz Davies	9.888s	10
9	Leon Haslam	11.325s	10
10	Michael Rinaldi	11.683s	10
11	Axel Bassani	11.979s	10
12	Tom Sykes	12.231s	10
13	Garrett Gerloff	12.502s	10
14	Lucas Mahias	21.597s	10
15	Tito Rabat	22.318s	10
16	Kohta Nozane	25.630s	10
17	Christophe Ponsson	26.090s	10
18	Jonas Folger	27.204s	10
19	Leandro Mercado	30.022s	10
20	Loris Cresson	33.524s	10
	Isaac Vinales	DNF	1

Fastest race lap: Rea on lap 6, 1m 36.374s, 102.38mph/164.77km/h.

Race 2: 21 laps, 57.558 miles/92.631km
Weather: Dry · Track 42°C · Air 28°C
Time of race: 34m 9.849s
Average speed: 101.085mph/162.681km/h

Pos.	Rider	Time & Gap	Laps
1	Toprak Razgatlioglu		21
2	Jonathan Rea	2.908s	21
3	Scott Redding	8.406s	21
4	Andrea Locatelli	10.329s	21
5	Chaz Davies	10.734s	21
6	Alvaro Bautista	11.467s	21
7	Michael Rinaldi	13.901s	21
8	Michael van der Mark	15.640s	21
9	Garrett Gerloff	16.254s	21
10	Tom Sykes	20.911s	21
11	Axel Bassani	39.410s	21
12	Christophe Ponsson	42.808s	21
13	Lucas Mahias	43.057s	21
14	Kohta Nozane	44.106s	21
15	Tito Rabat	48.202s	21
16	Jonas Folger	49.557s	21
17	Leandro Mercado	51.981s	21
18	Loris Cresson	1m 07.692s	21
	Leon Haslam	DNF	4
	Alex Lowes	DNF	1

Fastest race lap: Rea on lap 7, 1m 37.226s, 101.49mph/163.33km/h.

Superpole
1, Rea 1m 35.683s; 2, Razgatlioglu 1m 35.784s; 3, Sykes 1m 35.919s; 4, Lowes 1m 36.025s; 5, Locatelli 1m 36.201s; 6, Haslam 1m 36.258s; 7, Rinaldi 1m 36.415s; 8, Redding 1m 36.485s; 9, van der Mark 1m 36.736s; 10, Mahias 1m 36.814s; 11, Davies 1m 36.871s; 12, Gerloff 1m 36.926s; 13, Bassani 1m 37.114s; 14, Bautista 1m 37.269s; 15, Rabat 1m 37.719s; 16, Ponsson 1m 37.860s; 17, Vinales 1m 37.970s; 18, Nozane 1m 37.997s; 19, Folger 1m 38.184s; 20, Mercado 1m 38.357s; 21, Cresson 1m 38.862s.

Points
1, Razgatlioglu 370; 2, Rea 363; 3, Redding 298; 4, Locatelli 186; 5, Lowes 176; 6, Rinaldi 172; 7, Sykes 159; 8, van der Mark 154; 9, Gerloff 147; 10, Bautista 115; 11, Davies 114; 12, Bassani 100; 13, Haslam 78; 14, Mahias 41; 15, Rabat 38; 16, Nozane 32; 17, Vinales 20; 18, Ponsson 18; 19, Folger 14; 20, Laverty 14; 21, Mercado 8; 22, Fritz 6; 23, Cresson 3; 24, Mantovani 2; 25, Mossey 2.

Round 9 — CATALUNYA, Spain · 17–19 September, 2021 · 2.875-mile/4.627km circuit

Race 1: 20 laps, 57.875 miles/93.140km
Weather: Wet · Track 26°C · Air 23°C
Time of race: 39m 8.002s
Average speed: 88.734mph/142.804km/h

Pos.	Rider	Nat.	No.	Entrant	Machine	Time & Gap	Laps
1	Scott Redding	GBR	45	Aruba.it Racing - Ducati	Ducati Panigale V4 R		20
2	Axel Bassani	ITA	47	Motocorsa Racing	Ducati Panigale V4 R	1.577s	20
3	Michael Rinaldi	ITA	21	Aruba.it Racing - Ducati	Ducati Panigale V4 R	2.326s	20
4	Jonathan Rea	GBR	1	Kawasaki Racing Team WorldSBK	Kawasaki ZX-10RR	4.554s	20
5	Michael van der Mark	NED	60	BMW Motorrad WorldSBK Team	BMW M 1000 RR	6.518s	20
6	Alex Lowes	GBR	22	Kawasaki Racing Team WorldSBK	Kawasaki ZX-10RR	8.514s	20
7	Leon Haslam	GBR	91	Team HRC	Honda CBR1000 RR-R	12.695s	20
8	Tom Sykes	GBR	66	BMW Motorrad WorldSBK Team	BMW M 1000 RR	15.346s	20
9	Alvaro Bautista	ESP	19	Team HRC	Honda CBR1000 RR-R	16.938s	20
10	Chaz Davies	GBR	7	Team GoEleven	Ducati Panigale V4 R	33.386s	20
11	Kohta Nozane	JPN	3	GRT Yamaha WorldSBK Team	Yamaha YZF R1	33.394s	20
12	Andrea Locatelli	ITA	55	Pata Yamaha with Brixx WorldSBK	Yamaha YZF R1	34.169s	20
13	Lucas Mahias	FRA	44	Kawasaki Puccetti Racing	Kawasaki ZX-10RR	34.565s	20
14	Isaac Vinales	ESP	32	Orelac Racing VerdNatura	Kawasaki ZX-10RR	44.546s	20
15	Leandro Mercado	ARG	36	MIE Racing Honda Racing	Honda CBR1000 RR-R	58.200s	20
16	Samuele Cavalieri	ITA	76	Barni Racing Team	Ducati Panigale V4 R	1m 07.818s	20
17	Christophe Ponsson	FRA	23	Gil Motor Sport-Yamaha	Yamaha YZF R1	1m 22.762s	20
18	Loris Cresson	BEL	84	OUTDO TPR Team Pedercini Racing	Kawasaki ZX-10RR	1m 25.638s	20
19	Jonas Folger	GER	94	Bonovo MGM Racing	BMW M 1000 RR	1m 27.363s	20
20	Lachlan Epis	AUS	83	OUTDO TPR Team Pedercini Racing	Kawasaki ZX-10RR	1 Lap	19
	Toprak Razgatlioglu	TUR	54	Pata Yamaha with Brixx WorldSBK	Yamaha YZF R1	DNF	14
	Garrett Gerloff	USA	31	GRT Yamaha WorldSBK Team	Yamaha YZF R1	DNF	9

Fastest race lap: Redding on lap 17, 1m 56.166s, 89.68mph/144.32km/h.
Lap record: New layout.

Superpole: 5 laps, 14.469 miles/23.285km
Weather: Dry · Track 31°C · Air 19°C
Time of race: 8m 32.847s
Average speed: 101.564mph/163.452km/h

Pos.	Rider	Time & Gap	Laps
1	Jonathan Rea		5
2	Toprak Razgatlioglu	0.211s	5
3	Alvaro Bautista	2.771s	5
4	Alex Lowes	2.948s	5
5	Michael Rinaldi	3.428s	5
6	Axel Bassani	5.431s	5
7	Leon Haslam	5.729s	5
8	Garrett Gerloff	5.814s	5
9	Christophe Ponsson	9.514s	5
10	Leandro Mercado	9.818s	5
11	Samuele Cavalieri	10.767s	5
12	Isaac Vinales	12.713s	5
13	Jonas Folger	13.005s	5
14	Loris Cresson	14.513s	5
15	Scott Redding	19.893s	5
16	Lachlan Epis	28.773s	5
	Lucas Mahias	DNF	3
	Andrea Locatelli	DNF	1
	Kohta Nozane	DNF	0
	Tom Sykes	DNS	-
	Michael van der Mark	DNS	-

Fastest race lap: Razgatlioglu on lap 5, 1m 41.493s, 102.64mph/165.19km/h.

Race 2: 19 laps, 54.981 miles/88.483km
Weather: Dry · Track 43°C · Air 26°C
Time of race: 32m 48.622s
Average speed: 100.543mph/161.808km/h

Pos.	Rider	Time & Gap	Laps
1	Michael Rinaldi		21
2	Toprak Razgatlioglu	3.030s	21
3	Scott Redding	3.207s	21
4	Alvaro Bautista	3.415s	21
5	Andrea Locatelli	4.306s	21
6	Jonathan Rea	7.733s	21
7	Garrett Gerloff	11.098s	21
8	Axel Bassani	14.227s	21
9	Michael van der Mark	15.679s	21
10	Kohta Nozane	17.429s	21
11	Leon Haslam	21.211s	21
12	Samuele Cavalieri	26.533s	21
13	Christophe Ponsson	27.637s	21
14	Leandro Mercado	33.201s	21
15	Isaac Vinales	33.282s	21
16	Jonas Folger	36.090s	21
	Loris Cresson	DNF	15
	Lachlan Epis	DNF	7
	Lucas Mahias	DNF	5
	Alex Lowes	DNS	-
	Tom Sykes	DNS	-

Fastest race lap: Rinaldi on lap 2, 1m 42.566s, 101.57mph/163.46km/h.

Superpole
1, Sykes 1m 40.408s; 2, Razgatlioglu 1m 40.694s; 3, Rea 1m 40.921s; 4, Redding 1m 40.978s; 5, Lowes 1m 41.086s; 6, Locatelli 1m 41.129s; 7, Haslam 1m 41.253s; 8, Rinaldi 1m 41.275s; 9, van der Mark 1m 41.320s; 10, Gerloff 1m 41.405s; 11, Bassani 1m 41.632s; 12, Nozane 1m 41.744s; 13, Davies 1m 41.791s; 14, Cavalieri 1m 41.801s; 15, Mahias 1m 41.808s; 16, Bautista 1m 42.055s; 17, Mercado 1m 42.215s; 18, Folger 1m 42.257s; 19, Vinales 1m 42.446s; 20, Ponsson 1m 42.460s; 21, Cresson 1m 43.841s; 22, Epis 1m 45.732s.

Points
1, Razgatlioglu 399; 2, Rea 398; 3, Redding 339; 4, Rinaldi 218; 5, Locatelli 201; 6, Lowes 192; 7, van der Mark 172; 8, Sykes 167; 9, Gerloff 158; 10, Bautista 142; 11, Bassani 132; 12, Davies 120; 13, Haslam 95; 14, Mahias 44; 15, Nozane 43; 16, Rabat 38; 17, Vinales 23; 18, Ponsson 22; 19, Folger 14; 20, Laverty 14; 21, Mercado 11; 22, Fritz 6; 23, Cavalieri 4; 24, Cresson 3; 25, Mantovani 2; 26, Mossey 2.

Round 10 — JEREZ, Spain · 24–26 September, 2021 · 2.748-mile/4.423km circuit

Race 1: 20 laps, 54.966 miles/88.460km
Weather: Dry · Track 29°C · Air 22°C
Time of race: 33m 37.061s
Average speed: 98.103mph/157.881km/h

Pos.	Rider	Nat.	No.	Entrant	Machine	Time & Gap	Laps
1	Toprak Razgatlioglu	TUR	54	Pata Yamaha with Brixx WorldSBK	Yamaha YZF R1		20
2	Jonathan Rea	GBR	1	Kawasaki Racing Team WorldSBK	Kawasaki ZX-10RR	1.225s	20
3	Scott Redding	GBR	45	Aruba.it Racing - Ducati	Ducati Panigale V4 R	2.791s	20
4	Andrea Locatelli	ITA	55	Pata Yamaha with Brixx WorldSBK	Yamaha YZF R1	3.227s	20
5	Alvaro Bautista	ESP	19	Team HRC	Honda CBR1000 RR-R	8.652s	20
6	Loris Baz	FRA	11	Team GoEleven	Ducati Panigale V4 R	10.414s	20
7	Michael van der Mark	NED	60	BMW Motorrad WorldSBK Team	BMW M 1000 RR	12.294s	20
8	Axel Bassani	ITA	47	Motocorsa Racing	Ducati Panigale V4 R	12.384s	20
9	Alex Lowes	GBR	22	Kawasaki Racing Team WorldSBK	Kawasaki ZX-10RR	13.478s	20
10	Garrett Gerloff	USA	31	GRT Yamaha WorldSBK Team	Yamaha YZF R1	15.594s	20
11	Leon Haslam	GBR	91	Team HRC	Honda CBR1000 RR-R	24.783s	20
12	Eugene Laverty	IRL	50	BMW Motorrad WorldSBK Team	BMW M 1000 RR	26.917s	20
13	Kohta Nozane	JPN	3	GRT Yamaha WorldSBK Team	Yamaha YZF R1	27.252s	20
14	Jonas Folger	GER	94	Bonovo MGM Racing	BMW M 1000 RR	30.594s	20
15	Christophe Ponsson	FRA	23	Gil Motor Sport-Yamaha	Yamaha YZF R1	31.317s	20
16	Marvin Fritz	GER	17	IXS-YART Yamaha	Yamaha YZF R1	35.902s	20
17	Loris Cresson	BEL	84	OUTDO TPR Team Pedercini Racing	Kawasaki ZX-10RR	48.269s	20
18	Andrea Mantovani	ITA	9	Vince64	Kawasaki ZX-10RR	49.932s	20
19	Lachlan Epis	AUS	83	OUTDO TPR Team Pedercini Racing	Kawasaki ZX-10RR	4 Laps	16
	Leandro Mercado	ARG	36	MIE Racing Honda Racing	Honda CBR1000 RR-R	DNF	12
	Michael Rinaldi	ITA	21	Aruba.it Racing - Ducati	Ducati Panigale V4 R	DNF	4
	Samuele Cavalieri	ITA	76	Barni Racing Team	Ducati Panigale V4 R	DNF	4

Fastest race lap: Rea on lap 2, 1m 39.837s, 99.10mph/159.49km/h.
Lap record: Bautista, 1m 39.004s, 99.94mph/160.83km/h (2019).

Superpole: Cancelled following the death of WorldSSP300 rider Dean Berta Vinales.

Race 2: 20 laps, 54.966 miles/88.460km
Weather: Dry · Track 45°C · Air 28°C
Time of race: 33m 49.883s
Average speed: 97.483mph/156.884km/h

Pos.	Rider	Time & Gap	Laps
1	Toprak Razgatlioglu		20
2	Scott Redding	0.113s	20
3	Alvaro Bautista	4.247s	20
4	Andrea Locatelli	5.172s	20
5	Jonathan Rea	6.339s	20
6	Axel Bassani	7.780s	20
7	Michael Rinaldi	11.035s	20
8	Michael van der Mark	11.993s	20
9	Loris Baz	12.311s	20
10	Garrett Gerloff	16.651s	20
11	Eugene Laverty	27.224s	20
12	Leon Haslam	27.266s	20
13	Jonas Folger	27.713s	20
14	Samuele Cavalieri	33.438s	20
15	Leandro Mercado	46.941s	20
16	Marvin Fritz	47.308s	20
17	Andrea Mantovani	54.670s	20
18	Lachlan Epis	3 Laps	17
	Loris Cresson	DNF	4
	Kohta Nozane	DNF	3
	Christophe Ponsson	DNF	0
	Alex Lowes	DNS	0

Fastest race lap: Redding on lap 3, 1m 40.776s, 98.18mph/158.00km/h.

Superpole
1, Razgatlioglu 1m 38.512s; 2, Lowes 1m 38.539s; 3, Rea 1m 38.614s; 4, Redding 1m 38.661s; 5, Rinaldi 1m 38.860s; 6, Locatelli 1m 39.056s; 7, Baz 1m 39.322s; 8, Haslam 1m 39.423s; 9, Bautista 1m 39.609s; 10, Gerloff 1m 39.747s; 11, Mercado 1m 40.023s; 12, Bassani 1m 40.081s; 13, van der Mark 1m 40.092s; 14, Folger 1m 40.121s; 15, Laverty 1m 40.206s; 16, Vinales 1m 40.273s; 17, Nozane 1m 40.367s; 18, Cavalieri 1m 40.433s; 19, Fritz 1m 40.490s; 20, Mantovani 1m 40.795s; 21, Ponsson 1m 41.030s; 22, Cresson 1m 41.255s; 23, Epis 1m 42.626s.

Points
1, Razgatlioglu 449; 2, Rea 429; 3, Redding 375; 4, Rinaldi 227; 5, Locatelli 227; 6, Lowes 199; 7, van der Mark 183; 8, Gerloff 170; 9, Bautista 169; 10, Sykes 167; 11, Bassani 150; 12, Davies 120; 13, Haslam 104; 14, Nozane 46; 15, Mahias 44; 16, Rabat 38; 17, Laverty 23; 18, Ponsson 23; 19, Vinales 23; 20, Folger 19; 21, Baz 17; 22, Mercado 12; 23, Fritz 6; 24, Cavalieri 6; 25, Cresson 3; 26, Mantovani 2; 27, Mossey 2..

Round 11 — PORTIMAO, Portugal · 1–3 October, 2021 · 2.853-mile/4.592km circuit

Race 1: 20 laps, 57.067 miles/91.840km
Weather: Dry · Track 44°C · Air 25°C
Time of race: 34m 1.250s
Average speed: 100.644mph/161.971km/h

Pos.	Rider	Nat.	No.	Entrant	Machine	Time & Gap	Laps
1	Toprak Razgatlioglu	TUR	54	Pata Yamaha with Brixx WorldSBK	Yamaha YZF R1		20
2	Scott Redding	GBR	45	Aruba.it Racing - Ducati	Ducati Panigale V4 R	0.691s	20
3	Loris Baz	FRA	11	Team GoEleven	Ducati Panigale V4 R	10.628s	20
4	Michael Rinaldi	ITA	21	Aruba.it Racing - Ducati	Ducati Panigale V4 R	12.901s	20
5	Leon Haslam	GBR	91	Team HRC	Honda CBR1000 RR-R	13.305s	20
6	Garrett Gerloff	USA	31	GRT Yamaha WorldSBK Team	Yamaha YZF R1	13.596s	20
7	Axel Bassani	ITA	47	Motocorsa Racing	Ducati Panigale V4 R	26.961s	20
8	Leandro Mercado	ARG	36	MIE Racing Honda Racing	Honda CBR1000 RR-R	28.826s	20
9	Eugene Laverty	IRL	50	BMW Motorrad WorldSBK Team	BMW M 1000 RR	29.654s	20
10	Christophe Ponsson	FRA	23	Gil Motor Sport-Yamaha	Yamaha YZF R1	39.061s	20
11	Isaac Vinales	ESP	32	Orelac Racing VerdNatura	Kawasaki ZX-10RR	39.703s	20
12	Samuele Cavalieri	ITA	76	Barni Racing Team	Ducati Panigale V4 R	40.669s	20
13	Tito Rabat	ESP	53	Kawasaki Puccetti Racing	Kawasaki ZX-10RR	41.275s	20
14	Kohta Nozane	JPN	3	GRT Yamaha WorldSBK Team	Yamaha YZF R1	41.412s	20
15	Jonas Folger	GER	94	Bonovo MGM Racing	BMW M 1000 RR	52.815s	20
16	Loris Cresson	BEL	84	OUTDO TPR Team Pedercini Racing	Kawasaki ZX-10RR	52.894s	20
	Alvaro Bautista	ESP	19	Team HRC	Honda CBR1000 RR-R	DNF	19
	Michael van der Mark	NED	60	BMW Motorrad WorldSBK Team	BMW M 1000 RR	DNF	15
	Andrea Locatelli	ITA	55	Pata Yamaha with Brixx WorldSBK	Yamaha YZF R1	DNF	14
	Gabriele Ruiu	ITA	16	B-Max Racing Team	BMW M 1000 RR	DNF	8
	Lachlan Epis	AUS	83	OUTDO TPR Team Pedercini Racing	Kawasaki ZX-10RR	DNF	7
	Jonathan Rea	GBR	1	Kawasaki Racing Team WorldSBK	Kawasaki ZX-10RR	DNF	4

Fastest race lap: Redding on lap 7, 1m 41.507s, 101.20mph/162.86km/h.
Lap record: Bautista, 1m 39.004s, 99.94mph/160.83km/h (2019).

Superpole: 10 laps, 28.533 miles/45.920km
Weather: Wet · Track 25°C · Air 19°C
Time of race: 19m 17.562s
Average speed: 88.738mph/142.810km/h

Pos.	Rider	Time & Gap	Laps
1	Michael van der Mark		10
2	Scott Redding	5.330s	10
3	Loris Baz	7.066s	10
4	Andrea Locatelli	9.264s	10
5	Alvaro Bautista	9.753s	10
6	Toprak Razgatlioglu	16.745s	10
7	Axel Bassani	19.047s	10
8	Garrett Gerloff	19.115s	10
9	Eugene Laverty	20.901s	10
10	Isaac Vinales	28.977s	10
11	Leandro Mercado	31.057s	10
12	Samuele Cavalieri	38.997s	10
13	Jonas Folger	41.330s	10
14	Tito Rabat	51.079s	10
15	Gabriele Ruiu	55.894s	10
16	Christophe Ponsson	56.194s	10
17	Lachlan Epis	1m 23.343s	10
	Leon Haslam	DNF	9
	Kohta Nozane	DNF	5
	Jonathan Rea	DNF	0
	Michael Rinaldi	DNF	0
	Loris Cresson	DNF	0

Fastest race lap: van der Mark on lap 5, 1m 54.895s, 89.40mph/143.88km/h.

Race 2: 19 laps, 54.213 miles/87.248km
Weather: Dry · Track 38°C · Air 22°C
Time of race: 32m 21.137s
Average speed: 100.543mph/161.809km/h

Pos.	Rider	Time & Gap	Laps
1	Jonathan Rea		19
2	Scott Redding	5.425s	19
3	Andrea Locatelli	12.289s	19
4	Loris Baz	12.300s	19
6	Michael van der Mark	15.289s	19
7	Michael Rinaldi	20.639s	19
8	Leon Haslam	20.933s	19
9	Axel Bassani	26.031s	19
10	Eugene Laverty	26.276s	19
11	Leandro Mercado	31.493s	19
12	Isaac Vinales	41.117s	19
13	Kohta Nozane	42.583s	19
14	Christophe Ponsson	48.074s	19
15	Jonas Folger	51.009s	19
16	Samuele Cavalieri	57.467s	19
	Alvaro Bautista	DNF	17
	Gabriele Ruiu	DNF	10
	Toprak Razgatlioglu	DNF	9
	Tito Rabat	DNF	6
	Lachlan Epis	DNF	4
	Loris Cresson	DNF	2

Fastest race lap: Rea on lap 8, 1m 41.309s, 101.40mph/163.18km/h.

Superpole
1, Razgatlioglu 1m 40.219s; 2, Rea 1m 40.524s; 3, Haslam 1m 40.780s; 4, Redding 1m 40.874s; 5, van der Mark 1m 40.973s; 6, Bautista 1m 41.013s; 7, Locatelli 1m 41.146s; 8, Gerloff 1m 41.288s; 9, Baz 1m 41.384s; 10, Rinaldi 1m 41.405s; 11, Bassani 1m 41.593s; 12, Mercado 1m 41.599s; 13, Laverty 1m 41.871s; 14, Vinales 1m 41.909s; 15, Cavalieri 1m 42.167s; 16, Nozane 1m 42.208s; 17, Cresson 1m 42.931s; 18, Ponsson 1m 42.938s; 19, Folger 1m 43.264s; 20, Rabat 1m 44.000s; 21, Epis 1m 44.755s; 22, Ruiu 1m 44.836s.

Points
1, Razgatlioglu 478; 2, Rea 454; 3, Redding 424; 4, Rinaldi 249; 5, Locatelli 249; 6, van der Mark 211; 7, Lowes 199; 8, Gerloff 193; 9, Bautista 174; 10, Bassani 169; 11, Sykes 167; 12, Haslam 123; 13, Davies 120; 14, Baz 53; 15, Nozane 51; 16, Mahias 44; 17, Rabat 41; 18, Laverty 37; 19, Vinales 32; 20, Ponsson 31; 21, Mercado 25; 22, Folger 21; 23, Cavalieri 10; 24, Fritz 6; 25, Cresson 3; 26, Mantovani 2; 27, Mossey 2.

CHAMPIONSHIP RESULTS 281

Round 12 — SAN JUAN VILLICUM, Argentina · 15–17 October, 2021 · 2.657-mile/4.276km circuit

Race 1: 21 laps, 55.797 miles/89.796km
Weather: Dry · Track 45°C · Air 25°C
Time of race: 34m 29.479s
Average speed: 97.062mph/156.206km/h

Pos.	Rider	Nat.	No.	Entrant	Machine	Time & Gap	Laps
1	Toprak Razgatlioglu	TUR	54	Pata Yamaha with Brixx WorldSBK	Yamaha YZF R1		21
2	Jonathan Rea	GBR	1	Kawasaki Racing Team WorldSBK	Kawasaki ZX-10RR	5.295s	21
3	Michael Rinaldi	ITA	21	Aruba.it Racing - Ducati	Ducati Panigale V4 R	9.417s	21
4	Alex Lowes	GBR	22	Kawasaki Racing Team WorldSBK	Kawasaki ZX-10RR	12.808s	21
5	Axel Bassani	ITA	47	Motocorsa Racing	Ducati Panigale V4 R	13.980s	21
6	Michael van der Mark	NED	60	BMW Motorrad WorldSBK Team	BMW M 1000 RR	15.007s	21
7	Garrett Gerloff	USA	31	GRT Yamaha WorldSBK Team	Yamaha YZF R1	16.876s	21
8	Andrea Locatelli	ITA	55	Pata Yamaha with Brixx WorldSBK	Yamaha YZF R1	19.265s	21
9	Scott Redding	GBR	45	Aruba.it Racing - Ducati	Ducati Panigale V4 R	27.176s	21
10	Leon Haslam	GBR	91	Team HRC	Honda CBR1000 RR-R	31.571s	21
11	Tito Rabat	ESP	53	Kawasaki Puccetti Racing	Kawasaki ZX-10RR	34.474s	21
12	Chaz Davies	GBR	7	Team GoEleven	Ducati Panigale V4 R	36.241s	21
13	Eugene Laverty	IRL	50	BMW Motorrad WorldSBK Team	BMW M 1000 RR	37.072s	21
14	Samuele Cavalieri	ITA	76	Barni Racing Team	Ducati Panigale V4 R	41.103s	21
15	Kohta Nozane	JPN	3	GRT Yamaha WorldSBK Team	Yamaha YZF R1	43.220s	21
16	Leandro Mercado	ARG	36	MIE Racing Honda Racing	Honda CBR1000 RR-R	48.516s	21
17	Christophe Ponsson	FRA	23	Gil Motor Sport-Yamaha	Yamaha YZF R1	53.695s	21
18	Marco Solorza	ARG	39	OUTDO TPR Team Pedercini Racing	Kawasaki ZX-10RR	1m 39.426s	21
19	Luciano Ribodino	ARG	4	OUTDO TPR Team Pedercini Racing	Kawasaki ZX-10RR	1 Lap	20
	Isaac Vinales	ESP	32	Orelac Racing VerdNatura	Kawasaki ZX-10RR	DNF	8
	Alvaro Bautista	ESP	19	Team HRC	Honda CBR1000 RR-R	DNF	2

Fastest race lap: Razgatlioglu on lap 2, 1m 38.052s, 97.55mph/156.99km/h.
Lap record: Rea, 1m 37.462s, 98.14mph/157.94km/h (2019).

Superpole: 10 laps, 26.570 miles/42.760km
Weather: Dry · Track 35°C · Air 19°C
Time of race: 16m 20.713s
Average speed: 97.532mph/156.963km/h

Pos.	Rider	Time & Gap	Laps
1	Toprak Razgatlioglu		10
2	Scott Redding	0.046s	10
3	Jonathan Rea	3.419s	10
4	Axel Bassani	5.407s	10
5	Michael van der Mark	8.556s	10
6	Andrea Locatelli	9.608s	10
7	Garrett Gerloff	9.821s	10
8	Michael Rinaldi	10.415s	10
9	Alex Lowes	12.063s	10
10	Leon Haslam	15.170s	10
11	Alvaro Bautista	15.685s	10
12	Tito Rabat	18.017s	10
13	Chaz Davies	18.470s	10
14	Kohta Nozane	20.327s	10
15	Eugene Laverty	20.341s	10
16	Leandro Mercado	21.262s	10
17	Isaac Vinales	21.534s	10
18	Samuele Cavalieri	26.152s	10
19	Christophe Ponsson	27.693s	10
20	Luciano Ribodino	47.417s	10
	Marco Solorza	DNF	10

Fastest race lap: Redding on lap 6, 1m 37.345s, 98.26mph/158.13km/h.

Race 2: 21 laps, 55.797 miles/89.796km
Weather: Dry · Track 41°C · Air 22°C
Time of race: 34m 26.120s
Average speed: 97.220mph/156.460km/h

Pos.	Rider	Time & Gap	Laps
1	Scott Redding		21
2	Jonathan Rea	2.428s	21
3	Toprak Razgatlioglu	3.834s	21
4	Axel Bassani	5.390s	21
5	Michael Rinaldi	5.845s	21
6	Michael van der Mark	8.147s	21
7	Andrea Locatelli	12.040s	21
8	Garrett Gerloff	12.352s	21
9	Chaz Davies	19.409s	21
10	Alvaro Bautista	20.183s	21
11	Leon Haslam	23.993s	21
12	Tito Rabat	25.138s	21
13	Isaac Vinales	27.407s	21
14	Kohta Nozane	28.568s	21
15	Leandro Mercado	36.415s	21
16	Eugene Laverty	39.213s	21
17	Christophe Ponsson	40.746s	21
18	Samuele Cavalieri	56.034s	21
19	Luciano Ribodino	1m 36.692s	21
20	Marco Solorza	1m 36.776s	21

Fastest race lap: Redding on lap 13, 1m 37.615s, 97.99mph/157.70km/h.

Superpole
1, Razgatlioglu 1m 40.219s; 2, Rea 1m 40.524s; 3, Haslam 1m 40.780s; 4, Redding 1m 40.874s; 5, van der Mark 1m 40.973s; 6, Bautista 1m 41.013s; 7, Locatelli 1m 41.146s; 8, Gerloff 1m 41.288s; 9, Baz 1m 41.384s; 10, Rinaldi 1m 41.405s; 11, Bassani 1m 41.593s; 12, Mercado 1m 41.599s; 13, Laverty 1m 41.871s; 14, Vinales 1m 41.909s; 1 5, Cavalieri 1m 42.167s; 16, Nozane 1m 42.208s; 17, Cresson 1m 42.931s; 18, Ponsson 1m 42.938s; 19, Folger 1m 43.264s; 20, Rabat 1m 44.000s; 21, Epis 1m 44.755s; 22, Ruiu 1m 44.836s.

Points
1, Razgatlioglu 531; 2, Rea 501; 3, Redding 465; 4, Rinaldi 278; 5, Locatelli 270; 6, van der Mark 236; 7, Lowes 213; 8, Gerloff 213; 9, Bassani 199; 10, Bautista 180; 11, Sykes 167; 12, Haslam 134; 13, Davies 131; 14, Nozane 54; 15, Baz 53; 16, Rabat 50; 17, Mahias 44; 18, Laverty 40; 19, Vinales 35; 20, Ponsson 31; 21, Mercado 26; 22, Folger 21; 23, Cavalieri 12; 24, Fritz 6; 25, Cresson 3; 26, Mantovani 2; 27, Mossey 2.

Round 13 — MANDALIKA, Indonesia · 19–21 November, 2021 · 2.672-mile/4.300km circuit

Race 1: 20 laps, 53.438 miles/86.000km
Weather: Dry · Track 39°C · Air 30°C
Time of race: 32m 12.219s
Average speed: 99.562mph/160.230km/h

Pos.	Rider	Nat.	No.	Entrant	Machine	Time & Gap	Laps
1	Jonathan Rea	GBR	1	Kawasaki Racing Team WorldSBK	Kawasaki ZX-10RR		20
2	Toprak Razgatlioglu	TUR	54	Pata Yamaha with Brixx WorldSBK	Yamaha YZF R1	0.670s	20
3	Scott Redding	GBR	45	Aruba.it Racing - Ducati	Ducati Panigale V4 R	2.155s	20
4	Andrea Locatelli	ITA	55	Pata Yamaha with Brixx WorldSBK	Yamaha YZF R1	7.644s	20
5	Axel Bassani	ITA	47	Motocorsa Racing	Ducati Panigale V4 R	8.133s	20
6	Michael van der Mark	NED	60	BMW Motorrad WorldSBK Team	BMW M 1000 RR	9.809s	20
7	Alvaro Bautista	ESP	19	Team HRC	Honda CBR1000 RR-R	13.949s	20
8	Chaz Davies	GBR	7	Team GoEleven	Ducati Panigale V4 R	14.059s	20
9	Leandro Mercado	ARG	36	MIE Racing Honda Racing	Honda CBR1000 RR-R	22.907s	20
10	Tom Sykes	GBR	66	BMW Motorrad WorldSBK Team	BMW M 1000 RR	25.525s	20
11	Garrett Gerloff	USA	31	GRT Yamaha WorldSBK Team	Yamaha YZF R1	25.609s	20
12	Michael Rinaldi	ITA	21	Aruba.it Racing - Ducati	Ducati Panigale V4 R	26.267s	20
13	Isaac Vinales	ESP	32	Orelac Racing VerdNatura	Kawasaki ZX-10RR	27.168s	20
14	Samuele Cavalieri	ITA	76	Barni Racing Team	Ducati Panigale V4 R	43.748s	20
15	Kohta Nozane	JPN	3	GRT Yamaha WorldSBK Team	Yamaha YZF R1	50.244s	20
	Christophe Ponsson	FRA	23	Gil Motor Sport-Yamaha	Yamaha YZF R1	DNF	14
	Tito Rabat	ESP	53	Kawasaki Puccetti Racing	Kawasaki ZX-10RR	DNF	9
	Oliver Konig	CZE	15	OUTDO TPR Team Pedercini Racing	Kawasaki ZX-10RR	DNF	1
	Leon Haslam	GBR	91	Team HRC	Honda CBR1000 RR-R	DNS	-

Fastest race lap: Razgatlioglu on lap 19, 1m 34.288s, 102.02mph/164.18km/h.
Lap record: New circuit.

Superpole: Cancelled due to track conditions.

Race 2: 12 laps, 32.063 miles/51.600km
Weather: Wet · Track 29°C · Air 25°C
Time of race: 20m 53.598s
Average speed: 92.075mph/148.181km/h

Pos.	Rider	Time & Gap	Laps
1	Jonathan Rea		12
2	Scott Redding	0.283s	12
3	Michael van der Mark	7.437s	12
4	Toprak Razgatlioglu	10.641s	12
5	Tom Sykes	21.707s	12
6	Garrett Gerloff	24.555s	12
7	Kohta Nozane	27.772s	12
8	Andrea Locatelli	29.481s	12
9	Isaac Vinales	38.615s	12
10	Alvaro Bautista	47.233s	12
11	Christophe Ponsson	50.369s	12
12	Chaz Davies	50.591s	12
13	Tito Rabat	53.099s	12
14	Samuele Cavalieri	1m 00.069s	12
	Michael Rinaldi	DNF	11
	Axel Bassani	DNF	3
	Leandro Mercado	DNF	2
	Leon Haslam	DNS	-

Fastest race lap: Redding on lap 11, 1m 42.39s, 93.95mph/151.19km/h.

Superpole
1, Razgatlioglu 1m 32.877s; 2, Rea 1m 33.201s; 3, Redding 1m 33.256s; 4, Gerloff 1m 33.545s; 5, Locatelli 1m 33.588s; 6, Sykes 1m 33.672s; 7, Bassani 1m 33.775s; 8, Bautista 1m 34.051s; 9, van der Mark 1m 34.080s; 10, Mercado 1m 34.154s; 11, Davies 1m 34.427s; 12, Ponsson 1m 34.431s; 13, Vinales 1m 34.438s; 14, Rinaldi 1m 34.499s; 15, Cavalieri 1m 34.577s; 16, Nozane 1m 34.660s; 17, Rabat 1m 35.258s; 18, Konig 1m 35.864s.

Points
1, Razgatlioglu 564; 2, Rea 551; 3, Redding 501; 4, Locatelli 291; 5, Rinald 282; 6, van der Mark 262; 7, Gerloff 228; 8, Lowes 213; 9, Bassani 210; 10, Bautista 195; 11, Sykes 184; 12, Davies 143; 13, Haslam 134; 14, Nozane 64; 15, Baz 53; 16, Rabat 53; 17, Vinales 45; 18, Mahias 44; 19, Laverty 40; 20, Ponsson 36; 21, Mercado 33; 22, Folger 21; 23, Cavalieri 16; 24, Fritz 6; 25, Cresson 3; 26, Mantovani 2; 27, Mossey 2.

2021 FINAL WORLD SUPERBIKE POINTS TABLE

Position	Rider	Nationality	Machine	Aragon/1	Aragon/SPole	Aragon/2	Estoril/1	Estoril/SPole	Estoril/2	Misano/1	Misano/SPole	Misano/2	Donington/1	Donington/SPole	Donington/2	Assen/1	Assen/SPole	Assen/2	Most/1	Most/SPole	Most/2	Navarra/1	Navarra/SPole	Navarra/2	Magny-Cours/1	Magny-Cours/SPole	Magny-Cours/2	Catalunya/1	Catalunya/SPole	Catalunya/2	Jerez/1	Jerez/SPole	Jerez/2	Portimao/1	Portimao/SPole	Portimao/2	San Juan Villicum/1	San Juan Villicum/SPole	San Juan Villicum/2	Mandalika/1	Mandalika/SPole	Mandalika/2	Total Points
1	Toprak Razgatlioglu	TUR	Yamaha	16	4	10	20	9	16	20	9	25	25	4	25	16	7	-	25	12	20	16	7	25	25	9	25	-	9	20	25	-	25	25	4	-	25	12	16	20	-	13	564
2	Jonathan Rea	GBR	Kawasaki	25	12	20	16	12	25	16	7	16	20	12	-	25	12	25	-	7	16	20	9	16	20	12	20	13	12	10	20	-	11	-	-	25	20	7	20	25	-	25	551
3	Scott Redding	GBR	Ducati	13	2	25	25	7	-	13	6	13	-	-	13	20	5	20	20	9	25	25	12	20	4	5	16	25	-	16	16	-	20	20	9	20	7	9	25	16	-	20	501
4	Andrea Locatelli	ITA	Yamaha	6	-	7	6	-	11	7	1	7	-	1	5	11	6	16	16	6	13	13	6	13	16	6	13	4	-	11	13	-	13	-	6	16	8	4	9	13	-	8	291
5	Michael Ruben Rinaldi	ITA	Ducati	9	-	-	11	5	-	25	12	20	4	-	8	-	9	8	13	-	11	6	-	9	13	-	9	16	5	25	-	-	9	13	-	9	16	2	11	4	-	-	282
6	Michael van der Mark	NED	BMW	5	5	11	9	-	10	6	-	6	11	7	11	13	-	10	-	-	9	9	2	7	11	4	8	11	-	7	9	-	8	-	12	10	10	5	10	10	-	16	262
7	Garrett Gerloff	USA	Yamaha	7	7	9	13	6	-	4	2	11	9	5	20	10	2	-	10	4	8	7	1	-	5	-	7	-	2	9	6	-	6	10	2	11	9	3	8	5	-	10	228
8	Alex Lowes	GBR	Kawasaki	20	9	16	-	4	13	11	5	10	16	-	10	-	4	9	3	3	10	11	5	10	-	7	-	10	6	-	7	-	-	-	-	-	13	1	-	-	-	-	213
9	Axel Bassani	ITA	Ducati	4	-	2	5	-	5	9	4	9	6	-	3	6	-	7	11	2	-	8	-	6	8	-	5	20	4	8	8	-	10	9	3	7	11	6	13	11	-	-	210
10	Alvaro Bautista	ESP	Honda	-	3	5	8	-	9	10	-	8	8	-	6	-	-	11	9	1	6	-	-	8	10	3	10	7	7	13	11	-	16	-	5	-	-	-	6	9	-	6	195
11	Tom Sykes	GBR	BMW	10	-	13	2	3	8	8	3	4	13	9	16	9	3	1	7	5	7	10	4	11	7	-	6	8	-	-	-	-	-	-	-	-	-	-	-	6	-	11	184
12	Chaz Davies	GBR	Ducati	11	6	-	10	1	20	-	-	-	5	2	9	7	1	13	-	-	4	-	3	-	9	2	11	6	-	-	-	-	-	4	-	7	8	-	4	-	-	-	143
13	Leon Haslam	GBR	Honda	8	-	-	4	-	4	2	-	-	10	6	7	8	-	6	8	-	5	3	-	-	6	1	-	9	3	5	5	-	4	11	-	8	6	-	5	-	-	-	134
14	Kohta Nozane	JPN	Yamaha	2	1	4	1	-	3	3	-	3	-	-	-	-	-	-	4	-	2	5	-	-	-	-	2	5	-	6	3	-	-	2	-	3	1	-	2	1	-	9	64
15	Loris Baz	FRA	Ducati	-	-	-	-	-	-	-	-	-	-	-	-	-	-	-	-	-	-	-	-	-	-	-	-	-	-	-	10	-	7	16	7	13	-	-	-	-	-	-	53
16	Tito Rabat	ESP	Ducati/Kawasaki	-	-	-	7	-	6	1	-	2	-	-	2	-	-	5	-	-	3	-	5	2	-	1	-	-	-	-	-	-	-	3	-	-	5	-	4	-	-	3	53
17	Isaac Vinales	ESP	Kawasaki	3	-	3	-	-	1	-	-	-	1	-	-	5	-	2	-	-	-	-	-	-	1	-	-	2	-	1	-	-	-	5	-	4	-	-	3	3	-	7	45
18	Lucas Mahias	FRA	Kawasaki	1	-	6	3	-	2	5	-	5	7	3	4	-	-	-	-	-	-	-	-	-	2	-	-	3	-	3	-	-	-	-	-	-	-	-	-	-	-	-	44
19	Eugene Laverty	IRL	BMW	-	-	-	2	7	-	-	1	3	3	-	1	-	-	-	-	-	-	-	-	-	-	-	-	-	-	-	4	-	5	7	1	6	3	-	-	-	-	-	40
20	Christophe Ponsson	FRA	Yamaha	-	-	1	-	-	-	-	-	-	-	-	-	5	-	1	1	-	3	3	-	4	-	1	3	1	-	6	-	2	-	-	-	-	-	-	5	-	-	-	36
21	Leandro Mercado	ARG	Honda	-	-	-	-	-	-	-	-	-	4	-	3	-	-	-	-	-	-	-	-	1	-	-	-	1	-	2	-	-	1	8	-	5	-	-	1	7	-	-	33
22	Jonas Folger	GER	BMW	-	-	-	-	-	8	-	-	-	-	-	-	-	-	-	2	-	4	-	-	-	-	-	-	-	-	-	2	-	3	1	-	1	-	-	-	-	-	-	21
23	Samuele Cavalieri	ITA	Kawasaki/Ducati	-	-	-	-	-	-	-	-	-	-	-	-	-	-	-	-	-	-	-	-	-	-	-	-	4	-	2	4	-	-	2	-	-	-	-	-	2	-	2	16
24	Marvin Fritz	GER	Yamaha	-	-	-	-	-	-	-	-	-	-	-	-	6	-	-	-	-	-	-	-	-	-	-	-	-	-	-	-	-	-	-	-	-	-	-	-	-	-	-	6
25	Loris Cresson	BEL	Kawasaki	-	-	-	-	-	-	-	-	-	3	-	-	-	-	-	-	-	-	-	-	-	-	-	-	-	-	-	-	-	-	-	-	-	-	-	-	-	-	-	3
26	Andrea Mantovani	ITA	Kawasaki	-	-	-	-	-	-	-	-	-	2	-	-	-	-	-	-	-	-	-	-	-	-	-	-	-	-	-	-	-	-	-	-	-	-	-	-	-	-	-	2
27	Luke Mossey	GBR	Kawasaki	-	-	-	-	-	-	2	-	-	-	-	-	-	-	-	-	-	-	-	-	-	-	-	-	-	-	-	-	-	-	-	-	-	-	-	-	-	-	-	2

CHAMPIONSHIP RESULTS 283

94
YAMAHA
77
Ten Kate
YAMAHA
Ten Kate
RACING PRODUCTS
Putoline
PIRELLI
YAMAHA

WORLD SUPERSPORT REVIEW
THE LAST HURRAH

With so many machine, engine capacity and configuration changes due for the FIM Supersport World Championship for 2022, the 2021 season might well be the last recognisable version of its old self. GORDON RITCHIE covers the action...

Above: Formation braking – teammates Can Oncu and Philipp Oettl seem in perfect harmony.

Top right: Young Spanish star Manuel Gonzalez on the ParkinGO Team Yamaha.

Above right: Veteran Jules Cluzel ended the season with four wins in six races.

Right: Ten-times winner Dominique Aegerter celebrates his Supersport title victory.

Far right, top: Randy Krummenacher, champion in 2019, notched up a win in Barcelona.

Far right, bottom: Federico Caricasulo partnered Cluzel in the GMT94 Yamaha Team.

Opening spread: Dominique Aegerter and Steven Odendaal were the dominant contenders, Yamahas the dominant bikes. The similarly-mounted Caricasulo gives chase.

Photos: Gold & Goose

INTO the valley of marketing death rode the 600s? Just about everybody had a super-strong 600cc four-cylinder or 750cc V-twin back in 1999 when the first full world championship campaign was held, but now it is mostly Yamaha R6s versus a few Kawasaki Ninja ZX-6Rs, and the occasional MV Agusta F3 675 triple.

Despite too many bikes emanating from basically the same blue-hued lagoon, the 2021 championship fight for race wins was frequently volcanic, even if eventually there was only one clear title winner.

Dominique Aegerter (31) took his Ten Kate Yamaha R6 to the championship itself with one round to spare. Quite a remarkable performance considering that he had to miss one entire round mid-season, as he had signed a MotoE contract before he was given the WorldSSP ride. He missed out on a crown in MotoE, but ended up having almost the same kind of dominant Supersport season that Andrea Locatelli had had in 2020 on his Evan Bros Yamaha.

Initially, the inheritor of Locatelli's bike, Steven Odendaal, had looked good for the 2021 title, after winning the first three races of the year. It took until the fourth for Aegerter to win, and possibly for his Ten Kate team to really get the best out of their bike. They had scored all their previous nine WorldSSP riders' championship wins on Honda machinery, but the 2021 Ten Kate R6 was at least as fast as the rest.

Mostly, but not exclusively, it was all about the Yamaha riders, as second-year Kawasaki Puccetti Racing competitor Philipp Oettl was third on the Ninja ZX-6R at the first round in Aragon. Only winner Odendaal and Aegerter got the better of him. However, had the fast, but too fearless Niki Tuuli (MV Agusta Clienti Corse) not knocked off race leader Jules Cluzel (GMT94 Yamaha) under braking with seven laps to go, it could have been a different story.

Odendaal had engine enough and smarts enough to keep Aegerter behind across the line, by just 0.099 of a second.

In contrasting wet-weather conditions for race two, Tuuli had been ruled out with concussion before the sudden fall of rain. Odendaal won again, but fast-charging privateer Raffaele De Rosa (Orelac VerdNatura Kawasaki) was second, by a very thin sliver, while the experienced Cluzel took third ahead of Hannes Soomer (Kallio Racing Yamaha). All the top four were impressive on a greasy and changeable wet surface, but Cluzel had to come from the back of the grid for his podium spot, the result of a tyre-pressure infringement.

The first of two Portuguese weekends took place at Estoril, with Odendaal claiming the opening race on Saturday, from Oettl and Cluzel. The German rider had led for most of it before Odendaal passed at the end, while a brilliantly close fight for the final podium position ended with Cluzel just 0.015 of a second ahead of Aegerter over the line, less than a second from the win.

At this circuit near the sea, the overall tide was starting to turn just as news of the loss of Jason Dupasquier, Aegerter's young Swiss compatriot, came through from the GP weekend at Mugello. Thus Dominique's first WorldSSP win in race two became a poignant affair as much as a significant springboard for his push to the championship win several months later.

The second Estoril race had several dramatic moments that affected the final result. Leader De Rosa fell with three laps to go, Odendaal had a mechanical issue, while Cluzel also fell off. Thus young star Luca Bernardi (CM Racing Yamaha) was second, with Oettl third.

The next four races over two rounds went to Aegerter, who took the championship lead for the first time after race one at Misano.

Bernardi scored second and Odendaal was third in that first outing; Bernardi second again with Cluzel third in race two. De Rosa fell in the opener, as did fellow Italian Federico Caricasulo (GMT 94 Yamaha).

286 WORLD SUPERSPORT REVIEW

The second race was red-flagged for a crash, being restarted over only 12 laps. Odendaal was given a long-lap penalty for track-limits infringements, on the final lap, too, but he did not serve his sentence. He crossed the line ahead of Aegerter to 'win', but was demoted to fifth after receiving a three-second time penalty. Another compelling weekend of racing.

A welcome return to Assen was a biggie for the Ten Kate team, and lead rider Aegerter duly delivered – in show-stealing traditional yellow paint, just like the Ten Kate bikes of the early WorldSSP years.

In race one, Aegerter triumphed over Odendaal and Oettl. Then, in race two, he won again from Oettl and Randy Krummenacher, who was soon to jump ship from EAB Yamaha to the CM Yamaha team. Odendaal crashed out, restarted, and lost lots of available points, finishing 12th.

It was a whole new experience for the paddock when they took on Most in the Czech Republic, through all sorts of weather conditions. Odendaal regained some ground in the championship fight with a win in race one – passing no fewer than three riders in one go in the early stages – from the ever improving Manuel Gonzalez (ParkinGo Yamaha) and Oettl. A red flag was brought out with just enough laps completed to finish the race with full points. Aegerter was only fourth, almost a disaster by his standards.

Normal service – for Aegerter at least – was resumed in a dry race two, as he won from Odendaal and Gonzalez. A classy last-corner move gave Odendaal that second place.

Another new track, Navarra in Spain, was on the small side for Superbikes, but a great venue for this class. Strange then that we had the same top three in each race – Aegerter from Odendaal from the upwardly mobile Bernardi.

Navarra marked the halfway point in the championship and the round when we found out that Aegerter really was going to have to race at the MotoE final, not the Catalunya WorldSSP round. It complicated things, making every race result all the more important from here on in, despite

WORLD SUPERSPORT REVIEW 287

Aegerter's strong lead of 47 points. Almost two whole wins ahead of Odendaal.

Another border crossing, and relocation to France and the scene of many a championship decider, Magny-Cours. Not in 2021, though, not at round seven of 12.

The first contest – red-flagged and then restarted over only 12 laps – was won by Aegerter, from Odendaal and Cluzel, who had ended his relative podium dry spell. But he was about to become unlucky again.

Early in race two, pole-sitter Bernardi tried to pass Cluzel into the chicane, but he lost the front and collected Cluzel and Aegerter in a scary crash. Both Bernardi and Cluzel were taken to hospital. The latter would miss the Barcelona round; Bernardi's season was over.

Two small pieces of history were made after the restart, when former WorldSSP300 rider Gonzalez won his first race after a brilliant final two laps alongside Aegerter. Teenage Turkish rider Can Oncu (Kawasaki Puccetti Racing) was third, his career-first podium. Odendaal was only sixth, now 62 points behind.

With no Aegerter at Catalunya, the expectation was all on Odendaal to capitalise, but he left with an eighth place and a seventh. The writing was on the wall. Even if he had won both races in Barcelona, he would still have been 12 points adrift. As it turned out, he left Catalunya 45 points behind.

The first race was run under flag-to-flag wet rules, after the rain arrived. Krummenacher showed a flash of the form that had made him world champion in 2019, leading Gonzalez and De Rosa to the podium ceremony. Odendaal was given a huge 25.8-second pit time penalty.

In the second race, in the sunshine, Gonzalez scooped up another win after his Magny-Cours highpoint. De Rosa was second this time around, with Niki Tuuli finally getting the best out of the Corse Clienti MV Agusta in third place. The aggressive top three were covered by just 0.095 of a second.

A quick turnaround took WorldSSP down to Jerez, but

288 WORLD SUPERSPORT REVIEW

Above: Rising star Luca Bernardi on the CM Yamaha leads Kallio's Hannes Soomer (38) and Manuel Gonzalez (81).

Left: Gonzalez registered two victories to finish third overall.

Far left: Philipp Oettl leads Odendaal, Cluzel, Aegerter and Gonzalez in Portugal.

Below left: Veteran Raffaele De Rosa scored his first ever Supersport victory at the final round in Indonesia.

Below far left: South Africa's Steven Odendaal started out with three straight wins, but failed to fend off Aegerter at the finish.

Below: Adrian Huertas was the class of the field in Supersport 300 on the MTM Kawasaki.

Photos: Gold & Goose

there would be only one Andalusian race – on Sunday – following the death of WorldSSP300 rider Dean Berta Vinales on Saturday.

Aegerter won on his return, his tenth of his rookie season. Oettl was second and Tuuli third.

Portimao, the end of an intense run of four rounds in five weekends, was also the final event in Europe.

Few would have grudged Jules Cluzel his win in race one, not after a tough season and his recent injury. Gonzalez took second and championship leader Aegerter third.

Odendaal was clearly fired up by finishing just sixth in race one, and he won the second race from Cluzel and the resurgent Federico Caricasulo. The latter had started the year with the GMT94 Yamaha Team, but had left and joined the Biblion Iberica Yamaha MotoX racing team in time for his first 2021 podium.

There were some gaps in the grid after travel permission and other factors got in the way of a perfect attendance record at the penultimate round in Argentina. The Villicum track action was just as unruly as ever, but the head boy was Cluzel again, not once, but twice.

Behind him in race one came Gonzalez, with Oncu third.

Oncu was runner-up to Cluzel in race two, with Aegerter getting the final podium in one of those races that defy description. Odendaal was taken out in Turn One by Gonzalez, and the melee it caused pushed Aegerter down into the top six places. When Odendaal crashed again, it was all over – Aegerter became the championship winner in Argentina. It was a tenth WorldSSP riders' championship win for Ten Kate, their first with Yamaha.

A month passed before the next race in Indonesia and, of course, the rainy-season gamble did not pay off fully. As the weather broke at Mandalika, most riders stayed out on their slick tyres, most stayed vertical, and the rains abated.

After 89 WorldSSP races, De Rosa claimed his first win, from Aegerter and Caricasulo – the latter now riding for the VFT Yamaha team.

In the final race of 2021, held in the dry, four riders fought for the win. Odendaal crashed, creating a kinetic metaphor for his generally strong, but still disappointing season.

In the final action of the year, Aegerter and Caricasulo fought each other so hard in the last corners that they ran wide, leaving Cluzel and Tuuli space to go one, two, with Aegerter third.

Thus another ex-Moto2 rider became champion in 2021, the fourth in succession, in an epic epoch-defining season.

FIM Supersport 300 World Championship

Huertas Boxes Clever

The fifth season of WorldSSP300 racing at full FIM level delivered its fourth Spanish champion after a campaign full of incident, and the tragedy of losing Dean Berta Vinales in a race crash at Jerez.

Despite smaller entries than before, the action was as close as ever, making for too many faster riders unable to get away from the rest.

The most effective rider all year long was Adrian Huertas (MTM Kawasaki), who won six races, and with them the championship. He was almost always there or thereabouts on the podium and made few major mistakes.

Outgoing champion Jeffrey Buis (MTM Kawasaki) won three races and placed second, but only after a strong finish. Tom Booth Amos (Fusport RT Motorsports by SKM Kawasaki) was third overall and a two-times winner, with top Yamaha rider Bahattin Sofuoglu (Biblion Motoxracing Yamaha) fourth and also securing two wins.

Ana Carrasco, Victor Steeman and Samuel Di Sora each won a race apiece.

Once again, Kawasaki riders were in the ascendancy, but Sofuoglu's Yamaha and Steeman's KTM proved capable of wins if the circumstances were just so.

WORLD SUPERSPORT REVIEW 289

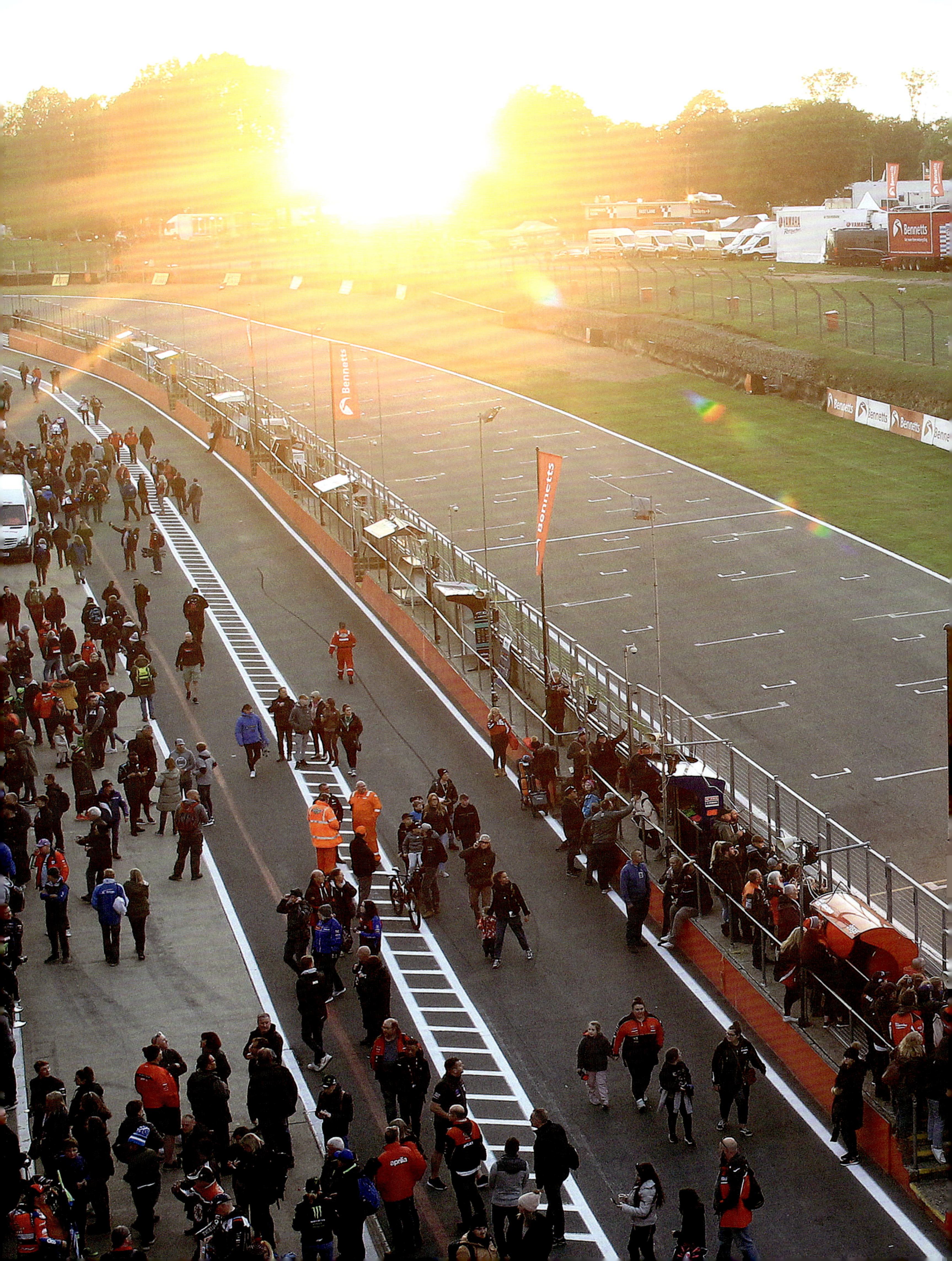
Bennetts
Bennetts

2021 BENNETTS BRITISH SUPERBIKE CHAMPIONSHIP REVIEW

RETURN OF THE MAC ATTACK

Having weathered the Covid storm, BSB returned with an expanded schedule, a nail-biting climax and a deserving champion. OLIVER BARSTOW recounts the action...

Stuart Higgs
Series Director,
Bennetts British Superbike Championship

The anticipation for the 2021 Bennetts British Superbike Championship season could not have been higher as we looked towards the 25th anniversary of the series.

However, the excitement for the start of the season was initially tempered by the uncertainty that remained following the global pandemic and sadly, the opening events were restricted on crowd numbers. That meant many of our loyal fans couldn't join us trackside but they continued to watch all the action from home across the Eurosport and free-to-air Quest channels.

We first welcomed a limited number of spectators back trackside at Oulton Park for the Official Test – 577 days since the season finale in 2019 and from there the atmosphere at each round continued to grow.

Bennetts BSB is without doubt a fans' sport, so there was nothing better than seeing fans flocking back to the tracks, and they were not disappointed.

Tens of thousands of spectators were treated to the grandstand finish that we have come to expect from Britain's leading motorsport series at the Brands Hatch season finale.

You couldn't have written the script for the 2021 season; Jason O'Halloran had a commanding lead heading into the Showdown, yet it all changed heading into the decider, with the top four contenders the closest they had been in the fight since 2010.

Over the season there were an impressive eight different race winners and a further seven podium finishers representing nine different teams and six manufacturers to finish inside the top three – showing just how competitive BSB is and the robustness of our technical regulations.

My congratulations to Tarran Mackenzie for sealing his first title 25 years after his father Niall had accomplished the feat. It was an iconic moment in the championship's history to have the pair on the grid as the sun set on finals day with the McAMS Yamaha alongside the 1996 Cadbury Boost Yamaha on the grid.

We also toast all of our support class champions – Jack Kennedy, Charlie Nesbitt, Casey O'Gorman, Tom Neave, Jack Nixon, Cameron Dawson and Josh Day.

We are already looking ahead to 2022 and have started the countdown to the opening round, which will kick off at Silverstone on April 15/16/17. We can't wait because if this season was anything to go by, we are in for another spectacular new season.

www.britishsuperbike.com

THE year is 1996: Mick Doohan collects the third of his eventual five 500GP World Championships, Troy Corser is top of the tree in WorldSBK, and a precocious mop-haired youngster by the name of Valentino Rossi is forging his first steps towards world domination on two wheels. It is also the year when Niall Mackenzie clinches the British Superbike Championship, the first of three domestic titles he'd attain on the bounce during the latter part of a career in which he'd already collected podiums at motorcycling's highest level.

The motorcycle racing scene has changed a lot in the 25 years since – measured, as it turns out, by the entire span of Rossi's spectacular racing career – but while the riders, the machinery and the technology of 2021 are a world away from 1996, one thing remains the same: full-throttle, elbows-out, wheel-to-wheel racing, the veritable signature of BSB as the world's most entertaining domestic series.

It's fitting, then, that on either side of this quarter-century time frame is Niall and his 2021 British Superbike Championship-winning son, Tarran Mackenzie. Not even a year old when his dad first had his name etched on the winner's trophy, Tarran's name sits proudly on the BSB roll call alongside his father and 16 other Superbike legends, a poignant compliment to his reward of being on the definitive side of a season told over two very distinct chapters.

That said, while Mackenzie Senior and Junior can certainly relate to one another's tales of bristling battles and energetic racing Yamahas around familiar circuits, the route by which the 2021 BSB title was won is a journey date-stamped in the modern era.

Now in its 11th season, the Title Showdown format will be familiar to even fairweather followers of BSB. It eschews the conventional 'points win prizes' approach in favour of a two-part season that places greater emphasis on the last three rounds to decide the champion.

This approach has divided opinions since its inception, but for the most part, the cream – that is the rider who scores the most points over a whole season regardless – has risen to the top while keeping the title race alive to the finale, as per its brief.

In 2021, though, it didn't – and by some margin, too. Instead, Jason O'Halloran scored more points than any other rider, including title-winning team-mate Mackenzie, over the entire 11-round, 33-race season, but ended up third under the Title Showdown format. This was a reflection of the vast advantage he'd built during the first eight events and the critical slump in form he experienced during the final three pivotal events. While it may bring the credibility of the Title Showdown into question, it's hard to deny that Mackenzie was anything less than a deserving champion.

Although Covid-19 had ravaged the BSB schedule in 2020, and its rippling effects still lingered into 2021, BSB returned to normality of sorts with an 11-round schedule – expanded to a triple-race format at each event – and the reappearance of the Title Showdown, after its single-year hiatus. That meant the season would comprise a record 33 races, setting a grand stage on which the championship would be played out. The teams dutifully supplied a diverse and hungry cast of esteemed veterans, hot tips with something to prove and fresh-faced newcomers, all primed to give

Above: Father and son. The Mackenzies celebrate their 25th-anniversary BSB win.
Photo: Bryn Williams

Top left: Niall Mackenzie took the first of three BSB titles in 1996.

Top: Brands Hatch, April, 2011. A young Tarran receives fatherly advice on the grid. Older brother Taylor watches on.
Photos: Clive Challinor Motorsport Photography

Opening spread: Flares fire in the sunset as the champions line up for a year-end photocall at the end of a dramatic season.
Photo: Bryn Williams

BRITISH SUPERBIKE REVIEW 293

Above: Jason O'Halloran was the long-time championship favourite, but it slipped away with a late-season slump.

Top: It was a long hard year without a single win for reigning champion Josh Brookes.

Above right: A late start. O'Halloran leads the pack as the compacted BSB schedule gets under way at Oulton Park in June.
Photos: Bryn Williams

Right: Christian Iddon, heading Tommy Bridewell and Peter Hickman, was three times second in the season-opener.
Photo: Ducati Corse

the audience what they hoped would be an award-winning performance.

Top of the bill was Paul Bird Motorsport's VisionTrack Ducati and defending champion Josh Brookes, the Australian seeking a third BSB title on the Panigale V4 R. Alongside him was Christian Iddon once again. Multiple race winner and fan favourite Tommy Bridewell, meanwhile, complemented the Ducati contingent on the single privateer Oxford Products Racing machine.

Runner-up in 2020 – a full decade after making his BSB debut – Jason O'Halloran stuck with McAMS Yamaha in his effort to go one better, with Mackenzie eyeing the same prize in his fourth season with the factory-backed outfit.

While Honda and Glenn Irwin didn't quite finish what they had started when the new CBR1000RR-R Fireblade burst out of the blocks and on to the top of the podium in 2020, the Ulsterman got a renewed shot for 2021. He was joined by Ryo Mizuno and Takumi Takahashi, two little-known products of the manufacturer's aspiration to emulate triple BSB champion Ryuichi Kiyonari by developing Japanese talent internationally. Alas, they remained barely a footnote to proceedings all year.

Kawasaki provided its factory support and the new ZX-10RR to FS-3 Racing, retaining Lee Jackson and winning the race to sign exciting talent Rory Skinner. The 18-year-old had stepped up to Superbikes after dominating the 2020 British Supersport Championship, while Ryan Vickers entered into his third campaign with Lee Hardy Racing.

Still winning races despite its ageing Suzuki GSX-R1000R, Buildbase Hawk Racing entrusted its effort to the retained Gino Rea. The former Moto2 rider was joined by another ex-GP standout, 2015 Moto3 world champion Danny Kent.

As ever, BMW – armed with the upgraded M 1000 RR – displayed strength in numbers with no fewer than seven teams running its wares. At the top of the tree was the TAS Racing Synetiq team, which had hired an all-new line-up of Danny Buchan and Andrew Irwin, while RICH Energy OMG Racing had poached Bradley Ray and 2020 standout Kyle Ryde for its fresh effort.

With Smiths Racing having bowed out of the sport, FHO Racing – helmed by Macanese entrepreneur and enthusiast Faye Ho – entered, holding on to TT star Peter Hickman and luring Xavi Fores from WorldSBK two years after his foray to BSB with Honda.

Keen to resist the requirement to race 'behind closed doors' with no spectators, as it had been forced to do in 2020, the new BSB season was delayed repeatedly until such time as crowds were allowed to return to enjoy live racing action. That meant the campaign didn't get under way until June – more than two months later than usual – with

294 BRITISH SUPERBIKE REVIEW

the crests and troughs of picturesque Oulton Park raising the curtain on a season that brimmed with anticipation, but boasted little in the way of an obvious title favourite.

That was until O'Halloran and McAMS Yamaha made a convincing pitch with a flawless hat trick of wins that were as skillfully attained as they were oozing in sheer confidence.

After a strong 2020 campaign that had yielded three wins (having achieved only one in the ten years prior to that), O'Halloran began the season in fine style by almost doubling his tally over a single weekend. Indeed, if there had been no clear favourite coming into the weekend, he certainly ended it as the standout, after swaggering the Yamaha around the Cheshire circuit like a man who'd spent the long off-season believing he was the one to beat and coolly repelling the challenge from an equally feisty-looking Christian Iddon in a heated battle.

Despite the VisionTrack Ducati rider muscling his way into the lead in each race, O'Halloran simply rolled with the punches before landing a decisive hook on all three occasions to secure triple victories. The most devastating of these was in race two after a sweetly judged overtake on the final corner of the final lap.

Tommy Bridewell completed the podium with a third in two of the races, only scuppering his chance of a hat trick when his hasty swipe across Tarran Mackenzie's bow into Hizzy's simply dragged the chain off his Ducati. Peter Hickman took advantage of the mishap to give FHO Racing a fine rostrum milestone on its debut outing.

BRITISH SUPERBIKE REVIEW 295

Above: Christian Iddon and Danny Buchan in front at Knockhill.

Top right: Iddon's Scottish victory cemented a strong start to his year, but the early points leader faced a dry spell in August and September.
Photos: Ducati Corse

Above right: Rookie Rory Skinner made his presence felt at Knockhill.
Photo: Bryn Williams

Above far right: Former world champion Danny Kent's comeback with Buildbase Suzuki was curtailed by injury at Donington Park.
Photo: www.suzuki-racing.com

Right: Pressed hard by Iddon, Mackenzie set the ball rolling with his first win at Brands Hatch in July.
Photo: Bryn Williams

BSB then headed north of the border into Scotland, where Knockhill marked round two, with Iddon initially succeeding in getting his own back on O'Halloran with a slick victory in race one. Although he only achieved one more over the season, nonetheless the consistent Iddon was considered a heavy hitter in the title race right up until its final moments.

Beyond race one, though, the weekend belonged to two riders on either end of the experience scale, Danny Buchan and Rory Skinner.

By rights, it could have been a trio of wins for double National Superstock 1000 champion Buchan, but he had nixed his hopes of victory in race one with an out-of-the-seat moment at the hairpin while leading Iddon, before bouncing back brilliantly to claim victory in races two and three.

Knockhill had been the scene of Buchan's long awaited maiden BSB victory two years before, and his affinity with the climbs and plunges of the track brought some much longed-for joy to his Synetiq TAS Racing squad by ending a victory drought that stretched back to 2016. In addition, it was the first BSB win for BMW since Ryuichi Kiyonari's title challenge with Buildbase Hawk Racing in 2017.

And yet, despite his achievements, Buchan was overshadowed by the event's homecoming prince, Skinner. Competing in only his second BSB event, but on beloved home soil, the 18-year-old put his local knowledge to supreme use by finishing second in race two, before coming remarkably close to a famous win in race three, having been overtaken by Buchan just prior to the race being red-flagged for a debris scattering accident in the pack.

Although Skinner wouldn't demonstrate such form on the FS-3 Racing Kawasaki ZX-10RR at any other stage of the season, the teenager acquitted himself more than ably throughout, confirming his status as one of the UK's brightest future prospects.

Having been forced to play second fiddle to Skinner in terms of vocal local support and silverware in Scotland, and after a lethargic start to his crowning season, Mackenzie stepped up the momentum of his campaign during round three at Brands Hatch with a convincing win from pole position amid a brace of podium results. However, his joy at the victory was tempered by an incident down the field involving iForce Lloyd & Jones PR Racing BMW rider Brad Jones, an accident so severe that it necessitated him being placed in an induced coma. Mercifully, after an uncertain seven weeks in hospital as he battled life-threatening injuries, he was reported to be on the road to recovery.

Having demonstrated his title credentials with a charging ride from 18th to fifth in race one – the outcome of a crash in qualifying – O'Halloran made the most of his loftier starting position in race two by picking off his rivals one by one to clinch a fourth victory in eight from Bridewell and a recovering Mackenzie. The last named had scuppered his victory hopes with a scary moment on lap one. It was Iddon, however, who retained his slim advantage at the head of the standings after the weekend, with a steely second (and final) win of the year in race three.

The race had got under way in damp and slippery conditions so variable that it led to combinations of tyre that ranged from full slicks all the way to full wets, plus everything in between. The order at the end of lap one bore scant resemblance to the riders' starting positions. Those who had selected full wets, hoping that the notoriously fickle British summer would reward them with another deluge, swiftly picked their way to the front, with Josh Brookes slaloming through the competition to lead.

A sight so familiar normally, the fillip of leading nonetheless came in the wake of a torrid start to his title defence that was as disappointing as it was apparently inexplicable.

296 BRITISH SUPERBIKE REVIEW

Bennet

PIRELLI
VISIONTRACK
DUCATI
:hager
aico
HJC
REISSER
YUASA
OMEGAPISTONS.COM
DUNSLEY HEAT
PLAY &
QUA
MONSTER

Racing Specialist

52
PHL

HJC
REISSER
WWW.OMEGAPISTONS.COM
SHOEI
McAMS
Bennetts
95
MONSTER
FINANCE
YUASA
hager

Above: Heading for another triple at Thruxton, O'Halloran leads away from (*from left*) Ryan Vickers (7), Peter Hickman (60), Glenn Irwin (2) and Dan Linfoot (4).
Photo: Bryn Williams

Right: Tommy Bridewell (*centre*) celebrates his race-three win at Donington with the Irwin brothers, Glenn (*left*) and Andrew.

Far right: Bridewell leads O'Halloran and Andrew Irwin out of Donington's shorter National Circuit chicane.
Photos: Ducati Corse

Brookes, arguably the most reliably successful BSB rider of the past decade, was not so much suffering from bad luck as simply lacklustre performance. His mental rain dance wouldn't bear fruit, however, and despite quickly opening up a healthy lead, he was soon being reeled in as those on slick tyres found the grip and with it their pace. Buchan was the first to pounce and grab the lead.

Fortunately for those regretting their tactical selections, the race was red-flagged after a pyrotechnic display of a Suzuki engine failure, which set up a seven-lap sprint to the flag, this time on a completely dry circuit.

From pole position, Buchan surged into the lead initially, but ceded it to Iddon soon afterwards, the first act of a thrilling exchange that went right down to the wire. With Buchan getting back ahead on the penultimate lap, Iddon swept through next time around before repelling his BMW rival to seal victory.

Buchan's all-out attempts to snatch the win had left him vulnerable to the advancing McAMS Yamahas, Mackenzie levering his rival aside so firmly that it invited O'Halloran through into third, demoting a disgruntled Buchan to fourth. As for the embattled Brookes, he made the most of the reset to collect fifth, one of his better results in what would turn out to be a rather limpid title defence.

Next it was on to the ultra-fast Thruxton circuit, where round four reasserted O'Halloran's status as both the title favourite and championship leader with another crushingly impressive trio of victories. While scrappy moments had tempered his results since bursting out of the blocks in round one, few doubted that he was the form-man in terms of raw speed, and he demonstrated that in formidable fashion.

Barely headed all weekend, O'Halloran controlled the pace to win both race one – ahead of Bridewell and Hickman – and race two from lights out. He impressed again in race three by managing sketchy conditions initially to work his way back to the front once it had dried to claim his seventh win of the year.

Erstwhile leader Iddon had kept him honest in race one with a run to second place, only to suffer a painful DNF in race two, when an out-of-shape Lee Jackson had misjudged his braking at Campbell and clattered into the Ducati rider. That allowed Mackenzie through to a one-two for McAMS Yamaha, Glenn Irwin redeeming himself with third a day after a similar result had been scuppered by a terrifying high-speed high-side at the fearsome Village bend.

While the evolving conditions of race three had resulted in a lottery on both tyres and nerves, O'Halloran didn't put a wheel wrong as he held off a charging Buchan, who secured his fourth podium of the year in second. They were joined on the rostrum for the first time by Buildbase Suzuki's Danny Kent, whose career recovery clicked off a key milestone at Thruxton, only for his season to be curtailed at the following event at Donington Park, where he suffered a hip injury in a crash.

With the compact National configuration of Donington Park – namely the flip-flop final-corner chicane – a reliable source of BSB entertainment, round five produced a trio of breathless, albeit crash-strewn races.

Reeling off his fourth BSB victory in succession, O'Halloran stamped his mark again with victory in race one. Although he won from pole position, he did it the hard way, adopting a cautious approach in damp conditions initially and hanging back in fourth, before once again calmly gathering momentum to reclaim the lead at three-quarters-distance and surge to the flag from Irwin and Mackenzie.

In race two, however, it was Mackenzie who snatched the spotlight from his team-mate in a thrilling fight for in-house supremacy that gave boss Steve Rodgers some heart-stopping moments as they swapped the lead and very nearly paint right up to the final lap. Ironically, their feud almost cost McAMS the win altogether when Bradley Ray sensed his opportunity to grab second from O'Halloran at the final corner with momentum that allowed him up alongside Mackenzie in the dash for the line. The RICH Energy OMG BMW rider was just 0.066 of a second shy of a stunning return to the top step.

With the great British weather once again doing its bit to splash some drama on the proceedings just in time for race

Above: Peter Hickman took his FHO Racing BMW to two popular wins at Cadwell Park.

Above right: Over the mountain. An airborne Josh Brookes displays the Ducati's PBM logo.

Right: The intrepid Hickman excelled at the technically difficult Cadwell Park track.

Far right: Lee Jackson leads Brookes at Cadwell. The Kawasaki rider was consistently in the points, with a single podium visit.

Photos: Bryn Williams

three, tyre choice was the critical factor again, with varying outcomes for the leading contenders.

After early leader Ryan Vickers commemorated his first ever spell in the lead by crashing out of it eight corners later, victory for the first time in 2021 went the way of Bridewell, who emerged from the gloom ahead of the brothers Irwin, Honda's Glenn chased home by Synetiq BMW's Andrew. Third for the latter was his one and only podium in a modest season for the former race winner.

O'Halloran and Mackenzie played it safe en route to seventh and ninth to firm up a one-two in the standings, benefiting from a torrid weekend for their two closest rivals, Iddon and Buchan. Iddon suffered a double DNF – the first at the hands of an over-zealous Andrew Irwin at Redgate, the second at Craner Curves and all his own doing – while Buchan's tumble out of race two resulted in a bump to the head that automatically ruled him out of the ensuing Cadwell Park round, under rules that stipulate any rider with a concussion cannot compete within the following seven days.

With the cut-off for the Title Showdown looming, round six at Cadwell Park proved as uplifting as a leap over The Mountain for some of the leading contenders as it was a painful crash-landing for others.

As one of the riders nestled neatly among the eight provisional Title Showdown spots, local favourite Peter Hickman cleared the path towards the final stages of the season with a tremendous weekend that very nearly yielded a clean sweep of wins. It was a veritable Party in the Park for Hickman, FHO Racing and his vast fanbase. He brushed aside his rivals around a circuit that – compared to any other on the BSB calendar – rewards those prepared to exhibit a daredevil-fuelled confidence akin to that required at the Isle of Man TT, the lap record of which is held by the 34-year-old.

With Covid scuppering the legendary road racing festival for the second year in succession, a fully BSB focused Hickman rediscovered his best form in 2021. His wins in races one and two represented his first trips to the top of the podium since 2017, not to mention only the fifth and sixth victories of a BSB tenure that stretches back to 2006.

By rights, it should have been a trio of wins but for a momentary error going into the final lap of race three. His mistake was punished by O'Halloran who, having followed the FHO rider home in races one and two, needed no second invitation to assure his Title Showdown place with a ninth win of the year. Bridewell, meanwhile, boosted his title aspirations with a steady brace of third-place finishes.

If O'Halloran was sky high at the summit of the standings, team-mate Mackenzie was sky high for entirely different reasons after the merest kiss of his Yamaha's rear wheel on the grass at Bend. The result was a violent high-side that sent the R1 over the barriers and Mackenzie to the medical centre. Fortunately, in the context of his title campaign, he escaped unharmed, but he played no further part in the race weekend.

300 BRITISH SUPERBIKE REVIEW

BRITISH SUPERBIKE REVIEW 301

Above: Down and out – O'Halloran looks bemused after being taken out by team-mate Mackenzie at Silverstone.

Above right: McAMS boss Steve Rogers was unimpressed by the over-ambitious Mackenzie putting both his riders on the ground.

Top: On a charge. Tommy Bridewell claimed two wins in the Oulton Park Showdown.

Top right: Glenn Irwin took full advantage of the McAMS collision for Honda's only win of the year.

Above far right: O'Halloran and Mackenzie ran in Yamaha retro livery at Oulton Park.
Photos: Bryn Williams

Right: Josh Brookes and team celebrate pole at Oulton.
Photo: Ducati Corse

The flat plains of Norfolk's Snetterton played host to round seven, and McAMS Yamaha confirmed its status as the new powerhouse with wins shared between Mackenzie and O'Halloran.

Bouncing back from his Cadwell Park misadventure, Mackenzie rediscovered his best form with a satisfying third win of the year in race one, having capitalised on Glenn Irwin's crash from the lead at mid-distance. He was followed home by Bridewell, who pipped O'Halloran on the run to the line in a blanket finish that covered the trio by a mere 0.095 of a second.

O'Halloran fought back in race two by prevailing in a heated battle with his team-mate, only for Mackenzie to strike again in a thrilling race-three sprint that made a convincing case for all encounters to be contested over no more than five laps. The compact distance was the result of Danny Buchan suffering his second wild crash of the weekend after his BMW's rear tyre struck oil deposited by his own expiring engine. It led to carnage behind when team-mate Irwin and Jackson found the same slick patch.

At the restart, Mackenzie, O'Halloran and Bridewell picked up where they had left off, before the Scot pulled clear with Oxford Ducati's Bridewell in hot pursuit. Despite the Devizes man's best efforts, though, he couldn't unseat his rival, but at least he did his bit to ensure his way through to the Title Showdown with one round to spare.

With O'Halloran, Mackenzie, Bridewell and Iddon booked into the Title Showdown, round eight at Silverstone turned attention towards the eight riders mathematically capable of filling the four remaining spots. Realistically, it was a seven-way fight over three spots, since Hickman was only a few digits away from sealing his place. The situation was much closer behind, however, with Buchan – despite his Cadwell Park absence and Snetterton acrobatics – Irwin and the consistent, but podium-less Jackson holding down a provisional six, seven and eight.

With 38 points covering sixth down to tenth, three riders with a point to prove were hot on their heels. Leading those on the cusp was Ray, whose challenge had been forged on solid points building. Behind him was defending champion Brookes, whose form had gathered momentum with a run of top-fives that recovered ground lost earlier in the year, and Vickers, who would have been better placed had podium-winning positions at Donington Park and Thruxton not ended on the ground.

Yet for all of the emphasis being placed on riders around them, there was no let up in McAMS Yamaha's momentum as O'Halloran and Mackenzie batted off all comers to work their way to the front in race one. That was until disaster struck two laps from home, when Mackenzie moved into the lead at Brooklands, only for the rear of the R1 to slide out from underneath him right into the path of his team-mate, who had nowhere to go but head-on into the stricken Yamaha, cartwheeling over the handlebars.

It was an alarming, but blameless accident that very easily could have had far reaching consequences in the context of the title battle. Fortunately, both escaped without injury and quickly put the incident behind them by taking a win apiece in races two and three.

The spoils in race one, meanwhile, had been inherited

302 BRITISH SUPERBIKE REVIEW

by a welcoming Glenn Irwin, who led home Bridewell and Iddon. Irwin and Honda's first win of the year meant that the Ulsterman and Hickman cemented the fifth and sixth Title Showdown spots.

Elsewhere, Jackson and Vickers' aspirations were all but ended by untimely DNFs in race one, leaving Buchan, Brookes and Ray to duke it out for the final two spots.

Faced with the ignominy of his title defence ending in failure to reach the Title Showdown, Brookes called upon his decades of experience to wring every ounce of form from his temperamental Ducati by scoring his first podium of the season in race two. However, fourth for Ray meant that he retained a slender advantage into the final encounter.

With it all to play for, each rider stepped up when it mattered, with Buchan – whose qualification had been jeopardised by two disappointing races so far in the weekend – Brookes and Ray taking their private fight to the upper echelons of the race order. Initially, Buchan and Ray appeared most likely to prevail, but a red-flag period swung the initiative back towards Brookes, who capitalised on the bunching effect of the restart to get ahead of his rivals and bring it home for third.

Ray was only seventh, which meant that Buchan and Brookes would progress to the final stages, and the OMG Racing rider was left to curse his luck, just four points shy of a Title Showdown berth.

Thus the 2021 BSB champion would come from the final eight: O'Halloran, Mackenzie, Bridewell, Iddon, Irwin, Hickman, Buchan and Brookes.

The points equalising format of the Showdown was certainly good news for all but the man at the top, O'Halloran, who had amassed a vast 106-point lead to that point. Indeed, with a career-defining 11 wins to his name from the eight rounds, he had good reason to be delighted and confident ahead of the Title Showdown, but surely frustrated that an advantage that in any other Superbike series would have put him on course for the title was largely obliterated.

While podium credits (five for a win, three for a second and one for a third) applied to an arbitrary 1,000-point starter, O'Halloran (1,071) still held a solid, but much depleted advantage over Mackenzie (1,041), followed by Iddon (1,026), Bridewell (1,024), Hickman (1,015), Buchan (1,014), Irwin (1,012) and Brookes (1,002).

Nine races across three events at Oulton Park, Donington Park and Brands Hatch awaited the title contenders, with the question mark looming over O'Halloran and whether he could sustain such a devastating run of fine form.

As it happens, Oulton Park couldn't have been more of a disaster for O'Halloran, whose 30-point lead was entirely wiped out by two DNFs, each the result of crashes. Worse still was the confidence-sapping manner in which they had occurred. In race one, having just moved into the lead three laps from home, he managed only a few more bends before slipping off at Knickerbrook. Then he made a curious showing in race three, running outside the top ten with tyre issues before dropping the Yamaha altogether.

A redeeming second-place finish in race two recovered some of the lost ground, but by the end of the weekend, not only had O'Halloran seen his once vast lead destroyed, but also he was two points down on team-mate and new leader Mackenzie.

The Scot enjoyed a strong weekend around the Cheshire circuit, capitalising on O'Halloran's fall to wrap up victory in race one, before claiming a third in race two. It would have been a hat trick of podiums in race three but for an impact with Lee Jackson that sent the FS-3 Kawasaki rider barrelling out of the race at Old Hall. The ensuing three-second penalty for Mackenzie dropped him to fifth.

The big winner of the weekend, however, was Bridewell, who delivered a masterclass performance to win races two and three with pace that was on a different level to his rivals. Having started the weekend on the back foot with 15th in qualifying, he scythed up to sixth in race one, before being made to do it all again in race two when a mistake left him

BRITISH SUPERBIKE REVIEW 303

13th on the opening lap. In a stunning fight back, however, he caught and passed O'Halloran on the final lap for his second win of the year, before delivering a third in race three after at times lapping more than a second quicker than the chasing pack. That put the Oxford Racing Ducati rider right back in contention, a mere nine points off the top spot.

As for the remaining Title Showdown contenders, Christian Iddon's bid got off to a stuttering start, with only a third-place finish the highlight of a disappointing weekend, while Vision-Track Ducati team-mate Josh Brookes enjoyed a more positive opening with two seconds marking his best results of the season, lifting him past Buchan and Irwin in the standings.

A return to Donington Park – this time for the full Melbourne Loop configuration – set the stage for the pivotal penultimate round, a pressure-laden encounter made all the more problematic by two of the three races being held in sodden conditions. With the stakes high and the grip low, perhaps it was no surprise that the weekend descended into a fight for survival rather than silverware, with only Iddon able to string a trio of strong results together among the Showdown contenders.

Even so, it was a crucial win for Mackenzie in a dry race two that set him on course for the crown. He had to work hard for it, though, keeping his cool in race one to finish seventh from 16th on the grid, before making the most of the optimum conditions in race two to pick his way to the front. Fortunately, he had lady luck on his side as well, after making contact with Iddon's Ducati, which flicked him out of his seat before he settled down and went on to win.

A DNF-inducing electrical problem in race three reined in his momentum, but otherwise Mackenzie benefited from main rivals O'Halloran and Bridewell failing to take advantage. Bridewell put himself on the back foot with a crash in race one – one of several riders to come off in the difficult conditions – before going on to finish seventh and fourth in the remaining encounters. A defeated-looking O'Halloran could only manage a fifth, ninth and eighth from his outings.

The others fared even worse, with Buchan showing sufficient pace in the wet and dry to secure second in race two, only to negate it with DNFs on either side, while Hickman, Brookes and Irwin posted middling results or retirements.

With the title contenders being tentative, the same couldn't be said for the weekend's star performer, Buildbase Suzuki's Gino Rea, who broke his BSB victory duck on a day for ducks with a confident run to victory amid the spray of race one, before doubling up in the similar conditions of race three.

Other standouts in the dreary conditions were Kyle Ryde, whose second place in race one marked the scant highlight of a disappointing season for the sophomore rider; Lee Jackson, also on the podium for the first and only time in 2021 in race three; and the precocious Storm Stacey, only 17, but already in his second season and very close to a podium in the wet on pure pace alone, only to fall before the flag.

Above: Gino Rea took advantage of wet conditions to claim two wins on Donington's full GP circuit in October.

Top left: Storm Stacey's Kawasaki leads Rea at Donington.

Above left: Tarran Mackenzie enjoyed his seventh win of the year at the Donington Showdown. Three more followed at Brands Hatch.

Right: Rea's Donington double was the high point of an otherwise downbeat season for Buildbase Suzuki.

Far right: Kyle Ryde was glowing after second place at Donington.
Photos: Bryn Williams

BRITISH SUPERBIKE REVIEW 305

Above: Tarran Mackenzie and Tommy Bridewell battle it out in the Brands Hatch finale.

Top right: Only one winner. Bridewell crestfallen, Mackenzie jubilant after securing the crown.

Above right: Rich Energy's Bradley Ray leads BSB Superbike returnee Luke Mossey on his TAG Honda.

Right: MotorSport Vision's Jonathan Palmer and Stuart Higgs crafted a compelling series for BSB in 2021.

Photos: Bryn Williams

Despite the differing fortunes of the lead contenders, six riders stood a mathematical chance of winning the 2021 BSB title heading to Brands Hatch. With Buchan and Hickman some way off, however, it was primarily considered a four-way showdown. Even so, with only 21 points covering those four riders and no defined trend having formed among them, it was arguably the most open championship finale for some years. Mackenzie held the advantage, ten points ahead of O'Halloran, despite his slump in performance, but with Bridewell only 15 points and Iddon only 21 points away from the top, it seemed plausible that a Ducati rider could still cause an upset by overhauling the Yamaha pair at the moment of truth.

With the title to gain, but everything else to lose, so began a high-stakes game of managing pressure. Yet again, Mother Nature threw in the curve ball of a wet qualifying, which threw up the bizarre outcome of pole position going the way of Luke Mossey, who made a headline-grabbing return to BSB on the TAG Honda he would campaign for a full season in 2022.

It was Mackenzie who sat prettiest on the grid in third position, however, a privilege he didn't waste by shrugging off the attentions of Iddon early on to establish a solid lead, before doing enough to resist the fast closing Bridewell on the run to the flag. The perfectly timed eighth win of the year extended Mackenzie's advantage going into the final Sunday to 25 points over Bridewell, who leapfrogged ahead of O'Halloran after he could only manage fourth.

That meant a win in race two would result in Mackenzie being crowned 2021 BSB champion. The McAMS Yamaha rider didn't put a wheel wrong, gritting his teeth through an entertaining tussle with Bridewell once more to get the drive through Clearways on the final lap and outdrag his Ducati rival to the finish line.

Without the pressure of having to hold his nerve into the final race of the year, a relaxed Mackenzie went on to toast his title with a third win of the weekend. His maiden BSB hat trick on a single weekend was a fitting landmark for a momentous achievement.

Having joined his father Niall on the BSB champion's trophy, Tarran's achievement simply added to the BSB success of a dynasty. Previously, he had won the 2016 British Supersport Championship, while brother Taylor had clinched the National Superstock 1000 Championship the same year.

A first title for McAMS (née Raceways), it was also the first BSB title for Yamaha since 2016, in a year when the Iwata marque largely dominated the racing scene, across MotoGP, WorldSBK, WorldSSP and MotoAmerica.

306 BRITISH SUPERBIKE REVIEW

If there was joy on one side of the garage for Mackenzie, no doubt there was sympathy for his team-mate, O'Halloran, who had scored the most points over the course of the year, but hadn't been able to maintain the momentum he'd built in what otherwise had been a stunning season for the Australian. Not that it should serve to diminish Mackenzie's achievement. His rapid run of form when it mattered had taken him to one win shy of O'Halloran's total in a year when McAMS Yamaha had stepped up to win 21 of the 33 races.

Such dominance across the board didn't quite get McAMS an overall one-two, however, with Bridewell arguably the rider who had made the most of the Title Showdown format to pip O'Halloran for a career-best runner-up spot.

Iddon ended up a fairly lonely fourth, but at the very least did what few riders had done before and grabbed the team-leader mantle from Josh Brookes, the Australian finishing the year a Showdown-assisted sixth for a final result that perhaps flattered to deceive.

Hickman won the battle of the BMWs in fifth overall, giving FHO Racing a satisfying maiden BSB season, while the factory-backed Synetiq BMW of Buchan settled for seventh and Honda's Irwin took eighth.

Beyond the Title Showdown, the BSB Riders' Cup – for the highest placed non-Showdown rider – went the way of Jackson. It was a welcome if scant reward for Kawasaki, which failed to reach the final stages for a second successive year.

Ray completed the top ten, ahead of double race winner Rea, the 2009 European Superstock 600 champion no doubt cursing the wayward reliability of his Suzuki for costing him a shot at a much better finish.

Vickers' third season in BSB demonstrated flashes of searing pace as well as an ongoing tendency for errors; he ended the year down in 12th, ahead of top rookie Skinner and Andrew Irwin, while Ryde rounded out the top 15.

As the sun set on another thrilling, action-packed season, it remained unclear whether Tarran Mackenzie would head for the bright lights of WorldSBK as rumoured. If he does stick around, he is likely to face a big threat to his crown from the likes of Tom Sykes and Leon Haslam, both of whom are expected to return to the domestic series in 2022. However, while high-profile names such as these certainly emphasise the gravitas of the enduringly popular BSB, there is no doubt that the action-packed racing remains the star of the show.

It is no coincidence that the British Superbike Championship is not only regarded as one of the best Superbike series in the world, but also one of the best motorcycling racing series period – and the 2021 season showed precisely no reason why anyone should dispute this.

Above: Jack Kennedy returned to the Supersport class to take seven wins and his third championship on the HEL Bournemouth Kawasaki.

Centre, from top: Ben Currie (Gearlink Kawasaki) was Kennedy's main rival; Currie and Kennedy sharing the podium at Donington; Lee Johnson was a consistent challenger to the pair; Eunan McLinchley (Kawasaki, 22) battles with Rhys Irwin (Yamaha).

Top far right: American Brandon Paasch on the Dynovolt Triumph.

Above far right: Fourteen wins took Charlie Nesbitt and his Kalex to a dominant GP2 title.

Far right: Bradley Perie gets his Appleyard MacAdam Yamaha out of shape at Oulton Park.

Photos: Bryn Williams

BSB Support Championships

THE main act of the British Superbike Championship swelled its set with three races per weekend, but there remained sufficient room for the support classes to share the high-profile stage.

Matching BSB for adrenaline-fuelled action and spectacle, precocious fresh faces measured up against esteemed veterans in the Supersport and Superstock classes, while MSV's quest to discover Britain's next motorcycling superstar in the Junior Supersport and Superstock series, and the Honda Talent Cup, suggested a rich vein of talent is being primed for tomorrow's headlines.

With 2021 BSB standout Rory Skinner proving that one can be 'junior' in age, but still collect the big prizes, the man who would succeed his **Quattro Group British Supersport Championship** title in 2021 was 2018 and 2019 winner Jack Kennedy, back in the category following a brief foray into the Superbike class. He picked up where he had left off with another convincing march towards a third career title, a feat matched only by the late Karl Harris.

Despite demonstrating an affinity with 600cc machinery, which ranks him as arguably the most adept British Supersport rider of the modern era, Kennedy didn't have it easy en route to reclaiming his crown, though he was never headed through the season. Seven wins kept the competition at arm's length.

Having achieved his previous two Supersport titles on Yamaha machinery, Kennedy won the third on the lesser fancied Kawasaki ZX-6R prepared by Bournemouth Kawasaki, the first non-Yamaha title winner since Tarran Mackenzie in 2016. In fact, it was a Kawasaki one-two, with Ben Currie clinching the runner-up spot for the stalwart Gearlink team in a campaign developed around steadfast consistency, which sustained his challenge until eventually he topped the podium in the very final race.

Flying the Yamaha flag highest was the experienced Lee Johnston on the Ashcourt Racing machine, his three wins, three seconds and three thirds putting him ahead of the rapid, but less-consistent Bradley Perie, whose quest to secure a fifth consecutive British Supersport title for Appleyard Macadam Yamaha fell short in fourth.

Harry Truelove and Euan McGlinchey rounded out the top six on the Truelove Brothers Yamaha and Gearlink Kawasaki respectively, ahead of Kyle Smith and American up-and-comer Brandon Paasch. The last named competed with Dynavolt Triumph, an intriguing entry that potentially set the blueprint for a new era of British Supersport.

Indeed, with the road-going Supersport class dwindling both in terms of sales and available models, an overhaul will permit motorcycles with larger engines – such as the Ducati Panigale V2 and MV Agusta F3 800 – to compete, at least at world championship level, in 2022.

Thus it was left to Triumph to take the lead in ensuring that 'balance of performance' is achieved with a faired Street Triple RS, equipped with the same 765cc triple-cylinder as found across the Moto2 World Championship grid. With PTR heading up the entry, Dynavolt Triumph were competitive, Smith achieving two wins in a campaign otherwise hampered by a period spent out through injury.

Elsewhere, the **British GP2 Championship** – which runs to Moto2 prototype-type regulations and competes within British Supersport races, albeit with their own separate points system – produced a clear champion in Charlie Nesbitt. Clinching the title with two rounds to spare, he and the RS Racing Kalex swept to 14 wins and seven podiums across 22 races.

Though unable to come close to Nesbitt in his efforts to defend his 2020 British GP2 title, Mason Law clicked off five wins en route to the runner-up spot, ahead of Cameron Horsman (Chassis Factory Racing), Dan Jones (Spirit) and Cameron Fraser (Chassis Factory Racing).

BRITISH SUPERBIKE REVIEW 309

310 BRITISH SUPERBIKE REVIEW

The **National Superstock Championship** mirrored the sister Superbike class with competitive, unpredictable action on 1000cc sportbikes that delivered nine different races and took the title fight right down to the wire. The championship had everyone guessing midway through the year, when just six points covered the entire top six, but a burst of form going into the second half proved just enough for Tom Neave to clinch title glory on the factory Honda Racing CBR1000RR-R Fireblade.

Indeed, a trio of wins in a row set Honda protégé Neave on course for going one better than his runner-up spot of the previous year, and he held his nerve in a tense final-round showdown to fend off the experienced Billy McConnell. The Australian – competing on the RICH Energy OMG BMW – had waited until the final round to achieve his one and only win of the year, but Neave's steady eighth place was enough to repel his advances by a mere five points.

Alex Olsen complemented Peter Hickman's BSB success with four wins and third overall for FHO Racing BMW, while Fraser Rogers proved that there was still pace in the ageing IN Competition Aprilia RSV4 with a race-winning turn that earned him fourth overall, ahead of BSB Title Showdown alumni Luke Mossey on the Bournemouth Kawasaki.

In the year his brother Tarran wrapped up the BSB title, Taylor Mackenzie, the 2016 National Superstock champion, announced his retirement from racing. However, the Bathams BMW rider still found time to score another three victories en route to sixth.

Defending champion Chrissy Rouse (STAUFF Fluid Power Kawasaki), Lewis Rollo (RAF Regular & Reserves Kawasaki) and Tim Neave (Buildbase Suzuki) – brother of champion Tom – ended the year seventh, eighth and ninth as the other riders to set foot on top of the podium.

Following a revamp of the BSB Support programme to develop a more systematic path through the domestic ranks towards BSB and beyond, the two 'Junior' series – Supersport and Superstock – continued to go from strength to strength in 2021. Boasting sizeable grids of youngsters, each was eager to demonstrate that it had the burgeoning talent that one day will follow in the wheel tracks of an illustrious roll-call of riders, which includes the likes of Jonathan Rea, Cal Crutchlow and Tarran Mackenzie, the new BSB champion just one example of the UK's fertile domestic proving ground.

Having charted the rise and successes of countless British and International superstars from grassroots racing right into the upper echelons of the sport over the past 46 years, MOTOCOURSE is proud to play its part in nurturing tomorrow's stars by backing the **HEL British Junior Supersport with MOTOCOURSE Championship**, which mirrors the regulations of the WorldSSP 300 Championship.

Cameron Dawson ended the year as title winner, following an eye-catching performance on the MSS Performance Kawasaki, which yielded seven wins en route to the summit, a dominant rout that allowed him to wrap up the title with a round to spare.

Ash Barnes, on the Barney Yamaha, made late inroads into Dawson's margin, despite just a single win to his name, and earned the runner-up spot, just ten points in arrears of his rival. Aron Davie (JDF Kawasaki) claimed four wins for third in the standings, ahead of Kam Dixon (Completely Motorbikes/Affinity Kawasaki) and Lucca Allen (Allen Yamaha) in fourth and fifth respectively.

Left: Tom Neave's Honda CBR1000RR-R Fireblade prevailed in National Superstock.

Below far left: Billy McConnell (BMW) was runner-up to Neave, just five points adrift.

Below left: Taylor Mackenzie's BMW leads Fraser Rogers and the champion's twin brother, Tim Neave, at Donington.

Bottom far left: Alex Olsen sweeps through the Thruxton chicane on his FHO Racing BMW.

Bottom left: Cameron Dawson (22) and Ash Barnes (46) were the main protagonists in the HEL British Junior Supersport series.

Below: Youngsters on the up: Ash Barnes, Cameron Dawson and Adon Davie were the best of the Junior Supersport field.
Photos: Bryn Williams

The **Pirelli Junior Superstock Championship** developed into a fierce battle for supremacy between Jack Nixon (Santander Salt Yamaha) and Joe Talbot (JR Performance Kawasaki), the pair heading into the final race of the season at Brands Hatch level on points. However, a second-place result allowed Nixon to clinch the title, seven points being the eventual winning margin between the youngsters. Zak Corderoy (Binch Yamaha) ended his year with six wins and third in the standings, from George Stanley (Ready4Racing Vision Kawasaki) and Eugene McManus (Completely Motorbikes/Affinity Kawasaki).

Founded with the primary aim of discovering the UK's future grand prix racing talents, the **Honda British Talent Cup** – a key component of the Road to MotoGP development programme – gained new perspective in a year when there were only three full-time British representatives in Moto2 and Moto3, with none in MotoGP itself. The situation looks more promising going forwards, however, with Casey O'Gorman powering to eight wins to clinch the title and with it a spot on the Red Bull Rookies grid for 2022. Carter Brown and Evan Belford picked up three wins apiece to round out the championship podium.

The one-make **Ducati TriOptions Cup** bulged with entries in 2021, the Italian firm having replaced the evergreen Ducati 959 with the new Panigale V2. Despite the change of weapon, Josh Day successfully defended his 2020 title with a dominant romp to 11 victories, which kept him well clear of experienced former WorldSBK and BSB race winner Chris Walker. David Shoubridge, Elliott Pinson and Isle of Man TT legend John McGuinness completed the top five.

The ever-popular **Molson Group British F1 Sidecar Championship** brought plenty of entertainment and close racing. Brothers Ben and Tom Birchall (Birchall Racing) charged to the title, taking 12 wins from 16 races.

Above: Defending champion Josh Day shares the Ducati TriOptions podium with old-stagers Chris Walker and John McGuinness.
Photo: Ducati Corse

Top: Carter Brown (67) and Casey O'Gorman 67 lead the Honda British Talent Cup pack at Oulton Park.

Left: Ben and Tom Birchall were the runaway sidecar winners.

Top far left: Honda British Talent Cup champion Casey O'Gorman receives the trophy from Shane Byrne.
Photos: Bryn Williams

Above centre far left: Jack Nixon (14) took the National Junior Superstock title by snitching second on the last lap of the last race.
Photo: Ian Hopgood Photography

Above far left: Joe Talbot (19) seemed to have the title sewn up until the last-lap drama.

Left: Ducati TriOptions champion Josh Day in action. He claimed 11 wins from 15 races.
Photos: Bryn Williams

2022 CALENDAR

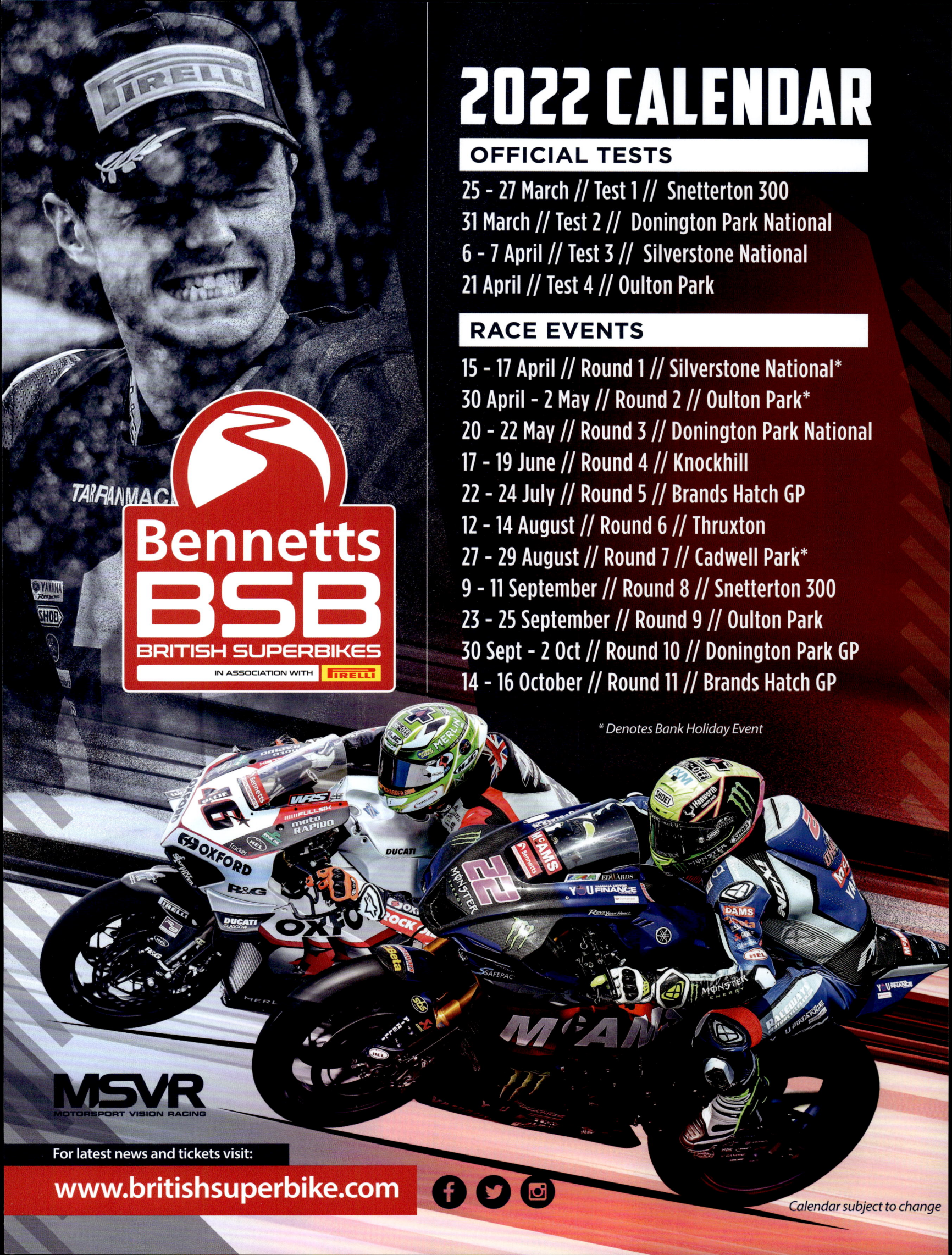

OFFICIAL TESTS

25 - 27 March // Test 1 // Snetterton 300
31 March // Test 2 // Donington Park National
6 - 7 April // Test 3 // Silverstone National
21 April // Test 4 // Oulton Park

RACE EVENTS

15 - 17 April // Round 1 // Silverstone National*
30 April - 2 May // Round 2 // Oulton Park*
20 - 22 May // Round 3 // Donington Park National
17 - 19 June // Round 4 // Knockhill
22 - 24 July // Round 5 // Brands Hatch GP
12 - 14 August // Round 6 // Thruxton
27 - 29 August // Round 7 // Cadwell Park*
9 - 11 September // Round 8 // Snetterton 300
23 - 25 September // Round 9 // Oulton Park
30 Sept - 2 Oct // Round 10 // Donington Park GP
14 - 16 October // Round 11 // Brands Hatch GP

Denotes Bank Holiday Event

Bennetts BSB
BRITISH SUPERBIKES
IN ASSOCIATION WITH Pirelli

MSVR
Motorsport Vision Racing

For latest news and tickets visit:
www.britishsuperbike.com

Calendar subject to change

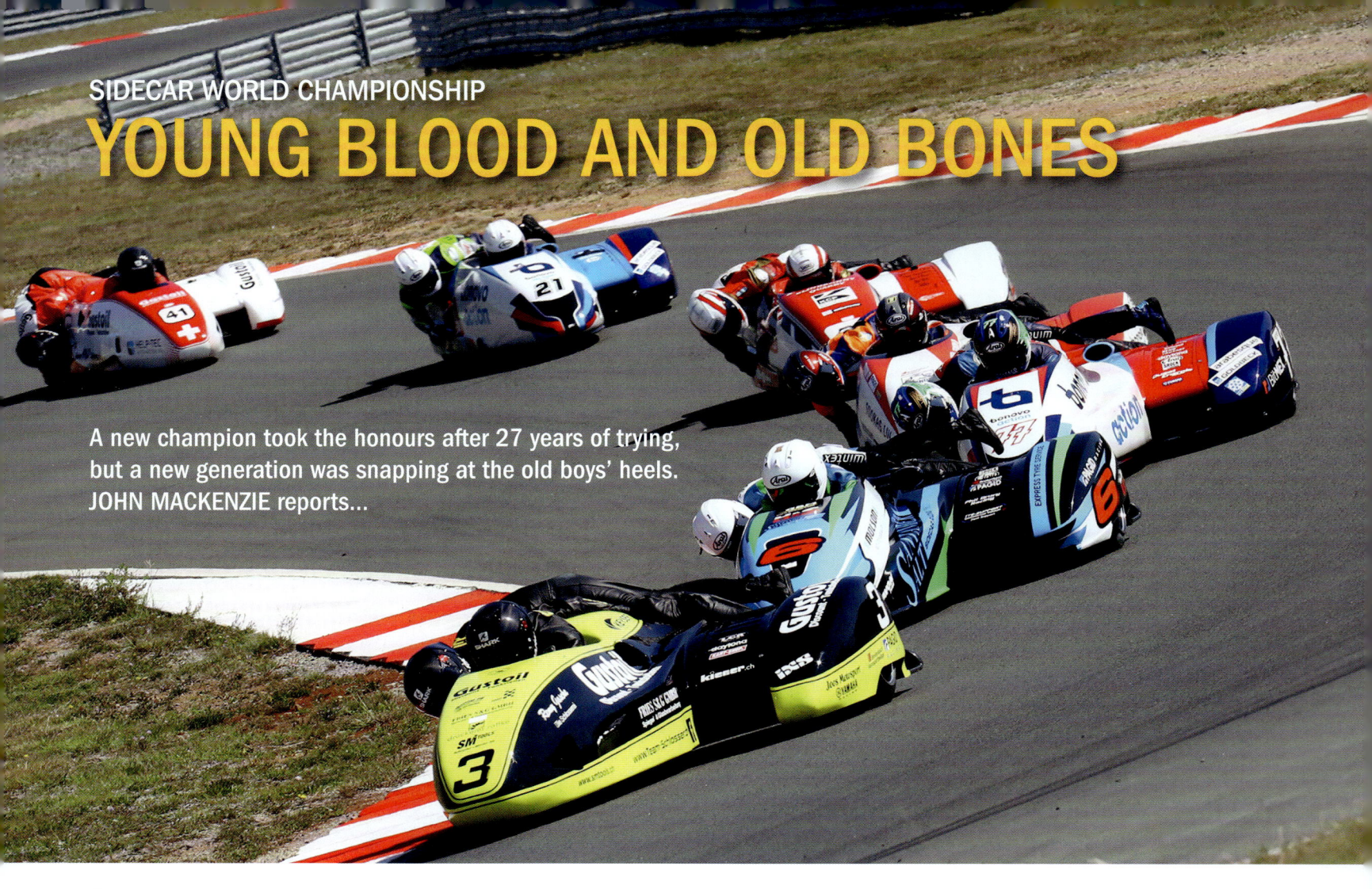

SIDECAR WORLD CHAMPIONSHIP
YOUNG BLOOD AND OLD BONES

A new champion took the honours after 27 years of trying, but a new generation was snapping at the old boys' heels. JOHN MACKENZIE reports...

LIKE everything else, the sidecars struggled with the shackles of Covid-19. The 2020 season had been cancelled, and plans for an April start to the 2021 series at Le Mans were deferred until June. Even then, special quarantine arrangements were in place: competitors from the UK required a PCR test and seven days' isolation, and the circuit became a 'bubble'. Not all crews were able to conform, and so missed the race.

Despite the difficulties, the organisers managed a 15-race calendar, and new for 2021 were two races of equal length at each round.

The usual protagonists lined up, led by 2019 and six-times world champion Tim Reeves and passenger Kevin Rousseau, and five-timer Pekka Paivarinta. Triple champions Ben and Tom Birchall were absent until the last round, concentrating instead on racing in the UK.

With 2015 champion Bennie Streuer recovering from a testing crash at Oschersleben, his passenger, Emmanuelle Clement, joined 2019 British champion Todd Ellis, the pair enjoying an excellent season.

Perennially fast Swiss rider Markus Schlosser, with Marcel Fries, fourth in 2019, committed to the full season, and his vast experience told as he went from bit-part player to domination.

Round 1 – Le Mans, France

Schlosser and Fries took pole on their Gustoil LCR Yamaha, with Ellis/Clement on the Santander Salt LCR Yamaha second, and Reeves/Rousseau (Bonovo Action Adolf RS Yamaha) third. Paivarinta was sixth fastest with late replacement passenger Ilse de Haas, after Kim Friman was injured late in qualifying.

It was close for the full 18 laps, with Reeves setting the pace. Schlosser found his way to second, past Ellis, but a mistake on the penultimate lap let in Ellis briefly, before Schlosser recovered. Just over a second covered the top three.

A great season-opener for Reeves, and his 63rd championship win took him past Steve Webster. Third-placed Ellis posted fastest lap at 1m 45.341s – a statement of intent from the young English driver.

Race two next day, with conditions slightly cooler, and Reeves, Ellis and Schlosser again dominated early. Schlosser led after four laps, pulling ten seconds clear of Ellis for his first win since 2016.

Paivarinta was third, after a tough battle with young French driver Ted Peugeot, passengered by his father, also Ted. Reeves was pleased just to finish in the points after dropping to fifth, stuck in fifth gear.

Schlosser took over at the top of the points table, a position he would never relinquish.

Round 2 – Pannoniaring, Hungary

A second pole for Schlosser, with Paivarinta/de Hass and Ellis/Clement making up the front row.

Paivarinta shot into the lead of the 15-lapper, with Schlosser and Reeves behind, then Ellis. By lap two, Reeves was leading, but by half-distance he had started to drop back, retiring after eight laps. Paivarinta took the lead again from Ellis, but Schlosser was waiting and watching.

As temperatures hit the high twenties, tyre management became decisive. Schlosser's decision to hold back won him the race, with a new lap record of 1m 57.722s. Ellis couldn't quite catch flying Finn Paivarinta.

In Sunday's race two, Reeves grabbed the early lead ahead of Schlosser, followed by Paivarinta and Ellis, with Sattler in fifth. The closest race of the season so far followed, with only Sattler dropping back slightly.

Tyres again became the ruling factor. Reeves managed to open a slight gap, and Ellis was pressing Paivarinta hard for third place, grabbing it almost on the line. Reeves took the flag by 0.052 of a second from Schlosser in an amazing race.

Reeves's joy was short-lived, as he was disqualified. Having blown up three engines after suffering issues with the water system, the only way he could make the grid was to use a spare 'emergency' Yamaha engine.

"We threw that in, but afterwards in technical inspection, it was found that one of the camshafts was not homologated. They didn't say we were cheating, but they had to disqualify us. I get it. It was a genuine mistake, but they have to stand by the rules. We have been just unlucky," lamented Reeves.

The win passed to Schlosser, the Swiss team rewarded with a 23-point lead over Ellis.

Round 3 – Donington Park, Great Britain

Back at Donington Park for the first time since 2016, and typically the talk was all about the threatening rain.

Pole went to Ellis with a stunning sub-record time of 1m 36.479s, but in the first race, Reeves/Rousseau streaked into Redgate, Ellis right behind. Determined to pull out a lead, Reeves posted fastest lap on the third, at 1m 37.251s, and seemed to be in control. But at the top of Craner curves, a brief shimmy and they were headed on to the grass, gifting Ellis a four-second lead.

Reeves regained the tarmac in sixth. Schlosser was second, but pressed by Paivarinta, who briefly took the position at the Melbourne loop, but he couldn't make it stick.

A joyous Ellis and Clement claimed their first World Championship win just over three seconds in front of Schlosser; Paivarinta was third.

Again, Sunday's race two was threatened by rain, but after a short delay, and despite a few drops, the race was declared dry, reduced to 17 laps, with two warm-up laps.

Championship leader Schlosser didn't make the grid after his engine failed in the pit lane. Reeves led

Left: Markus Schlosser and Marcel Fries lead Todd Ellis/Emmanuelle Clement (6), Tim Reeves/Kevin Rousseau and the rest of the sidecar pack.

Right: Old bones. Schlosser and Fries earned their gongs.

Far right: Pekka Paivarinta and Ilse de Haas lead Todd Ellis and Emmanuelle Clement.
Photos: Mark Walters

into Redgate once more, with Steve Kershaw/Ryan Charlwood (Quattro Yamaha) in second, Ellis third, but soon up to second.

Ellis was relentless in his pursuit, and as the two leading outfits parried and blocked, Kershaw was able to close up, awaiting an error.

Into the last lap, Reeves looked secure until Ellis tried to force the issue at the Foggy Esses. Hurtling into the Melbourne hairpin, Reeves tried for the inside line past Ellis, while Kershaw went wide, attempting to stay out of trouble. The move dropped Reeves to third, but as the outfits thrashed up to Goddard's, Ellis went in too fast, giving Kershaw the inside line and the lead. Reeves arrived as Ellis tried to get back on the racing line, and the two outfits barged together, each refusing to give way. Kershaw took the flag, with Reeves just managing to grab second – a brutal and spectacular finish to a classic race. Despite the bumping and grinding, it was all smiles in the paddock afterwards. It's tough at the top.

Round 4 – Assen, Netherlands

Todd Ellis's 1m 43.127s was enough for pole, just pipping Schlosser, with Reeves making up the front row. It was pleasing to see local hero Bennie Streuer back on the track, and a respectable sixth on the grid.

Reeves won the sprint to the first corner for race one, and used the clear track to full advantage as he tried to pull a gap on Ellis and Schlosser, who had passed Kershaw for third.

With five of 18 laps left, Schlosser was second from Ellis and pressing Reeves, with Kershaw and Streuer closing – five outfits bunching up. With three laps to go, chasing towards Stekkenwal, Schlosser just took the lead, and Ellis went for the same imperceptible gap. Not surprisingly, Reeves would not yield, and the two outfits made contact, which was enough to put Ellis into the gravel.

Kershaw and Streuer were able to take advantage of the melee, and Reeves lost two more places.

Schlosser held on to win by seven-tenths from Kershaw, Streuer third and Reeves, who had recovered to fourth.

However, the post-race technical inspection found Streuer's machine to be in breach of minimum weight regulations, and he was disqualified.

In race two, Ellis was away first, Paivarinta in his tracks. Then Schlosser and Reeves demoted Paivarinta to fourth, before forcing Ellis back to third.

With four laps left, an electrical gremlin halted Reeves, leaving an empty road in front of Schlosser, who posted fastest race lap. Ellis took second, Kershaw third.

The win gave the Swiss crew a useful 32-point lead in the standings.

Round 5 – Rijeka, Croatia

A 16th consecutive trip for the sidecars to an almost always hot and sunny 4.168km Grobnik was next. With temperatures hitting the mid-30s and two 18-lap races, it was going to be a gruelling weekend.

Schlosser's third pole of the season, just ahead of Reeves, with Ellis third, came on his first visit to the track. He led away in torrid conditions in race one, challenged by Reeves, briefly in front. But for a second race in a row, the Englishman was forced to retire, with just four laps remaining. That left Schlosser unchallenged. Ellis just couldn't do enough to catch up, despite posting fastest lap. Kershaw was a grateful third.

For Sunday, Schlosser was away again, Reeves and Ellis in tow. Reeves managed to impose his dominance, just holding off Ellis. Then, with two laps to go, Schlosser made his move on Ellis to take second in an incredible finish, with only 0.160 of a second separating the three outfits. Kershaw followed them home for fourth place, a lonely six seconds in arrears.

Round 6 – Oschersleben, Germany

Ellis and Clement got the jump at the start of the 21-lapper, just containing Schlosser at the first corner. The Swiss driver stayed close and the two outfits opened a gap. As the race progressed, Ellis's tyre wear began to tell and Schlosser took over. He posted fastest lap on his way to a 4.5-second win.

An uncharacteristically poor start meant that Reeves had to battle through for third.

Sunday's second race benefited from a welcome drop in temperature. Again, Ellis was the instant pace-setter, this time with Reeves tucked in behind, determined to make up for his race-one lapse. On lap nine, he found a way through, followed by Schlosser, who then harried Reeves before sweeping into an unassailable lead.

Another perfect weekend for Schlosser, with pole, two wins, and fastest laps. Ellis and Clement were happy with third, Streuer fourth.

Round 7 – Estoril, Portugal

It had been the intention to run a mixed British/World round at Brands Hatch in mid-October, but there was no time for separate events in an already packed BSB programme, and there were FIM licensing and insurance issues. For the final round at Estoril, already carrying double points, a third race (with normal points) was added to make up for the disappointment.

That meant 125 points in one weekend – Schlosser's 55-point lead looked a bit less comfortable. The return to the World Championship of triple champions Ben and Tom Birchall, after dominating in the British championship, also complicated matters.

Reeves took pole ahead of Ellis, with surprise package Harry Payne third on a Steinhausen-supplied Adolf RS Yamaha. Rain had played havoc, and Schlosser was down in ninth.

With race-one weather looking iffy, the Birchalls gambled on slicks, most of the rest on wets.

Ellis and Reeves shot away, Reeves getting the upper hand before the Birchalls' slicks began to pay off for a clean break. Reeves lost a safe second, pitting with a failed fuel pump relay after 12 laps.

Then French pair Leglise and Lavorel crashed, bringing out the red flags, and the race was declared after 13 of the planned 18 laps. Birchall won by a huge 40-second margin, Streuer was second, Ellis third.

A couple of hours later, in the double-points race two, Reeves shot away, knowing that first would be the only position not affected by spray from the saturated track. In shocking conditions, he built his lead, setting fastest lap on the second. Ellis was close behind, but struggling for grip, and he dropped back after a couple of spins. Wild-card Harry Payne was now second; meanwhile, as Ellis struggled, Schlosser was improving, passing Ellis for fifth. With double points, if Ellis couldn't move up, the title would go to Schlosser.

As the conditions worsened, Ellis spun again, letting Paivarinta through. Then, with two laps to go, a slipping clutch forced Reeves into the pits. That left a surprise win for Payne and Mark Wilkes, who'd passengered for Reeves's 2019 title following a remarkable comeback from injuries sustained in a New Zealand crash. They'd been offered a last-minute ride by Rolf Steinhausen after good showings at Donington and Assen, and had wanted to gauge their chances before committing to the 2022 campaign.

Kershaw was second, while Schlosser's third was enough to secure him a hugely popular and well-deserved 2021 World Championship. At 49, he might provide a new definition of 'slow burner': Schlosser had begun his GP career in the era of 500cc two-strokes at Assen, in June, 1994, when he had placed 13th among such titans of the sport as Rolf Biland, Steve Webster, Klaus Klaffenbock, Darren Dixon and Steve Abbott. In 1998, he had finished third overall and had been third again in 2007, when he had won his first grand prix at Schleiz. A staggering 27 years from that nervous afternoon in Holland to a richly deserved top prize.

Schlosser had dominated with four poles and eight wins from 15 races, while meticulous preparation had left only one non-scoring race.

There were other places still to be settled in race three. Again, Reeves led away, Ellis and Payne in pursuit, but the determined leader was never headed. Even Birchall, up through the field and faster in the closing stages, couldn't catch him.

Schlosser was third, Ellis hanging on to fourth and runner-up in the title chase.

Defending champion Reeves's hopes had been torpedoed by six no-scores, but this final win took his total to 65. Only Biland, on 82, had more.

Paivarinta finished third overall, but appeared to have dropped away slightly from the pace with a string of fourth and fifth places.

Following success with the British championship, ex-driver Roger Body's RKB-F1 Motorsport had taken over series management, and enjoyed the most dramatic and action-packed championship for years. Young challengers like Ellis, Kershaw and Payne emerged to tackle Reeves, Paivarinta, Birchall and Schlosser, dominant for the previous 15 years.

Runner-up in his first season, Ellis was a revelation. The 2019 British champion managed one win, but his consistency and quality can be measured with 12 rostrum finishes, two poles and a full house of top-three qualifying. Never fazed when the going got tough, he showed massive potential.

The sidecar world, with its close friendships, and generational and family bonds, is as strong as ever. And we can look forward to some immense racing in 2022.

SIDECAR WORLD CHAMPIONSHIP 315

US RACING REVIEW

REWRITING THE RECORD BOOKS

Jake Gagne was unstoppable – literally. LARRY LAWRENCE reports…

WHEN Cameron Beaubier completed his stunning 16-win season during the 2020 MotoAmerica Superbike Championship, it was thought that his performance would live long in the record books as the most dominating in the 45-year history of the series. Then came 2021 and Jake Gagne, riding for the same Fresh N' Lean Attack Performance Yamaha squad.

Gagne won 17 of the 20 rounds and scored 445 points, compared to Beaubier's 436. He not only set a new MotoAmerica/AMA Superbike record for the most wins in a single season, but also shattered the winning-streak record. Sixteen consecutive victories easily eclipsed the 11 straight wins set jointly by four-times champion Josh Hayes and five-timer Beaubier.

All from a rider who, in four previous seasons, had not won a single race. Amazingly, Gagne went from zero wins straight into the top ten on the all-time MotoAmerica/AMA Superbike wins list in a single season! Seventeen tied him with Nicky Hayden for eighth.

Gagne's run did not come about because of weak competition. He lined up every week against talented rivals, including Yamaha team-mate Josh Herrin, a former AMA Superbike champion; multiple MotoAmerica Superbike race winner Mathew Scholtz of South Africa; 2020 MotoAmerica Superstock champion Cameron Petersen, also of South Africa; another multi-Superbike race winner in Suzuki's Bobby Fong; ten-times grand prix race winner Hector Barbera; former MotoAmerica Superbike and Moto2 world champion Toni Elias, who raced part-time in 2021; and former Superbike World Championship race winner and MotoGP rider Loris Baz on a factory Ducati.

"What a year," Gagne said after wrapping it up by winning the season finale. "I'm so happy for what we've accomplished. Again, thanks to the whole team. We've got such a great crew, and everybody works so hard."

Richard Stanboli, the Fresh N' Lean Attack Performance Yamaha Racing team manager, summed up the 2021 campaign at the series finale: "We were able to finish the season properly today with a win and a new record. Our 2021 championship season is another success to add to our 2020 championship results. It has been an amazing experience! We can't thank the staff at Yamaha enough for giving us the opportunity and the trust in what is now two of our best seasons in Superbike racing."

Stanboli's Attack Performance managed to build Yamaha Superbikes that proved to be on a par, or possibly even better, than the factory R1s that had won races and championships in seasons past. And the bad news for other teams and riders looking forward is that there does not seem to be another squad in MotoAmerica that can even approach the same levels of speed and consistency. Attack Racing appears to be well on its way to building a dynasty to challenge the all-time best in the history of the series.

Inset: Fresh N' Lean Attack Performance Yamaha riders Josh Herrin and Jake Gagne celebrate their double one-two finish at The Ridge.

Main: Gagne takes charge at the start in Pittsburgh.
Photos: MotoAmerica/Brian J. Nelson

Above: Early championship leader Mathew Scholtz (Westby Yamaha) heads Gagne and the pack in the Road Atlanta opener.

Top right: First-timer Loris Baz brought fresh stimulus to the series on the Warhorse Ducati.
Photos: MotoAmerica/Brian J. Nelson

Above centre right: Suzuki's Bobby Fong (50) scored a couple of podiums on his way to fifth in the final standings.
Photo: www.suzuki-racing.com

Above right: Herrin leads Baz and Petersen at The Ridge.

Right: South African rider Cameron Petersen took his M4 ECSTAR Suzuki to third overall.
Photos: MotoAmerica/Brian J. Nelson

Road Atlanta – 1–2 May

On the Saturday, Westby Racing's Mathew Scholtz got the soaking-wet monkey off his back with his first dry-race HONOS Superbike victory in bright sunshine at Road Atlanta's Michelin Raceway. He led 18 of the 19 laps for a perfect start to his campaign.

Scholtz's previous two Superbike wins had occurred in wet conditions in 2017 and 2018. This victory came in his first race since sustaining serious leg injuries at Indianapolis Motor Speedway in October, 2020.

Warhorse HSBK Racing Ducati New York's Loris Baz battled for the lead, but tucked the front end of his Ducati and crashed out. Pole-qualifier Gagne was the unluckiest in the race, however. He was at the front of the pack on the opening lap when his YZF-R1 imploded on the front straight.

On the Sunday, there was a change in fortune, with Gagne's career-first MotoAmerica Superbike victory, achieved in style. The grid had been set by Saturday's results, and he started from the middle of the third row, then worked his way through to pull clear by almost five seconds. Once he'd adjusted the play out of his slipping clutch, his rampaging pace was unmatchable.

It was his first win since 2015, his victorious Superstock 1000 Championship season. "It feels good to get something like that off the back," he said. "Last year, [there were] a lot of second places, and it wears you down."

Scholtz held on for second, well clear of Gagne's teammate, Herrin, who was third for a second straight day.

Thus Scholtz led the series from Herrin 45–32.

Virginia International Raceway – 22–23 May

Gagne turned in an ominously strong performance in the first of two MotoAmerica HONOS Superbike races at Virginia International Raceway. He had broken Beaubier's lap record earlier in the day during final qualifying and shot from pole position to the lead, never to be headed.

Scholtz was the next best, staying on top of the points with second. Herrin was third again in the race, and now also in the points.

Then Gagne took his third straight win in impressive fashion. On the Saturday, he'd won by 11.8 seconds. On Sunday, that gap swelled to 13.9 seconds, after he had led from Turn One to the flag. He was well clear of Ducati's Baz, the Frenchman earning his first MotoAmerica podium.

Scholtz was roughed up in Turn One off the start and finished the opening lap in 14th, but the South African didn't give up and pushed his way through the pack, eventually making his way to the heels and then ahead of the battle for third, maintaining his perfect season of podium finishes and preserving his championship lead from the fast closing Gagne by six points.

Road America – 12–13 June

Gagne's domination continued with three carbon copies, leading all the way from pole. He was the only rider to lap in the 2m 11s, and on Saturday he pulled away by almost six seconds.

There was a good fight for second, Baz storming through

318 US RACING REVIEW

in the last few laps to pass both M4 ECSTAR Suzukis, after making dramatic changes to his Ducati Panigale V4 R prior to the race. Fong and Petersen passed the flag within just 0.073 of a second, with Petersen claiming third and his first MotoAmerica Superbike podium from his team-mate.

On Sunday, Gagne swept to yet another win. To say he was on a roll would be a gross understatement. At this stage, nobody could predict how long it would last.

He fought off Petersen's early attack with a second lap as hot as the Wisconsin sun, a 2m 10.998s, while Petersen clicked off a 2m 12.114s. End of contest.

Nonetheless, the South African delivered a strong weekend, adding second place in race two to his earlier third. His compatriot, Scholz, was third in race two, having barely held off Fong after the Suzuki rider had finally rid himself of Herrin's Yamaha.

Kyle Wyman (Panera Bread Ducati), lying seventh overall, suffered elbow injuries in an apparently innocuous Sunday crash that put him out for two races.

The Ridge Motorsports Park – 26–27 June

In record-setting heat at the second visit to Ridge Motorsports Park outside Seattle, Gagne broke the track record during Q2 on Saturday morning and was unstoppable again in the race, leading every lap.

His team-mate, Herrin, found a faster and more comfortable setting to take second, his best of the year, 4.49 seconds behind Gagne after 17 laps. He'd had his hands full with Petersen for most of the race, until the South African ran wide in the Turn One chicane, dropping some four seconds behind.

Gagne took his seventh straight win on Sunday, again beating Herrin, this time by better than five seconds.

Laguna Seca Raceway – 10–11 July

Gagne's eighth win was different. It was close – just a tick over a second, and that was the biggest lead of the race, after Baz had applied relentless pressure for the duration of the red-flag-interrupted event.

Petersen, in third, was another 2.4 seconds away for a podium of three different manufacturers (Yamaha, Ducati and Suzuki) and three different nationalities (American, French and South African).

Sunday's race in California was one of the most exciting of the season. Gagne went off the track on the run from Turn Five to Turn Six on the opening lap, which allowed Baz to get ahead. What followed was a frenzied 20 or so seconds as Gagne, Baz and Scholtz rubbed elbows and motorcycles through the Corkscrew and Rainey Curve. When the dust had settled, Gagne was back in front.

Despite constant pressure from Baz for the duration, Gagne kept his composure to win by less than two seconds. The ninth victory increased his championship points lead to 65 points over Scholtz, 225–160.

Toni Elias, 2016 champion, who had retired at the end of 2020, made a one-off return, finishing eighth and seventh on the injured Wyman's Ducati.

Brainerd International Raceway – 31 July–1 August

On Saturday at Brainerd, Gagne crashed, but still managed to win the first AMA Superbike race held at BIR in 17 years.

Leading on the second lap, Gagne fell and was marooned in the middle of the track as the field motored by on both sides. He finally ran to safety, but with his bike still on track, a red flag was thrown, stopping the race. Fortunately for him, his Yamaha suffered only minor damage and he was able to ride back to the pit for repairs prior to the restart.

From that point on, it was typical Gagne: he grabbed the lead and pulled away, ultimately besting Bobby Fong's Su-

US RACING REVIEW 319

Above: Gagne leads stand-in teammate Toni Elias at Pittsburgh. Behind, the pursuing Baz tumbles from his Ducati.

Top: Jake Lewis celebrates his Supersport win at Pittsburgh.

Top right: Petersen (46) leads Scholtz (11) and Baz (76) in the rain-lashed race at Barber.

Right: All three fell and got up again to complete a remarkable podium.

Far right: Wayne Rainey with Jake Gagne, the runaway 2021 MotoAmerica champion.

Photos: MotoAmerica/Brian J. Nelson

zuki by 4.675 seconds. His tenth win tied him with Mike Baldwin for 19th on the all-time AMA Superbike win list.

The next day, he made history with an 11th straight win, beating the record of ten set by four-times AMA Superbike champion Josh Hayes and five-times MotoAmerica Superbike champion Cameron Beaubier.

The win was like most of Gagne's other victories – dominating. He shot away from pole position and was never headed, finishing 5.2 seconds ahead of Scholtz, who'd been battling for the duration with Baz's Ducati. The Frenchman made a last-lap mistake, however, which let Scholtz escape by just over a second.

Pittsburgh International Race Complex – 14–15 August

Jake's records continued to build as he made it an even dozen on Saturday at Pittsburgh. As had become the norm for the runaway leader, he hit the front from pole position, was never headed and ended up crossing the finish line 11.3 seconds over second place.

It takes a lot to overshadow 12 wins in a row, but on a sunny Saturday, Toni Elias came close, substituting for Herrin, who had tested positive for Covid-19. In just his second outing of the year, and his first ever on a Yamaha YZF-R1 (he had first thrown his leg over the bike on the Friday), the Spaniard came off the couch to finish second on the Fresh N' Lean Attack Performance machine. He was three seconds ahead of Mathew Scholtz.

In Sunday's race two, Gagne continued his complete domination with a 13th successive win. But this one was closer, with Scholtz halving Saturday's gap.

Fong took third ahead of Elias, Baz and Petersen.

New Jersey Motorsports Park – 11–12 September

The season's first of two triple-headers started on Saturday in familiar fashion, as Gagne again made a mockery of the rest. He led all 20 laps to win by 7.6 seconds. Scholtz took his fifth second place of the year; Elias was third, on his third outing on the Yamaha.

On Sunday came Gagne's clincher, securing the championship with his second and third wins of the weekend, for a total of 16, equalling that joint Hayes/Beaubier wins-per-season record, and tying with triple world champion and MotoAmerica chief Wayne Rainey's AMA career tally.

Scholtz added two more second places to secure second overall ahead of Petersen, whose best of the weekend was fifth in race three.

And Josh Herrin was back, finishing sixth, third and third to move back ahead of Baz (twice fourth) on points.

Barber Motorsports Park – 18–19 September

One of the most dramatic races in AMA Superbike history took place in a rainstorm at Barber Motorsports Park on Saturday, and it won't be forgotten soon, especially by Cameron Petersen. Or Mathew Scholtz. Or Loris Baz.

Suzuki's Petersen earned his first MotoAmerica Superbike win after surviving a crash in the downpour. Scholtz placed his Yamaha second after doing the same. Oh, and Ducati-mounted Baz finished third after also surviving a crash in the deluge. A podium of fallen and remounted riders was a first in AMA Superbike history.

Despite an Alabama weekend of horrendous weather and difficult racing conditions, the 2021 MotoAmerica Superbike Series ended appropriately, with Jake Gagne taking a record 17th win to put an exclamation mark on a season like no other. He'd been third in race two, which was won by Scholtz from Baz, and had been red-flagged early after a deer ran across the track in front of the leader.

MISSION POSSIBLE

Wayne Rainey's aim to revitalise US racing talent is starting to bear fruit.

WAYNE RAINEY has been around racing his entire life, so there's not much he hasn't seen. Yet even he was surprised by how Jake Gagne was practically untouchable in 2021.

"Gagne kind of came out of nowhere," Rainey said. "I think being teamed with [Cameron] Beaubier, who was really dominant, gave Gagne the insight on what makes the Yamaha work, how to work inside that team, and I think it gave him confidence because he could run close with Beaubier. So when Beaubier went to the world championships, Gagne had a real opportunity. He's had a good deal of experience, and then you mix that with great lap times and results, that breeds confidence.

"Fast from the first every weekend, in the races he opened gaps early, and it caused a lot of the other riders to panic and forced them into mistakes."

MotoAmerica president Rainey, like many observers, had thought Loris Baz on the factory Ducati might have been the rider to beat. After all, another MotoGP/World Superbike transfer, Toni Elias, had begun winning races right out of the gate.

That Baz didn't demonstrated the improved level of MotoAmerica competition. Rainey pointed out that the Frenchman had gone back to the Superbike World Championship as a fill-in rider after the MotoAmerica season was over and immediately had been able to earn podium finishes. "And Baz earned his way back into a solid world championship ride next year," Rainey added.

"That's exactly what we wanted to do in MotoAmerica, to get riders up to the level, or in Baz's case, back to the level where they could step right into a world championship and be competitive."

Rainey is happy that the pipeline of American riders going into the world championships is beginning to flow again. Joe Roberts and Cameron Beaubier are showing sparks in Moto2. In 2022, they'll be joined by MotoAmerica Supersport champion Sean Dylan Kelly. And then there's Garrett Gerloff in World Superbike, who scored a podium result in 2021.

"At CoTA, Beaubier showed he has the talent to run up front," Rainey said. "I think that performance will up his confidence tremendously. I think SDK [the nickname for Sean Dylan Kelly] is a young aggressive rider with a lot of desire to show he deserves to be in the world championships. I think he could surprise a lot of people."

Rainey was bullish on the future of MotoAmerica. "We continue to make progress," he said. "There was a pretty long period there where American racing didn't provide a lot of opportunities for riders. Now we see that if a rider comes in and can be competitive here, that opportunities to step up to the next level are available, and we're pumped about that."

Above: The view that only the best of rivals had of Gagne during 2021.

Top right: Superstock champion Jake Lewis took six wins from 12 races.

Top far right: Kaleb De Keyrel took his Aprilia to a clear Twins Cup win.

Above right: Sean Dylan Kelly (*left*) after one of 12 wins in a dominant season. He follows Beaubier to Moto2 in 2022; (*centre*) Tyler Scott (70) and Benjamin Gloddy (72) fought for honours in the Junior Cup; (*right*) the KTM rider took 11 victories in his successful Junior campaign.

Right: Richie Escalante on the HONOS HVMC Racing Kawasaki side by side with M4 ECSTAR Suzuki's Sean Dylan Kelly.

Photos: MotoAmerica/Brian J. Nelson

Mathew Scholtz had his best weekend of the year, taking a fourth career win on Sunday morning, and second again in race three – another wet race.

The conditions threw up some surprises, with a pair of fourth places for Ashton Yates (Jones Honda), son of four-times AMA champion Aaron Yates; and two fifths for Altus Suzuki's Jake Lewis.

With the top three championship places already settled for Gagne, Scholtz and Petersen, two podiums for Baz moved him back up to fourth; while two no-scores for Herrin meant that he ceded fifth overall to Fong by just seven points.

Hector Barbera was seventh on the Scheibe BMW, having taken three fifth places in a year of solid top-tens; Lewis was eighth and Kyle Wyman ninth, having missed three rounds. Corey Alexander (HONOS Kawasaki) completed the championship top ten.

Supersport

Sean Dylan Kelly had been chasing a championship since he was five. On Sunday at the New Jersey round, aged 19, he finally claimed one, wrapping up the Supersport Championship. He didn't need to win Sunday's race. Second to rookie M4 ECSTAR Suzuki team-mate Sam Lochoff was enough.

"I've been working really hard for this. My family have given literally everything … they left everything behind in the US. They took me to Spain. They lived there with pennies. Everything for me, for this passion, for this dream."

Kelly will join the American Racing team for the 2022 and 2023 Moto2 World Championships, riding alongside Cameron Beaubier.

Superbike Cup & Stock 1000

Rain at Barber Motorsports Park in Birmingham, Alabama, could not dampen the spirits of the Altus Motorsports team. For the second year running, the Suzuki squad won the MotoAmerica Stock 1000 and Superbike Cup Championships.

After clinching Stock 1000 the previous weekend, Jake Lewis came into the final round looking to do the same with the Superbike Cup. And he did. Fifth in the first wet and crash-laden race, he was the second fastest Stock 1000 bike, but it was good enough to take the title. In the second Superbike race, he finished fifth again.

Jake also won the last Stock 1000 race of the year, and was only off the podium three times, including six wins.

Twins Cup

Kaleb De Keyrel was on the verge of clinching his first MotoAmerica No.1 plate at the start of the New Jersey round, and the Aprilia rider wasted no time in wrapping up the 2021 MotoAmerica Twins Cup title on Saturday. The Minnesotan piloted his Aprilia RS 660 to a podium finish that also secured Aprilia's first MotoAmerica crown in its maiden year competing in the Twins Cup.

Junior Cup

Fifteen-year-old Tyler Scott wrapped up the 2021 MotoAmerica Junior Cup Championship with an impressive double victory sweep at the Barber Motorsports Park season finale. The KTM-supported rider was officially crowned on Saturday, following a title-clinching victory aboard his Scott Powersports KTM RC 390 R, and he didn't stop there, as he charged his way to another dominant performance at the final race on Sunday.

Entering the weekend with a 30-point lead in the Junior Cup Championship, Scott knew that he only needed to finish race one within five points of the second-place rider and the title was his. The Pennsylvanian did just that, taking the title with one race to spare.

After two seasons primarily in Europe, in the Red Bull Rookies Cup and then the European Talent Cup in Spain, Scott's rookie MotoAmerica season brought 11 career victories, as well as four podium finishes, in 18 races.

HenryUSA.com

MOTOAMERICA

DUNLOP
MOTOAMERICA
KTM

Ninja
hudson valley
DUNLOP
Arai
SUZUKI
ECSTAR
DUNLOP

MAJOR RESULTS

OTHER CHAMPIONSHIP RACING SERIES WORLDWIDE

Compiled by PETER McLAREN

MOTOAMERICA Superbike Championship

ROAD ATLANTA, Braselton, Georgia, 1-2 May, 19 Laps, 48.45 miles/77.97km
Race 1
1 Mathew Scholtz (Yamaha); **2** Bobby Fong (Suzuki); **3** Josh Herrin (Yamaha); **4** Cameron Petersen (Suzuki); **5** Kyle Wyman (Ducati); **6** Hector Barbera (BMW); **7** Travis Wyman (BMW); **8** Danilo Lewis (BMW); **9** Geoff May (Honda); **10** Michael Gilbert (Kawasaki).

Race 2
1 Jake Gagne (Yamaha); **2** Mathew Scholtz (Yamaha); **3** Josh Herrin (Yamaha); **4** Cameron Petersen (Suzuki); **5** Bobby Fong (Suzuki); **6** Kyle Wyman (Ducati); **7** Hector Barbera (BMW); **8** Travis Wyman (BMW); **9** Jake Lewis (Suzuki); **10** Jayson Uribe (Suzuki).

VIRGINIA INTERNATIONAL RACEWAY, Danville, Virginia, 22-23 May, 20 Laps, 45 miles/72.42km
Race 1
1 Jake Gagne (Yamaha); **2** Mathew Scholtz (Yamaha); **3** Josh Herrin (Yamaha); **4** Loris Baz (Ducati); **5** Cameron Petersen (Suzuki); **6** Hector Barbera (BMW); **7** Kyle Wyman (Ducati); **8** Jason Uribe (Suzuki); **9** Jake Lewis (Suzuki); 10. Travis Wyman (BMW).

Race 2
1 Jake Gagne (Yamaha); **2** Loris Baz (Ducati); **3** Mathew Scholtz (Yamaha); **4** Josh Herrin (Yamaha); **5** Bobby Fong (Suzuki); **6** Kyle Wyman (Ducati); **7** Cameron Petersen (Suzuki); **8** Hector Barbera (BMW); **9** Corey Alexander (Kawasaki); **10** Andrew Lee (Kawasaki).

ROAD AMERICA, Elkhart Lake, Wisconsin, 12-13 June, 12 Laps, 48 miles/77.2485km
Race 1
1 Jake Gagne (Yamaha); **2** Loris Baz (Ducati); **3** Cameron Petersen (Suzuki); **4** Bobby Fong (Suzuki); **5** Josh Herrin (Yamaha); **6** Mathew Scholtz (Yamaha); **7** Kyle Wyman (Ducati); **8** Hector Barbera (BMW); **9** David Anthony (Suzuki); **10** Geoff May (Honda).

Race 2
1 Jake Gagne (Yamaha); **2** Cameron Petersen (Suzuki); **3** Mathew Scholtz (Yamaha); **4** Bobby Fong (Suzuki); **5** Josh Herrin (Yamaha); **6** Hector Barbera (BMW); **7** David Anthony (Suzuki); **8** Jake Lewis (Suzuki); **9** Travis Wyman (BMW); **10** Corey Alexander (Kawasaki).

THE RIDGE MOTORSPORTS PARK, Shelton, Washington, 26-27 June, 17 laps, 42.5 miles/ 68.4km
Race 1
1 Jake Gagne (Yamaha); **2** Josh Herrin (Yamaha); **3** Cameron Petersen (Suzuki); **4** Loris Baz (Ducati); **5** Mathew Scholtz (Yamaha); **6** Corey Alexander (Kawasaki); **7** David Anthony (Suzuki); **8** Bobby Fong (Suzuki); **9** Jake Lewis (Suzuki); **10** Jayson Uribe (Suzuki).

Race 2
1 Jake Gagne (Yamaha); **2** Josh Herrin (Yamaha); **3** Loris Baz (Ducati); **4** Mathew Scholtz (Yamaha); **5** Hector Barbera (BMW); **6** Cameron Petersen (Suzuki); **7** Bobby Fong (Suzuki); **8** David Anthony (Suzuki); **9** Corey Alexander (Kawasaki); **10** Jayson Uribe (Suzuki).

LAGUNA SECA RACEWAY, Monterey, California, 10-11 July, 17 Laps, 38.05 miles/61.24km
Race 1
1 Jake Gagne (Yamaha); **2** Loris Baz (Ducati); **3** Cameron Petersen (Suzuki); **4** Mathew Scholtz (Yamaha); **5** Josh Herrin (Yamaha); **6** Hector Barbera (BMW); **7** Bobby Fong (Suzuki); **8** Toni Elias (Ducati); **9** Jake Lewis (Suzuki); **10** Travis Wyman (BMW).

Race 2
1 Jake Gagne (Yamaha); **2** Loris Baz (Ducati); **3** Mathew Scholtz (Yamaha); **4** Cameron Petersen (Suzuki); **5** Josh Herrin (Yamaha); **6** Bobby Fong (Suzuki); **7** Toni Elias (Ducati); **8** Hector Barbera (BMW); **9** Travis Wyman (BMW); **10** Bryce Prince (Yamaha).

BRAINERD INTERNATIONAL RACEWAY, Brainerd, Minnesota, 31 July-1 August, 15 Laps, 37.5 miles/ 60.35km
Race 1
1 Jake Gagne (Yamaha); **2** Bobby Fong (Suzuki); **3** Mathew Scholtz (Yamaha); **4** Cameron Petersen (Suzuki); **5** Hector Barbera (BMW); **6** JD Beach (Yamaha); **7** Jake Lewis (Suzuki); **8** Andrew Lee (Kawasaki); **9** David Anthony (Suzuki); **10** Bradley Ward (Suzuki).

Race 2 (18 laps, 45 miles/72.42km)
1 Jake Gagne (Yamaha); **2** Mathew Scholtz (Yamaha); **3** Loris Baz (Ducati); **4** Bobby Fong (Suzuki); **5** Cameron Petersen (Suzuki); **6** JD Beach (Yamaha); **7** Hector Barbera (BMW); **8** Jake Lewis (Suzuki); **9** Bradley Ward (Suzuki); **10** Corey Alexander (Kawasaki).

PITTSBURGH INTL RACE COMPLEX, Wampum, Pennsylvania, 14-15 August, 17 laps, 47.26 miles/ 76.06km
Race 1
1 Jake Gagne (Yamaha); **2** Toni Elias (Yamaha); **3** Mathew Scholtz (Yamaha); **4** Cameron Petersen (Suzuki); **5** Hector Barbera (BMW); **6** Kyle Wyman (Ducati); **7** Bradley Ward (Suzuki); **8** Bobby Fong (Suzuki); **9** Jake Lewis (Suzuki); **10** Hayden Gillim (Suzuki).

Race 2
1 Jake Gagne (Yamaha); **2** Mathew Scholtz (Yamaha); **3** Bobby Fong (Suzuki); **4** Toni Elias (Yamaha); **5** Loris Baz (Ducati); **6** Cameron Petersen (Suzuki); **7** Hector Barbera (BMW); **8** Kyle Wyman (Ducati); **9** Jake Lewis (Suzuki); **10** Hayden Gillim (Suzuki).

NEW JERSEY MOTORSPORTS PARK, Millville, New Jersey, 11-12 September, 20 Laps, 45 miles/ 72.42km
Race 1
1 Jake Gagne (Yamaha); **2** Mathew Scholtz (Yamaha); **3** Toni Elias (Yamaha); **4** Bobby Fong (Suzuki); **5** Loris Baz (Ducati); **6** Josh Herrin (Yamaha); **7** Cameron Petersen (Suzuki); **8** Kyle Wyman (Ducati); **9** Jake Lewis (Suzuki); **10** Bradley Ward (Suzuki).

Race 2
1 Jake Gagne (Yamaha); **2** Mathew Scholtz (Yamaha); **3** Josh Herrin (Yamaha); **4** Loris Baz (Ducati); **5** Cameron Petersen (Suzuki); **6** Hector Barbera (BMW); **7** Kyle Wyman (Ducati); **8** Jake Lewis (Suzuki); **9** Ashton Yates (Honda); **10** Michael Gilbert (Kawasaki).

Race 3
1 Jake Gagne (Yamaha); **2** Mathew Scholtz (Yamaha); **3** Josh Herrin (Yamaha); **4** Loris Baz (Ducati); **5** Cameron Petersen (Suzuki); **6** Toni Elias (Yamaha); **7** Hector Barbera (BMW); **8** Kyle Wyman (Ducati); **9** Bobby Fong (Suzuki); **10** Danilo Lewis (BMW).

BARBER MOTORSPORTS PARK, Birmingham, Alabama, 18-19 September, 17 Laps, 40.46 miles/ 65.11km
Race 1
1 Cameron Petersen (Suzuki); **2** Mathew Scholtz (Yamaha); **3** Loris Baz (Ducati); 4.Ashton Yates (Honda); **5** Jake Lewis (Suzuki); **6** Danny Eslick (Suzuki); **7** David Anthony (Suzuki); **8** Hector Barbera (BMW); **9** Josh Herrin (Yamaha); **10** Bobby Fong (Suzuki).

Race 2 (12 Laps, 28.56 miles/45.96km)
1 Mathew Scholtz (Yamaha); **2** Loris Baz (Ducati); **3** Jake Gagne (Yamaha); **4** Cameron Petersen (Suzuki); **5** Jake Lewis (Suzuki); **6** Ashton Yates (Honda); **7** Kyle Wyman (Ducati); **8** Bobby Fong (Suzuki); **9** Danny Eslick (Suzuki); **10** Hector Barbera (BMW).

Race 3 (15 Laps, 35.7 miles/57.45km)
1 Jake Gagne (Yamaha); **2** Mathew Scholtz (Yamaha); **3** Loris Baz (Ducati); **4** Ashton Yates (Honda); **5** Cameron Petersen (Suzuki); **6** Kyle Wyman (Ducati); **7** Corey Alexander (Kawasaki); **8** Bobby Fong (Suzuki); **9** Jake Lewis (Suzuki); **10** Josh Herrin (Yamaha).

2021 Honos MotoAmerica Superbike Championship points:

1	Jake Gagne	445
2	Mathew Scholtz	357
3	Cameron Petersen	264
4	Loris Baz	238
5	Bobby Fong	207
6	Josh Herrin	200

7 Hector Barbera, 157; **8** Jake Lewis, 131; **9** Kyle Wyman, 111; **10** Corey Alexander, 83.

Final Stock 1000 Championship Points:

1	Jake Lewis	232
2	Travis Wyman	175
3	Corey Alexander	173
4	Michael Gilbert	170
5	Ashton Yates	153
6	Andrew Lee	107

7 Geoff May, 78; **8** Danilo Lewis, 75; **9** Wyatt Farris, 64; **10** Maximiliano Gerardo, 57.

Final Supersport Championship Points:

1	Sean Dylan Kelly	410
2	Richie Escalante	315
3	Samuel Lochoff	233
4	Rocco Landers	182
5	Benjamin Smith	178
6	Stefano Mesa	175

7 Kevin Olmedo, 106; **8** Dominic Doyle, 97; **9** Carl Soltisz, 95; **10** Jaret Nassaney, 91.

Final Twins Championship Points:

1	Kaleb De Keyrel	234
2	Hayden Schultz	166
3	Jackson Blackmon	158
4	Teagg Hobbs	156
5	Anthony Mazziotto	130
6	Jody Barry	128

7 Chris Parrish, 118; **8** Toby Khamsouk, 89; **9** John Knowles, 76; **10** Trevor Standish, 70.

Sportbike Trackgear.com Junior Cup Championship Points:

1	Tyler Scott	390
2	Benjamin Gloddy	346
3	Gus Rodio	218
4	David Kohlstaedt	212
5	Cody Wyman	186
6	Blake Davis	135

7 Max VanDenBrouck, 133; **8** Kayla Yaakov, 117; **9** Maxwell Toth, 109; **10** Joseph LiMandri Jr, 99.

Endurance World Championship

24 HEURES MOTOS, Le Mans Bugatti Circuit, France, 12-13 June 2021.
FIM Endurance World Championship, Round 1.
855 laps of the 2.600-mile/4.185km circuit, 2223.4 miles/3578.2km
1 Yoshimura Sert Motul: 24h 0m 26.817s.
2 Webike SRC Kawasaki France Trickstar: 847 laps; **3** BMW Motorrad World Endurance Team: 842 laps; **4** National Motos: 830 laps; **5** BMRT 3D Maxxess Nevers: 828 laps; **6** No Limits Motor Team: 827 laps; **7** VRD Igol Experiences: 826 laps; **8** ERC Endurance Ducati: 819 laps; **9** F.C.C. TSR Honda France: 816 laps; **10** Pitlane Endurance - JP3: 812 laps; **11** Maco Racing Team: 812 laps; **12** Motobox Kremer Racing #65: 810 laps; **13** Players: 810 laps; **14** Team space moto: 808 laps; **15** Team LH Racing: 806 laps.
Fastest lap: Tati Team Beringer Racing, 1m 36.743s, 96.75mph/155.7km/h, on lap 273.
Championship points: 1 Yoshimura Sert Motul, 64; **2** Webike SRC Kawasaki France Trickstar, 48; **3** BMW Motorrad World Endurance Team, 44; **4** F.C.C. TSR Honda France, 36; **5** VRD Igol Experiences, 32; **6** ERC Endurance Ducati, 29.

12 HOURS OF ESTORIL, Estoril, Portugal, 17 July 2021.
FIM Endurance World Championship, Round 2.
417 laps of the 2.599-mile/4.182km circuit, 1083.6 miles/1743.9km
1 F.C.C. TSR Honda France: 12h 0m 32.811s.
2 Webike SRC Kawasaki France Trickstar: 416 laps; **3** BMW Motorrad World Endurance: 416 laps; **4** VRD Igol Experiences: 415 laps; **5** Moto Ain: 412 laps; **6** BMRT 3D Maxxess Nevers: 410 laps; **7** ERC Endurance Ducati: 410 laps; **8** Team Bolliger Switzerland #8: 409 laps; **9** National Motos: 407 laps; **10** YART - Yamaha Official Team EWC: 407 laps; **11** Wójcik Racing Team: 406 laps; **12** 3ART Best Of Bike: 405 laps; **13** Team 18 Sapeurs Pompiers: 402 laps; **14** Team 33 Louit April Moto: 401 laps; **15** Slider Endurance: 401 laps.
Fastest lap: Yoshimura Sert Motul, 1m 39.155s, 94.32mph/151.8km/h, on lap 342.
Championship points: 1 Webike SRC Kawasaki France Trickstar, 87; **2** F.C.C. TSR Honda France, 82; **3** BMW Motorrad World Endurance Team, 80; **4** Yoshimura Sert Motul, 76; **5** VRD Igol Experiences, 61; **6** ERC Endurance Ducati, 49.

BOL D'OR, Paul Ricard Circuit, France, 18-19 September 2021.
FIM Endurance World Championship, Round 3.
704 laps of the 3.525-mile/5.673km circuit, 2481.6 miles/3993.8km
1 Yoshimura Sert Motul: 24h 1m 11.531s.
2 Moto Ain: 685 laps; **3** BMRT 3D Maxxess Nevers: 681 laps; **4** RAC41-Chromeburner: 679 laps; **5** No Limits Motor Team: 676 laps; **6** VRD Igol Experiences: 674 laps; **7** OG Motorsport by Sarazin: 672 laps; **8** Falcon Racing: 671 laps; **9** Motobox Kremer Racing #65: 664 laps; **10** Maco Racing Team: 656 laps; **11** ADSS 97: 649 laps; **12** Team space moto: 645 laps; **13** Pitlane Endurance 86: 645 laps; **14** TRT27 Bazar 2 La Becane: 641 laps; **15** Metiss JBB: 633 laps.
Fastest lap: Tati Team Beringer Racing, 1m 53.707s, 111.60mph/179.6km/h, on lap 125.
Championship points: 1 Yoshimura Sert Motul, 141; **2** VRD Igol Experiences, 105; **3** F.C.C. TSR Honda France, 89; **4** Webike SRC Kawasaki France Trickstar, 87; **5** BMW Motorrad World Endurance Team, 84; **6** Moto Ain, 72.

6 HOURS OF MOST, Most, Czech Republic, 9 October 2021.
FIM Endurance World Championship, Round 4.
213 laps of the 2.617-mile/4.212km circuit, 557.5 miles/897.2km
1 BMW Motorrad World Endurance Team: 6h 1m 31.007s.
2 YART - Yamaha Official Team EWC: +0.070s; **3** Yoshimura Sert Motul: 212 laps; **4** Webike SRC Kawasaki France Trickstar: 212 laps; **5** Wójcik Racing Team: 211 laps; **6** ERC Endurance Ducati: 211 laps; **7** No Limits Motor Team: 208 laps; **8** TME Racing: 207 laps; **9** Energie Endurance 91: 203 laps; **10** Team Aviobike: 203 laps; **11** JMA Motos Action Bike: 202 laps; **12** Falcon Racing: 202 laps; **13** Motobox Kremer Racing #65: 202 laps; **14** Tati Team Beringer Racing: 201 laps; **15** Team Bolliger Switzerland #8: 201 laps.
Fastest lap: YART - Yamaha Official Team EWC, 1m 33.875s, 100.35mph/161.5km/h, on lap 212.

FIM Teams' Endurance World Championship:

1	Yoshimura Sert Motul	175.5
2	BMW Motorrad World Endurance Team	133
3	Webike SRC Kawasaki France Trickstar	115.5
4	VRD Igol Experiences	105
5	F.C.C. TSR Honda France	91
6	YART - Yamaha Official Team EWC	88

7 Moto Ain, 84; **8** Motobox Kremer Racing #65, 83.5; **9** ERC Endurance Ducati, 78; **10** Maco Racing Team, 69; **11** Wójcik Racing Team, 57.5; **12** Tati Team Beringer Racing, 44; **13** Team LRP Poland, 42.5; **14** Team Bolliger Switzerland #8, 35.5; **15** EMRT Endurance Monaco Racing Team, 22.

MotoE World Cup

Round 1, JEREZ, Spain, 2 May 2021, 2.748-mile/4.423km circuit
(7 laps, 19.238 miles/ 30.961 km)
1 Alessandro Zaccone, ITA (Energica); 14m 33.776s, 90.5mph/145.7km/h.
2 Dominique Aegerter, SWI (Energica); **3** Jordi Torres, SPA (Energica); **4** Mattia Casadei, ITA (Energica); **5** Miquel Pons, SPA (Energica); **6** Matteo Ferrari, ITA (Energica); **7** Hikari Okubo, JPN (Energica); **8** Andrea Mantovani, ITA (Energica); **9** Maria Herrera, SPA (Energica); **10** Yonny Hernandez, COL (Energica); **11** Jasper Iwema, NED (Energica); **12** Andre Pires, POR (Energica); **13** Eric Granado, BRA (Energica); **14** Kevin Zannoni, ITA (Energica); **15** N/A.
Fastest lap: Eric Granado, 1m 47.473s, 92.0mph/ 148.1km/h.
Championship points: 1 Zaccone, 25; **2** Aegerter, 20; **3** Torres, 16; **4** Casadei, 13; **5** Pons, 11; **6** Ferrari, 10.

Round 2, LE MANS, France, 16 May 2021, 2.600-mile/4.185km circuit
(7 laps, 18.203 miles/ 29.295 km)
1 Eric Granado, BRA (Energica); 12m 23.012s, 88.2mph/141.9km/h.
2 Mattia Casadei, ITA (Energica); **3** Alessandro Zaccone, ITA (Energica); **4** Dominique Aegerter, SWI (Energica); **5** Jordi Torres, SPA (Energica); **6** Yonny Hernandez, COL (Energica); **7** Lukas Tulovic, GER (Energica); **8** Matteo Ferrari, ITA (Energica); **9** Corentin Perolari, FRA (Energica); **10** Maria Herrera, SPA (Energica); **11** Kevin Zannoni, ITA (Energica); **12** Andre Pires, POR (Energica); **13** Xavi Cardelus, AND (Energica); **14** Jasper Iwema, NED (Energica); **15** Fermín Aldeguer, SPA (Energica).
Fastest lap: Matteo Ferrari, 1m 43.951s, 90.0mph/144.9km/h.
Championship points: 1 Zaccone, 41; **2** Casadei, 33; **3** Aegerter, 33; **4** Granado, 28; **5** Torres, 27; **6** Ferrari, 18.

Round 3, BARCELONA, Spain, 6 June 2021, 2.894-mile/4.657km circuit
(6 laps, 17.362 miles/ 27.942 km)
1 Miquel Pons, SPA (Energica); 11m 15.075s, 92.6mph/149.0km/h.

2 Dominique Aegerter, SWI (Energica); **3** Jordi Torres, SPA (Energica); **4** Alessandro Zaccone, ITA (Energica); **5** Yonny Hernandez, COL (Energica); **6** Fermín Aldeguer, SPA (Energica); **7** Matteo Ferrari, ITA (Energica); **8** Lukas Tulovic, GER (Energica); **9** Hikari Okubo, JPN (Energica); **10** Corentin Perolari, FRA (Energica); **11** Maria Herrera, SPA (Energica); **12** Kevin Zannoni, ITA (Energica); **13** Andre Pires, POR (Energica); **14** Andrea Mantovani, ITA (Energica); **15** N/A.
Fastest lap: Eric Granado, 1m 50.769s, 94.0mph/151.3km/h.
Championship points: 1 Zaccone, 54; **2** Aegerter, 53; **3** Torres, 43; **4** Pons, 36; **5** Casadei, 33; **6** Granado, 28.

Round 4, ASSEN, The Netherlands, 27 June 2021, 2.822-mile/4.542km circuit
(7 laps, 19.756 miles/ 31.794km)
1 Eric Granado, BRA (Energica); 12m 10.143s, 97.4mph/156.7km/h.
2 Jordi Torres, SPA (Energica); **3** Alessandro Zaccone, ITA (Energica); **4** Matteo Ferrari, ITA (Energica); **5** Lukas Tulovic, GER (Energica); **6** Mattia Casadei, ITA (Energica); **7** Fermín Aldeguer, SPA (Energica); **8** Hikari Okubo, JPN (Energica); **9** Yonny Hernandez, COL (Energica); **10** Miquel Pons, SPA (Energica); **11** Corentin Perolari, FRA (Energica); **12** Xavi Cardelus, AND (Energica); **13** Kevin Zannoni, ITA (Energica); **14** Andrea Mantovani, ITA (Energica); **15** Maria Herrera, SPA (Energica).
Fastest lap: Eric Granado, 1m 43.184s, 98.4mph/158.4km/h.
Championship points: 1 Zaccone, 70; **2** Torres, 63; **3** Granado, 53; **4** Aegerter, 53; **5** Casadei, 43; **6** Pons, 42.

Round 5, RED BULL RING, Austria, 15 August 2021, 2.683-mile/4.318km circuit
(5 laps, 13.415 miles/ 21.590km)
1 Lukas Tulovic, GER (Energica); 8m 6.619s, 99.2mph/159.7km/h.
2 Eric Granado, BRA (Energica); **3** Dominique Aegerter, SWI (Energica); **4** Fermín Aldeguer, SPA (Energica); **5** Hikari Okubo, JPN (Energica); **6** Alessandro Zaccone, ITA (Energica); **7** Jordi Torres, SPA (Energica); **8** Matteo Ferrari, ITA (Energica); **9** Kevin Zannoni, ITA (Energica); **10** Yonny Hernandez, COL (Energica); **11** Andrea Mantovani, ITA (Energica); **12** Miquel Pons, SPA (Energica); **13** Corentin Perolari, FRA (Energica); **14** Jasper Iwema, NED (Energica); **15** Stefano Valtulini, ITA (Energica).
Fastest lap: Eric Granado, 1m 35.161s, 101.5mph/163.3km/h.
Championship points: 1 Zaccone, 80; **2** Granado, 73; **3** Torres, 72; **4** Aegerter, 69; **5** Tulovic, 53; **6** Ferrari, 48.

Round 6, MISANO, San Marino, 18-19 September 2021, 2.630-mile/4.200km circuit
Race 1 (7 laps, 18.381 miles/ 29.582km)
1 Jordi Torres, SPA (Energica); 12m 11.858s, 90.4mph/145.5km/h.
2 Dominique Aegerter, SWI (Energica); **3** Mattia Casadei, ITA (Energica); **4** Matteo Ferrari, ITA (Energica); **5** Miquel Pons, SPA (Energica); **6** Kevin Zannoni, ITA (Energica); **7** Fermín Aldeguer, SPA (Energica); **8** Lukas Tulovic, GER (Energica); **9** Yonny Hernandez, COL (Energica); **10** Xavi Cardelus, AND (Energica); **11** Andrea Mantovani, ITA (Energica); **12** Corentin Perolari, FRA (Energica); **13** Maria Herrera, SPA (Energica); **14** Jasper Iwema, NED (Energica); **15** Andre Pires, POR (Energica).
Fastest lap: Kevin Zannoni, 1m 43.081s, 91.7mph/147.5km/h.

Race 2 (8 laps, 21.007 miles/33.808km)
1 Matteo Ferrari, ITA (Energica); 13m 54.140s, 90.7mph/145.9km/h.
2 Mattia Casadei, ITA (Energica); **3** Miquel Pons, SPA (Energica); **4** Kevin Zannoni, ITA (Energica); **5** Eric Granado, BRA (Energica); **6** Hikari Okubo, JPN (Energica); **7** Fermín Aldeguer, SPA (Energica); **8** Xavi Cardelus, AND (Energica); **9** Andrea Mantovani, ITA (Energica); **10** Corentin Perolari, FRA (Energica); **11** Maria Herrera, SPA (Energica); **12** Dominique Aegerter, SWI (Energica); **13** Jordi Torres, SPA (Energica); **14** Jasper Iwema, NED (Energica); **15** Lukas Tulovic, GER (Energica).
Fastest lap: Dominique Aegerter, 1m 42.660s, 92.0mph/148.1km/h.

Final MotoE World Cup points:

1	Jordi Torres,	100
2	Dominique Aegerter,	93
3	Matteo Ferrari,	86
4	Eric Granado,	84
5	Alessandro Zaccone,	80
6	Mattia Casadei,	79

7 Miquel Pons, 73; **8** Lukas Tulovic, 62; **9** Fermín Aldeguer, 51; **10** Yonny Hernandez, 47; **11** Hikari Okubo, 45; **12** Kevin Zannoni, 44; **13** Corentin Perolari, 31; **14** Andrea Mantovani, 29; **15** Maria Herrera, 27.

British Championships

OULTON PARK, 26-27 June 2021, 2.692-mile/4.332km circuit.
Bennetts British Superbike Championship, Round 1
Race 1 (14 laps 37.688 miles/60.653km)
1 Jason O'Halloran (Yamaha), 22m 15.857s, 101.56mph/163.44km/h.
2 Christian Iddon (Ducati); **3** Tommy Bridewell (Ducati); **4** Peter Hickman (BMW); **5** Tarran Mackenzie (Yamaha); **6** Glenn Irwin (Honda); **7** Kyle Ryde (BMW); **8** Lee Jackson (Kawasaki); **9** Ryan Vickers (Kawasaki); **10** Josh Brookes (Ducati); **11** Gino Rea (Suzuki); **12** Danny Buchan (BMW); **13** Rory Skinner (Kawasaki); **14** Dean Harrison (Kawasaki); **15** Bjorn Estment (Suzuki).
Fastest lap: O'Halloran, 1m 34.715s, 102.32mph/164.66km/h.

Race 2 (18 laps 48.456 miles/77.982km)
1 Jason O'Halloran (Yamaha), 28m 38.583s, 101.50mph/163.35km/h.
2 Christian Iddon (Ducati); **3** Peter Hickman (BMW); **4** Danny Buchan (BMW); **5** Bradley Ray (BMW); **6** Tarran Mackenzie (Yamaha); **7** Josh Brookes (Ducati); **8** Lee Jackson (Kawasaki); **9** Glenn Irwin (Honda); **10** Kyle Ryde (BMW); **11** Ryan Vickers (Kawasaki); **12** Rory Skinner (Kawasaki); **13** Gino Rea (Suzuki); **14** Danny Kent (Suzuki); **15** Andrew Irwin (BMW).
Fastest lap: Hickman, 1m 34.803s, 102.22mph/164.51km/h.

Race 3 (18 laps 48.456 miles/77.982km)
1 Jason O'Halloran (Yamaha), 28m 37.270s, 101.58mph/163.48km/h.
2 Christian Iddon (Ducati); **3** Tommy Bridewell (Ducati); **4** Tarran Mackenzie (Yamaha); **5** Peter Hickman (BMW); **6** Josh Brookes (Ducati); **7** Lee Jackson (Kawasaki); **8** Danny Buchan (BMW); **9** Ryan Vickers (Kawasaki); **10** Glenn Irwin (Honda); **11** Gino Rea (Suzuki); **12** Kyle Ryde (BMW); **13** Rory Skinner (Kawasaki); **14** Luke Hopkins (Honda); **15** Dan Linfoot (Honda).
Fastest lap: Mackenzie, 1m 34.563s, 102.48mph/164.93km/h.
Championship points: 1 Jason O'Halloran, 75; **2** Christian Iddon, 60; **3** Peter Hickman, 40; **4** Tarran Mackenzie, 34; **5** Tommy Bridewell, 32; **6** Danny Buchan, 25.

Quattro Group British Supersport Championship, Round 1
Race 1 (12 laps 32.304 miles/51.988km)
1 Jack Kennedy (Kawasaki), 19m 53.604s, 97.43mph/156.8km/h.
2 Bradley Perie (Yamaha); **3** Ben Currie (Kawasaki); **4** Lee Johnston (Yamaha); **5** Mason Law (Spirit); **6** Charlie Nesbitt (Kalex); **7** Korie McGreevy (Yamaha); **8** Harry Truelove (Yamaha); **9** Jack Scott (Harris); **10** Jamie Perrin (Spirit); **11** Rhys Irwin (Yamaha); **12** Cameron Fraser (Chassis Factory); **13** Eunan McGlinchey (Kawasaki); **14** Sam Munro (Yamaha); **15** Kyle Smith (Triumph).
Fastest lap: Kennedy, 1m 38.490s, 98.39mph/158.35km/h.

Race 2 (15 laps 40.380 miles/64.985km)
1 Bradley Perie (Yamaha), 24m 49.602s, 97.58mph/157.04km/h.
2 Jack Kennedy (Kawasaki); **3** Lee Johnston (Yamaha); **4** Ben Currie (Kawasaki); **5** Charlie Nesbitt (Kalex); **6** Harry Truelove (Yamaha); **7** Mason Law (Spirit); **8** Jack Scott (Harris); **9** Brandon Paasch (Triumph); **10** Kyle Smith (Triumph); **11** Sam Munro (Yamaha); **12** Cameron Horsman (Chassis Factory); **13** Jake Archer (Kalex); **14** Dan Jones (Spirit); **15** Eunan McGlinchey (Kawasaki).
Fastest lap: Currie, 1m 38.585s, 98.30mph/158.20km/h.
Championship points: 1 Jack Kennedy, 45; **2** Bradley Perie, 45; **3** Ben Currie, 29; **4** Lee Johnston, 29; **5** Harry Truelove, 21; **6** Eunan McGlinchey, 15.

Honda British Talent Cup, Round 1
Race 1 (10 laps 26.920 miles/43.324km)
1 Casey O'Gorman (Honda), 18m 25.835s, 87.63mph/141.03km/h.
2 Evan Belford (Honda); **3** Carter Brown (Honda); **4** Ryan Hitchcock (Honda); **5** Johnny Garness (Honda); **6** Ollie Walker (Honda); **7** Harrison Crosby (Honda); **8** Jamie Lyons (Honda); **9** Mason Johnson (Honda); **10** Rossi Dobson (Honda); **11** Rhys Stephenson (Honda); **12** Troy Jeffrey (Honda); **13** Harrison Mackay (Honda); **14** Lucas Brown (Honda); **15** Luca Hopkins (Honda).
Fastest lap: O'Gorman, 1m 49.164s, 88.77mph/142.87km/h.

Race 2 (10 laps 26.920 miles/43.324km)
1 Casey O'Gorman (Honda), 18m 21.067s, 88.01mph/141.64km/h.
2 Carter Brown (Honda); **3** Evan Belford (Honda); **4** Johnny Garness (Honda); **5** Cormac Buchanan (Honda); **6** Harrison Crosby (Honda); **7** Jamie Lyons (Honda); **8** Sullivan Mounsey (Honda); **9** Troy Jeffrey (Honda); **10** Bailey Stuart-Campbell (Honda); **11** James Cook (Honda); **12** Mason Johnson (Honda); **13** Harrison Mackay (Honda); **14** Luca Hopkins (Honda); **15** Rhys Stephenson (Honda).
Fastest lap: Brown, 1m 47.979s, 89.75mph/144.44km/h.
Championship points: 1 Casey O'Gorman, 50; **2** Evan Belford, 36; **3** Carter Brown, 36; **4** Johnny Garness, 24; **5** Harrison Crosby, 19; **6** Jamie Lyons, 17.

KNOCKHILL, 10-11 July 2021, 1.268-mile/2.042km circuit.
Bennetts British Superbike Championship, Round 2
Race 1 (20 laps 25.338 miles/40.778km)
1 Christian Iddon (Ducati), 15m 59.903s, 95.03mph/152.94km/h.
2 Jason O'Halloran (Yamaha); **3** Danny Buchan (BMW); **4** Bradley Ray (BMW); **5** Rory Skinner (Kawasaki); **6** Tarran Mackenzie (Yamaha); **7** Ryan Vickers (Kawasaki); **8** Tommy Bridewell (Ducati); **9** Lee Jackson (Kawasaki); **10** Josh Brookes (Ducati); **11** Kyle Ryde (BMW); **12** Glenn Irwin (Honda); **13** Gino Rea (Suzuki); **14** Dan Linfoot (Honda); **15** Andrew Irwin (BMW).
Fastest lap: Buchan, 47.534s, 95.95mph/154.42km/h.

Race 2 (30 laps 38.007 miles/61.166km)
1 Danny Buchan (BMW), 24m 1.494s, 94.92mph/152.76km/h.
2 Rory Skinner (Kawasaki); **3** Tarran Mackenzie (Yamaha); **4** Christian Iddon (Ducati); **5** Tommy Bridewell (Ducati); **6** Ryan Vickers (Kawasaki); **7** Peter Hickman (BMW); **8** Lee Jackson (Kawasaki); **9** Bradley Ray (BMW); **10** Gino Rea (Suzuki); **11** Glenn Irwin (Honda); **12** Josh Brookes (Ducati); **13** Dan Linfoot (Honda); **14** Andrew Irwin (BMW); **15** Kyle Ryde (BMW).
Fastest lap: Skinner, 47.628s, 95.76mph/154.11km/h.

Race 3 (24 laps 30.406 miles/48.934km)
1 Danny Buchan (BMW), 19m 14.271s, 94.83mph/152.61km/h.
2 Rory Skinner (Kawasaki); **3** Tarran Mackenzie (Yamaha); **4** Christian Iddon (Ducati); **5** Bradley Ray (BMW); **6** Jason O'Halloran (Yamaha); **7** Tommy Bridewell (Ducati); **8** Peter Hickman (BMW); **9** Ryan Vickers (Kawasaki); **10** Lee Jackson (Kawasaki); **11** Gino Rea (Suzuki); **12** Dan Linfoot (Honda); **13** Josh Brookes (Ducati); **14** Danny Kent (Suzuki); **15** Andrew Irwin (BMW).
Fastest lap: Ray, 47.584s, 95.85mph/154.26km/h.
Championship points: 1 Christian Iddon, 111; **2** Jason O'Halloran, 105; **3** Danny Buchan, 91; **4** Tarran Mackenzie, 76; **5** Rory Skinner, 61; **6** Tommy Bridewell, 60.

Quattro Group British Supersport Championship, Round 2
Race 1 (20 laps 25.338 miles/40.778km)
1 Bradley Perie (Yamaha), 16m 40.025s, 91.21mph/146.79km/h.
2 Jack Kennedy (Kawasaki); **3** Lee Johnston (Yamaha); **4** Ben Currie (Kawasaki); **5** Charlie Nesbitt (Kalex); **6** Jamie Perrin (Spirit); **7** Jack Scott (Harris); **8** Eunan McGlinchey (Kawasaki); **9** Brandon Paasch (Triumph); **10** Harry Truelove (Yamaha); **11** Dan Jones (Spirit); **12** Scott Swann (Yamaha); **13** Rhys Irwin (Yamaha); **14** Jamie Van Sikkelerus (Yamaha); **15** Mason Law (Spirit).
Fastest lap: Johnston, 49.404s, 92.32mph/148.57km/h.

Race 2 (26 laps 32.939 miles/53.01 km)
1 Bradley Perie (Yamaha), 21m 43.189s, 90.99mph/146.43km/h.
2 Lee Johnston (Yamaha); **3** Jack Kennedy (Kawasaki); **4** Charlie Nesbitt (Kalex); **5** Jack Scott (Harris); **6** Kyle Smith (Triumph); **7** Eunan McGlinchey (Kawasaki); **8** Jamie Perrin (Spirit); **9** Harry Truelove (Yamaha); **10** Brandon Paasch (Triumph); **11** Ben Currie (Kawasaki); **12** Mason Law (Spirit); **13** Rhys Irwin (Yamaha); **14** Cameron Horsman (Chassis Factory); **15** Jamie Sikkelerus (Yamaha).
Fastest lap: Perie, 49.655s, 91.85mph/147.82km/h.
Championship points: 1 Bradley Perie, 95; **2** Jack Kennedy, 81; **3** Lee Johnston, 65; **4** Ben Currie, 50; **5** Harry Truelove, 40; **6** Eunan McGlinchey, 37.

Honda British Talent Cup, Round 2
Race 1 (20 laps 25.338 miles/40.778km)
1 Evan Belford (Honda), 18m 25.672s, 82.50mph/132.77km/h.
2 Johnny Garness (Honda); **3** Harrison Crosby (Honda); **4** Cormac Buchanan (Honda); **5** James Cook (Honda); **6** Troy Jeffrey (Honda); **7** Bailey Stuart-Campbell (Honda); **8** Ollie Walker (Honda); **9** Kiyano Veijer (Honda); **10** Jamie Lyons (Honda); **11** Rossi Banham (Honda); **12** Lucas Hill (Honda); **13** Luca Hopkins (Honda); **14** Rossi Dobson (Honda); **15** Mason Johnson (Honda).
Fastest lap: Belford, 54.635s, 83.48mph/134.35km/h.

Race 2 (24 laps 30.406 miles/48.934km)
1 Evan Belford (Honda), 22m 4.371s, 82.65mph/133.01km/h.
2 Johnny Garness (Honda); **3** Cormac Buchanan (Honda); **4** James Cook (Honda); **5** Carter Brown (Honda); **6** Ollie Walker (Honda); **7** Bailey Stuart-Campbell (Honda); **8** Kiyano Veijer (Honda); **9** Ryan Hitchcock (Honda); **10** Jamie Lyons (Honda); **11** Mason Johnson (Honda); **12** Luca Hopkins (Honda); **13** Rossi Dobson (Honda); **14** Harley McCabe (Honda); **15** Lucas Brown (Honda).
Fastest lap: Belford, 54.665s, 83.43mph/134.27km/h.
Championship points: 1 Evan Belford, 86; **2** Johnny Garness, 64; **3** Casey O'Gorman, 50; **4** Carter Brown, 47; **5** Cormac Buchanan, 40; **6** Harrison Crosby, 35.

BRANDS HATCH GP, 24-25 July 2021, 2.433-mile/3.916km circuit.
Bennetts British Superbike Championship, Round 3
Race 1 (12 laps 29.196 miles/46.986km)
1 Tarran Mackenzie (Yamaha), 17m 15.766s, 101.48mph/163.32km/h.
2 Tommy Bridewell (Ducati); **3** Christian Iddon (Ducati); **4** Danny Buchan (BMW); **5** Jason O'Halloran (Yamaha); **6** Lee Jackson (Kawasaki); **7** Bradley Ray (BMW); **8** Rory Skinner (Kawasaki); **9** Josh Brookes (Ducati); **10** Danny Kent (Suzuki); **11** Glenn Irwin (Honda); **12** Andrew Irwin (BMW); **13** Xavi Forés (BMW); **14** Dan Linfoot (Honda); **15** Ryan Vickers (Kawasaki).
Fastest lap: Buchan, 1m 25.607s, 102.32mph/164.67km/h.

Race 2 (20 laps 48.660 miles/78.311km)
1 Jason O'Halloran (Yamaha), 28m 48.394s, 101.36mph/163.12km/h.
2 Tommy Bridewell (Ducati); **3** Tarran Mackenzie (Yamaha); **4** Danny Buchan (BMW); **5** Christian Iddon (Ducati); **6** Rory Skinner (Kawasaki); **7** Lee Jackson (Kawasaki); **8** Glenn Irwin (Honda); **9** Peter Hickman (BMW); **10** Gino Rea (Suzuki); **11** Xavi Forés (BMW); **12** Bradley Ray (BMW); **13** Kyle Ryde (BMW); **14** Andrew Irwin (BMW); **15** Ryan Vickers (Kawasaki).
Fastest lap: O'Halloran, 1m 25.670s, 102.25mph/164.55km/h.

Race 3 (7 laps 17.031 miles/27.409km)
1 Christian Iddon (Ducati), 10m 11.517s, 100.27mph/161.37km/h.
2 Tarran Mackenzie (Yamaha); **3** Jason O'Halloran (Yamaha); **4** Danny Buchan (BMW); **5** Josh Brookes (Ducati); **6** Glenn Irwin (Honda); **7** Peter Hickman (BMW); **8** Lee Jackson (Kawasaki); **9** Rory Skinner (Kawasaki); **10** Danny Kent (Suzuki); **11** Xavi Forés (BMW); **12** Dan Linfoot (Honda); **13** Bradley Ray (BMW); **14** Dean Harrison (Kawasaki); **15** Ryan Vickers (Kawasaki).
Fastest lap: O'Halloran, 1m 25.755s, 102.14mph/164.39km/h.
Championship points: 1 Christian Iddon, 163; **2** Jason O'Halloran, 157; **3** Tarran Mackenzie, 137; **4** Danny Buchan, 130; **5** Tommy Bridewell, 100; **6** Rory Skinner, 86.

Quattro Group British Supersport Championship, Round 3
Race 1 (10 laps 24.330 miles/39.155km)
1 Kyle Smith (Triumph), 16m 17.108s, 89.65mph/144.28km/h.
2 Jack Kennedy (Kawasaki); **3** Eunan McGlinchey (Kawasaki); **4** Mason Law (Spirit); **5** Charlie Nesbitt (Kalex); **6** Ben Currie (Kawasaki); **7** Cameron Horsman (Chassis Factory); **8** Rhys Irwin (Yamaha); **9** Jack Scott (Harris); **10** Dan Jones (Spirit); **11** Lee Johnston (Yamaha); **12** Korie McGreevy (Yamaha); **13** Jake Archer (Kalex); **14** James Hind (Yamaha); **15** Conor Wheeler (Harris).
Fastest lap: Nesbitt, 1m 36.024s, 91.22mph/146.81km/h.

Race 2 (8 laps 19.464 miles/31.324km)
1 Jack Kennedy (Kawasaki), 13m 20.785s, 87.51mph/140.83km/h.
2 Kyle Smith (Triumph); **3** Eunan McGlinchey (Kawasaki); **4** Ben Currie (Kawasaki); **5** Lee Johnston (Yamaha); **6** Charlie Nesbitt (Kalex); **7** Korie McGreevy (Yamaha); **8** Mason Law (Spirit); **9** Brandon Paasch (Triumph); **10** Bradley Perie (Yamaha); **11** Rhys Irwin (Yamaha); **12** Dan Jones (Spirit); **13** Cameron Horsman (Chassis Factory); **14** Jamie Van Sikkelerus (Yamaha); **15** Sam Munro (Yamaha).
Fastest lap: Kennedy, 1m 38.351s, 89.06mph/143.33km/h.
Championship points: 1 Jack Kennedy, 126; **2** Bradley Perie, 103; **3** Lee Johnston, 86; **4** Ben Currie, 76; **5** Kyle Smith, 73; **6** Eunan McGlinchey, 69.

Honda British Talent Cup, Round 3
Race 1 (14 laps 34.062 miles/54.817km)
1 Carter Brown (Honda), 23m 15.193s, 87.90mph/141.46km/h.
2 Evan Belford (Honda); **3** James Cook (Honda); **4** Ryan Hitchcock (Honda); **5** Johnny Garness (Honda); **6** Cormac Buchanan (Honda); **7** Sullivan Mounsey (Honda); **8** Jamie Lyons (Honda); **9** Ollie Walker (Honda); **10** Harrison Crosby (Honda); **11** Rossi Banham (Honda); **12** Bailey Stuart-Campbell (Honda); **13** Kiyano Veijer (Honda); **14** Rossi Dobson (Honda); **15** Rhys Stephenson (Honda).
Fastest lap: Cook, 1m 38.52s, 88.91mph/143.09km/h.

Race 2 (12 laps 29.196 miles/46.986km)
1 Evan Belford (Honda), 19m 53.016s, 88.10mph/141.78km/h.
2 James Cook (Honda); **3** Johnny Garness (Honda); **4** Carter Brown (Honda); **5** Ryan Hitchcock (Honda); **6** Ollie Walker (Honda); **7** Jamie Lyons (Honda); **8** Rossi Banham (Honda); **9** Sullivan Mounsey (Honda); **10** Bailey Stuart-Campbell (Honda); **11** Harrison Crosby (Honda); **12** Kiyano Veijer (Honda); **13** Lucas Brown (Honda); **14** Rhys Stephenson (Honda); **15** Luca Hopkins (Honda).
Fastest lap: Belford, 1m 38.227s, 89.17mph/143.52km/h.
Championship points: 1 Evan Belford, 131; **2** Johnny Garness, 91; **3** Carter Brown, 85; **4** James Cook, 65; **5** Cormac Buchanan, 50; **6** Casey O'Gorman, 50.

THRUXTON, 31 July-1 August 2021, 2.356-mile/ 3.792km circuit.
Bennetts British Superbike Championship, Round 4
Race 1 (13 laps 30.628 miles/49.291km)
1 Jason O'Halloran (Yamaha), 17m 1.710s, 107.91mph/173.66km/h.
2 Christian Iddon (Ducati); **3** Peter Hickman (BMW); **4** Ryan Vickers (Kawasaki); **5** Lee Jackson (Kawasaki); **6** Danny Kent (Suzuki); **7** Bradley Ray (BMW); **8** Gino Rea (Suzuki); **9** Tarran Mackenzie (Yamaha); **10** Tommy Bridewell (Ducati); **11** Andrew Irwin (BMW); **12** Xavi Forés (BMW); **13** Danny Buchan (BMW); **14** Rory Skinner (Kawasaki); **15** Storm Stacey (Kawasaki).
Fastest lap: Jackson, 1m 15.334s, 112.58mph/ 181.19km/h.

Race 2 (20 laps 47.120 miles/75.832km)
1 Jason O'Halloran (Yamaha), 25m 26.379s, 111.13mph/178.85km/h.
2 Tarran Mackenzie (Yamaha); **3** Glenn Irwin (Honda); **4** Bradley Ray (BMW); **5** Peter Hickman (BMW); **6** Kyle Ryde (BMW); **7** Danny Buchan (BMW); **8** Andrew Irwin (BMW); **9** Danny Kent (Suzuki); **10** Gino Rea (Suzuki); **11** Rory Skinner (Kawasaki); **12** Tommy Bridewell (Ducati); **13** Xavi Forés (BMW); **14** Dan Linfoot (Honda); **15** Takumi Takahashi (Honda).
Fastest lap: O'Halloran, 1m 15.159s, 112.84mph/ 181.61km/h.

Race 3 (20 laps 47.120 miles/75.832km)
1 Jason O'Halloran (Yamaha), 27m 16.033s, 103.68mph/166.86km/h.
2 Danny Buchan (BMW); **3** Danny Kent (Suzuki); **4** Ryan Vickers (Kawasaki); **5** Andrew Irwin (BMW); **6** Glenn Irwin (Honda); **7** Tarran Mackenzie (Yamaha); **8** Peter Hickman (BMW); **9** Christian Iddon (Ducati); **10** Bradley Ray (BMW); **11** Gino Rea (Suzuki); **12** Lee Jackson (Kawasaki); **13** Dan Linfoot (Honda); **14** Josh Brookes (Ducati); **15** Storm Stacey (Kawasaki).
Fastest lap: Buchan, 1m 19.830s, 106.24mph/ 170.98km/h.
Championship points: 1 Jason O'Halloran, 232; **2** Christian Iddon, 190; **3** Tarran Mackenzie, 173; **4** Danny Buchan, 162; **5** Tommy Bridewell, 110; **6** Peter Hickman, 108.

Quattro Group British Supersport Championship, Round 4
Race 1 (12 laps 28.272 miles/45.499km)
1 Charlie Nesbitt (Kalex), 15m 41.086s, 108.15mph/ 174.05km/h.
2 Bradley Perie (Yamaha); **3** Lee Johnston (Yamaha); **4** Jamie Perrin (Spirit); **5** Kyle Smith (Triumph); **6** Korie McGreevy (Yamaha); **7** Ben Currie (Kawasaki); **8** Mason Law (Spirit); **9** Eunan McGlinchey (Kawasaki); **10** James Hind (Yamaha); **11** Cameron Horsman (Chassis Factory); **12** Brandon Paasch (Triumph); **13** Harry Truelove (Yamaha); **14** Jamie Van Sikkelerus (Yamaha); **15** Cameron Fraser (Chassis Factory).
Fastest lap: Nesbitt, 1m 17.553s, 109.36mph/ 176.00km/h.

Race 2 (15 laps 35.340 miles/56.874km)
1 Kyle Smith (Triumph), 20m 40.253s, 102.57mph/ 165.07km/h.
2 Ben Currie (Kawasaki); **3** Charlie Nesbitt (Kalex); **4** Jack Kennedy (Kawasaki); **5** Brandon Paasch (Triumph); **6** Eunan McGlinchey (Kawasaki); **7** Mason Law (Spirit); **8** Jack Scott (Harris); **9** Bradley Perie (Yamaha); **10** Rhys Irwin (Yamaha); **11** Jamie Perrin (Spirit); **12** Cameron Horsman (Chassis Factory); **13** Harry Rowlings (ABM Evo); **14** Conor Wheeler (Harris); **15** Jamie Van Sikkelerus (Yamaha).
Fastest lap: Smith, 1m 21.793s, 103.69mph/ 166.88km/h.
Championship points: 1 Jack Kennedy, 142; **2** Bradley Perie, 138; **3** Kyle Smith, 114; **4** Ben Currie, 107; **5** Lee Johnston, 106; **6** Eunan McGlinchey, 90.

Honda British Talent Cup, Round 4
(14 laps 32.984 miles/53.083km)
1 Carter Brown (Honda), 19m 53.192s, 99.51mph/ 160.15km/h.
2 Jamie Lyons (Honda); **3** Cormac Buchanan (Honda); **4** Ollie Walker (Honda); **5** James Cook (Honda); **6** Evan Belford (Honda); **7** Troy Jeffrey (Honda); **8** Kiyano Veijer (Honda); **9** Sullivan Mounsey (Honda); **10** Lucas Brown (Honda); **11** Rhys Stephenson (Honda); **12** Rossi Banham (Honda); **13** Harley McCabe (Honda); **14** Luca Hopkins (Honda); **15** Harrison Mackay (Honda).
Fastest lap: Brown, 1m 23.664s, 101.37mph/ 163.15km/h.
Championship points: 1 Evan Belford, 141; **2** Carter Brown, 110; **3** Johnny Garness, 91; **4** James Cook, 76; **5** Cormac Buchanan, 66; **6** Jamie Lyons, 66.

DONINGTON PARK NATIONAL, 15-16 August 2021, 1.979-mile/3.185km circuit.
Bennetts British Superbike Championship, Round 5
Race 1 (20 laps 39.580 miles/63.698km)
1 Jason O'Halloran (Yamaha), 22m 48.014s, 104.06mph/167.47km/h.
2 Glenn Irwin (Honda); **3** Tarran Mackenzie (Yamaha); **4** Christian Iddon (Ducati); **5** Tommy Bridewell (Ducati); **6** Ryan Vickers (Kawasaki); **7** Andrew Irwin (BMW); **8** Lee Jackson (Kawasaki); **9** Peter Hickman (BMW); **10** Bradley Ray (BMW); **11** Kyle Ryde (BMW); **12** Dan Linfoot (Honda); **13** Danny Buchan (BMW); **14** Xavi Forés (BMW); **15** Gino Rea (Suzuki).
Fastest lap: O'Halloran, 1m 6.137s, 107.72mph/ 173.36km/h.

Race 2 (28 laps 55.412 miles/89.177km)
1 Tarran Mackenzie (Yamaha), 31m 46.011s, 104.59mph/168.32km/h.
2 Bradley Ray (BMW); **3** Jason O'Halloran (Yamaha); **4** Peter Hickman (BMW); **5** Tommy Bridewell (Ducati); **6** Kyle Ryde (BMW); **7** Ryan Vickers (Kawasaki); **8** Xavi Forés (BMW); **9** Andrew Irwin (BMW); **10** Josh Brookes (Ducati); **11** Dan Linfoot (Honda); **12** Storm Stacey (Kawasaki); **13** Dean Harrison (Kawasaki); **14** Rory Skinner (Kawasaki); **15** Ryo Mizuno (Honda).
Fastest lap: Hickman, 1m 6.081s, 107.81mph/ 173.51km/h.

Race 3 (20 laps 39.580 miles/63.698km)
1 Tommy Bridewell (Ducati), 23m 5.903s, 102.71mph/165.3km/h.
2 Glenn Irwin (Honda); **3** Andrew Irwin (BMW); **4** Josh Brookes (Ducati); **5** Joe Francis (BMW); **6** Storm Stacey (Kawasaki); **7** Tarran Mackenzie (Yamaha); **8** Dean Harrison (Kawasaki); **9** Dan Linfoot (Honda); **10** Gino Rea (Suzuki); **11** Rory Skinner (Kawasaki); **12** Jason O'Halloran (Yamaha); **13** Ryo Mizuno (Honda); **14** Peter Hickman (BMW); **15** Lee Jackson (Kawasaki).
Fastest lap: Iddon, 1m 8.008s, 104.76mph/ 168.59km/h.
Championship points: 1 Jason O'Halloran, 277; **2** Tarran Mackenzie, 223; **3** Christian Iddon, 203; **4** Danny Buchan, 165; **5** Tommy Bridewell, 157; **6** Peter Hickman, 130.

Quattro Group British Supersport Championship, Round 5
Race 1 (20 laps 39.580 miles/63.698km)
1 Charlie Nesbitt (Kalex), 23m 6.040s, 102.70mph/ 165.28km/h.
2 Bradley Perie (Yamaha); **3** Jack Kennedy (Kawasaki); **4** Brandon Paasch (Triumph); **5** Ben Currie (Kawasaki); **6** Lee Johnston (Yamaha); **7** Korie McGreevy (Yamaha); **8** Harry Truelove (Yamaha); **9** Kyle Smith (Triumph); **10** Mason Law (Spirit); **11** Jamie Van Sikkelerus (Yamaha); **12** Eunan McGlinchey (Kawasaki); **13** Cameron Horsman (Chassis Factory); **14** Jake Archer (Kalex); **15** James Hind (Yamaha).
Fastest lap: Johnston, 1m 8.472s, 104.05mph/ 167.45km/h.

Race 2 (24 laps 47.496 miles/76.437km)
1 Harry Truelove (Yamaha), 28m 15.540s, 100.76mph/162.16km/h.
2 Ben Currie (Kawasaki); **3** Charlie Nesbitt (Kalex); **4** Brandon Paasch (Triumph); **5** Mason Law (Spirit); **6** Eunan McGlinchey (Kawasaki); **7** Jack Scott (Harris); **8** Cameron Horsman (Chassis Factory); **9** Dan Jones (Spirit); **10** Kyle Smith (Triumph); **11** Jamie Van Sikkelerus (Yamaha); **12** Sam Munro (Yamaha); **13** James Hind (Yamaha); **14** Scott Swann (Yamaha); **15** Jake Archer (Kalex).
Fastest lap: Nesbitt, 1m 8.367s, 104.21mph/ 167.71km/h.
Championship points: 1 Bradley Perie, 163; **2** Jack Kennedy, 162; **3** Ben Currie, 140; **4** Kyle Smith, 133; **5** Lee Johnston, 117; **6** Eunan McGlinchey, 109.

Honda British Talent Cup, Round 5
Race 1 (20 laps 39.580 miles/63.698km)
1 Johnny Garness (Honda), 25m 21.813s, 93.54mph/150.54km/h.
2 Casey O'Gorman (Honda); **3** James Cook (Honda); **4** Ollie Walker (Honda); **5** Carter Brown (Honda); **6** Evan Belford (Honda); **7** Kiyano Veijer (Honda); **8** Jamie Lyons (Honda); **9** Sullivan Mounsey (Honda); **10** Harrison Crosby (Honda); **11** Rossi Banham (Honda); **12** Troy Jeffrey (Honda); **13** Mason Johnson (Honda); **14** Rossi Dobson (Honda); **15** Josh Bannister (Honda).
Fastest lap: Brown, 1m 15.265s, 94.66mph/ 152.34km/h.

Race 2 (20 laps 39.580 miles/63.698km)
1 Casey O'Gorman (Honda), 25m 27.589s, 93.19mph/149.97km/h.
2 Johnny Garness (Honda); **3** James Cook (Honda); **4** Jamie Lyons (Honda); **5** Bailey Stuart-Campbell (Honda); **6** Ollie Walker (Honda); **7** Carter Brown (Honda); **8** Kiyano Veijer (Honda); **9** Evan Belford (Honda); **10** Troy Jeffrey (Honda); **11** Harrison Crosby (Honda); **12** Sullivan Mounsey (Honda); **13** Rossi Banham (Honda); **14** Rhys Stephenson (Honda); **15** Corey Tinker (Honda).
Fastest lap: Stuart-Campbell, 1m 15.185s, 94.76mph/152.50km/h.

Race 3 (22 laps 43.538 miles/70.068km)
1 Casey O'Gorman (Honda), 28m 0.468s, 93.19mph/149.97km/h.
2 Kiyano Veijer (Honda); **3** Johnny Garness (Honda); **4** Bailey Stuart-Campbell (Honda); **5** Ollie Walker (Honda); **6** Jamie Lyons (Honda); **7** Sullivan Mounsey (Honda); **8** Carter Brown (Honda); **9** Evan Belford (Honda); **10** Corey Tinker (Honda); **11** Harrison Crosby (Honda); **12** Rhys Stephenson (Honda); **13** Lucas Brown (Honda); **14** Troy Jeffrey (Honda); **15** Mason Johnson (Honda).
Fastest lap: Mounsey, 1m 15.379s, 94.51mph/ 152.11km/h.
Championship points: 1 Evan Belford, 165; **2** Johnny Garness, 152; **3** Carter Brown, 138; **4** James Cook, 108; **5** Jamie Lyons, 97 **6** Casey O'Gorman, 95;

CADWELL PARK, 21-22 August 2021, 2.180-mile/ 3.508km circuit.
Bennetts British Superbike Championship, Round 6
Race 1 (14 laps 30.520 miles/49.117km)
1 Peter Hickman (BMW), 20m 21.062s, 89.98mph/ 144.81km/h.
2 Jason O'Halloran (Yamaha); **3** Tommy Bridewell (Ducati); **4** Glenn Irwin (Honda); **5** Christian Iddon (Ducati); **6** Lee Jackson (Kawasaki); **7** Andrew Irwin (BMW); **8** Ryan Vickers (Kawasaki); **9** Rory Skinner (Kawasaki ; **10** Josh Brookes (Ducati); **11** Storm Stacey (Kawasaki); **12** Dan Linfoot (Honda); **13** Bradley Ray (BMW); **14** Xavi Forés (BMW); **15** Tim Neave (Suzuki).
Fastest lap: Hickman, 1m 26.350s, 90.88mph/ 146.26km/h.

Race 2 (18 laps 39.240 miles/63.151km)
1 Peter Hickman (BMW), 26m 10.023s, 89.97mph/ 144.79km/h.
2 Jason O'Halloran (Yamaha); **3** Tommy Bridewell (Ducati); **4** Lee Jackson (Kawasaki); **5** Josh Brookes (Ducati); **6** Glenn Irwin (Honda); **7** Andrew Irwin (BMW); **8** Bradley Ray (BMW); **9** Ryan Vickers (Kawasaki); **10** Storm Stacey (Kawasaki); **11** Tim Neave (Suzuki); **12** Xavi Forés (BMW); **13** Dan Linfoot (Honda); **14** Dean Harrison (Kawasaki); **15** Joe Sheldon-Shaw (Kawasaki).
Fastest lap: Bridewell, 1m 26.588s, 90.63mph/ 145.86km/h.

Race 3 (18 laps 39.240 miles/63.151km)
1 Jason O'Halloran (Yamaha), 26m 7.054s, 90.14mph/145.07km/h.
2 Peter Hickman (BMW); **3** Tommy Bridewell (Ducati); **4** Lee Jackson (Kawasaki); **5** Josh Brookes (Ducati); **6** Glenn Irwin (Honda); **7** Christian Iddon (Ducati); **8** Bradley Ray (BMW); **9** Andrew Irwin (BMW); **10** Ryan Vickers (Kawasaki); **11** Gino Rea (Suzuki); **12** Rory Skinner (Kawasaki); **13** Xavi Forés (BMW); **14** Dan Linfoot (Honda); **15** Tim Neave (Suzuki).
Fastest lap: Jackson, 1m 26.373s, 90.86mph/ 146.22km/h.
Championship points: 1 Jason O'Halloran, 342; **2** Christian Iddon, 223; **3** Tarran Mackenzie, 223; **4** Tommy Bridewell, 205; **5** Peter Hickman, 200; **6** Danny Buchan, 165.

Quattro Group British Supersport Championship, Round 6
Race 1 (12 laps 26.160 miles/42.1km)
1 Harry Truelove (Yamaha), 18m 3.759s, 86.89mph/ 139.84km/h.
2 Jack Kennedy (Kawasaki); **3** Ben Currie (Kawasaki); **4** Jack Scott (Harris); **5** Brandon Paasch (Triumph); **6** Lee Johnston (Yamaha); **7** Charlie Nesbitt (Kalex); **8** Eunan McGlinchey (Kawasaki); **9** Cameron Horsman (Chassis Factory); **10** James Hind (Yamaha); **11** Kyle Smith (Triumph); **12** Cameron Fraser (Chassis Factory); **13** Jamie Van Sikkelerus (Yamaha); **14** Scott Swann (Yamaha); **15** Phil Wakefield (Yamaha).
Fastest lap: Kennedy, 1m 29.329s, 87.85mph/ 141.39km/h.

Race 2 (16 laps 34.880 miles/56.134km)
1 Harry Truelove (Yamaha), 24m 6.660s, 86.79mph/ 139.67km/h.
2 Ben Currie (Kawasaki); **3** Charlie Nesbitt (Kalex); **4** Bradley Perie (Yamaha); **5** Lee Johnston (Yamaha); **6** Kyle Smith (Triumph); **7** Dan Jones (Spirit); **8** Cameron Horsman (Chassis Factory); **9** James Hind (Yamaha); **10** Jamie Van Sikkelerus (Yamaha); **11** Sam Munro (Yamaha); **12** Cameron Fraser (Chassis Factory); **13** Conor Wheeler (Harris); **14** Jake Archer (Kalex); **15** Scott Swann (Yamaha).
Fastest lap: Kennedy, 1m 29.634s, 87.55mph/ 140.90km/h.
Championship points: 1 Jack Kennedy, 182; **2** Bradley Perie, 179; **3** Ben Currie, 176; **4** Kyle Smith, 152; **5** Lee Johnston, 141; **6** Harry Truelove, 138.

SILVERSTONE GP, 27-29 August 2021, 3.666-mile/5.900km circuit.
Honda British Talent Cup, Round 6
Race 1 (11 laps 40.326 miles/64.898km)
1 Jamie Lyons (Honda), 26m 2.159s, 92.62mph/ 149.06km/h.
2 Casey O'Gorman (Honda); **3** Carter Brown (Honda); **4** Sullivan Mounsey (Honda); **5** Bailey Stuart-Campbell (Honda); **6** Corey Tinker (Honda); **7** Cormac Buchanan (Honda); **8** Rhys Stephenson (Honda); **9** Evan Belford (Honda); **10** Ollie Walker (Honda); **11** Rossi Banham (Honda); **12** Harley McCabe (Honda); **13** Lucas Brown (Honda); **14** Kiyano Veijer (Honda); **15** Julian Correa (Honda).
Fastest lap: N/A.

Race 2 (11 laps 40.326 miles/64.898km)
1 Casey O'Gorman (Honda), 26m 8.933s, 92.52mph/148.9km/h.
2 Jamie Lyons (Honda); **3** Evan Belford (Honda); **4** Harrison Crosby (Honda); **5** Carter Brown (Honda); **6** Sullivan Mounsey (Honda); **7** Corey Tinker (Honda); **8** Rhys Stephenson (Honda); **9** Lucas Brown (Honda); **10** Harley McCabe (Honda); **11** Kiyano Veijer (Honda); **12** Julian Correa (Honda); **13** Luca Hopkins (Honda); **14** Johnny Garness (Honda); **15** Alexander Rowan (Honda).
Fastest lap: N/A.
Championship points: 1 Evan Belford, 188; **2** Casey O'Gorman, 165; **3** Carter Brown, 165; **4** Johnny Garness, 154; **5** Jamie Lyons, 142; **6** James Cook, 108.

SNETTERTON, 3-5 September 2021, 2.969-mile/ 4.778km circuit.
Bennetts British Superbike Championship, Round 7
Race 1 (12 laps 35.628 miles/57.338km)
1 Tarran Mackenzie (Yamaha), 21m 41.072s, 98.57mph/158.63km/h.
2 Tommy Bridewell (Ducati); **3** Jason O'Halloran (Yamaha); **4** Josh Brookes (Ducati); **5** Lee Jackson (Kawasaki); **6** Ryan Vickers (Kawasaki); **7** Peter Hickman (BMW) **8** Rory Skinner (Kawasaki); **9** Bradley Ray (BMW); **10** Danny Buchan (BMW); **11** Dan Linfoot (Honda); **12** Xavi Forés (BMW); **13** Storm Stacey (Kawasaki); **14** Takumi Takahashi (Honda); **15** Joe Francis (BMW).
Fastest lap: Bridewell 1m 47.245s, 99.66mph/ 160.38km/h.

Race 2 (16 laps 47.504 miles/76.450km)
1 Jason O'Halloran (Yamaha), 28m 58.211s, 98.38mph/158.33km/h.
2 Tarran Mackenzie (Yamaha); **3** Tommy Bridewell (Ducati); **4** Josh Brookes (Ducati); **5** Gino Rea (Suzuki); **6** Lee Jackson (Kawasaki); **7** Ryan Vickers (Kawasaki); **8** Andrew Irwin (BMW); **9** Rory Skinner (Kawasaki); **10** Peter Hickman (BMW); **11** Christian Iddon (Ducati); **12** Bradley Ray (BMW); **13** Danny Buchan (BMW); **14** Glenn Irwin (Honda); **15** Kyle Ryde (BMW).
Fastest lap: Mackenzie, 1m 47.642s, 99.29mph/ 159.79km/h.

Race 3 (5 laps 14.845 miles/23.891km)
1 Tarran Mackenzie (Yamaha), 9m 9.255s, 97.29mph/156.57km/h.
2 Tommy Bridewell (Ducati); **3** Jason O'Halloran (Yamaha); **4** Gino Rea (Suzuki); **5** Christian Iddon (Ducati); **6** Josh Brookes (Ducati); **7** Peter Hickman (BMW); **8** Dan Linfoot (Honda); **9** Bradley Ray (BMW); **10** Kyle Ryde (BMW); **11** Glenn Irwin (Honda); **12** Andrew Irwin (BMW); **13** Ryan Vickers (Kawasaki); **14** Luke Stapleford (Suzuki); **15** Rory Skinner (Kawasaki).
Fastest lap: Brookes, 1m 48.148s, 98.82mph/ 159.04km/h.
Championship points: 1 Jason O'Halloran, 399; **2** Tarran Mackenzie, 293; **3** Tommy Bridewell, 261; **4** Christian Iddon, 239; **5** Peter Hickman, 224; **6** Danny Buchan, 174.

Quattro Group British Supersport Championship, Round 7
Race 1 (10 laps 29.690 miles/47.781km)
1 Lee Johnston (Yamaha), 18m 52.091s, 94.41mph/ 151.94km/h.
2 Ben Currie (Kawasaki); **3** Jack Kennedy (Kawasaki); **4** Kyle Smith (Triumph); **5** Bradley Perie (Yamaha); **6** Charlie Nesbitt (Kalex); **7** Rhys Irwin (Yamaha); **8** Jack Scott (Harris); **9** Mason Law (Spirit); **10** Jamie Perrin (Spirit); **11** Harry Truelove (Yamaha); **12** Sam Munro (Yamaha); **13** Eunan McGlinchey (Kawasaki); **14** Cameron Horsman (Chassis Factory); **15** Dan Jones (Spirit).
Fastest lap: Paasch, 1m 51.626s, 95.74mph/ 154.09km/h.

Race 2 (15 laps 44.535 miles/71.672 km)
1 Jack Kennedy (Kawasaki), 28m 14.085s, 94.63mph/152.29km/h.
2 Ben Currie (Kawasaki); **3** Kyle Smith (Triumph); **4** Charlie Nesbitt (Kalex); **5** Cameron Horsman (Chassis Factory); **6** Mason Law (Spirit); **7** Lee Johnston (Yamaha); **8** Eunan McGlinchey (Kawasaki); **9** Sam Munro (Yamaha); **10** Conor Wheeler (Harris); **11** Cameron Fraser (Chassis Factory); **12** Harry Rowlings (ABM Evo); **13** Harvey Claridge (Chassis Factory); **14** Jake Archer (Kalex); **15** Phil Wakefield (Yamaha).
Fastest lap: Currie, 1m 51.809s, 95.59mph/ 153.84km/h.
Championship points: 1 Jack Kennedy, 223; **2** Ben Currie, 216; **3** Bradley Perie, 190; **4** Kyle Smith, 181; **5** Lee Johnston, 179; **6** Harry Truelove, 147.

Honda British Talent Cup, Round 7
Race 1 (12 laps 35.628 miles/57.338km)
1 Casey O'Gorman (Honda), 25m 8.280s, 85.03mph/136.84km/h.
2 Carter Brown (Honda); **3** Evan Belford (Honda); **4** Harrison Crosby (Honda); **5** Rhys Stephenson (Honda); **6** James Cook (Honda); **7** Jamie Lyons (Honda); **8** Kiyano Veijer (Honda); **9** Corey Tinker (Honda); **10** Harrison Dessoy (Honda); **11** Mason Johnson (Honda); **12** JJ Cunningham (Honda); **13** Julian Correa (Honda); **14** Josh Bannister (Honda); **15** Alexander Rowan (Honda).
Fastest lap: Garness 2m 4.449s, 85.88mph/ 138.21km/h.

326 OTHER CHAMPIONSHIP RESULTS WORLDWIDE

Race 2 (12 laps 35.628 miles/57.338km)
1 Johnny Garness (Honda), 25m 13.593s, 84.73mph/136.36km/h.
2 Casey O'Gorman (Honda); **3** Evan Belford (Honda); **4** Carter Brown (Honda); **5** James Cook (Honda); **6** Harrison Crosby (Honda); **7** Cormac Buchanan (Honda); **8** Ollie Walker (Honda); **9** Jamie Lyons (Honda); **10** Corey Tinker (Honda); **11** Harley McCabe (Honda); **12** Harrison Dessoy (Honda); **13** Alexander Rowan (Honda); **14** Luca Hopkins (Honda); **15** Kiyano Veijer (Honda).
Fastest lap: Crosby, 2m 4.788s, 85.64mph/137.84km/h.
Championship points: 1 Evan Belford, 220; **2** Casey O'Gorman, 210; **3** Carter Brown, 198; **4** Johnny Garness, 179; **5** Jamie Lyons, 158; **6** James Cook, 129.

SILVERSTONE NATIONAL, 17-19 September 2021, 1.640-mile/2.640km circuit.
Bennetts British Superbike Championship, Round 8
Race 1 (23 laps 37.743 miles/60.741km)
1 Glenn Irwin (Honda), 21m 2.781s, 107.56mph/173.1km/h.
2 Christian Iddon (Ducati); **3** Tommy Bridewell (Ducati); **4** Josh Brookes (Ducati); **5** Bradley Ray (BMW); **6** Gino Rea (Suzuki); **7** Rory Skinner (Kawasaki); **8** Kyle Ryde (BMW); **9** Xavi Forés (BMW); **10** Luke Stapleford (Suzuki); **11** Andrew Irwin (BMW); **12** Ryo Mizuno (Honda); **13** Dan Linfoot (Honda); **14** Bjorn Estment (Suzuki); **15** Storm Stacey (Kawasaki).
Fastest lap: Rea, 53.503s, 110.38mph/177.63km/h.

Race 2 (30 laps 49.230 miles/79.228km)
1 Tarran Mackenzie (Yamaha), 26m 56.075s, 109.62mph/176.42km/h.
2 Jason O'Halloran (Yamaha); **3** Josh Brookes (Ducati); **4** Bradley Ray (BMW); **5** Tommy Bridewell (Ducati); **6** Gino Rea (Suzuki); **7** Christian Iddon (Ducati); **8** Ryan Vickers (Kawasaki); **9** Rory Skinner (Kawasaki); **10** Peter Hickman (BMW); **11** Lee Jackson (Kawasaki); **12** Danny Buchan (BMW); **13** Glenn Irwin (Honda); **14** Luke Stapleford (Suzuki); **15** Kyle Ryde (BMW).
Fastest lap: Mackenzie, 53.379s, 110.63mph/178.05km/h.

Race 3 (15 laps 24.615 miles/39.614km)
1 Jason O'Halloran (Yamaha), 13m 28.557s, 109.55mph/176.3km/h.
2 Tarran Mackenzie (Yamaha); **3** Josh Brookes (Ducati); **4** Danny Buchan (BMW); **5** Tommy Bridewell (Ducati); **6** Christian Iddon (Ducati); **7** Bradley Ray (BMW); **8** Lee Jackson (Kawasaki); **9** Glenn Irwin (Honda); **10** Ryan Vickers (Kawasaki); **11** Andrew Irwin (BMW); **12** Peter Hickman (BMW); **13** Dan Linfoot (Honda); **14** Xavi Forés (BMW); **15** Ryo Mizuno (Honda).
Fastest lap: Mackenzie, 53.503s, 110.38mph/177.63km/h.
Championship points (Start of Showdown): 1 Jason O'Halloran, 1071; **2** Tarran Mackenzie, 1041; **3** Christian Iddon, 1026; **4** Tommy Bridewell, 1024; **5** Peter Hickman, 1015; **6** Danny Buchan, 1014; **7** Glenn Irwin, 1012; **8** Josh Brookes, 1002.

Quattro Group British Supersport Championship, Round 8
Race 1 (18 laps 29.538 miles/47.537km)
1 Lee Johnston (Yamaha), 16m 56.916s, 104.53mph/168.22km/h.
2 Charlie Nesbitt (Kalex); **3** Bradley Perie (Yamaha); **4** Rhys Irwin (Yamaha); **5** Ben Currie (Kawasaki); **6** Mason Law (Spirit); **7** Dan Jones (Spirit); **8** Cameron Horsman (Chassis Factory); **9** Scott Swann (Yamaha); **10** Eunan McGlinchey (Kawasaki); **11** Jamie Van Sikkelerus (Yamaha); **12** Sam Munro (Yamaha); **13** Cameron Fraser (Chassis Factory); **14** James Hind (Yamaha); **15** Harvey Claridge (Chassis Factory).
Fastest lap: Johnston, 55.889s, 105.66mph/170.05km/h.

Race 2 (25 laps 41.025 miles/66.023km)
1 Charlie Nesbitt (Kalex), 23m 30.807s, 104.65mph/168.42km/h.
2 Mason Law (Spirit); **3** Bradley Perie (Yamaha); **4** Lee Johnston (Yamaha); **5** Dan Jones (Spirit); **6** Rhys Irwin (Yamaha); **7** Jack Kennedy (Kawasaki); **8** Cameron Horsman (Chassis Factory); **9** Ben Currie (Kawasaki); **10** Harry Truelove (Yamaha); **11** Jamie Van Sikkelerus (Yamaha); **12** Eunan McGlinchey (Kawasaki); **13** Scott Swann (Yamaha); **14** Jake Archer (Kalex); **15** James Hind (Yamaha).
Fastest lap: Nesbitt, 55.852s, 105.73mph/170.16km/h.
Championship points: 1 Ben Currie, 240; **2** Jack Kennedy, 236; **3** Bradley Perie, 235; **4** Lee Johnston, 224; **5** Kyle Smith, 181; **6** Harry Truelove, 157.

Honda British Talent Cup, Round 8
Race 1 (22 laps 36.102 miles/58.101km)
1 Ollie Walker (Honda), 23m 6.725s, 96.69mph/155.61km/h.
2 Sullivan Mounsey (Honda); **3** Harrison Crosby (Honda); **4** Jamie Lyons (Honda); **5** Carter Brown (Honda); **6** Troy Jeffrey (Honda); **7** Harley McCabe (Honda); **8** Kiyano Veijer (Honda); **9** Josh Bannister (Honda); **10** Harrison Dessoy (Honda); **11** Lucas Brown (Honda); **12** Julian Correa (Honda); **13** Rossi Banham (Honda); **14** Luca Hopkins (Honda); **15** Rhys Stephenson (Honda).
Fastest lap: Walker, 1m 2.240s, 94.88mph/152.70km/h.

Race 2 (22 laps 36.102 miles/58.101km)
1 Carter Brown (Honda), 22m 54.449s, 94.52mph/152.12km/h.
2 Jamie Lyons (Honda); **3** Johnny Garness (Honda); **4** Casey O'Gorman (Honda); **5** Sullivan Mounsey (Honda); **6** Harrison Crosby (Honda); **7** Rhys Stephenson (Honda); **8** Evan Belford (Honda); **9** Ollie Walker (Honda); **10** James Cook (Honda); **11** Harley McCabe (Honda); **12** Kiyano Veijer (Honda); **13** Julian Correa (Honda); **14** Lucas Brown (Honda); **15** Luca Hopkins (Honda).
Fastest lap: Belford, 1m 1.689s, 95.73mph/154.06km/h.
Championship points: 1 Carter Brown, 234; **2** Evan Belford, 228; **3** Casey O'Gorman, 223; **4** Johnny Garness, 195; **5** Jamie Lyons, 191; **6** Ollie Walker, 138.

OULTON PARK, 24-26 September 2021, 2.692-mile/4.332km circuit.
Bennetts British Superbike Championship, Round 9
Race 1 (14 laps 37.688 miles/60.653km)
1 Tarran Mackenzie (Yamaha), 22m 19.960s, 101.25mph/162.95km/h.
2 Josh Brookes (Ducati); **3** Christian Iddon (Ducati); **4** Lee Jackson (Kawasaki); **5** Peter Hickman (BMW); **6** Tommy Bridewell (Ducati); **7** Danny Buchan (BMW); **8** Glenn Irwin (Honda); **9** Bradley Ray (BMW); **10** Storm Stacey (Kawasaki); **11** Rory Skinner (Kawasaki); **12** Dan Linfoot (Honda); **13** Kyle Ryde (BMW); **14** Dean Harrison (Kawasaki); **15** Bjorn Estment (Suzuki).
Fastest lap: O'Halloran, 1m 34.777s, 102.25mph/164.56km/h.

Race 2 (18 laps 48.456 miles/77.982km)
1 Tommy Bridewell (Ducati), 28m 39.981s, 101.42mph/163.22km/h.
2 Jason O'Halloran (Yamaha); **3** Tarran Mackenzie (Yamaha); **4** Christian Iddon (Ducati); **5** Peter Hickman (BMW); **6** Lee Jackson (Kawasaki); **7** Bradley Ray (BMW); **8** Danny Buchan (BMW); **9** Andrew Irwin (BMW); **10** Gino Rea (Suzuki); **11** Rory Skinner (Kawasaki); **12** Dean Harrison (Kawasaki); **13** Ryan Vickers (Kawasaki); **14** Michael Dunlop (Suzuki); **15** Josh Owens (Kawasaki).
Fastest lap: Bridewell, 1m 34.670s, 102.36mph/164.74km/h.

Race 3 (18 laps 48.456 miles/77.982km)
1 Tommy Bridewell (Ducati), 28m 31.689s, 101.91mph/164.01km/h.
2 Josh Brookes (Ducati); **3** Bradley Ray (BMW); **4** Peter Hickman (BMW); **5** Tarran Mackenzie (Yamaha); **6** Danny Buchan (BMW); **7** Glenn Irwin (Honda); **8** Andrew Irwin (BMW); **9** Gino Rea (Suzuki); **10** Rory Skinner (Kawasaki); **11** Christian Iddon (Ducati); **12** Ryan Vickers (Kawasaki); **13** Dean Harrison (Kawasaki); **14** Storm Stacey (Kawasaki); **15** Kyle Ryde (BMW).
Fastest lap: Bridewell, 1m 34.031s, 103.06mph/165.86km/h.
Championship points: 1 Tarran Mackenzie, 1093; **2** Jason O'Halloran, 1091; **3** Tommy Bridewell, 1084; **4** Christian Iddon, 1060; **5** Peter Hickman, 1050; **6** Josh Brookes, 1042; **7** Danny Buchan, 1041; **8** Glenn Irwin, 1029.

Quattro Group British Supersport Championship, Round 9
Race 1 (12 laps 32.304 miles/51.988km)
1 Jack Kennedy (Kawasaki), 19m 50.817s, 97.66mph/157.17km/h.
2 Ben Currie (Kawasaki); **3** Harry Truelove (Yamaha); **4** Lee Johnston (Yamaha); **5** Bradley Perie (Yamaha); **6** Charlie Nesbitt (Kalex); **7** Dan Jones (Spirit); **8** Jamie Perrin (Spirit); **9** Mason Law (Spirit); **10** Jamie van Sikkelerus (Yamaha); **11** Rhys Irwin (Yamaha); **12** Scott Swann (Yamaha); **13** Brandon Paasch (Triumph); **14** Sam Munro (Yamaha); **15** Cameron Horsman (Chassis Factory).
Fastest lap: Currie, 1m 38.221s, 98.66mph/158.79km/h.

Race 2 (14 laps 37.688 miles/60.653km)
1 Jack Kennedy (Kawasaki), 24m 2.584s, 94.05mph/151.36km/h.
2 Harry Truelove (Yamaha); **3** Mason Law (Spirit); **4** Scott Swann (Yamaha); **5** Dan Jones (Spirit); **6** Jamie Perrin (Spirit); **7** Ben Currie (Kawasaki); **8** Lee Johnston (Yamaha); **9** Brandon Paasch (Triumph); **10** Jamie van Sikkelerus (Yamaha); **11** Cameron Horsman (Chassis Factory); **12** Danny Webb (Triumph); **13** Korie McGreevy (Yamaha); **14** Sam Munro (Yamaha); **15** Eunan McGlinchey (Kawasaki).
Fastest lap: Kennedy, 1m 38.379s, 98.50mph/158.53km/h.
Championship points: 1 Jack Kennedy, 286; **2** Ben Currie, 273; **3** Lee Johnston, 248; **4** Bradley Perie, 246; **5** Harry Truelove, 193; **6** Kyle Smith, 181.

DONINGTON PARK INTERNATIONAL, 1-3 October 2021, 2.822-mile/4.452km circuit.
Bennetts British Superbike Championship, Round 10
Race 1 (16 laps 39.792 miles/64.039km)
1 Gino Rea (Suzuki), 30m 10.868s, 79.04mph/127.2km/h.
2 Kyle Ryde (BMW); **3** Christian Iddon (Ducati); **4** Lee Jackson (Kawasaki); **5** Jason O'Halloran (Yamaha); **6** Joe Francis (EMW); **7** Tarran Mackenzie (Yamaha); **8** Ryan Vickers (Kawasaki); **9** Bradley Ray (BMW); **10** Rory Skinner (Kawasaki); **11** Bjorn Estment (Suzuki); **12** Andrew Irwin (BMW); **13** Takumi Takahashi (Honda); **14** Josh Owens (Kawasaki); **15** Brian McCormack (BMW).
Fastest lap: Rea, 1m 50.058s, 81.36mph/130.93km/h.

Race 2 (20 laps 49.740 miles/80.049km)
1 Tarran Mackenzie (Yamaha), 30m 12.526s, 98.73mph/158.89km/h.
2 Danny Buchan (BMW); **3** Christian Iddon (Ducati); **4** Gino Rea (Suzuki); **5** Lee Jackson (Kawasaki); **6** Kyle Ryde (BMW); **7** Tommy Bridewell (Ducati); **8** Andrew Irwin (BMW); **9** Jason O'Halloran (Yamaha); **10** Glenn Irwin (Honda); **11** Josh Brookes (Ducati); **12** Bradley Ray (BMW); **13** Naomichi Uramoto (Suzuki); **14** Ryo Mizuno (Honda); **15** Ryan Vickers (Kawasaki).
Fastest lap: Mackenzie, 1m 29.767s, 99.75mph/160.53km/h.

Race 3 (15 laps 37.305 miles/60.037km)
1 Gino Rea (Suzuki), 26m 54.981s, 83.08mph/133.7km/h.
2 Christian Iddon (Ducati); **3** Lee Jackson (Kawasaki); **4** Tommy Bridewell (Ducati); **5** Andrew Irwin (BMW); **6** Ryan Vickers (Kawasaki); **7** Peter Hickman (BMW); **8** Jason O'Halloran (Yamaha); **9** Joe Francis (BMW); **10** Glenn Irwin (Honda); **11** Storm Stacey (Kawasaki); **12** Rory Skinner (Kawasaki); **13** Naomichi Uramoto (Suzuki); **14** Bradley Ray (BMW); **15** Kyle Ryde (BMW).
Fastest lap: Rea, 1m 45.148s, 85.16mph/137.05km/h.
Championship points: 1 Tarran Mackenzie, 1127; **2** Jason O'Halloran, 1117; **3** Christian Iddon, 1112; **4** Tommy Bridewell, 1106; **5** Danny Buchan, 1061; **6** Peter Hickman, 1059; **7** Josh Brookes, 1047; **8** Glenn Irwin, 1041.

Quattro Group British Supersport Championship, Round 10
Race 1 (12 laps 29.844 miles/48.029km)
1 Lee Johnston (Yamaha), 23m 23.572s, 76.45mph/123.03km/h.
2 Mason Law (Spirit); **3** Scott Swann (Yamaha); **4** Charlie Nesbitt (Kalex); **5** Jack Kennedy (Kawasaki); **6** Bradley Perie (Yamaha); **7** Rhys Irwin (Yamaha); **8** Barry Burrell (Kramer); **9** Cameron Horsman (Chassis Factory); **10** Phil Wakefield (Yamaha); **11** Harry Truelove (Yamaha); **12** Brandon Paasch (Triumph); **13** Cameron Fraser (Chassis Factory); **14** Elliott Lodge (Yamaha); **15** Jake Archer (Kalex).
Fastest lap: Johnston, 1m 54.041s, 78.51mph/126.36km/h.

Race 2 (18 laps 44.766 miles/72.044km)
1 Jack Kennedy (Kawasaki), 28m 3.039s, 95.68mph/153.98km/h.
2 Mason Law (Spirit); **3** Ben Currie (Kawasaki); **4** Charlie Nesbitt (Kalex); **5** Jamie van Sikkelerus (Yamaha); **6** Danny Webb (Triumph); **7** Brandon Paasch (Triumph); **8** Dan Jones (Spirit); **9** Eunan McGlinchey (Kawasaki); **10** Harry Truelove (Yamaha); **11** Rhys Irwin (Yamaha); **12** Jamie Perrin (Spirit); **13** James Hind (Yamaha); **14** Cameron Fraser (Chassis Factory); **15** Scott Swann (Yamaha).
Fastest lap: Kennedy, 1m 32.797s, 96.49mph/155.29km/h.
Championship points: 1 Jack Kennedy, 327; **2** Ben Currie, 293; **3** Lee Johnston, 273; **4** Bradley Perie, 259; **5** Harry Truelove, 21?; **6** Kyle Smith, 181.

Honda British Talent Cup, Round 9
Race 1 (12 laps 29.844 miles/48.029km)
1 Casey O'Gorman (Honda), 24m 14.454s, 73.78mph/118.74km/h.
2 Cormac Buchanan (Honda); **3** Jamie Lyons (Honda); **4** Carter Brown (Honda); **5** Rhys Stephenson (Honda); **6** Harrison Crosby (Honda); **7** James Cook (Honda); **8** Johnny Garness (Honda); **9** Kiyano Veijer (Honda); **10** Julian Correa (Honda); **11** Sullivan Mounsey (Honda); **12** Maik Duin (Honda); **13** Evan Belford (Honda); **14** Mason Johnson (Honda); **15** Harrison Mackay (Honda).
Fastest lap: Brown, 1m 59.524s, 74.91mph/120.56km/h.

Race 2 (15 laps 37.305 miles/60.037 km)
1 Casey O'Gorman (Honda), 25m 52.822s, 86.41mph/139.06km/h.
2 Carter Brown (Honda); **3** Jamie Lyons (Honda); **4** Evan Belford (Honda); **5** Johnny Garness (Honda); **6** Rhys Stephenson (Honda); **7** Bailey Stuart-Campbell (Honda); **8** Harrison Crosby (Honda); **9** Rossi Banham (Honda); **10** Harley McCabe (Honda); **11** Kiyano Veijer (Honda); **12** Corey Tinker (Honda); **13** Luca Hopkins (Honda); **14** Ryan Hitchcock (Honda); **15** Lucas Hill (Honda).
Fastest lap: O'Gorman, 1m 42.666s, 87.21mph/140.36km/h.

BRANDS HATCH GP, 15-17 October 2021, 2.433-mile/3.916km circuit.
Bennetts British Superbike Championship, Round 11
Race 1 (16 laps 38.928 miles/62.649km)
1 Tarran Mackenzie (Yamaha), 23m 39.642s, 98.72mph/158.87km/h.
2 Tommy Bridewell (Ducati); **3** Christian Iddon (Ducati); **4** Jason O'Halloran (Yamaha); **5** Peter Hickman (BMW); **6** Andrew Irwin (BMW); **7** Josh Brookes (Ducati); **8** Lee Jackson (Kawasaki); **9** Glenn Irwin (Honda); **10** Bradley Ray (BMW); **11** Danny Buchan (BMW); **12** Gino Rea (Suzuki); **13** Kyle Ryde (BMW); **14** Joe Francis (BMW); **15** Luke Mossey (Honda).
Fastest lap: Bridewell, 1m 25.129s, 102.90mph/165.6km/h.

Race 2 (20 laps 48.660 miles/78.311km)
1 Tarran Mackenzie (Yamaha), 28m 44.261s, 101.60mph/163.51km/h.
2 Tommy Bridewell (Ducati); **3** Jason O'Halloran (Yamaha); **4** Christian Iddon (Ducati); **5** Peter Hickman (BMW); **6** Josh Brookes (Ducati); **7** Danny Buchan (BMW); **8** Gino Rea (Suzuki); **9** Glenn Irwin (Honda); **10** Kyle Ryde (BMW); **11** Joe Francis (BMW); **12** Bradley Ray (BMW); **13** Luke Mossey (Honda); **14** Storm Stacey (Kawasaki); **15** Takumi Takahashi (Honda).
Fastest lap: Bridewell, 1m 25.086s, 102.95mph/165.68km/h.

Race 3 (20 laps 48.660 miles/78.311km)
1 Tarran Mackenzie (Yamaha), 28m 40.521s, 101.82mph/163.86km/h.
2 Tommy Bridewell (Ducati); **3** Jason O'Halloran (Yamaha); **4** Josh Brookes (Ducati); **5** Peter Hickman (BMW); **6** Lee Jackson (Kawasaki); **7** Rory Skinner (Kawasaki); **8** Bradley Ray (BMW); **9** Andrew Irwin (BMW); **10** Gino Rea (Suzuki); **11** Kyle Ryde (BMW); **12** Ryan Vickers (Kawasaki); **13** Storm Stacey (Kawasaki); **14** Dean Harrison (Kawasaki); **15** Bjorn Estment (Suzuki).
Fastest lap: Mackenzie, 1m 25.218s, 102.79mph/165.42km/h.

Quattro Group British Supersport Championship, Round 11
Race 1 (12 laps 29.196 miles/46.986km)
1 Jack Kennedy (Kawasaki), 17m 58.575s, 97.46mph/156.85km/h.
2 Bradley Perie (Yamaha); **3** Ben Currie (Kawasaki); **4** Lee Johnston (Yamaha); **5** Jamie Perrin (Spirit); **6** Charlie Nesbitt (Kalex); **7** Mason Law (Spirit); **8** Harry Truelove (Yamaha); **9** Rhys Irwin (Yamaha); **10** Eunan McGlinchey (Kawasaki); **11** Brandon Paasch (Triumph); **12** Dan Jones (Spirit); **13** Jamie van Sikkelerus (Yamaha); **14** Cameron Horsman (Chassis Factory); **15** Scott Swann (Yamaha).
Fastest lap: Johnston, 1m 28.714s, 98.74mph/158.91km/h.

Race 2 (5 laps 12.165 miles/19.578 km)
1 Ben Currie (Kawasaki), 7m 29.304s, 97.48mph/156.88km/h.
2 Jack Kennedy (Kawasaki); **3** Mason Law (Spirit); **4** Lee Johnston (Yamaha); **5** Charlie Nesbitt (Kalex); **6** Eunan McGlinchey (Kawasaki); **7** Jamie Perrin (Spirit); **8** Harry Truelove (Yamaha); **9** Brandon Paasch (Triumph); **10** Rhys Irwin (Yamaha); **11** Dan Jones (Spirit); **12** Cameron Horsman (Chassis Factory); **13** Harry Rowlings (ABM); **14** Jamie van Sikkelerus (Yamaha); **15** Phil Wakefield (Yamaha).
Fastest lap: Nesbitt, 1m 28.225s, 99.28mph/159.79km/h.

Final British Superbike Championship points:

1	Tarran Mackenzie,	1202
2	Tommy Bridewell,	1166
3	Jason O'Halloran,	1162
4	Christian Iddon,	1141
5	Peter Hickman,	1092
6	Josh Brookes,	1079

7 Danny Buchan, 1075; **8** Glenn Irwin, 1055; **9** Lee Jackson, 248; **10** Bradley Ray, 245; **11** Gino Rea, 202; **12** Ryan Vickers, 180; **13** Rory Skinner, 178; **14** Andrew Irwin, 169; **15** Kyle Ryde, 118.

Final British Supersport Championship points:

1	Jack Kennedy,	372
2	Ben Currie,	334
3	Lee Johnston,	302
4	Bradley Perie,	279
5	Harry Truelove,	233
6	Eunan McGlinchey,	192

7 Kyle Smith, 181; **8** Brandon Paasch, 158; **9** Rhys Irwin, 142; **10** Jamie Van Sikkelerus, 140; **11** Scott Swann, 112; **12** James Hind, 99; **13** Phil Wakefield, 96; **14** Sam Munro, 85; **15** Korie McGreevy, 60.

Final British Talent Cup points:

1	Casey O'Gorman,	273
2	Carter Brown,	267
3	Evan Belford,	244
4	Jamie Lyons,	223
5	Johnny Garness,	214
6	James Cook,	144

7 Harrison Crosby, 142; **8** Ollie Walker, 138; **9** Sullivan Mounsey, 110; **10** Kiyano Veijer, 107; **11** Cormac Buchanan, 104; **12** Bailey Stuart-Campbell, 78; **13** Rhys Stephenson, 78; **14** Troy Jeffrey, 52; **15** Ryan Hitchcock, 46.

Supersport World Championship

Round 1, ARAGON, Spain, 21-23 May 2021, 3.155-mile/5.077km circuit
Race 1 (15 laps, 47.321 miles/76.155km)
1 Steven Odendaal, RSA (Yamaha), 28m 53.622s, 98.265mph/158.142km/h.